D0930071

A
CHECKLIST of
AMERICAN IMPRINTS
for
1830

Items 1–5609

Compiled by
Gayle Cooper

The Scarecrow Press, Inc.
Metuchen, N.J.   1972

Copyright 1972 by Mrs. Richard H. Shoemaker

ISBN 0-8108-0520-2

A. & C. A. Warren's Northern almanack for 1831. Ballston Spa, A. & C. A. Warren [1830] 12 1. MWA; NHi. 1

The A. B. C. with verses... New-York, Pr. and sold by Mahlon Day [1830?] 8 p. NN. 2

Abaellino. See Zschokke, Heinrich.

Abbot, Gorham Dummer, 1807-1874.
Memoir of Nathan W. Dickerman, who died at Boston, Mass., Jan. 2, 1830 in the eighth year of his age. New York, D. Fanshaw, print. American Tract Society [1830] 140 p. CLCM; CSmH; ICU; M; MB; MBC; MH; MWA; MdBE; RPB. 3

Abbott, Benjamin, 1732-1796.
Experience and gospel labours of the Rev. Benjamin Abbott, to which is annexed a narrative of his life and death. By John Ffirth... New York, Pub. by J. Emory and B. Waugh for the Methodist Episcopal Church [J. Collard, pr.] 1830. 211 p. CSmH; DLC; ICN; MBC; MiD-B; NjR. 4

[Abbott, Jacob] 1803-1879
Biography for young persons. Designed to illustrate the triumphs of genius and perseverance... Boston, Leonard C. Bowles, 1830. 2 vols. KU; MWA; NNU; NhHi; RP. 5

---- The corner-stone, or, A familiar illustration of the principles of Christian truth... By Jacob Abbott ... Boston, W. Peirce [183-] 2 p. 1., [3]-360 p. DLC; MH. 6

[----] The little philosopher, or the infant school at home. No. I [-IV] By Erodore. Boston, Carter and Hendee, 1830 [pt. 2 dated 1829] 36, 36, 36, 36 p. CtY; DLC; KU; MB; NNC; RPAt. 7

Abbott, John Emery.
Extracts from sermons by the late Rev. John Emery Abbott, of Salem, Mass. With a memoir of his life, by Henry Ware, jr. Boston, Wait, Green & co., 1830. 139 p. CtY; ICMe; IEG; MAnP; MH; MWA; NNUT; Nh-Hi; PPLT. 8

Abercrombie, John, 1780-1844
Pathological and practical researches on diseases of the stomach, the intestinal canal, the liver, and other viscera of the abdomen. Philadelphia, Carey & Lea; E. & G. Merriam, printer, 1830. 416 p. ArU-M; CU; DNLM; GEU-M; KyLxT; ICJ; MB; MdBJ; MdUM; MiDW-M; MoSW-M; MsU; NIC; NNS; NbU-M; NjR; PPC; TxU-M; ViRMC; VtU; WU-M. 9

Abernethy, John, 1764-1831.
Lectures on the theory and practice of surgery. New York, C. S. Francis... Munroe & Francis - Boston [Clayton & Van Nor-

den, printer] 1830. 191 p.
CSt-L; LNT-M; MBCo; MdBJ;
MiDW-M; MoSMed; NBMS;
OCGHM; PU; ScCMeS; ViNoM.
                                    10
Abraham, Richard. See Ameri-
can Academy of the Fine Arts.

Account of Meh Shway-ee: a Burman slave girl. Philadelphia
[1830?] 24 p. PHi.   11

An account of the destruction of
the city of Jerusalem, by the
Roman army under Titus. Ro-
chester, N. Y. , Pr. by Marshall,
Dean & Co. , 1830. 32 p. NRU.
                                    12
An account of the last illness of
Hannah Dudley. See Dudley,
Elizabeth.

Adam, Alexander, 1741-1809.
    Adam's Latin grammar, sim-
plified, by means of an introduction, designed to facilitate the
study of Latin grammar by
spreading before the student on
the compass of a few pages, what
is most essentially necessary to
be remembered, with appropriate exercises to impress on the
memory the declensions and in-
flections of the parts of speech,
and to exemplify and illustrate
the rules of syntax, by Allen
Fisk... 5th ed. from the 2d ed. ,
rev. and cor. New York, Pub.
and sold by White, Gallaher &
White, 1830. 190, 16 p. MH;
NRU; NjR; OkU.   13

---- Adam's Latin grammar,
with some improvements... By
Benjamin A. Gould... Boston,
Hilliard, Gray, Little, and Wilk-
ins; and Richardson and Lord,
1830. 299 p. At head of title:
Stereotype edition. AU; CtHT-W;
IGK; IaHi; MBC; MH; MeB; MeHi;
NN; NNC; OClW; RPB.   14

---- Adam's Latin grammar, with

the following additions; the ancient
and modern pronunciation of the Latin language; observations on the declinable parts of speech, rules for
the govt. of the subjunctive mood;
and with various improvements and
corrections. By David Patterson...
New-York, Collings & Co. , Collins
& Hannay [etc.] 1830. 272 p. NNC;
ViU.   15

---- Roman antiquities; or, An
account of the manners and customs of the Romans... Revised,
corrected, and illustrated with
notes and additions, by P. Wilson. New York, Pub. by Collins & Hannay, W. E. Dean,
printer, 1830. 496 p. CBPac;
CS; ICU; LNL; MB; NGH;
NbCrD; TWcW; ViRU.   16

[Adams, Catherine (Lyman)] d. 1879.
    Parlor lecture on Scripture
history, by a Mother. Augusta,
Pub. by P. A. Brinsmade, at the
depository of Kennebec Co. , S.
S. Union [Eaton and Severance,
printers] 1830. 2 v. MA; MBC;
MH-AH; RPR.   17

Adams, Daniel, 1773-1864.
    Adams' New arithmetic. Arith-
metic, in which the principles of
operating by members are analytically explained and synthetically applied.   Keene, New Hampshire, John Prentiss, Stereotyped at the Boston Type and
Stereotype Foundry, 1830. 264 p.
CSt; CtHT-W; MB; MH; NNC;
TxU.   18

---- Arithmetic, in which the
principles of operating numbers
are analytically explained and
synthetically applied... Utica,
N. Y. , Hastings & Tracy, 1830.
262+ p. OClWHi (Imperfect) 19

---- Geography: or, A description of the world. In three parts
... accompanied with an atlas.

For use in schools and acade-
mies. 12th ed. Boston, Lincoln
& Edmonds, 1830. 323 p. ICU;
MH; NNC; OClWHi; OSW.   20

---- Scholar's arithmetic. Keene,
N. H., Pr. by John Prentiss,
1830. 224 p. MH; MWHi; RP.
21

Adams, John, 1786-1856.
A treatise on the principles
and practice of the action of
ejectment, and the resulting action for mesne profits... From
the last London ed. To which
are added, notes of the decisions
made by the Supreme and circuit
courts of the United States... Albany, W. & A. Gould & Co.; New
York, Gould, Banks & co., 1830.
lxx p., 1 l., 568 p. C-L; CU;
CoU; DLC; GU; MH-L; MiD-B;
MsU; NjP; TU; WU-L; WaU-L.
22

Adams, Robert H.
Speech of Mr. Adams of Mississippi, on the bill to remove
the Indians west of the Mississippi. Delivered in the Senate of the
United States, April, 1830. Washington, Pr. by Duff Green, 1830.
31 p. PPL.   23

Adams, Solomon, 1797-1870.
An address, delivered at
North-Yarmouth, April 28, 1830,
before the Cumberland co. temperance society. Portland [Me.]
Shirley, Hyde and company, 1830.
21 p. CSmH.   24

---- ---- Second edition. Portland, Shirley, Hyde and Company,
1830. 23, [1] p. CBPac; CtY;
MB; MBC; MH; MWA; MeHi; N;
NN; PPPrHi.   25

Adams County, Mississippi.
Citizens.
Public dinner, given in honor
of the Chickasaw and Choctaw
treaties, at Mr. Parker's hotel,
in the city of Natchez, on the
10th day of October, 1830. [Na-
tchez, 1830] 16 p. CSmH; LNHT;
OCHP; OkHi; PPL.   26

An address, occasioned by the
opposition... See MacDill, David.

Address submitted for consideration. See Carey, Mathew.

An address to a youth at school.
Stereotyped by James Connor,
New York. New York, Pr. at
the Protestant Episcopal Press,
1830. 8, [1] p. MBD.   27

Address to the citizens of Baltimore, relative to the contemplated extension of the rail road,
down Pratt street, to the city
block. Adopted at an adjourned
meeting of citizens of the western and southwestern section of
the city, held at the Union Engine Committee Room, Thursday
evening, September 30, 1830.
Baltimore, Pr. at the Office of
the Baltimore Republican, 1830.
8 p. DLC; MdHi.   28

An address to the citizens of New
York, on the claims of Columbia
College and the new university to
their patronage. New York, 1830.
10 p. CtHT; CtY; DLC; IC; MB;
MH; N; NNU; PHi.   29

Address to the clergy, of all
ranks, and of every persuasion,
throughout the United States, by
one of the people. Boston, 1830.
12 p. MBC.   30

An address to the Columbian Institute. See Law, Thomas.

An address to the inhabitants of
Nantucket. See Peirce, Cyrus.

An address to the leaders of political anti-masonry. See Brutus,
Lucius Junius.

Address to the Mayor and city council. See Winchester, George.

An address to the people of North Carolina, on the evils of slavery. By the friends of liberty and equality. ... Greensborough, N. C., William Swaim, printer, 1830. 2 p. l., [3]-68 p., 1 l. ArU; CSmH; DLC; MH; MWA; MdBP; NIC-L; NcD; NcU; Nh-Hi; RP; TNF; Vi; WHi.   31

An address to the people of the county of Salem. See Jeffers, William N.

An address to the people of the United States. See Lathrop, John Hiram.

Address to the voters of Morgan County. See Thomas, William.

Addresses delivered at Chestertown, Kent County, Md. at the dinner given to Gen. Ezekiel F. Chambers. Baltimore [1830?] 16 p. PHi.   32

Advice to the young Christian, on the importance of aiming at an elevated standard of piety. By a village pastor. With an introductory essay, by the Rev. Dr. Alexander, of Princeton, N. J. ... Third edition, revised and corrected. New York, G. & C. & H. Carvill [Ludwig & Tolefree, printers] 1830. 196 p. CtHC; CtY-D; DLC; NGH; BrMus. 33

The Aeolian harp; or, Songster's cabinet; being a selection of the most popular songs and recitations; patriotic, sentimental, humorous etc. ... Albany, Pr. for the purchaser, 1830. 124, [4] p. DLC; NjP.   34

Aetna Insurance Company. Instructions for the direction

of agents of the Aetna Insurance Company of Hartford, Connecticut. Hartford, Pr. by Hanmer and Phelps, 1830. 30, [1] p. CtHi.
                         35
An affectionate address, to every sincere inquirer after truth. By a Catholic Clergyman. Monroe, M. T., Pr. for Edw. D. Ellis, 1830. 36 p. InNd; OCX.   36

African Education Society of the United States.
  Report of the proceedings at the formation of the African Education Society: instituted at Washington, December 28, 1829. With an address to the public, by the board of managers. Washington, Pr. by James C. Dunn, Georgetown, D.C., 1830. 16 p. DLC; MB; MH; MMeT-Hi; MdBJ; MiU; Ms-Ar; Nh; OClWHi; PHi; PPL; PPPrHi; TNF; TxH.   37

---- ---- Washington city, Pr. by Rothwell & Ustick, 1830. 16 p. CtY; DLC; MiU; NNUT; OCHP; BrMus.   38

The age of rhyme. See Duke, Seymour R.

The age of steam. See Whiting, Henry.

Agricultural almanac for 1831. Lancaster, John Bear [1830] 18 l. MiU-C; NjR; PHi; PPeSchw.   39

Aiken, Solomon, 1758-1833.
  A Thanksgiving sermon, delivered in the South Village in Starksborough, Vt., December 3, 1829. Middlebury, J. W. Copeland, 1830. 31 p. NNUT; RPB.   40

[Aikin, John] 1747-1822.
  The arts of life, described in a series of letters ... 1st Amer-

ican ed. Boston, Carter and Hendee, and Waitt and Dow, 1830. 158 p. MB; MH; MnU; RPB.
41

Ainsworth, Luther.

Conversation on practical arithmetic, comprising a collection and familiar explanation of the most important rules of practical arithmetic, in a series of questions and answers, designed for the use of schools. Providence, Cory, Marshall and Hammond, 1830. 84 p. CtHT-W; NN; RPB.
42

Alabama.

Acts passed at the eleventh annual session of the General Assembly of the state of Alabama, begun and held in the town of Tuscaloosa, on the third Monday in November, one thousand eight hundred and twenty-nine. Tuscaloosa, Pr. by M'Guire, Henry and Walker, State Printers. 1830. 95 p. A-SC; AB; ABCC; AU-L; DLC; ICLaw; IU; In-SC; MH-L; Ms; NNB; NNLI; OClW; BrMus.
43

---- Executive Department, Tuscaloosa... [Tuscaloosa, 1830] 4-page folder, printed on first page only. Title from McMurtrie.
44

---- Journal of the House of Representatives, of the state of Alabama. Begun and held at the town of Tuscaloosa, on the third Monday in November, 1829. Being the eleventh annual session of the General Assembly of said state. Tuscaloosa, Pr. by McGuire, Henry and Walker, 1830. 296 p. A-SC; AB; BrMus.   45

---- Journal of the Senate of the state of Alabama. Begun and held at the town of Tuscaloosa, on the third Monday in November, 1829, Being the eleventh annual session of the General Assembly of said state. Tuscaloosa, Pr. by

M'Guire, Henry & Walker, state printer, 1830. 214 p. A-SC; AB; BrMus.   46

---- Reports of cases argued and determined in the Supreme Court of Alabama, embracing the decisions made in the years 1827 and 1828. With an appendix, containing the rules of practice in the courts of Alabama. By George N. Stewert. Vol. I. Tuscaloosa, Pub. by the Author. Wiley, M' Guire and Henry, Printers, 1830. 650 p. ABB; DLC; F-SC; IaDaGL; LNL-L; MH-L; Ms; N; NN; NNB; NcS; Nj; PPiAL; PU-L; RPL; BrMus.   47

Albany Argus, Extra. See Democratic Republicans. New York.

The Albany directory for 1830-31. Albany, Pr. by Edmund B. Child, 1830. 148 p. MBNEH; N.   48

Alcott, Amos Bronson, 1799-1888.

Observations on the principles and methods of infant instruction. Boston, Pub. by Carter and Hendee [Pr. by I. R. Butts, Boston] 1830. 27 p. CtHT-W; CtY; DLC; MB; MBAt; MBC; MH; MHi; MWA; NN; NhD; PPAmP; PPL; ViU; WU; BrMus.   49

Alexander, Archibald, 1772-1851.

Evidences of the authenticity, inspiration, and canonical authority of the Holy Scriptures. Philadelphia, Presbyterian board of publication, [183-?] 308 p. CBPac; DLC; ICU; MB; MH; NjP; P; ViR; ViU.   50

---- Objections obviated, and God glorified by the success of the Gospel among the heathen; a sermon preached at Albany,

N.Y., Oct. 7, 1829, at the twentieth annual meeting of the American Board of Commissioners for Foreign Missions. Boston, Crocker and Brewster, 1830. 35 p. CtY; ICMe; MB; MBC; MH-AH; MWA; MeB; NCH; OO; PHi; PPPrHi; WHi.   51

---- A pocket dictionary of the Holy Bible. Containing a historical and geographical account of the persons and places mentioned in the Old and New Testaments. ... Revised by the Committee of Publication. Philadelphia, American Sunday School Union [Stereotyped by L. Johnson] 1830. 4th ed. 546 p. CBCDS; ICU; MWA; NN; OO; PPL; ViU.   52

Alexander, James Waddell, 1804-1859.
A geography of the Bible, compiled for the American Sunday School Union, by J. W. and J. A. Alexander. Rev. by the committee of publication of the American Sunday School Union. Philadelphia, American Sunday School Union [Stereotyped by L. Johnson] 1830. 180 p. CtMW; CtY; GDC; GHi; ICU; IEG; KyBgW; MB; MBAt; MH; MiU; NNG; NNUT; NcD; NhD; NjPT; NjR; O; OHi; OO; PLT; PPL; PPPrHi; ViAlTh; WHi; BrMus.   53

Alexander the great. See Kenney, Lucy.

Alicia and her aunt; or, Think before you speak. A tale for young persons... new ed. New York, W. B. Gilley, 1830. 175 p. CtHT-W; ICMe; MH; NN.   54

Alison, Archibald, 1757-1839.
Essays on the nature and principles of taste. ... With corrections and improvements by Abraham Mills. New York, G. C. and H. Carvill [Sleight & Rob-

inson, printers] 1830. 418 p. CtY; ICJ; IG; IGK; MNF; MdBE; NN; NjP; OMC; PPL.   55

[Alken, Henry Thomas] 1784-1851.
The beauties and defects in the figure of the horse... Boston, Carter & Hendee, 1830. 2 p., front, 18 pl. CtY; ICJ; MW; MiU-C; PPA.   56

...All for the best. Boston, Pub. by the Doctrinal Book and Tract Society; Perkins & Marvin, Agents [183-?] 12 p. (Doctrinal Tract, No. 18.)   WHi.   57

Allegheny County (Pa.)
Rules for regulating the practice in the courts of Common Pleas and other courts of Allegheny County. Pittsburgh, Johnston & Stockton, 1830. 160 p. PHi.   58

Alleine, Joseph, 1634-1668.
An alarm to unconverted sinners in a serious treatise on conversion. New York, American Tract Society [183-?] 164 p. [Evangelical Family Library Vol. 3]   ViU. 59

Allen, Ethan, 1796-1879.
Discourse delivered in Christ Church, Washington, D. C. in April last, at the request of the Board of Managers of the Washington City Temperance Society, in aid of its cause. Published by the Washington City Temperance Society. Washington, Pr. by Gales & Seaton, 1830. 27 p. MB; OCHP; RPB.   60

Allen, Joseph, 1790-1893.
Questions on select portions of the four Evangelists [Part first] By Joseph Allen ... Boston, Gray and Bowen, 1830. 112 p. MB.   61

---- ---- 2d ed. Boston, Gray
and Bowen, publishers, 1830.
114 p. CtY; InND; MH.   62

Allen, Samuel Clesson, 1772-
1842.
  An address delivered at North-
ampton before the Hampshire,
Franklin & Hampden Agricultural
Society, October 27, 1830. North-
ampton, T. Watson Shephard,
printer, 1830. 32 p. CSmH; CtY;
DLC; MBAt; MBHo; MH; MWA;
MiD-B; N.   63

Allen, William
  Plan of the city of Philadelphia and adjoining districts, shewing the existing and contemplated
improvements. Compiled from
original documents by William Allen. Philadelphia, H. S. Tanner,
1830. Col. map engraved by W.
Allen and E. B. Dawson. ____In-
dex. vi, 44 p. DeGE; PHi.   64

Allen, William, 1784-1868.
  A decade of addresses, delivered from 1820 to 1829, to the
senior classes at Bowdoin College. Together with an inaugural
address to which is added a Dudleian lecture, delivered May 12,
1830, at Harvard University. Boston, Hilliard, Gray & Co.,
[Brunswick, Pr. by Joseph Grif-
fin] 1830. 272 p. CtMW; CtY;
DLC; GDC; IC; ICU; MA; MB;
MBAt; MBC; MH; MHi; MWA;
NN.   65

---- ---- Concord, Horatio Hill
& Co. [Pr. by Joseph Griffin,
Brunswick, Me.] 1830. 272 p.
CtHT-W; DLC; MB; MH; MeB;
MeHi; MoSpD; NN; NNUT; Nh;
OO.   66

---- ---- Portland, Samuel Col-
man, 1830. 272 p. DLC; G;
GDC; MH; MiD; MnU; NN; RNR.
      67
---- Ordination by elders vindi-

cated. A discourse, delivered
May 12, 1830, at the Dudleian
Lecture at Harvard University.
Boston, Pub. by Peirce and Wil-
liams, 1830. 43 p. CtY; DLC;
KWiU; MA; MB; MBAt; MBC;
MH-AH; MHi; MeBaT; RPB;
BrMus.   68

Allen, William S.
  An oration, delivered in New-
buryport, on the fifty-fourth an-
niversary of the Declaration of
American Independence. New-
buryport, Pr. at the Herald Of-
fice, 1830. 20 p. CSmH; CtY;
ICN; MBAt; MH; MHi; MWA; NCH;
OClWHi; PHi; PPAmP; BrMus.
      69
Allen's almanac for 1831. [Hart-
ford, H. Burr, Jun.] 1830. Bdsd.
CtHi.   70

Almanac for 1831. Peekskill. Advertised in the "Westchester &
Putnam Sentinel," October 14,
1830. Drake 7070.   71

Almanac, for the states of Ohio,
Kentucky, and Indiana for 1831.
By Oner R. Powell. Cincinnati,
William Conclin [1830] 12 l.
OClWHi.   72

Alonzo and Melissa. See Mitchell, Isaac.

The alphabet, or, The child's
first look; with a catechism of
Walker's pronunciation of the letters. Concord, M. G. Atwood,
1830. 36 p. DLC.   73

[Althans, Henry]
  Scripture natural history of
quadrupeds. With reflections.
New-Haven, S. Babcock, Publisher, ...Sidney's Press, 1830.
23 p. CtHi.   74

Alumnus, pseud.
  Professor Hale and Dartmouth
College. [Hanover? N.H.,

183-?] MH.   75

An American, pseud.   See Biddle, Richard.

An American, pseud.   See Hunt,
Freeman.

An American, pseud.   See Pickering, Henry.

American Academy of the Fine
Arts, New York.
   A catalogue of Italian, Flem-
ish, Spanish, Dutch, French,
and English pictures; which have
been collected in Europe and
brought to this country by Mr.
Richard Abraham of New Bond
Street, London and are now exhibiting at the American Academy
of Fine Arts. New York, Pr. by
Christian Brown, 1830. 53 p. On
cover: Ninth Edition. CtHT-W;
CtY; DLC; MBMu; MH; NN; PHi;
PPL (cover wanting); PPPM. 76ι

---- A catalogue of Italian, Flem-
ish, Spanish, Dutch, French, and
English Pictures... now exhibiting
at the American Academy of Fine
Arts. March, 1830. New York,
Pr. by R. & G.S. Wood [1830]
54 p. PPL.   77

The American almanac and re-
pository of useful knowledge for
1831. Boston, Gray & Bowen
[1830] 156 l. CSmH; CtHT-W;
CtSoP; CtW; DLC; IEN; KyU;
MH-AH; MoHi; NNE; Nc-Ar; O;
PPT; PPiHi; ScU-S; TU; UPB;
ViHi; WyU.   78

---- (Second edition) Boston,
Gray & Bowen [etc.] [1830] 168 l.
CtY; MH; MHi; MWA; MdBJ;
NNA; NNC; OClWHi; OMC; PPL;
PPiU; T; ViL.   79

---- (Third Edition) Boston,
Gray & Bowen [1830] 156 l.
MdBP.   80

---- (Third Edition) Boston,
Gray & Bowen [1830] 156 l.
[Cover error: "Second Edition"]
Drake 3974.   81

American anecdotes. See Hunt,
Freeman.

The American annual register;
For the years 1827-8-9. Or,
the fifty-second and fifty-third
years of American Independence.
New York, Pub. by E. G. W.
Blunt, 1830. 622, 169, [1] p.
CSfCW; DLC; KWiU; KyBC;
MeHi; MoSpD; RNR; RP.   82

American Bible Class Society.
   Second annual report of the
American Bible Class Society,
presented in Philadelphia, May
26, 1829; together with the Pres-
ident's address, and an appendix.
Williamstown, Pr. by Ridley Ban-
nister, 1830. 16 p. CBPac;
CSmH; MB; MiD-B; PPHi;
PPPrHi.   83

American Bible Society.
   An abstract of the American
Bible Society, containing an account of its principles and operations, and of the manner of organizing and conducting auxiliary
and branch Bible societies. Published by the direction of the
board of managers, and under
the inspection of a committee appointed by the same. New York,
Pr. by Daniel Fanshaw, 1830.
48 p. MBAt; MHi; MNtcA; NCH;
NcD; NjPT; NjR; PHi; PPAmP;
PPL.   84

---- A brief analysis of the system of the American Bible Society, containing a full account of
its principles and operations, and
of the manner of organizing and
conducting auxiliary, branch,
and ladies' Bible societies. New
York, Pr. by Daniel Fanshaw,

1830. vii, [5], 144 p. CSmH;
Ct; CtY; KyLoS; M; MBAt; MNe;
MeBaT; OClWHi; PPAmP; PPL
(vii, [5]-140 p., with wrappers);
PPPrHi; PU; BrMus.   85

---- Fourteenth annual report of
the American Bible Society, presented May, 1830... New York,
Pr. by Daniel Fanshaw, 1830.
xii, 154 p. MeBaT; NjR; WBB.
                                86
American Board of Commissioners for Foreign Missions.
   Report of the American Board
of Commissioners for Foreign
Missions... Twenty-first meeting,
1830. Pr. by Crocker and Brewster, Boston [1830] 131 p. MA;
MeB; MeBaT; TxU.   87

American Colonization Society.
   A few facts respecting the
American Colonization Society,
and the colony at Liberia. For
gratuitous distribution. Boston,
Pr. by Peirce and Williams,
1830. 16 p. ICN; MBC; MWA;
MdBJ; MsJS; TxDaM; WHi.   88

---- ---- Pub. by the American
Colonization Society. Washington,
Pr. by Way and Gideon, 1830.
16 p. DLC; GDC; M; MB; MH-
AH; MWA; OClWHi; PHC; TNJ.
                                89
---- The thirteenth annual report
of the American Society for Col-
onizing the Free People of Color
of the United States. With an ap-
pendix. Washington, Pr. by
James C. Dunn, Georgetown,
D.C., 1830. xv, [1], 50, [6] p.
CSmH; DLC; KHi; MA; PPL;
TxHuT.   90

---- 2nd ed. Washington, Pr.
by James C. Dunn, Georgetown,
D.C., 1830. xv, [1], 55, [1] p.
MA; PPL.   91

The American comic almanac for
1831. Boston, Charles Ellms;

Hooton, Teprell & Hart, printers
[1830] 18 l. DLC; InU; MB; MHi;
MWA (3 varieties); MiD-B; NHi;
NN; NcD; TxU; WHi.   92

The American comic almanack
for 1831. Boston, Charles Ellms;
Working Man's Advocate Office
[1830] 18 l. Drake 3976.   93

American Convention for Promoting the Abolition of Slavery, and
Improving the Condition of the
African Race.
   Minutes of the twenty-first bi-
ennial American Convention for
Promoting the Abolition of Slavery, and Improving the Condition
of the African Race. Convened at
the city of Washington, December
8, A.D. 1829. And an appendix,
containing the addresses from
various societies, together with
the constitution and by-laws of
the convention. Philadelphia, Pr.
by order of the convention.
Thomas B. Town, pr., 1829. 72
p. Imprint date on cover, 1830.
MNS.   94

American Education Society.
   Fourteenth annual report of
the directors of the American Ed-
ucation Society, presented at the
annual meeting held in the city of
New York, May, 1830, to which
are prefixed the constitution and
rules of the Society. New York,
Pub. by Jonathan Leavitt, for the
Society [Pr. by Sleight & Robin-
son] 1830. 80 p. CBPac;
CtMW; ICMcC; MA; MNE; MeB;
MeBaT; MiD-B; NjR; OOxM; PCA;
PP.   95

---- Northwestern Branch.
   Tenth annual meeting of the
North-western Branch of the
American Education Society. Held
at Rutland, Sept. 14, 1830. [n.p.
n.d.] 12 p. DHEW; MBC.   96

American Farmers' almanac for

1831. By Charles F. Egelmann. Hagers-Town, John Gruber [1830] 15 l. CLU; MWA; MdBE; NcD; PYHi. 97

American Home Missionary Society.
The fourth report of the American Home Missionary Society, presented by the executive committee, at the anniversary meeting, May 12, 1830, with an appendix.... New York, Pr. by Clayton & Van Norden, 1830. 73, [7] p. MA. 98

American Institute of Instruction.
Constitution of the American Institute of Instruction. Adopted August 21, 1830. [Boston? 1830] 8 p. PPL. 99

American Institute of the City of New York.
Charter of "The American Institute of the city of New-York." Incorporated May 2, 1829. Accompanied with the By-Laws. ...New York, Pr. by John M. Danforth, 1830. 8 p. NIC. 100
---- Report of the third annual fair of the American Institute of the City of New-York, held at Masonic Hall, October, 1830; with a list of premiums, and a catalogue of all the articles exhibited, by whom made and sold, with the duties imposed on similar imported commodities. New-York, Pr. by J. Seymour, 1830. 32 p. MH; NCH; NbU; OCHP; PHi. 101
The American landscape. See Bryant, William Cullen.

American military biography; containing the lives and characters of the officers of the Revolution. ...Pub. for Ross Houck, Cincinnati, Pr. at the Chronicle Office, 1830. 615 p. CSmH; DLC; GDC; InU; MnHi; NjR;

OClWHi; PPL. 102
---- Published for subscribers. New York, Pr. by Edward J. Swords, 1830. 607 p. CSmH; MnHi; NjR; OkU; ScCliTo; Vi. 103

American Peace Society.
A congress of Nations, for the peaceful adjustment of all international disputes. [Boston, Mass., American Peace Society, 183-?] 12 p. WHi. 104

---- Sketch of the peace cause; or, A brief exposition of the American Peace Society.... [Boston, 183-!] 4 p. WHi. 105

American popular lessons. See Robbins, Eliza.

The American primary class-book; or, Lessons in reading, for younger classes of children ... Providence, Cory, Marshall and Hammond [etc.] 1830. 144p. DLC; RHi; RPB. 106

The American primer. See Lamb, Jonathan.

American Seaman's Friend Society.
Second annual report of the American Seamen's Friend Society, presented at the meeting May 10, 1830. New York, J. Seymour, printer, 1830. 42 p. MeBaT; PPL; WHi; BrMus. 107

American Society for Encouraging the Settlement of the Oregon Territory.
The Oregon country; a circular to the citizens of the U. States. [Boston, 1830] Broadsid. MBAt. 108

American Stenographic Academy. See Gould, Marcus Tullius Cicero.

American Sunday School Union.
Constitution of the American Sunday School Union; with by laws of the Board, list of officers, managers and committees. Philadelphia, 1830. 8 p. OClW. 109

---- A help to the Gospels; containing harmony exercises, illustrations, and practical lessons from the history and miracles contained in the four Gospels. 2d ed., rev. by the committee of publication... Philadelphia, American Sunday School Union, 1830. 243 p. CBPac; CtHC; GDC; MH; NCH; NjP (252 p.); WHi; BrMus. 110

---- Hints to aid in the organization and support of Sabbath Schools in the country. 4th ed. Philadelphia, American Sunday-School Union, 1830. 10, 2 p. NbU; PHi. 111

---- Sixth annual report... May 25, 1830. Philadelphia, Depository of the American Sunday School Union, 1830. 48 p. WHi. 112

---- The sixth report of the American Sunday-School Union; presented at their annual meeting in Philadelphia, May 25, 1830. Philadelphia, No. 146 Chestnut Street, 1830. 68 p. ICU (59, [1] p.); PPL. 113

---- ---- Philadelphia, No. 146 Chestnut Street, 1830. 34 p. MA; PPL. 114

The American system exemplified by a reference to the duties on some of the most necessary and substantial articles of life. By a citizen of Sumter District. Summerville, S.C., James S. Bowen, 1830. 11 p. ScU. 115

American Temperance Society.
Third annual report of the executive committee of the American Society for the Promotion of Temperance. Presented Dec. 30, 1829. Andover, Pr. for the Society by Flagg and Gould, 1830. 32 p. OC; VtMidbC. 116

The American time-piece; or, almanac for 1831. By Charles F. Egelmann. Baltimore, Richard J. Matchett [1830] 28 l. MdBE. 117

American Tract Society. Boston.
Sixteenth annual report of the American Tract Society, Boston, read May 26, 1830. Boston, T. R. Marvin, pr., 1830. 47, [1] p. DLC. 118

---- Connecticut.
Fourteenth report of the Connecticut branch of the American Tract Society, January, 1830. Hartford, Pr. by Goodwin & Co., 1830. 24 p. Ct. 119

---- New York.
"Fetch them in, and tell them of Jesus," a true narrative. New York, American Tract Society [183-?] 32 p. RPB. 120

---- Fifth annual report of the American Tract Society, Instituted at New York 1825. Presented May, 1830. ...Printed at the Society's house,... by D. Fanshaw, New York, 1830. 96 p. MeBaT. 121

---- The fourth commandment, or, Some account of Jack Riot and Will Mindful. New York, 150 Nassau St. [183-?] 15 p. RPB. 122

---- The fourth of July. A tale. New York, 150 Nassau St. [183-?] 36 p. RPB. 123

---- The history of Ann Lively and her Bible... New York, Pub. by the American Tract Society, 1830. 8 l. MB; PP. 124

---- The history of Anna Emery, exemplifying the power of divine grace through a long period of great suffering. New York, 144 Nassau St. [183-?] 36 p. RPB. 125

---- The history of Peter Thomson. In two parts. New York, 144 Nassau St. [183-?] 34 p. RPB. 126

---- ..."I am an infidel!" An authentic narrative. [New York, Pub. by the American Tract Society, 183-?] 4 p. [i. e. p. 158-160] No. 267. PPL. 127

---- ..."I am no hypocrite. [Pub. by the American Tract Society, New York, 1830?] 4 p. ([61]-64 p.) No. 391. PPL. 128

---- Tom Steady, a pretty history for good children. New York, 150 Nassau St. [183-?] 15 p. RPB. 129

---- Tommy Wellwood; or, A few days of incident and instruction. New York, 144 Nassau St. [183-?] RPB. 130

---- The vine. New York, 150 Nassau St. [183-?] RPB. 131

---- The wonderful cure of Naaman a general in the Syrian army. New York, 150 Nassau St. [183-?] RPB. 132

---- Pennsylvania.
Third annual report of the Pennsylvania branch of the American Tract Society, with lists of auxiliaries and benefactors. Philadelphia, Pr. by Wm. F. Geddes, 1830. 34 p. MiU-C. 133

American Unitarian Association.
... The divinity of Jesus Christ. 2d ed. Boston, Gray & Bowen [Pr. by I. R. Butts] 1830. 28 p. (Tracts, American Unitarian Association. 1st ser. No. 34). CtHC; ICU; MB; MBAU; MH-AH;

MHi; MeLB. 134

---- Fifth annual report made to the American Unitarian Association, May 25, 1830, with the addresses at the annual meeting. Boston, Gray and Bowen [Pr. by I. R. Butts] 1830. 60 p. M; MMeT-Hi; MNF; MiD-B; WHi. 135

---- ... Excuses for the neglect of the communion considered. 2d ed. Pr. for the American Unitarian Association. Boston, Gray & Bowen, [Pr. by I. R. Butts] 1830. 24 p. (1st series. No. 22.) MH-AH; MNBedf; OClWHi. 136

---- Suggestions respecting the formation of auxiliaries to the association. April, 1830. Boston, [1830] 14 p. (2d Series, No. 6) CtY; MB; MH-AH; OClWHi. 137

Americanischer stadt und land calender auf 1831. Philadelphia, Conrad Zentler [1830] 18 l. CLU; CtY; DLC; InU; MWA; NHi; NN; NjP; NjR; PHi; RPB. 138

The American's guide: comprising the Declaration of independence; the Articles of confederation; the Constitution of the United States, and the constitutions of the several states composing the Union... Philadelphia, Towar, J. & D. M. Hogan; Pittsburg, Hogan & co. [Sherman & Co., printers] 1830. 428 p., 1 l. CLCL; DLC; KyDC; KyU; MB; MH-L; MeBa; MiD; OClWHi; ScC; ScU. 139

Americanus, pseud. See The Military Academy at West Point.

Der Amerikanisch-Teutsche hausfreund und Baltimore calender auf 1831. von Carl F. Egelmann. Baltimore, Johann T. Hanzsche [1830] 18 l. DeWint; MWA; NjR; PHi. 140

[Ames, Nathaniel] d. 1835
A mariner's sketches, originally pub[lished] in the Manufacturer's and Farmer's Journal, Providence, Rev., corr. and enl. by the author. Providence, Cory, Marshall and Hammond, 1830. 312 p. CSmH; DLC; MB; MH; MWA; MeBaT; NhD; NjP; OClWHi; P; PU; RJa; WHi; BrMus. 141

Amherst Academy.
Amherst academy. Catalogue of the trustees, instructors and students; during the fall term, ending November 23d, 1830. Amherst, J. S. and C. Adams, printers, 1830. 6, [1] p. MA-H; MAJ; MH. 142

---- Amherst academy, Mass. This institution has been in successful operation for several years, ...Amherst, Nov. 5th, 1830. [Amherst] J. S. and C. Adams, printers [1830] Bdsd. MAJ. 143

Amherst College.
Amherst college. Order of exercises at commencement, MDCCCXXX. August 25, --10 o' clock, A. M. Amherst, Mass. [Amherst] John S. & Charles Adams, printers [1830] 4 p. MA; MBC; MH. 144

---- Catalogue of the corporation, faculty and students. October, 1830. Amherst, J. S. and C. Adams & co., printers [1830] 16 p. Cover title. CoU; ICU; MeB; NN. 145

Amicus Sabbati, pseud.
Sabbath miscellany. Boston, 1830. 77, [2] p. MH. 146

Amos, Andrew, 1791-1860.
A treatise on the law of fixtures and other property partaking of both a real and personal nature: comprising the law relative to annexations to the freehold in general...With an appen- dix, containing practical rules and directions respecting fixtures By A. Amos & J. Ferard, 1st. Am. ed. New York, Gould and Banks, Albany, W. Gould & Co., 1830. xxviii, 342 p. CLSU; CU; DLC; LNT-L; MBS; MH-L; NIC-L; NNLI; NNU; NRAL; OU; RPL; TU. 147

Zum Andenken des Confirmations-Bundes. [ca. 1830] Bdsd. PPL. 148

Anderson, James.
The pulpit assistant: containing three hundred skeletons of sermons: chiefly extracted from various authors. With an essay on the composition of a sermon; and a copious and accurate index, prepared expressly for this edition. Boston, Langdon Coffin, 1830. 2 v. CBPac; CtHC; GDC; ICN; ICU; LNB; MB; MH-AH; MoS; ViL. 149

Anderson, Rufus, 1796-1880.
Observations upon the Peloponnesus and Greek Islands, made in 1829, by Rufus Anderson, one of the secretaries of the American Board of Commissioners for Foreign Missions. Boston, Pub. by Crocker and Brewster; New York, Jonathan Leavitt, 1830. viii, 21-334 p. CU; CtMW; CtY; GDC; ICMcC; IaU; MA; MB; MBAt; MBC; MH-AH; MHi; MdBE; MeB; MiU; MnHi; NNUT; NcU; NjPT; OMC; PHC; PP; PPPrHi; BrMus. 150

Anderton, Samuel G., b. 1780.
"Masonry the same, all over the world." Another Masonic murder. Boston, 1830. 8 p. CtY; DLC; IaCrM; MB; MH; MHi; MWA; NR; NjP; RPB; WHi; BrMus. 151

---- ---- Philadelphia, 1830. CtY. 152

Andover Theological Seminary.
Catalogues of the libraries, belonging to the Porter Rhetorical Society, and the Society of Inquiry, in the Theological Seminary, Andover. [Andover] Flagg and Gould, printers, 1830. 36 p. CtY; MH.
153

---- General catalogue of the Theological Seminary. Andover, Pr. by Flagg and Gould, 1830. 23, [1] p. MNtcA.   154

Andrews, Charles C.
The history of the New-York African free-schools, from their establishment in 1787, to the present time; embracing a period of more than forty years: also a brief account of the successful labors, of the New-York Manumission Society: with an appendix... New York, Pr. by M. Day, 1830. 2 p. l., [7]-148 p. CSmH; DLC; MH; MHi; NNQ; OClWHi; PHi; PSC-Hi; BrMus.
155

Andros, Thomas, 1759-1845.
The temperance society vindicated and recommended. A discourse...preached to his own charge, soon after the formation of the Bristol County Temperance Society, January 5, 1830. Taunton, Pr. by Edmund Anthony, 1830. 22 p., 1 l. CSmH; M; BrMus.   156

Angell, Oliver, 1787-1858.
The union, no. 1; or, Child's first book. Being the first of a series of spelling and reading books, in six numbers... Providence, Cory, Marshall and Hammond, 1830. 71, [1] p. [Angell's union series of common school classics, no. 1] DLC.   157

---- The union, no. II; or Child's second book. Being the second of a series of spelling and reading books, in six numbers... Providence, Cory, Marshall and Ham-

mond, 1830. 144p. [Angell's union series of common school classics, no. 2] DLC; RHi; RPB.   158

---- The union, no. III; or, Child's third book. Being the third of a series of spelling and reading books, in six numbers. ...Providence, Cory, Marshall and Hammond, 1830. 216 p. [Angell's union series of common school classics, no. 3] DLC; RPB; BrMus.   159

---- The union, no. V. Containing a brief system of English grammar; together with lessons for reading, mental arithmetic, abbreviations and definitions, being the fifth of a series of spelling and reading books, in six numbers. Providence, Pub. by Cory, Marshall and Hammond, 1830. 82 p. [Angell's union series of common school classics, no. 5] [DLC has a 1831 imprint] NNC; RPB (imperfect).   160

Ein Angriff auf das Afterreden oder die Verlaumdung. Ephrata, Pr. by Joseph Baumann, 1830. Seidensticker p. 245.   161

Anonymous, esq. See Whiting, Henry.

Anthon, Henry.
The wise and faithful steward. A sermon preached in St. Stephen's Church, New-York, on the 15th Sunday after Trinity, September 19, 1830, being the Sunday after the decease of the Right Rev. Bishop Hobart. New York, Pub. by T. and J. Swords; Edward J. Swords, printer, 1830. 19 p. CtHT; CtY; MB; NNG; NjPT; RPB.   162

Anthony Rollo. See Baptist General Tract Society.

An Anti-Episcopal Methodist, pseud. See An exposition of the government.

Anti-Masonic almanac for 1831. Philadelphia, Pa., J. Clarke [1830] MWA. 163

---- By Edward Giddins. Utica, William Williams [1830] 36 l. DLC; IaCrM; MB; MBFM; MWA; MiD-B; MnU; NHi; NN; NRU; OClWHi; PHi; PPFM; WHi. 164

Anti Masonic pamphlet no. 3. See History of the outrage...

Anti-Masonic Party. Alabama. The proceedings of the first Anti-Masonic meeting, held on North-River, Tuscaloosa County, Alabama, September 18th, 1830. Accompanied by an appropriate address. Tuscaloosa, Pr. by Hampton & Mitchell, 1830. 15 p. PHi. 165

---- Connecticut. Proceedings of the Anti-masonic state convention of Connecticut, held at Hartford, Feb. 3 and 4, 1830. Hartford, Packard & Butler, 1830. 32 p. CtHi; CtY; DLC; IaCrM; MB; MWA; MnU; NNFM; PPFM. 166

---- Massachusetts. An abstract of the proceedings of the Anti-masonic state convention of Massachusetts, held in Faneuil Hall, Boston, Dec. 30 & 31, 1829 and Jan. 1, 1830. Boston, John Marsh, Jan. 1830. 32 p. CSmH; CtY; DLC; IaCrM; MB; MHi; MWA; MdHi; MeB; MiD-B; MoSU; NR; NjP; NjR; OClW; PHi; PPFM; PPL; BrMus. 167

---- A brief report of the debates in the Anti-masonic state convention of the commonwealth of Massachusetts, held in Faneuil Hall, Boston, December 30, 31, 1829,

and January 1, 1830. Boston, Pub. by John Marsh, 1830. 48 p. CSmH; CtY; IaCrM; MB; MBAt; MBC; MH; MHi; MWA; MdHi; MeB; MiD-B; MnU; MsJMC; NN; NjR; PHi; PPFM; PPL; TxU; BrMus. 168

---- National Convention. The address of the national Anti-Masonic convention held in Philadelphia, September 11, 1830, to the people of the United States. Philadelphia, 1830. 24 p. InHi; MBC; MBFM; MH; MiD-B; MiU; NjR; OClW; P; PHi; PPFM; PPL; RPB; WHi. 169

---- New York. Proceedings of the Anti Masonic Convention for the state of New York, held at Utica, August 11, 1830, with the address and resolutions. Utica, Pr. by Wm. Williams, 1830. 16 p. CtY; IaCrM; MA; MB; MBC; MHi; NN; NNC. 170

---- Proceedings of the Young Men's Anti-Masonic State Convention for the state of New York. Held at Utica, September 16 and 17, 1830. Utica, Press of William Williams, 1830. 18 p. NHi. 171

---- Ohio. Proceedings of the Ohio Anti-Masonic State Convention, held at Canton, Ohio, on the 21st and 23d days of July, 1830. 16 p. MB; MBFM; PPFM. 172

---- United States. The address of the United States Anti-Masonic Convention held in Philadelphia, September 11, 1830. To the people of the United States. Philadelphia, Pub. by John Clarke; New York, Skinner & Dewey; Albany, L. B. Packard and Co.; Utica, William Williams; Hartford, Conn., Strong; Boston, John Marsh and

Co., 1830. 22 p. CSmH; ICN;
IaCrM; MB; MBFM; MHi; MWA;
MdHi; MeB; MiU; MoSpD; N;
NNS; NbO; PPFM.   173

---- The proceedings of the
United States Anti-Masonic Convention, held at Philadelphia,
September 11, 1830. Embracing
the journal of proceedings, the
reports, the debates, and the address to the people. Philadelphia,
Pub. by I. P. Trimble, Skinner
and Dewey; New York, D. B.
Packard; Albany, William Williams; Utica, D. D. Spencer; Ithaca,
N. D. Strong; Hartford, Conn.,
John Marsh & Co., office of the
Boston Christian Herald, and of
the Free Press Boston, Mass.,
1830. [4], 142, [2] bl., 22 p.
[last 22 p. "To the People of the
United States" also numbered
[145]-164] CSmH; MBFM; PPFM;
PPL.   174

---- Vermont.
    Proceedings of the Anti-masonic
State Convention holden at Montpelier, June 23, 24, & 25, 1830.
With reports, addresses, etc. Pub.
by order of the Convention. Middlebury, Pr. by O. & J. Miner, 1830.
35 p. DLC; PPFM; BrMus.
                            175
Anti-Masonic Republican Convention.
    Proceedings of the Anti-Mason-
ic Republican convention of the
County of Cayuga, held at Auburn,
January 1, 1830. With their address to the farmers and mechanics of the county. Auburn, Thomas M. Skinner, printer, 1830. 21,
[1] p. MB; N; NRU; NjPT; WHi.
                            176
Anti-masonry, first published in
the American Quarterly Review.
1830. 32 p. NjR.   177

Anti-Masonry in its true colors.
Addressed to all who love their
country. [Albany? 1830] 8 p.

NbU.   178

An apology for uniting with the
Methodists; designed to point out
the misrepresentations, contained
in a late publication, entitled
"Candid reasons, for not uniting
with the Methodists; by Bernard."
By a Methodist preacher. Middlebury, Vt., Pr. by J. W. Copeland, 1830. 24 p. VtHi.   179

Appeal to American Christians.
See Hamilton, Alexander.

An appeal to Matter of fact. See
Fletcher, John William.

Appeal to the people of Vermont.
...See Freemasons. Vermont.

The Arabian nights' entertain-
ments, carefully revised and oc-
casionally corrected, from the
Arabic. To which is added a selection of new tales... Philadelphia, J. J. Woodward, 1830. 546
p. CtHT; MdBS.   180

Arch, Royal, pseud.
    The principles of anti-masonry,
illustrated in a series of letters
addressed to Rev. David Pease...
Belchertown, Mass., Pr. at the
Hampshire Sentinel Office, 1830.
32 p. CSmH.   181

Archbald, William A.
    Prospectus d'une mode perfec-
tionné de fabrication pour le sucre
Brut. d'apres les Brevets de William A. Archbald. [New Orelans,
1830] [2] p. PPL.   182

Archbold, John Frederick.
    A summary of the law relative
to pleading and evidence in criminal cases: with precedents of in-
dictments, &c. And the evidence
necessary to support them... 2d
American from the third London
ed., with very considerable alterations, including Lord Lansdowne's

Notes, &c. Waterford [N. Y.],
John C. Johnson, printer, 1830.
viii, 337, [4] p. CSfLaw; ICLaw;
In-SC; LNB; LNT-L; MoKB;
NbCrD.   183

Archer, William Segar, 1789-
1855.
  Speech of Mr. Archer of Virginia, on the bill proposing to
construct a national road from
Buffalo to New Orleans. Delivered in the House of Representatives of the United States, April,
1830. Washington, Pr. by Duff
Green, 1830. 20 p. PPL.   184

The archer's manual; or, The
art of shooting with the long-bow,
as practised by the United Bow-
men of Philadelphia. Philadelphia, R. H. Hobson, 1830. 66 p.
DLC; ICHi; LNHT; MB; MdBP;
PHi.   185

Arden, the Unfortunate stranger
... New York, S. King [1830?]
1 p. l., [7]-28, [23]-26 p. CtY;
PU; BrMus.   186

An argument in support of the
claims of James Hamilton. See
Hamilton, James.

Arkansas (Territory)
  Acts, passed at the sixth ses-
sion of the General Assembly of
the territory of Arkansas: Which
was begun and held at the town of
Little Rock, on Monday, the fifth
day of October, and ended on
Saturday, the twenty first day of
November, one thousand eight
hundred and twenty-nine. Little
Rock, Pr. by William E. Wood-
ruff, printer to the territory,
1830. 137, [4] p. Ar-SC; ArL;
ArU; DLC; ICLaw; Ia-L; InU-L;
LU-L; M; MH-L; OCLaw; Or-
SC; RPL.   187

---- Journals of the General Assembly of the territory of Ar-

kansas, begun and held at Little
Rock, in said territory, on Monday, the fifth day of October,
and ended on Saturday, the twen-
ty-first day of November, one
thousand eight hundred and twenty-
nine. Little Rock, Pr. by William
E. Woodruff, printer to the terri-
tory, 1830. 294 p. ArU; DLC.
                                188
[Armroyd, George]
  A connected view of the whole
internal navigation of the United
States... By a citizen of the
United States. Philadelphia, Pub.
by the author. Pr. by Lydia R.
Bailey, 1830. 617 p. CU; CtY;
DeGE; ICJ; ICN; IaU; InU; LNHT;
MBAt; MH; Md; MeU; MiD; MnU;
MoSM; NN; NjP; OO; PHi;
PPAmP; PPF; PPL; PU; RP;
BrMus.   189

Armstrong, Lebbeus, 1775-1860.
  Masonry proved to be a work of
darkness, repugnant to the Christian religion and inimical to a republican government... Delivered
in Philadelphia, New York and
Newark and other places, Sept.,
1830. New York, Pr. for the author, 1830. 24 p. CtHT-W;
CtY; IaCrM; PPFM; PPPrHi.
                                190
Arndt, Johann.
  Des hocherleuchteten Lehrers
Herrn Johann Arndts,...Sechs
Bücher vom wahren Christenthum
...nebst dessen Paradiesgärtlein.
Nach der accuratesten Edition
aufs neue collationirt und unver-
ändert herausgegeben. Philadelphia, in der deutsch-europäischen
Buch- und Kunsthandlung von
Joh. G. Ritter, 1830. 711, [17],
80, 192, [8] p.   PPeSchW.
                                191
Arnold, Samuel. An astonishing
affair. See Philandros.

The art of making money plenty
in every man's pocket; by Doctor
Franklin. [n.p., 1830?] sheet.

(Binder's title dated 1830.) DLC.
192

An article on the American Sunday School Union, extracted from the Biblical Repertory and Theological Review for April 1830. Philadelphia, Pr. by James Kay, Jun. & Co., 1830. 35, 8 p. ICMcC; NNUT.   193

The arts of life.   See Aikin, John.

Ashfield, Mass. Congregational Church.
Articles of faith and covenant adopted by the Congregational Church in Ashfield, January 29, 1830. Greenfield, Mass., Phelps & Ingersoll, 1830. 10 p. MBC; MHi.   194

Ashmead, William.
Sermons by the late Rev. William Ashmead, with a memoir of his life. Philadelphia, Pub. by Towar, J. & D. M. Hogan, 1830. 438 p. CtSoP; CtY; GAuY; GDC; ICN; NcMHi; NjPT; PPPrHi.
195

Ashtabula County Republican Union Society.
Constitution and address of the Ashtabula County Republican Union Society. Ashtabula, Pr. at the Journal office, 1830. 10 p., [1] l. MiU-C; OClWHi.   196

Associate Reformed Church in North America. General synod.
The judicial acts of the General synod, of the Associate Reformed church of North America, emitted, from time to time, as occasional testimonies against prevailing errors: together with a warning against Hopkinsian and other allied errors, addressed by the Associate Reformed synod of the West to the churches under their care; with a short narrative prefixed of the state and progress of such errors...

Washington, Ohio, Pr. by Hamilton Robb, 1830. 98, [2] p. CSmH; DLC; NN; NNUT; NcMHi; OCHP; OClWHi.   197

---- Synod of the West.
Extracts from the minutes, of the proceedings of the Associate Reformed Synod of the West; which met in Chillicothe, October 27th, A. D. 1830.   Office of the Religious Examiner, Washington, Ohio, Pr. by Hamilton Robb, 1830. 30 p. NcMHi.   198

Associate Society of West Point, N. Y.
Exposition of the objects and views of the Associate Society of West Point.   New York, Pr. by J. & J. Harper, 1830. 31 p. CSmH; DLC; MB; MH; MiU-C.
199

Association for the Relief of Respectable Females.
The seventeenth annual report of the Association for the Relief of Respectable, Aged, Indigent Females.... New York, Seymour, printer, 1830. 12 p. NNG; NjR.
200

Association of Mechanics and Other Working Men of Washington City.
Address of the Association of Mechanics and Other Working Men, of the City of Washington, to the operatives throughout the United States. Washington, Pr. by W. Duncan, 1830. 15 p. DLC
201

Association of Young Men for the Gratuitous Instruction of Male Coloured Persons.
Constitution... Philadelphia, Pr. by Joseph Rakestraw, 1830. 8 p. MiD-B.   202

An astonishing affair.   See Philandros.

[Atkins, Sarah]
Memoirs of John Frederic Ob-

erlin, pastor of Waldbach, in the
Ban de la Roche. Compiled from
authentic sources, chiefly French
and German. 1st American edition, with a dedication and translation. By the Rev. Luther Halsey, professor of theology in the
Western Theological Seminary.
Pittsburgh, Pub. by Luke Loomis, D. & M. Maclean, printers,
1830. 255 p. KTW; OO; PPi;
RPB.   203

The Atlantic souvenir for 1830.
Philadelphia, Carey, Lea &
Carey [Pr. by James Kay, Jun.
& Co.] 1830. 328 p. DLC; MB;
MWA; NNC; PPL.   204

Atwater, Caleb.
    The far west region. Letter
written by Caleb Atwater, esq.,
one of the Commissioners on the
part of the U.S., appointed to
treat with the Indians of the upper Mississippi, descriptive of
the region of the Wisconsin Territory. January 1st, 1830. W.B.
Thrall, printer, Circleville, O.,
[1830?] Broadside. CtY.   205

Atwood, Moses G.
    The American definition spell-
ing book improved. Carefully rev.
and adapted to Walker's Principles of English orthoepy with progress reading lessons. Designed
for the use of schools in the
United States. Concord, N.H.,
Hoag & Atwood, 1830.   DLC;
MH; OClWHi.   206

Auburn Theological Seminary.
    Catalogue of the officers and
students of the Theological Seminary, at Auburn, New-York, January, 1830. Auburn, Pr. by
Thomas M. Skinner, 1830. 8 p.
MBC; MWA; N; NAuT.   207

Augustine, St.
    The meditations of Saint Au-
gustine. Revised and corrected.

Baltimore, Pub. by F. Lucas,
Jr. (J. Robinson, printer)
[183-?] 202 p. MdW; PV.   208

Auner, (J.G.), bookseller, Philadelphia.
    J. G. Auner's catalogue of
books in the various departments
of literature and science... Philadelphia, J. G. Auner, 1830. 22 p.
DeGE.   209

Austin, James Trecothick, 1784-
1870.
    An address delivered before
the Massachusetts Society for the
Suppression of Intemperance,
May 27, 1830. Boston, Press
of John H. Eastburn, 1830. 32 p.
CSmH; CtSoP; CtY; DLC; ICU;
MBAt; MBC; MH; MWA; MeBaT;
MiD-B; NjPT; OO; PPAmP; WHi;
BrMus.   210

---- Speech delivered at Faneuil
Hall on 21st. Oct. 1830, before
the citizens convened to take
measures for electing a member
of Congress for the district of
Suffolk. [Boston, 1830] Broadside. MH.   211

Austin, Stephen Fuller, 1793-
1836.
    Map of Texas with parts of the
adjoining states, compiled by
Stephen F. Austin. Philadelphia,
H.S. Tanner, 1830. map. NNF;
PHi; TxU.   212

An authentic account of the fatal
duel fought on Sunday the 21st
March 1830, near Chester, Penna.
between Mr. Charles G. Hunter,
late midshipman of the U.S.
navy, and Mr. William Miller,
jun., late attorney at law of
Philadelphia; containing an impartial investigation of all the circumstances and correspondence
which preceded the meeting...
with some observations on the
custom of duelling considered as

to its effects on society... Washington city, Jonathan Elliot, 1830. 81 p. DLC; MB; MeBaT; N; NjR; PHi; PPL; PU; RPB.   213

An authentic historical memoir of the Schuylkill Fishing Company. See Milnor, William.

Authorship. See Neal, John.

Autobiography of an almost septuagenarian: with remarks on the opinions and manners of the age. Boston, Carter & Hendee, Press of Putnam & Hunt, 1830. 178 p. RPB.   214

Auxiliary Foreign Mission Society of Brookfield.
    Proceedings of the Auxiliary Foreign Mission Society of the Brookfield Association, at their seventh annual meeting, October 19, 1830. Brookfield, E. & G. Merriam, prs., 1830. 16 p. MBC.   215

Auxiliary Foreign Mission Society of Essex County.
    Proceedings at the third annual meeting of the ...held at Haverhill, April 21, 1829. Salem, Pr. by W. Palfray, Jr., 1830. 32, [1] p. Ct; MBC.   216

Auxiliary Foreign Mission Society of Franklin County, Mass.
    Seventeenth annual report. ... Shelburns, Oct. 14, 1829. Greenfield, Mass., Phelps & Ingersoll, printers, 1830. 14 p. MHi; WHi.   217

Auxiliary New York Bible and Common Prayer-Book Society.
    The fifteenth annual report of the Board of Managers of the Auxiliary New York Bible and Common Prayer Book Society read before the society in St. John's Chapel, Oct. 7, 1830. With an appendix. New York, Pr. at the Protestant Episcopal Press, 1830. 11 p. MBD; NNG; WHi.   218

Avery, S. W.
    The dyspeptic's monitor; or The nature, causes, and cure of the diseases called dyspepsia, indigestion, liver complaint...etc. New York, E. Bliss, 1830. 152 p. CtHT; GU-M; MBCo; MWA; NNNAM; OMC; PPC.   219

---- ---- 2d ed. New York, E. Bliss, 1830. 164 p. MA.   220

The aviary, and Bird breeder's companion... New York, G. Thoburn & Sons, 1830. 72 p. DLC; MeB.   220a

Award in the case of the Pole-Boat New-Jersey, on a claim for contribution in the way of general average. Savannah, Pr. by T. M. Driscoll, 1830. 8 p. ScHi.   221

Ayars, James B.
    A discourse on the mode of Baptism, delivered at Harrisburg, Sept. 2, 1830. Harrisburg, Pr. by John T. Bobbs, 1830. 32 p. LNB; NNUT; NjPT; NRAB. 222

B

Babylon the Great. See Cresson, Warder.

Bacheler, Origen.
    Address on the subject of universalism by Origen Bacheler, editor of the Anti-universalist. Delivered in various places. Boston, Pr. for the author, 1830. 24 p. ICMe; MMeT-Hi; MNtcA; TxU.   223

Backhouse, Hannah Chapman (Gurney), 1787-1850.
    Discourse delivered at Henry Street Meeting New York. New York, 1830. PPFr; PSC-Hi;

BrMus.   224

Bacon, Joel Smith, 1802-1869.
An inaugural address, delivered in Georgetown, Ky. July 26, 1830... Georgetown, Ky., Pr. by N. L. Finnell, 1830. 13 p. CSmH; DLC; ICU; MNtcA; NHC-S; PPPrHi.   225

Bacon, Leonard, 1820-1881.
A manual for young church members. New Haven, Stephen Cooke, 1830. 216 p. VtU.   226

A Baconian Biblist. See A practical view.

The bad boy reformed. Or The morning walk. Concord, N. H., Robert H. Sherburne & Co., 1830. 12 p. NhHi.   227

[Badcock, John] fl. 1816-1830.
The veterinary surgeon; or, Farriery taught on a new and easy plan; being a treatise of all the diseases and accidents to which the horse is liable... by John Hinds, [pseud.] Philadelphia, John Grigg [Mifflin & Parry, printers] 1830. xiv, 284 p. CSmH; CU; DLC; GDC; KyBgW; LNHT; MdUM; MeB; NGH; NNC-M; NRHi; NjR; PPC; PPL; PPeSchW; PU-V; TNJ; Vi.   228

Baldwin, Elihu Whittlesey, 1789-1840.
The Young Freethinker reclaimed. Written for the American Sunday School Union... Revised by the Committee of Publication, Philadelphia, American Sunday School Union [1830] 5-166 p. ViU; BrMus.   229

Baldwin, Henry.
An address delivered before the subscribers to the Mechanics' Institute, on Thursday evening, July 22, 1830, by the Hon. Henry Baldwin. Pittsburgh, Pr.

by Joseph Snowden, 1830. 8 p. NjR.   230

Baldwin & Treadway's sheet almanac for 1831. [New Haven, Baldwin & Treadway, 1830] Broadside. CtY.   231

Ballou, Adin, 1803-1890.
The inestimable value of souls. A sermon, delivered before the Universalist Society in Medway, (Mass.) May, 1830. Pub. by request of the hearers. Boston, Pr. at the Trumpet Office, 1830. 23 p. Cover title. DLC; MMeT; MWA; NNUT.   232

---- Oration delivered before the citizens of Blackstone Village and its vicinity, at Mendon, Mass., July 5, A.D. 1830. Providence, Cranston and Knowles, printers, 1830. 18 p. MWA; RPB.   233

Baltimore.
Journal of the proceedings of the first [-2nd] branch of the city council of Baltimore. January session, 1830. Baltimore, Pr. by John D. Toy, 1830. Bd. in 1 vol; (1st) - 286 p.; (2d) - 154 p. MdBJ.   234

---- Journal of the proceedings of the Second branch of the City Council of Baltimore. Extra session. Wednesday, June 16, 1830. [Baltimore, Pr. by Sands & Neilson, 1830?] 9 p. DLC; MdHi.   235

---- Report and proceedings on the subject of a House of refuge, at a meeting of the citizens of Baltimore, held at the City Hall, on the Sixteenth October, 1830. Baltimore, Benjamin Edes, printer, 1830. 17 p. MB; MdHi.
                                236
---- Report of the Commissioners of Public Schools, to the City Council of Baltimore. 1830. 17 p.

DLC; MdAS; OO; PP; PPAmP.
                                    237
---- Report of the visitors and
governors of the jail of Balto.
County, 1830. Md.   238

Baltimore & Harford Turnpike
Road Company.
   Report of the Baltimore and
Harford Turnpike Road Company,
to the Legislature of Maryland.
In obedience to an order of the
House of delegates of the 14th
January, 1830. Annapolis, Jere-
miah Hughes, printer, 1830. 7 p.
MdHi.   239

Baltimore & Harve-de-Grace
Turnpike Co.
   Report of the Baltimore and
Harve-de-Grace Turnpike Com-
pany, to the Legislature of
Maryland. Annapolis, Jeremiah
Hughes, printer, 1830. [4] p.
MdHi.   240

Baltimore & Ohio Railroad Company.
   Fourth annual report, of the
president and directors, to the
stockholders of the Baltimore
and Ohio Rail Road Company.
Baltimore, Pr. by William Wooddy, 1830. 153 p. CtY; DLC;
ICJ; LNHT; MBAt; MH; MdHi;
MiU-T; NN; O; PPL; BrMus.
                                    241
---- Information and directions,
relative to laying a single track
of wood rail way, on the Baltimore and Ohio Rail Road. [Bal-
timore, W. Wooddy, printer,
183-?] 8 p. MH-BA.   242

---- Letter and documents from
the Baltimore and Ohio Rail
Road Company, in refutation of
the charges contained in a pamphlet laid before Congress by the
Chesapeake and Ohio Canal Company.   [Baltimore, 1830] 8 p.
CtY; DBRE; DLC; MiU-T; NN.
                                    243

---- ---- [Baltimore, 1830] 7
p. CtY; DLC; MdHi; NN. 244

The Baltimore and Ohio Rail
Road Company, vs. The Chesapeake and Ohio Canal Company,
and others. n. t.-p. [Annapolis,
1830] 71 p. PPF.   245

Baltimore & Susquehanna Railroad Company.
   Address to the mayor and
city council. See Winchester,
George.

---- Third annual report of the
directors to the stockholders of
the Baltimore and Susquehanna
Rail Road Company. Together
with the report of the engineers.
18th October, 1830. Baltimore,
Pr. by James Lucas & E. K.
Deaver, 1830. 27 p. CSt; CtY;
DBRE; DLC; DeGE; MdHi; PPL.
                                    246
Baltimore Temperance Society.
   The constitution and address
of the Baltimore Temperance So-
ciety; to which is added an ad-
dress, delivered before the so-
ciety, by N. R. Smith. Baltimore,
Pr. by J. D. Toy, 1830. 39 p.
DLC; MdBE; MdHi; PPL; BrMus.
                                    247
Bancroft, Luther S.
   An address delivered to the
Prescott Guards, and to the in-
habitants of Pepperell. June 17,
1830. Groton, Stacy and Rogers,
printers, 1830. 17, [2] p. MB.
                                    248
Bangor. Theological Seminary.
Bangor, Me.
   A survey of the Theological
Seminary, at Bangor, Me. Pub.
by order of the trustees. Bangor,
Burton & Carter, printers, 1830.
20 p. DLC; MH; MWA; NNUT.
                                    249
Bangs, Nathan.
   The life of the Rev. Freeborn
Garrettson: compiled from his
printed and manuscript journals,

and other authentic documents.
By Nathan Bangs, D.D. ...2d ed.,
rev. and cor. New York, Pub. by
J. Emory and B. Waugh, at the
conference office... J. Collord,
printer, 1830. xii, 335 p. DLC;
MnHi; NNC; NcU; NhHi; NjPT;
TNJ.   250

----The reviewer answered: or,
The discipline and usages of the
Methodist Episcopal Church de-
fended against the attacks of The
Christian Spectator. New-York,
Pub. by J. Emory and B. Waugh,
at the Conference Office, J. Col-
lord, printer, 1830. 124 p. IEG;
MBAt; MWA; MnHi; MsJS;
PPPrHi.   251

Bank of Pennsylvania.
   Charters and laws... Phila-
delphia, 1830. 28 p. NjP; PHi.
                                   252
---- Charters, laws, and by-
laws of the Bank of Pennsylvania.
Philadelphia, Clark & Raser,
prs., 1830. 49 p. MH-BA; NNC.
                                   253
[Banim, John] 1798-1842.
   The denounced. By the au-
thors of "Tales by the O'Hara
family" ... New York, Pr. by J.
& J. Harper, 1830. 2 v. in 1.
DLC; MB; NN; PV; RJa; WU.
                                   254
[Baptist, Edward] 1790-1863.
   A series of letters addressed
to the Pamphleteer, by Wickliffe
[pseud.] in reply to an essay on
baptism. First published in the
Religious Herald. Richmond, Pr.
for the author, by Wm. Sands,
1830. 74 p. CSmH; MB; MnU;
NjPT; RPB; Vi.   255

Baptist Board of Foreign Missions.
   Report of the Baptist Board of
Foreign Missions, at its annual
meeting, in Hartford, April 28,
1830. 30 p. NRAB; BrMus.
                                   256

Baptist General Tract Society.
   ...Anthony Rollo, the Converted Indian. Pub. by the Baptist General Tract Society. Philadelphia, [1830] 12 p. [also pp.
[181]-192 of Vol. III] No. 60.
PPL.   257

Baptist Literary and Theological
Seminary, Hamilton.
   Order of exercises of the Baptist Literary and Theological
Seminary, Hamilton. At the anniversary, June 2, 1830. Hamilton, Pr. by Williams & Orton
[1830] Broadside. MNtcA. 258

Baptists. Alabama. Cahawba
Association.
   Minutes of the thirteenth anni-
versary of the Cahawba Baptist
Association, held at the meeting
house of Mount Moriah Church,
Bibb County, Alabama, from the
twenty third to the twenty sixth
October, eighteen hundred and
thirty, inclusive. Selma, Ala.,
Thomas J. Frow, printer, 1830.
8 p. NRAB.   259

---- ---- Mount Zion Association.
   Minutes of the seventh annual
session of the Mount Zion Baptist Association. Convened at Big
Spring Meeting House, Shelby
County, Ala. from the eighteenth
to the twentieth September, inclusive, A.D. 1830. Huntsville,
P. Woodson, printer, 1830. 13 p.
NRAB.   260

---- Connecticut. Ashford Association.
   Minutes of the Ashford Baptist Association held at Willing-
ton, Conn. June 2 and 3, A.D.
1830 Sixth anniversary, 1830.
11 p. NRAB.   261

---- ---- Hartford Association.
   Minutes of the forty-first anniversary of the Hartford Bap-

tist Association, holden in the
Meeting House of the Baptist
Church in Windsor. (Wintonbury)
Conn., Oct. 13, and 14, 1830.
15 p. NRAB.   262

---- ---- New Haven Association.
Minutes of the fifth anniver-
sary of the New Haven Baptist
Association, held with the Bap-
tist Church in Bristol, Oct. 6th
and 7th, 1830. 11 p. NRAB.
                               263
---- ---- State Convention.
Proceedings of the Connecticut
Baptist convention. Hartford,
1830. 20 p. MWA.   264

---- Delaware. Delaware Baptist Association.
Minutes of the Delaware Baptist Association, held at London
Tract, on the 5th, 6th, and 7th
of June, 1830. 8 p. NRAB. 265

---- Illinois. Edwardsville Association.
[Periodical] Extracts from the
minutes of the Baptist Conference, which organized the Edwardsville Baptist Association,
held at Edwardsville, Illinois, October 16th, and days following,
1830; with an address to the Baptists throughout Illinois. [Rock
Spring? 1830] 4 p. NRAB. 266

---- ---- Illinois Association.
Minutes of the Illinois United
Baptist Association, begun and
held at Wood River Church Meeting House, Madison County, Illinois, September 25th, 26th, and
27th, 1830. [Kaskaskia? 1830]
4 p. ISBHi.   267

---- ---- Wabash Association.
Minutes of the annual meeting
of the Wabash District Association, of Regular Baptists. Held
at Embarrass Church, Clark
county, Illinois; on the second
day of October, 1830, and days

following. [Pr. at the office of
the Western Sun, Vincennes, Indiana, 1830] 8 p. ICU; ISB; In.
                               268
---- Illinois and Missouri.
Friends to Humanity.
Minutes of three separate associations, held by the Baptised
[sic] Churches of Christ, Friends
to Humanity, in Missouri & Illinois, for the year 1830. Pioneer office, Rock-Spring, Illinois.
Pr. by A. Smith, 1830. 8 p.
ISBHi; NRAB.   269

---- Indiana. Coffee Creek As-
sociation.
Minutes. The Coffee Creek As-
sociation of Baptists met at Free-
dom meeting house, 4th day of
September, 1830. [Pr. by Arion
& Lodge, Madison] 3 p. InFrlC;
NRAB.   270

---- ---- Eel River Association.
Minutes of the Eel River District Association of Baptists,
held at Reserve meeting-house,
Parke county, Indiana, August
20th, 21st, & 22nd, 1830: together with their circular letter.
Lafayette, Pr. by J. B. Semans,
1830. 8 p. In.   271

---- ---- Flat Rock Association.
Minutes of the Flat-Rock Association of Baptists, began and
held at Blue River meeting house
Johnson county Ind. on the first
second and third days of October
A.D. 1830. 4 p. In; InFrlC.
                               272
---- ---- Lost River Association.
Minutes of the fifth annual
meeting of the Lost-River Association, held at Clifty-Church
meeting house, Washington county, Indiana, on the first Saturday,
Lord's Day, and Monday in
September, 1830. [J. Allen,
printer, Salem, Indiana, 1830]
4 p. InFrlC; NRCR-S.   273

---- ---- Union Association.

Minutes of the Union Association of Baptists, convened at Union meeting-house, Vigo county, Indiana, on the 18th of September, A.D. 1830. [Pr. at the office of the Vincennes Gazette, 1830] 3 p. InFrlC.   274

---- ---- White River Association.

Minutes of the White River Association, held at Salt Creek meeting house Lawrence county, Ia. on the 2d Saturday in August 1830. 4 p. InFrlC; TxDaHi.   275

---- Kentucky. Bethel Association.

Minutes of the sixth Bethel Baptist Association, held at Lebanon, Todd County, Ky. on the 25th, 26th and 27th days of September 1830. Russellville, Ky., Pr. by Charles Rhea, at the office of "The Weekly Messenger." 1830. 8 p. NRAB.   276

---- ---- Bracken Association.

Minutes of the Bracken Association of Baptists, held at Washington, Mason County, Kentucky, on the first Saturday in September, 1830, and continued by adjournment until the Monday following, inclusive. Maysville, Ky., Pr. at the Eagle Office, 1830. 8 p. NRAB.   277

---- ---- Drake's Creek Association.

Minutes of the tenth annual Drake's Creek Association; held at Mount Pleasant Meeting House, Warren County, Ky. on the 25th, 26th & 27th days of Sept. 1830. Gallatin, Pr. by Watlington & Word, 1830. 3 p. KyBgW.   278

---- ---- Elkhorn Association.

A narrative, of the proceedings of the last Elkhorn Association, held at Silas Meeting House, Bourbon County, Ky. on the 14th, 15th, and 16th days of August, 1830. 8 p. KyLoS. 279

---- ---- Franklin Association.

Minutes of the Franklin Association of Baptists, convened in Frankfort, Kentucky, on the second Friday and Saturday in July, 1830. Frankfort, A.G. Hodges, printer, Commentator office, 1830. 16 p. NRAB; OCHP; MWA.   280

---- ---- Gasper River Association.

Minutes of the nineteenth annual meeting of the Gasper's River Association, of United Baptists. Held at Providence Meeting House, (Warren County, Kentucky) on the 21st, 22d, and 23d days of August 1830. Russellville, Pr. by Chas. Rhea, 1830. 7 p. NRAB.   281

---- ---- Goshen Association.

Minutes of the 14th annual Goshen Association of Baptists; held at Mount Pleasant Meeting House, Ohio county, Ky. commencing on the 2nd Friday in October, 1830. 4 p. NRAB.   282

---- ---- Green River Association.

Minutes of the thirty first Green River Baptist Association, holden at Doughty's Creek Church, in Barren county on the second Saturday in August, 1830. ... Bowling-Green, Ky., Pr. by Samuel A. Atchison, at the office of the "Bowlinggren public advertiser," 1830. 7 p. CSmH.   283

---- ---- Licking Association.

Minutes of the Licking Association of Particular Baptists, held at Friendship Meeting-House, Clarke County, Ky. on the second Saturday in September 1830, and two succeeding days. [Pr. by H. Miller, 1830]

8 p. NRAB.   284

---- ---- Long Run Association.
Minutes of the Long Run Association of Baptists, held at
Drennon's Creek Meeting-House,
in the town of New-Castle, on
the 1st Friday and Saturday in
September, 1830. 4 p. NRAB.
                          285

---- ---- Nolynn Association.
Minutes. The Nolynn Associ-
ation of Separate Baptists; was
begun and held at the Republican
Meeting-House, in the county of
Hardin, and state of Kentucky,
on the 11th day of September, in
the year of our Lord, 1830.
Elizabethtown, Ky., Pr. by J.
Eliot, 1830. 4 p. NRAB.   286

---- ---- North Bend Association.
Minutes of the twenty-eighth
annual meeting of the North-Bend
Association of Baptists, 1830.
At the North-Bend Association of
Baptists, begun and held at Middle Creek meeting house, Boone
county, Kentucky, on the 3d Friday in August, 1830... [Gregg &
Dowling, printers, Lawrenceburgh
[sic] 1830] 4 p. ICU.   287

---- ---- South District Association.
Minutes of the South District
Association of Baptists convened
at Shawneyrun Meeting House,
Mercer County, Kentucky, the
3rd Saturday in August, 1830.
4 p. NRAB.   288

---- ---- Sulphur Fork Association.
Minutes. Of the 9th annual
meeting of the Sulphur Fork Association of Baptists held at
Friendship Meeting-House, Old-
ham County, Ky., on the 4th Friday, Saturday and Sunday, in
September, 1830. 4 p. NRAB.
                          289

---- Maine. Bowdoinham Association.
Minutes of the Bowdoinham
Association, held with the First
Baptist Church in Lisbon, on
Wednesday and Thursday, September 22 and 23, 1830; together
with their circular and corresponding letters. 8 p. NRAB.
                          290

---- ---- Cumberland Association.
Minutes of the nineteenth anniversary of the Cumberland Baptist Association, held at the Baptist Meeting House in New Gloucester, on Wednesday and Thursday, August 25 & 26, 1830.
Portland, Pr. at the Advocate
Office, 1830. 12 p. MeHi; NRAB.
                          291

---- ---- Kennebec Association.
Minutes of the Kennebec Association, held at the Center
Meeting-House, in Industry, on
Wednesday and Thursday, September 1st and 2nd, 1830. Being its first anniversary. Portland, Pr. at the Advocate Office,
1830. 8 p. NRAB.   292

---- ---- Oxford Association.
Minutes of the second anniversary of the Oxford Baptist Association, held at the Baptist Meeting-House in Bridgton, Wednesday and Thursday, Sept. 29 & 30,
1830. Norway, Pr. at the Observer Office, by Goodnow &
Phelps, 1830. 8 p. NRAB. 293

---- ---- Penobscot Association.
Minutes of the fifth anniversary of the Penobscot Association, held with the Baptist Church
in Dover, September 7th & 9th,
1830. Portland, Pr. at the Advocate Office, 1830. 16 p. NRAB.
                          294

---- ---- State Convention.
(Sixth Anniversary. Minutes
of the Maine Baptist Convention,
held at North Yarmouth, 1830)

24 p. Williamson, 683.   295

---- ---- Waldo Association.
(Minutes of the Waldo Association. 1830) Williamson, 683.
296
---- ---- York Association.
Minutes of the York Baptist Association, holden at the Baptist meeting-house in Lyman, Me. June 9 and 10, 1830. Portland, Day & Fraser, prs., 1830. 16 p. MNtcA; NRAB.   297

---- Maryland.   Baltimore Association.
Minutes of the Baltimore Baptist Association, held by appointment, in the meeting-house of the church at Upper Seneca, Montgomery County, Maryland, May 13, 14 & 15, 1830. 12 p. NRAB.   298

---- Massachusetts. Boston Association.
Minutes of the nineteenth anniversary of the Boston Baptist Association, held at the Second Baptist Meeting-House, Boston, on Wednesday and Thursday, Sept. 15 & 16, 1830. Boston, Lincoln and Edmands, prs. [1830] 24 p. MiD-B; NRAB.
299
---- ---- Convention.
Minutes of the Massachusetts Baptist Convention, held in Southbridge, October 27 & 28, 1830. Sixth anniversary. Worcester, Moses W. Grout, pr., 1830. 27 p. CBBD; MHi.   300

No entry.   301

---- ---- Old Colony Association.
Eighth anniversary. Minutes of the Old Colony Baptist Association, holden with the Central Church in Middleborough, Wednesday and Thursday, October 6th and 7th, 1830. Plymouth, Allen Danforth [1830] 16 p. MWA; NRAB.   302

---- ---- Salem Association.
Minutes of the first anniversary of the Salem Baptist Association, held at the Second Baptist meeting-house in Haverhill, on Wednesday and Thursday, Sept. 23 & 24, 1829. Boston, Pr. by Lincoln & Edmands, No. 59 Washington-St. [1830?] 20 p. MB; MNtcA.   303

---- ---- Worcester Association.
Minutes of the Worcester Baptist Association, held at Princeton, Mass. August 18 & 19, 1830. Eleventh anniversary. Worcester, Moses W. Grout, pr., 1830. 20 p. CBBD; MB; MWA.   304

---- Mississippi. Mississippi Association.
Minutes of the Mississippi Baptist Association, held at Jerusalem, Amite County, Oct. 16, 17, 18, 1829. [n.p., 1830] 3, 9 p. (printed with the minutes of 1830) LNB.   305

---- ---- Pearl River Association.
[Minutes of the Pearl River Baptist Association, ...1830] 15 p. LNB (t. p. wanting)   306

---- Missouri. Salem Association.
Minutes of the Salem Association, held at Samuel Boone's, in Callaway County, Mo. on the 4th, 5th and 6th September, 1830. [Columbia? Pr. by W.

Patton? 1830] 4 p. MoHi. 307

---- New Hampshire. Newport Association.

Minutes of the second anniversary of the Newport Baptist Association, held at Acworth, August 25 and 26, 1830. Newport, Pr. by French & Brown, 1830. 12 p. NRAB.   308

---- ---- Portsmouth Baptist Association.

Minutes of the second anniversary of the Baptist Association held at the Baptist Meeting House in Newtown, N. H. On Wednesday and Thursday Oct. 6 & 7, 1830. Exeter, J. C. Gerrish [1830] NhHi.   309

---- ---- Salisbury Association.

Minutes of the twelfth anniversary of the Salisbury Baptist Association, held at the Baptist Meeting House in Gilmanton, on Wednesday and Thursday, Oct. 13 & 14. Concord, N. H., Fisk & Chase, prs., 1830. 16 p. Nh.   310

---- ---- State Convention.

Proceedings of the fifth annual meeting of the Baptist Convention of the state of New Hampshire, held at the Baptist Meeting House in Cornish, on Wednesday and Thursday, June 23 & 24, 1830. Concord, Pr. by Henry Eaton Moore, for the Convention, 1830. 44 p. NRAB.   311

---- ---- Wendell Association.

Minutes of the Wendell Baptist Association, held at the Baptist Meeting House in Winchendon, Mass. ... Keene [N. H.], Pr. by J. & J.W. Prentiss, 1830. 12 p. MWA; MiD-B (15 p.)   312

---- New Jersey. New Jersey Association.

Minutes of the New-Jersey Baptist Association, held agree-ably to appointment with our sister church at Cape May, Sept. 7th, 8th & 9th, A. D. 1830. [Bridgeton, S. S. Sibley, pr., 1830] 12 p. NjR.   313

---- New York. Baptist Education Society of the State of New York.

Annual meeting of the Baptist Education Society of the state of New York, held at Hamilton, June 1, 1830. Syracuse [N. Y.], Pr. by L. H. Redfield, 1830. 24 p. CSmH; NN.   314

---- ---- Berkshire Association.

Minutes of the seventh annual meeting... held with the First Baptist Church in Lisle, on the 9th and 10th of June, 1830, with their circular and corresponding letters. Ithaca, Pr. by Mack & Andrus, 1830. 8 p. NRAB. 315

---- ---- Chemung Association.

Minutes of the Chemung Baptist Association, held at Milltown, Bradford County, Pa. with the Athens and Ulster Baptist Church. August 6th and 7th, 1830. Milton, Pa., Pr. at the office of the State's Advocate, 1830. 8 p. NRAB.   316

---- ---- Cortland Association.

Minutes of the third anniversary of the Cortland Baptist Association, held at Marcellus, Onondaga Co., Thursday and Friday, September 9 & 10, 1830. Utica, From the press of D. Bennett & Co., 1830. 12 p. NRAB.   317

---- ---- Franklin Association.

Minutes of the Franklin Baptist Association, convened at the Baptist Meeting House, in Huntsville, Otsego County, N. Y. June 16th and 17th, 1830. Cooperstown, N. Y., Pr. by Chauncy E. Dutton's Press, 1830. 16 p.

NRAB.   318   NRAB.   323

---- ---- Holland Purchase As-   ---- ---- Niagra Association.
sociation.   Minutes of the Niagra Baptist
   Minutes of the annual meeting   Association, convened at Shelby,
of the Holland Purchase Baptist   June 9th and 10th, 1830; With
Association. Held by appointment   their corresponding and circular
with the Baptist Church in Sar-   letter. Lockport, Pr. originally
dinia. Aug. 25 & 26, 1830.   by M. Cadwallder, 1830. 8 p.
Buffalo, Pr. by H. A. Salisbury,   NRAB.   324
1830. 12 p. MWA; NBu; NRAB.
                         319   ---- ---- Oneida Association.
---- ---- Hudson River Associ-   Minutes of the tenth anniver-
ation.   sary of the Oneida Baptist Asso-
   The fifteenth anniversary of   ciation, held with the church at
the Hudson River Baptist Associ-   Bridgewater, N. Y. , on Wednes-
ation...held in the Meeting-   day and Thursday, September 1
House of the Baptist Church,   & 2, 1830. Organized at the
Troy, August 4 & 5, 1830. New   church in Vernon Sept. 1820.
York, Pr. by George F. Bunce,   Utica, Pr. by D. Bennett & Co. ,
1830. 20 p. NRAB.   320   1830. 16 p. NRAB.   325

---- ---- Madison Association.   ---- ---- Otsego Association.
   Minutes of the twenty-second   Minutes of the thirty-fourth
anniversary of the Madison Bap-   anniversary of the Otsego Baptist Association, held at Manlius   tist Association, held at South
Square, Madison Co. , Tuesday   New Berlin, Chenango Co. , N. Y. ,
and Wednesday, September 7 & 8,   on Wednesday and Thursday,
1830. Utica, From the press of   August 25 & 26, 1830. Utica,
D. Bennett & Co. , 1830. 16 p.   From the press of D. Bennett &
NRAB; PPL.   321   Co., 1830. 16 p. NRAB.   326

---- ---- Missionary Convention.   ---- ---- St. Lawrence Associ-
   Proceedings of the ninth annual   ation.
meeting of the Baptist Missionary   The sixteenth anniversary of
Convention of the state of New   the ... convened at Gouveneur
York, held at Palmyra, Oct. 20   September 7 - 8, 1830. ...Can-
& 21, 1830, with the proceedings   ton, N. Y. , Pr. by W. W. Wy-
and report of the board, an ad-   man, 1830. 8 p. NRAB.   327
dress to the churches, constitu-
tion, list of life directors and   ---- North Carolina. Nawhunty
life members. Utica, Pr. by   Baptist Association.
Bennett & Bright, 1830. 24 p.   Minutes. [Halifax, Office of
IaHi; MWA; NRAB.   322   the Free Press, 1829-30] Tar-
                                        boro, 1830. NcU.   328
---- ---- New York Association.
   Minutes of the fortieth anniver- ---- ---- State Convention.
sary of the New-York Baptist As-   Proceedings of the Baptist
sociation, held in the meeting-   State Convention of North Caro-
house of the First Church in New-   lina; held in Greenville, March,
ark, May 25, 26, 27, 1830. New   1830. Newbern, John I. Pasteur,
York, Pr. at the Office of the   1830. 23 p. NcU.   329
Baptist Repository, 1830. 24 p.

---- ---- Toisnot Baptist Association.
Minutes. [Halifax, Office of the Free press] 1830. NcU.
330

---- ---- Tuckasiegee Baptist Association.
Minutes. Rutherfordton, 1830. NcU.
331

---- Ohio.
Minutes of the association of Baptists, held at Union Church, Jackson county, Ohio, Saturday, August 7, 1830. Portsmouth, Pr. at the office of the Western Times, 1830. 8 p. OClWHi.
332

---- ---- Eagle Creek Association.
Minutes, of the Eagle Creek Baptist Association: held at Bethel, on the 17th, 18th & 19th of September, 1830; together with their circular letter. Batavia, Ohio: David Morris, pr., 1830. 7 p. OClWHi.
333

---- ---- East Fork Association.
Minutes of the East Fork of the Little-Miami Baptist Association, held at the Bethel Meeting House, in Cincinnati, Ohio, on the 4th, 5th, and 6th September, 1830. Saturday, September 4, 1830. [Wm. J. Ferris, pr., Cincinnati, 1830] 8 p. NRAB; OClWHi.
334

---- ---- Grand River Association.
Minutes of the Grand River Baptist Association, held at Euclid, Ohio, September 8th and 9th, 1830; together with their circular & corresponding letter. Jefferson, O., Pr. by L. B. Edwards, 1830. 12 p. NRAB; OClWHi.
335

---- ---- Huron Association.
Minutes of the ninth annual meeting of the Huron Baptist Association, with the Eldredge

Church, Huron County, Ohio. August 13 & 14, 1830. Norwalk, Ohio, Pr. by Preston & Buckingham, 1830. 8 p. NRAB; OClWHi.
336

---- ---- Mad-River Association.
Minutes of the Mad-River Baptist Association, held at Buck-Creek, Champaign County, Ohio, September 18, 19 & 20, 1830. Piqua, O., Pr. at the Gazette Office, 1830. 8 p. OClWHi. 337

---- ---- Miami Association.
Minutes of the Miami Baptist Association, held at Tapscott's M. H. Warren county, Ohio, Sept. 10th, 11th, and 12th, 1830. Lebanon, Ohio, 1830. 7 p. NRAB; OClWHi.
338

---- ---- Owl Creek Association.
Minutes of the Owl Creek Baptist Assocation, Held at Bucyrus Church, Bucyrus Township, Crawford County, Ohio. Bucyrus, Pr. at the office of the "Western Journal." William Crosby, pr., 1830. 8 p. NRAB.
339

---- ---- Oxford Association.
Minutes of the Oxford Regular Baptist Association. Held at Oxford, Butler County, state of Ohio, on Friday the 30th of July 1830, and the two following days. 8 p. NRAB.
340

---- ---- Salem Association.
Minutes, of the Salem Baptist Association, held at Troy, Athens County, Ohio, on the 2d, 3d & 4th days of October, 1830. 8 p. NRAB.
341

---- Pennsylvania. General Association for Missionary Purposes.
Minutes of the third annual meeting of the Baptist General Association of Pennsylvania, for Missionary Purposes, held at the meeting house of the Fifth

Baptist Church, Phil. June 1, 1830, with the constitution and the annual report of the board of managers, &c. Philadelphia, Pr. by John Gray, 1830. 12 p. NRAB; PHi; ViRU.   342

---- ---- Juniata Association.
Minutes of the Juniata Baptist Association held in the meeting house of the Tonoloway Church, Bedford County, Pa., October 14, 15 and 16, 1830. Chambersburg, Pa., Pr. by J. Pritts [1830?] 15 p. NRAB.   343

---- Rhode Island. State Convention.
Minutes of the Baptist Convention of the state of Rhode Island and vicinity, held with the First Baptist Church. Providence, April 14, 1830. [Providence, H. H. Brown, pr. 1830] 8 p. ICN; NRAB; RHi; RPB.   344

---- ---- Warren Association.
Sixty-third anniversary. Minutes of the Warren Baptist Association held at the Second Baptist Meeting House in Newport, Wednesday and Thursday, September 8 and 9, 1830. Providence, Pr. by H. H.Brown, 1830. 15, [1] p. MB; NRAB; RHi.   345

---- South Carolina. State Convention.
Minutes of the State convention of the Baptist denomination in South Carolina at it's tenth annual meeting, held in Robertville, December 11, and continued to December 14, 1830. [William Riley, pr., Charleston, 1830?] 56 p. NN.   346

---- Tennessee. Concord Association.
Minutes of the Concord Baptist Association, held at Spencer's Lick Meeting House, Wilson County, September 4, 5 & 6, 1830.

[Nashville? 1830] 8 p. MWA.
                                    347
---- ---- Elk River Association.
Minutes of the Elk River Association Baptists, began [sic] and held at Mount Moriah Meeting House, Lincoln County, Ten. on the 2d Saturday in September, 1830, and days following. Fayetteville, T, Pr. by Ebenezer and J. B. Hill, 1830. [11] p. OCHP.
                                    348
---- ---- Nolachucky Association.
Minutes, of the Nolachucky Baptist Association, held at Slate Creek Meeting House, Cocke County, E. T. on the fourth Friday in Sept. 1830, and following days. Broadsheet.   TKL.
                                    349
---- ---- Salem Association.
Minutes of the Baptist Salem Association, began [sic] and held at Brawley's Fork Meeting House, Rutherford County, Ten., Saturday preceding the first Lord's day in October 1830, and two days following. [Murfreesborough, Pr. by Joshua D. Hill, 1830] 12 p. KyLoS.   350

---- Vermont. State Convention.
Proceedings of the fifth annual meeting of the Baptist Convention of the state of Vermont, held at the Baptist Meeting-House in Hinesburgh. Brandon, Vermont Telegraph Office, 1830. 28 p. MNtcA; NRAB; Nh; VtMiS. 351

---- ---- Woodstock Association.
Minutes of the Woodstock Baptist Association held at the Baptist Meeting-House in Grafton, on Wednesday and Thursday, September 29 & 30, 1830. Brandon, Vermont Telegraph Office, 1830. 12 p. Not located.   352

---- Virginia. Albemarle Association.
The minutes of the Baptist As-

sociation, in the Albemarle Dis-
trict; Met at the Pine Grove
Meeting-House, Albemarle County.
The second Saturday in May 1830.
Charlottesville, Va., Pr. by C.
P. & J. H. McKennie, 1830. 8 p.
ViRVB.   353

---- ---- Dover Association.
Minutes of the Dover Baptist
Association, held at Salem Meeting-House, Caroline County, Saturday, Sunday and Monday, the
9th, 10th, and 11th of October,
1830. 12 p. CSmH; DLC; NRAB.
                              354
---- ---- Ebenezer Association.
Minutes of the proceedings, at
the third annual meeting...22d &
23d days of October, 1830. 8 p.
NRAB.   355

---- ---- General Association for
Missionary Purposes.
Minutes of the General Associ-
ation of Virginia, for Missionary
Purposes. (Held in the Second
Baptist Church of the city of Rich-
mond, Saturday June 5th, 1830)
[Richmond, 1830?] 16 p. NRAB
                              356
---- ---- Goshen Association.
Minutes of the Goshen Baptist
Association, held at South Anna
Meeting-house, Louisa County,
Virginia: commencing on the 14th
of August, 1830. Pr. at the Her-
ald Office, Fredericksburg, Va.
15 p. NRAB; ViRVB; ViU. 357

---- ---- Ketocton Association.
The 64th annual publication.
Minutes of the Ketocton Baptist
Association, held by appointment
at Upperville, Fauquier County,
Va. August 12, 13 & 14, 1830.
[Samuel H. Davis, pr., Winches-
ter, 1830] 8 p. ViRVB.   358

---- ---- Portsmouth Association.
Minutes of the Virginia Ports-
mouth Baptist Association, held at
London Bridge Meeting House,

Princess Anne County, Virginia,
May 21, 22 and 23, 1830. Norfolk, Va., Pr. by Shields & Ash-
burn, 1830. 8 p. NRAB.   359

---- ---- Strawberry Association.
Minutes of the Strawberry District Baptist Association, convened at Moody's Meeting-House,
in the county of Bedford, October
3d, 1829... and, likewise, the
minutes of the same Association,
convened at Lynchburg, in the
meeting house of the First Baptist Church, May 29th, 1830...
Lynchburg, Pr. at the office of
The Virginian, 1830. 8 p. ViRU.
                              360
---- Washington, D.C. Columbia Association.
Minutes of the eleventh annual
session, of the Columbia Baptist
Association held by appointment,
at the Meeting-house of the First
Church in the city of Washington.
Aug. 19, 20, & 21, 1830. Washington, D.C., Pr. by Stephen C.
Ustick, 1830. 16 p.   ViRVB.
                              361
A Baptizer's letter. Boston,
Sabbath School Society [183-?]
4 p. LNB; MBAt.   362

Barbauld, Anna Laetitia (Aikin)
A discourse on being born
again. 2d ed. Pr. for the American Unitarian Association. Boston, Gray and Bowen, 1830. 12
p. (Tracts, 1st series, v. 2, no.
13).   MBAt; MH; MHi; BrMus.
                              363
---- Lessons for children. In
four parts. Part 2, being the
first for children of three years
old. Providence, Pub. by J.
Hutchens, 1830. 35 p. CtY. 364

---- ---- In four parts. Part 3,
being the second for children of
three years old. Providence,
1830. 41 p. RHi.   365

Barbé-Marbois, François Marquis de, 1745-1837.
The history of Louisiana, particularly of the cession of that colony to the United States of America; with an introductory essay on the Constitution and government of the United States. Tr. from the French by an American citizen. Philadelphia, Carey & Lea, [Griggs and Dickinson, prs.] 1830. xviii p., 1 l. [17]-455 [1] p. ABBS; CU; CoCsC; CtSoP; DeGE; FSa; GU; ICHi; ICN; IaU; In; KU; KyLo; LNHT; LU; MB; MBAt; MH; MHi; MWA; MdBE; MdHi; MeB; MiD-B; MoSU; NCH; NNS; NcD; NcU; NhHi; NjP; OClWHi; OkU; OrHi; PPL; RPB; ScU; TNJ; TxU; ViU; Wv; BrMus.   366

Barber, Edward Downing, 1806-1855.
"Popular excitements." An address delivered before the Antimasonic Convention holden at Middlebury, Vt., Feb. 26th, 1830. Pub. at the request of the Convention. Middlebury, 1830. 19 p. DLC; MB; VtHi.   367

Barber, John Warner, 1798-1885.
Interesting events in the history of the United States: being a selection of the most important and interesting events which have transpired since the discovery of this country to the present time. (2d improved ed. ?) New Haven, J. W. Barber, 1830. 312 p. Ct; CtSoP; CtY; IcHi; MB; MBAt; MH; MiD-B; RPB.   368

Barber, Jonathan, 1784-1864.
A grammar of elocution; containing the principles of the arts of reading and speaking. Illustrated by appropriate exercises and examples. Adapted to colleges, schools, and private instruction; the whole arranged in the order in which it is taught in

Yale College. New Haven, Pub. by A. H. Maltby [Baldwin & Treadway, prs.] 1830. [2], 344 p. CU; CtHi; CtHT-W; CtY; MB; MH; MWA; MWHi; NPV; NjP; OMC; PPL; RPA; VtNN.   369

Barbour, Philip Pendleton, 1783-1841.
Speech of Mr. Philip P. Barbour, of Virginia on the national road bill delivered in the House of Representatives, March, 1830. Washington, Pr. by Duff Green, 1830. 15 p. DeGE.   370

Barclay, Robert.
A treatise on church government, formerly called Anarchy of the ranters... Philadelphia, Pr. by Joseph Rakestraw, 1830. [1], 102 p. CSmH; CtHT; InRE; MH; NIC; OClWHi; PHC; PHi; PSC-Hi.   371

Barnard, Frederick Augustus Peter, 1809-1889.
A treatise on arithmetic, designed particularly as a text book for classes, in which the principles of the science are inductively developed, and rendered simple by modes of illustration. Hartford, Pub. by Packard & Butler, [George F. Olmstead, pr.] 1830. x, [2], 288 p. CSmH; CtHT-W; CtSoP; CtY; DLC; MH; NCH; PU.   372

Barnes, Albert, 1798-1870.
Questions on the historical books of the New Testament, designed for Bible classes and Sunday schools. New York, J. Leavitt, 1830-34. 4 v. NN.   373

---- The way of salvation; a sermon delivered at Morristown, N. J. Feb. 8, 1829. 2d edition. Philadelphia, Pr. by William F. Geddes, 1830. 24 p. CBPac; CtY; DLC; ICMcC; MBC; MH; NjPT; NjR; PHi; PPL; PPPrHi.   374

---- ---- Morris-town, N. J.,
Pr. by Jacob Mann, 1830. 33 p.
CSmH; CtY; MB; MiU; NN; NjPT;
NjR; OClWHi; PHi; PPPrHi.
                                    375
Barnes, John Harbeson.
    Tariff or rates of duties for
the year 1828, with all the alter-
ations made in the year 1830 on
tea, coffee, salt and molasses...
Collated and compiled by J. Har-
beson Barnes & Elijah A. Carroll.
Philadelphia, The proprietors,
1830. viii, [5]-9, [9]-131 p.
MB.   376

Barney, Mary.
    Letter from Mrs. Mary Bar-
ney of Baltimore, to Andrew Jack-
son, President of the United
States. Washington, Pr. by Peter
Force, 1830. 16 p. MB; MdBP.
                                    377
---- Mrs. Barney's letter to
President Jackson. Baltimore,
June 13th, 1830. 4 p. DLC; MB.
                                    378
Barney, William B.
    William B. Barney to his fel-
low citizens. [Baltimore, September, 1830] 19 p. MB; MWA.
                                    379
Barrett, Ezra.
    Sabbath school psalmody. Com-
prising an analysis of the rudiments of music, with directions
for the reading of verse and musical expression adapted to the
mutual or monotonal mode of instruction... 2d ed. Boston, Pub.
by Richardson, Lord and Holbrook, 1830. 55, [1] p. CtMW;
ICN; MB.   380

Barrett, G., Chaplain of the Connecticut State Prison.
    The boy in prison. Written
for the American S. Union and
revised by the Committee of Publication. Philadelphia, American Sunday-School Union [1830?]
22 p. BrMus.   381

Barrett, Solomon.
    A full grammatical analysis of
British classical poetry adapted
to Murray's English grammar,
exercise and key, and intended
as a supplement to the same.
Milton, Gazette Office, 1830.
24 p. NcU.   382

Barry, the dog of Saint Bernard.
New York, Munroe and Francis,
1830. 24 p. MH.   383

Barstow, Zedekiah Smith.
    A sermon preached at Dunbar-
ton, N. H. July 8, 1830, at the
installation of Rev. John M. Putnam, as pastor of the Congregational Church in that place...
Pub. by request of the people in
Dunbarton.   Concord, Pr. by Luther Roby, 1830. 32 p. CtY;
DLC; ICMcC; ICN; MBC; MH-AH;
MWA; MiD-B; NNUT; Nh; RPB.
                                    384
Bartlett, Montgomery Robert.
    The Clinton primer: a series
of first lessons, with cuts for
little children; designed to prepare them for entering upon the
study of the first part of the
Common school manual... By
M. R. Bartlett... New York, Pub.
for the author, 1830. 48 p. DLC;
MH.   385

---- The common school manual: a regular and connected
course of elementary studies...
In four parts. Compiled from
the latest and most approved authors. By M. R. Bartlett ... 2d
ed., rev. and cor. ... New
York, Pub. for the author, 1830.
CtHT-W; DLC; MH; NCH; NPV;
NRMA.   386

Bartlett, Robert.
    Restitution sermon. A ser-
mon delivered at Bradford, N.H.
Sabbath afternoon, October 3,
1830. Newburyport, French &
Brown, 1830, 12 p. MMeT-Hi. 387

Barton, David, 1785-1837.
In the Senate of the United
States. --March 17, 1830. Executive Session. Speech of Mr.
Barton, of Missouri, upon the
power of the President to remove federal officers; and upon
the restraining power and duty
of the Senate over an abusive
exercise of that power; and in
reply to the arguments of several members of the majority.
St. Louis, Pr. by Charless &
Pascall, 1830. 16 p. MoHi;
MoSHi; NN.   388

---- Mr. Barton's speech in Sen-
ate--February 20, 1830. St.
Louis, Charless & Paschall, prs.
[1830] 18 p. MoHi.   389

---- ... Speech of Mr. Barton,
of Missouri, upon the power of
the President to remove federal
officers; and upon the restraining
power and duty of the Senate over
an abusive exercise of that power;
and in reply to the arguments of
several members of the majority.
Washington, Office of the National Journal, 1830. 28 p. CSmH.
                                    390
---- Speech of Mr. Barton, of
Missouri. In Senate United
States. --Feb. 9, 1830. [Wash-
ington, 1830] 42 p. CSmH; DLC.
                                    391
---- Speech of Mr. D. Barton, of
Missouri; delivered in the Senate
of the United States, February
9th, 1830, in the debate which
arose upon Mr. Foot's resolution relative to the public lands.
2d ed. Washington, The National
Journal, 1830. 36 p. CSmH;
DLC.   392

Barton, Seth.
To the voters of the middle
congressional district of the state
of Alabama. [183-?] 1 p.
Broadside. DLC.   393

Barton, William Paul Crillon,
1787-1836.
Hints for naval officers cruis-
ing in the West Indies. Philadel-
phia, E. Littell; Carter & Hendee,
Boston; G. & C. & H. Carvill,
New York; E. J. Coale, Balti-
more; P. Thompson, Washington;
C. Hall, Norfolk; E. Thayer,
Charleston, 1830. 222, [1] p.
DLC; ICJ; MBCo; NIC; NNNAM;
NjP; PHi; PPC; PPL; PU. 394

Bates, Barnabas, 1785-1853
An address delivered at a general meeting of the citizens of
the city of New-York... Held at
Tammany Hall, Dec. 28, 1829.
To express their sentiments on
the memorials to Congress to
prevent the transportation of the
mail, and the opening of the post
offices on Sunday. New York,
Gospel Herald, 1830. 12 p. DLC;
NN; BrMus.   395

---- Character and exertions of
Elias Hicks in abolition of slavery. New York, 1830. PSC-Hi.
                                    396
---- Remarks on the character
and exertions of Elias Hicks in
the abolition of slavery, being
an address delivered... in Zion's
chapel New York, March 15,
1830... New York, Mitchell &
Davis, 1830. 20 p. MWA; MdHi;
NNFL; OClWHi; PHi; PSC-Hi.
                                    397

Bates, Elisha.
The retrospect: or, Reflections on the goodness of Providence, in the works of creation,
redemption, &c. Mountpleasant,
Pub. by the author, 1830. 24 p.
OClWHi.   398

Bates, Isaac Chapman, 1780-
1845.
Speech of Mr. Bates, of Massachusetts, on the Indian Bill.
House of Representatives, May
[19], 1830. [Washington, 1830]

24 p. CSmH; GU-De; MNt; MnH;
NN. 399

The battle of the Potomac with
the Malays. Written by one of
the crew... Boston, Hunt
[183-?] Bdsd. CSmH; MB.
400
Der Bauern calender auf 1831.
Von Samuel Burr. Cincinnati, N.
und G. Guilford; Oliver Farnsworth; Lancaster, Johann Herman, pr. [1830] 18 l. PPL (Imperfect) 401

Baxter, Richard, 1615-1691.
A call to the unconverted. To
which are added, several valu-
able essays. By Richard Baxter.
With an introductory essay, by
Thomas Chalmers, D. D. Boston,
Pub. by Lincoln and Edmands
[Stereotyped by Lyman Thurston
& Co.] 1830. 240 p. IC;
NRAB. 402

---- ---- Revised and slightly
abridged. New York, American
Tract Society [183-?] 135 p.
CSmH. 403

---- ---- New-York, Pub. by
the American Tract Society, D.
Fanshaw, pr. [183-?] 159 p.
CSmH. 404

---- ---- New York, The American Tract Society, [183-?] 176
p. CSmH; GAU; InCW; LNB;
MnU; ScU; BrMus. 405

---- ---- Richmond (Va.), Pub.
by Arial Works, stereotyped by
L. Johnson, Philadelphia, 1830.
240 p. IaDaU-Sem; NcU; Vi.
406
---- The dying thoughts of the
Rev. Richard Baxter... New-
York, Pub. by the American
Tract Society, D. Fanshaw, pr.
[183-?] 132 p. CSmH. 407

---- ---- Abridged by Benjamin

Fawcett... New York, American
Tract Society [183-?] 132 p.
CSmH. 408

---- Plain scriptural directions
to sinners how to attain salva-
tion: being an abridgement of
Baxter's Christian directory, vol.
I, chap. I. ... By Nathaniel Bur-
ton. Portsmouth, N. H., J. T.
Shepard, 1830. 47 p. CtY; GDC;
MB; MWA; MeBaT; Nh; BrMus.
409
---- The saints' everlasting rest,
by the Rev. Richard Baxter.
Abridged by Benjamin Fawcett,
A.M. New York, American Tract
Society [183-?] 453 p. DLC; IEG;
NIC; OO; PSC; PU; ViU. 410

---- ---- New York, American
Tract Society [183-?] 540 p.
MoU; NcWsW; ViU. 411

---- ---- D. Fanshaw, pr.
[183-?] 540 p. ViU. 412

---- ---- New York, American
Tract Society [183-?] 445 p.
CSmH. 413

---- ---- New York, American
Tract Society, Fanshaw, pr.,
[183-?] 271 p. ViU. 414

---- ---- Philadelphia, Stoddart
and Atherton, 1830. 288 p.
GU; NN; OC. 415

The Bay of Biscay. Friend dear
Friend. [A parody on Home]
Poor sailor boy. The lads of
the village. And Behave yourself
before folk. Philadelphia, Sold
by R. Swift [1830?] 8 p. DLC.
416
Baylies, Francis, 1783-1852.
An historical memoir of the
colony of New Plymouth... Bos-
ton, Hillard, Gray, Little and
Wilkins [Boston Classic Press -
I. R. Butts] 1830. 4 pt. in 2 v.
C; CtHT; CtSoP; CtY; DLC; GU;

ICU; Ia; In; KHi; MB; MH; MHi;
MNtcA; MWA; MdHi; MeB; MiD-
B; MnM; NBLiHi; NNUT; NjP;
OCHP; OClWHi; PHi; PPL;
RPJCB; Vi; VtU; BrMus.   417

Bayly, Thomas M.
The substance of several
speeches of Thomas M. Bayly,
delivered in the convention of Virginia; reported by A. J. Stanbury.
Richmond, Pr. by Samuel Shephard & co., 1830. 39 p. NcD.
418
Bayly, William.
A collection of the several
writings of that true prophet,
faithful servant of God, and suf-
ferer for the testimony of Jesus.
...Printed in the year 1676. Reprinted 1830: Philadelphia, Marcus T. C. Gould; New York,
Isaac T. Hopper, J. Harding, pr.
1830. viii, 24, 400 p. AU;
DLC; ICN; MH; MiU-C; NN;
NNUT; NcGuG; PHC; PHi; PSC-
Hi; PU; TxU; BrMus.   419

Bazeley, C. W.
The elements of analytical and
ornamental penmanship: To which
are added a variety of specimens,
calculated to inspire a true taste
for useful and elegant writing. 4th
ed., rev. and augmented. Philadelphia, Pr. for the author, and
sold by Robert Desilver; Carey &
Hart, and J. Grigg, 1830. 101 p.
KyBC; BrMus.   420

---- The juvenile scholar's geography; designed only for the
younger classes of learners but
calculated to advance them, by
natural and easy gradations, to a
perfect acquaintance with the elements of the science...Accompan-
ied with a miniature, but complete atlas.... Philadelphia, Pr.
for the author, 1830. 324 p.
MdBS; NNC; PPL.   421

Bean, James.

The Christian minister's affectionate advice to a married
couple. ...New York, The American Tract Society [Fanshaw, pr.]
[1830?] 28 p., 1 l. (No. 67)
MiU; PPL.   422

Beasley, Frederick.
A vindication of the fundamental principles of truth and order,
in the Church of Christ, from the
allegations of the Rev. William
E. Channing, D.D. Trenton, Pr.
by Joseph Justice, 1830. 144 p.
CtHT; CtY; DLC; MBAt; MWA;
NNG; NjPT; NjR; PHi; BrMus.
423
Beaumont, Augustus Hardin.
Adventures of two Americans
in the siege of Brussels, Sept.,
1830. ... Boston, 1830. MBAt.
424
The beauties and defects in the
figure of the horse. See Alken,
Henry Thomas.

[Beazley, Samuel] 1786-1851.
... The lottery ticket. And
Lawyer's clerk; a farce. In one
act. Correctly printed from the
most approved acting copy ...
To which are added, properties
and directions, as performed in
the principal theatres. New York,
and Philadelphia, Turner & Fish-
er [ca. 1830] 30 p. CtY; DLC.
425
[----] The Oxonians; a glance at
society, by the author of "The
roue." New York, Pr. by J. &
J. Harper, Sold by Collins and
Hannay, Collins & Co., G. and
C. and H. Carvill, O. A. Roar-
bach, White, Gallaher, and White,
A. T. Goodrich, W. B. Gilley, E.
Bliss; - Boston, Richardson,
Lord, and Holbrook, Hilliard,
Gray, and Co., Crocker and
Brewster, Carter and Hendee, R.
P. and C. Williams, and Wells
and Lilly; - Baltimore, Cushing
and sons, W. and J. Neal, Joseph
Jewett, and F. Lucas, Jr., 1830.

2 vols. CtY; MH; NCH; WU.
426

Beck, John Brodhead, 1794-1851.
An introductory lecture, de-
livered at the College of Physi-
cians and Surgeons of the City of
New York, Nov. 5, 1830. New
York, G. & C. & H. Carville,
1830. 30 p. CtHT-W; CtY; DLC;
DNLM; MdBM; NNNAM. 427

Bèclard, Pierre Auguste, 1785-
1825.
Elements of general anatomy;
or, A description of every kind
of organ composing the human
body. By P.A. Bèclard... Pre-
ceded by a critical biographical
memoir of the life and writings
of the author, by Oliver, M. D.
Tr. from the French, with notes
by Joseph Togno. Philadelphia,
Carey & Lea, 1830. 541 p. CSt;
CtY; GEU-M; GHi; ICJ; InU-M;
KU; KyLxT; LNOP; MBCo;
MdBJ; MnU; MoSW-H; MsCliM;
NBMS; NBuU-M; NNNAM;
NRAM; Nh; PPC; PU; ScCMe;
ViRA; ViRMC. 428

Bedell, Gregory Townsend,
1793-1834.
The life and travels of St.
Paul: written for the American
Sunday School Union. Philadel-
phia, American Sunday School
Union [1830] 197 p. GEU; ICU;
MB; MBC; MiU; NcWsM; NjP;
OO; PHi; ScCliTO; BrMus. 429

Beecher, Lyman.
A sermon, against the doctrine of Universalism, delivered
in the New Calvinistic Meeting-
House in Dorchester, Mass.
Wednesday Evening, March 7,
1830. Boston, Pub. at the Trumpet Office, G. W. Bazin, pr.
[1830] 18 p. MWA; BrMus. 430

---- Six sermons on the nature,
occasions, signs, evils, and
remedy of intemperance... 10th

ed. Boston, Pub. by Perkins &
Marvin [etc., etc.] 1830. 107
p. MB; MW; MWA; OMC; OU.
431

Beers Carolinas and Georgia almanack for 1831. By Elijah Middlebrook. Charleston, S. Babcock & Co. [1830] 18 l. MWA.
432

Beers' Louisiana and Mississippi
almanac for 1831. By Elijah Mid-
dlebrook. Natchez, F. Beaumont;
H. Millard; New Orelans, Geo.
W. Clark [1830] 18 l. LNSM;
MWA; Ms-Ar; NcD. 433

Beers's (Revived) almanac for
1831. By David Young. Poughkeepsie, P. Potter & Co. [1830]
N (22 l., t. p. wanting) 434

Bell, John.
An address delivered at Nash-
ville, T. October 5th, 1830, be-
ing the first anniversary of the
Alumni Society of the University
of Nashville. Pub. by request of
the Society. Nashville, Hunt
Tardiff & Co., 1830. 37 p.
CSmH; DNLM; KyDC; MH;
PPAmP; PPPrHi; T; WHi. 435

Bell, Solomon, pseud. See
Snelling, William Joseph.

Bell, Thomas, 1792-1880.
Anatomy, physiology and dis-
eases of the teeth. Philadelphia,
Carey and Lea [William Sharp-
less, pr.] 1830. [ii], xiv, 352,
[iv] p. CSt-L; CU-M; MBCo;
MdBJ; MdBM; MoS; NNNAM;
NRU-M; NbU; Nh; OU; PPiAM;
PPiU-D; TU-M; ViU. 436

Bellini, Vincenzo, 1801-1835.
Overture to the opera of La
Norma by V. Bellini arranged
for the piano forte by Ch. Zeu-
ner. With a flute, or violin,
accompaniment, ad libitum. Boston, Pub. by Parker & Ditson,
107 Washington st. [183-] 1 p.

1., 10 p. CSmH. 437

Belliol, Jean Alexis, b. 1799.
Memoir on a new mode of
treatment for the cure of herpet-
ic affections. Translated from
the 3d Paris ed., considerably
enl. Baltimore, J. D. Toy & W.
R. Lucas [John D. Toy, pr.]
1830. 94 p., 1 l. DLC; DNLM;
ICJ; MBCo; MdHi; NNNAM;
PPC. 438

Benedict, David, 1779-1874.
Historical and biographical
sketches of some of the early and
succeeding inhabitants of Pawtucket. [Providence? 1830?] 14
p. RHi; RPB. 439

Benjamin, Asher, 1773-1845.
The practical house carpenter.
Being a complete development of
the Grecian orders of architec-
ture... Boston, The author [etc.]
1830. 119 p. 64 plates. CSmH;
CtY; DLC; MBAt; MNE; MWA;
PPF; RPAt; ViU. 440

Bennett, Alfred.
The kingdom of Christ, distinguished from the kingdom of Caesar, in a discourse delivered on
the fourth of July, 1830, before
the Baptist Church and congregation in Homer Village. Utica,
Pr. by D. Bennett & Co., 1830.
16 p. NjPT; WHi. 441

Bennett, John, curate of St.
Mary's, Manchester.
Letters to a young lady, on a
variety of useful and interesting
subjects, calculated to improve
the heart, to form the manners,
and enlighten the understanding...
9th American ed., corr. New-
York, Pub. by J. A. Clusman,
1830. 3 p. l., [5]-288 p. MB;
NN; RPB; TNJ; WHi. 442

Bennett & Walton's almanack for
1831. By Joseph Cramer. Phil-

adelphia, Bennet & Walton; W.
Pilkington & Co., prs. [1830] 18
l. DLC; InU; MWA (2 varieties);
NN; PHC; PHi; PPL. 443

Bennington, Vermont. Bennington Academy.
Academy catalogue for summer
and fall term ending Nov. 23,
1830. Bennington, 1830. 8 p.
MH; OCHP. 444

---- Catalogue for the term ending April 1830. [Bennington] E.
C. Purdy, pr., April 27, 1830.
8 p. MH. 445

Bennington, Vermont. Bennington Seminary.
Bennington Seminary. Catalogue for the summer term, ending Nov. 16, 1830. [Bennington?
1830] 8 p. VtU. 446

Bentham, Jeremy, 1748-1832.
The ballot. Care for ballot-
ophobia--a species of pseustophob-
ia or morbid tenderness of con-
science. By J.B., M.D., S.P.
Prescribed to Henry Brougham,
esq., M.P. and other patients
driven to the verge of mental de-
rangement by terror of the ballot. [Richmond? 1830?] Bdsd.
ViU. 447

---- Jeremy Bentham to Henry
Brougham. May 22, 1830. Old
and familiar friend, The administration of justice in England
needs improvement... [New
York? 1830] folder ([1] p.) [At
head of title: From the Globe of
May 25, 1830] MB. 448

---- Principles of legislation
from the ms. of Jeremy Bentham
... By M. Dumont... Tr. from
the 2d cor. and enl. ed., with
notes and a biographical notice of
Jeremy Bentham and M. Dumont.
By John Neal. Boston, Wells &
Lilly; New York, G. & C. & H.

Carvill, [etc., etc.] 1830. 310 p.
AU; AZ; CU; IU; GU; KyLx; L;
LNHT; MB; MH; MWA; Mi; MoK;
NBu; NhD; NjN; NjR; O; PPi;
PU; VtB.   449

Benton, Thomas Hart, 1782-1858.
   Speech of Mr. Benton of Missouri, in reply to Mr. Webster:
the resolution offered by Mr.
Foot, relative to the public lands,
being under consideration. Delivered in the Senate, session 1829-
30. Washington, Pr. by Gales &
Seaton, 1830. 74 p. CSmH; DLC.
                             450
---- Speech ... on the bill to
provide for the abolition of unnecessary duties, to relieve the
people from sixteen millions of
taxes and to improve the conditions of the agriculture, commerce, and navigation of the
United States. Delivered in the
Senate of the United States, Feb.
23, 1830. Washington, Pr. by
D. Green, 1830. 12 p. CSmH.
                             451
Bentz, Louis.
   Elements of agriculture. Boston, 1830. MB.   452

Berean, pseud.
   A respectful appeal from the
injurious charge of a wish to
"pluck with unhallowed hands, the
crown from the head of the eternal," by a Berean. Raleigh,
Gales, 1830. 12 p. NcU.   453

Berington, Joseph.
   The faith of Catholics on certain points of controversy, confirmed by scripture, and attested
by the Fathers of the five first
centuries of the Church. Baltimore, Pub. by Fielding Lucas,
Jr. [John D. Toy, pr., 1830]
404 p. MdW; MoSU.   454

Berkshire Gymnasium.
   Catalogue... March, 1830.
[Pittsfield, 1830] 11 p. MBC;

MHi.   455

Bernard.
   Candid reasons, for not uniting with the Methodists, in five
letters to a brother. By Bernard. Utica, Pr. by Hastings &
Tracy, 1830. 24 p. NCH. 456

[Berquin, Arnaud] 1749?-1791.
   Louisa's tenderness to the little birds in winter... Concord
(N.H.), Pub. by Hoag & Atwood,
1830. 16 p. CtY; NhHi.   457

The best bargain (From Houls-
ton's series of tracts, London)
Boston, Peirce and Williams,
1830. 26 p. DLC.   458

[Bethune, Mrs. Joanna Graham)]
   The infant school grammar,
consisting of elementary lessons
in analytical method... New-
York, Sold by R. Lockwood, and
A. W. Corey, 1830. x, [9]-132 p.
NNC; NNG; RPB; BrMus.   459

The betrothed of Wyoming. See
McHenry, James.

Beveridge, Thomas.
   A sermon on the duties of
heads of families... 3d ed. Philadelphia, Griggs & Dickinson,
prs., 1830. 24 p. NbOP; PHi;
PPPrHi.   460

Beverstoc, George.
   The silver key, or A fancy to
truth and a warning to youth.
Boston, Leonard Deming [1830?]
Bdsd. KU.   461

Bible.
   Das apokryphische Neue Testament, eine sammlung aller
evangelien, episteln und anderer
schriften, welche in den ersten
vier jahrhunderten Jesu Christo,
seinen aposteln und deren gefähr-
ten zugeschrieben wurden, und in
dem eigentlichen Neuen Testa-

ment nicht enthalten sind. Aus den ursprünglichen manuscripten übersetzt und in einen band zusammen getragen. Nebst einem anhang. 1. amer. aufl. Lancaster, J. Bär, 1830. 484 p. DLC; MWA; MiGr; MiU-C; PHi; PLFM; PP; PPG; PPL; PPeSchw. 462

---- ... Assuring promises of Scripture. Baltimore, J. Harrod, 1830. 242 p. NN. 463

---- Die Bibel, oder die ganze Heilige Schrift des alten und neuen Testaments. Nach Dr. Martin Luther's ubersetsung. Philadelphia, Herausgegeben von Georg B. Mentz und Sohn Buchhandler, 1830. 900, 311 p. IaCrM; MB; NN; OO; P. 464

---- Biblia, das ist, Die ganze Heilige Schrift des Alten und Neuen Testaments, nach der deutschen uebersetzung D. Martin Luthers... Philadelphia, Kimber, 1830. 2 v. PU. 465

---- Crumbs from the Master's table; or Select sentences... New York, By W. Mason, [1830] 192 p. IU. 466

---- Devotional extracts from the Book of Psalms... See Bible. Selections from the Scriptures...

---- The Gospel of St. John, in Greek and English, interlined and literally translated; with a transposition of the words into their due order of construction... By E. Freiderici. New York, Pub. by G. F. Bunce, 1830. 176 p. CLCM; IEG; MB; MBC; MH-AH; NjPT; BrMus. 467

---- The Hieroglyphick Bible; or, Select passages in the Old and New Testaments, represented with emblematical figures, for the amusement of youth: De-

signed chiefly to familiarize tender age, in a pleasing and diverting manner, with early ideas of the Holy Scriptures. To which are subjoined, a short account of the lives of the Evangelists, and other pieces... 4th ed. Hartford, Pub. by Silas Andrus, 1830. 129, [4] p. CtHi. 468

---- The Holy Bible, translated from the Latin Vulgate: diligently compared with the Hebrew, Greek, and other editions, in various languages... With annotations, by the Rev. Dr. Challoner; together with references, and an historical and chronological index. Rev. and corr. according to the Clementine edition of the Scriptures. Baltimore, Lucas [1830] 2 v. in 1. DLC; MdBS; BrMus. 469

---- The Holy Bible, containing the Old and New Testaments, according to the authorized version, with explanatory notes, practical observations and copious marginal references by Thomas Scott. Stereotype edition, from the 5th London ed., with the author's last corrections and improvements. Boston, Pub. by Samuel T. Armstrong, and Crocker and Brewster. New York, J. Leavitt. Stereotyped by T. H. Carter and Co., Boston Type and Stereotype Foundry, 1830-32. 6 v. CtMW; DLC; ICU; IEG; MB; MH; Md; MeB; MiU; MoSW; NN; NbU; PPPrHi; TxU; ViU. 470

---- The Holy Bible containing the Old and New Testaments ... with explanatory notes, practical observations, and copious marginal references by Thomas Scott. Stereotype edition, from the 5th London edition, with the author's last corrections and improvements. Boston, S. T. Armstrong, 1830-31. 6 v. v. 5, has

imprint: stereotype ed. , with
the author's last corrections...
newly arranged and carefully
revised.   Exeter, N. H. , A.
Poor and J. Derby, 1830. v. 6,
Exeter, N. H. , J. Derby, 1831.
NN.   471

---- ---- Stereotype ed.   Boston,
Pub. by S. Bicknell.   T. Bed-
lington, agent. 1830. 486, 162 p.
PPL.   472

---- ---- Boston, Richardson,
Lord & Holbrook, 1830.   792 p.
NN.   473

---- ---- Stereotyped by B. and
J. Collins, New York.   Boston,
Pr. by John H. A. Frost, for
West Richardson and Lord, 1830.
Stereotype ed. 604 p. NBatHi.
                                 474
---- ---- Boston, Pub. by Waitt
& Dow, 1830.   486, 102 p.
MWHi.   475

---- The Holy Bible, containing
the Old and New Testaments: together with the Apocrypha.
Translated out of the original
tongues, and with the former
translations diligently compared
and revised.   With Canne's marginal notes and references to
which are added, an appendix.
Stereotyped by E. White, New
York.   Cincinnati, Pub. and sold
by N. & G. Guilford and Morgan
& Sanxay, and by the principal
booksellers of the western states,
1830.   [2], 570, 112, [2], 573-
770 p.   OC; OUrC.   476

---- ---- Claremont, N. H.,
Claremont Press [1830?] 486,
162 p.   NN; NNAB.   477

---- ---- Coopertown, (N. Y.),
Stereotyped, pr. and pub. by H.
& E. Phinney, 1830. 768 p.
NCooHi; NNAB; RNHi; WGr. 478

---- ---- Stereotype ed.   Exeter,
N. H. , Andrew Poor and James
Derby, 1830. 6 v.   See above no.
471. NhHi; OO.   479

---- ---- Hartford, Ct. , 1830-
31.   2 v. in 1.   MB; NIC.   480

---- ---- Hartford, Pub. by Si-
las Andrus, Stereotyped by J.
Howe, Philadelphia, 1830.   x,
729, 225 p.   MB; NN; NNAB.
                                 481
---- ---- Stereotyped by J.
Howe... Andrus and Judd, Hart-
ford [1830?] 681, [7] p. NNAB.
                                 482
---- ---- Hartford, Hudson &
Skinner, 1830. NN.   483

---- ---- New York, Stereotyped
by A. Chandler, for the American Bible Society, 1830. 832 p.
NHunt; Nj.   484

---- ---- Stereotype ed.   New
York, Stereotyped by A. Chandler, for the American Bible Society, D. Fanshaw, pr., 1830.
852 p. IEG; KyU; LNB; MWA;
MdHi; NN; NNG; NT; OHi.   485

---- ---- Stereotype ed.   Pr. by
D. Fanshaw, for the American
Bible Society, New-York, 1830.
669, [1] p.   NNAB.   486

---- ---- |Stereotype ed.] Aux-
iliary New York Bible and Common Prayer Book Society, New
York, 1830. 884 p.   487

---- ---- Stereotyped by J. Conner, Pub. by J. Emory and B.
Waugh for the Methodist Episcopal Church, at the Conference
Office, New York, 1830.   814,
[2], [247], [4] p. OC.   488

---- ---- [Stereotyped by J. Howe,
Philadelphia] Daniel D. Smith,
New York, 1830. 615, 192 p.
NN; NNAB; PPL.   489

---- Holy Bible with notes, by
George D'Oly... and Richar Mant
... New York, Society for Promoting Christian Knowledge, 1830.
2 v. NjMD.   490

---- ---- With Canne's Margin-
al References... Together with the
Apocrypha and Index. Also ref-
erences...Key Sheet of Questions
...Harmonies...and Highly Useful
Tables... By Hervey Wilbur...
The text corr. according to the
Standard of the American Bible
Society. [Stereotyped by James
Conner, New York] Pub. by
White, Gallaher and White, New
York, 1830. [2], 527, [1], 78,
168, 54, 32 p. InNovJ.   491

---- ---- Stereotyped by J. Howe,
Philadelphia. Philadelphia, Pub.
by Joseph M'Dowell and Kimber
& Sharpless, 1830. 660 p. PPL;
PPeSchw.   492

---- ---- Pub. by George W.
Mentz & Son, Philadelphia, 1830.
NN.   493

---- ---- Philadelphia, Towar,
J. & D.M. Hogan, and Hogan &
Co., Pittsburgh, C. Sherman &
Co., prs. 1830. 750, 238 p. Ct;
MH-AH; NN; NRHi; PU.   494

---- ---- Stereotyped ed. Wood-
stock, R. Colton and G. W.
Smith, 1830. 486, 162 p. MB;
NN (imperfect); VtMiS.   495

---- An index to the Holy Bible.
Hartford, Conn. [183-?] 11 p.
NN.   496

---- ---- New York [183-?] 10 p.
NN.   497

---- A manual. The Apostolic
epistles with amendments in conformity to the Dutch version.
Pub. by the translator, New
York, 1830. 189-295 [1] p.

NN; NT; NjP.   498

---- Das Neue Testament unsers
Herrn und Heilandes Jesu Christi
nach der Deutschen Uebersetzung
von Dr. Martin Luther... Zehnte
mit Stereotypen gedruckte auflage. Harrisburg, Pa., Gedruckt
und zu haben bey Gustav S. Peters, 1830. 511, 5 p. DLC;
OClWHi; PHi; PPL; PPeSchw.
                                   499

---- ---- Harrisburg, Herausgegeben von T. und F. Wyeth
[Stereotypirt Jon J. Howe, Phila-
delphia] 1830. 472 p. MiU;
MiU-C; PPL.   500

---- ---- Philadelphia, Georg
W. Mentz und Sohn [Stereotypirt
von J. Howe] 1830. 472 p. PPL.
                                   501

---- ---- Philadelphia, Heraus-
gegeben von Georg W. Mentz,
Buchhändler, Stereotyprit von J.
Howe, 1830. 504 p. CLCM;
CtMW; IEG; PPL; PPeSchw;
PRHi.   502

---- The new book of Chronicles.
(As rendered from the original
Hebrew, by a learned Rabbi.)
New York, Office of the Free En-
quirer, 1830. (In Owen's Popular
Tracts, No. 14) 24 p. In.   503

---- A new hieroglyphic Bible,
with 400 cuts. Munroe and Francis' edition, Boston, who are
publishers of a great variety of
books for children. Boston,
Sold by J. H. Francis, and C.S.
Francis and Co. New York
[183-?] 106 p. NN.   504

---- The New Testament of our
Lord and Saviour Jesus Christ.
With references, and a key sheet
of questions, historical, doctrinal, and practical, designed to
facilitate the acquisition of Spiritual knowledge, in Bible classes,
Sunday schools, common schools,

and private families. By Hervey
Wilbur. 13th ed., with harmony
and tables. Boston, Carter &
Hendee, 1830. 463 p. CBPac.
505

---- The New Testament of our
Lord and Saviour Jesus Christ:
translated out of the original
Greek; with the former translations diligently compared and revised. Stereotyped by B.& J.
Collins, New York. Boston, Pub.
by G. Clark, 1830. 312 p.
MBuT; NNC; PP.   506

---- ---- Boston, Pub. by
Charles Gaylord, 1830. 335, [1]
p. MHi.   507

---- The New Testament in the
common version, conformed to
Griesback's standard Greek text.
Boston, Gray & Bowen, 1830.
viii, 491 p. CBPac; CtY; GAGTh;
ICMcC; IEG; KyLxT; MB; MBC;
MH-AH; MWA; MoSpD; OClWHi;
WHi; BrMus.   508

---- The New Testament... [The
Pronouncing Testament] To which
is applied in numerous words,
the orthoepy of the Critical Pro-
nouncing Dictionary... by J.
Walker... To which is added an
explanatory key. By I. Alger,
Jun... [Stereotyped by T. H. & C.
Carter] Pr. and pub. by Lincoln
& Edmands, Boston, 1830. 292 p.
ICMcC; NN.   509

---- ---- Gardiner, 1830. 290,
[1] p. MWA.   510

---- ---- S. Andrus, Hartford,
1830. 222 p. (Appears to be NT
from 1830 Andrus Bible (No. 481)
without contents at end.) NN.
511

---- ---- Lunenburg, Mass.,
1830. 310 p. MWA.   512

---- ---- S. Babcock, New
Haven, [1830?] 288 p. CtY;

NN; NNAB.   513

---- ---- New York, American
Bible Society, 1830. 429 p. MWA.
514

---- ---- New York, Pr. by
Daniel Fanshaw for the American
Bible Society, 1830. 254 p. DLC;
NRAB; Nj.   515

---- ---- Philadelphia, Clark &
Raser, 1830. 416 p. CBPac;
PHi.   516

---- ---- Stereotyped by H. & H.
Wallis, New York, Pr. and pub.
by Wm. F. Geddes, Philadelphia,
1830. 201 p.   517

---- ---- Stereotyped by J. Howe,
J. M'Dowell, and Kimber &
Sharpless, Philadelphia [183-?]
270 p. NN.   518

---- A practical harmony of the
four Gospels arranged according
to the most approved harmonies
in the world of authorized version and accompanied with notes.
By Joseph Muenscher. Hartford,
D. F. Robinson and Co., 1830.
[8], 326 p. CBPac; RP.   519

---- The Psalms of David in
metre; translated and diligently
compared with the original text
... allowed by the authority of
the General Assembly of the Kirk
of Scotland, and appointed to be
sung in congregations and families. Albany, B.D. Packard,
1830. PP; PPPrHi.   520

---- The Psalms of David, imi-
tated in the language of the New
Testament, and applied to the
Christian state and worship.
Elizabethtown, N. J., Pub. by T.
C. Sayre, 1830. 282 p. MiToC;
NjP; OO.   521

---- ---- A new ed. in which
the Psalms omitted by Dr. Watts

are versified, local passages are altered...To the Psalms is added a selection of hymns. By Timothy Dwight, D.D. 2nd ed. Hartford, P. B. Gleason & Co., 1830. 342 p. MA; PPPrHi. 522

---- ---- Hartford, Pr. by P. B. Gleason and co. for Collins & Hannay, 1830. 580 p. CSmH; CtHT-W; CtY; IEG; MH; OCl. 523

---- ---- Stereotyped by Wm. Hager & Co., New York. New London, W. & J. Bolles and Collins and Hannay, 1830. NGH; NRMA. 524

---- Psalms, carefully suited to the Christian worship in the United States. ...A new edition, corrected. New York, Pub. by Daniel D. Smith, 1830. CSmH. 525

---- ---- Peekskill, N.Y., S. Marks & Son, 1830. 455, [1] p. CSmH; MoS; PSC-Hi; ViRUT. 526

---- The Psalms and hymns of Dr. Watts. Arranged by Dr. Rippon in one volume. Philadelphia, Clark & Raser, 1830. 906 p. PPPrHi. 527

---- La Sainte Bible, qui contient le Vieux et le Nouveau Testament... Edition Stéréotype revue et corrigée avec soin d'après les textes Hebreu et Grec. A. New-York, Imprimé avec des planches solides, aux Frais de la Société Biblique Americaine, Par Daniel Fanshaw, 1830. 788, [1], 207 p. KyBC; MeLB; NjPT; PPL. 528

---- Selections from the Holy Scriptures. Intended as Sabbath exercises for children. [Josiah Willard Gibbs] New Haven, H. Howe, 1830. 88 p. CtY; DLC; OO. 529

The Bible against slavery. See Weld, Theodore Dwight.

Bible anecdotes, illustrative of the value and influence of divine truth. Revised by the Committee of Publication of the American Sunday School Union. Philadelphia, American Sunday School Union, 1830. 34, [2] p. ICBB. 530

Bible Association of Friends in America.
First annual report of the Bible Association of Friends in America, read at the annual meeting held on the evening of the nineteenth of fourth month, 1830. Philadelphia, Wm. Brown, pr. [1830] 13 p., 1 l. PPL. 531

Bible biography, in the form of questions with references to the Scripture for the answers... 1st American ed. Boston, Pub. by Munroe and Francis, 1830. [3], 112 p. MBNEH; NjPT. 532

Bible history. J. Metcalf. Wendell, Mass., 1830. 18 p. DLC; NPV. 533

Bible pictures. Philadelphia, American Sunday-School Union [1830?] 16 p. BrMus. 534

Bible Society of Philadelphia.
Twenty-second report of the Bible Society of Philadelphia, 5th May, 1830. Philadelphia, Pr. by order of the Society, by John W. Allen, 1830. 29 p. MWA; PPAmP. 535

The Bible story book; taken from the Old and New Testaments. New-York, M'Elrath, 1830-31. 2 v. KU. 536

Bickersteth, Edward.
The Christian student, designed to assist Christians in general in acquiring religious knowledge; with a list of books suitable

for a minister's library by... E.
Bickersteth. From the 2d London
ed. Boston, Perkins & Marvin,
1830. vii, [1], 362, [1] p.
CBCDS; CtHT; CtSoP; GAGTh;
ICMcC ; KyDC; MBAt; MBC;
MWA; MoSpD; MsJMC; NBLiHi;
NCH; NNG; NNUT; NjPT; OO;
PPLT; PU; ViU.   537

[Biddle, Richard] 1796-1847.
Captain Hall in America. By
an American. Philadelphia,
Carey & Lea [Griggs & Dickin-
son, prs.] 1830. 120 p. CtY;
DLC; ICN; LNHT; MB; MH; MiD-
B; MnU; NN; NjP; OC; PHi;
PPAmP; PPL; BrMus.   538

Bigelow, Andrew.
Dispositions requisite for
Christian communion. A discourse, preached at Framingham,
Mass., March 12, 1830. at a
lecture, preparatory to a celebration of the Lord's supper.
Boston, Leonard C. Bowles,
1830. 19 p. MH.   539

Biglow, William.
History of Sherburne, Mass.
from its incorporation,
MDCLXXIV, to the end of the
year MDCCCXXX; including that
of Framingham and Holliston, so
far as they were constituent parts
of that town... Milford, Ballou
& Stacy, 1830. 80 p. DLC.   540

---- History of the town of Natick, Mass., from the days of
the apostolic Eliot, MDCL, to the
present time M. DCCC. XXX. Boston, Pub. by Marsh, Capen, &
Lyon, [Waitt & Dow's print.]
1830. 87 p. CtHT-W; CtSoP;
DLC; ICN; MBAt; MBC; MH;
MWA; MiD-B; MnHi; NBLiHi;
NN; Nh; OO; RPJCB; WHi;
BrMus.   541

The bijou minstrel: containing
all the choice, fashionable and

popular songs, as sung at the
concerts, in private circles, etc.
... Philadelphia, Turner &
Fisher [183-?] vii, [3]-446,
[28] p. RPB.   542

Bingham, Caleb.
The American preceptor im-
proved... Stereotype ed., Rev.
and corr. Boston, Hilliard,
Gray, Little, and Wilkins, 1830.
CtHT-W.   543

---- Child's companion... a concise spelling-book... Boston,
1830. CtHT-W.   544

Biographical sketch of General
John Adair. Washington, Pr. by
Gales & Seaton, 1830. 23 p.
CSmH; CtY; DLC; ICN; MB; MHi;
MWA; MdBE; PHi; PPAmP; PPL
(attributed to Adair, Robt.);
PPiU; ScC.   545

A biographical sketch of the celebrated Salem murderer, who for
ten years past has been the terror of Essex County, Mass.
Boston, Pr. for the author, 1830.
24 p. DLC; ICN; MB; MBAt; MH;
MoSpD; MoU; NIC-L; Nh.   546

Biographical sketches of eccen-
tric characters. Cooperstown,
N. Y., H. & E. Phinney, [183-?]
CtY; MH; NBuG.   547

Biography for young persons.
See Abbott, Jacob.

Biography of Master Burke the
Irish Roscius: The wonder of
the world; and the paragon of ac-
tors... Philadelphia, Shakspeare
press [1830] 11, [1] p. CSmH;
DLC; ICU; MB; MH; NN.   548

Birckhead, (James) and Co.
Pro-forma sales and invoices
of imports and exports at Rio de
Janeiro, with tables, remarks,
&c. By Birckhead & Co. Balti-

more, Pr. by James Lucas &
E. K. Deaver, 1830. 54 p. MH-
BA. 549

Birth-day present; from an affectionate friend. New-Haven, S.
Babcock, Sidney's Press, 1830.
[18] p. CtHi. 550

[Bishop, Sir Henry Rowley],
1786-1855.
Home! sweet home! Philadelphia, Pub. & sold by G. Willig,
171 Chesnut st. [183-?] Bdsd.
CSmH. 551

Bishop, John W. D. F.
Conversations holden between
a new and an old church clergy-
man. Watertown [N. Y.], Pr. by
W. Woodward, 1830. 34 p.
CSmH. 552

Bishop, Robert Hamilton.
An address to the graduates of
Miami University, September 30,
1830. Oxford, Ohio, Pub. by W.
W. Bishop, 1830. 12 p. ICU;
OCHP; OOxM. 553

---- A manual of logic. Oxford,
Ohio, Pr. at the Societies' Press,
1830. iv, 109 p. OOxM. 554

Blackstone, Sir William.
Commentaries on the laws of
England; to which is added an an-
alysis by Baron Field. New ed.
with practical notes, by Chris-
tian, Archbold, and Chitty; to-
gether with additional notes and
references, by a gentleman of
the New York bar. New York,
Collins & Hannay, Collins & Co.,
O. A. Roarbach, White, Gallaher
& White, G. & C. & H. Carvill,
Philadelphia; John Grigg [W. E.
Dean, pr.] 1830. 2 v. GS;
ICLaw; NcD; RPL; TxU-L. 555

Blair, Hugh.
An abridgement of lectures on
rhetoric and belles lettres, by

Hugh Blair, D.D. Greatly im-
proved by the addition of appro-
priate questions, by Rev. J. L.
Blake, A.M. ... Stereotyped by
David Hills, Boston. Concord,
N. H., Pub. by Marsh, Capen &
Lyon, 1830. 342, [2] p. ABBS;
CLSU; CtY; ICHi; KU; KyLoS;
MB; MH; MeHi; NNG; NjMD; OO;
TxU-T. 556

---- Cheap stereotype edition.
Lectures on rhetoric and belles
lettres, by Hugh Blair... To
which are added copious questions
and an analysis of each lecture.
By Abraham Mills. New York,
G. & C. & H. Carvill, 1830. 557
p. KU; KyDC; MH; NSyU; NjP;
NjR; PU. 557

Blake, John Lauris, 1788-1857.
A geography for children...
Boston, Richardson, Lord & Hol-
brook, 1830. 64 p. DLC. 558

---- The historical reader, designed for the use of schools and
families. On a new plan... Stereotyped by T. H. Carter & Co. Rochester, N. Y., Pr. by E. Peck
& Co., 1830. 372 p. MWA;
OClWHi. 559

---- ---- Concord, H. Hill &
Co., 1830. 372 p. ICN; ICU; MH.
560
Blessington, [Marguerite (Power)
Farmer Gardiner] countess of,
1789-1849.
Ella Stratford; or, The orphan
child. A thrilling novel, founded
on facts, by the Countess of
Blessington... Philadelphia, T. B.
Peterson [1830?] 1 p. l., 7-
116 p. DLC. 561

Bliss, Elam, ed.
Psalmodia evangelica A collection of Psalm and hymn tunes,
adapted to all the various metres
used in sacred poetry, to which
is prefixed an introduction to the

art of sacred music. New York,
E. Bliss, 1830. 352 p. CtHT-
W; PU.   562

Bloede, Karl August.
   Dr. F. J. Gall's system of the
function of the brain. New York,
1830. 92 p. PPCP.   563

Blomfield, C. J.
   A manual of family prayers.
2d American from the 8th London
ed. New York, Pr. and pub. by
the New York Protestant Episcopal Press, 1830. 36 p. Ct; MB;
NNG; NSyU.   564

Bluebeard, or, The fatal effects
of curiosity and disobedience.
Embellished with elegant copper-
plate engravings. Providence,
Cory, Marshall and Hammond
[1830?] 16 p. RPB.   565

Blunt, Edmund.
   Long Island Sound from New
York to Montock Point, surveyed
in the years 1828, 29, & 30.
[New York, Blunt, 1830]
[Chart] MB.   566

Blunt, E. & G.W., firm publish-
ers, New York.
   Blunt's charts of the north &
south Atlantic oceans, the coast of
North and South America, and the
West Indies. New York, E. & G.
W. Blunt, 1830. 1 pl., 14 maps
on 29 sheets.   DLC.   567

Boardman, Charles Adolph, 1788-
1860.
   The duties and embarrassments
of rulers. A sermon, addressed
to the legislature of the state of
Connecticut, at the annual election
in New-Haven, May 5, 1830. New
Haven, L. H. Young, pr. 1830.
20 p. CSmH; CtHi; CtY; DLC;
M; MB; NN.   568

Boardman, Henry Augustus.
   The almost Christian. A

premium tract. New York,
American Tract Society [1830?]
16 p. BrMus.   569

Bockius, Jacob, firm, Philadelphia.
   List of prices at Jacob Bockius's brush manufactory, no. 204,
North Second Street, Philadelphia.
Philadelphia, Pr. by D. Schneck
[ca. 1830] Bdsd. DeGE.   570

Bolmar, Antoine.
   A collection of colloquial
phrases on every topic necessary
to maintain conversation. With
remarks on pronunciation and use
of various words. By A. Bolmar.
A new ed. New York, Sheldon &
Co., 1830. ix, 280 p. CtHT-W;
ICMcC; KyLoS; TNJ.   571

---- ---- The whole so disposed
as considerably to facilitate the
acquisition of a correct pronunciation of the French. Philadelphia,
Carey and Lea; Richmond, C.
Bonsal and C. Hall; Norfolk, W.
H. Barrett [etc., etc.] 1830. vi,
216 p. DLC; LN; NcD; ViU.   572

---- Key to the first eight books
of the Adventures of Telemachus,
the son of Ulysses. Philadelphia,
Carey & Lea, 1830. [3], 273 p.
PPL.   573

Bolton, Mass. Evangelical Church.
   The confession of faith and
covenant, adopted by the Evangel-
ical church of Bolton, Lancaster,
Sterling, and Stow, March, 1830.
Lancaster, Carter, Andrews, and
company, prs., 1830. 15, [1] p.
CSmH.   574

A book full of pictures. With in-
teresting explanations to each.
New-Haven, S. Babock, publisher;
Charleston, S. Babcock & Co.,
Sidney's press, 1830. 23 p. (New-
Haven toy books - no. 2's. New
series. 2) CtHi; CtY.   575

Book of accidents; designed for young children. New-Haven, S. Babcock, publisher; Charleston, S. Babcock & Co., Sidney's Press, 1830. 23 p. [Toy books 1830 & 1. Sidney's Press] CtHi. 576

The book of famous kings and queens. Philadelphia, Peck and Bliss [183-?] 191 pp. MB; P. 577

The book of health; a compendium of domestic medicine, deduced from the experience of the most eminent modern practitioners... 1st American from the second London ed. Boston, Richardson, Lord & Holbrook, 1830. xii, 9, 179 p. CtY; ICJ; KyLx; MB; MWA; MeB; NGH; NNNAM; OClM. 578

Book of Mormon.
The book of Mormon: an account written by the hand of Mormon, upon plates taken from the plates of Nephi. ... By Joseph Smith, junior, Author and proprietor. Palmyra [N.Y.], Pr. by E. B. Grandin, for the author, 1830. 588, [2] p. ArCH; CSmH; CtHi; DLC; ICN; IHi; IaHi; KU; MH; MWA; MeLB; MiD; MnSJ; NN; NRHi; NbOP; OCHP; OClWHi; PP; PPL; PU; UU; BrMus. 579

Book of nullification. See Memminger, Christopher Gustavus.

Booth, Abraham.
Vindication of the Baptists from the charge of bigotry in refusing Communion at the Lord's table to Paedobaptists. (Tract No. 126) Abridged for the Baptist general tract society. Philadelphia, Baptist General Tract Society [183-?] 76 p. NN; NRAB. 580

Borgo, C., S.J.
Meditations on the Sacred Heart of Jesus Christ, being those taken from A Novena in preparation for the feast of the same, by Father C. Borgo, S.J. Translated from the Italian. Baltimore, Pub. by Lucas Bros., [ca. 1830] 48 p. MdW. 581

Bossuet, Jacques Bénigne, pb.
An exposition of the doctrines of the Catholic Church... With notes by the Rev. John Fletcher. Baltimore, Fielding Lucas, Jr., 1830. 248 p. MB. 582

---- ---- Philadelphia, Pub. by Eugene Cummiskey, 1830. 128 p. MdW; NNG. 583

Boston, Thomas, 1676-1732.
The crook in the lot; or, The sovereignty and wisdom of God, in the afflictions of men, displayed; together with a Christian deportment under them. Being the substance of several sermons on Eccl. VII. 13, Prov. XVI. 19, and Peter V. 6. Pittsburgh, Johnston & Stockton, 1830. 132 p. NNG; OClWHi; PPi. 584

---- Human nature in its fourfold state. Philadelphia, [3d. Philadelphia ed.] Towar and J. & D.M. Hogan; Russel & Martien, prs., 1830. 400 p. ArBaA; CBPac; MB; MH; NCH; OrU; P. 585

Boston.
An address to the Board of aldermen, and members of the Common council, of Boston, on the organization of the city government, January 4, 1830... Boston, J.H. Eastburn, city printer, 1830. 11 p. CSmH. 586

---- An address to the members of the city council on the removal of the municipal government to the old state house. Boston, John H. Easturn, city pr., 1830. 15 p. CSmH; Ct; CtHT-W; CtSoP; DLC; DeGE; ICME; MB;

MBAt; MBC; MH; MHi; MMeT;
MeHi; MiD-B; MoS; NNC; OCHP;
OClWHi; PHi; PPL; BrMus. 587

---- Eighteenth annual report of
the receipts and expenditures of
the city of Boston, and county of
Suffolk, May 1, 1830. Boston,
J. H. Eastburn, 1830. 52 p.
MiD-B; NCH.   588

---- General abstract of the bill
of mortality for the city of Boston, from January 1, 1829, to
January 1, 1830. Agreeably to
the records kept at the Health
Office... Samuel H. Hewes, Superintendent of Burial Grounds
[Boston, 1830] Bdsd. MB. 589

---- Rules and orders of the
Common council of the city of
Boston. Boston, J. H. Eastburn,
city pr., 1830. 46 p. CU. 590

---- Rules and regulations for
the pilotage of Boston Harbor,
1830. Boston, Dutton & Wentworth, 1830. 15 p. DLC; MWA.
591
---- Ward No. 10. A list of
qualified voters. 1830-31. [Bos-
ton, 1830] 2 p. DLC.   592

Boston Athenaeum. Gallery.
Catalogue of pictures in the
Athenaeum Gallery. [Boston,
John H. Eastburn, pr., 1830]
24 p. Cover titie: The fourth ex-
hibition in the Gallery of the
Boston Athenaeum, 1830. Note.
Lists 224 items. MB; MBAt;
MHi; MWA; NjR.   593

---- ---- [Boston, John H. Eastburn, pr., 1830] 24 p. Cover
title: The fourth exhibition in the
Gallery of the Boston Athenaeum,
1830. Note. Lists 225 items.
MBAt.   594

---- Illustrations of the Athenaeum Gallery of paintings. Bos-

ton, Frederic S. Hill, 1830. 42
p. MBAt; NBuG.   595

Boston Baptist Female Society
for Missionary Purposes.
Constitution of the Boston Baptist Female Society for Missionary Purposes. Organized Oct. 9,
1800. Constitution altered and
amended, December, 1829. Boston, Pr. by True & Greene,
1830. 8 p. MiD-B.   596

Boston Baptist Sabbath School
Union.
First annual report of the
board of the Boston Baptist Sab-
bath School Union. Presented
Thursday evening, March 11,
1830. Boston, Press of Putnam
& Hunt, 1830. 23, [1] p. NRAB;
NjR.   597

Boston. Conservative Fire Society.
Conservative Fire Society.
[List of members] [Boston] Dutton & Wentworth, prs., January
1, 1830. Bdsd. MB.   598

The Boston directory. Boston,
Charles Stimpson, Jr., 1830.
30, 330 p. MB; MBAt; MBNEH;
MHi; MWA.   599

Boston Evening Bulletin.
New year's address, from the
carriers of the Boston Evening
Bulletin and United States Republican... January, 1st, 1830. [Bos-
ton, 1830] Bdsd. MB.   600

Boston Female Monitorial School.
Third report of the instructer
of the Female Monitorial School,
communicated to the trustees and
proprietors, at their sixth annual meeting, July 6, 1830. Boston, Pub. by Munroe & Francis,
1830. 23 p. MBAt; NIC.   601

Boston Free Press.
The carrier of the Boston

Free Press, to its friends and
patrons, respectfully presents
the compliments of the season,
with the following address...
January 1, 1830. [Boston, 1830]
Bdsd. MB.   602

Boston. House of Industry.
Seventh annual report of the
directors of the House of Industry, April 1, 1830. [Boston,
1830] 23 p. MHi.   603

---- House of Reformation.
Rules for the House of Reformation, at South Boston. Reported by the Chaplain, E. M. P.
Wells, to the Board of Directors,
and by them approved. Boston,
John H. Eastburn, city printer,
1830. 12 p. PPL.   604

Boston Library Society.
Catalogue of books in the Boston Library, June, 1830, kept in
the room over the arch in Frank-
lin-place. Boston, Pr. by John
H. Eastburn, 1830. 107 p. MB;
MH; OClWHi; RPAt; WHi.   605

Boston Masonic Mirror.
Strictures on seceding Masons,
with reviews of the anti-masonic
characters of Pliny Merrick...
Rev. Joel Mann...Rev. Thos. M.
Smith...Elder David Bernard...
from Boston Masonic Mirror.
Boston, Pr. and pub. by Carr &
Page, 1830. 32 p. DLC; IaCrM;
MH; MWA; PPFM.   606

Boston Mechanics Institution.
The third annual report of the
Board of managers of the Boston
Mechanics Institution; with the
Constitution; by-laws, and a list
of members. Boston, Pr. by
Samuel N. Dickinson, 1830. 23
p. MB; MBAt; MWA.   607

Boston Medical Association.
Boston medical police; rules
and regulations of the Boston

Medical Association. Boston,
Press of J. H. Eastburn, 1830.
26 p. CtHT-W; MBCo; MHi;
NNNAM; WHi.   608

Boston. Old South Church.
Centennial celebration. Order
of exercises in the Old South
Church, Sept. 17, 1830. [Boston]
J. H. Eastburn, city pr., [1830]
Bdsd. MB.   609

Boston Patriot and Chronicle.
The carrier's address to the
patrons of the Patriot and Chronicle, on the commencement of
the year 1830... Boston, January
1, 1830. [Boston, 1830] Bdsd.
MB.   610

Boston. Penitent Female's Refuge. See Refuge in the city of
Boston.

The Boston picture books. [Bos-
ton] Pr. by Munroe and Francis
[1830?] [16] p. DLC; MB; NN.
                            611

Boston reading lessons for primary schools. Boston, Richardson, Lord & Holbrook, 1830.
142, [2] p. CSmH; M.   612

Boston Sabbath School Union.
Celebration of American Inde-
pendence by the Boston Sabbath
School Union, at Park Street
Church, July 5, 1830, Order of
Exercises [Boston, 1830] Bdsd.
MHi.   613

Boston Society for the Diffusion
of Useful Knowledge.
The first annual report of the
board of managers of the Boston
Society for the Diffusion of Useful Knowledge. Presented at the
annual meeting April 2, 1830.
Boston, Office of the Daily Advertiser, W. L. Lewis, pr., 1830.
16 p. MBAt; MH; MHi; MWA;
MoS; NIC; PPL.   614

Boston Society for the Moral and Religious Instruction of the Poor.
Thirteenth annual report of the directors to the Boston Society for the Religious and Moral Instruction of the Poor. Dec. 30, 1829. Boston, Pr. by Crocker & Brewster, 1830. 8 p. MB. 615

Boston Sunday School Union.
The annual reports of the Boston Sunday School Society for the year 1829. Boston, Leonard C. Bowles, Press of M. Pratt, 1830. 36 p. ICU. 616

Boston two hundred years ago; or, The romantic story of Miss Ann Carter, (Daughter of one of the first settlers,) and the celebrated Indian chief, Thundersquall; with many humorous reminiscences and events of olden time. Boston, 1830. 16 p. CSmH; DLC; MH; MWA; NN; PU. 617

Boston. Union Church.
Confession of faith and covenant. Also a brief history of Union Church, Essex Street... Boston, Pr. by E. K. Allen, 1830. 36 p. CtY; ICN; MB; MH-AH; MHi; MWA; MiD-B; NjPT; WHi. 618

---- West Church.
Catalogue of the Library of the West Parish Association in Boston. Boston, 1830. MHi. 619

Bostwick, Henry.
A geographical chart of ancient Italy and Rome exhibiting their various names and divisions, with an account of its inhabitants, colonies, subjugations, &c. New York, Sleight & Robinson, prs., 1830. 1 p. DLC. 620

[Botsford, Margaret] fl. 1812-1828.
The reign of reform, or, Yankee Doodle court. By a lady. Baltimore, Pr. for the authoress, 1830. 146 p. CSmH; CtY; DLC; IU; MB; MBAt; MH; MdHi; NNG; OClWHi; PPL; RPB; TxU. 621

[----] ---- Continuation of Vol. II. Philadelphia, Pr. for the authoress, 1830. 24 p. OClWHi. 622

The Bouquet, or Spirit of English poetry. 3d ed. Philadelphia, T. T. Ash [183-?] 256 p. CtY; DLC; MH; RPB. 623

Bourdaloue, Louis, S.J., 1632-1704.
A spiritual retreat, for eight successive days: with meditations and considerations, for ecclesiastics, religious, and all Christians in every state of life. Translated from the French by Bourdaloue, a Father of the Society of Jesus. Baltimore, Pub. by F. Lucas, Jun. [183-?] xii, 327 p. DGU; MWH; MiD. 624

Bourne, George.
The picture of Quebec...2d ed. New York, Bourne, Depository of arts, 1830. 109 p. ICN; MB; MWA; NNA; PHi; RHi; BrMus. 625

Bowdoin College. Brunswick, Me.
Catalogue of the library of the Medical School of Maine, at Bowdoin College, February, 1830. Brunswick, Pr. at the Bowdoin Press by J. Griffin, 1830. 84, [1] p. MeHi; WU. 626

---- Catalogue of the officers and students of Bowdoin College and the Medical School of Maine. Brunswick, Me., Joseph Griffin, pr., 1830. 20 p. Me; MeB; MeHi. 627

---- Laws of Bowdoin College, in the state of Maine. Brunswick, Bowdoin Press, J. Griffin, 1830. 30 p. MH-AH; MeHi. 628

---- Athenaean Society.
Catalogue of the library of the Athenaean Society of Bowdoin College, August, 1830. Brunswick, Joseph Griffin, 1830. 48 p. MeB. 629

[Bowen, Abel], 1790-1850, comp.
The naval monument, containing official and other accounts of all the battles fought between the navies of the United States and Great Britain during the late war; and an account of the war with Algiers. Boston, Pub. by George Clark, 1830. xiv, [2], 326, [2] p. CSmH; CtSoP; IC; ICHi; KyLoF; LN; LNHT; NIC; NN; PHi. 630

Boyer, Abel, 1667-1720.
Boyer's French [French-English. English-French] dictionary: comprising all the additions and improvements of the latest Paris and London editions, with a very large number of useful words and phrases now first selected from the modern dictionaries of Boiste, Wailly, Catineau and others... Boston, Hilliard, Gray, Little and Wilkins, 1830. 530, 250 p. C-S; DLC; MNBedf; NcD; OClW. 631

Boylston, Mass. Congregational Church.
The confession of faith and covenant of the Congregational Church in Boylston... Worcester [Mass.] Pr. by S. H. Colton & Co., 1830. 12 p. CSmH; MBC. 632

Bracebridge Hall. See Irving, Washington.

Bradburn, Eliza Weaver.
The story of Paradise Lost, for children. By Eliza W. Bradburn. Portland, Shirley and Hyde, 1830. 143 p. IU; MH; NNC; PU. 633

Bradford, Alden, 1765-1843.
A discourse delivered before the Society for Propagating the Gospel among the Indians and Others, in North America. Nov. 4, 1830. Boston, John Putnam, 1830. 51, [2] p. CBPac; CtHT-W; CtY; ICMe; MB; MBAt; MBC; MH-AH; MHi; MWA; MeB; MeHi; MiD-B; OClWHi; PHi; PPAmP; RPB; WHi; BrMus. 634

Bradford, Samuel, pub.
Prospectus. History of the Indian tribes of North America, with biographical sketches and anecdotes of the principal chiefs. Embellished with 120 portraits, from the Indian gallery in the Department of War at Washington. Philadelphia, Samuel Bradford, 1830. 2 p. PPAmP. 635

Brainard, John Gardiner Calkins, 1796-1828.
...Fort Braddock letters; by J. G. C. Brainard. Washington, D. C., Pr. & pub. by Charles Galpin, 1830. iv, [7]-97 p. (Fugitive tales, no. 1) CtY; DLC; NN. 636

Brainard, William Fowler.
Masonic lecture, spoken before the brethren of Union Lodge, New-London, on the nativity of St. John the Baptist, June 24, A. L. 5825. 3rd ed. Boston, Repr. for John Marsh, 1830. 16 p. CtY; MH; MWA; NNFM; PPFM; PPL; BrMus. 637

Braintree, Mass. First Congregational Church.
Historical notices of the First Congregational Church in Braintree. From its organization in 1707, to the beginning of 1830... Boston, T. R. Marvin, pr., 1830. 24 p. CtY; MB; MBC; MHi; NBLiHi. 638

Brashears, Noah.
Columbia's wreath; or, Miscellaneous poems, composed between the years 1814, and 1830,

by N. Brashears. 2d ed., with
corrections and additions... City
of Washington, Pub. for the author by S. A. Elliot, pr., 1830.
120 p. DLC; MWH; PU; RPB.
639
Brereton, John A.
Florae columbianae prodromus, exhibens enumerationem
plantarum quae hactenus explor-
atae sunt; or A prodromus of the
Flora columbiana, exhibiting a
list of all the plants which have
as yet been collected. Comp. by
John A. Brereton... Washington,
Pr. by Jonathan Elliot, 1830.
86 p. CtHT-W; CtY; DLC; DeWi;
IU; InNd; KU; MB; MH; MdBJ;
MoSB; NBLiHi; NNNAM; NjR;
OClM; OO; PPL (Cover dated
1831, Pr. for George Temple-
man); PU; RPB; WHi.   640

Brewer, Josiah, 1796-1872.
A residence at Constantinople
in the year 1827 with notes to the
present time. 2nd ed. New Haven,
Durrie & Peck [Pr. by Baldwin
& Treadway] 1830. 372 p. CU; Ct;
CtHT; CtY; KyDC; MA; MBL;
MDeeP; MWA; MdBE; NCH; NR;
RHi.   641

---- ---- 2d ed. New-Haven,
Durrie and Peck, 1830. 384 p.
CSmH.   642

Bridgen, Thomas Attwood.
The office of surrogate, and
executors and administrators
guide; containing the whole ecclesiastical law, and practice of
the state of New York; also an
entire new set of forms, adapted
to all cases of practice in the
Surrogate courts. Albany, G. J.
Loomis, [etc.] 1830. 128, xii,
78, v, p. CU; CU-Law; MWA;
NN; NUtSC; NjR.   643

A brief compendium of mythology,
for the use of children and
schools. By a lady, authoress

of a Compendium of geography.
Reading [Pa. ?], C. Ingall, etc.
[183-?] MH.   644

A brief history and defence of
the drama. See Jewell, Isaac
Appleton.

A brief investigation of the
causes which created the late
controversy on the election of
mayor [Walter Bowne]. By a
Democratic member of the Common Council... New-York, 1830.
24 p. DLC; KyDC; MB; MiD-B;
NBuG; OCHP.   645

A brief memoir of Horace Bassett Morse, designed for Sabbath
School Libraries; by a teacher.
Portsmouth, N.H., J. W. Shepard, 1830. 96 p. MBC.   646

A brief sketch of the trial of
William Lloyd Garrison. See
Garrison, William Lloyd.

Brinley, Francis, Jr., b. 1800.
An address delivered before
the Franklin Debating Society in
Chauncy Hall, January 17, 1830,
being the celebration of their
seventh anniversary and the birth-
day of Franklin. Boston, I. R.
Butts, 1830. 16 p. MB; MH;
MWA; NCH; BrMus.   647

Brinsmade, Horatio Nelson, 1798-
1879.
Early history of New England,
containing a brief account of the
most interesting events connected
with the settlement of the country. Adapted to the capacities
of children. Hartford, Pub. by
Goodwin & Co., 1830. 71 p.
CtHi.   648

---- Memoir of Isabella Campbell of Rosneath, Scotland.
Abridged for Sabbath schools...
Hartford, Packard & Butler,
1830. 161 p. Ct; PPAmS;

RPB.   649

British opinions. See Everett,
Alexander Hill.

Brooklyn directory for the year
1830. By Lewis Nichols. Brooklyn, A. Spooner, pr., June 1830.
87, 1 p. NB; NBLiHi; NHi; NN.
                             650
Brooklyn. St. Cecilia Society.
Constitution and by-laws of
the St. Cecelia Society of Brooklyn. Brooklyn, Pr. by A. Spooner, 1830. 8 p. NBLiHi.   650a

Brown, Alling, [fl. 1823], comp.
Musical cabinet, or New Haven
collection of sacred music. 2nd
ed. New Haven, Durrie & Peck,
1830. xix, 230 p. CtHT-W;
CtY; MHi; RPB.   651

[Brown, Bartholomew]
Templi Carmina. Songs of the
Temple, or Bridgewater collec-
tion of sacred music. 20th ed.
Boston, Richardson & Lord, 1830.
349 p. CSmH; ICN; OO; VtVe.
                             652
Brown, David Paul, 1795-1872.
Sertorius: or, The Roman
patriot. A tragedy. By David
Paul Brown. Philadelphia, E. L.
Carey & A. Hart; Mifflin &
Parry, prs., 1830. 87 p. CSmH;
CtHT; DLC; ICU; MB; MBAt;
MHi; MdBE; MiD; MnU; NIC;
NcU; PHi; PPDrop; PPL; TxU.
                             653
---- ---- Philadelphia, Pr. by
Mifflin & Parry, 1830. 87 p.
DLC; ICN; ICU; IaU; KU; MH;
MdBE; MiU; NNC; NjP; NjR; OCl;
P; PP; PPL; PSC-Hi; PU; RPB.
                             654
Brown, Goold, 1791-1857
The institutes of English
grammar, methodically ar-
ranged; ... and a key to the oral
exercises: to which are added
four appendixes... 4th ed. New-
York, Pub. by Samuel Wood &

Sons, R. & G. S. Wood, prs.,
1830. 311, [1] p. CtHT-W; CtY;
DLC; LU; MH; MWHi; NNC;
OMC; PSC-Hi.   655

Brown, Jacob.
Catalogue of garden and flower
seeds, green house plants, etc.
for 1830. New Haven, Baldwin
& Treadway, 1830. MiD-B (not
loc., 1971).   656

Brown, James.
The American grammar...
Philadelphia, Pub. by James
Anderson. Wm. Sharpless, pr.,
1830. xliv, [2], 15-144 p. NNC.
                             657
---- The American system of
English grammar. Abridged and
simplified. Printed from the
Philadelphia edition. Cincinnati,
Pub. for the author by R.I.
Fleming & I. D. Rupp, 1830.
157 p. ArCH.   658

Brown, John, 1722-1787.
A brief concordance to the
Holy Scriptures. Rev. and corr.
Philadelphia, Towar and Hogan,
1830. 85 p. DLC; MH; NN; Nh.
                             659
---- ---- Stereo. by B. & J.
Collins. Boston, Langdon Cof-
fin, 1830. 56 p. MBD; MMeT-Hi;
NN; ViU (bd. with Bible 1831).
                             660
---- A short catechism, for
young children. Pittsburgh, Pub.
by Luke Loomis and co. D. & M.
Maclean, prs. 1830. 23 p. DLC;
PPPrHi.   661

---- Two short catechisms, mutu-
ally connected. The questions of
the former being generally supposed and omitted in the latter
... To which is added the Gospel
Catchism... by John Brown. Philadelphia, J. Grigg, Wm. Sharpless, pr., 1830. 138 p. GDC;
OOxM (rep. as 140 p.).   662

Brown, John, 1771-1850.
Eine kurze Unterweisung
Christlichen Religion, nach dem
Heidelbergischen Catechismus,
in den Deutschen und Englischen-
Sprachen. bey Johannes Braun,
Diener des Evangelii. A short
instruction according to the
Heidelberg Cateschism [!] in Ger-
man and English. Harrisonburg,
Pr. by Lawrence Wartmann,
Rockingham County, Virginia,
1830. 72 p. PPL.   663

Brown, John Thompson.
J. T. Brown, respectfully informs the citizens of Harrison
...[Will not be candidate for the
legislature] Clarksburg, March
15, 1830. Bdsd. ViW.   664

[Brown, Rezeau]
Memoirs of Augustus Hermann
Franke. Prepared for the American Sunday School Union, and
revised by the Committee of Publication. Philadelphia, American
Sunday School Union [c 1830] 185
p. MBC; MWA; NNUT; NcMHi;
PPL; ScCliTO.   665

Brown, Thomas, 1778-1820.
Lectures on the philosophy of
the human mind. Corrected from
the last ed. Stereotyped by T.
H. Carter and Co., Boston.
Hallowell, Pr. and pub. by Glazier, Masters & Co., 1830. 2
vols. CtHT-W; DLC; MsJMC;
MtHi; NjP; PHC; PPLT; TNJ.
                           666
Brown University.
Catalogue of the officers and
students of Brown University, for
the academical year 1829-30.
Providence, H. H. Brown, pr.,
1830. 20 p. RPB.   667

---- Catalogue of the officers
and students of Brown University,
for the academical year 1830-31.
Providence, H. H. Brown, pr.,
1830. 24 p. CSt; TNJ.   668

---- Catalogus Senatus Academici, eorum qui munera et officia gesserunt, quique alicujus
gradus laurea donati sunt in Universitate Brownensi, Providentiae,
in Republica Insulae Rhodienis.
Providentiae, Typis H. H. Brown,
1830. 30 p. IC; MBNEH; MiU;
PPL; RPB.   669

---- Exhibition in the chapel, by
a part of the junior class, on
Saturday, May 8, 1830. Order of
exercises. [Providence, 1830]
Bdsd. RNHi.   670

Brownell, Thomas Church, 1779-
1865.
A sermon, preached in St.
John's Chapel, New York, on the
26th of November, 1830, at the
consecration of the Rt. Rev.
Benjamin T. T. Onderdonk. And
also an address by the Rt. Rev.
William White. New York, Protestant Episcopal Press, 1830.
27 p. CtHT; DLC; InID; MH;
MiD-B; NCH; NGH; NjR; PHi;
BrMus.   671

Brunton, Robert, 1796-1852.
A compendium of mechanics;
or, Text book for engineers,
mill-wrights, machine-makers,
founders, smiths, &c. ... 1st
American from 4th London ed.,
with plates. Edited by James
Renwick... New York, G. & C. &
H. Carvill, [Pr. by G. F. Bunce]
1830. 228 p. CtY; DeGE; GU;
PPL; PU-P; VtU.   672

---- ---- 1st American, from
the 2d English ed. Boston, Hilliard, Gray, Little, and Wilkins,
1830. 11, [3], [13]-148 p. DLC;
MNBedf; MnU.   673

Brutus, pseud.
Brutus continued. Letters to
George M'Duffie, esq. chairman
of the committee of ways and
means, in the House of Repre-

sentatives of the United States, in answer to his report, sustaining the Bank of the United States. Philadelphia, Pr. and pub. by T. S. Manning, 1830. 48 p. PPL. 674

---- ---- 2d ed. Philadelphia, Pr. and pub. by T. S. Manning, 1830. 39 p. NNC; PPL; PU; WHi. 675

Brutus, Lucius Junius, pseud. An address to the leaders of political anti-masonry. An exposition of the new political system under the guise of anti-masonry. Signed Brutus. New Haven, Herald office, 1830. CtY. 676

Bryan, Daniel, 1795-1866 Thoughts on education in its connexion with morals, a poem recited before the literary and philosophical society of Hampden Sidney college, Va. At the fifth anniversary meeting of the institution, held in September, 1828. Richmond, T. W. White, 1830. 40 p. CSmH; DLC; KyDC; KyLx; MB; MBAt; MH; NIC; NjPT; PHi; PPPrHi; PU; RPB; Vi; ViU. 677

Bryan, John Herritage, 1798-1870. An oration, delivered at Chapel Hill, on Wednesday, the 23d June, 1830; the day preceding commencement, at the University of North Carolina; according to the annual appointment of the two literary societies belonging to the University. By the Hon. John H. Bryan. Newbern, Pr. by J. I. Pasteur, 1830. 19 p. CSmH; CtY; DLC; MH; NcU; OClW; PHi. 678

[Bryant, William Cullen], 1794-1878. The American landscape, no. 1. Containing the following views: Weehawken, Catskill Mountains, Fort Putnam, Delaware Water- gap, Falls of the Sawkill, Winnipiseogee Lake. Engraved from original and accurate drawings; executed from nature expressly for this work, and from well authenticated pictures; with historical and topographical illustrations. New-York, Pub. by Elam Bliss, 1830. 16 p. CSmH; CtHT-W; CtY; RPB; BrMus. 679

---- Selections from the American poets... New York, 1830. MeB. 680

---- Song of the Greek amazon ... Philadelphia, Kretschmar & Nunns [183-] 5 p. CSmH. 681

Buck, Charles, 1771-1815. Models of female character, from scripture history. Boston, Pub. by James Loring, 1830. 107 p. NNC. 682

---- Kay's improved and enl. ed. A theological dictionary. New American, from the latest London ed., rev. and imp. By the Rev. Geo. Bush, A.M. With an appendix, containing a late account of the Methodist Episcopal Church in America, and of the associated Methodists. Philadelphia, James Kay, Jun. & Co. Pittsburg, John I. Kay & Co., 1830. 463 p. CBPac; CtHT; DLC; IU; LNB; MB; MWA; MoS; NbCrD; NjMD; OClW; PPL; TxU. 683

---- ----(Stereotype ed.) Philadelphia, Pub. by Joseph J. Woodward, 1830. 615 p. GAGTh; IU; KyLxT; LNHT; MA; MMeTHi; MdW; NPV; NbOP; OC; PU; ViRUT. 684

---- ---- Woodward's new edition. Pub. from the last London ed.; to which is added an appendix. Philadelphia, Pub. by Joseph J. Woodward [Stereotype ed.]

1830. 624 p. CtHT; CtMW; MB;
MH; NjR; OClWHi; ViU.   685

---- The young Christian's guide,
or, Suitable directions, cautions,
and encouragements, to the believer. On his first entrance into the divine life. Harrisburg,
John Winebrenner, 1830. 154,
[3], 4 p. P.   686

Buckingham, D. W.
   Map of the city of New Haven
from actual survey, by D. W.
Buckingham, country-surveyor.
[New Haven?] Pub. by Jocelyn,
Darling & Co., 1830. CtY.   687

Buckingham, Joseph Tinker,
1779-1861.
   An address delivered before
the Massachusetts Charitable Association at the celebration of
their eighth triennial festival, October 7, 1830. Boston, Pr. for
the Association, [John Cotton, pr.]
1830. 30 p., 1 l. CSmH; DLC.
MB; MBAt; MH; MHi; MWA;
MiD-B; NbHi; NcD; OClWHi;
PHi; WHi; BrMus.   688

The budget of stories; intended
for little boys and girls. New-
Haven, S. Babcock, publisher...
Charleston, S. Babcock & Co.,
Sidney's Press, 1830. 23 p.
CtHi; CtY.   689

Budlong, Ann Maria.
   Memoirs of the life and happy
death of Ann Maria Budlong,
daughter of Mr. John Budlong, of
Warwick, R.I. 2d ed. Repr. by
Elder Thomas Tillinghast. Providence, H. H. Brown, pr., 1830.
12 p. MBNEH; MWA; RHi. 690

Buds and blossoms gathered from
a Sabbath school, ...by the author of "The young disciple."
Boston, Perkins and Marvin, 1830.
108 p. GDC.   691

...The bufforanian songster.
New York, Elton's theatrical,
play, print and song store, 1830.
33 p. (At head of title: Elton's
edition) MH.   692

[Bulfinch, Stephen Greenleaf]
1809-1870.
   A dialogue, occasioned by a
pamphlet entitled, "A conversation on an important subject."
Augusta, Pr. by W. Lawson,
1830. 47 p. CSmH; CtY (attri-
bution); DLC.   693

---- A sermon, delivered in the
Unitarian Church, in Augusta,
Geo. on Sunday, July 4, 1830.
[Published by the Augusta Unitar-
ian Book Association] Augusta,
Pr. at W. Lawson's Job Office,
1830. 27 p. ICMe; MA; MABt;
MH; MWA; NN; NcD; PPAmP;
PPL.   694

Bunker Hill Monument Association.
   Act of incorporation, by-laws,
and a list of the original members of the Bunker Hill Monument Association: with a statement, shewing the magnitude and
progress of the work, and a copy
of the original estimate. Compiled for the use of the members.
Boston, Pr. by Samuel N. Dickinson, 1830. 74 p. DLC; MB;
MBAt; MBNEH; MH; MHi; MMeT;
MWA; MdHi; MiD-B; PHi; PPL;
WHi.   695

---- Address to the public relative to the progress of the monument. [Charlestown, 1830] MHi.
                          696

Bunyan, John, 1628-1688.
   Kay's stereotype ed. The holy
war made by King Shaddai upon
Diabolus; to regain the metropolis of the world. Or the losing
and taking again of the town of
Mansoul. A new edition, with
explanatory, experimental and

practical notes. By the Rev. G.
Burder. Philadelphia, James
Kay, Jun. & Co. Pittsburg,
John I. Kay and Co., 1830. 252
p. ICMcC; KWiU; MBC; MWA;
OMC; PPL. 697

---- The pilgrim's progress
from this world to that which is
to come. Delivered under the
similitude of a dream. In two
parts... with original notes by
Thomas Scott. Hartford, S. Andrus, 1830. 360 p. CtHT;
CtHi; DLC; MWA; NN; PV. 698

---- ---- Hartford, Con., Andrus & Judd [183-?] 368 p.
CtY. 699

---- ---- By John Bunyan. New
York, American Tract Society,
[1830?] 376 p. CSt; CtY; DLC;
MB; MH; MdAS; MiDU; NN; NhD;
OHi; ViU. 700

---- ---- Pub. by R. W. Pom-
eroy, Philadelphia, 1830. 249 p.
GU; MWA; MeBaT; NN; OMC;
PU. 701

---- The works of that eminent
servant of Christ, John Bunyan,
minister of the gospel, and formerly pastor of a congregation at
Bedford [England]. New Haven,
Pr. and pub. by Nathan Whiting,
1830. 3 v. ArCH; CSmH; CtY-D;
GDC; MB; PPL (Vol. III only) 702

Burder, George, 1752-1832.
Twelve sermons to the aged...
New York, American Tract So-
ciety [1830?] v. p. CtY. 703

---- Village sermons: or, Fifty-
two plain and short discourses on
the principal doctrines of the Gospel: intended for the use of families, Sunday-schools, or companies assembled for religious instruction in country villages...
Revised. New York & Boston

[183-?] 571 p. CtY. 704

Burder, Henry Forster, 1783-
1864.
Mental discipline; or Hints on
the cultivation of intellectual and
moral habits... 3d ed., considerably enl., to which is appended
an address on pulpit eloquence,
by Rev. Justin Edwards, D.D.
also a course of study in Christian theology by Rev. Leonard
Woods, D.D. New York, Pub.
by Jonathan Leavitt; Boston,
Crocker & Brewster [New York,
Pr. by William A. Mercein] 1830.
254 p. CBPac; CSmH; CtMW;
DLC; GDC; ICMcC; IEG; KyLoP;
MB; MeB; NNUT; NjPT; OMC;
PU; ViAl. 705

Burford, Robert, 1791-1861.
Description of the panorama
of the superb city of Mexico,
and the surrounding scenery,
painted on 2700 square feet of
canvas by Robert Burford, esq.,
from drawings made on the spot
at the request of the Mexican
government, by Mr. W. Bullock,
jr. Now open for public inspection. [Charleston? S.C.] Pr. by
A. E. Miller, 1830. 16 p. DLC;
KyDC. 706

Burges, Tristam, 1770-1853.
Address, delivered before the
American Institute of the City of
New York, at their third annual
fair, held at Masonic Hall, Oc-
tober 1830. Pr. by request of
the Institute. New York, Pub.
by John M. Danforth, 1830. 34 p.
CtHT-W; CtY; MH; PHi; PPAmP;
PPL. 707

---- The speech of Tristam Burges, in the House of Representatives of the United States, when
in committee of the whole, May
10, 1830, on the bill for the more
effectual collection of the duties
on imports, Mr. M'Duffie's

amendment to repeal the tariff
being under consideration. Providence, Pr. by Marshall and Hammond [1830] 28 p. MWA; MdHi;
MiD-B; MiU-C; NN; RP; RPB;
WHi; BrMus.   708

Burgess, Dyer.
Solomon's temple haunted, or
Free masonry, the man of sin,
in the temple of God. An ad-
dress delivered by the Rev. Dyer
Burgess, at the anti-masonic
meeting, held at the Court House,
West Union, Adams County,
Ohio, on the 1st of June 1830.
[West Union? 1830] 12 p.
ICMcC.   709

Burhans, Hezekiah.
The young tyro's instructor;
or, The necessary rudiments of
the English language; comprising
all that is really useful in a
spelling-book to instruct a child
in his native tongue, and prepare
him for more advanced books, in
the progress of his education.
Written for the use of schools in
the United States, Great Britain,
and her colonies... New York,
The Author, 1830. 1 p. l., [5]-
180 p. CtY; DLC.   710

Burlamaqui, Jean Jacques, 1694-
1748.
The principles of natural and
politic law... By J. J. Burla-
maqui... Tr. into English by Mr.
Nugent. 7th ed. cor. Philadel-
phia, Carey & Lea [E. & G.
Merriam, prs.] 1830. 2 v. C-L;
DLC; ICJ; IaU-L; MdW; NjP; OO;
PU-L; TMeB; ViU.   711

Burnap, Uzziah Cicero, 1794-
1854.
Priestcraft exposed. A lecture, delivered in Chester, April
9, 1830. Being the annual fast;
together with an essay on the
clergy of the United States. Windsor [Vt.] Pr. at the Chronicle

Press, by John C. Allen, 1830.
28 p. CSmH; CtHT; IEG; MWA;
MiD; MiD-U; NjPT; PHi; VtMiM;
VtU; BrMus.   712

Burns, Robert, 1759-1796.
The works of Robert Burns:
with an account of his life, and
criticism on his writings. To
which is prefixed, some observations on the character and condition of the Scottish peasantry.
By James Currie, M.D. A new
ed., four volumes complete in
one. With many additional poems
and songs, and an enl. and corr.
glossary. From the latest London ed. of 1829. New-York, S.
& D. A. Forbes, prs., 1830. 2 v.
in 1. DLC; MH; MWA.   713

---- ---- Philadelphia, J. Crissy
and J. Grigg, 1830. 2 p. l.,
[iii]-xv, 180, x, 258 p. AMob;
DLC; GU; MB; MdBS; NjR; RPAt.
                                 714

Burritt, Elijah Hinsdale, 1794-
1838.
Burritt's universal multipliers
for computing interest, simple
and compound; adapted to the various rates in the United States.
By Elijah Hinsdale Burritt, ...
1st stereotype ed. Hartford,
1830. 32, [1] p. DLC; Nh; PU.
                                 715

---- ---- 1st pocket ed. New
York, Henry C. Sleight, 1830.
72 p. PPL.   716

Burroughs, Charles, 1787-1868.
A sermon, delivered in St.
Paul's Chapel, New York, July 29,
1830. On occasion of the fourth
anniversary of the General Prot-
estant Episcopal Sunday School
Union. New York, Pr. at the
Protestant Episcopal Press, 1830.
29 p. CtHT; DLC; KU; MB; MBC;
MH; NCH; NGH; NNG; NcU; NjR;
PHi; RPB; WHi.   717

Burrowes, John Freckleton,
1787-1852.
The piano-forte primer; containing the rudiments of music:
calculated either for private tuition, or teaching in classes. 3rd
American, from the 4th London
ed. New York, Dubois & Stod-
art, 1830. 60, 12 p. MB.   718

Burt, John.
An address delivered before
the Cumberland County Temperance Society, at Bridgeton, N. J.
September 28, 1830. by John
Burt, Furnished for publication
at the request of the Executive
Committee of said Society [1830]
8 p. MB; MdHi.   719

[Bury, Lady Charlotte Campbell]
1775-1861.
The exclusives. In two vol-
umes.... New-York, Pr. by J.
& J. Harper, 82 Cliff street.
Sold by Collins and Hannay, Col-
lins and co., G. and C. and H.
Carvill, O. A. Roarbach, White,
Gallaher, and White, A. T. Good-
rich, W. B. Gilley, E. Bliss; C.
S. Francis, G. W. Bleecker, W.
Burgess, M. Bancroft and N. E.
Holmes; - Philadelphia, Carey
and Lea, E. L. Carey and A.
Hart; - Albany, O. Steele, and
W. C. Little, 1830. 2 v. CtHT;
MH; MeB; NhD; PU; RPAt; TNJ.
                             720
Bush, George, 1796-1859.
Harper's stereotype edition.
The life of Mohammed; founder
of the religion of Islam, and of
the empire of the Saracens. By
the Rev. George Bush...New-
York, Pr. by J. & J. Harper,
Sold by Collins & Hannay [etc.]
1830. 261 p. CU; CtY; DLC;
IU; LNHT; MB; NCH; NNS; NhD;
NjP; OrPD; PHi; PPL; PPPrHi;
PU; PV; TNJ; VtU.   721

---- Scripture questions, designed principally for adult Bible
classes by George Bush, Pastor
of the Presbyterian Church at Indianapolis, Ind., 5th ed., imp.
New York, Pub. by John P. Hav-
en, American Tract Society
House [Pr. by Sleight & Robin-
son] 1830. 179 p. CtY; MWA;
NNUT; NRAB; NjP; P; PPPrHi.
                             722
Butler, Benjamin Franklin, 1795-
1858.
Anniversary discourse, delivered before the Albany Institute,
April 23, 1830. ... Pub. at the
request and under the direction of
the Institute. Albany [N. Y.] Pr.
by Webster and Skinners, 1830.
88 p. CSmH; DLC; MB; MBAt;
MF; MH; MHi; MdHi; MiD-B;
N; NCH; NbU; NjP; PPL; ScU;
BrMus.   723

Butler, Joseph, 1692-1752.
The analogy of religion, natur-
al and revealed, to the constitu-
tion and course of nature. 2d ed.
Cambridge, Pub. by Hilliard &
Brown [etc.] 1830. 348 p. KyLoS;
MB; MH; MnU; MoS; MoSpD;
NRU.   724

---- ---- To which are added,
two brief dissertations: I. Of
personal identity; II. Of the nature of virtue. By Joseph Butler
... To which is prefixed a life
of the author, by Dr. Keppis;
with a preface, giving some account of his character and writings, by Samuel Halifax...New
Haven, A. H. Maltby & co.
[183-?] 299 p. CSmH.   725

Butler, S. Worcester.
A biographical sketch of the
late Nathaniel Chapman, M.D.,
Reprinted from the New Jersey
Medical Reporter. Philadelphia,
Joseph M. Wilson, [T. K. and
P. G. Collins, prs., 183-?]
NNNAM.   726

Butler, Samuel.

Hudibras... written in the time
of the late wars... By Samuel
Butler...with a life of the author,
annotations, and an index...Hart-
ford, Andrus [183-?] 312 p.
NjP.   727

[----] Journal of the heart.
Edited by the authoress of "Flirtation" ... Philadelphia, Carey
and Lea, 1830. 239 p. DLC; ICU;
LU; RPAt; VtU.   728

[----] The separation. A novel,
by authoress of "Flirtation" ...
New York, Pr. by J. & J. Harper, 1830. 2 v. in 1. CtHT; DLC;
IaHi; LU; NRMA; RPAt; TNJ.
                                     729
Buy a broom a celebrated Bavar-
ian song as sung by Mrs. Sharpe
at the Park theatre with the most
unbounded approbation. Arranged
with an accompaniment for the
piano forte. New York, Pub. by
Firth & Hall [183-?] fragment:
1 l. (Apollo, No. 4) CSmH. 730

Byerly, Stephen.
   Byerly's new American spell-
ing-book... Compiled by Stephen
Byerly... Stereotyped by J. Howe,
New-York. Philadelphia, Pub. by
M'Carty & Davis, 1830. 167 p.
MiU-C; NNC.   731

Byron, George Gordon Noël Byron, 6th baron, 1788-1824.
   The beauties of Lord Byron,
selected from his works. To
which is prefixed, a biographical
memoir of his life and writings
... By B. F. French...10th ed. --
enl. Philadelphia, Pr. by W. F.
Geddes, 1830. xi, 204 p. DLC;
OCl.   732

---- Harper's stereotype edition.
Letters and journals of Lord By-
ron: with notices of his life.
By Thomas Moore. New-York,
Pr. and pub. by J. & J. Harper
[etc.] 1830-31. 2 vols. CLU;

CSmH; CtHT; ICN; KyLo; MB;
MBC; MH; MWA; MdBP; MoSU;
NCH; NIC; NN; Nh; NjP; P;
PPL; PU; TNJ; USlW; ViU.
                                     733

C

Cabinet literature, the Presi-
dent's consistency, &c. [Balti-
more, Md.? 1830?] 18 p. MB.
                                     734
Cadwallader, Priscilla.
   Sermon, delivered by Priscilla
Cadwallader, in the Meeting-
House at Waynesville, Miami, on
1st day, 26th of 9th mo. 1830;
being the first day preceding the
Yearly Meeting. Reported by
Robert Way, stenographer. Leb-
anon, O., 1830. 12 p. PSC-Hi.
                                     735
Calamy, Edmund, 1671-1732.
   History of Jonathan Brown.
New York, American Tract So-
ciety [1830?] 12 p. DLC.   736

Caldwell, Charles, 1772-1853.
   Thoughts on the original unity
of the human race. New-York,
E. Bliss, [Brown, pr.] 1830.
x, 178 p. DLC; DNLM; ICN; MH;
MnH; NNNAM; OC; PU; ScU;
WHi; BrMus.   737

---- A valedictory address on
some of the duties and qualifica-
tions of a physician, delivered
to the graduates of the medical
department of Transylvania Uni-
versity, on the 17th day of
March, 1830. [Lexington, The
University, 1830] 22 p. MBCo.
                                     738
Der Calender Eines Christen für
1831. Philadelphia, Conrad
Zentler [1830]. Drake 11705.
                                     739
Calender, Für den Westliche
Büerger und Landmann auf 1831.
Von dem ehrw. Johann Taylor.
Pittsburgh, H. Holdschip und

Sohn; Gedruckt bey D. und M.
Maclean [1830] 18 1. PHi.   740

Calhoun, George Albion.
The means and preeminent ad-
vantages of God's dwelling with
a people. A sermon, preached
at Andover, Conn. June 24, 1829,
at the installation of the Rev.
Alpha Miller; and also in York,
Maine, February 17, 1830. at
the ordination of the Rev. Eber
Carpenter. Portland, Shirley and
Hyde, 1830. CtY; DLC; MBC;
MH-AH; MWA; NjR.   741

Callcott, John Wall.
A musical grammar, in four
parts... By Dr. Callcott, organ-
ist of Covent Garden Church...
Loring's 2d ed. Boston, James
Loring, 1830. 274 p. CtHT; MB;
MH; NNS.   742

Calvin, John, 1509-1564.
A selection of the most celebrated sermons of John Calvin,
minister of the gospel, and one
of the principal leaders in the
Protestant reformation. (Never
before published in the United
States.) To which is prefixed, a
biographical history of his life.
New York, S. & D. A. Forbes,
prs., 1830. 200 p. MoSU;
NNUT; PPLT; PPPrHi; TxU.
                          743
Cambreleng, Churchill Caldom,
1786-1862.
Merchants second edition of
Mr. Cambreleng's report on com-
merce and navigation, New York,
March 1830... [Pr. by J. M. Dan-
forth, for the merchants of New-
York, 1830] 63 p. ICU; MBAt;
MH-BA; MWA; PHi; ScU.   744

Cambridge, Mass. Infant School.
(Circular) 1830. MH.   745

Camden; a tale. See McClung,
John Alexander.

[Cameron, Lucy Lyttleton (Butt)]
1781-1858.
The caskets: or, The palace
and the church. By the author
of 'The raven and the dove, '
'The two lambs, ' &c. Stereotyped by James Conner. New-
York, General Protestant Episcopal Sunday School Union Pr. at
the Protestant Episcopal Press,
1830. 24 p. DLC; MB.   746

[----] Religion and its image.
By the author of "The two
lambs," &c., &c. Rev. by the
Committee of publication. Phila-
delphia, American Sunday School
Union [1830?] 49 p. CSmH;
BrMus.   747

The Camp-Meeting Chorister, or,
A collection of hymns and spiritual songs, for the pious of all
denominations. To be sung at
camp meetings, during revivals
of religion, and other occasions.
Philadelphia, W. A. Leary & Co.,
1830. 320 p. NcD.   748

Campbell, George, 1718-1796.
The philosophy of rhetoric...
A new edition with the author's
last additions and corrections.
Boston, Pub. by Thomas B.
Wait & Co. [183-?] xii, 517 p.
MB.   749

Campbell, James, comp.
Tariff; or, Rates of duties
payable on goods, wares & merchandise imported into the U. S. A.
with the rates of duty of the tariff of 1828. New York, Mahlon
Day, 1830. 164 p. PU.   750

Campbell, Thomas, 1763-1854.
Prospectus of a religious reformation; the object of which is
the restoration of a primitive
apostolic Christianity in letter
and spirit--in principle and practice. [Bethany? c. 1830] 12 p.
TNDC.   751

Campbell, Thomas, 1777-1844.
Pleasures of hope; in two
parts with a memoir. Petersburg, Pub. by J. W. Campbell
[ca. 1830?] 60 p. CtHT-W.   752

---- The poetical works of
Thomas Campbell including The-
odric. New York, S. & D. A.
Forbes, prs.] 1830. 183, 38 p.
GEU; MH; NBuG; NIC; Nh; OMC;
RPB; TxU.   753

---- ---- And many other pieces
not contained in any former editions. Philadelphia, J. Crissy,
and J. Grigg, 1830. 183, 38 p.
MiU.   754

Campbell, Z.
Lazorus in Abraham's bosom.
[Boston? Mass., 1830?]
BrMus.   755

Canal, John B. E.
To the public... [Signed:] J. B.
E. Canal. Edwardsville, May 20,
1830. Bdsd. DLC.   756

Candid examination of the Protestant Episcopal Church, in two
letters to a friend, with an appendix. Nashville, Tenn., Pr. by
John S. Simpson, 1830. 32 p.
Signed with the initials "T. S."
T.   757

Candid reasons for not uniting.
See Bernard.

Canfield, John Spencer.
An abstract of the most important alterations, of general interest, introduced by the revised
statutes: the principal part of
which originally appeared in numbers published in the Ontario
Messenger; collected and examined by the author of those numbers, with the addition of notes,
marginal references, forms of
conveyances, &c., and an index.
Canandaigua, Pr. by Day and

Morse, at the office of the Ontario Messenger, 1830. [4], 137
p. DLC; MH-L; NN.   758

Cannon, James Spencer.
Lectures on history and chron-
ology introductory to the reading
of ancient, sacred, and profane
history... New Brunswick, N. J.,
Rutgers press, Pr. by Terhune
& Letson, 1830. 27 p. NjR;
PPL; PPPrHi.   759

Captain Hall in America. See
Biddle, Richard.   760

Cardell, William S.
The analytical spelling-book
... By William S. Cardell...
Revised by M. T. Leavensworth,
esq. Philadelphia, Uriah Hunt,
Stereotyped by L. Johnson, 1830.
144 p. NNC.   761

Carden, Allen D.
The Missouri harmony; or, A
choice collection of psalm tunes,
hymns, and anthems, selected
from the most eminent authors
and well adapted to all Christian churches, singing schools,
and private societies. Together
with an introduction to grounds
of music and plain rules for beginners. Cincinnati, Pr. and
pub. by Morgan and Sanxay;
stereotyped by Oliver Wells and
Co., 1830. 199 p. KHayF;
MPiB.   762

Carey, E. L. and A. Hart (Firm)
Catalogue of a valuable collection of books in the English,
French, Spanish and Italian Languages...for sale by E. L. Carey
& A. Hart... Philadelphia, 1830.
272 p., 2 l. NRAM; PU.   763

---- Catalogue of a valuable collection of books, recently imported,
and for sale by E. L. Carey and
A. Hart... Philadelphia, 1830.

16 p. MoSW; RNR; TxH.   764

[Carey, Mathew] 1760-1839.
    Address submitted for consideration to the Board of managers of the Impartial Humane Society [delivered May 15, 1830. Baltimore, n.p., 1830] 2 p. MB; MWA; MdBJ; PHi; <u>PU.</u>   765

---- A brief account of the malignant fever which prevailed in Philadelphia, in the year 1793... 5th ed., improved. Philadelphia, Clark & Raser, prs., 1830. 1 p. l., [ix]-xii, [13]-97 p. CU; PHi; <u>PPL;</u> PU.   766

---- Case of the seamstresses... [Philadelphia, 1830] 4 p. MHi; <u>PU.</u>   767

---- Essay on Rail Roads. [Signed: Hamilton. Philadelphia, 1830] 26 p. DBRE; DLC; MB; MH-BA; MWA; MiU-T; NN; NNC; PHi; PPAmP; <u>PU.</u>   768

[----] Second Edition. - Gratuitous. Essay on railroads. [Philadelphia, 1830] 26 p. MHi; <u>PU.</u>   769
---- Essay on the protecting system. 1830.   72 p. MWA.   770

---- Essays on the public charities of Philadelphia, intended to vindicate benevolent societies from the charge of encouraging idleness... 5th ed., gratuitous. Philadelphia, Clark & Raser, prs., 1830. 2 l., 51 p. DLC; IU; KU; MB; MH; MWA; MnHi; NNG; PHi; <u>PPL;</u> WHi.   771

---- Maxims for the promotion of the wealth of nations, being a manual of political economy, extracted from the writings of Franklin, Jefferson, Madison, Hamilton... &c. &c. Philadelphia, Clark & Raser, 1830. 32 p. MBAt; MBL; PPAmP; PU.   772

---- Miscellaneous essays... by M. Carey... Philadelphia, Pr. for Carey & Hart, Nov. 13, 1830. 472 p. AU; CSmH; CtY; DGU; DLC; DeGE; ICN; IU; InNd; LNHT; MB; MBAt; MH; MWA; MdHi; MeB; MnU; NBu; NIC; NNC; NbU; NjP; OClW; OO; PHi; RPB; TNJ; Vi; WU; BrMus. 773

[----] ... The new olive branch. A solemn warning on the banks of the Rubicon. No. 1. [Philadelphia, 1830] [52] p. At head of title: 2d ed. [Signed: Hamilton. July 24 - Nov. 19, 1830] CSmH; DLC; ICN; MWA; MdHi; <u>PPL;</u> PU.   774

[----] Prospects on and beyond the Rubicon. No. 1-[2]. [Philadelphia, 1830] 8 p. Caption title. Signed: Hamilton, and dated September 15th and 20, 1830 respectively. DeGE; MB; MH; MHi; MWA; MdHi; <u>PPL;</u> <u>PU;</u> WHi.   775
---- Review of the evidence of the legendary tale of a general conspiracy of the Roman Catholics of Ireland, "to massacre all the Protestants that would not join with them," on the twenty-third of October, 1641. Extracted from the Vindiciae hibernicae... By M. Carey. 3rd ed. Philadelphia, Clark and Raser, prs., 1830. 24 p. CU; MWA; MdBS; NNUT; PU.   776

---- To the editor of the New-York Daily Sentinel. [Philadelphia, 1830] Caption title. Letter on the rate of wages paid to women. MA; MBL; PPAmP; <u>PU.</u>   777
---- To the ladies who have undertaken to establish a House of Industry in New York. [Philadelphia, May 11, 1830] 4 p. PHi; <u>PU.</u>   778

[----] To the printer of the Del-

aware Advertiser, [Philadelphia, March 30, 1830] 4 p. DeGE; MWA; PPAmP; PU.   779

[----] To the public. Baltimore, May 10, 1830 "The undersigned, having received from a number of ladies..." [Baltimore? 1830] 2 p. PU.   780

[----] To the Public [on various charitable organizations] [Philadelphia? 1830?] Signed: Hamilton, dated 12 April 1830. 4 p. PU.   781

---- "We ought never to forget that in alleviating the immediate sufferings of the poor [women], we are only palliating, not eradicating the evils of poverty." ... Philadelphia, July 1, 1830. [22] p. On the plight of women shirtmakers. PU.   782

Carnahan, James, 1775-1859.
Filial duty. A discourse, delivered in the chapel of Nassau-Hall, on the sabbath, December 27, 1829... Princeton, N. J., Pr. by J. Madden, 1830. 32 p. CSmH; DeU; MH-AH; PHi; PPLT; PPPrHi.   783

The Carolina and Georgia almanac for 1831. By David Young. Augusta, Richards and Ganahl [1830] 18 l. GEU; GU.   784

Carpenter, Lant.
...The beneficial tendency of Unitarianism. Printed for the American Unitarian Association. Boston, Gray and Bowen [Pr. by I. R. Butts] 1830. 32 p. 1st series, No. 43. DLC; MBAt; MMeT-Hi; MeB; Nh; PPL; RP.   785
The carpenter's standard price book. Carefully revised by a competent hand. Washington, 1830. 18 l. ICU.   786

Carr, Benjamin, 1768-1831.
A new edition with an appendix of masses, vespers, litanies, hymns, psalms, anthems & motetts, composed, selected and arranged for the use of the catholic churches in the United States of America ... Baltimore [Pr. at Carr's Music Store, ca. 1830?] iv p., 1 l., 136 p. PU.   787

---- Sacred airs, in six numbers ... Philadelphia, Pr. for Benjamin Carr [c1830] 25 p. NBuG.
                                    788

[Carrick, John D.]
Life of Sir William Wallace, the governor general of Scotland, and hero of the Scottish chiefs. Containing his parentage, adventures, heroic achievements, imprisonments and death... By Peter Donaldson [pseud.] Hartford, Pub. by Silas Andrus, 1830. 132 p. CtHi.   789

Carter, James Gordon, 1795-1849.
A geography of Essex county. Boston, Carter and Hendee, 1830. 118 p. MB; MHi; MWA.
                                    790
---- A geography of Massachusetts; for families and schools... With a new map of the state. Boston, Hilliard, Gray, Little and Wilkins [Press of Carter, Andrews & Co., Lancaster] 1830. x, 224 p. CtHi; CtY; DLC; MB; MBAt; MH; MHi; MWA; NNC; OClWHi; BrMus.   791

---- A geography of Middlesex county for young children... Cambridge [Mass.] Hilliard and Brown, 1830. 106 p. CSmH; DLC; MB; MH; MHi; MWA; MiD-B; MnHi; NNC; BrMus.   792

---- A geography of Worcester county; for young children. Lancaster, Carter, Andrews, and company, 1830. vii, 61 p.

DLC.   793

---- A lecture on the development of the intellectual faculties
as the proper purpose of elementary studies, and on teaching geography; delivered in the Representatives' Hall, Boston, August
23, 1830, before the American
Institute of Instruction. Boston,
Hilliard, Gray, Little and Wilkins, 1830. 42 p. CtHT-W; DLC;
MB; MBC; MH; MHi; MWA; PPL.
                               794
Carter, Jesse.
Observations on Mania A Potu
... Extracted from the American
Journal of the Medical Sciences,
for August, 1830. Philadelphia,
Pr. by Joseph R. A. Skerrett,
1830. 18 p. PHi.   795

Carter, Richard.
Valuable vegetable medical
prescriptions, for the cure of all
nervous and putrid disorders.
Cincinnati, Pub. by Nathaniel
Lewis. Lodge, L'Hommedieu &
Hammond, prs., 1830. 178 p.
DNLM; OCLloyd.   796

Cary, Virginia [Randolph], 1786-
1852.
Letters on female character,
addressed to a young lady, on
the death of her mother. By Mrs.
Virginia Cary. 2d. ed., enl.
Richmond, Va., Pub. by Ariel
Works; Philadelphia, Towar, J. &
D. M. Hogan, 1830. [2], 220 p.
CSmH; CtY; GMW; IU; MWA;
MdBE; NcD; NjP; PP; PPL; PU;
TxU; ViR; ViU; BrMus.   797

The case of the Albany and Schenectady Turnpike Company considered. [183-?] 2 p. NN. 798

The casket; or, Youth's pocket
library. 3d ed., improved. Boston, Geo. Davidson, 1830. 254 p.
MBAt; NIC; RPB; TNJ.   799

The caskets. See Cameron,
Lucy Lyttleton (Butt).

Cass, Lewis, 1782-1866.
Address of Lewis Cass, of
Michigan, LL. D. Delivered, by
appointment, before the associa-
tion of the alumni of Hamilton
College, at their anniversary
meeting, August 25, 1830. Pub-
lished by request of the associa-
tion. Utica, Press of William
Williams, 1830. 40 p. CSmH;
CtHT-W; CtY; DLC; ICN; MB;
MBC; MH; MWA; MiD-B; MiU;
MnHi; NIC; NN; NbU; NjR; OO;
PPL; PPPrHi; ScCC; WHi;
BrMus.   800

[----] Considerations on the present state of the Indians, and
their removal to the west of the
Mississippi. (From the North
American Review, No. LXVI for
January, 1830). Boston, Gray
and Bowen, 1828 [i. e. 1830] 61
p. MdHi; N; ScU; WHi.   801

---- Discourse delivered at the
first meeting of the Historical
Society of Michigan, September
18, 1829... Detroit, Pr. by Geo.
L. Whitney, 1830. 52 p. CtY;
ICN; MH; MHi; MiD-B; PHi;
PPAmP.   802

---- Examination of Lewis Cass
on the subject of the removal of
the Indians. With an article
from the American Monthly Magazine. Boston, 1830. 72 p. PHi.
                               803
Castle Garden grand aerostatic
ascension, of Charles F. Durant
... Joseph C. Spear, printer.
[New York, 1830] Bdsd. NN.
                               804
Catalogue of the extensive and
valuable collection of pictures,
engravings, and works of art...
collected by M. Paff, esq., of
this city, dec'd... The whole of
which will be disposed of at pub-

lic auction. [New York, 1830]
42 p. DLC; MH; PPPM.   805

Catholic Church.
    Pastoral letter of the Most
Reverend the Archbishop of Baltimore, and other right reverend
and very reverend prelates of the
Roman Catholic Church of the
United States, in council assembled at Baltimore, in October,
1829 to the Roman Catholic Laity
of the United States of America.
Baltimore, Pub. by James Myres.
Bailey & Francis, prs., 1830.
28 p. DLC.   806

---- Translation of the form for
conferring orders in the Roman
Catholic Church, according to the
Latin rite. Published by the au-
thority of the Right Rev. John
England, D.D., Bishop of Charl-
eston. Charleston, William S.
Blain, 1830. 54 p. DGU; MdBS;
MoSU; ScU.   807

A Catholic clergyman. See An
affectionate address.

[Cazotte, Jacques], 1720-1792.
    The devil in love. Translated
from the French. From the last
London ed. Boston, N. H. Whitaker, 1830. MH.   808

Cecil, Richard.
    ...A friendly visit to the house
of mourning. Pub. by the American Tract Society [Fanshaw, pr.]
[1830?] 32 p. No. 3. PPL.   809

---- ---- New York, Pub. by the
American Tract Society, D. Fan-
shaw, pr., [1830] 79 p. PPL.
                            810
The celebrated dance in Tekeli.
See Hook, James.

Celebration in Baltimore of the
triumph of liberty in France with
the address delivered on that occasion, by Wm. Wirt, on Monday,

October 25, 1830. Baltimore,
John D. Toy, pr. 1830. 42 p.
DLC; KyDC; MBAt; MBC; MH;
MdBE; MdHi; MiD-B; N; NjP;
OCLaw; PPL; BrMus.   811

The cerebro-spinal axis of man.
With the origin and first division
of its nerves. From the French
of M. Manec, D.M.P. ...
Trans. and rev. by J. Pancost,
M.D. Philadelphia, Pub. by Towar and Hogan, Adam Waldie,
pr. [1830] Bdsd. PPL.   812

Cervantes Saavedra, Miguel de,
1547-1616.
    The life and exploits of the in-
genious gentleman Don Quixote
de la Mancha. Translated from
the original Spanish of Miguel
de Cervantes Saavedra by Charles
Jarvis, esq. To which is prefixed, a life of the author...
Philadelphia, J. Crissy and J.
Grigg, 1830. 4 v. DeGE; THi.
                            813

Chadwick, Jabez.
    Two discourses on Christian
baptism: showing reasons for
renouncing the baptism of infants
and for limiting that ordinance to
believers in Christ. Ithaca,
Mack & Andrus, 1830. 42, [1]
p. CSmH; CtY; N; NAuT.   814

Chahta holisso. See Wright, Alfred.

The chain of affection. See
Stringer, Mrs.

Challoner, Richard, bp.
    Considerations upon Christian
truths and Christian duties, digested into Meditations for every
day in the year. Part I For the
first six months. Philadelphia,
Pub. by Eugene Cummiskey,
1830. 296 p. DGU; ICN; MdW.
                            815
---- ---- Part II. For the last
six months. Philadelphia, Pub.

by Eugene Cummiskey. Boston Type and Stereotype Foundry, 1830. 312 p. MdW. 816

Chalmers, Thomas, 1780-1847.
  The works of Thomas Chalmers... Complete in one volume. Philadelphia, Towar, J. & D. M. Hogan; and Hogan & Co. Pittsburg. Sold also by J. P. Haven, New-York; and Pierce & Williams, Boston. Stereotyped by L. Johnson. 1830. 469 p. CBPac; CSmH; CtY; ICT; KyDC; MBC; MH; MMeT-Hi; MWA; MdBS; MeB; MiD; MnU; MoSpD; NSyU; NdHi; NjP; PP; RPB. 817

[Chandler, A.]
  The Scripture directory to baptism, or A faithful citation of the principal passages of the Old & New Testaments, which relate to the mode of administering this ordinance: with the sacred text ... By a Layman. New York, Pr. by D. Fanshaw, 1830. 45 p. Ct; MB; PPLT. 818

Channing, Walter, 1786-1876
  Cases of inflammation of the veins, with remarks on the supposed identity of phlebitis and phlegmasia dolens. [Boston, 1830] 41 p. CtHT-W; MBCo. 819

Channing, William Ellery, 1780-1842.
  Discourses, reviews, and miscellanies. Boston, Carter and Hendee [Stereotyped by Lyman Thurston & Co.] 1830. ix, 603 p. CBPac; CU; CtHT; CtY; GDC; IU; KyDC; MB; MBC; MH; MHi; MeB; MeU; MiU; MoSpD; NCH; NIC; NNG; NbCrD; NhD; NjPT; O; PHi; PP; PPi; PPL; PSC; PU; RHi; RPAt; RPB; TNJ; TxH; BrMus. 820

[----] Remarks on physical education. [Boston? ca. 1830?] 8 p. MB. 821

---- A sermon, preached at the annual election, May 26, 1830, before His Excellency Levi Lincoln... His Honor Thomas L. Winthrop... the honorable Council, and the Legislature of Massachusetts. Boston, Pub. by Carter and Hendee, Dutton and Wentworth, prs., 1830. 46 p. (5 lines in imprint.) CBPac; CSmH; CtY; DLC; ICU; MB; MBAU; MH; MWA; MdHi; MeB; MiD-B; NIC; NNG; NNUT; NbHi; NjPT; OCHP; OClWHi; PHi; PPAmP; PPL; PU; RHi; RPB; ScHi; ViU; BrMus. 822

---- A sermon, preached at the annual election, May 26, 1830 ... Boston, Dutton and Wentworth, 1830. 46 p. (Imprint 3 lines, no dotes in 2d line, Boston in roman.) CSmH; PPL. 823

---- ---- Boston, Dutton and Wentworth... 1830. 46 p. (Imprint 3 lines, dotes in 2d line, Boston in black letter.) CSmH. 824

Chapin, Stephen.
  Series of letters on the mode and subjects of baptism. Addressed to the Christian public. 2d ed. With an appendix, containing strictures on Mr. Moore's reply. Boston, Pr. and pub. by Lincoln & Edmands, 1830. 68 p. KyLoS. 825

Chapman, Isaac A.
  A sketch of the history of Wyoming. By the late Isaac A. Chapman, esq. To which is added, an appendix, containing a statistical account of the valley, and adjacent country. By a gentleman of Wilkesbarre. Wilkesbarre, Pa., Pr. & pub. by Sharp D. Lewis, 1830. 209 p. CSmH; CtHT-W; CtSoP; DeGE; ICN; IaHA; MBAt; MH; MWA; MdBE; MdBJ; MiD-B; MnHi; MoS; NBLiHi; NNUT; NcAS; NjPT; OCHP; OClWHi; PHi; PPL; PU; RPB;

Vt; BrMus.   826

Chapman, James.
Historical notices of Saint
Peter's Church, in the city of
Perth-Amboy, New Jersey, con-
tained in two discourses deliv-
ered...by James Chapman ...
Elizabeth-Town, Sanderson &
Brookfield, 1830. 28 p. MB;
NBLiHi; NNG; NjR; PHi;
PPPrHi; BrMus.   827

Chapone, Hester (Mulso), 1727-
1801.
Chapone on the improvement of
the mind. Dr. Gregory's legacy
to his daughters. Lady Pennington's advice to her absent daughters... Philadelphia, Pub. by L.
Johnson. S. Probasco, pr., 1830.
[viii], 208 p. CtHi; KyHi; MDeeP.
                              828
---- Letters on the improvement
of the mind. Addressed to a lady.
By Mrs. Chapone. A father's
legacy to his daughter, by Dr.
Gregory. A mother's advice to
her absent daughter, with an additional letter on the management
and education of infant children by
Lady Pennington. New York, W.
Marks, 1830. 279 p. NPV.
                              829
Charless' Missouri almanac for
1831. By Samuel Burr. St.
Louis, Charless & Paschall
[1830] 12 l. MoSM; NN.   830

The Charleston mercury.
Essays on the origin of the
federal government; tending to
shew that it emanates not from
the people collectively, but from
the people of the respective
states, acting as confederate
sovereignties. Selected from a
series of essays published at
various times in the Charleston
mercury... Charleston [S. C.]
Pr. by A. E. Miller, 1830. 28 p.
CtHT-W; DLC; MB; MBAt; MH;
MHi; PPL.   831

Charleston Protestant Episcopal
Sunday School Society.
The eleventh annual report of
the board of managers of the
Charleston Protestant Episcopal
Sunday School Society, made at
the Anniversary of the Society,
on Whitsun Tuesday, June 1st,
1830. To which is annexed, a
list of the officers and members
of the society. Charleston, Pr.
by A. E. Miller, 1830. 23 p.
NNG.   832

Charleston, S. C. College of
Charleston.
Catalogue of the trustees, fac-
ulty, and students, of Charleston
College, February 8th, 1830.
Charleston, S. C., W. Riley, pr.
1830. 12 p. ScU.   833

Charlestown, N. H. Public Library.
Regulations and catalogue of
the First Public Library, in
Chalestown [!] N.H. Charlestown [N. H.] Pub. by Webber &
Bowman, 1830. 16 p. MB. 834

Cheever, George Barrell, 1807-
1890.
The American common place
book of prose, a collection of
eloquent and interesting extracts
from the writings of American
authors. By G. B. Cheever.
Boston, Pub. by Carter and Hendee, 1830. 468 p. CSmH; Ct;
ICU; PP; RNR.   835

---- Studies in poetry. Embracing notices of the lives and writings of the best poets in the English language. Boston, Carter
and Hendee, 1830. xvi, 480 p.
CtY; KyDC; MB; MBAt; MBC;
MH; MWA; MeB; MiD; MoSU;
NIC; NbU; NjP; PPL.   836

Cherokee Nation.
Cherokee Phoenix-Extra. Address of the Committee and coun-

cil of the Cherokee nation in general council convened, to the
people of the United States. [New
Echota, Ga., 1830] Bdsd. DLC.
                                  837
---- Address of the "Committee
and council of the Cherokee Nation in general council convened,"
to the People of the United
States. [n.p., 1830] 11 p. DLC;
PPL.   838

Chesapeake and Delaware Canal
Co.
    Eleventh general report of the
president and directors... June 7,
1830. [Baltimore? 1830] 17 p.
NbU; PPL.   839

Chesapeake and Ohio Canal Company.
    Correspondence between the
Chesapeake and Ohio Canal Company and the Baltimore and Ohio
Rail Road Company. In relation
to the disputes between those
companies concerning the right
of way for their respective
works along the Potomac River.
Baltimore, Pr. by Wm. Wooddy,
1830. 80 p. CSt; DBRE; DLC;
DeGE; MH; MWA; MdHi; PPF;
PPi; WU; BrMus.   840

---- Memorial from the ... to
the Legislature of Maryland.
Annapolis, 1830. 12 p. MdBP.
                                  841
---- Second annual report of the
president and directors of the
Chesapeake and Ohio Canal Company, together with the proceedings of the stockholders, at their
second annual meeting, begun,
on the seventh day of June, 1830.
Washington, Pr. by Gales & Seaton, 1830. 42 p. CtY; DLC;
MiU-T; NN; NNE.   842

---- Second annual report of the
president and directors of the
Chesapeake and Ohio Canal Company, together with the proceed-

ings of the stockholders, at their
second annual meeting, begun on
the 7th day of June, 1830, and
held, by adjournment, on the 8th,
9th, 10th, and 12th days of June.
Washington, Pr. by Gales & Seaton, 1830. 38 p.   DIC; ICJ; NN.
                                  843
Chester County Cabinet of Natural Science.
    Third report of the Chester
County Cabinet of Natural Science. March 20, 1830. West-
Chester, Pa., Pr. by Dodson &
Price, 1830. 10 p. PHi.   844

Chesterfield [and other counties]
Va.
    To the General Assembly of
Virginia: The petition of the
undersigned, citizens of the
county of [Blank] respectfully
represents: that the people of
a large and wealthy portion of
this commonwealth being on the
south side of James River, carry
on their whole trade in the city
of Richmond [Text continues]
[Petersburg? 1830?] Bdsd. Vi.
                                  845
[Child, Mrs. Lydia Maria (Francis)]
    The frugal housewife. Dedi-
cated to those who are not
ashamed of economy. By the author of Hobomok...2d ed. cor.
and arranged by the author. To
which is added Hints to persons
of moderate fortune. Boston,
Carter and Hendee, 1830. 128 p.
KU; MNBedf; MdBJ.   846

[----] ---- 3d ed. Boston, Pub.
by Carter & Hendee [Waitt & Dow's
Print. ...Boston] 1830. 128 p.
PPL.   847

Children in the wood.
    The children in the wood, to
which is added, My mother's
grace, a pathetic story. New
York, Pr. and sold by Mahlon
Day at the New Juvenile Book-

store [1830?] 22 p. DLC.   848

...Children of the forest. [New
York, American Tract Society,
1830?] 20 p. Tract no. 245 DLC;
MH.   849

The children's Robinson Crusoe.
See Farrar, Eliza Ware (Rotch)
"Mrs. John Farrar."

The Children's week. By the author
of 'The Morals of pleasure'...
Boston, Carter & Hendee, 1830.
2 l., 135 p. DLC; MH; NN.   850

Childs, Henry Halsey.
   Eulogy on the death of John
Doane Wells, M.D., late professor in the Berkshire Medical Institution, delivered before the
faculty and medical class, September, 1830. Pittsfield, Phinehas Allen & son [1830] 14 p.
MHi; NBMS; BrMus.   851

The child's book of nature; being
figures and descriptions illustrative of the natural history of
beasts, birds, insects, fishes, &c.
Lancaster, Pub. by Carter, Andrews and Co. [1830?] 16 p.
DLC; MdBP.   852

The child's botany. See Goodrich, Samuel Griswald.

The child's diadem. By a lady.
Philadelphia, Fisher [183-?] 120,
[4] p. MB.   853

The child's first step up the ladder of learning; or, Easy lessons
for the infant mind. New York,
Pr. and sold by M. Day [c 1830]
8 l. PP.   854

The child's guide. See Merriam,
George.

The child's instructer. See Ely,
John.

The child's instructor and picture
book. 1st ed. Woodstock, John
Wilcox, 1830. Tingelstad 280.
                            855
Child's instructor; or, A present
for sister. New Haven, S. Babcock. Sidney's Press, 1830.
[18] p. CtHi.   856

The child's own book; or, Spelling and reading illustrated by
emblematic figures. Part I. Boston, Pub. by Munroe and Francis, 1830. 64 p. CtY; DLC;
MBMu.   857

Child's scripture question book.
Philadelphia, [183-?] MBAt.
                            858
Child's song book. See Peabody,
Augustus.

Chinese Museum.
   Unprecedented novelty! The
Chinese lady. [Philadelphia] Jes-
per Harding, pr. [1830] Bdsd.
PPL.   859

Chittenango, N.Y. Polytechny.
   Catalogue of the officers and
students of the Polytechny. Chittenango, Pr. by Isaac Lyon,
1830. 8 p. NjR.   860

Chitty, Joseph, 1776-1841.
   A practical treatise on bills
of exchange, checks on bankers,
promissory notes, bankers' cash
notes, and bank notes...7th
American from the 7th imp. London ed. To which are added the
cases decided in the courts of the
United States, and of the several
states to the present time. by
Thomas Huntington. New York,
Collins & Hannay, 1830. 3 p. l.
[xi]-lxii p., 1 l., 702 (i.e. 644)
p. DLC; ICLaw; KyLoU-L;
MnU; N-L.   861

The choice of a free people.
n.p., 1830. 8 p. [Concerns presidential campaign of H. Clay

"...Jackson scarcely has reign'd
A short year o'er his conquest
..."] <u>PPL</u>.   862

A choice selection of hymns,
from various authors, recommended to all denominations for
the worship of God. 1st edition.
Canton, O. , Pr. by John Sax-
ton, 1830. 256 p. KWiF.   863

Choules, John Overton, 1801-1856.
    A sermon, preached Novem-
ber 26, 1829, being the day of
Thanksgiving; containing a history
of the origin and growth of the
Second Baptist Church in New-
port, [R.I.] Providence, H. H.
Brown, 1830. 27 p. ICMe; ICU;
MB; MBC; MH; MHi; MWA; NN;
PHi; RHi; RPB; BrMus.   864

The Christian almanac, for Connecticut for 1831. Hartford, Connecticut Branch of American
Tract Society; Charles Hosmer
[1830] 20 l. Ct; CtB; CtHi; InU;
MWA; MiD-B; NN; WHi.   865

The Christian almanac for 1831.
Charleston, South Carolina Tract
Society; S. Babcock & Co. [1830]
24 l. ScCC.   866

---- Natchez, American Tract Society [1830] Drake 4529.   867

The Christian almanac, for Kentucky for 1831. Lexington, American Tract Society; Abraham T.
Skillman; Danville, Michael G.
Young; Louisville, William Mix
[1830] 18 l. KyLx; KyU.   868

The Christian almanac, for Maryland and Virginia for 1831. Baltimore, American Tract Society
[1830] 20 l. MWA.   869

The Christian almanac for New
England for 1831. Boston, Lin-
coln & Edmands [1830] 24 l.
CLU; Ct; DLC; ICU; MB; MBAt;

MH; MWA (2 varieties); NN;
NjR; OClWHi; RPB; WHi.   870

The Christian almanac for New
Orleans for 1831. New Orleans,
American Tract Society [1830]
20 l. MWA.   871

The Christian almanac, for New-
York, Connecticut, and New-Jer-
sey for 1831. New-York, Amer-
ican Tract Society [1830] 18 l.
CLU; CtHi; CtY; InU; MWA;
MnU; NHi; NN; NjR; OO; <u>PPL</u>.
                              872
The Christian almanac, for New-
York, Vermont, and Massachu-
setts for 1831. Albany, Ameri-
can Tract Society; Duncan Mc
Kercher [1830] 18 l. N.   873

The Christian almanac for Pennsylvania, Delaware, and West
New-Jersey for 1831. Philadelphia, Pennsylvania branch of the
American Tract Society [1830]
20 l. InU; MWA; NjP; PPi. 874

---- Philadelphia, Pennsylvania
branch of the American Tract Society; Rev. Joel T. Benedict
[1830] 18 l. DLC; MWA; NHi.
                              875
The Christian almanac, for the
state of Connecticut for 1831.
New Haven, S. Babcock [1830] 18
l. MB.   876

The Christian almanac for the
states of Ohio, Kentucky, and Indiana for 1831. Cincinnati, American Tract Society; George T.
Williamson [1830] 18 l. OCHP;
OHi.   877

The Christian almanac for the
Western District for 1831. Ro-
chester, American Tract Society;
Levi A. Ward [1830] 18 l. NR;
NRU.   878

---- Utica, American Tract Society; Edward Vernon [1830] 18 l.

N; NN; NRU; NUtHi.   879

The Christian almanac for the
Western Reserve for 1831.
Cleaveland [sic], American Tract
Society [1830] 18 l. MWA;
OClWHi.   880

The Christian almanac, for Virginia for 1831. Richmond, American Tract Society; Collins & Co.
[1830] 18 l. MWA; Vi; ViU. 881

The Christian almanack for 1831.
By Charles Frederick Egelmann.
Philadelphia, Pennsylvania branch
of the American Tract Society
[1830] 18 l. NjP.   882

The Christian & farmers' almanack for 1831. By Zadock Thompson. Burlington, E. & T. Mills
[1830] 24 l. CLU; DLC; MWA;
VtHi; VtU.   883

The Christian economy: translated from the original Greek of
an old manuscript, found in the
island of Patmos, where St. John
wrote the Book of the Revelation.
Georgetown, D. C., Samuel S.
Rind, 1830. 76 p. CSmH; DLC;
NjP; NjPT.   884

The Christian's companion; or A
new selection of spiritual songs;
designed to be used at camp
meetings... Westfield, N. Y., Pr.
by Hull & Newcomb, for the publishers, 1830. 128 p. CSmH.
                            885
...Christmas day. Published by
the "Episcopal Female Tract Society of Philadelphia," for the
"Society of the Protestant Episcopal Church for the Advancement
of Christianity in Pennsylvania."
Philadelphia, Pr. by William
Stavely, 1830. 8 p. Religious
tracts - No. 76. PPL.   886

Chronicles of the city of Gotham.
See Paulding, James Kirke.

The churchman's almanac for
1831. By David Young. New-
York, New-York Protestant Epis-
copal Press [1830] 18 l. CLU;
MB; MWA; NHi; NNG; NR;
NRHi; OrPD; PPL; ViW; WHi.
                            887
---- By David Young [and] F. R.
Hassler. New-York, New-York
Protestant Episcopal Press
[1830] [Imprint ends with line of
prices.] 18 l. N; NNA.   888

The churchman's reasons for
bringing his children to baptism,
or, Arguments in favor of in-
fant baptism. Stereotyped by
James Conner. New York, New
York Protestant Episcopal Tract
Society, Pr. at the Protestant
Episcopal Press, 1830. 8 p.
CtHT; KyU; MBC; NNG; NjPT.
                            889

Cincinnati.
    The book of prices of the
house carpenters and joiners of
the city of Cincinnati. Adopted:
Monday, January 4, 1819. Cincinnati, Pr. at the Chronicle Office, 1830. 48, [2] p. ICU. 890

Cinderella.
    Cinderella and her glass slip-
pers. New-York, Pub. by Solomon King, 1830. 16 p. MH;
MHi.   891

Circular. See Classical, English, and Agricultural Institute.

(Circular.) Baltimore August,
1830. The undersigned has
rented the Rooms known by the
name of Wentworth Academy,
Baltimore street, No. 132. 4 p.
MdHi.   892

Circular in reference to a Society for the Dissemination of Useful Knowledge. Philadelphia,
1830. Bdsd. MHi.   893

A citizen of Albany, pseud. See
Southwick, John B.

A citizen of Massachusetts,
pseud. See Free masonry; A
poem.

A citizen of New York. See
Lathrop, John Hiram.

A citizen of the United States,
pseud. See Armroyd, George.

Citizens' almanack for 1831.
Philadelphia, Griggs & Dickinson
for L. B. Clarke [1830] 18 1.
MWA; PPL.   894

---- Philadelphia, Griggs & Dickinson, for John Grigg [1830] 18 1.
MWA; PHi; PP.   895

The citizens' and farmers' almanac for 1831. By Charles F. Egelmann. Baltimore, J. T.
Hanzsche [1830] 18 1. MWA;
MdBE; NBLiHi; PHi.   896

Citizens and farmers' almanack
for 1831. Philadelphia, L. B.
Clarke [1830] 18 1. MWA.   897

---- Philadelphia, Griggs & Dickinson [1830] 18 1. PDoBHi. 898

---- Philadelphia, Griggs & Dickinson, for John Grigg [1830] 18 1.
PHi.   899

The citizens' and farmers' yearly
messenger, or New town & country almanac for 1831. By Charles
F. Egelmann. Baltimore, John
T. Hanzsche [1830] 18 1. MWA
(two varieties); OClWHi; PDoBHi.
                                 900
---- By Charles F. Egelmann.
Baltimore, G. McDowell & Co.
[1830] 18 1. MdBE.   901

---- ---- Baltimore, J. Plaskitt
& Co. [1830] 18 1. MdBE. 902

Claiborne, John F. H.
    Speech, on the bill "for the
relief of Jefferson College," delivered in the house of Representatives, of ... Mississippi,
December, 1830... [Washington,
Miss., Cadet Office] 8 p. Ms-
Ar; MsJS.   903

Clarence. See Sedgwick, Catharine Maria.

Clark, George.
    Ladies amusement... Poetry
made without studying and the
best that was ever accomplished
by the 45th degree East Longi-
tude. [183-?] 1 p. DLC.   904

Clark, L. F.
    Questions for Sabbath schools
and Bible classes, adapted to the
Child's expositor and Sabbath
school teacher's assistant. Belchertown, Ms., Pr. and pub. by
S. Wilson, 1830. 36 p. CSmH.
                                 905
Clark, Schuyler.
    The American linguist; or,
Natural grammar. Explaining in
a series of social lessons, the
first elements of language. The
whole interspersed with directions
and questions, for the assistance
of teacher and pupil. Designed to
be a guide to a perfect command
of voice, and proper use of
words. Providence, Pub. by Cory,
Marshall and Hammond, 1830.
240 p. CtHT-W; CtY; DLC; MB;
MH; MeB; NNC; BrMus.   906

Clarke, Adam, 1760?-1832.
    Discourses on various subjects
relative to the being and attributes of God, and his works in
creation, providence, and grace
... 3rd ed. New York, M'Elrath and Bangs. Stereotyped by
James Conner. 1830. 2 v. GEU-
T; MtHi; OMC; PPLT; TxDaM;
ViU (vol. 1 only); WM.   907

Clarke, Francis G.
The seamans manual; containing a variety of matters useful to the navigator... Portland, Shirley, Hyde & Co., 1830. 367 p. DeGE; MH-BA; MeHi. 908

Clarke, John.
An address to the people of Pennsylvania, read to the Antimasonic convention, held at Harrisburg, Feb. 25th, 1830: and offered as a substitute for an address which had previously been read to it... Lancaster [Pa.] Pub. by Theo. Fenn, office of the Anti-masonic Herald, 1830. 34 p. CSmH; DLC; IaCrM; MB; MWA; PHi. 909

Clarke, Samuel.
Address delivered at the State Communication of the Grand Chapter of Mass. June 8, 1830. By the Rev. Samuel Clarke, M.P. and Rev. Paul Dean, G.G. K. Boston, Marsh, Capen & Lyon [Waitt and Dow's, prs.] 1830. 23 p. DLC; IaCrM; MH; MMeT-Hi; MWA; MeB; MiD-B; NNFM; PPFM; WHi; WMFM; BrMus. 910

---- A collection of the sweet assuring promises of Scripture, or The believers' inheritance.... Rev. by J. S. Harrod ... Baltimore, Pub. by Joseph N. Lewis [183-?] 250 p. MB; MdHi; PP. 911

Clarke, Saul.
Saints' perseverance. A sermon preached at Chester, Mass., April 25, 1830. Northampton, Pr. by T. Watson Shepard, 1830. 20 p. MA; MBAt; MBC; BrMus. 912

Clarkson, Thomas, 1760-1846.
Abolition of the African slave-trade, by the British Parliament. Abridged from Clarkson, together with a brief view of the present state of the slave-trade and of slavery... Augusta, Pub. by P. A. Brinsmade at the Depository of Kennebec Co. S. S. Union [Glazier, Masters & Co., pr., Hallowell] 1830. 2 v. CU; CtHT; DLC; GDC; KHi; MB; MeB; NIC; NcD; NjR; OClWHi; OO; RP; TxH; ViU. 913

Clarkstown, N. Y. Reformed Church.
Clarkstown Reformed Sabbath-school anniversary hymns. [Haverstraw? ca. 1830] Bdsd. NN. 914

... Classical, English, and Agricultural Institute, at Bolton Farm, Bucks County, Pa. [Bristol, 1830] 12 p. At head of title: "[Circular.]" PPAmP; PPL. 914a

Claxton, Timothy.
Concise decimal tables, for facilitating arithmetical calculations... Boston, Pr. by Samuel N. Dickinson, at the office of the Mechanicks Magazine, 1830. 23 p. CtHT-W; MB; MH; MWA; PPAmP; PPF; PPL; WU. 915

Clay, Henry, 1777-1852.
An address delivered to the Colonization Society of Kentucky, at Frankfort, Dec. 17, 1829. by the Hon. Henry Clay, at the request of the Board of Managers. Frankfort, Ky., J. H. Holeman, 1830. 24 p. KyDC; MoSHi; NIC. 916

---- Mr. Clay's speech, delivered at the mechanics' dinner, in the Appollonian garden, Cincinnati, on the third of August, 1830. Baltimore, Pr. and for sale at the Baltimore patriot office, 1830. 12 p. DLC; OClWHi. 917

---- Speech of Henry Clay, delivered at the Mechanics' Collation, in the Apollonian Garden, in Cincinnati, (Ohio,) on the 3d of August, 1830. [Cincinnati? 1830] 24 p. DLC; OCHP; PHi;

WHi. 918

---- Speech of the Hon. Henry
Clay, late Secretary of State. delivered, in reply to a toast given
at a public dinner, got up by the
citizens of Washington City, out
of respect for his great public
service, on the 7th of March,
1830. Xenia, Ohio, Pr. by Richard C. Langdon [1830?] 1 p.
DLC. 919

Claybaugh, Joseph.
Discourse delivered at the
first meeting of the Presbytery of
Ohio, in April, 1830, by Rev.
Joseph Claybaugh [Chillicothe?
1830?] 14 p. OCHP; PPPrHi.
920

---- The genius of the gospel,
the genius of universal freedom;
or, The influence of the Christian religion, in improving the
civil and political condition of
mankind. A discourse... Fourth
of July, 1830, in the Associated
Reformed Church, Chillicothe...
Chillicothe, Pr. by Robert Ker-
cheval, 1830. 16, iv p. WHi.
921

Clayton, Augustin Smith.
Review of the report of the
committee of ways and means,
to whom was referred so much of
the message of the president, as
related to the Bank of the United
States, which report was, in the
House of Representatives of the
United States, read and laid on
the table, April 13, 1830. Milledgeville [Ga.], Camak & Ragland, prs., 1830. 43, [1] p.
CSmH; MB; MWA; PHi. 922

Clayton, John Middleton, 1796-
1856.
Speech of Mr. Clayton, of
Delaware, in the Senate of the
United States, on the fourth day
of March, in reply to Mr. Grundy of Tennessee, Mr. Woodbury
of New Hampshire, and others;

the resolution of Mr. Foot, of
Connecticut, being under consideration. Washington, Pr. and
pub. at the Office of the National journal, 1830. 56 p. CSmH;
DeGE; PPL. 923

Clinton, De Witt, engineer.
Correspondence on the importance & practicability of a rail
road, from New York to New Orleans, in which is embraced a
report on the subject, by De
Witt Clinton ... New York, Vanderpool and Cole, prs., 1830.
2 p. l., 23 p. DBRE; DLC;
MB; MHi; MWA; NN; NNC; Nh;
NjR; PPAmP; PPL; WU. 924

Clinton, George W.
An address, delivered at Canandaigua, June 22, 1830, before
the Domestic Horticultural Society of the western parts of the
state of New-York. Published
at the request of the society.
Canandaigua, Pr. by Morse,
Ward and co., 1830. 23 p. MB;
MBHo; NGH; NN; NRHi. 925

Clinton Hall Association.
Proceedings and report at the
opening of Clinton Hall, on Tuesday, November 2, 1830. New
York, Pr. by Elliott and Palmer,
1830. 16 p. DLC. 926

Cloquet, Hippolyte, 1787-1840.
A system of human anatomy,
translated from the fourth edi-
tion of the French of H. Clo-
quet... With notes and a correct-
ed nomenclature, by Robert Knox
... Boston, Wells & Lilly, [etc.]
1830. viii p., 1 l., 836 p. CSt-
L; CtY; GEU-M; ICU-R; KyLxT;
MB; MdUM; MeB; MiDW-M;
MnU; NNNAM; NRAM; NjR;
PPC; PPiU-Med. 927

Cloudesley. See Godwin, William.

Coates, Benjamin H[ornor]
An oration on certainty in
medicine. Delivered before the
Philadelphia Medical Society,
February 10, 1830. Philadelphia,
Pr. by James Kay, jun. & co.,
1830. 29 p. DLC; DNLM; MWA;
PHi; PPL; PU.   928

Cobb, Lyman, 1800-1864.
Cobb's first book; or, Introduction to the spelling-book, designed for the use of small children. Charleston, J. J. Mc-
Carter, 1830. 35 p. NN.   929

---- Cobb's juvenile reader No.
1; containing interesting, moral,
and instructive reading lessons,
composed of easy words of one
and two syllables. Designed for
the use of small children, in
families and schools. Pittsburgh,
Luke Loomis & co. [1830] 72 p.
OClWHi.   930

---- Cobb's series of reading
books, in five numbers. Cobb's
new juvenile reader. No. III. or,
third reading book, containing interesting, historical, moral, and
instructive reading lessons, composed of words of a greater number of syllables than the lessons
in Nos. I and II. ... designed for
the use of larger children in
schools and families. New York,
John C. Riker, 1830. 216 p. NN.
                                  931
Cobb, Sylvanus, 1798-1866.
A sermon (on James iii. 13)
delivered in Malden, Mass., etc.
[Boston? Mass. 1830?] BrMus.
                                  932
Cobbin, Ingram.
The child's arithmetic, on a
plan entirely new, for families
and infant schools. 1st American
from 2d London edition. Hartford, H. & F. J. Huntington [etc.,
etc.] 1830. 138 p. MH.   933

Cochin, M.

Instructions on the progress
and ceremonies of the holy sacrifice of the Mass. Translated
from the French of M. Cochin,
and arranged for each Sunday
throughout the Year, by W. Joseph Walter. Baltimore, Pub. by
Fielding Lucas, Jr.; J. Robinson, pr. [183-?] 352 p. DGU;
MoSU.   934

Cock Robin.
Cock Robin and Jenny Wren.
Published by Turner and Fisher.
Philadelphia [183-] 8 p. MB;
MHi.   935

---- The death and burial of
Cock Robin. New York, George
W. Burgess [183?] 13 l. RPB.
                                  936
Cogswell, William.
A valedictory discourse,
preached to the South Church
and parish in Dedham, Dec. 20,
1829... Boston, Perkins & Mar-
vin, 1830. 28 p. CBPac;
CtSoP; ICN; MB; MBC; MH-AH;
MHi; MWA; MiD-B; MnHi;
NhHi; NjPT; NjR; PHi; RPB;
BrMus.   937

Colburn, Warren.
Arithmetic upon the inductive
method of instruction: being a
sequel to intellectual arithmetic.
...Stereotyped at the Boston
Type and Stereotype Foundry.
Boston, Hilliard, Gray, Little
and Wilkins, 1830. 245, [5] p.
MDeeP; MH; MHi; MeHi; MiHi;
NNC; BrMus.   938

---- ---- Stereotyped at the Bos-
ton Type and Stereotype Foundry.
Philadelphia, Pub. by Uriah
Hunt. Boston, Hilliard, Gray,
Little and Wilkins, 1830. 245 p.
MH; MeHi; BrMus.   939

---- Colburn's first lessons.
Intellectual arithmetic, upon the
inductive method of instruction.

Stereotyped at the Boston Type and Stereotype Foundry. Boston, Hilliard, Gray, Little and Wilkins, 1830. 172 p. MH; MeHi; MiGr; NjR; OClWHi; TxU-T.   940

---- ---- Watertown, N.Y., Pub. by Knowlton & Rice, 1830. 178 p. CtHT-W; NN.   941

---- An introduction to algebra upon the inductive method of instruction. Boston, Hilliard, Gray, Little and Wilkins, 1830. 276 p. MB; MH; MiU; NjR; PPi.
                                    942
---- A key containing answers to the examples in the Sequel to Intellectual arithmetic. Boston, Hilliard, Gray, Little, and Wilkins, 1830. 70 p. MB; MH; MiU; NN.   943

Cole, John, 1774-1855, comp.
   Cole's pocket edition of psalm and hymn tunes. 6th ed. Albany, 1830. NjPT.   944

Coleman, George.
   The circle of anecdote and wit, to which is added a choice selection of toasts and sentiments. New York, S. & D. A. Forbes, pr., 1830. 256 p. NjR.   945

A collection of psalms, hymns, anthems, &c. (With the Evening Office) for the use of the Catholic Church. Throughout the United States. Washington, Pr. by J. F. Haliday, 1830. iv, 289 p. DGU; IEG; MdW; NWM.   946

A collection of strange figures of speech, expressive terms and old phrases used in the leading cities of the world. Their origin meaning and application. Collected and arranged by a well known detective. Containing portraits of celebrated criminals, with sketches of their lives.

Published at the National Police Gazette Office, New York, 1830. 54 p. IU.   947

College of Physicians and Surgeons of the Western District of the State of New York. See Fairfield, N.Y.

Collins, Robert.
   An address, delivered in Brunswick, September 22, 1830, before the Brunswick Temperance Society. Troy, N. Tuttle, pr., 1830. 16 p. PPL.   948

Collyer, Mary. The death of Cain. See Gessner, Salomon.

Colman, George, 1762-1836.
   ... Blue Beard; or Female curiosity: a dramatic romance in two acts. By G. Colman, the younger. As altered..., with additional songs, by W. Dunlap, Esq. New York, E. B. Clayton [Clayton & Van Norden, prs.] 1830. 41 p. ICU; MH; NR.
                                    949
---- The mountaineers; an opera, in three acts. As performed in the Philadelphia theatres. Philadelphia, C. and J. C. Neal, 1830. 58 p. MH; NCH; NIC; PU.   950

Colton, Asa S.
   Successful mission, or, A history of the missions conducted by the London Missionary Society in the Society & Georgian Islands, together with an account of the unsuccessful attempt at the Friendly Islands. Philadelphia, Pub. by William Stavely, New York, John P. Haven, 1830. 174 p. CtMW; GDC; MB; MH-AH; NjPT; PU.   951

Colton, Simeon.
   The claims of anti-masonry, and duty of Masons. An address delivered before the Central lodge of Free-masons in Dudley,

Mass., June 24, A. L. 5830...
Southbridge, J. Snow, pr., 1830.
24 p. CSmH; DLC.   952

Colton's Vermont miniature register and gentleman's almanac for
1831. Woodstock, R. & A. Colton
[1830] 60 l. Drake 13656.   953

Colton's Vermont miniature register and gentleman's pocket almanac for 1831. By Marshall
Conant. Woodstock, R. & A. Colton [1830] 60 l. MHi; NN; VtHi;
VtU.   954

Columbia College.
     Claims of the new university.
New York, 1830. MB.   955

---- Columbia College. New
York, 23d January 1830.   The
faculty of Columbia hereby give
notice to the public... Course of
instruction... 4 p. MB.   956

---- A statute, passed at a meeting of the board of trustees of
Columbia College, on the 16th
January, 1830. [New York, 1830]
4 p.   MH.   957

Columbia, S.C. State Rights'
Meeting.
     Proceeding [sic] of the State
rights' meeting.   Columbia, S.C.
on the twentieth of September,
1830.   Columbia, S.C., Pr. at
the "Times & Gazette" Office,
1830.   46 p. DLC; ICN; MHi;
RP; ScU.   958

Columbian almanac for 1831. By
William Collom.   Philadelphia,
Joseph M'Dowell [1830] 18 l. InU;
MWA; MiU-C; NHi; NN; NjR;
PHi; PPL.   959

The Columbian calendar, or New-
York and Vermont almanack for
1831.   Troy, Francis Adancourt
[1830] 12 l. CLU; MWA; N; NCH;
NT; OClWHi; PHi; VtHi.   960

The Columbus almanac for 1831.
By William Lusk.   Columbus,
Olmsted & Bailhache [1830] 12 l.
MWA; OHi.   961

---- Issue with 24 l. [Cover
title: "Magazine Almanac for
1831"] N.   962

Come rest in this bosom.   The
soidier's [!] return.   Old Adam.
The rose tree.   And Jessie, the
flower of Dumblane.   Philadelphia,
Sold by R. Swift [1830?]   8 p.
DLC.   963

The commandment with promise.
By the author of "The Last Day
of the Week." ... Pub. by Perkins & Marvin, Boston, 1830.
288 p. MA; MH; MeBa.   964

The complete fortune-teller and
dream book; a new system for
foretelling future events by
dreams, etc., by Madam Connoisseur [pseud.] Providence, 1830.
RPB.   965

The complete New-England almanac for 1831. By Marshall Conant.   Woodstock, R. & A. Colton
[1830] 18 l. CtY; DLC; MB; MWA;
VtHi.   966

Comstock, Andrew.
     Practical elocution; or, The
art of reading simplified: Being a selection of pieces in prose
and verse.   Philadelphia, Uriah
Hunt [William Brown, pr.] 1830.
xiii, [1], 300 p. MWA; PPAmP;
PPL; PSC-Hi.   967

Comstock, John Lee, 1789-1858.
     Natural history of birds; with
engravings, on a new plan, exhibiting their comparative size;
adapted to the Capacities of
youth.... Hartford, D. F. Robinson and Co., 1830. 216 p.
ArBaA; CtHT-W; NBLiHi; Nh;
OClW; WBB.   968

---- A system of natural philosophy; in which the principles of mechanics, hydrostatics, hydraulics, pneumatics, acoustics, optics, astronomy, electricity, and magnetism are familiarly explained. Hartford, D. E. Robinson, 1830. 295 p. CtHT-W; GU; ICU; KyDC; MBC; MH; MdU; MiU; NjR; TNJ.   969

Comstock, Joshua, comp.
The whole duties of men and women, in two parts. With an appendix, containing The polite philosopher, and Dr. Franklin's Way to wealth. New York, S. Hoyt & Co., 1830. 162 p. CtY.
970

Concert. Signorina Giulia Da Ponte's vocal and instrumental concert will take place at the Musical Fund Society's hall, on Friday evening, May 21st, 1830. [Philadelphia] Pr. at the office of the Daily Chronicle [1830] Bdsd. PPL.   971

Concise history of the First Church of Christ in Ipswich... Boston, Crocker and Brewster, 1830. 22 p. MBC; MHa; MWA.
972

The Concord directory, containing the names of the legal voters and householders, belonging to the Centre village, and its adjacent neighborhood; ... Concord [N. H.] Pr. by Hoag and Atwood, 1830. 24 p. CSmH; DLC; MiD-B.   973

Concord, Mass.
Regulations of the school committee of the town of Concord. Revised and adopted March, 1830. ... Concord, Herman Atwill, 1830. 8 p. MB; MH; MWA. 974

Concord Mechanic's Association. Concord, N. H.
Report submitted to the Concord Mechanics' Association, at

a quarterly meeting, April 6, 1830. 8 p. DLC.   975

Concord, N. H. First Congregational Church.
A list of the pastors, deacons, and members of the First Congregational Church, in Concord, New-Hampshire, from 18 November, 1730, to 18 November, 1830. Concord, Pr. by Asa M' Farland, 1830. 21 p. CSmH; CtY; DLC; MBC; NBLiHi.   976

Condition and character of females in pagan and Mohammedan countries. [Boston? 1830?] 16 p. PPL.   977

Congregational Churches in Connecticut. Eastern district of Fairfield County. Auxiliary Foreign Mission Society.
Fifth annual report... October 20, 1829. New Haven, Pr. by Hezekiah Howe, 1830.   978

Congregational Churches in Maine. General Conference.
Minutes of the General Conference of Maine at their annual meeting, Winthrop, June 22, 1830. Portland, Shirley, Hyde & Co., 1830. 24 p. MeBaT; NhHi.
979

Congregational Churches in Massachusetts. General Association.
Minutes of the General Association of Massachusetts, at their meeting in Groton, June, 1830. Boston, Pr. by Crocker & Brewster, 1830. 32, [14] p. DLC; M.   980

Congregational Churches in New Hampshire. General Association.
Minutes of the ... at their annual meeting at Portsmouth, September 7, 1830. ... Concord, Asa M'Farland, pr. [1830] 24 p. CtHi.   981

Congregational Churches in Vermont. General Convention.

Extracts from the minutes of
the General Convention of Congregational and Presbyterian ministers in Vermont, at their session
at East Rutland, September 1830.
Windsor, Pr. at the Chronicle
Press, 1830. 20 p. MiD-B.
982

---- Montpelier Association.

Proceedings of the "Mont-
pelier Association," in reply to
annexed statements of Henry
Jones, one of that body, in relation to the influence of freemasonry in the churches. Danville,
Pr. by E. Eaton, 1830. 22 p.
MB; VtHi.   983

A connected view. See Armroyd, George.

Connecticut (Colony).

The code of 1650, being a
compilation of the earliest laws
and orders of the General court
of Connecticut: also, the Constitution, or civil compact...to
which is added some extracts
from the laws and judicial proceedings of New Haven Colony
commonly called blue laws. Hartford, Silas Andrus, 1830. 119 p.
Ct; CtSoP; CtY; DLC; GDC; MnU;
NIC; NN; Nv; OMC; PU.   984

Connecticut (State).

[Arms] By His Excellency Gideon Tomlinson, governor of the
State of Connecticut, a proclamation. The continuance of our
lives, during another revolution
of favorable seasons, the general prevalence of health...I do,
therefore appoint Thursday, the
twenty-fifth day of November next
to be observed as a day of public thanksgiving and prayer,
throughout this state... Given under my hand, at Fairfield, this
thirteenth day of October, in the
year of our Lord one thousand,
eight hundred and thirty... Gide-

on Tomlinson. 1 p. DLC. 985

---- Message of Governor Tomlinson to the legislature of Connecticut, May session, 1830.
New Haven, J. Barber, 1830. 1
l. (fold) Ct.   986

---- The public statute laws of
the state of Connecticut, passed
at the session of the General Assembly in 1830. Published by authority of the General Assembly,
under the direction and superintendence of the secretary of this
state. Hartford, Pr. by Charles
Babcock, 1830. [3], 254-317 p.
Ar-SC; CtSoP; IaU-L; MdBB;
NNLI; Nb; Nv; Wa-L.   987

---- Report, [Committee of the
School fund.] May 1830. New
Haven, J. Barber, 1830. 15 p.
NRHi.   988

---- Report of the directors and
warden of the Connecticut State
Prison. Submitted to the Legislature May session, 1830... New
Haven, Pr. by Hezekiah Howe,
1830. 28 p. CSmH; Ct; CtHT;
DNLM.   989

---- Reports of cases argued and
determined in the Supreme Court
of Errors, of the State of Connecticut. In the years 1802, 1803,
and 1804. Vol. I. 2d. ed., with
notes and references. Philadelphia, P. H. Nicklin & T. Johnson, 1830. [2], 7, 339, [2] p.
C; CoU; Ct; F-SC; In-SC; KU;
KyLxT; MdBB; MeU; Ms; NNU;
P; BrMus.   990

The Connecticut annual register,
and United States' calendar for
1831. New-London, Samuel
Green [1830] 78 l. Ct; CtHi;
CtY; InU; MB; MHi; MWA; N;
Nh.   991

Connecticut. Colonization Society.

Third annual report of the managers of the Colonization Society of the state of Connecticut. With an appendix. May, 1830. New Haven, Baldwin & Treadway, 1830. 28 p. CtHT; GDC; MA; MBAt; MH-AH; MHi; NjP; OO; RP. 992

Connecticut Medical Society.
Report of a committee of the Connecticut Medical Society, respecting an asylum for inebriates, with the resolutions of the Society, adopted at their annual meeting, May 1830. New Haven, Pr. by Hezekiah Howe, 1830. 1 p. l., 9 p. CtY; DLC; MH-M. 993

Connecticut. Retreat for the Insane.
Report of the medical visitors of the Connecticut Retreat for the Insane, presented to the society May 13, 1830. With tables for three years commencing 1st April 1827, and ending 1st April 1830. Hartford, Hudson and Skinner, prs., 1830. 22 p. Ct; CtHT-W; IEN; MB; N; NjR; TxU. 994

Connecticut Sunday School Union.
The annual report of the Connecticut Sunday School Union, presented at the sixth annual meeting of the Society, holden in New-Haven, May 6, 1830. New-Haven, Pr. by Charles Adams [1830] 40 p. CtHi. 995

Connoisseur, Madam, pseud. See The complete fortune-teller.

Considerations on the practicability, and utility, of immediately constructing a rail way, from Pottsville to Sunbury and Danville, through the coal region of Mahonoy & Shamokin; with the proceedings of a meeting at Sunbury, December, 1830. [Milton, Pa., Pr. at the office of the "State's advocate," 1830] 24 p. CSmH; DBRE; DLC; DeGE; ICJ; MB; MH-BA; MWA; PPL; WU. 996

Considerations on the practicability and utility of immediately constructing a central railway, from Pottsville to Sunbury and Danville, through the coal region of Mahanoy and Shamokin, with the proceedings of a meeting at Sunbury, Dec. 1830. Republished with additions by the Philadelphia committee... [Philadelphia] 1830. 1 p. l., 37 p. DBRE; DLC; DeGE; MH-BA; MWA; MiU-T; N; NN; PPL (34+ p.). 997

Considerations on the present state of the Indians. See Cass, Lewis.

Considerations upon the expediency and the means of establishing a university in the city of New-York. Addressed to the citizens. New-York, Grattan, pr., 1830. 29 p. CoU; CtHT-W; DLC; DNLM; IC; MBAt; MBC; MH; MnHi; NNU; PU; ScCC. 998

Consolation, An offering of sympathy to parents bereaved of their children. Being a collection of manuscripts. Boston, Pr. and pub. by Samuel N. Dickinson, 1830. 224 p. MBAU. 999

The contemplated plan of the Franklin Railroad Company, to commence with a route through the counties of Middlesex, Worcester and Franklin, to the line of Vermont; from thence to lake Champlain and to lake Ontario, with branches convenient to accommodate the inhabitants of Massachusetts. etc. Boston, J. H. Eastburn, 1830. 7 p. DLC; MBAt. 1000

Contestacion a las Observaciones sobre las instrucciones que dió

el Presidente de los Estados
Unidos del Norte America ... a
los representantes de aquella republica en el Congreso de Panama en 1826: sobre la conducta
del Senor Poinsett... Filadelfia,
Impr. de Guillelmo Stavely, 1830.
27 p. C-S; DLC; BrMus.   1001

Conversations on chemistry.
See Marcet, Jane (Haldimand).

Conversations on common things;
or, Guide to knowledge. With
questions.... By a teacher. 3d
ed. Boston, Munroe & Francis,
1830. 288 p. KyBC; ScCliTO.
                                 1002
Conversations on natural philosophy. See Marcet, Mrs. Jane
(Haldimand.)

Conversations on the Burman
mission, by a lady of New Hampshire. Revised by the publishing
committee. Boston, Mass., Sabbath School Union, 1830. 160 p.
GDC; MB; MH-AH; NhHi.   1003

Conversations on the Choctaw
mission. See Tuttle, Sarah.

Conversations on vegetable physiology. See Marcet, Mrs. Jane
(Haldimand).

The conversion of an infidel, being the confession and exhorta-
tion of an old man, who wishes
well to his fellow mortals, near
the close of his life. Enfield,
Mass., Pr. for the Proprietor,
John Howe, pr., 1830. 43 p.
CSmH; CtHT-W; MWA; NN. 1004

Cook, Charles.
    A brief account of the African
Christian Church, in New-Bed-
ford. Being the first of the
Christian denomination in the
United States formed by people of
colour. New-Bedford, Benjamin
T. Congdon, 1830. 8 p.

NHi.   1005

Cook, Zebedee.
    An address, pronounced before
the Massachusetts Horticultural
Society. In commemoration of
its second annual festival, the
10th of September, 1830. Boston, Pr. by Isaac R. Butts,
1830. 54 p. CU; DLC; MBAt;
MH; MHi; MWA; MiD; NCH; NN;
BrMus.   1006

The cook not mad, or, Rational
cookery;... Watertown, Knowlton
& Rice, 1830. "From NN imprint catalog but not in NN."
                             1007
Cooke, Bates.
    Remarks of Mr. Bates Cooke,
of New York, made in the U.
States Anti-Masonic Convention
held at Philadelphia, September
11, 1830. Providence, H. H.
Brown, pr., 1830. 12 p.
MNBedf.   1008

Cooke, John Esten, 1783-1853.
    Answer to the review of an
essay on the invalidity of Presbyterian ordination published in
the January number of the Biblical Repertory & Theological Review, of Princeton, New Jersey.
Lexington, Ky., Pr. at the Reporter office, 1830. 136 p.
CSmH; CtHT; DLC; GDC; ICU;
KyLxT; KyU; MiU-C; NNG; NhD;
NjPT; NjR; PHi; PPPrHi; RPB;
TxU; BrMus.   1009

Cooke, Thomas Simpson, 1782-
1848.
    Singing exemplified, in a se-
ries of solfeggi and exercises,
progressively arranged with an
accompaniment for the piano
forte. To which are affixed explanatory observations composed
& written by T. Cooke. ... New
York, Pub. by Geib & Walker,
[183-] 97 p. CSmH.   1010

Cooley, E.
Description of the etiquette at Washington city. [Philadelphia, L. B. Clarke, 1830] 112 p. DLC; MB. 1011

Cooper, James Fenimore, 1789-1851.
Greenough's marble group of chanting cherubs now exhibiting at the American Academy of Fine Arts, New York. [New York, J. W. Bell, 1830] 4 p. MH. 1012

---- Lionel Lincoln; or, The leaguer of Boston... by the author of "The Spy," in two volumes. 5th ed. Philadelphia, Carey & Lea, 1830. 2 vols. PU. 1013

Cooper, Joab Goldsmith.
The North American spelling-book; or The youth's instructor in the art of spelling and reading: methodically arranged, and calculated to lead to a correct pronunciation of the English language. By Rev. J. G. Cooper, A.M. author of A new and improved system of practical arithmetic, &c. Philadelphia, Towar, J. & D. M. Hogan; Pittsburgh, Hogan & Co., 1830. 148 p. DLC; MH; NH. 1014

---- The scholar's assistant; or, A plain, comprehensive, and practical system of arithmetic: To which is prefixed an introduction, containing a practical illustration of the primary rules, and of the tables of money, weights, and measures. Designed for the use of schools in the United States. Philadelphia, Towar, J. & D. M. Hogan; Pittsburg, Hogan & Co., C. Sherman & Co., prs., 1830. 288 p. CtHT-W; LU; BrMus. 1015

Cooper, Samuel, 1780-1848.
...A dictionary of practical surgery; comprehending all the most interesting improvements from the earliest times down to the present period... From the 6th London ed., rev., corr. & enl. with numerous notes... embracing improvements...by American surgeons... by David Meredith Reese. New York, J. & J. Harper, 1830. 2 v. CSt-L; DLC; ICJ; MBCo; MdW; NBMS; OClM; PPC; ViU; (At head of title: Harper's Stereotype edition. Uniform with Hooper's[!] Medical Dictionary.) 1016

---- The first lines of the practice of surgery designed as an introduction for students and a concise book of reference for practitioners, by Samuel Cooper. With notes by Alexander H. Stevens, and additional notes by Samuel McClellan. 3d American from the 5th London ed. Philadelphia, Pub. by John Grigg; L. H. Bailey, pr., 1830. 2 v. CSt-L; CtY; GU-M; ICJ; ICU-R; IU; MBCo; MdBJ; MdBM; MoS; NBMS; NBuU-M; NNNAM; PPC; PPF; TxU; ViU. 1017

Cooper, Thomas, 1759-1840.
Consolidation. An account of parties in the United States, from the Convention of 1787, to the present period. 2d. ed. Columbia, S.C., Pr. at the "Times and Gazette" office, 1830. 37 p. A-Ar; CtY; DLC; IEN-M; MHi; MdBJ; NNNAM; ScC; ScU. 1018

---- A treatise on the law of libel and the liberty of the press; showing the origin, use, and abuse of the law of libel, with copious notes and references to authorities in Great Britain and the United States; as applicable to individuals and to political and ecclesiastical bodies and principles. New York, Pr. by G. F. Hopkins & son, 1830. 184 p. CSmH; DLC; ICLaw; IU;

IaU; InU; MH-L; MeB; MoU;
NNS; NcD; OCLaw; P; PPL;
PPiAL; PU-L; ScU; TxU; BrMus.
                                1019
[Coote, Clement T.] d. 1849.
   A discourse on the principle
and practice of charity: delivered in the Central masonic hall,
in the city of Washington, on the
8th of March, 1830, before the
members and visitors of Federal
lodge no. 1, by the R. W. Master... Washington, Pr. by W.
Greer, 1830. 24 p. DLC; PPL;
ScU.   1020

Corporation for the Relief of the
Widows and Children of Clergy-
men in the Communion of the
Protestant Episcopal Church in
the Commonwealth of Pennsylvania.
   The charter of the Corporation...and an act of the Assembly altering and confirming it.
Philadelphia, Jesper Harding,
pr. 1830. 24 p. PHi.   1021

Corrector, pseud.
   Letters addressed to Martin
van Buren, esq., Secretary of
State: correcting many important
errors in a late biography of
that gentleman. By Corrector.
New York, Pr. October first,
1830. 15 p. DLC; MB; MH;
PPL; ScU; BrMus.   1022

A cosmopolite, pseud.   See
Lawson, James.

Cosmopolite - A listener, pseud.
See Dow, Lorenzo.

The cottage boy, or, The history
of Peter Thompson. Revised by
the Committee of publication.
Philadelphia, American Sunday
School Union, 1830. 36 p. DLC;
NNC.   1023

Cottom's constitutional almanack
for 1831. By Joseph Cave.

Richmond, Peter Cottom [1830]
18 l. DLC; ViHi.   1024

Cottom's Virginia & North Caro-
lina almanack for 1831. By
Joseph Cave. Richmond, Peter
Cottom [1830] 18 l. DLC; ICN;
MWA; NcD.   1025

The country curate. See Gleig,
George Robert.

Cousin Elizabeth, by the author
of "A visit to the sea-side."
... Boston, Leonard C. Bowles,
1830. 210 p. DLC; KU; MH.
                                1026
Cowles, Eber.
   A sermon, on the danger and
possibility of falling from grace
... Taunton [Mass.] Repub. by
Abijah Baker; Edmund Anthony,
pr., 1830. 24 p. CSmH.   1027

[Cox, Richard] 1808-1860.
   The duty of Christians with
respect to war... [New York?
1830?] 16 p. NNG.   1028

Coxe, John Redman, 1773-1864.
   American dispensatory containing the natural, chemical,
pharmaceutical, and medical history of the different substances
employed in medicine; together
with the operations of pharmacy;
... 8th ed. imp. and greatly enl.
Philadelphia, Carey & Lea [Sker-
rett] 1830. iv, 808 p. ICU-R;
IEN-M; LNOP; MBCo; MdBJ;
MdUM; NBMS; NNNAM; PPC;
PPL; PPiU; WU.   1029

---- Observations on the subject
of the Jalap plant. ... [Extracted
from the American Dispensatory,
eighth edition, and from the February number of the American
Journal of the Medical Sciences.]
[Philadelphia, 1830] 12 p. PPL.
                                1030
Coxe, Richard Smith, 1792-1865.
   Address delivered by Richard

S. Coxe, before the mechanics and other citizens of the city of Washington, friends of Henry Clay, on Monday, July 5, 1830. Washington, Pr. by Peter Force, 1830. 15 p. CSmH; DLC; DeGE; LNHT; MHi; MiU; NCH; OClWHi; OO; PHi; PPL; RPB.   1031

Crabb, George, 1778-1851.
Dictionary of general knowledge, or explanation of words and things connected with all the arts and sciences. American ed., with many improvements. Boston, Gray and Bowen, 1830. 368 p. MH; MWA; MoSU.   1032

---- ---- New York, White, Gallaher and White, 1830. [Stereotyped by Lyman Thurston & Co., Boston] iv, 368 p. CLCM; CSansS; IC; MBAt; MDeeP; Mi; NcA-S; PPL.   1033

---- Harper's Stereotype edition. English synonymes... A new edition enlarged. New York, Pub. by J. & J. Harper, Sold by E. Duyckinck [etc.] 1830. 535, [1] p. Ct; LNHT; MWA; NBuG; NN; PPL; RPAt; ScC.   1034

[Craik, George Lillie] 1789-1866.
The library of entertaining knowledge. The New Zealanders. Boston, Lilly & Wait, G. & C. & H. Carvil, and E. Bliss; New York, Carey & Hart; Philadelphia, W. & J. Neal; Baltimore, P. Thompson; Washington, R. Cruikshank, Georgetown, 1830. 424 p. CSmH; CtY; IEG; KyDC; MB; NCH; NN; Nh; Nj; WHi.   1035

---- The library of entertaining knowledge. The pursuit of knowledge under difficulties. Illustrated by anecdotes. Revised edition. With preface and notes, by F. Wayland. Boston, Wells & Lilly, 1830-1831. 2 vols. CtHT; CtY; KyDC; MB; MeB; MoSW; NCH;

NRU; Nh; Nj.   1036

Cramer's magazine almanack for 1831. By Sanford C. Hill. Pittsburgh, Cramer & Spear [1830] 36 l. OClWHi; PPi.   1037

Cramer's Pittsburgh almanack for 1831. By Sanford C. Hill. Pittsburgh, Cramer & Spear [1830] 18 l. CLU; OFH; PPi.   1038

Crayon, Geoffrey, pseud. See Irving, Washington.

Cresson, Elliot.
What can colonization do? From the Boston Daily Advertiser ... Elliot Cresson. Tremont Hotel, Dec. 31 [183-?] 1 p. DLC.   1039

[Cresson, Warder]
Babylon the Great is falling! The morning star, or, Light from on high. Written in defence of the rights of the poor and oppressed ... Philadelphia, Pr. by Garden & Thompson, 1830. 67, [1], 3 p. NNUT; OClWHi; PHi; PPL; PSC-Hi.   1040

Crockett, David.
Col. Crockett's exploits and adventures in Texas: ... written by himself. Philadelphia, T. K. and P. G. Collins, [Stereotyped by L. Johnson, Philadelphia] 1830. 216 p. NNS.   1041

Croly, George, 1780-1860, comp.
The beauties of the British poets. With a few introductory observations. By the Rev. George Croly. New-York, Charles Wells; Piercy & Reed, prs., [183-?] CSmH.   1042

Crosby, Eliza Leland.
Chronological rhymes prepared for the aid and comfort of a class of little girls, battling with Blair's Outlines, in the School in the garden on Harlow Street.

Bangor, 1830. 4 p. Williamson, 2552.   1043

Crosby, Jaazaniah, 1780-1864.
The tendency of religious obedience to promote national prosperity. A sermon, preached at Concord... June 3, A. D. 1830. Being the anniversary election. Concord [N.H.] Pr. by Hill & Barton for the state, 1830. 16 p. CSmH; DLC; MBC; MNtcA; MW; MiD-B; NhHi; BrMus.   1044

Cruden, Alexander, 1701-1770.
A complete concordance to the Holy Scriptures of the Old and New Testament: or, A dictionary and alphabetical index to the Bible ... From the 10th London ed., carefully rev. and cor. by the Holy Scriptures ... Philadelphia, T. Wardle, 1830. 856 p. CBCDS; CtHT; CtY; ICU; IEG; Ia; MB; MH; MnSH; NjPT; PV; TNJ. 1045

A cry from the wilderness. See Dow, Lorenzo.

Cumberland almanac for 1831. By William L. Willeford. Nashville, Hunt, Tardiff & Co. [1830] 18 l. DLC.   1046

Cumberland Fire Engine Company, Cumberland, Md.
Constitution of the Cumberland Fire Engine Company. Cumberland [Md.] Pr. by Samuel Charles, 1830. 11 p. CSmH.   1047

Cumberland Law Library. Cumberland, Me.
Catalogue of the Cumberland Law Library. Portland, Shirley and Hyde, 1830. 22 p. MeHi.   1048

Cumberland Presbyterian Church.
The constitution of the Cumberland Presbyterian Church, in the U. States of America. Containing the confession of faith; a catechism; the government and discipline; a directory for the worship of God. 2d ed. Rev. and adopted by the General Assembly, at Princeton, Ky. May 1829. Fayetteville, Pr. by Ebenezer & J. B. Hill, 1830. [3], 177, [3] p. KyHb; KyLoF; NNG; NcMHi; PPPrHi.   1049

Cummings, Asa, 1791-1856.
A memoir of the Rev. Edward Payson, D. D. Late pastor of the second church in Portland. By Asa Cummings... 2d ed. Boston, Pub. by Crocker and Brewster, New York, J. Leavitt, [Stereotyped at the Boston Type and Stereotype Foundry] 1830. viii, 400 p. CU; CtSoP; IC; MB; MBAt; MH; MHi; MeHi; MoSpD; PPPrHi; ScClTO; ViRUT.   1050

---- ---- 3rd ed. Boston, Pub. by Crocker and Brewster; New York, J. Leavitt [Stereotyped at the Boston Type and Stereotype Foundry] 1830. viii, 400 p. CtY; DLC; GDC; ICN; InNd; KyLoS; MBC; MH; MWA; MeB; NN; NNUT; NjP; RNHi; ScCC.   1051

---- A memoir of the Rev. Edward Payson, D. D., late of Portland, Maine. New York, Pub. by the American Tract Society, D. Fanshaw, pr. [c1830] 486 p. (Vol. XII of the Evangelical family library) ArU; CBPac; CSmH; CtHT; CtY; IU; IaDuU; KWiU; LNHT; LU; MB; MH; MeB; MiD; MoSpD; NBuU; NN; NPV; NcU; NjR; OClWHi; PHC; PPPrHi; RPAt; RPB; ScU; TNJ.   1052

---- ---- Portland, Pub. by Ann L. Payson, Shirley and Hyde, prs., 1830. 444 p. ArCH; CtY; DLC; ICN; KyLoS; MB; MBAt; MH; MHi; MWA; MiU; NN; NNUT; NhHi; NjP; RPB.   1053

Cummings, Jacob Abbot, 1773-1820.

First lessons in geography and
astronomy. 14th ed. New Haven,
S. Babcock, 1830. 82 p. MH.
1054
---- An introduction to ancient
and modern geography... 10th ed.
rev. and improved. Boston, Hilliard, Gray, Little and Wilkins,
1830. 204 p. CtHT-W. 1055

---- The pronouncing spelling
book, adapted to Walker's criti-
cal pronouncing dictionary...
Rev. & imp. from 4th ed. Ster-
eotyped by T. H. Carter & Co.,
Boston. Boston, Hilliard, Gray,
Little and Wilkins, 1830. 166 p.
MWA; OClWHi. 1056

---- ---- New York, Pub. by
Collins & Hannay, and Cummings,
Hilliard, & Co., Boston, 1830.
[2], 166 p. PPL. 1057

---- ---- Rev. from 4th ed.
Concord, N. H., Horatio Hill &
co., 1830. 168 p. MBAt; RPB.
1058
---- School atlas to Cummings'
Ancient and modern geography.
Boston, Pub. by Cummings &
Hilliard, [183-?] 10 maps. WHi.
1059

Cunningham, John William.
Address on confirmation, to
young persons, by the Rev. J. W.
Cunningham. Boston, Putnam &
Hunt, 1830. 12 p. MBD. 1060

---- Sermons. By Rev. J. W.
Cunningham, A. M. Vicar of Har-
row; 1st American, from the 2d
London ed. New York, Pub. by
T. & J. Swords; Edward J.
Swords, pr., 1830. viii, 317 p.
CBCDS; CSansS; MH; OMC;
ViRUT. 1061

Curr, Joseph.
Familiar instructions in the
faith of the Catholic Church.
Boston, Donahoe [1830] 150 p.
OHi. 1062

Curtis, Jonathan.
Character and reward of the
wise, who turn many to right-
eousness. A sermon delivered
before the Auxiliary Education
Society of Norfolk County, at
their annual meeting, in Dedham,
South Parish, June 9, 1830. Boston, T. R. Marvin, pr., 1830.
36 p. CtY; MBC; MHi; MWA;
NhHi; NhD; RPB; BrMus. 1063

Custis, George Washington Parke,
1781-1857.
Pocahontas; or, The settlers
of Virginia, a national drama; in
three acts... Philadelphia ed.
[Philadelphia] C. Alexander, pr.,
1830. 47 p. CSt; CtY; DLC;
ICU; MB; NIC; NNC; OClW; PHi;
PPAmP; PU; RPB. 1064

Cuthbert, James.
An address delivered in
Charleston, before the Agricultur-
al Society of South-Carolina, at
the anniversary meeting, on Tues-
day, 18th August, 1830 ...
Charleston [S. C.] Pr. by A. E.
Miller, 1830. 16 p. CSmH. 1065

D

[Dabney, Jonathan Peele] ed.
A selection of hymns and
psalms, for social and private
worship. 10th ed. Boston, Munroe and Francis, 1830. [342] p.
"Stereotype edition." DLC;
NNUT. 1066

Daboll, George P.
Original American poetry.
Troy, N. Y., Pub. for the au-
thor, 1830. 48 p. CSmH. 1067

Daboll, Nathan.
Daboll's schoolmaster's as-
sistant. Improved and enlarged.
Being a plain practical system of
arithmetick. Adapted to the
United States. By Nathan Daboll.

With the addition of the Farmers'
and mechanicks' best method of
book-keeping. Designed as a
companion to Daboll's arithmetick.
By Samuel Green. Ithaca, N.Y.,
Pub. by Mack & Andrus. Stereotyped by A. Chandler, New-York,
1830. 228, 12 p. CLCM; CtHT-
W; DLC; ICU; MWA; NIC; NNC;
OClWHi; PU.   1068

Daily Chronicle, Philadelphia,
Pa.
   Address of the carriers of
The Daily Chronicle, to their patrons, on the commencement of
the New Year 1830. [Philadel-
phia, Pa., 1830] 1 p. DLC.
                               1069
Daily food for Christians. Being
a promise, and another Scriptural portion, for every day in
the year. Together with the
verse of a hymn... 1st American
from the 8th London ed. Boston,
Perkins & Marvin, 1830. 192 p.
MB; MH; MWA; RPB.   1070

---- New York, The American
Tract Society [183-?] 192 p.
CSmH; DLC.   1071

Daily texts, with verses of
hymns; adopted for general use,
and suited for every day. New
York, American Tract Society
[1830] 128 p. NN.   1072

Dalzel, Andrew, 1742-1806.
   ... Collectanea Graeca Minora:
with notes, partly compiled, and
partly written by Andrew Dalzel
... 2d New York ed. New York,
Pr. by W. E. Dean, Pub. by Collins and Hannay, Collins & Co.
[etc.] 1830. vi, 338 p. CtMW;
ViU.   1073

Danforth, Joshua Noble, 1798-
1861.
   An alarm to the citizens of
Washington; or An exposure of
the evils of intemperance; being

a discourse delivered in the
Fourth Presbyterian Church,
Ninth St., Washington. Washing-
ton, Pr. by Way and Gideon,
1830. 20 p. CSmH; OCHP; PHi.
                               1074
Danger of bad company; or The
unfortunate market boy. An in-
structive story for youth. New-
Haven, S. Babcock, Publisher;
Charleston, S. Babcock & Co.
Sidney's Press, 1830. 23 p.
CtHi.   1075

... The danger of revenge; or The
idiot boy. Published by the
"Episcopal Female Tract Society
of Philadelphia," for the "Society
of the Protestant Episcopal
Church for the Advancement of
Christianity in Pennsylvania."
Philadelphia, Pr. by William
Stavely, 1830. 8 p. Religious
tracts - No. 74. PPL.   1076

Danvers, Mass.
   Bye-laws of the fire department of the town of Danvers.
Salem, Pr. by W. and S. B. Ives,
1830. 8 p. MPeaHi.   1077

Da Ponte, Lorenzo, 1749-1838.
   Alcune poesie di Lorenzo Da
Ponte. Publicate da lui in New-
York, l'anno 1830. 31 p. DLC;
MH.   1078

[Darby, William] 1775-1854.
   The United States reader, or
Juvenile instructor. no. 1 [-3] 2d
ed. rev. Baltimore, Plaskitt &
co., [J. D. Toy, pr.] 1830-[-31].
3 vols. DLC; ICU; MdHi.   1079

Darnley. See James, George
Payne Rainsford.

Darrach, William, 1796-1865.
   Drawings of the anatomy of
the groin, with anatomical remarks. Philadelphia, Littell;
James Kay Jun. & Co., prs.,
1830. 28 p. DNLM; MBCo;

MdBM; OClM; PPC; PPL; PU.
                                    1080
Dartmouth College.
   A catalogue of the officers
and students of Dartmouth Col-
lege, October, 1830. Haverhill,
John R. Reding, pr., 1830. 23 p.
CSmH; MeB.   1081

---- Commencement. Order of
exercises. Concord, Aug. 18,
1830. 4 p. MHi.   1082

Darusmont, Frances (Wright),
1795-1852.
   Address, containing a review
of the times, as first delivered
in the Hall of Science, New-
York, on Sunday, May 9, 1830,
by Frances Wright. New York,
Pub. at the office of the Free
Enquirer, 1830. 20 p. DLC;
ICMcC; LNHT; MB; NN; PHi;
RPB.   1083

---- An address to young mechanics, as delivered in the Hall
of Science, June 13, 1830, by
Frances Wright. New York, Pub.
at the office of the Free Enquirer, Hall of Science, 1830.
13 p. ICMcC; MB; MWA; NN.
                             1084
---- Course of popular lectures,
as delivered by Frances Wright
... 3d ed. New York, Pub. at
the Office of the Free Enquirer,
1830. 239 p. NN; NNC; PPL;
RPB.   1085

---- Parting address, as delivered in the Bowery Theatre, to
the people of New York, in June,
1830, by Frances Wright. New
York, Pub. at the office of the
Free Enquirer, 1830. 22 p.
ICMcC; MB; MH; NN; PPL.
                             1086
Davenport, Bishop.
   Chronological table of remarkable events, discoveries and
inventions, etc., from the creation of the world to the year

A.D. 1830 for the use of Bible
classes, Sabbath and other
schools. 1st ed. Wilmington,
Del., R. Porter, 1830. 36 p.
DeWi; PPDrop.   1087

---- English grammar simplified on philosophical principles.
1st ed. Wilmington, Del., Pr.
for the author, by R. Porter &
Son, 1830. 138+ p. CtHT-W;
DLC; DeWI; ICMcC; MB.   1088

---- History of the United States,
containing all the events necessary to be committed to memory;
with the Constitution of the
United States, and a valuable
table of chronology, for the use
of schools. By B. Davenport. 1st
ed. Wilmington, Del., R. Porter
& Son [1830] 143 p. DeU; DeWI.
                             1089

---- 3d ed., corr. and imp.
Philadelphia, T. T. Ash and U.
Hunt [1830] 144 p. DLC.   1090

Davenport, Rufus.
   The Free Debt Rules under
Copy Right for the present.
Equitable principles for free debt
rules. Boston [1830] [4] p.
MBAt.   1091

[David, J. B.], bp.
   True piety, or, The day well
spent: A manual of fervent
prayers, pious reflections, and
solid instructions calculated to
answer the use of the members,
of all ranks and conditions, of
the Roman Catholic Church.
Baltimore, Pub. by Fielding Lucas, Jr., [183-?] 186 p. MdBS.
                             1092
Davidson, Henry.
   Specimen number. An ecclesiastical register, being a collection of facts relative to the
churches and clergy of New-
England... Portland, Shirley

and Hyde, 1830. 10, [2] p.
CSmH; CtHT; MHi; MWA; MeB;
MiD; NjPT.   1093

Davies, Charles, 1798-1876.
Elements of surveying. With
the necessary tables... New
York, Pr. and pub. by J. & J.
Harper, Sold by Collins and Han-
nay, [etc.] 1830. 147, 62, 91 p.
CSt; CtY; DLC; DeGE; MH; MiU;
NN; NcD; NjR; PU.   1094

Davis, A. H.
Observations on the religious
instruction of youth, principally
with a reference to Sunday
schools. Philadelphia, American
Sunday School Union, 1830. 179 p.
GDC; NCanHi.   1095

Davis, Emerson.
Intellectual philosophy for children and youth. In schools and
families. Boston, Munroe &
Francis; and Charles S. Frances,
New-York, 1830. vi, [1], 32, 3
p. MH.   1096

Davis, Gustavus Fellows, 1797-
1836.
A lecture on the necessary
qualifications of teachers in common schools, delivered before
the Connecticut Convention of
Teachers and the Friends of Education, assembled at the city hall
in Hartford, Nov. 10, 1830.
Hartford, Pub. by D. F. Robinson & Co., P. Canfield, pr.,
1830. 16 p. CtSoP; CtY; MBC;
MH; MWA; NjPT.   1097

Davis, John.
Remarks on the Julian and
Gregorian styles, in reference to
the day appointed for a centennial celebration of the first settlement of Boston. [Boston,
1830] Bdsd. (From the Mechanicks magazine, for April, 1830.)
MH; MHi.   1098

Davis, John, 1789-1854.
Speech of Mr. Davis, of
Mass. on the bill for the more
effectual collection of impost du-
ties. Delivered in Committee of
the Whole on the state of the
Union. House of Representatives,
May 4, 1830. Washington, Of-
fice of the National Journal;
Peter Force, pr., 1830. 28 p.
CSmH; CtY; DeGE.   1099

Davis, Seth.
The pupils' arithmetic. Where-
by the practical use of figures is
demonstrated in a series of original questions. Boston, Lincoln &
Edmands, 1830. MH.   1100

Davison, Gideon Miner, 1791-
1869.
Canada. The fashionable tour:
a guide to travellers visiting the
middle and northern states, and
the provinces of Canada. 4th ed.,
enl. and imp. Saratoga Springs,
G. M. Davison; New York, G. &
C. & H. Carvill, 1830. 434 p.
CSmH; CtY; DLC; MBAt; MWA;
MiD-B; NBuG; NN; NUtHi; NjR;
OClWHi; OHi; P; PPFHi; WHi;
BrMus.   1101

Davy, Sir Humphry, bart, 1778-
1829.
Consolations in travel, or The
last days of a philosopher...
With a sketch of the author's life,
and notes, by Jacob Green, M.D.
Philadelphia, John Grigg, Clark
and Raser, prs., 1830. 252 p.
CtY; GDC; ICU; KyDC; MB;
MBC; MH; MdBS; MeB; MiD;
NGH; NNS; NjP; O; PHC; PPL;
PU; RPB; TxH; ViU.   1102

Dawes, Rufus, 1803-1859.
The valley of the Nashaway:
and other poems. By Rufus
Dawes. Boston, Carter & Hen-
dee, 1830. 96 p. CSmH; CtY;
DLC; MB; MH; MWA; MeB;
MoSW; NIC; NhD; PHi; RPB;

WHi; BrMus.   1103

Day, Thomas.
The history of Sandford and
Merton, by Thomas Day, Esq.
A new edition; revised through-
out and embellished with very
numerous engravings. New York,
Charles S. Francis [183-?] 380 p.
MB.   1104

Day's New-York pocket almanac
for 1831. New York, M. Day
[1830] 12 l. NHi.   1105

Dayton, Ohio.
The book of prices of the
House Carpenters and Joiners,
of the town of Dayton, adopted
Friday, July 10, 1830. Dayton,
Pr. at the Journal office, 1830.
28, [1] p. ODa.   1106

Dean, Christopher C.
Conversations on the Bombay
mission, by the author of "Conversations on the Sandwich Island mission," Boston, Pr. by
T. R. Marvin, for the Massachusetts Sabbath School Union, 1830.
viii, 156 p. GDC; ICMcC; MNF;
NjP; OCl.   1107

[----] The Stanwood family: or
The history of the American
Tract Society... Revised by the
publishing committee. Boston,
Pr. by T. R. Marvin, for the
Massachusetts Sabbath School
Union, and sold at their deposi-
tory, 1830. 158 p. NN; TNJ;
ViRUT.   1108

Deane, Samuel, 1784-1834.
A discourse delivered at the
dedication of a house of public
worship, erected by the Second
Congregational Society in Cituate,
Oct. 13, 1830. Boston, Carter
& Hendie, 1830. 19 p. CBPac;
ICMe; MB; MBC; MHi; MWA;
MiD-B; RPB; BrMus.   1109

Dearborn, Henry Alexander
Scammell, 1783-1851.
An address delivered on the
viii of October, MDCCCXXX,
the second centennial anniversary,
of the settlement of Roxbury.
Roxbury, Pub. by Charles P.
Emmons.   J.H. Eastburn, pr.,
1830. 40, 25 p. A-Ar; CSmH;
CtHT-W; CtY; DLC; ICU; InU;
LNHT; MB; MBAt; MH-AH;
MHi; MdHi; MiD-B; MnHi;
NBLiHi; NIC; NN; NjPT; OClWHi;
PHi; RHi; RPB; WHi.   1110

Death. Published by the American Tract Society. New York.
No. 6. [1830] Bdsd. PPL. 1111

The death and burial of Cock
Robin.   See Cock Robin.

Death of Crowninshield, The Salem Murderer. Who hung himself in prison, June 15, 1830...
Sold wholesale and retail N.W.
corner of Cross and Mercantile
streets, Boston [1830] Bdsd.
MB; MHi.   1112

Decatur, Mrs. Susan [Wheeler]
Documents relative to the
claim of Mrs. Decatur, with her
earnest request that the gentlemen of Congress will do her the
favor to read them. Georgetown,
D.C., James C. Dunn, pr., 1830.
51 p. CtHT-W; MdHi; PHi. 1113

Deering, Nathaniel, 1791-1881.
Carabasset, a tragedy...in
five acts, by M. Deering. Portland, Pub. by S. Colman [Pr.
by Thomas Todd] 1830. 54 p.
DLC; ICU; MH; MHi; NRU; PU;
RPB; WaU.   1114

A defence of the institution of
Freemasonry; being a series of
letters addressed to Col. Pliny
Merrick. (Originally published
in the Southbridge register.) By
a Royal arch mason. South-

bridge, Mass., Pr. by Josiah
Snow, 1830. 11 p. CSmH.　1115

[Defoe, Daniel] 1661?-1731.
　The history of the great
plague in London in the year
1665 with an introduction by the
Rev. H. Stebbing, M.A. ... Philadelphia, Pr. from the last London ed. [183-] CtHT-W.　1116

---- Life and most surprising
adventures of Robinson Crusoe
... Peekskill, N.Y., Samuel
Marks, 1830. 144 p. CSmH;
MWA.　1117

---- Robinson Crusoe adaptations.
The little Robinson Crusoe. New
Haven, Durrie & Peck, 1830.
191 p. CtHT-W; CtY; MB; MW.
　1118

Degelos, Pierre A.
　Statement of sugar made in
Louisiana in 1828 and 1829... by
Pierre A. Degelos. New Orleans,
Pr. by Benjamin Levy [1830]
Bdsd. PPL.　1119

Dejean, Pierre François Auguste.
　Anichinabek amisinahikaniwa,
kicheanameatchick, catonik, Ota-
wak wakanakesssi. Dejean macate
okonoye... Wyaotenong [i.e. Detroit, Mich.] Geo. L. Whitney
manda mesenahiken hauseton,
1830. 106 p. CSmH; ICN-Ayer;
MiDC.　1120

De Lancey, William Heathcote,
1797-1865.
　An address delivered before
the trustees, faculty, and students, of the University of Pennsylvania, on opening the collegi-
ate session of 1830-31, in the
new college hall. Pub. at the request of the Board of trustees.
Philadelphia, Pr. by Joseph R.
A. Skerrett, 1830. 56 p. CSmH;
CtHT; CtY; DLC; DeGE; GHi;
InID; MH-AH; MWA; MdUM;
MiD-B; MnHi; NIC; NjP; PHi;

PPAmP; PPL; PPPrH; PU;
ScCC; BrMus.　1121

---- Ministerial perils; a ser-
mon preached at the opening of
the annual convention of the dio-
cese of Pennsylvania, in St.
Peter's Church, Philadelphia,
May 19, 1830.　Philadelphia, J.
Harding, 1830. 22 p. InID; MH;
NBuDD: NGH; NjR; PHi; PPAmP;
RPB; BrMus.　1122

Delaware.
　Journal of the House of Representatives of the state of Delaware, at a session commenced
and held at Dover, on Tuesday
the fifth day of January 1830;
and in the fifty-fourth year of
the independence of the United
States. Dover, Del., Pr. by A.
M. Schee, 1830. DLC.　1123

---- Journal of the Senate of the
state of Delaware, at a session
commenced & held at Dover, on
Tuesday, the fifth day of January, 1830; and in the fifty-
fourth year of the independence
of the United States. Dover, Del.,
Pr. by H. W. Peterson, 1830.
109 p. DLC.　1124

---- Laws of the state of Dela-
ware; passed at a session of the
General Assembly, commenced
and held at Dover, on Tuesday
the fifth day of January, in the
year of our Lord 1830, and of
the independence of the United
States the 54th. By authority.
Dover, Pr. by Augustus M.
Schee, 1830. 40, 8 p. In-SC;
Mi-L; Mo; Ms; Nb; Nj; Nv; R;
T; Wa-L.　1125

---- A supplement to "An act
for the establishment of free
schools." [1830] 4 p. DeWi. 1126

Delaware and Maryland almanac
for 1831. Wilmington, Robert

Porter & Son [1830] 18 l. DeU;
MWA.   1127

Delaware Coal Company.
   Act of incorporation and by-
laws. Wilmington, R. Porter &
son, 1830. 13 p. IU; N; NN.
                              1128
The deluge. See Featherstonhaugh, George William.

Demme, Karl R.
   Philadelphia den 23sten Nov:
1830. Herrn Georg W. Mentz
und Sohn ... Bdsd. PPL.   1129

A Democratic member of the
Common Council. See A brief
investigation.

Democratic Party. Kentucky.
   Proceedings, resolutions and
address of the Jackson convention, held in Frankfort, 13th Dec.
1830. [Frankfort? Ky., 1830?]
22 p. ICU.   1130

---- Maryland.
   Address of the Jackson central committee to the people of
Maryland, on subjects connected
with the approaching elections in
the state. Baltimore, Pr. at the
office of the Baltimore Republican, 1830. 16 p. MdHi.   1131

---- New Jersey.
   Proceedings of the Jackson
Republican convention with an address to the Jackson Republican
electors of New Jersey. Trenton, New Jersey, December 8,
1830. 1 p. DLC.   1132

---- Pennsylvania.
   Democratic celebration of the
third Congressional district.
Regular toasts. [13 toasts includ-
ing toasts to Andrew Jackson,
President of the U.S. Martin
Van Buren, Vice-president,
Pennsylvania and Henry A. Muh-
lenburg, (n.p., 183-)] 1 p.

DLC.   1133

---- List of delegates to the
Democratic General Ward Com-
mittee. City of Philadelphia,
September 13, 1830. Bdsd.
PPL.   1134

---- Private circular. A plan
for the more effectual organization of the Democratic party of
Pennsylvania. [183-?] 1 p.
DLC.   1135

Democratic Republicans. New
York.
   ...Election, 1st, 2d & 3d
days of November. Republican
State Convention [1830] 8 p. (Al-
bany Argus, Extra.) NN.   1136

---- Republican Legislative meeting. At a meeting of the Republican members of the Legislature of the state of New-York,
held in the Assembly Chamber,
Tuesday Evening, April 13, 1830;
Hon. Wm. M. Oliver, President
of the Senate, in the Chair, and
Hon. J. B. Gosman, of the County of Tompkins, Secretary. [Al-
bany, 1830] 8 p. (Albany Argus,
Extra.) NbU.   1137

The denounced. See Banim,
John.

DeSaussure, W. F.
   Address to the citizens of
Richland district. By W. F. De-
Saussure, Columbia, S.C., Pr.
at the "Times and Gazette" of-
fice, 1830. 12 p. ScU.   1138

A description and history of vegetable substances, used in the
arts, and in domestic economy.
Timber trees: fruits. Illustrated with wood engravings.
Boston, Wells & Lilly, [etc.]
1830. [3], 6, 422 p. (The Library of Entertaining Knowledge)
CtHT; CtY; KyDC; MB; MdW;

NRU; NT; Nh; Nj; OU; <u>PPL.</u>
1139
Description of the picture. The
departure of the Israelites out of
Egypt. Open at the Diorama
from 9 o'clock 'till dusk. ...
Boston, From the press of W. W.
Clapp [183-?] 18 p.   CSmH. 1140

Description of the ten ancient
Javan Deities, now exhibiting at
the New-York Museum, corner of
Broadway and Anthony-street.
New York, Pr. by J. Seymour,
1830. 8 p. CtY; MWA; <u>PPL.</u>1141

A description of the Tremont
House. See Eliot, William Harvard.

Description of the view of Athens,
and surrounding country; with an
improved explanation, giving a
complete outline of the whole picture, with numbers and references... [n. p., ca. 1830] 12 p.
CSmH; MH.   1142

The design of the Lord's Supper;
the obligation to receive it, and
answers to the excuses commonly made for not coming thereto.
New-York, New-York Protestant
Episcopal Tract Society, 1830.
20 p. MH; MHi; NNG.   1143

Desilver's Philadelphia directory
and stranger's guide, 1830. Containing a plan of the city and sub-
urbs, the names of the citizens
alphabetically arranged, with
their occupations and places of
abode... Philadelphia, Robert Desilver, 1830. 4, 10, [4], 220,
[14], 56 p. DLC; MBNEH; MWA;
NN; P; PHi; PP; PPL.   1144

Desilver's United States register
and almanac for 1831. Philadel-
phia, R. Desilver; T. Desilver;
J. Grigg; William Sharpless, pr.
(By Seth Smith) [1830] 28 l. CtY;
DLC; MWA; PPAmP.   1145

---- Issue with 32 l. NHi; PPL.
1146
Desruelles, Henri Marie Joseph,
1791-1858.
    Memoir on the treatment of
venereal diseases without mercury... Philadelphia, Carey &
Lea [Skerrett, pr.] 1830. x, [5]-
217 p. CtY; GEU-M; IEN-M;
MdUM; MeB; MoSMed; NNNAM;
Nh; NjR; PPC; RPM; TNJ.   1147

The devil and Tom Walker. See
Irving, Washington.

The devil in love. See Cazotte,
Jacques.

Dew-drops. Published by the
American Tract Society, New
York. [D. Fanshaw, pr.,
183-?] [128] p. MWA.   1148

Dewees, William Potts, 1768-
1841.
    A compendious system of mid-
wifery. Chiefly designed to facilitate the inquiries of those
who may be pursuing this branch
of study. Illustrated by occasional cases. With many engravings. 4th ed., with additions,
and improvements. Philadelphia,
Carey & Lea, 1830. 640 p.
CSt-L; CtY; ICU-R; InU-M; KU;
MnU; MoSU-M; NNNAM; NbU-
M; Nh; OU; PPiAM; RPM; ViRA.
1149
---- A practice of physic, comprising most of the diseases not
treated of in "Diseases of females," and "Diseases of children," by William P. Dewees...
Philadelphia, Carey & Lea [Sker-
rett, pr.] 1830. 2 v. ArU-M;
CU; DNLM; ICU; KyLxT; MBCo;
MdBJ; MdUM; MoSpD; NBuU-M;
NIC; NNC; NNNAM; NbU; NhD;
PPC; PPiU; PU; RPM; ViU;
BrMus.   1150

Dewey, Orville, 1794-1882.
    The deep things of the gospel.

A discourse, delivered at the ordination of the Rev. George Putnam, as colleague pastor with Rev. Eliphalet Porter, D.D. over the First Church and Religious Society in Roxbury, July 7, 1830. Boston, Gray, and Bowen [Pr. by I.R. Butts] 1830. 32 p. CBPac; CtY; ICN; MB; MBAU; MBC; MH; MWA; MeBaT; PPL; RPB; BrMus.   1151

---- An oration delivered at Cambridge before the society of Phi Beta Kappa, Aug. 26, 1830. Boston, Pub. by Gray & Bowen [Cambridge, E. W. Metcalf & Co.] 1830. 32 p. CBPac; CSmH; CtY; DLC; MBAt; MBC; MH-AH; MHi; MWA; MiD-B; MnHi; NCH; NjP; NjR; NNC; OCHP; PPL; PPPrHi; PU; RPB; BrMus. 1152

---- The Unitarian's answer...
5th ed. Boston, Pr. for the American Unitarian Association by Gray and Bowen, 1830. 47 p. MB; MH-AH.   1153

DeWitt, John.
The necessity of atonement. A sermon at New York, May 23, 1830. New York, 1830. 34 p. MH-AH.   1154

DeWitt, William Radcliffe, 1792-1867.
Ministerial influence. A sermon delivered at the opening of the synod of Philadelphia, in Lancaster, Pa. October 27, 1830. Harrisburg [Pa.] F. Wyeth, pr., 1830. 20 p. CSmH; MiU; NjPT; NjR; PPPrHi. 1155

D'Homergue, John.
Essays on American silk, and the best means of rendering it a source of individual and national wealth. With directions to farmers for raising silk worms. By John D'Homergue... and Peter Stephen Duponceau. Philadelphia,

John Grigg, 1830. xxii, 120, [1] p. CtY; DLC; IU; MB; MWA; NNC; PPAmP; PPL; PU; RPB; TxU; Vi; BrMus.   1156

A dialogue, occasioned by a pamphlet. See Bulfinch, Stephen Greenleaf.

Dick, Thomas, 1774-1857.
The philosophy of a future state. 2d Brookfield ed. Brookfield, Mass., Pr. and pub. by E. & G. Merriam, 1830. xii, 17-308 p. DLC; MB; OClW.   1157

Dickinson, Austin, 1791-1849.
Appeal to American youth on temperance. (A premium tract.) Pub. by the Franklin Temperance Society. Frankfort, Ky., Pr. by A. G. Hodges, 1830. 12 p. DLC; WHi.   1158

---- ---- [New York, The American Tract Society 1830?] 12 p. ([American Tract Society. Publications] No. 233) CSmH.
1159
---- Scripture argument for temperance. New York, American Tract Society [183-?] 16 p. (American Tract Society [Publications] no. 276) CSmH. 1160

Dickinson, Baxter, 1795-1875.
Alarm to distillers and their allies. New York, 1830. MH-AH.   1161

Dickinson College, Carlisle, Pa.
A narrative of the proceedings of the Board of trustees of Dickinson College, from 1821 to 1830. Setting forth the true history of many events which have been made the themes of public animadversion. Prepared by a committee appointed by the Board, and read at their sessions, May 14, 17, 18, and 19, and now published by order of the same. Carlisle, Pr. by G. Fleming,

1830. 83 p. CSmH; CtY; DLC; KyDC; MHi; MdBP; MiU; MnHi; N; NNUT; NjR; OClWHi; P. 1162

---- The statutes of Dickinson College, as revised and adopted by the Board of Trustees, April 16, 1830. Carlisle, Pr. by George Fleming, 1830. 30 p. CSmH; DLC; MH; MdBLC; PCarlD.   1163

Dickson, Samuel Henry, 1798-1872.
    Address before the South Carolina Society for the Promotion of Temperance, April 6th, 1830. To which is annexed the constitution of the South Carolina Temperance Society, and the report of the Columbia Temperance Society. Charleston [S. C.] Observer office press [1830] 72 p. CSmH; CtY; DLC; M; NNNAM; ScHi; ScU; TxU.   1164

---- Syllabus of part of the course of lectures of S. Henry Dickson, M.D., Professor of the Institutes and Practice of Medicine. In the Medical College of South Carolina. Charleston, Pr. by James S. Burges, 1830. 106 p. NcWsW; ScCM.   1165

Dillaway, Charles Knapp.
    The classical speaker. Boston, Pub. by Lincoln & Edmands, 1830. viii, [5]-272 p. CSt; CtHT-W; DLC; ICU; KyLoS; MB; MBAt; MH; MWA; MiU; N; NH.
                                   1166
Disciples of Christ. Wabash Christian Conference.
    Circular letter. The elders and brethren of the Wabash Christian conference, assembled at Union meeting house, in P[osey coun]ty, Indiana, October 8th, 1830, to all Christia[ns it] may concern. 4 p. WHi.   1167

Disclosures relating to the "A.

B. C." affair. From the Essex Register [Salem, 1830?] 8 p. DLC.   1168

A discourse on the principle and practice of charity. See Coote, Clement T.

Distress for rent in Virginia... [n.p. 1830?] 30 p. DLC; MBAt; MH-L; MHi.   1169

The divinity of Jesus Christ. See American Unitarian Association.

Dixon, George Washington, 1808-1861.
    Oddities and drolleries of Mr. G. Dixon, the celebrated American Buffo Singer; with the likeness of Mr. G. Dixon, in the characters of Billy Grizzel, Major Longrow, &c. Also, several popular songs as sung by the celebrated Miss C. Fisher. New ed. New York, George G. Sickels, 1830. 140, [4], 34, [1] p. MH.   1170

Doane, George Washington, 1799-1858.
    The missionary argument; a sermon preached, by appointment, before the board of directors of the Domestic and Foreign Missionary Society of the Protestant Episcopal Church, in the U.S. of America; in St. Andrew's Church, Philadelphia, on Tuesday evening, May 11, 1830... Boston, Samuel H. Parker [Press of Putnam & Hunt] 1830. 24 p. DLC; ICMe; InID; MB; MBAt; MiD-B; NcD; PPAmP; RPB; WHi; BrMus.   1171

---- The voice of the departed: A sermon preached in Trinity Church, Boston, on Sunday, September 12, 1830 on occasion of the death of the late rector the Reverend John Sylvester John

Gardiner. Boston, Pub. by Samuel H. Parker [J.H. Eastburn, pr.] 1830. 27 p. CSmH; CtHT; CtSoP; ICMe; ICN; MB; MBAt; MBC; MHi; MWA; MiD-B; NBLiHi; NNG; NjPT; NjR; PHi; PPL; RPB; WHi; BrMus.   1172

Doddridge, Philip.
The rise and progress of religion in the soul, illustrated in a course of serious and practical addresses suited to persons of every character and circumstance; with a devout meditation, or prayer, subjoined to each chapter. New-York, American Tract Society [183-?] MB; MH.   1173
---- ---- Philadelphia, Pub. by L. Johnson, J. Clarke, pr., 1830. 273 p. MB; NBuDD; NbOM; OClW; PPF.   1174

---- The rise and progress of religion in the soul; with a devout meditation or prayer added to each chapter. ...To which is prefixed The Life of the Author. Baltimore, Pub. by John J. Harrod, 1830. xxiii, 304 p. MB; MH-AH.   1175

[Dodsley, Robert] 1703-1764.
The economy of human life. Translated from an Indian manuscript, written by an ancient Bramin. To which is prefixed an account of the manner in which said manuscript was discovered; in a letter from an English gentleman residing in China, to the Earl of *** Providence, John Tillinghast [John Hutchens] [ca 1830] 200 p. MBC.   1176

Domestic and Foreign Missionary Society.
Proceedings of the board of directors of the Domestic and Foreign Missionary Society of the Protestant Episcopal Church... at a meeting, held in Philadel-

phia May 11th, 1830. Philadelphia, Pr. by William Stavely, 1830. 42 p. InlD; MBD; MHi; MnHi; PPL.   1177

Donaldson, Peter, pseud. See Carrick, John D.

Doolittle, Giles.
Gambling, especially horse racing, contrary to law, both civil and divine. Erie, Pa., Joseph M. Sterrett, 1830. 18 p. IU.   1178

Dorchester, Mass.
Commemoration of the settlement of the First Church in Dorchester. At the close of the second century from the arrival of the Puritans; Lord's day, June 20, 1830. [Dorchester? 1830] Bdsd. MHi.   1179

Dorchester, Mass.
Order of exercises, at the celebration of the second century from the settlement of Dorchester ... June 17, 1830. Boston, True & Greene, prs., [1830] Bdsd. MHi; NN.   1180

Dorr, Benjamin, 1796-1869.
A sermon, preached in Trinity Church, New York, at the opening of the convention of the Protestant Episcopal Church in the state of New York, on Thursday, October 7, 1830. New York, Pr. at the Protestant Episcopal Press, 1830. 35 p. CtHT; DLC; ICU; InlD; MBAt; MH; MWA; NCH; NGH; NN; NcU; NjR; WHi.   1181

[----] The history of a pocket prayer book. Written by itself ... Philadelphia, G.W. Donohue; New York, Scofield & Voorhies, 1830. 192 p. NNG.   1182

[----] ---- Stereotyped by James Conner. New-York, General

Protestant Episcopal Sunday
School Union Pr. at the Protestant Episcopal Press, 1830.
94 p. MB; MBD.   1183

[Dorsey, John Larkin]
    To the voters of St. Mary's
County. [Baltimore, Md. ?
1830] 19 p. DLC; MB.   1184

Douglas, James.
    The advancement of society in
knowledge and religion... 1st
American, from the 2d Edin-
burgh ed. Hartford, Cooke &
Co. [etc.] 1830. 315 p.
CSmH; CtHi; CtSoP; CtY; DLC;
ICMe; MBAU; MBC; MeB; MiOC;
NCH; NGH; NN; NNG; NhD; NjP;
NjR; OC; OClW; RNR; WBB.
                             1185
The Dover directory. Dover
[N. H.] Samuel C. Stevens, 1830.
96 p. MWA; NN; NhHi.   1186

[Dow, Lorenzo] 1777-1834.
    A cry from the wilderness:
A voice from the East, A reply
from the West. ... By Cosmopo-
lite--A Listener. United States
Pr. for the Purchaser and the
Public, 1830. 65, [1] p. ICN;
MWA.   1187

[----] ---- 2d ed., rev. and enl.
United States, Pr. for the purchaser and the public, 1830. 71
p. CSmH; CtHT-W.   1188

---- ---- 3d ed. rev. and enl.
United States, Pr. for the purchaser and the public, 1830. 70,
[2] p. MWA.   1189

---- Chain of reason, consisting
of 5 links, 2 hooks, 1 swivel.
34th ed. rev. and imp. Lockport, Pub. & sold by C. Marsh,
M. Cadwallader, pr., 1830. 72
p. MWA.   1190

---- Omnifarious law exemplified. How to curse and swear,

lie, cheat, and kill; according to
law. By Lorenzo Dow. 2nd ed.
enl. Georgetown, D. C. , Pr. by
James C. Dunn, Bridge Street,
1830. 58 p. DLC.   1191

---- Wisdom displayed, and Lorenzo's villany detected. Or, The
second trial, confession and con-
demnation of Lorenzo Dow, before the Superior court, held at
Norwich, Conn. , January, term,
1829. ... 2d ed., imp. Baltimore, Pr. for the author, 1830.
23 p. CSmH; NcD.   1192

Downing, Jack, pseud. See
Smith, Seba.

Doyle, James.
    An abridgment of the Chris-
tian doctrine, with proofs of
scripture on points controverted
... Philadelphia, E. Cummiskey
[1830] 107 p. NNF.   1193

[Drake, Daniel]
    The people's doctors; a re-
view, by 'The People's Friend. '
Cincinnati, O. , Pr. and pub. for
the use of the people, 1830. 60
p. (t. p. dated 1829 - cover title
dated 1830.) DNLM; MH; O;
OCHP; OClWHi; PPL.   1194

[Drake, R. Dillon]
    The late duel, being the en-
tire correspondence between the
parties which led to that melan-
choly event. Philadelphia, Pub.
at the office of the Pennsylvania
Inquirer, 1830. 35 p. PPL. 1195

[----] Sir, - A printed paper,
signed H. Wharton Griffith, having been circulated among my
friends, I consider it my duty to
them to explain the reason of the
punishment which I have inflicted
on that individual ... [Philadel-
phia, 1830] 8 p. PPL.   1196

Draper, Bourne Hall.

Bible histories. Philadelphia, 1830. BrMus.   **1197**

---- Scripture stories. Philadelphia, 1830. BrMus.   **1198**

---- The youth's instructor. Philadelphia, American Sunday School Union [1830] 35 p. ICU; BrMus.   **1199**

Drayton, William, 1776-1846.
Col. Drayton's dinner speech, "A Whig." Extracts from Mr. McDuffie's Pamphlet "One of the People" and Washington's Farewell Address. [O. H. Wells, pr., Greenville, S. C., 1830] 42 p. NN.   **1200**

The drunkard's fate. See Jerrold, Douglas.

Dryden, John.
The hind and the panther. In three parts. Baltimore, Fielding Lucas, Jr. [1830?] 124 p. PPL.   **1201**

Drysdale, Isabel.
Evening recreations: A series of dialogues. On the history and geography of the Bible. Revised by The Committee of Publication. Philadelphia, American Sunday School Union [c 1830] 106 p. GEU; IU.   **1202**

---- Scenes in Georgia. Written for the American Sunday School Union. Philadelphia, 1830. BrMus.   **1203**

Ducoudray-Holstein, H. La Fayette Villaume, 1763-1839.
Memoirs of Simon Bolivar, President liberator, of the republic of Colombia; and of his principal generals; secret history of the revolution, and the events which preceded it, from 1807 to the present time. Boston, S. G. Goodrich & co. [Waitt & Dow,

prs.] 1830. 383 p. DLC; MiJa; OClWHi.   **1204**

[Dudley, Elizabeth]
An account of the last illness of Hannah Dudley. Philadelphia, Pub. by The Tract Association of Friends [1830] 8 p. (No. 50) PPL.   **1205**

Duffin, Edward Wilson, 1800-1874.
The influence of modern physical education of females; in producing and confirming deformity of the spine. New York, Chas. S. Francis; Munroe & Francis, Boston [Clayton & Van Norden, prs.] 1830. 140 p. CSt-L; MWA; MeB; MoSW-M; NNNAM; NbU-M; OO; PPC.   **1206**

[Duke, Seymour R.]
The age of rhyme; or A glance at the poets. By a Southerner. Charleston, Pub. by S. Babcock and Co. [Pr. by A. F. Cunningham] 1830. 30 p. NN; RPB.   **1207**

Duncan, James M.
James M. Duncan's address to the people of Illinois. Fellow citizens ... [signed:] James M. Duncan. Vandalia, June 3d, 1830. Illinois Intelligencer--Extra. [Vandalia] June 9, 1830. ICHi.   **1208**

Dunlap, William, 1766-1839.
A trip to Niagara; or, Travellers in America. A farce, in three acts. Written for the Bowery Theatre, New York. By William Dunlap. New York, Pr. and pub. by E. B. Clayton, 1830. 54 p. CSmH; CtY; DLC; ICU; KU; MB; MBAt; MH; MWA; MiU; MnM; NIC; NN; NcU; PHi; PPL; PU; RPB; TxU; WU.   **1209**

Du Pont de Nemours (E. I.) and Company, Wilmington, Del.
[Circular explaining the in-

validity of a recent test of powder of various manufacturers, and announcing the company had begun to manufacture orange stain powder.] [Wilmington?] 1830. 1 p., blank leaf. (Dated at end: Wilmington, Nov. 8th, 1830.) DeGE. 1210

Dutchess County Anti-Slavery Society.
County convention. Liberty and justice. The Dutchess County Anti-Slavery Society, will meet at the house of Daniel P. Eghmie, Washington Hollow, on Monday, the 7th of October inst. [183-?] 1 p. DLC. 1211

Dutchess County farmers' almanack for 1831. By David Young. Poughkeepsie, W. M. Parsons [1830] 18 l. DLC; NBuG. 1212

Duties of children. [New York, American Tract Society, 183-?] 12 p. (American Tract Society, New York [Publications. (Separates)] no. 39) CSmH. 1213

The duty of Christians with respect to war. See Cox, Richard.

Dwight, Edwin Welles.
Memoir of Henry Obookiah; a native of the Sandwich Islands, who died at Cornwall, Connecticut, Feb. 17, 1818, aged 26. New York, American Tract Society, 1830. 126 p. DLC; P. 1214

Dwight, Nathaniel.
Scriptural answer to the question, how may I know that I am an adopted child of God? ...Norwich, Pr. by J. Dunham, 1830. 208, [3] p. CtHi. 1215

Dwight, Nathaniel, 1770-1831.
Sketches of the lives of the signers of the Declaration of independence, intended principally for the use of schools. New York, Pr.

by J. & J. Harper, 1830. 2 p. l., 373 p. CtHT; CtHi; CtY; DLC; MB; MBAt; MeBa; MiD-B; PHi; PP; RHi; ScC; TNJ; ViR. 1216

Dwight, Sereno Edwards, 1786-1850.
The life of President Edwards: by S. E. Dwight. New York, G. & C. & H. Carvill, 1830. 766 p. CBCDS; CSmH; CtY; DLC; GU; ICN; InU; KyDC; MBC; MH; MWA; MoS; NNC; NNUT; NWM; NjPT; NjR; PHi; RPB; ViRUT; WHi. 1217

[Dwight, Theodore] 1796-1866.
The northern traveller, and Northern tour; with the routes into the Springs, Niagara, and Quebec, and the coal mines of Pennsylvania; also, the tour of New-England. Embellished with thirty-two copperplate engravings. 4th ed., rev. and extended. New-York, Pr. by J. & J. Harper, Sold by Collins & Hannay [etc.] 1830. 444 p. CSmH; CtY; DLC; IC; MH; MdBP; MiD-B; NIC; NN; NRU; NSyHi; OClWHi; PPL; PSC. 1218

Dwight, Timothy, 1752-1817.
Theology; explained and defended, in a series of sermons ... with a Memoir of the life of the author... 7th ed. New York, G. & C. & H. Carvill, 1830. 4 v. CtY; GDC; ICMcC; KyLoS; MH-AH; MiD; MsJMC; NR; NjPT; ViRU. 1219

Dwyer, Alexander, b. 1798?
A discourse on the structure of the poetry of the Hebrews. Utica, Pr. by Hastings and Tracy, 1830. iv, 40 p. CSmH; NN. 1220

Dyer, Samuel.
Choruses, solos, duets, and recitatives from the works of Handel, Haydn, Mozart, Beethoven, and other composers of the

first eminence, arranged in full
vocal score, and interspersed
with notes and explanatory remarks... New York, Pr. for the
pub. by Daniel Fanshaw, 1830.
[vi], 240 p. CtHT-W; RPB. 1221

---- ---- Philadelphia, Pub. by
J. G. Auner, [c1830] [6], 240 p.
CtY; MH; MHi; PHi; PPL. 1222

Dymond, Jonathan, 1796-1828.
An inquiry into the accordancy
of war with the principles of
Christianity, and an examination
of the philosophical reasoning by
which it is defended. Philadelphia, Uriah Hunt and son [etc.]
Joseph Snowden; New York, Collins and brother [183-?] 158 p.
DLC; ICU; MnU; NcD; OClWHi;
PPL; ViU. 1223

E

Earle, Thomas.
A treatise on rail-roads and
internal communications. Com-
piled from the best and latest au-
thorities, with original sugges-
tions and remarks. Philadelphia,
Sold by John Grigg, Towar, J.
& D. M. Hogan; Miffin & Parry,
prs., 1830. 120 p. CSt; CtY;
DBRE; DLC; DeGE; ICJ; MB;
MH-BA; MWA; MdBP; MiU-T;
MnSJ; N; NN; OHi; PHi; PPF;
PPL; WHi; BrMus. 1224

[Earle, William, jr.]
Obi; or, The history of
Threefingered Jack. ... Boston,
N. H. Whitaker, 1830. 140 p.
ICN. 1225

Eastman, Francis Smith, 1803-
1846.
A history of the state of New
York, from the first discovery
of the country to the present
time: with a geographical account of the country, and a view

of its original inhabitants. New
York, Augustus K. White, 1830.
456 p. NIC; NNA; NR; NSyU;
OO. 1226

Easy lessons in perspective. Including instructions for sketch-
ing from nature. Boston, Hilliard, Gray, Little and Wilkins,
1830. [4], 66 p. CSmH; CtHT-
W; CtMW; DLC; KWiU; MB; MH;
NNC; PU; RNR. 1227

Eaton, Amos, 1776-1842.
Art without science: or, Men-
suration, surveying and engineer-
ing, divested of the speculative
principles and technical language
of mathematics. 2d ed., much
enl. Albany, Pr. by Websters
and Skinners, 1830. 96 p. CSmH;
MMeT; NCH; NNC; Nh; RPB.
1228
---- Geological text-book, prepared for popular lectures on
North American geology; with applications to agriculture and the
arts. Albany, Pr. by Websters
and Skinners, 1830. 63, [1] p.
CtY; ICN; MB; MdBJ; MiU;
MnSM; MsU; NBLiHi; NCH; NIC;
NN; NjP; OClW; OO; PPF; PPL;
PU; BrMus. 1229

Eberle, John, 1787-1838.
A treatise of the materia med-
ica and therapeutics... 3d ed.,
enl. and corr. Philadelphia,
John Grigg; William Brown, pr.,
1830. 2 v. CtMW; CtY; DLC;
GHi; IaU; InU-M; KyLxT; LU;
MNF; MdBJ; MdUM; MeB;
NNNAM; NRAM; NjPT; OCHP;
OU; PPC; TxU-M; ViU; WU.
1230
---- A treatise on the practice
of medicine. Philadelphia, John
Grigg, William Brown, pr.,
1830. 2 v. CSt-L; DNLM; GU-
M; IU-M; IaU; KyLxT; LU;
MBCo; MdUM; MeB; NNNAM;
NbU-M; Nh; OCU-M; PPC; ViU.
1231

The economy of human life. See
Dodsley, Robert.

Eddy, Ansel Doan.
   An address to young men, on
the subject of temperance, de-
livered before the young men of
Canandaigua and East-Bloomfield,
N. Y. and published at their re-
quest... Canandaigua, Pr. by
Day and Morse, at the Messen-
ger office, 1830. 24 p. CSmH;
NAuT; NN.   1232

The Edgefield hive. See Landrum, Abner.

Edgeworth, Maria, 1767-1849.
   Harry and Lucy. To which
are prefixed An address to moth-
ers, and the stories of Little dog
Trusty, The orange man, and
The cherry orchard. Boston,
Munroe and Francis, etc., etc.
[183-?] (Front cover: Juvenile
classicks. Munroe & Francis.
Back cover: Munroe & Francis!
Juvenile library.) MH.   1233

---- The parent's assistant, or
Stories for children. Boston,
Munroe & Francis, etc., etc.
[183-?] MH.   1234

The editor of the Masonic mirror. See Moore, Charles Whitlock.

[Edmands, B. F.]
   Maps from the Boston school
geography. [Boston] Pub. at the
office of the Boston Daily Advertiser, 1830. MH.   1235

Edson, William J.
   Musical monitor, ... Together
with the elementary class-book,
introductory to the science of
musick... 6th ed., corr., enl.
and greatly imp. Ithaca, Pr.
and pub. by Mack and Andrus,
1830. 256 p. WHi.   1236

Edwards, Charles, 1797-1868.
   The antique statues. Lec-
tures delivered at the National
Academy of Design, New York
... [New York, Pr. by Osburn
& Buckingham, 1830?] 111 p.
DLC; MH; RPB.   1237

Edwards, George Cunningham,
1787-1837.
   Treatise on the powers and duties of justices of the peace and
town officers in the state of New
York under the revised statutes.
With practical forms. Bath, Pr.
by D. Rumsey, 1830. 2 p. l.,
[9]-411 p. CtHT; DLC; LNT;
N-L; WMM.   1238

Edwards, Jonathan, 1703-1758.
   The life of Rev. David Brainerd chiefly extracted from his
diary by President Edwards.
Somewhat abridged. Embracing
in the chronological order Brainerd's Public Journal of the most
successful year of his missionary labors. New York, American Tract Society. D. Fanshaw,
pr. [183-?] 360, 105 p. [Evan-
gelical Family Library Vol. 7;
bound with Flavel's A Treatise
on Keeping the Heart.] ViU.
                             1239
---- The treatise on religious affections, by the late Rev. Jonathan Edwards, A.M. Somewhat
abridged. New-York, American
Tract Society, D. Fanshaw, pr.,
[183?] 276 p. ViU.   1240

---- The works of President Ed-
wards: with a memoir of his
life... New York, G. & C. & H.
Carvill, 1830. 10 v. CBCDS;
CtHT; CtY; GEU; ICMcC; LU;
MBAt; MBC; MHi; MeBaT;
NNUT; NcD; OU; PPiW; RPAt;
TNJ; BrMus.   1241

Eichelberger, Lewis, 1801-1859.
   Two sermons on national
blessings and obligations. In

which are pointed out the advantages we enjoy as a nation, in consequence of our free and liberal institutions; and the religious duties and obligations these blessings impose... Preached in the Lutheran Church, July 4, 1830. Winchester, Pr. by Samuel H. Davis. And to be had at the office of the Republican, at the stores of Messrs. Slagle and John W. Miller, and at the different bookstores in town, 1830. 32 p. PPL; PPLT; ViWn.   1242

Elder, Irene S.
   Katy Keen. [A poem. New York, American Tract Society, 183-?] 16 p. RPB.   1243

Eldridge, Richard.
   A sermon, delivered in the Baptist meeting-house, in Hyannis, (Mass.) July 18, 1830... Published by request. New Bedford, B. Lindsey & son, prs. 1830. 35 p. MNBedf; NRAB.
                                     1244
The election of president... See Fox.

An elementary treatise. See Oliver, Henry Kemble.

Elements of mythology. See Robbins, Eliza.

[Eliot, William Harvard]
   A description of the Tremont House, with architectural illustrations. Boston, Pub. by Gray and Bowen. Cambridge, Pr. by E. W. Metcalf and Company, printers to the University, 1830. CtY; ICJ; MB; MHi; NBLiHi; NBU; NNC; PU; RPAt; BrMus.
                                     1245
Elliot, Jonathan, 1784-1846.
   Historical sketches of the ten miles square forming the District of Columbia; ... Washington, Pr. by J. Elliot, jr., 1830.

554 p. CSmH; CtY; DGU; DLC; MB; MH; MdHi; MiU; MnHi; NIC; NjP; OMC; P; PHi; RP; Vi; WHi; BrMus.   1246

Elliot, William.
   The patentee's manual; containing a list of patents granted by the United States for the encouragement of arts & sciences, alphabetically arranged, from 1790 to 1830. [To be continued by supplements.] Also, the laws of Congress for granting patents; with a digest of all the decisions which have taken place in the courts of the United States respecting patents. Washington, Pr. by S. A. Elliot, 1830. xviii, 3-118, [137]-153 p. CSmH; DLC; PPL [iv], [3]-118, [137]-153 p.   1247

Elliot, William, Jr.
   Address delivered before the Columbian Society, at Marblehead, on the sixth anniversary, January 8, 1830. ... Boston, True & Greene, prs., 1830. 16 p. MBAt; MH; MHi; NhHi; BrMus.   1248

Elliot's Washington pocket almanac for 1831. Washington, J. Elliot [1830] NCH.   1249

Elliott, Mary (Belson), 1794?-1894.
   Matthew and John; or Truth our best friend. New-Haven, S. Babcock, Publisher, ... Charleston, S. Babcock & Co. Sidney's press, 1830. 23 p. CtHi.   1250

[----] My sister. A poem ... New-York, Pr. and sold by Mahlon Day, at the New Juvenile Bookstore, [c1830] 8 p. CSmH; NN; PP.   1251

Ely, Aaron.
   A school dictionary of selected words, according to the orth-

ography of Webster. With a key
to etymology, being introductory
to a system of practical analysis.
New York, M. Day, 1830. 142 p.
CtHT-W; DLC; MB.   1252

[Ely, John]
   The child's instructer; consisting of easy lessons for children,
on subjects which are familiar to
them, in language adapted to their
capacities. By a teacher of little
children in Philadelphia. Stereotyped by William Hagar and Co.
New-York. Bridgeport (Conn.),
Pr. and pub. by J. B. and L.
Baldwin, 1830. 108 p. CtHT-W;
CtHi; MWA; NRivHi.   1253

Emerson, Benjamin Dudley, 1781-
1872.
   The academical speaker; a selection of extracts in prose and
verse, from ancient and modern
authors; adapted for exercises in
elocution, by B. D. Emerson.
Boston, Richardson, Lord and
Holbrook, 1830. xii, 321 p. MH;
MWA; MiD; N; NNC-T; NhHi;
NjP; RPB.   1254

---- An introduction to the national spelling book... Boston, Richardson, Lord and Holbrook, 1830.
NNC-T.   1255

---- The national spelling-book,
and pronouncing tutor; containing
rudiments of orthography and
pronunciation on an improved
plan. By which the sound of every syllable is distinctly shown
according to Walker's principles
of English orthoepy... Concord,
N. Y., H. Hill & Co., 1830. 164
p. CtHT-W; CtY; MH; MWA;
RPB.   1256

Emerson, Eleanor.
   ... Conversion of Mrs. Eleanor Emerson. From an account
written by herself. Pub. by the
American Tract Society. [Fan-

shaw, pr., 1830? N.Y.] 20 p.
No. 133. PPL.   1257

Emerson, F.
   Private school. Boston, August 17, 1830. [1] p. [Prospectus
for a private school for boys.]
OClWHi.   1258

Emerson, Frederick, 1788-1857.
   North American arithmetic.
Part first, containing elementary
lessons. Baltimore, Joseph Jew-
ett, pub., 1830. 48 p. RPB.
                           1259
---- ---- Philadelphia, Pub. by
Uriah Hunt; Lincoln & Edmunds.
Boston [Lyman Thurston Co.,
stereotypers] 1830. 4, 4, 48 p.
CtY; KU; MB; MH; MWHi.   1260

---- ---- Stereotyped. Concord,
Marsh, Capen & Lyon, etc.,
1830. MH.   1261

Emerson, Joseph, 1777-1833.
   The evangelical primer, containing... Doctrinal catechism...
historical catechism... Westminster Assembly's Shorter catechism. Boston, Pr. and sold
wholesale and retail by Crocker
& Brewster. New York, By Jonathan Leavitt, 1830. 70 p.
OO.   1262

---- Lectures on the millinnium.
2d ed. Boston, Philip Shaw,
publisher, 1830. vi, 288 p. ICM;
MH.   1263

---- Questions adapted to Whelpley's Compend of History. 10th
ed. Boston, Pub. by Richardson, Lord and Holbrook, 1830.
69 p. MWA; NjPT.   1264

---- Questions and supplement to
Goodrich's History of the United
States. 3d ed., stereotyped. Bos-
ton, Richardson, Lord and Hol-
brook, 1830. 208 p. CSt; MH;
NNC; TxU-T.   1265

Emma and her nurse. Rev. by
the Committee of Publication of
the American Sunday School
Union.   Philadelphia, American
Sunday School Union [183-?] 105
p. DLC; BrMus.   1266

Emmons, Richard, b. 1788.
The fredoniad; or Independence preserved. An epic poem
on the late war of 1812. In
four volumes. 2d ed. Philadel-
hia, Pub. by William Emmons.
Adam Waldie, pr., 1830. 4 vols.
CSmH; CSt; CtSoP; ICU; KyU;
LNHT; MB; MH; MdHi; MiD-B;
MnU; OC; P; PHi; PPAmP; PPL
(vol. 1 only); RPB; ViU; WHi.
                            1267
---- The national jubilee. And
other miscellaneous poems...
Washington, F. S. Myer, pr.,
1830. 47 p., 16 l. CSmH;
CtHT-W; CtY; MH; NBuG; PPL
(47 p.)   1268

England, John, bp., 1786-1842.
Examination of evidence and
report to the Most Reverend
James Whitfield, D.D. Archbish-
op of Baltimore upon the miracu-
lous restoration of Mrs. Ann
Mattingly of the city of Washing-
ton, D.C. Charleston, James S.
Burges, 1830. 90 p. DLC;
MdBL; PHi.   1269

---- ---- Together with the doc-
uments. Charleston [Pr. by
James S. Burges] 1830. 42 p.
DGU; InNd; MH; MdBS; MdW;
PPL.   1270

[Engles, William Morrison]
A true and complete narrative
of all the proceedings of the Phil-
adelphia Presbytery, and of the
Philadelphia Synod, in relation to
the case of the Rev. Albert
Barnes, Philadelphia, Pr. by
Russell & Martien, 1830. 48 p.
ICU; MB; MH-AH; MWA; MiD-B;
NN; NjPT; NjR; OClW; PPPrHi;

ViRUT.   1271

An enquiry into the present system. See McNaughton, James.

Episcopacy tested by Scripture.
See Onderdonk, Henry Ustick.

Erie County, N. Y.
Report of a county convention
of delegates, from the several
towns in the county of Erie, held
at the court house, in Buffalo, on
the eleventh of February, eighteen hundred and thirty, for the
purpose of inquiring into the title
of the Holland Land Company to
the lands claimed by them in
this state.   Buffalo, Republican
press, S. H. Salisbury, 1830. 22
p. NBu; NBuHi; O.   1272

Erläuterung für herrn Caspar
Schwenckfeld, und die zugethanen
seiner lehre, wegen vielen stü-
cken, beydes aus der historie
und theologie; allen aufrichtigen
nachforschern und liebhabern der
wahrheit zum dienste ans licht zu
stellen beabsichtiget und verfas-
set worden, durch etliche der
ehemaligen gottseeligen auswan-
derer aus schlesien nach Pennsylvanien in Nord-Amerika.
Zweyte auflage ... Sumnytaun
[Pa.] Gedruckt bey E. Benner,
1830. 2 p. l., [iii]-xiv, 507 [i. e.
508], [2] p. CSmH; P; PHi;
PPG; PPLT.   1273

Erodore, pseud. See Abbott,
Jacob.

Erskine, Thomas.
Essay on faith. Philadelphia,
E. Littell, Stereotyped by L.
Johnson, 1830. 89 p. CtMW;
GDC; MeB.   1274

An essay on duelling. New York,
G. & C. & H. Carvill [Ludwig &
Tolefree, prs.] 1830. 29 p. CtHT;
CtY; NNC; PPL; TxU.   1275

Essays, devoted principally to
the discussion of the great meta-
physical problem of "How we acquire a knowledge of eternal objects." [1830?] 16+ p. PPL
(imperfect).   1276

Essays on the origin of the federal government. See The
Charleston mercury.

Essays on the present crisis in
the condition of the American
Indians. See Evarts, Jeremiah.

Essays on the protecting system.
. . . I. Three of the addresses
of the Philadelphia Society for
the Promotion of National Industry. - Published in Philadelphia,
in the year 1819. II. Essay on
the maxims of free trade, prom-
ulgated by Adam Smith. - From
the London Quarterly Review.
III. Essay on free trade. -
From Blackwood's Magazine for
May, 1825. IV. Extract from a
message of Governor Wolcott, of
Connecticut. Philadelphia, Pr.
by Mifflin & Parry, 1830. 72 p.
DeGE; LU; MH-BA; MWA;
MdHi; PHi; PPAmP; PPPrHi;
PU.   1277

Essex Agricultural Society.
   Essex Agricultural Society.
Reports of committees and premi-
ums awarded in 1829; And a list
of premiums offered in 1830;
with remarks and hints to farm-
ers, &c. Pamphlet No. ix, 1829.
Salem, W. & S. B. Ives, prs.,
Observer office, 1830. 88 p.
MBAt; MH; MHi.   1278

Evangelical Lutheran Church in
the U. S. Synod of Ohio.
   Minutes of the proceedings of
the thirteenth session of the Synod and Ministerium of the Evangelical Lutheran Church, in the
state of Ohio, convened at Zanes-

ville, Ohio, in Trinity week,
A. D. 1830. [Lancaster? John
Herman? 1830] 20 p. OCoC.
                                1279
---- Synod of Ohio and Adjacent
States.
   Liturgy, or formulary, for
the use of Evangelical Lutheran
Churches. Compiled by a com-
mittee, appointed by the Synod
of Ohio, and ordered to be
printed. Lancaster, O., Pr. by
John Herman, 1830. 12 p. OCoC;
PPLT.   1280

---- Verhandlungen der dreyzehn-
ten Synodal-Versamlung der Ev.
Lutherischen Prediger von Ohio,
und den angränzenden Staaten;
gehalten zu Zanesville, Muskin-
gum Caunty, Ohio, in der Trini-
tatis-Woche, 1830. Lancaster,
O., Gedruckt bey Johann Herman
[1830] 24 p. OCoC; PPLT. 1281

---- Synod of Pennsylvania.
   Verhandlungen der Deutschen
Evangelisch-Lutherischen Synode
von Pennsylvanien, gehalten zu
Lancaster... 1830. Easton, Ge-
druckt bey Heinrich und Wilhelm
Huetter, 1830. 16 p. NN.   1282

---- Synod of South Carolina.
   Proceedings.... convened at St.
Paul's Church, Newberry Dis-
trict, South Carolina November,
1830. Charleston, S. C., Pr. by
James S. Burges, 1830. 28 p.
ScCoT.   1283

Evangelical Lutheran Ministerium
of Pennsylvania and adjacent
states.
   Erbauliche Lieder-sammlung
zum Gottesdienstlichen Gebrauch
in den Vereinigten Evangelisch-
Lutherischen Gemeinen in Pennsylvanien und den benbenachten
Staaten... Die Neunte vermehrte
und mit einen Melodien Register
versehene Auflage. Germantaun,

Gedruckt bey M. Billmeyer,
1830. 12 1., 463, [8], 26 p.
PPL; RPB.   1284

---- Minutes of the German
Evangelical Lutheran Synod of
Pennsylvania convened in the city
of Lancaster from the fifth to
the ninth of June, in the year of
our Lord 1830. Easton [Pa.],
Pr. by C. J. Hütter, 1830. 11 p.
PPLT.   1285

An evangelical view. See Winslow, Hubbard.

Evangelus Pacificus, pseud. See
Winslow, Hubbard.

Evans, Charles.
    Account of the Asylum for the
Relief of Persons deprived of
their Reason, near Frankford. ...
Philadelphia, 1830. Sabin 23142.
                             1286
Evans, Thomas.
    Examples of youthful piety,
principally intended for the instruction of young persons...
Philadelphia, Pr. and pub. for
the author by Thomas Kite, 1830.
215, [1] p. InRE; MBC; MWA;
NNUT; PHC; PPF; PPL; PSC-Hi.
                             1287
[Evarts, Jeremiah]
    Essays on the present crisis
in the condition of the American
Indians; first published in the National Intelligencer, under the signature of William Penn. Philadelphia, Thomas Kite, 1830. 116
p. ICN; MHS; NbHi; NjP; NjR;
PHi; PPL; PU; BrMus.   1288

Events in Paris, during the 26,
27, 28 and 29 of July, 1830, by
several eye witnesses. Continued
until the oath of Louis Philip I,
and augmented by the Charter,
with the new modifications, by
several interesting articles, and
the Marche parisienne, by Mr.
Casimir Delavigne, with the mu-

sic, and his latest Messénienne.
Tr. from the 4th Paris ed. Boston, Carter and Hendee [etc.,
etc.] [Pr. by I. R. Butts] 1830.
197 p. CSmH; CtY; MB; MBAt;
MH.   1289

[Everett, Alexander Hill] 1790-
1847.
    British opinions on the protect-
ing system being a reply to strictures on that system which have
appeared in several recent British publications. Reprinted with
a few alterations from an article
in the North American Review
for January 1830. Boston, Nathan Hale and Gray & Bowen,
W. L. Lewis, pr., 1830. 85 p.
CtY; DeGE; ICN; ICU; MB; MHi;
MWA; NbU; PHi; PPL; ScC;
WHi; BrMus.   1290

[----] ---- 2d ed. Boston, Na-
than Hale and Gray & Bowen
[W. L. Lewis, pr.] 1830. 43 p.
CSmH; MH.   1291

---- An oration delivered at the
request of the city government,
before the citizens of Boston on
the 5th of July 1830... Boston,
Press of John H. Eastburn, city
pr., 1830. 47 p. CSmH; CU;
CtHT; CtSoP; KHi; M; MBAt;
MH; MHi; MWA; MiD-B; NCH;
NIC; NNC; NbO; Nh; NjPT; NjR;
PHi; PPL; BrMus.   1292

Everett, Edward, 1794-1865.
    An address delivered on the
28th of June, 1830, the anniver-
sary of the arrival of Governor
Winthrop at Charlestown. Deliv-
ered and published at the request
of the Charlestown Lyceum.
Charlestown, Pub. by William W.
Wheildon; Boston, Carter and
Hendee [From the Aurora Press,
William H. Wheildon] 1830. 51 p.
CBPac; CSmH; CtSoP; DLC;
MBAU; MBAt; MDeeP; MH; MHi;
MdBJ; MiD-B; NCH; NbU; NhHi;

NjR; OClWHi; OO; PP; PPL; RPB; T; WHi; BrMus.   1293

---- A lecture on the working men's party, first delivered October sixth, before the Charlestown Lyceum, and published at their request. Boston, Pub. by Gray and Bowen [Pr. by W. L. Lewis] 1830. 27 p. CSmH; CtSoP; CtY; IU; MBAU; MBAt; MH; MHi; MWA; MiD-B; NbO; PHi; PPAmP; PPL; T; BrMus.   1294

---- Remarks on the public lands and on the right of a state to nullify an act of Congress... Boston, Pub. by Gray & Bowen, 1830. 86 p. MB; NbO; PPL.   1295

---- Speech of Mr. Everett, of Massachusetts, on the bill for removing the Indians from the east to the west side of the Mississippi. Delivered in the House of Representatives, on the 19th of May, 1830. Boston, From the office of the Daily Advertiser [W. L. Lewis, pr.] 1830. 46 p. ICN; MBAt; MH; MHi; MWA; MdHi; N; OCHP; PPAmP; PPL; WHi; BrMus.   1296

---- ---- Washington, Pr. by Gales & Seaton, 1830. 32 p. CSmH.   1297

---- Speech of Mr. Everett, of Mass., on the proposal of Mr. McDuffie to repeal the laws of 1828 and 1824, imposing duties on imports. Delivered in the House of Representatives, on the 7th and 8th May, 1828. Washington, Pr. by Gales & Seaton, 1830. 34 p. CSmH.   1298

Every man's lawyer: Or, Every man his own scribner and conveyancer... Laid down in so plain a manner... By a gentleman of the Bar... Philadelphia, Pr. and pub. by J. Boyer, 1830. 120 p.

PPL (imperfect in beginning) 1299

The evil of theft: exhibited in the history of James Forrest, a penitent sabbath scholar. By the author of Sabbath school scenes. Boston, J. Loring [c 1830] 108 p. DLC; MB.   1300

Ewing, Greville.
    A memoir of Barbara Ewing; by her husband, Greville Ewing. Revised by the Committee of Publication of the American Sunday School Union. Philadelphia, American Sunday School Union, 1830. 143 p. P; BrMus.   1301

Examination of Dr. Tyler's vindication. See Winslow, Hubbard.

The exclusives. See Bury, Lady Charlotte (Campbell).

Excuses for the neglect of the communion considered. See American Unitarian Association.

An exhibition of unitarianism: in quotations from its standard authors and works with scriptural extracts. 2d ed. rev. and abridged. Boston, Pub. by Peirce and Williams, 1830. 40 p. CtSoP; CtY; DGU; DLC; ICMe; ICN; LU; MB; MBC; MH; MMeT; MeBaT; MeHi.   1302

An experienced teacher. See Questions for the examination of scholars...

An expose of the rise and proceedings of the American Bible Society, during the thirteen years of its existence, by a member. 2d ed. New York, 1830. 32 p. ICMe; MBBC; MH; MMeT; MNBedf; WHi.   1303

An exposition of the government of the Methodist Episcopal conference: with reflections on the

nature and tendency of its system... Also, a serious address
to the Methodist community of
New-England. By an anti-Episcopal Methodist. Boston, Pr.
by Edgar W. Davis, 1830. 16 p.
KBB; MB; MBC; PPL; TxDaM;
TxU.   1304

An exposition of the principles of
the Roman Catholic religion.
See Philalethes.

An exposition of the reasons for
the resignation of some of the
professors in the University of
the city of New York. New York,
Jas. Van Nordon, 1830. KyDC.
                              1305
Extracts for translation. See
Kingsley, James Luce.

Extracts from pamphlets originally published in England and relating to the Rev. George Montgomery West, intended to accompany
his printed reply to the late report delivered by Bishop Chase
before the annual convention in
Gambier, Ohio. Sept. 8th, 1830.
[Gambier? 1830?] 32 p. MBD;
OCHP.   1306

                    F

Faber, George Stanley.
    The difficulties of Romanism.
2d Philadelphia ed. Philadelphia,
Towar, J. & D. M. Hogan, and
Hogan and Co. Pittsburg, 1830.
305 p. MH; MNF; NNG; NjPT;
OClW; OMC; ViRUT.   1307

Fairchild, Ashbel Green, 1795-
1864.
    Letters on the mode and sub-
jects of Christian baptism addressed to the members of the
United Congregations of George's
Creek and the Tent. Uniontown,
Pr. by William H. Whitton, 1830.
32 p. DGU; NjPT; NjR.   1308

---- The opposition made to the
great moral enterprizes of the
day. An address delivered in
New-Geneva, Pa. at the formation of the Spring-Hill Temperance Society, and, subsequently,
by request, in Greensburgh,
Greene County, April 11th, 1830.
Pub. by request. Pittsburgh, Pr.
at the "Statesman" office, 1830.
20 p. NjPT.   1309

Fairchild, James Harris.
    The essential doctrines of the
gospel: A sermon, by J. H.
Fairchild... Published by request.
2d ed. Boston, Peirce and Williams, 1830. 36 p. CtHT; CtY;
MWA; MiD-B; RPB; WHi.   1310

Fairfax County, Va.
    To the General Assembly of
Virginia. The petition of the undersigned freeholders and citizens
of the county of [Blank] in the
state of Virginia, respectfully
sheweth: ... [Alexandria? 1830?]
Bdsd. Vi.   1311

Fairfield, Sumner Lincoln, 1803-
1844.
    Abaddon. The spirit of de-
struction; and other poems. New
York, Sleight and Robinson,
1830.   157 p., 1 l. CSmH; CtY;
ICN; MB; MBAt; MWA; MeB;
MiD; NBuDD; NCH; NIC; NNUT;
NRU; NjP; PPL; PU; RPB; TxU;
ViU; BrMus.   1312

Fairfield, N. Y. College of Phys-
icians and Surgeons of the West-
ern district of the State of New
York.
    Circular and catalogue [of the
faculty and students...] Little
Falls, N.Y., Pr. by Edward M.
Griffins, 1830. 22 p. NNNAM;
NUtHi.   1313

Falconer, William, 1732-1769.
    The shipwreck and other po-
ems... New York, G. G. Sickles,

1830. 142 p. MWH.   1314

---- ---- Philadelphia, L. Johnson, 1830. 162 p. CSmH; CtY; DLC; MWA; MoSU; OClW; OO; TNJ.   1315

Falkland, Lucius.
A review of the article in the Southern Review, for 1830, on the several speeches made during the debate on Mr. Foote's resolution, by Mr. Hayne of South Carolina, and Mr. Webster of Massachusetts. Baltimore, Pr. by Sands & Neilson, 1830. 46 p. CtY; MdHi; N; PPL; ScCC.   1316

Falkland. See Lytton, Edward George Earle Lytton Bulwer-Lytton.

Familiar instructions for the public worship of Almighty God, agreeably to the services of the Protestant Episcopal Church. 2d ed. Stereotyped by James Conner. New York, New York Protestant Episcopal Tract Society, 1830. 16 p. MBD; MH; NNG.   1317

Family conversations on the evidences of Revelation, etc. Philadelphia, American Sunday School Union, 1830. BrMus.   1318

Faneuil Hall convention, or Masonry unveiled... Entered according to act of Congress, February 18, 1830. 1 p. DLC.   1319

Fansher, Sylvanus.
Concise treatise on electricity; with directions for constructing and applying lightning rods, used for the purpose of shielding houses, ships, etc., against the dangerous effects of electrical fluid from the thunder-cloud. New-Haven, Pr. for the author, 1830. 36, [3] p. CtHi; CtY; MH; MWA.   1320

Farley, Frederick Augustus, 1800-1892.
Two discourses on the Lord's Supper, preached in Westminster Church, Providence, R.I., Sunday, Feb. 28. Providence, Pub. by M. Robinson, Arcade; Pr. by F. Y. Carlile, 1830. [5]-31 p. ICMe; MBC; MMeT; MWA; MiD-B; NBLiHi; PPAmP.   1321

Farmer, John, 1789-1838.
A catechism of the history of New-Hampshire, from its first settlement to the present period; for the use of schools and families. 2d ed. Concord, Hoag and Atwood, 1830. 108 p. DLC; MB; MH; NhD; BrMus.   1322

---- The emigrants' guide; or, Pocket gazetteer of the surveyed part of Michigan. Albany [N.Y.] Pr. by B. D. Packard and co., 1830. 32 p. CSmH; ICN; MiD-B; N; NIC; NhHi.   1323

---- Map of the territories of Michigan and Ouisconsin. Albany, 1830. col. map. "Map separately sold but inserted in some copies of The emigrants guide." NIC.   1324

Farmer's almanac for 1831. By Thomas Sharp. Baltimore, J. N. Toy & W. R. Lucas [1830] 18 l. MWA.   1325

---- By James W. Palmer. Louisville, J. W. Palmer [1830] 12 l. KyLo.   1326

---- By James W. Palmer. Louisville, J. W. Palmer; J. A. Frazer; Lexington, M. Kennedy [1830] 12 l. ICU; KyBgW; OC; PPiU.   1327

---- By David Young. New-York, Caleb Bartlett [1830] 18 l. NHi.   1328

---- By John Ward. Philadelphia, M'Carty & Davis [1830] 18 l. DeU; InU; MWA; NjR; PHi; PPL.   1329

The Farmer's almanack for 1831. By Robert B. Thomas. Boston, Richardson, Lord & Holbrook; Lyman Thurston and Co., prs. [1830] 30 l. CU; CtY; DLC; GU; In; MHi; MeB; MiD-B; NN; NcD; NbHi; NhHi; NjR; OClWHi; RPB; TxU; WHi.   1330

---- By Robert B. Thomas. Boston, Richardson, Lord & Holbrook; H. Hill & Co. [etc.]; Lyman Thurston & Co., prs. [1830] 30 l. MWA.   1331

---- By Zadock Thompson. Burlington, E. & T. Mills [1830] 12 l. MWA; VtU.   1332

---- By Samuel Burr. Cincinnati, N. & G. Guilford; Oliver Farnsworth; O. & P. M. Farnsworth, prs. [1830] 18 l. DLC; OClWHi.   1333

---- By Robert B. Thomas. Hallowell, Glazier, Masters & Co. [1830] 24 l. MeP.   1334

---- Ithaca [1830] 18 l. Drake 7082.   1335

---- By Samuel Burr. Louisville, W. W. Worsley [1830] 18 l. MWA.   1336

---- By David Young. New York, Daniel D. Smith [1830] 18 l. MHi; MWA; NN.   1337

---- By Robert B. Thomas. Portland, Shirley, Hyde & Co. [1830] 24 l. MWA; MeHi.   1338

---- By David Young. Poughkeepsie, P. Potter [1830] 18 l. MB; MWA; NHi; NP.   1339

Farmer's almanack, for the middle states for 1831. By Thomas Spofford. New-York, David Felt; Boston, Willard Felt & Co. [1830] 18 l. Ct; CtLHi; InU; MB; MWA; MnU; NN; NjR; PHi; ViHi.   1340

---- By Thomas Spofford. Utica, Hastings & Tracy [1830] 18 l. AU; NSyOHi.   1341

The farmers & mechanics almanack for 1831. Easton, Henry Hamman [1830] 18 l. MWA.   1342

---- By Charles Frederick Egelmann. Philadelphia, George W. Mentz & Son [1830] 18 l. MWA; N; NHi; NN; P; PLF; PYHi; ViU.   1343

---- Issue with 19 l. NNU-H; NjR; PHi; PPL.   1344

Farmers' diary; or Catskill almanack for 1831. By Edwin E. Prentiss. Catskill, Faxon & Elliott. [1830] 18 l. MWA; N; NHi; NN; NbO; NjR; WHi. 1345

The farmer's diary, or Ontario almanac for 1831. Canandaigua, Bemis and Ward [1830] 12 l. N; NIC; NRU.   1346

---- Canandaigua, Morse & Harvey [1830] 12 l. NBuG; NCooHi; NR; NRMA; NSyOHi.   1347

---- By Andrew Beers. Canandaigua, Morse & Harvey [1830] 12 l. MWA; MiD-B; NCanHi; WHi.   1348

The farmer's, mechanic's and gentleman's almanack for 1831. By Nathan Wild. Amherst, J. S. & C. Adams [1830] 24 l. CtY; DLC; MWA; N; NRMA; NhHi; WHi.   1349

A farmer's narrative, of his conversion, in a series of letters,

which originally appeared in the
Auburn (Cayuga County, New
York) Gospel Messenger, for
1827. Stereotyped by James Conner. New York, General Protestant Episcopal Sunday School
Union, Depository. Pr. at the
Protestant Episcopal Press, 1830.
40 p. MBD.   1350

Farmington Academy. Farmington, Conn.
   Catalogue of the trustees, instructors, and students of Farmington Academy, during the winter of 1829, '30. Hartford, Pr.
by George F. Olmsted, 1830.
12 p. CtHi.   1351

Farr, Jonathan.
   "These four days meetings."
What are they for? and what will
be the cost and fruit of them?
By Jonathan Farr, minister of
Gardner, Mass. [Gardner?
183-?] 18 p. CBPac; BrMus.
                                    1352
[Farrar, Eliza Ware (Rotch)
"Mrs. John Farrar,"] 1791-1870.
   The children's Robinson Crusoe; or The remarkable adventures of an Englishman who lived
five years on an unknown and un-
inhabited island of the Pacific
Ocean. By A Lady... Boston,
Hilliard, Gray, Little and Wilk-
ins, 1830. 367 p. CtY; MB.
                                    1353
Farrell, John, d. 1848.
   ... The dumb girl of Genoa;
or, The bandit merchant: a
melo-drama, in three acts. By
John Farrell. The only edition
correctly marked from the
prompter's book; with the stage
business situations, and directions. As performed at the New-
York theatres. New-York, R.H.
Elton [1830] 35 p. DLC.   1354

Faulkner, Charles James, 1806-
1884.
   Sketch of an argument deliv-

ered by Charles James Faulkner,
in the House of Delegates of Virginia, in support of the claims of
the supernumerary officers of the
Virginia state line, to the compensation of half pay for life.
February 2, 1830. Richmond,
Pr. and pub. by T. W. White,
1830. 25 p. MB; NcD; NcU;
ScU.   1355

Featherstonhaugh, George Willi-
am, 1780-1866.
   The death of Ugolino. A
tragedy. Philadelphia, Pub. by
Carey & Lea [Pr. by James Kay,
jun. & co.] 1830. 116 p. CSmH;
CSt; ICU; MB; MBAt; MH; NCH;
PHi; PPAmP; PPL; PU; RPB;
ScU; BrMus.   1356

[----] The deluge. A demi-
serious poem. ...By a Mr. Smith.
Philadelphia, Pr. for the Author,
1830. 50 p. MH; MdBP; PPL;
TxU.   1357

The federal ready reckoner, in
dollars and cents; for the use of
persons who have not the convenience, or are not expert, in making calculations in figures. To
which is added, a number of valuable tables, forms, &c. &c.
Cincinnati, Pr. and pub. by William Conclin, 1830. 144 p. OC.
                                    1358
Fellows, Willis.
   A friendly warning to the public. ... Willis Fellows, July 2d,
1830. [Vincennes? 1830] Bdsd.
                                    1359
Female Cent Institution.
   Seventeenth annual report on
the concerns of the Female Cent
Institution, Auxiliary to the New
Hampshire Missionary Society,
for the year 1830. Concord, Pr.
by Asa M'Farland, 1830. 12 p.
MBC.   1360

Female wages. The following
is one of a series of articles

published in the New York Mir-
or. [New York, 1830?] 11 p.
PPL.   1361

Fénelon, François de Salignac de
La Mothe, 1651-1715.
   Les aventures de Télémaque,
fils d'Ulysse. Nouv. éd. avec
la signification des mots les plus
difficles en anglais au bas de
chaque page. A laquelle on a
ajouté, un petit dictionnaire.
Mythologique et géographique...
d'après l'édition de Mr. Charles
Le Brun. ... New York, Leavitt
and Allen [1830?] 395 p. GEU.
                                        1362
---- Les aventures de Télémaque,
fils d'Ulysse...From the last and
best Paris edition. Accompanied
by a key to facilitate the translation of this work by A. Bolmar.
Philadelphia, Carey & Lea, Sold
by E. L. Carey & A. Hart,
[etc.] 1830. iv, 355 p. MB; OO;
PU.   1363

---- ---- From the last Paris
edition... Philadelphia, Pub. by
H. L. Carey and I. Lea, 1830.
2 v. MB.   1364

---- ---- Nouvelle edition. A
laquelle on a ajouté, un petit
dictionnaire d'après l'édition de
Mr. Charles Le Brun, Le tout
soigneusement revu et corrigé
sur l'edition Stéréotype de Didot
à Paris. A Philadelphia, Towar,
J. & D. M. Hogan; Pittsburg-
Hogan & Co., 1830. 420 p.
CtHT-W; DGU; DLC; MB; MeLB;
MiDSH; MoS; NN; Nh; P.   1365

Ferguson, Adam.
   History of the progress and
termination of the Roman republic. Philadelphia, Thomas
Wardle, Pr. by James Kay, jr.
& co., [Stereotyped by L. John-
son] 1830. 493 p. AMob; CtHT;
GDC; InU; KyLoP; KyU; MB; MH;
MWA; MdBS; MiU; MoSW; NNC;

NbCrD; NjP; OHi; PHi; PU; ScCC;
TNJ; WHi.   1366

Ferguson, John.
   Memoir of the life and char-
acter of Rev. Samuel Hopkins,
D.D. formerly pastor of the
First Congregational church in
Newport, Rhode Island. With an
appendix. Boston, L. W. Kimball;
New York, J. P. Haven, 1830.
196 p. CtHT-W; CtSoP; CtY;
DLC; ICU; KyDC; MB; MBAt;
MH-AH; MWA; MdBE; MiD-B;
NNUT; PPPrHi; RNHi.   1367

Fessenden, Samuel, 1784-1869.
   An address delivered at the
annual communication of the
Grand Lodge of Maine, Jan. 28,
1830. Portland, Shirley and Hyde,
1830. 11 p. IaCrM; NNFM;
PPFM.   1368

Fessenden, Thomas G.
   The new American gardener;
containing practical directions on
the culture of fruits and vege-
tables; including landscape and
ornamental gardening grape-vines,
silk, strawberries, &c. &c. 4th
ed. Boston, Pub. by Carter and
Hendee. Stereotyped at the Boston Type and Stereotype Foundry,
1830. [1], 16-306 p. IU; MNBedf;
MWA.   1369

"Fetch them in..." See American Tract Society. New York.

Fete Civique.
   Célébrée A Charleston, South
Carolina En Commemoration de
la Glorieuse Revolution Fran-
çaise de 1830. Charleston, A. E.
Miller, Imprimateur [1830] 18 p.
ScCC.   1370

A few reasons for being members of the Roman Catholic
Church. Republished by the Catholics of Pittsburgh, 1830.
Not located.   1371

Field, Hannah.
Memorial of Hannah Field.
New York, Tract Association,
1830. (Tract No. 32) PSC-Hi.
                                   1372
Field, Timothy.
A sermon, preached November
12, A.D. 1829, in Westminster,
West Parish, Vermont, at the
dedication of a new meeting-
house. Pastor of the Church is
said. Brattleboro, Pr. for the
author, 1830. 15 p. MWA; N;
OCHP.   1373

Field, William.
A series of questions comprising the history of the four Gospels and the Acts of the Apostles;
with reference to the scriptures
instead of answers. Boston, 1830.
95 p. MH-AH; MHi.   1374

Fifty-five reasons for not being
a Baptist. By Timothy. Printed
in New-England, by Titus. 1830.
12 p. DLC.   1375

Finley, Anthony.
Indiana [map]. Philadelphia,
A. Finley [1830?] ICN (photostat)
                                 . 1376
---- A new general atlas, comprising a complete set of maps,
representing the grand divisions
of the globe, together with the
several empires, kingdoms and
states in the world; compiled
from the best authorities, and
corrected by the most recent discoveries. Philadelphia, A. Finley, 1830. 3 l. 60 maps. GU;
MH; OClWHi; PPL.   1377

---- Virginia [map]. Philadelphia, A. Finley, 1830. ICN.
                                   1378
Finn, Matthew D.
Theoremetrical system of
paintings; or, Modern plan fully
explained in six lessons... to
which is added the theory and
practice of the old school...

New York, James Ryan, 1830.
60 p. NjR.   1379

Fire-side conversations on some
of the principal doctrines of the
Bible. Philadelphia, American
Sunday School Union, 1830. 123
p. BrMus.   1380

First impressions on reading the
message of the governor of
Georgia, 1830, relative to the
Indians. [1830] 4 p. PHi; PPL.
                                   1381
First lessons in grammar. See
Peabody, Nathaniel.

The first part of the comical
sayings. See Graham, Dougal.

Fisher, Edward, 1627-1655.
The marrow of modern divinity, in two parts. Part I, touch-
ing both the covenant of works
and covenant of grace...To which
is added the twelve queries,
which were proposed to the twelve
marrow men, by the commission
of the general assembly of the
church of Scotland, 1721... 1st
American rev. from the 8th
Scottish ed. Pittsburgh, Pub. by
William Paxton, D. & M. Maclean, prs., 1830. 418 p. MiU;
NcMHi; NjPT; PPiPT.   1382

Fisher, John.
Masonic address, delivered in
West Union, Ohio, on June 24,
A. L. 5830 A.D. 1830, being the
anniversary of Saint John the
Baptist... Maysville, Ky., Collins
and Co., prs. 1830. 16 p. IaCrM;
MBFM.   1383

Fisk, Benjamin Franklin, d. 1832.
A grammar of the Greek lan-
guage... Boston, Hilliard, Gray,
Little & Wilkins. [Cambridge,
E. W. Metcalf & co.] 1830. xi,
240 p., 1 l. DLC; MdU; NNC;
NjR.   1384

Fitch, Charles.
The safety of this nation, A sermon delivered in Holliston on the day of the annual Thanksgiving, November 26, 1829. Boston, T. R. Marvin, pr., 1830. 14 p. CBPac; MBAt; MBC; MW; BrMus. 1385

Fitch, Eleayar Thompson, 1791-1871.
A review of Dr. Wood's letters to Dr. Taylor on the permission of sin; together with remarks on Dr. Bellamy's treatise on the same subject. New Haven, [Baldwin & Treadway] 1830. 50 p. MH-AH. 1386

Fitch, Samuel Sheldon.
Remarks on the importance of the teeth. On their diseases & modes of cure; with direction for forming regular and beautiful sets of teeth, and for the preservation of their helath and beauty. 3d ed. Philadelphia, Carey & Lea, (Philadelphia, Jesper Harding, Pr., 1830.) 24 p. KyDC; PHi; PPC; PPL. 1387

Fitz, John.
Modern Presbyterianism unmasked, and arrant bigotry and rank fanaticism exposed, in a review of the administration of church government in the session of the First Presbyterian Church in Newburyport; ... Boston, Pr. for the Author, by John H. Eastburn, 1830. 72 p. CtSoP; CtY; MBC; MH; MH-AH; MHi; MWA; NcMHi; PPPrHi; RPB; BrMus. 1388

Flavel, John, 1627?-1691.
The fountain of life; or, A display of Christ in His essential and mediatorial glory. New York, American Tract Society, [183-?] 559 p. DLC; GMM; OCl; TxD-T; WHi. 1389

---- Keeping the heart: or The saint indeed... New York, Pub. by the American Tract Society, 1830. 192 p. DLC; N; PPeSchw. 1390

---- The touchstone of sincerity; or, The signs of grace, and symptoms of hypocrisy. New York, Pub. by the American Tract Society [183-?] 96 p. (Evangelical family library; issued with Wilberforce, A practical view.) DLC; NcD; ViU. 1391

---- A treatise on keeping the heart. Selected from the works of the Rev. John Flavel. New York, American Tract Society [183-?] 108 p. (Evangelical family library; issued with David Brainerd, The life of David Brainerd.) CU; CtHT; DLC; ICU; IU; ViU. 1392

Fleetwood, John.
The life of our Lord and Saviour Jesus Christ; containing a full, accurate, and universal history. New Haven, Nathan Whiting, 1830. 708 p. CtHi; CtSoP; CtY; MH; MiD-B; NBuDD; NIC; OO; PPeSchw; TxU. 1393

[Fletcher, John William] 1729-1785.
An appeal to matter of fact and common sense or a rational demonstration of man's corrupt and lost state... New York, J. Emory and B. Waugh, for the Methodist Episcopal Church, 1830. 165 p. DLC; ICMcC; LNB; MB; NRMA; ScDuE; TxD-T. 1394

---- The portrait of St. Paul; or, The true model for Christians and pastors; translated from a French manuscript of the late Rev. John William Fletcher, by Rev. Joshua Gilpin... New York, J. Emory & B. Waugh, 1830. 342 p. ArL; CBPac; MiU; NR; NjMD. 1395

Flint, Abel, 1765-1825.

A system of geometry and
trigonometry, with A treatise on
surveying. ... With a complete
series of mathematical tables
and necessary explanations... 6th
ed., rev. and enl. by the addition of copious notes and illustrations, and a concise treatise
on Logarithms, by Frederick A.
R. Barnard. Hartford, Pub. by
Cooke and Co., 1830. Ct; ICJ;
MH; OClWHi; TxU.   1396

Flint, Timothy, 1780-1840.
The lost child... Boston,
Carter & Hendee, and Putnam &
Hunt, 1830. 121 p. CtY; ICN;
MiU.   1397

---- ---- Boston, Putnam &
Hunt, Peirce & Williams and
Wait, Greene & Co., 1830. 121 p.
CSmH; CtY; ICN; MBAt; MoKU;
TN.   1398

[----] The Shoshonee Valley; a
romance... By the author of
Francis Berrian. Cincinnati, E.
H. Flint, 1830. 2 v. CSmH;
CtHT; DLC; ICN; IU; Ia; MB;
MBAt; NN; NR; OC; OCHP;
OClWHi; PHi; PU; TN; WaU;
BrMus.   1399

Flora, pseudonym.
The Chaplet a waltz by Flora.
Philadelphia, Pub. by R. H. Hob-
son; Washington City, Pishey
Thompson [183-?] Bdsd. CSmH.
                           1400
Flora's dictionary. See Wirt,
Mrs. Elizabeth W. G.

Folsom, George, 1802-1869.
History of Saco and Biddeford,
with notices of other early settlements, and of the proprietory
governments, in Maine, including the provinces of New Somer-
setshire and Lygonia. Saco, Pr.
by Alex C. Putnam, 1830. 331 p.
CL; CtSoP; DLC; ICU; InCW;
KHi; MB; MBAt; MBC; MWA;

MeHi; MeU; MiD-B; MnHi; MoK;
NIC; NhD; NhHi; OClWHi; PPL;
RPJCB; WHi.   1401

Fonblanque, John.
A treatise of equity with the
addition of marginal references
and notes. 3rd Amer. ed. Additional notes by Anthony Lous-
sat. Philadelphia, John Grigg,
1830, 1831. 2 v. in 1. GU;
MoKB.   1402

Fontaine, Edward.
Address of E. Fontaine to the
voters of the district composed
of the counties of Fluvanna,
Goochland, Louisa and Hanover.
Richmond, Bailie & Gallagher,
prs. [1830] 7 p. Sabin 24984.
                           1403
Food for fun, or The humorist's
almanack for 1831. Boston, E.
L. Bell [1830] 28 l. DLC; MHi;
MWA.   1404

Foot, Joseph Ives, 1796-1840.
A sermon preached at the or-
dination of Rev. Lucius W. Clark,
as pastor of the church in South
Wilbraham. December 9, 1829.
Brookfield [Mass.] E. and G.
Merriam, prs., 1830. 22 p.
CSmH.   1405

Foot, Samuel Augustus, 1780-
1846.
Speech of Mr. Foot, of Connecticut, on the resolution offered by him on the 29th December, 1829, on the subject of the
public lands. Delivered in the
Senate of the United States, on
the 20th May, 1830. Washington,
Pr. by Gales & Seaton, 1830.
28 p. CSmH.   1406

Footsteps to natural history.
[No. 2] Boston, Leonard C.
Bowles, 1830. 44 p. MH.   1407

For the benefit of the heirs of
Fulton. [Philadelphia, 1830?]

Bdsd. PPL.   1408

Force, Peter.
My present engagements render it necessary that all accounts
connected with the newspaper I
lately published should be settled
as promptly as practicable. En-
closed is a bill for the amount
due on your subscription to the
National Journal... Your obedi-
ent servant. Washington, D. C.
1830. 1 p. DLC.   1409

Foreign Mission Society for the
County of Litchfield.
Annual report of the Foreign
Mission Society for the county of
Litchfield, for the year 1830.
[Litchfield? 1830?] 12 p. MBC.
                          1410
The form book: containing nearly
three hundred of the most ap-
proved precedents for conveyanc-
ing, arbitration, bills of exchange,
promissory notes, receipts for
money, letters of attorney, bonds,
copartnerships, leases, petitions,
and wills; besides many other
subjects referred to in the index.
By a member of the Philadelphia
Bar. Philadelphia, Towar, J. &
D. M. Hogan; Pittsburgh, Hogan
& Co., Stereotyped by L. John-
son, 1830. 288 p. CSmH; Ct;
GDC; ICLaw; MH-L; MdU; MiU;
NIC; NN; NbHi; NcD; NjP; OCHP;
OO; PHi; PPF; PPL; PU-L; TN;
TxU; ViU; WHi.   1411

Forster, Josiah.
Piety promoted in brief bio-
graphical memorials, of some of
the Religious Society of Friends,
commonly called Quakers. The
eleventh part. 2d Philadelphia ed.
Philadelphia, Pr. and pub. by
Thomas Kite, 1830. 368 p. CL;
CoU; CtY; DeWi; MBC; MH; OO;
RNHi.   1412

Forsyth, John, 1780-1841.
Speech of Mr. Forsyth, of

Georgia, on the bill providing
for the removal of the Indians.
Delivered in the Senate of the
United States, May, 1830. Washington, Pr. by D. Green, 1830.
32 p. DLC.   1413

Foscarini. See Saluces, Mme.
de.

Foster, Benjamin Franklin.
Practical penmanship, being
a development of the Carstarian
system. Albany, Little and Cummings, 1830. 112 p. ICJ; LNHT;
MeB; NRU; PPF.   1414

Foster, E.
Two letters on the terms of
communion at the Lord's table,
to a Pedobaptist. Dover, Pub.
by E. French, 1830. 24 p. DLC.
                          1415
Foster, John.
An appeal to the young on the
importance of religion. New-
York, American Tract Society
[183-?] 69 p. MH.   1416

Foster, John, 1770-1843.
Essay on decision of character; from the latest edition. Burlington, C. Goodrich, 1830.
105 p. Ct; ICU; InRE; MH; NGH;
NN; NNC; OMC; VtHi; VtU. 1417

---- Decision of character and
other essays. In a series of
letters. New York, Robert Carter & Bros., 1830. 352 p. LNB.
                          1418

Foster, Thomas C., auctioneer.
Will be sold at auction on the
premises, the farm lately owned
and improved by Zebediah Shat-
tuck, situated in Andover, West
Parish, near Merrimack River,
and within about six miles of
Lowell... Thomas C. Foster,
Auc'r. Andover, April 13, 1830.
Bdsd. MHi.   1419

Foster, Thomas Flournoy, 1790-1847.

Speech of Thomas F. Foster, of Georgia, on the Bill providing for the removal of the Indians west of the Mississippi. Delivered in the House of Representatives of the United States, May 17th, 1830. [1830]. 40 p. GU-De; PPAmP. 1420

The four seasons; pretty stories for good children; An alphabet of lessons for children; Good child's soliloquy; The journey; The hymn-book; Morning and evening. New York, The American Tract Society, 1830. 16, 16, 16, 16, 14, 16, 16 [Plus Child's Devotions, p. 5-12 (incomplete) 1421

The fourth commandment. See American Tract Society, New York.

The fourth of July. See American Tract Society. New York.

Fourth of July! A meeting of the citizens of Brandon was held at the Inn of A. W. Titus, on the 18th of June, when it was resolved that the approaching anniversary of our national independence should be appropriately commemorated, and that our fellow citizens of the adjoining towns be invited to join in such celebration. [Brandon 183-?] 1 p. DLC. 1422

Fowle, William Bentley, 1795-1865.

The child's arithmetic, or, The elements of calculation, in the spirit of Pestalozzi's Method. ... [3d ed.] Boston, Pub. by the author, 1830. 60 p. MB; BrMus. 1423

---- Modern practical geography, on the plan of Pestalozzi.

3d ed. Boston, Pub. by Lincoln & Edmands, 1830. 162, 24 p. CtHT-W; ICU; MBAt; MH; MHi; NNC. 1424

Fox.

[From the National Journal.] The election of President in the House of Representatives. To the people of the United States. [Signed: Fox] [1830] 8 p. PPL. 1425

Foxe, John, 1516-1587.

Allgemeine geschichte des Christlichen marterthums... Philadelphia, Mentz und Rovoudt [183-] 934 p. ViU. 1426

---- Book of martyrs; or, A history of the lives, sufferings, and triumphant deaths of the primitive as well as Protestant martyrs... Hartford, Pr. by Philemon Canfield, 1830. 597 p. Ct; NN; PP; RPB. 1427

---- Fox's Book of Martyrs; or The acts and monuments of the Christian Church; being a complete history of the lives, sufferings, and deaths of the Christian martyrs... Rev. and imp. by the Rev. John Malham. Re-edited by the Rev. T. Pratt, D.D. Philadelphia, J. J. Woodward, 1830. 2 v. in 1. AMob; CBPac; CtY; GAGTh; GU; InRE; KyBgW; LNHT; MH; MWA; MdAN; MsJMC; NBLiHi; NIC; NbU; OCl; PBa; PPLT; PPi; PRHi; RBr; ScDuE; ScP; TU; ViRU. 1428

---- Geschichte der märtyrer, nach dem ausführlichen original des ehrw. Johann Fox und anderer. Kurz gefasst und, besonders für den gemeinen deutschen mann in den Vereinigten Staaten von Nordamerica, aus dem englischen übersetzt von I. Daniel Rupp... Cincinnati, Robinson und Fairbank, 1830. 2 v. in 1. CSmH;

DLC; MWA; MiU-C; P; PHi;
PLT; PPL.   1429

Fragen eines Lehrers an seine
Unterrichts-Kinder. [Jos. Hartman, Drucker, Libanon] [1830?]
23, [1] p. PPL.   1430

Francis, Convers, 1795-1863.
    An historical sketch of Water-
town, in Massachusetts, from
the first settlement of the town
to the close of its second century. Cambridge, E. W. Metcalf
and company, 1830. 151 p.
CBPac; CtSoP; ICN; M; MB;
MBNEH; MH-AH; MWA; MiD-B;
MiU; MnHi; N; NBLiHi; Nh; NhD;
OClWHi; PHi; RHi; RPB; WHi.
                            1431
Francis, John Wakefield, 1789-
1861.
    An address delivered before
the New-York Horticulture Society, at their anniversary, on the
eighth of September, 1829. Published at the request of the Society. New-York, Pr. by E.
Conrad, 1830. 31 p. CtY; MBHo;
MH; MHi; MiD-B; NNNAM; PHi;
PPL.   1432

Francoeur, Louis Benjamin,
1773-1849.
    An introduction to linear draw-
ing: translated from the French
of M. Francoeur; with alterations
and additions to adapt it to the
use of schools in the United
States. To which are added, The
elements of linear perspective;
and questions on the whole. By
William B. Fowle. 3d ed. Boston, Hilliard, Gray, Little &
Wilkins, 1830. vi, [2], 86 p.
CtY; MB; MH; MdBL; MoS; NNC;
NbHi; BrMus.   1433

Franklin, Benjamin, 1706-1790.
    The life of Dr. Benjamin
Franklin. Written by himself.
Cincinnati, Pub. by Morgan &
Sanxay, and Robinson & Fair-

bank, 1830. 192 p. DLC; (132
p.); MiD-B.   1434

---- The way to wealth. By Dr.
Franklin. Northampton, Mass.
A. R. Merrifield. [183-?] 18 p.
PU.   1435

---- The works of Dr. Benja-
min Franklin, consisting of es-
says, humorous, moral, and lit-
erary, with his life, written by
himself. New York, G. G. Sick-
els, 1830. [Added t. p. Life and
Writings...1831] 290 p. Ct
(Added t. p. The life of...1829);
CtY; DLC (Added t. p. "Life and
writings...1831); MWA; OClWHi.
                            1436
Franklin almanac for 1831. By
Nathan Bassett. Baltimore,
Geo. McDowell & Son; William
Wooddy, pr. [1830] 18 l. MH;
PHi.   1437

---- By John Ward. Philadelphia, Joseph M'Dowell [1830] 18
l. MWA; NBuG; PDoBHi.   1438

---- ---- Philadelphia, M'Carty
& Davis [1830] 18 l. DLC; InU;
PHi; PPL.   1439

---- By John Armstrong. Pittsburgh, Johnson & Stockton [etc.]
[1830] 18 l. OClWHi; OHi; OMC.
                            1440
---- Issue with added "Magazine." 30 l. DLC; MWA; OC;
OClWHi; PPiU; WvU.   1441

---- Issue with added "Magazine,"
no "Hogan & Co." in imprint.
30 l. PPiU.   1442

Franklin Institute. Philadelphia.
    Address of the Committee on
Premiums and Exhibitions of the
Franklin Institute of the state of
Pennsylvania. With a list of the
premiums offered to competitors
at the exhibition to be held in
September, 1830. Philadelphia,

J. Harding, pr., 1830. 8 p.
DLC; MH-BA; PHi; PPAmP.
1443
Franklin Institution, New Haven.
  Outline of the Franklin Institu-
tion of New Haven. [New Haven,
Baldwin and Treadway, prs.,
183-] 10 p. CtY; DLC.   1444

The Franklin primer.   See
School Convention of Franklin
County, Mass.

Franklin Railroad Company.
  The contemplated plan of the
Franklin Rail Road Company, to
commence with a route through
the counties of Middlesex, Wor-
cester and Franklin to the line
of Vermont. Boston, Press of
John H. Eastburn, 1830. 8 p.
DLC; ICJ; M; MBAt; MH-BA;
MHi; MWA; NN; RPB.   1445

---- Great publick improvement.
Franklin Rail-Road Company.
[Boston, Pr. at the office of the
Mechanicks Magazine, and Journal of Publick Internal Improvement, 1830?] 8 p. CtY; DLC;
ICJ; MB; MH; MH-BA; WHi.
1446
Frederick County, Va. Citizens.
  To the General Assembly of
the commonwealth of Virginia
the memorial and petition of the
undersigned, citizens residing in
the tenth judicial district, respectfully represents:... [Win-
chester? 1830] Bdsd. Vi. 1447

---- To the General Assembly of
Virginia the memorial of the undersigned, citizens of [blank]
county, respectfully represents:
[Winchester? 1830] Bdsd. Vi.
1448
---- To the honorable, the General Assembly of Virginia, the
undersigned, citizens of the county of [blank] respectfully repre-
sent: ...[Winchester? 1830]
Bdsd. Vi.   1449

Fredonia Academy, Fredonia,
N. Y.
  Catalogue of the officers and
students of Fredonia Academy,
for the year ending Oct. 1st,
1830. Fredonia, N.Y., Henry
C. Frisbee, pr., [1830] 8 p.
NFred.   1450

Free and Independent German
Reformed Church of Pennsyl-
vania.
  Constitution of the Synod of
the Free and Independent German
Reformed Church of Pennsylvania.
Philadelphia, Pr. by A. A.
Blumer, 1830. 8 p. PLERC-Hi;
PLT.   1451

---- Proceedings of the Synod of
the Free and Independent German
Reformed Church of Pennsylvania,
convened in the city of Philadelphia, in the year of our Lord,
1830. Philadelphia, A. A. Blumer, pr., 1830. 16 p. PLT. 1452

Free Baptist Church. General
Conference.
  Free-will Baptist Denomination in North America. Minutes
of the Fourth General Conference
...at Greenville, Smithfield,
R.I., Oct. 1830, etc. Providence, Marshall and Hammond,
1830. 24 p. CSmH.   1453

Free Baptists. New York. Black
River Meeting.
  Constitution and articles of
faith of the Free Communion Bap-
tist Black River Yearly Meeting,
as adopted at their meeting in
Russia, in September, 1830. Al-
so the church covenant. Utica,
From the press of D. Bennett
& Co., 1830. 8 p. MeLB; NN.
1454
Freeman, T. B.
  Address on the principles of
Masonry, delivered on the twen-
ty-second of June, 1821, before
Hiram Lodge, No. 81, in the

English Presbyterian Church at
Germantown. Philadelphia, Pub.
by Robert Desilver, 1830. 43,
[1] p. blank, 4 p. IaCrM; MiD-B;
PHi; PPAmP; PPFM; PPL; PU.
1455

The freeman's almanack for 1831.
By Samuel Burr. Cincinnati,
N. & G. Guilford; Oliver Farns-
worth; O. & P. M. Farnsworth,
prs. [1830] 12 l. In; OCHP;
OClWHi.   1456

---- Issue with 24 l. ICN; KyHi;
MWA; NN; O; OClWHi; OHi;
OMC; WHi.   1457

Free masonry: a poem. In
three cantos. Accompanied with
notes, illustrative of the history,
policy, principles, &c. of the masonic institution, shewing the
coincidence of its spirit and design with ancient Jesuitism... By
a citizen of Massachusetts. Lei-
cester [Mass.] S. A. Whittemore,
1830. 216 p. CSmH; PU.   1458

Free-Masonry, in reply to Anti-
Masonry, in the American Quarterly Review, for March, 1830.
Boston, John Marsh & Co., 1830.
40 p. MB; MBC; MH; MHi; WHi.
1459

Freemasons. Alabama. Grand
Lodge.
Proceedings of the Grand
Lodge of the state of Alabama, at
its annual communication in December 1829. Tuscaloosa, Pr.
by M'Guire, Henry and Walker,
1830. 30 p. AMFM; IaCrM;
MBFM.   1460

---- Florida. Grand Lodge.
Constitution laws and regula-
tions, for the government of the
Grand Lodge of Florida... July 5,
A. L. 5830, A. D. 1830. Talla-
hassee, Pr. at the Floridian and
Advocate office, 1830. 23 p.
NNFM.   1461

---- Georgia. Grand Lodge.
Proceedings of the Grand
Lodge of the state of Georgia, at
the annual communication, held
at Milledgeville, Monday, December 7, A. L. 5829... Milledgeville, Office of the Statesman &
Patriot, 1830. 37 p. NNFM.
1462

---- Kentucky. Grand Lodge.
Proceedings of the Grand
Lodge of Kentucky, at a grand
annual communication, in the
town of Lexington, commencing
on the 30th August, 5830. Lexington, Pr. by Bradford and
Herndon, 1830. 36 p. ICU;
KyLxFM; MBFM; NNFM.   1463

---- Louisiana. Grand Lodge.
Extract from the proceedings
of the Grand Lodge of Free and
Accepted Masons of the state of
Louisiana... New Orleans, Pr.
by Buisson & Boimare, 1830.
14 p. OCM; NNFM.   1464

---- Maine. Grand Lodge.
Grand Lodge of the most an-
cient and honorable fraternity of
Free and Accepted Masons of the
state of Maine... Portland,
Shirley & Hyde, 1830. 32 p.
IaCrM; NNFM.   1465

---- Maryland. Royal Arch Ma-
sons. Grand Chapter.
Proceedings of the G. R. A.
chapter of the state of Maryland,
at a communication held at the
Masonic hall, in the city of Bal-
timore, May 19th, A. T. 2830.
Baltimore, Pr. by Lucas and
Deaver...1830. 16 p. MdBP;
NNFM.   1466

---- Massachusetts. Grand
Chapter.
Proceedings of Grand Chapter
of Masonic lodge, in Massachusetts; meeting held in 1830. Boston, Comp. E. G. House, 1830.
12 p. IaCrM.   1467

---- ---- Grand Lodge.
Annual communication. Boston, Masonic Mirror, 1830. MB.
1468

---- Proceedings of the Grand Lodge of Massachusetts 1829. Boston, Moore & Sevry, 1830. 15 p. IaCrM.   1469

---- ---- Royal Arch Masons. Grand Chapter.
Grand royal arch chapter of Massachusetts... Boston, October 1830. Boston, Pr. by companion, E. G. House, 1830. 12 p. NNFM.
1470

---- St. Alban's Lodge, Wrentham.
A report of the committee of St. Alban's Lodge. Wrentham, Mass. Appointed to investigate the proceedings of Rev. Moses Thacher, relative to the Masonic institution. Boston, Press of the Masonic Mirror, Moore & Sevry, 1830. 27 p. IaCrM; MH; MWA; PHi; PPFM.   1471

---- Mississippi. Grand Lodge.
Constitution and by-laws of the Grand Lodge of the state of Mississippi, as amended. Natchez, Pr. by William C. Grissam, 1830. 10 p. DSC; IaCrM; NNFM.
1472

---- Extract from the proceedings of the Grand Lodge of the state of Mississippi, at a grand annual communication, held at their hall in the city of Natchez on the 15th February, A. L. 5830, A. D. 1830. Natchez, Pr. by William C. Grissam, 1830. 34 p. ICS; MBFM; MsMFM; NNFM; PPFM.   1473

---- Missouri. Grand Lodge.
Proceedings of the Grand Lodge of the state of Missouri, at their several communications, begun and held in the city of St. Louis, on the fifth day of April, and fourth day of October, eighteen hundred and thirty. St. Louis, Pr. by C. Keemle, 1830.

20 p. DSC; IaCrM; MBFM; NNFM; PPFM.   1474

---- New Hampshire. Grand Lodge.
Proceedings of Grand Lodge of Masonic Lodge, in New Hampshire; meeting held in 1830. Charlestown (N. H.), Webber-Bowman, 1830. 36 p. IaCrM.   1475

---- New Hampshire. Royal Arch Masons. Grand Chapter.
A journal of the proceedings of the Grand Royal Arch Chapter of the state of New Hampshire, at their annual communication, holden in Concord, June 10, A. L. 5830. Concord, Asa M'Farland, pr., 1830. 11 p. LNMas; NNFM.
1476

---- New Jersey. Grand Lodge.
Proceedings of the Grand Lodge of the most ancient and honourable fraternity of Free and Accepted Masons, of the state of New Jersey, held at their hall, in the city of Trenton, on Tuesday the tenth day of November A. L. 5829. Trenton, Pr. by Br. Joseph Justice, 1830. 8, 4 p. IaCrM.   1477

---- New York. Grand Lodge.
Abstract of the proceedings of the Grand Lodge of the most ancient and honorable fraternity of Free and Accepted Masons of the state of New York, at the annual communication, held at the Grand Lodge room in the city of New York, on Wednesday the 2d June, and the special meeting on the 24th June, A. L. 5830. New York, Pr. by William A. Mercein, 1830. 25 p. NNFM; OCM.
1478

---- ---- Independent Royal Arch Masons. Lodge.
By-laws of the Independent Royal Arch Lodge, no. 2, held in the city of New York. Revised

and adopted on January 12, A. L.
5824; and amended to 5830. New
York, Thomas Longworth, pr.,
1830. 16 p. IaCrM. 1479

---- ---- Minerva Lodge.
By-laws of Minerva Lodge,
no. 371, of the city of New York.
New York, Pr. by Bro. Geo. G.
Sickels, 5830 [1830] 12 p. NNFM.
1480

---- ---- Royal Arch Masons.
Grand Chapter.
Extracts from the proceedings
of the Grand Chapter (Royal Arch
Masons) of the state of New York,
at its annual meeting, February
5830 (1830). Albany, (N. Y.), E.
B. Child, 1830. 14 p. IaCrM.
1481

---- North Carolina. Grand
Lodge.
Proceedings of the Grand
Lodge of ancient York masons of
North Carolina... Raleigh, Pr.
by Lawrence & Lemay, 1830. 15
p. LNMas; MH; OCM. 1482

---- Ohio. Grand Council.
Proceedings of a convention of
select masters, held at Worthington, together with the constitution
and by-laws, of the Grand Council
of the state of Ohio, and the general regulations of councils of
royal and select masters. Y. D.
2830. Rev. Robert Punshon,
Grand Puissant. Lancaster, Pr.
by Companion George Sanderson,
1830. 12 p. MBFM. 1483

---- ---- Grand Lodge.
Proceedings of the Grand
Lodge of the most ancient and
honorable fraternity of Free and
Accepted Masons, in the state of
Ohio: at the annual Grand Com-
munication, A. L. 5830. Most
worshipful William Fielding, Grand
Master. Columbus, Pr. by
Bros. Olmsted & Bailhache, 1830.
12 p. IaCrM; MBFM; OCM. 1484

---- Rhode Island. Grand Lodge.
Proceedings [of the worshipful
Grand Lodge of the state of Rhode
Island and Providence Planta-
tions, at the annual meeting...]
Providence, Bro. William Simons,
Jr., 1830. 8 p. IaCrM. 1485

---- Tennessee. Grand Lodge.
Proceedings of the Grand
Lodge of the state of Tennessee,
at its annual meeting, held in the
town of Nashville for the year
1830. Nashville, Pr. at the Republican and Gazette Office, 1830.
23 p. IaCrM; MBFM; NNFM; T.
1486

---- ---- Royal Arch Masons.
Grand Chapter.
Proceedings of the Grand Royal Arch Chapter of Tennessee, at
a grand annual convocation, begun and held at the Masonic Hall,
Nashville, Tenn. on Monday the
eleventh October, A. D. 1830--
Y. D. 2370--A. L. 5830. Nashville, Tenn., Hunt, Tardiff & Co.,
prs., 1830. 18 p. IaCrM; MBFM;
NNFM. 1487

---- Vermont.
Appeal to the people of Vermont on subject of Anti-masonic
excitement by lodges of Freemasons in the county of Orange, and
Valley of White River. Chelsea,
Pr. at Advocate Office [1830] 23
p. IaCrM. 1488

---- ---- Grand Lodge.
Journal of the most worshipful Grand Lodge of Vermont at
communication, holden at Montpelier, Oct. 6, A. L. 5829, with
the constitution, by-laws and general regulations of the same.
Chester, Pr. by D. Winslow,
1830. 44 p. DSC; IaCrM; MBFM;
NNFM; VtBFM. 1489

---- ---- Royal Arch Masons.
Grand Chapter.
Extracts from the proceedings

of the Grand Royal Arch Chapter
of the state of Vermont, at its
annual communication, June 17,
A. L. 5830. Rutland, Pr. by E.
Maxham, 1830. 18 p. CSmH;
DLC; IaCrM; MBFM; NNFM;
VtBFM.   1490

---- Virginia.
Proceedings of Grand Com-
mandery of Masonic lodge, in
Virginia: meeting held in 1830.
Winchester, Samuel H. Davis,
1830. 8 p. IaCrM.   1491

---- ---- Royal Arch Masons.
Grand Chapter.
Proceedings of the Grand Roy-
al Arch Chapter of Virginia...
Richmond... December, A. D.
1830. Richmond, Pr. by John
Warrock, 1830. 15 p. IaCrM;
NNFM.   1492

The Freewill Baptist register,
and Saint's annual visitor... for
the year of Our Lord, 1831.
Limerick, Me. , Pub. by Elder
Samuel Burbank, William Burr,
pr. [1830] 54 p. MHa; MeLB.
                               1493
Freligh, Martin, 1813-1889.
An address, delivered in Watervliet, February 23, 1830, before the Watervliet & Niskayuna
Temperance Society. West Troy,
N. Y. , A. & C. A. Warren, prs. ,
1830. 27 p. N.   1494

Frelinghuysen, Theodore, 1787-
1862.
Speech of Mr. Frelinghuysen,
of New Jersey, delivered in the
Senate of the United States, April
6, 1830, on the bill for an exchange of lands with the Indians
residing in any of the states or
territories, and for their removal west of the Mississippi. Washington, Pr. and pub. at the Office of the National journal,
1830. 44 p. CSmH; DLC; PPL.
                               1495

---- Speech of Mr. Frelinghuy-
sen on his resolution concerning
Sabbath mails in the Senate of
the United States, May 8, 1830.
Washington, Pr. by Rothwell &
Ustick--Spectator & chronicle
office, 1830. 15 p. CSmH; DLC;
PPL.   1496

Frenaye, Mark Anthony.
The following pages exhibit the
merits of a transaction which has
been made the subject of atten-
tion by the legislature of Pennsylvania, for two successive sessions... [concerning divorce pro-
ceedings] [Harrisburg, 1830] 48
p. PPL.   1497

French exercises. See Longfellow, Henry Wadsworth.

... French spoliations, prior to
1800. [Washington? 1830?] 32 p.
At head of title: From the American Quarterly Review. PPL.
Washington, 1830).   1498

---- 24 p. PPL.   1499

Frey, George.
Last will and testament of
George Frey, deceased. [Mont-
gomery and Dexter, prs. , Har-
risburg, Pa. , 1830] 14, [2] p.
P.   1500

Frey, Joseph Samuel Christian
Frederick, 1771-1850.
Essays on Christian baptism.
2d ed. , rev. and much enl.
Newark, N. J. , Pr. for the au-
thor, Pr. at the Office of the
Eagle, 1830. 165, [2] p. ABS;
CtMW; MB; PCC; PPPrHi;
TxDaM.   1501

A friend of Sabbath schools. See
The life of the Rev. John Wesley.

Friends of Education.
Proceedings of a general con-

vention of the Friends of Education, held at Utica, Nov. 28th &
29th, 1830, with an Address to
the public. Utica, Northway &
Porter, prs., 1830. 8 p. PPL.
1502

Friends' Academy.
A catalogue of the trustees,
instructors and pupils of Friends'
Academy, New-Bedford, Mass.
for the year ending July 1st,
1830. New-Bedford, (Mass.), S.
S. Smith, pr., 1830. 16 p. M;
MH; MNBedf.   1503

Friends' almanac for 1831. Philadelphia, M. T. Gould [1830] 18 l.
CtY; ICN; MWA (two varieties).
1504

Friends, Society of.
The memorial of the Society
of Friends, to the legislature of
the state of New-York on the subject of imprisonment, for non-
compliance with military requisi-
tions, to which is added, a letter
from Benjamin Bates, to a member of the legislature of Virginia,
on the subject of military fines.
New York, Pr. by Mahlon Day,
1830. 12 p. ICN; OC; PSC-Hi;
Vi.   1505

---- The testimony of the Society
of Friends, on the continent of
America. Pr. in Mount Pleasant,
Ohio, 1830. 36 p. OHi.   1506

---- ---- New York, Pr. by
Richard & George S. Wood at the
office of The Medico-Chirurgical
Review, 1830. 36 p. CLCM;
CSmH; NGH; PSC-Hi.   1507

---- ---- Philadelphia (Joseph
Rakestraw, pr.] 1830. 39 p.
CSmH; CtY; DLC; ICU; InRE;
MB; NjR; PHC; PHi; PPAmP;
PPL; PPPrHi; PU; WHi.   1508

---- Indiana Yearly Meeting.
Indiana yearly meeting of
Friends, held at White-Water, in
Wayne county, Indiana, on the
4th day of the 10th month, 1830.
[Smith & Bulla, prs., Centre-
ville, Ia., 1830] 24 p. In; InHi;
InU; WHi.   1509

---- Jericho Monthly Meeting.
A testimony from the Monthly
Meeting of Friends of Jericho
concerning Elias Hicks, deceased.
New York, Pr. by Isaac T. Hop-
per, 1830. 8 p. CSmH; CtY; ICU;
MB; MBC; MH-AH; MWA; PSC-
Hi; WHi.   1510

---- London Yearly Meeting.
The epistle from the yearly
meeting, held in London, by adjournments, from the 19th of the
fifth month, to the 28th of the
same, inclusive, 1830. [Pr. by
Smith & Bulla, Centreville, Ia.,
1830] 4 p. RPB.   1511

---- ---- Pr. and pub., Mt.
Pleasant, Ohio, 1830. 8 p. ICN
(lack t.p.)   1512

---- ---- Providence, H. H.
Brown, pr., [1830] [3]-12 p.
MiD-B.   1513

---- The epistle from the yearly
meeting of the religious Society
of Friends, held in London, by
adjournments, from the twentieth
of the fifth month, to the twenty-
ninth of the same, inclusive,
1829. Philadelphia, Pr. by Timothy A. Conrad, 1830. 8 p. InRE;
PPL.   1514

---- New York Monthly Meeting.
Statement of the efforts made
by Friends, to effect an amicable
settlement with the orthodox, in
relation to property belonging to
the monthly meeting of New
York. [New York, 183-?] 8 p.
MH.   1515

---- New York Preparative
Meeting.

The rules and catalogue of the library of the Preparative Meeting of Friends of New York. [New York] Pr. by R. & G. S. Wood, 1830. 16 p. MH.   1516

---- New York. Yearly Meeting.
Discipline of the Yearly Meeting of Friends, held in New-York, for the state of New-York, and parts adjacent, revised in the sixth month, 1810. New-York, Pr. by John F. Sibell, 1830. 105, [2] p. NNFL; PSC; PSC-Hi.   1517

---- Ohio Yearly Meeting.
Extracts, from the minutes of Ohio Yearly Meeting, (held by adjournments from the 6th of the 9th month, to the 11th of the same inclusive) 1830. Mountpleasant, Ohio, Pr. by Ezekiel Harris, 1830. 12 p. OClWHi.
                                   1518

---- Philadelphia Yearly Meeting.
Extracts from the minutes of the Yearly Meeting of Friends held in Philadelphia... Philadelphia, Pr. for the Yearly Meeting, by William Sharpless, 1830. 12 p. MBC; NNFL; PSC-Hi. 1519

---- ---- Education Committee.
Report of the committee on education, appointed by the Yearly Meeting of Friends, held in Philadelphia, Pr. by Timothy A. Conrad, 1830. 7 p. PHC.   1520

---- Purchase Monthly Meeting, Westchester Co., N.Y.
The testimony of Purchase Monthly Meeting of Friends, concerning Hannah Field. New-York, M. Day, pr., 1830. 12 p. MH; PHi; WHi.   1521

---- Washington Preparative Meeting.
Inventory of books belonging to the Washington Preparative Meeting of Friends... Washington, Duncanson, pr. [183-?] 1 p. DLC.   1522

Frieze, Jacob.
A brief examination of the orthodox doctrine of future punishment, a sermon, delivered at Pawtucket, R.I. and repeated at Franklin, Mass. [Pawtucket, R.I., Meacham & Fowler, prs. (1830?)] 20 p. CSmH.   1523

Froeligh, Solomon, 1749-1827.
God's marvellous thunder. A sermon preached in the church at Hackensack. ...On occasion of the ligtning [!] and thunder striking and rending the steeple of said church, on Friday, July 10, 1795. Translated from the Dutch. New York, Pr. by M' Elrath & Bangs, 1830. 20 p. PPL.   1524

Frost, Henry Rutledge, 1790-1866.
Syllabus of a course of lectures on the materia medica. By Henry R. Frost, M.D. Charleston, Pr. by A. E. Miller, 1830. 64 p. NNNAM; ScCM.
                                   1525

Frost, John, 1800-1859.
The easy reader. Designed to be used next in course after the spelling book, in schools and families... 2d ed., with a few additional lessons. Boston, Carter & Hendee [etc., etc.] 1830. 176 p. MnU; OMC.   1526

---- Elements of English grammar: with progressive exercises in parsing. 2d ed. Boston, Richardson, Lord & Holbrook, 1830. MB; MH.   1527

---- Questions for the examination of students in Paley's Moral and political philosophy... Boston, N. H. Whitaker, 1830. 35

p. AMob; NNC.   1528

Frothingham, Nathaniel Langdon,
1793-1810.
  Two hundred years ago. A
sermon preached to the First
Church, on the close of their sec-
ond century, 29 August, 1830.
By N. L. Frothingham. Boston,
Pr. for the Society, 1830. 20 p.
CBPac; CtHT-W; CtY; DLC; IU;
MB; MBAt; MBC; MH; MHi;
MWA; MiD-B; NCH; OClWHi; OO;
WHi.   1529

Frothingham, William.
  A sermon delivered in Belfast,
on the day of annual thanksgiving,
December 2, 1830. Pub. by re-
quest. Belfast, Pr. by John
Dorr, 1830. [3]-12 p. Me; MiD-
B.   1530

The frugal housewife. See
Child, Mrs. Lydia Maria (Francis).

Fry, Caroline.
  The Scripture reader's guide
to the devotional use of the Holy
Scripture. New York, T. & J.
Swords, 1830. 123 p. NNG.
                            1531
A full-length portrait of Calvin-
ism. By an old-fashioned churchman. 3d ed., with additions and
corrections. Canandaigua, Pr.
by Morse and Harvey, 1830. 59
p. N.   1532

Fuller, Zelotes.
  The tree of liberty. An ad-
dress in celebration of the birth
of Washington, delivered at the
Second Universalist Church in
Philadelphia, Sunday morning,
February 28, 1830. By Zelotes
Fuller. Philadelphia, 1830. 15
p. CSmH; MMeT-Hi; MWA; NNC.
                            1533
Furness, William H.
  The genius of Christianity. By
William H. Furness. Pr. for

the American Unitarian Associa-
tion. Boston, Gray and Bowen
[Pr. by I. R. Butts] 1830. 24 p.
(Also numb. [241]-264. 1st se-
ries. no. 35. CBPac; ICU; MB;
MBC; MH-AH; PPL; BrMus.
                            1534

G

G., G. E.
  Memoir of Anna Louisa Camp-
bell. Revised by the Committee
of Publication of the American
Sunday-school Union. Philadel-
phia, American Sunday-School
Union [1830] No. 516, 5th series.
[Wrapper title: A star of Vir-
ginia. By. E. G. G.] 31 p. PPL.
                            1535
G., W. L. S. See Gregory,
William.

Gahan, William.
  A compendious abstract of
the history of the Church of
Christ, from its first foundation
to the eighteenth century. Bal-
timore, Pub. by Fielding Lucas,
Jun'r, [183-?] 348 p. MdW;
MChB.   1536

The galaxy of wit: or, Laughing
philosopher: being a collection
of choice anecdotes many of
which originated in or about "The
Literary emporium." Embellished
with several engravings. Boston, Pr. by J. H. A. Frost, 1830.
2 v. in 1. CtY; ICU; MB; MBAt;
RPB; BrMus.   1537

Gales and Seaton.
  Letter to the Library Com-
mittee of Congress. Washington,
Feb. 20, 1830. 10 p. PPL.
                            1538
Gales's North-Carolina almanac
for 1831. By Dr. Hudson M.
Cave. Raleigh, J. Gales & Son
[1830] 18 l. NN; NcU.   1539

Gallagher, Bp.
   The sermons of the Right Rev.
Dr. Gallagher, translated from
the original Irish by James Byrne.
Revised and corr. by a Catholic
clergyman. Baltimore, Pub. by
Fielding Lucas, Jr. [183-?] 208
p. MdW.   1540

Gallaudet, Thomas Hopkins, 1787-
1851.
   The child's picture defining
and reading book. Hartford, Pub.
by H. & F. J. Huntington, Richardson, Lord & Holbrook, and
Carter & Hendee, Boston; Jonathan Leavitt, New York, 1830.
52 p. CtHT-W; CtHi; DLC; MB;
MH; MWA.   1541

---- The story of Isaac; or, The
first part of a conversation between Mary and her mother.
Prepared for the American Sunday School Union. Philadelphia,
American Sunday School Union,
1830. v, [1], 88 p. PMA;
ScCliTO; BrMus.   1542

Galt, John, 1779-1839.
   Lawrie Todd; or, The settlers
in the woods. New York, Pr. by
J. & J. Harper; Sold by Collins
and Hannay, [etc.] 1830. 2 vols.
CSmH; CtY; LNHT; MB; MBAt;
NN; PPL; PU; RPB; ScC; WU.
                                1543
---- ...The life of Lord Byron.
By John Galt, Esq. New York,
Pr. by J. & J. Harper, Sold by
Collins & Hannay [etc., etc.]
1830. 334, 6 p. advts. (Harper's
stereotype ed.) ArCH; CtHT-W;
CtY; IEG; InGrD; MB; MH; MWA;
MdBE; NN; NcGC; NjMD; OMC;
PPL; PV; RPB; ScC; VtU.   1544

---- ---- Philadelphia, E. Littell, Stereotyped by L. Johnson,
1830. 257 p. CSmH; MB; NRU;
NjP; PPL; PU.   1545

---- Southennan. New-York, Pr.

by J. & J. Harper; Sold by Collins and Hannay [etc., etc.]
1830. [14], 4-207 p. CtHT;
DLC; MBAt; MH; NGH; NNS;
PPi; RP.   1546

Galusha, Elon.
   An address, delivered before
the Rome Temperance Society,
on the Fifth of July, 1830. Utica,
From the Press of D. Bennett
& Co., 1830. 15 p. DLC.   1547

The games of the match at chess,
played by the London and Edinburgh Chess Clubs, in 1824,
1825, 1826, 1827 & 1828... New
York, Pr. for the Publisher by
A. Ming, Jr. 1830. 8 p. NjP;
OCl; PPL.   1548

Ganilh, Anthony.
   Odes, and fugitive poetry. By
Rev. Anthony Ganilh. Boston,
Pr. by W. Smith, 1830. 36 p.
LNHT; MH; RP TxU.   1549

Gannett, Ezra Stiles, 1801-1871.
   A discourse, delivered in the
Federal Street Church, on Thanks-
giving day, December 2, 1830.
By Ezra S. Gannett, Junior Pas-
tor. Pr. by request. Boston,
Office of the Christian Register
[Hiram Tupper, pr.] 1830. 24 p.
CSmH; CtHT-W; DLC; ICN; MB;
MBAt; MH-AH; MHi; MWA; NCH;
NGH; OClWHi; PPAmP; PPL;
RPB; BrMus.   1550

---- Unitarian Christianity suited
to make men holy. A discourse
delivered at the ordination of
Rev. Artemas B. Muzzey as pas-
tor of the First Church & Society
in Framingham, June 10, 1830.
Boston, Pub. by Gray & Bowen
[Pr. by I. R. Butts] 1830. 43 p.
CtY; ICMe; MB; MBC; MH-AH;
MWA; MiD-B; NjPT; OClWHi;
PPAmP; PPL; RPB; BrMus.
                                1551
Garnett, James Mercer, 1770-

1843.
Token of regard presented to
the pupils of the Elmwood school,
by their friend James M. Garnett.
Richmond, Pr. and pub. by T. W.
White, 1830. 1 p. CSmH; CtY; DE;
NNC; NcAS; NcD; PHi; Vi; ViU.
1552

[Garrison, William Lloyd]
A brief sketch of the trial of
William Lloyd Garrison, for an
alleged libel on Francis Todd, of
Massachusetts. [Baltimore, 1830]
8 p. MdHi; PHi; PPL. 1553

Gaston, Hugh.
A Scripture account of the
faith and practice of Christians;
consisting of an extensive collec-
tion of pertinent texts of scrip-
tures... 3d Philadelphia ed.
Philadelphia, Towar, J. & D.M.
Hogan, 1830. 370 p. CSt; CtHT-
W; GDC; ICU; InGrD; KyBC;
LNB; MB; MoSpD; NNG; NNUT;
PPPrHi; ViAlTh. 1554

Gayarré, Charles Étienne Arthur.
Essai historique sur la Lou-
isiana... Nouvelle-Orléans, Ben-
jamin Levy, 1830-31. 2 v. ICN;
ICU; LNHT; LU; MiU; NN;
OClWHi; TxU; Vi. 1555

Gayle, John.
An address to the public, by
John Gayle, speaker of the House
of Representatives; repelling the
attack made upon him by the
Aristocratic party in this state,
at the close of the late session of
the General Assembly: and expos-
ing the true objects and principles
of said Party, and containing the
proceedings of the House and the
evidence taken before the committee in relation to the investigation instituted at his request.
Tuscaloosa, Pr. by M'Guire,
Henry and Walker, 1830. 42 p.
AU. 1556

Geddings, Eli, 1799-1878.

Introductory lecture delivered
on the 15th of November, 1830.
Published by the class. Charleston, Pr. by J. S. Burges, 1830.
22 p. MdBMA; NNNAM; ScCC;
ScCM. 1557

Der Gemeinnützige Landwirth-
schafts Calender auf 1831. Lancaster, Wm. Albrecht [1830] 18
l. CLU; CtY; DLC; InU; MH;
MWA; NjP; OC; PHi; PPL;
PPeSchw; WHi. 1558

The general class book. See
Willard, Samuel.

General Protestant Episcopal
Sunday School Union.
Fourth annual report of the
executive committee of the board
of managers of the General Protestant Episcopal Sunday School
Union. Presented to the board of
managers, at their fourth annual
meeting, held in the city of New
York, July 29, 1830. With appendixes. New York, Pr. at the
Protestant Episcopal Press,
1830. 95, [1] p. MBD; NCH;
NNG; PPL. 1559

General Union for Promoting the
Observance of the Christian Sab-
bath.
Second report of the General
Union, and proceedings at the
annual meeting. [New York,
1830] 16 p. CtHT-W; CtY;
MBAt; MH; PPL. 1560

Genesee Consociation.
A reply of the Genesee Consociation to the letter of the Rev.
Joseph Emerson, of Westers-
field, Conn. addressed to them
on the subject of their resolution
relative to Masonic ministers and
masonic candidates for the ministry. Rochester, N. Y., pr.
Philadelphia, Repr. at No. 7
Franklin Place [At the office of
the Sun] 1830. 31, [1] p.

PHi.   1561

Geneva College.
    Address to the public, by the
trustees of Geneva College. [Pr.
by James Bogert] Nov. 10, 1830.
10 p. MH; N; NGH.   1562

---- Circular address of the
medical faculty of Geneva College,
New-York... New-York, November 1, 1830. Bdsd. NjR.   1563

A geographical present; being descriptions of the several countries of Europe. ...New York,
Pub. by William Burgess, Juvenile Emporium [R. & G. S. Wood,
prs.] 1830. [4], 140 p. CSmH;
KU; PP; PPL.   1564

Geometry. See Holbrook, Josiah.

George Wilson and his friend. (A
tale.) By the author of Jane and
her teacher. Philadelphia, 1830.
BrMus.   1565

The Georgetown directory for the
year 1830: to which is appended
a short description of the
churches, public institutions, &c.,
the original charter of Georgetown, and extracts from laws relating to the Chesapeake and Ohio
Canal Company. Georgetown,
D.C., Pr. by B. Homans, 1830.
48 p. DLC.   1566

Georgia.
    Acts of the General Assembly
of the state of Georgia, passed in
Milledgeville at an annual session
in November and December, 1829.
Milledgeville, Pr. by Camak &
Ragland, 1830. 299 p. GHi; IaU-L;
L; MdBB; Mi-L; Mo; Ms; NNLI;
Nb; Nj; Nv; R; T; W; Wa-L.1567

---- Journal of the Senate of the
state of Georgia, at an annual
session of the General Assembly,
begun and held at Milledgeville,

the seat of government, in November and December, 1829.
Milledgeville, Camak and Ragland,
1830. 432 p. G-Ar; GMiW.
                          1568
The Georgia and South Carolina
almanack for 1831. By Robert
Grier. Augusta, W. J. Bunce
[1830] GA.   1569

Georgia. University.
    Announcement. Athens, 1830-.
MH.   1570

Gérando, Joseph Marie de,
baron, 1772-1842.
    Self-education; or, The means
and art of moral progress. Tr.
from the French of M. le baron
Degerando. Boston, Carter &
Hendee, 1830. xi, 456 p. CtY;
ICMe; IEG; KWiU; LNHT; MB;
MBAt; MDeeP; MH-AH; MWA;
MeB; NNC; NNU; OO; PU; RPB;
TxAbH; VtU.   1571

Gerdil, Giacinto Sigismondo,
Cardinal, 1718-1802.
    A short exposition of the marks
of the true church; by Cardinal
Gerdil. Translated from the
French, for the first time; to
which is prefixed a brief and interesting sketch of the life of the
illustrious writer. Boston, Pub.
for the editors of "The Jesuit" by
William Martin, 1830. Parsons,
1031.   1572

Gerhard, William Wood, 1809-
1872.
    Observations on the endermic
application of medicines... Philadelphia, Pr. by James Kay, Jun.
& Co., 1830. 27 p. NNNAM; PHi;
PPAN; PPL.   1573

Gessner, Salomon, 1730-1788.
    The death of Abel, in five
books. Attempted from the German of Mr. Gessner, by Mary
Collyer. To which is added, The
death of Caine in five books.

Woodstock, Vt., Pub. by Colton
& Smith, Rufus Colton, pr.,
1830. 133, 58 p. DLC.   1574

Gibbons, William, 1781-1845.
An exposition of modern scep-
ticism, in a letter, addressed to
the editors of the Free Enquirer.
By William Gibbons, M. D. 2d
ed. Wilmington, Pr. and sold by
R. Porter and son [1830] 48 p.
DLC; DeU; LU; PHC; PPAmP;
PPL; PSC-Hi.   1575

---- ---- 3d ed., rev. and enl.
Wilmington, R. Porter and Son
[1830] 52 p. CSmH; and DeHi
(3d ed., corr. and enl.); NN.
      1576
---- ---- From the 3d Wilmington ed., corr. and enl. Repr.
by R. I. Curtis, Wheeling, for
the representative committee of
the Ohio Yearly Meeting of
Friends, 1830. 47 p. CSmH;
OCHP.   1577

Giddings, Edward.
An account of the savage
treatment of Captain William
Morgan, in Fort Niagara, who
was subsequently murdered by the
Masons, and sunk in Lake Ontario, for publishing the secrets
of Masonry. 6th ed. Boston,
Pub. and sold at the Anti-Masonic Bookstore, 1830. 24 p. MH;
NCanHi; BrMus.   1578

Gift of piety; or, Divine breath-
ings in one hundred meditations.
Stereotyped ed. Boston, Pub. by
J. Buffum [183-?] MB.   1579

[Gilbert, Ann (Taylor)], 1782-
1866.
My mother. A poem... New-
York, Baker, Crane & Day
[183-?] 8 p. CSmH.   1580

[----] Original poems, for infant
minds. By Ann and Jane Taylor,
and others. Philadelphia, L. B.

Clarke, 1830. 144 p. MB; MH;
NN; TxU.   1581

Gillett, Francis, 1807-1879.
An address, delivered at Windsor, (Wintonbury) Con., February 10th, 1830, before the annual meeting of the Temperance
Society, Hartford, A. Bolles
[Philemon Canfield, pr.] 1830.
32 p. CtHC; CtHT; CtHi; CtSoP;
CtY; MdBJ; NNUT.   1582

Gillitzin, Demetrius A.
The Bible, truth and charity:
A subject for meditation for the
editors of certain periodicals,
miscalled religious publications.
Ebensburg, Pr. by J. J. Canan.
1830. 45 p. DGU.   1583

Gillmore, Calvin, comp.
A collection of hymns, and
spiritual songs. Selected from
various authors... Geneva, Pr.
for the compiler, by J. Bogert,
1830. 144 p. CSmH.   1584

[Gilman, Samuel] 1791-1858.
Memoirs of a New England
Village choir... 2d ed. Boston,
Crosby, Nichols & co. [183-]
2 p. l., 152 p. DLC.   1585

Gilmore, Robert.
Memoir; or, Sketch of the history of Robert Gilmor of Baltimore. [Baltimore? 1830?] 46 p.
MdBE.   1586

Gilpatrick, James, 1801-1865.
A sermon delivered Sept. 8,
1830 at the ordination of Rev.
Wilson C. Ryder, over the First
Baptist Church in Mariaville.
Pub. by request. Bluehill [Me.],
Beacon Press, B. F. Bond, pr.
1830. 12 p. CSmH.   1587

[Gilpin, Joshua]
State of the application to
Congress for aid to complete the
post road from Philadelphia to

Baltimore, and observations thereupon. [Philadelphia, 1830] 3 p. PPL. 1588

Gilpin, Richard Arthington, d. 1887.
An oration on biography, delivered by Richard A. Gilpin, A. B. on receiving his degree at the public commencement of the University of Pennsylvania. July 31, 1830. [Wilmington, R. Porter and son, prs.] 8 p. PHi; PU. 1589

Gilpin & Co.
Pro patria. Gilpin & Co. Brandywine. Fine, Quarto, Post, Hot pressed. Broadside engraved by J. W. Steel advertising paper manufactured by Gilpin & Co., ca. 1830. Bdsd. DeGE. 1590

Girault, A. N.
The French guide; or, An introduction to the study of the French language. Philadelphia, Garden and Thompson, 1830. vi, [3]-135, 36 p. PHi; PMA. 1591

The girl and her pets and other stories. New York, Leavitt & Allen [183-?] 16 p. NN. 1592

The gleaner; or, Selections in prose and poetry from the periodical press. Boston, Office of the New-England galaxy, 1830. 238 p. CSmH; DLC; KWiU; MB; MBAt; NNC; RPB; TxU. 1593

Gleig, George Robert, 1796-1888.
...The history of the Bible. New York, Pr. by J. & J. Harper, Sold by Collins & Hannay, 1830-1831. 2 vols. Harper's stereotype ed. NNS; PPL (vol. I only); PU. 1594

[----] The country curate. By the author of "The Subaltern," and "The Chelsea Pensioners." New

York, Pr. by J. & J. Harper, 1830. 2 vols. CtHT; ICMe; LNHT; MBL; RJa; RPAt; WU. 1595

Gobinet, Charles.
Gobinet's Instructions of youth in Christian piety. A new edition, abridged, by the Rev. Edward Damphoux, D. D. Baltimore, Pub. by Fielding Lucas, Jun'r [183-?] 304 p. DGU; MdBS. 1596

Gock, Carl.
Meine religiöse und darauf Bezug habende Politische Aňsicht. von Nord-Amerika und Fortsetzung der "Bertheidigung der freyen Kirche" verfasst in drey Theilen. Gedruckt auf Kosten des verfassers, 1830. 119 p. PPL. 1597

Goddard, Henry, 1785-1871.
Ambition, an historical and argumentative poem. [Portland, 1830?] 25 p. MHi. 1598

Godman, John Davidson, 1794-1830.
...Description of a new genus and new species of extinct mammiferous quadruped. [Philadelphia, 1830] [478]-485 p. DLC. 1599

Godwin, Parke, 1816-1904.
The history of Frence. (Ancient Gaul). New York, Harper & Brothers, 1830. xxiv, p., 1 l., [9]-495 p. ArU; CS; CtY; DLC; GU; InRE; LN; NRU; NWM; O; PMA; TNJ. 1600

[Godwin, William]
Cloudesley: a tale. By the author of Caleb "Williams." New York, J. & J. Harper, 1830. 2 v. in 1. CtHT; CtY; MB; MBL; MW; NGH; NNS; PU; RPAt; RPB; WU. 1601

Goldsmith, Oliver, 1728-1774.
An abridgement of the History of England, from the invasion of

Julius Caesar to the death of George the Second ... And continued, by an eminent writer, to the end of the year 1823. With heads, by Bewick. A new ed. with upwards of a thousand questions for exercises. New-York, Pub. by C. Wells, 1830. 346, 20 p. NCH; PHi; PWW; TNJ.
1602

---- The Grecian history, from the earliest state to the death of Alexander the Great. By Dr. Goldsmith; revised, etc., by William Grimshaw. Stereotyped by J. Howe. Philadelphia, John Grigg [Pr. by Pilkington and Hannay] 1830. 322 p. DeWI; FTU; MiDSH; ViU.   1603

---- A history of the earth and animated nature. By Oliver Goldsmith... A new ed. In four volumes. Philadelphia, Pub. by J. Grigg, 1830. 4 vols. ArBaA; DLC; InCW; LNHT; MWA; MeBaT; MoS; NBuDD; NNC; NcAS; Nh; Nj; OClW; OO; ScCC; TNJ; ViR; ViRU.   1604

---- ---- New York, Pub. by J. & J. Harper; James Smith, pr., 1830. 4 vols. MWA; OMC; PU; TMSC; TxDaM.   1605

---- Goldsmith's Roman history for the use of schools; Revised and corrected, and a vocabulary of proper names appended... by William Grimshaw. Improved ed. Philadelphia, J. Grigg, 1830. 235 p. DLC; KyLo; LNHT; MoS.
1606

---- The miscellaneous works of Oliver Goldsmith, with an account of his life and writings. Stereotyped from the Paris ed., edited by Washington Irving. Complete in one volume. Philadelphia, Pub. by J. Crissy and J. Grigg, 1830. 527 p. CSmH; CoD; CtMW; GDC; IU; InGrD; InHi; LNB; MH; MeBaT; NNC;

NcW; NjR; OClW; TNJ.   1607

---- The vicar of Wakefield; a tale. By Oliver Goldsmith. With the life of the author, by Dr. Johnson. Philadelphia, J. Locken, 1830. 252 p. DLC; MWA.
1608

Good, John Mason.
   The book of nature... with a sketch of the author's life. New York, J. & J. Harper, 1830. 467 p. NjT.   1609

Good, Peter Peyto, 1789-1875.
   Exercises designed to assist young persons to pronounce and spell correctly, also to practice writing and acquire punctuation, with accuracy and effect. Upon an efficacious and approved principle, being easy, instructive and important lessons, selected from the most approved writers, and particularly adapted for these purposes. To which is added an index, containing the false orthography correctly spelled, and grammatical rules for punctuation. Woodstock, Stereotyped by David Watson, 1830. 120 p. CtSoP; DLC; MH; NCH; OO; VtMiS.   1610

The good child's A. B. C. Book. Wendell, Mass., J. Metcalf, 1830. 18 p. NN.   1611

The good child's little hymn book ... New York, Pr. and sold by Mahlon Day, 1830. 18 p. RPB.
1612

Goodell, William.
   Reasons why distilled spirits should be banished from the land. An address delivered (June, 1830) before the Temperance Association of the American Bible Society House, in the city of New-York. New York, Daniel Fanshaw, 1830. 12 p. MBC.   1613

Goodrich, Charles Augustus, 1790-1862.

A history of the United States of America, on a plan adapted to the capacity of youths and designed to aid the memory by systematic arrangement and interesting association. Bellows Falls, J. I. Cutler & Co.; Pr. by Cook & Taylor, 1830. 296, 20 p. KU; MH; NN. 1614

---- ---- 14th ed. Greenfield, Mass., A. Phelps, 1830. 296, 20 p. OClWHi. 1615

---- A history of the United States of America ... with engravings in which the historical events are brought down to the year 1827, and to which is added a geographical view of the United States. Cincinnati (Ohio), Robbins & Deming, 1830. 432, 119, [1] p. LNHT; OC; TxGR. 1616

---- ---- New York, Pub. by William W. Reed, 1830. 432, 120 p. MsMer. 1617

---- Lives of the signers to the Declaration of Independence. By the Rev. Charles A. Goodrich. New York, Mather & D. M. Jewett, 1830. 460 p. GS; MBL; MnU; NNF; NRU. 1618

---- Outlines of modern geography on a new plan... Boston, Richardson, Lord & Holbrook, 1830. 252 p. MH. 1619

Goodrich, Chauncey Allen, 1790-1860.

A brief notice of Dr. Tyler's vindication of his strictures. (Taken from the Quarterly Christian Spectator.) New Haven, [Baldwin & Treadway, prs.] 1830. 7 p. CtY; MA. 1620

---- Exercises in elocution. New Haven [Durrie & Peck] 1830. 16 p. CtY. 1621

---- Lessons in Greek parsing; or An outline of the Greek grammar. New Haven, Durrie & Peck, 1830. 138 p. CtY. 1622

Goodrich, Samuel Griswold, 1793-1860.

Atlas designed to illustrate the Malte-Brun School Geography, by S. Griswold Goodrich. Boston, Carter and Hendee, Hartford, H. & F. J. Huntington, 1830. 11 maps, 3 charts, 1 p. of text. CtHT-W; MWA. 1623

[----] The child's botany. 3d ed. Boston, Carter & Hendee, 1830. 103 p. MH; NRHi; NRU-W. 1624

[----] Peter Parley's juvenile tales. A New Year's present for children. Boston, Carter & Hendee, 1830. various pagings. MB; MWA. 1624a

[----] Peter Parley's method of telling about geography to children. With nine maps and seventy-five engravings. Boston, Carter & Hendee & co., 1830. MH. 1625

[----] ---- Hartford, H. & F. J. Huntington, 1830. 122 p. DLC; KU; MH; NCH. 1626

[----] ---- Philadelphia, Towar, J. and D. M. Hogan, 1830. 114 p. P. 1627

[----] Peter Parley's poetical present. Worcester, Pub. by J. Grout, Jr. [183-?] 24 p. MH. 1628

[----] Peter Parley's story of the mocking bird. Boston, Carter and Hendee, 1830. 16 p. CtY; ViU. 1629

[----] Peter Parley's story of

the soldier and his dog. Boston, Carter and Hendee, 1830. 16 p. ViU.   1630

[----] Peter Parley's story of the storm. Boston [Waitt and Dow for] Carter & Hendee, 1830. 9 l. PP.   1631

[----] Peter Parley's story of the truants. Boston, Carter and Hendee, 1830. 13 p. MnU.   1632

[----] Peter Parley's story of the unhappy family. Boston, Carter & Hendee, 1830. MB.   1633

[----] Peter Parley's tales about Asia. ... Boston, Gray and Bowen, and Carter & Hendee, 1830. 116 p. MB; MH; TxD-T.   1634

[----] Peter Parley's tales about the sun, moon, and stars. [2d ed.] Boston, Gray & Bowen [1830] 116 p. CSmH.   1635

[----] Peter Parley's tales of animals; containing descriptions of three hundred quadrupeds, birds, fishes, reptiles and insects, with numerous engravings. Boston, Carter & Hendee [Pr. by I. R. Butts] 1830. 342 p. CSmH; ICMe; MBAt; OClWHi.   1636

[----] Peter Parley's winter tales. Boston, Carter and Hendee, 1830. 112 p. CSmH; CtY; MH.   1637

---- The story of Alice Green. One of Peter Parley's winter evening tales. Boston, Carter & Hendee, 1830. 16 p. MB.   1638

[----] ---- Boston, S. G. Goodrich [Waitt & Dow, prs.] 1830. 16 p. (Imprint slip pasted on.) MB; PU.   1639

---- A system of school geography, chiefly derived from Malte-Brun, and arranged according to the inductive plan of instruction. By S. Griswold Goodrich. Hartford, H. & F. J. Huntington; New York, Collins & Hannay, [etc., etc.] 1830. 320 p. + atlas. DLC; MH (Atlas); OMC.   1640

[----] ---- Hartford, H. & F. J. Huntington; Collins & Hannay, New York; Carter & Hendee, Boston [etc., etc.] [P. Canfield, pr.] 1830. 308 p. CtSoP; ICU; MB; MH; RPB.   1641

[----] The tales of Peter Parley about Africa. ... Boston, Gray & Bowen, 1830. [128] p. KU; MdBJ; NNC; PU.   1642

[----] The tales of Peter Parley about America. 3d ed. Boston, Carter & Hendee, 1830. 160 p. Ia-HA; MH; ViU.   1643

[----] The tales of Peter Parley about Europe. 3d ed. Boston, Pub. by Carter & Hendee & Gray & Bowen [Waitt & Dow's pr.] 1830. 152 p. CtSoP; MWA; PHi (146+ p.)   1644

Goodwin, Isaac, 1786-1832.
    New England sheriff: Digest of the duties of civil officers: being a compendium of the laws of Massachusetts, with reference to those of the neighboring states, upon those subjects. With copious forms. Worcester, Dorr & Howland; Boston, Richardson, Lord & Holbrook, 1830. vi, 312 p. Ct; CtY; ICN; MB; MBAt; MH; MWA; MiD-B; MoSpD; NNC; NcD; NjP; RPB.   1645

Gospel sonnets. See Lamb, Jonathan.

[Gould, Marcus Tullius Cicero] 1793-1860.
    American Stenographic Academy, No. 6, North Eighth

Street, Philadelphia. [Philadel-
phia, 1830] ix, [3] p. PPL.
                                    1646
---- The art of short-hand writing; comp. from the latest Euro-
pean publications, with sundry
improvements, adapted to the
present state of literature in the
United States. By M. T. C.
Gould... Stereotype ed., with
seventeen new engravings. Philadelphia, 1830. 47 p. 17 pl.
CSmH; DLC;   1647

---- ---- Rev. stereotype ed.,
with new engravings. Philadelphia, The author, 1830. 60 p.
MB; MBC; MH; NjR; OHi; P;
WGr.   1648

Gould, Nathaniel Duren, 1781-
1864.
    Musical prosody; containing a
selection of hymns, with concise
directions for the appropriate
application of music to words: designed for the use and improve-
ment of individuals and singing
choirs... Boston, Richardson,
Lord & Holbrook, 1830. 40 p.
CtY; MBC; MH; MWA; PPPrHi.
                                    1649
Gouverneur, Samuel L.
    Oration delivered by Samuel
L. Gouverneur, esq. on the 26th,
November, 1830, at Washington
Square, before the citizens of
New-York: in commemoration of
the revolution in France, 1830.
New York [Pr. by Thos. Snow-
den, 1830] 21 p. DLC; MiU-C;
NNC; PP; PPL; PPPrHi; BrMus.
                                    1650
Gow, Niel.
    A practical treatise on the law
of partnership. By Niel Gow...
2d American from the 2d London
ed. by Edward D. Ingraham...
Philadelphia, Robert H. Small
[Russell & Martien, prs.] 1830.
xxix, 638 p. ICLaw;
KyBgW; MH-L; Ms; NIC; N-L;
NNLI; NcD; Nv; OClW; PPB;

PU-L; ViU; BrMus.   1651

Grace Seymour. See Lee, Mrs.
Hannah Farnham (Sawyer).

Grafton, Joseph.
    A sermon, exhibiting the ori-
gin, progress and present state
of the Baptist Church and Society
in Newton, Mass. Boston, Pr.
by William R. Collier, 1830. 16
p. CtSoP; MBC; MBD; MH;
MHi; MiD-B; NHC-S; OClWHi;
PHi; BrMus.   1652

[Graham, Dougal] 1724-1779.
    The first [-second] part of the
comical sayings of Paddy from
Cork, with his coat button'd be-
hind. Being a laughable conference between English Tom and
Irish Teague. New York, 1830.
38 p. (2nd part, New York 1840,
- p. 19-31). DLC.   1653

Graham, Isabella.
    The power of faith, exempli-
fied in the life and writings of
the late Mrs. Isabella Graham,
of New York. 7th ed. New
York, Pub. by Jonathan Leavitt.
Wm. A. Mercein, pr., 1830.
304 p. MNBedf; MeBa; NcMHi.
                          1654

[Graham, Thomas John]
    The manual for invalids. By a
physician. Boston, Wells and
Lilly, 1830. 232 p. CtHT-W;
DLC; DNLM; ICJ; MBCo; PP;
PPC; RPM.   1655

Grand Masonic bobalition. At de
consecratium ob de Masonic
tumble. Bosson, May Dirty, Five
Tousan eight hundred and sump-
tin. Dialogue between Cuffiee
and Sambo. [Boston, 183-?]
Bdsd. WHi.   1656

No entry.   1657

Gray, Thomas Jr.
Change: A poem pronounced at Roxbury, October VIII, MDCCCXXX, in commemoration of the first settlement of that town. Roxbury, Pub. by Chas. P. Emmons. J. H. Eastburn, pr. Boston, 1830. (in Dearborn Henry Alexander Scummel, An Address... Roxbury, 1830). 25 p. CSmH; CtHT-W; CtSoP; CtY; DLC; ICMe; ICN; IU; LNHT; MB; MBAt; MH; MdHi; MWA; MiD-B; N; NN; NNC; Nh; PHi; PU; RPB; WHi; BrMus.   1658

---- The vestal: or, A tale of Pompeli... Boston, Gray and Bowen, 1830. xii, 220 p. CSmH; DLC; MB; MH; MHi; MWH; RPB; TxU; BrMus.   1659

Graydon, William.
The justices & constables assistant, Being a general collection of forms of practice, interspersed with various observations and directions, together with a number of adjudged cases, relative to the office of justice and constable. Philadelphia, U. Hunt, 1830. 487 [8] p. NIC; NcD. 1660

Grayson, P. W.
Vice unmasked, an essay: being a consideration of the influence of law upon the moral essence of man. With other reflections. New York, George H. Evans, 1830. 168 p. CtHT; ICLaw; InGrD; MH-AH; NNC;

OCLaw; PU.   1661

Great Britain.
Reports of cases argued and determined in the English courts of common law... Philadelphia, Phili H. Nicklin, 1830. v. 14-17. Ia; In-Sc; LNT-L; MdBB; MdUL; Ms; PScrLL; U.   1662

Great rail road meeting. Boston, 1830. Bdsd. MB.   1663

Greatrake, Lawrence.
The parallel and pioneer; or A pocket mirror for Protestant Christendom. New Lisbon, Pr. at the office of the Paladium, 1830. 100 p. IEdS.   1664

Green, Jacob, 1790-1841.
Notes of a traveller, during a tour through England, France, and Switzerland, in 1828. Philadelphia, J. Dobson, 1830. 2 vols. NjP; PPA.   1665

Green, Richard W.
Inductive exercises in English grammar: designed to give young pupils, a knowledge of the first principles of language... 2d ed. New York, Pub. by M'Elrath & Bangs; Boston, Hilliard, Gray & co.; Philadelphia, J. Grigg; Baltimore, Cushing & sons, 1830. 119 p. NNC.   1666

Greene, Richard Ward, 1792-1875.
The legal opinion of Richard W. Greene, esq., on the question of the town's interest in the ancient grist mill. Providence, H. H. Brown, pr., 1830. 14 p. DLC; MWA; OCLaw; RHi; RP; RPB.   1667

Greene, Roscoe Goddard.
A practical grammar of the English language, in which the principals established by Lindley Murray, are inculcated, and his

theory of the moods clearly illustrated by diagrams, representing the number of tenses in each
mood, their signs, and the manner in which they are formed. 2d
ed., imp. Portland, Pub. by
Shirley and Hyde, 1830. 111 p.
CSmH; CtHT-W; DLC; MeHi;
MnU.   1668

Greenleaf, Jonathan, 1785-1865.
    A sermon, preached in Mill-
bury, Mass. January 13, 1830.
At the installation of Rev. George
W. Campbell, as pastor of the
Presbyterian Church in that place.
Worcester, Spooner and Church,
prs., 1830. 19 p. IEG; MB;
MWA; MiD-B; NN.   1669

Green's anti-intemperance almanack for 1831. By Nathan Daboll.
New-London, Samuel Green
[1830] 16 l. CtHi; CtY; InU; MH;
MWA.   1670

Greenwood, Francis William
Pitt, 1797-1843.
    The classical reader. A se-
lection of lessons in prose and
verse... Boston, Lincoln & Edmonds, and Carter & Hendee
[Stereotyped at the Boston Type
and Stereotype Foundry] 1830.
408 p. MB; MWA; MeHi; BrMus.
                              1671
---- A collection of psalms and
hymns for Christian worship selected by F. W. P. G. Boston,
Pub. by Carter and Hendee, 1830.
xxvi, [3], [420] p. CtY; DLC;
IEG; MB; MBC; MDeeP; MHi;
MWA.   1672

---- Comprehensiveness of charity. A discourse delivered at the
ordination of the Rev. William
Newall as pastor of the First
parish in Cambridge, May 19,
1830... Published by request.
Cambridge, Pub. by Hilliard and
Brown, 1830. 40 p. CtY; ICMe;
ICU; MBAU; MH-AH; MHi; MWA;

MiD-B; MiU; NGH; NjR; OClWHi;
PPAmP; RPB; WHi; BrMus.
                              1673
---- ... The theology of the
Cambridge divinity school. 2d ed.
Pr. for the American Unitarian
Association. Boston, Gray and
Bowen, 1830. 20 p. 1st series,
no. 32. CBPac; ICMe; ICU; IEG;
MB; MBAt; MH-AH; MHi; MMeT-
Hi; MWA; MeB; NNUT; NjPT;
PPAmP; RP.   1674

Gregory, George.
    Elements of the theory and
practice of physic, designed for
the use of students. 1st New
York from 3d London ed. New
York, M. Sherman, 1830. xviii
p. 1 l., 9-738 p. ArU-M; CtY;
ICJ; KyLoJM; MBCo; MdBM;
MoSU-M; NBMS; NNNAM; NhD;
NjP; OCGHM; PPC; PU; RPM;
ViRA.   1675

Gregory, John.
    A father's legacy to his daugh-
ters by the late Dr. Gregory of
Edinburgh. Albany, Pr. & pub.
by J. G. Shaw, 1830. viii, 96 p.
MWA.   1676

---- ---- A new ed. with additions. Baltimore, Pub. by M.
Stewart. R. J. Matchett, pr.,
1830. 90 p. MdHi.   1677

[Gregory, William]
    ...Trial of Anti-Christ; other-
wise, The man of sin, for high
treason against the Son of God;
tried at the sessions house of
truth before the Right Hon. Divine Revelation, lord chief justice of his majesty's court of
Equity; the Hon. Justice Reason
of said court; and the Hon. Justice History, one of the justices
of his majesty's court of information; taken in short-hand, by
the Rev. W. L. S. G., a friend of
St. Peter; professor of stenogra-
phy; and author of "Four dia-

logues between the Apostle St. Peter and His Holiness, the Pope of Rome." Pittsburgh, Pub. by Robert Wilson, D. & M. Maclean, prs., 1830. 187, [2] p. At head of title: By special commission. CSmH; ICMcC; MWA; NN; PHi; PPDrop; PPi; ViAl.   1678

Greppo, J. G. Honore.
Essay on the hieroglyphic system of M. Champollion, jun., and on the advantages which it offers to sacred criticism... Translated from the French by Isaac Stuart... Boston, Perkins & Marvin [Pr. by T. R. Marvin] 1830. xii, 276 p. ArCH; CBPac; CU; CtHT-W; CtY; GDC; GU; ICN; IU; IaCrM; LNHT; MBAt; MBC; MH; MWA; MiD; MnU; MoSU; NBLiHi; NN; NNNAM; NSyU; NcU; NjR; OClW; P; PP; PPL; PU; RPAt; ScCC; Vi; ViAlTh; WHi; BrMus.   1679

Griffin, Edward Dorr, 1770-1837.
An address delivered May 26, 1829, at the second anniversary of the American Bible Class Society, in the city of Philadelphia; on the author's taking the chair as president of the institution... Williamstown, Ridley Bannister, 1830. 11 p. ICMe; MBAt; MWA; MWiW.   1680

---- God exalted and creatures humbled by the Gospel. A sermon preached on sabbath evening, May 30, 1830, in Murray Street Church, New York, (on Cor. i. 31)... being one of a course of Lectures on the Evidence of Divine Revelation by different preachers appointed for that purpose... New York, Sleight & Robinson, 1830. 33 p. NN; OO; BrMus.   1681

[Griffin, Gerald] 1803-1840.
The rivals. Tracy's ambition. By the author of "The collegians" ... New-York, Pr. by J. & J. Harper, 1830. 2 v. CtY; MBL; MH; NjR.   1682

Griffith, H. Wharton.
Sir, It is with the greatest reluctance that I lay before the public a statement of certain recent transactions... Philadelphia, February 25, 1830. [2] p. PPL.   1683

Grigg, John.
John Grigg's Catalogue of books, in the various departments of literature and science. Philadelphia, John Grigg, 1830. KyDC.   1684

Griggs & Dickinson's American primer improved: being a selection of words the most easy of pronounciation; adapted to the capacities of young beginners. Philadelphia, Griggs & Dickinson, 1830. 36 p. PPeSchw.   1685

Grigg's city and country almanack for 1831. By Joseph Cramer. Philadelphia, John Grigg; W. Pilkington & Co., prs. [1830] 18 l. CLU; DLC; InU; MWA; N; PHi; PPL.   1686

Grimke, Thomas Smith, 1786-1834.
Address on the expediency and duty of adopting the Bible: as a class book: in every scheme of education, from the primary school to the university: delivered at Columbia S. C. in the Presbyterian church, on Friday evening, 4th of December, 1829. Before the Richland school: By T. S. Grimke... Charleston, Observer office press [1830] 96 p. DLC; KHi; MBC; MiD-B; MnU; NNC; NcD; NjR; PPAmP; PPL; ScCC; ScU; WU.   1687

---- Oration on the advantages to be derived from the introduction of the Bible, and of sacred

literature as essential parts of all
education, in a literary point of
view merely. New Haven, Pr.
by Hezekiah Howe, 1830. 76 p.
CSmH; CtHC; CtHi; CtY; DLC;
IEG; KHi; MB; MBC; MH-AH;
MWA; NjN; PPAmP; TxU.   1688

Grimshaw, William, 1782-1852.
    History of England, from the
first invasion by Julius Caesar,
to the accession of George the
Fourth in eighteen hundred and
twenty... Philadelphia, J. Grigg,
1830. iv, 292 p. MdW; NjMD;
P; PLF; ViU.   1689

---- The history of France, from
the foundation of the monarchy,
to the death of Louis XVI. Interspersed with entertaining anecdotes, and biographies of eminent men. Philadelphia, Towar,
J. & D.M. Hogan, 1830. 302 p.
KHi; NjP; PLF; PWW.   1690

---- The history of South America,
from the discovery of the new
world by Columbus, to the conquest of Peru by Pizarro; interspersed with amusing anecdotes, and containing a minute
description of the manners and
customs, dress, ornaments, and
mode of warfare of the Indians.
New York, Collins & Hannay;
Stereotyped by L. Johnson, 1830.
252 p. GEU; IU; MB; MdU; NR;
NcU; PWW.   1691

---- History of the United States
from their first settlement as
colonies, to the cession of Florida, in eighteen hundred and
twenty-one: comprising every
important political event, with a
progressive view of the aborigines... Revised ed.   Philadelphia,
Stereotyped by J. Howe, Pub. by
John Grigg; Pr. by Wm. Pilkington & Co., 1830. [2], 308 p.
CtY; GU; IEG; IHi; InU; LNT;
MWA; NNUT; NhHi; PHi; PPL;

THi; TN.   1692

---- The gentlemen's lexicon or
A pocket dictionary containing
nearly every word in the English
language.   Philadelphia, John
Grigg. Stereotyped by J. Howe,
1830.   406+ p. MB; ViU.   1693

---- The ladies' lexicon and par-
lour companion, containing nearly
every word in the English language... Philadelphia, Pub. by
John Grigg, 1830. 407, iv p.
MiD-B.   1694

---- The life of Napoleon, with
the history of France, from the
death of Louis XVI to the year
1821. Philadelphia, Towar, J.
& D. M. Hogan; Pittsburg, Hogan & Co.   Stereotyped by J.
Howe, 1830. 285 p. CtHC; MiD-
B; NmU; TNJ.   1695

---- Questions adapted to Grim-
shaw's History of the United
States. Revised and improved.
Philadelphia, Pub. and sold by
John Grigg. Pr. by Wm. Pilking-
ton & Co., 1830. [Cover title:
- title dated 1824] 84 p. CtHT-W;
PPL.   1696

Grimshawe, Thomas Shuttleworth,
1778-1850.
    A memoir of the Rev. Legh
Richmond... 6th American, from
the last London ed. New York,
G. & C. & H. Carvill, Stereotyped by James Connor, 1830.
362 p. MWA; NNUT; PPL.   1697

---- Memoirs of the Rev. Legh
Richmond of Trinity College,
Cambridge, by Thomas S. Grim-
shaw. 6th American from the
Last London ed. New York, Pub.
by Jonathan Leavitt, G. L. Aus-
tin & Co., prs., 1830. 371 p.
CtHC; CtHT; ICU; MB; MDeeP;
MH; NjPT; PPLT; RNR; TNJ.
                            1698

Griswold, Alexander Viets,
1766-1843.

Discourses on the most important doctrines and duties of the Christian religion. Philadelphia, Pub. by William Stavely, 1830. 472 p. CtY; GEU-T; ICU; IaCrM; LNT; MBC; MH; MdBS; MnHi; NNG; NNUT; NjMD; PP; PPL; RHi; RPB; ViW; BrMus.   1699

Griswold, Henry A.

An address delivered in the Second Presbyterian Church, on the 22nd February, 1830, in behalf of Transylvania Whig Society. Lexington, Pr. at the Office of the Kentucky Gazette, 1830. 15 p. KyLx; KyU.   1700

Gross, Samuel David, 1805-1884.

The anatomy, physiology, and diseases of the bones and joints. Philadelphia, John Grigg, 1830. 5, [2], 389 p. CSt; CU; CtMW; GU-M; ICU-R; LNOP; MBCo; MdBJ; MnU; MoSMed; NBMS; NBuU-M; NNNAM; OCGHM; PU.
                              1701

Grosvenor, Moses G.

An address delivered at Alstead, N. H. ...January 1, 1830. By Moses G. Grosvenor... Boston, Perkins & Marvin, 1830. 16 p. MWA; Nh; NhHi.   1702

Groves, John.

A Greek and English dictionary, comprising all the words in the writings of the most popular Greek authors. Boston, Hilliard, Gray and company, 1830. vii, 616, 74, 617-644 p. MiD; WU.   1703

Grund, Francis Joseph, 1805-1863.

An elementary treatise on geometry, simplified for beginners not versed in algebra. Boston, Carter, Hendee & Babcock, 1830. 238 p. CtHT-W; GU; ICU; InU; KyLoB; MB; MH; MiD-B; NNC; OMC; OrU; PHC; PU.   1704

---- First lessons in plane geometry. Together with an application of them to the solution of problems... Boston, Carter & Hendee, 1830, iv, 255 p. CtMW; MB; MBAt; MH; MHi; NWM; OMC; PPF; BrMus.   1705

Grundy, Felix, 1777-1840.

Speech of Mr. Grundy, of Tennessee, on Mr. Foot's resolution, proposing an inquiry into the expediency of abolishing the office of surveyor general of public lands, and for discontinuing further surveys, &c. Delivered in the Senate of the United States, February 29, 1830. Washington, Pr. by D. Green, 1830. 16 p. CSmH; DLC; MWA.   1706

Guion, John Marshall.

The obligations of Christians to a remembrance of their spiritual rulers. A sermon, preached in St. Mark's Church, New-York, September 19th, 1830, on occasion of the death of the Right Rev. John Henry Hobart, D. D. New-York, Pub. by T. & J. Swords; Edward J. Swords, pr., 1830. CtY; InID; MBD; NGH; NNG; PHi.   1707

Gumbo Chaff as sung at the different theatres. Baltimore, Pub. by G. Willig Jr. [183-?] [3] p. CSmH.   1708

Gummere, Samuel R.

Elementary exercises in geography, for the use of schools. 7th ed., corr. and improved. Philadelphia, Kimber & Sharpless, Adam Waldie, pr., 1830. OSW.   1709

Gunn, John C.

Gunn's Domestic medicine, or Poor man's friend. In the hours of affliction, pain and sickness, This book points out, in plain language, free from Doctor's terms the diseases of men, women and children, and the latest and most approved means used in their cure, and is expressly written for the benefit of families in the western and southern states. Knoxville, Pr. under the immediate superintendence of the Author, a physician of Knoxville. 1830. [9]-440 p. NcAS; T; TKL.   1710

Gunton, William, of Washington.
An exposition of the circumstances which gave rise to suits instituted by Joseph Pearson, esq., against the Patriotic bank, Dr. P. Bradley, and William Gunton: and of the conduct of Dr. Bradley and his son, Mr. William A. Bradley, during the prosecution of those suits. By William Gunton... Washington, Pr. by P. Force, 1830. 56 p. DLC; ScU.   1711

Gurney, Joseph John, 1788-1847.
Essay on the habitual exercise of love of God, condensed as a preparation for Heaven. New York, Pub. by the American Tract Society [183-] 242 p. IU.   1712

H

H., A. C.
Tales for Thomas, containing The soldier, The present, The return, The mouse, The dog. Little Harry, The garden, Strawberries, The kite, and The black man, by A. C. H. of Newport, R. I. ... New York, Pr. and sold by Mahlon Day at the New Juvenile book-store, 1830. 17 p. DLC; NPV.   1713

The Hackney-coachman, etc. Philadelphia, American Sunday School Union, [1830?] BrMus.
                                  1714
The Hagerstown town and coun-

try almanack for 1831.   By Charles F. Egelmann.   Hagerstown, J. Gruber [1830] Drake 2601.   1715

Hale, Benjamin.
A sermon, preached at the opening of the convention of the Protestant Episcopal Church, in the state of New-Hampshire, holden in Saint Andrew's Church, Hopkinton, Wednesday, September 8, 1830.   Concord, Pr. by Asa M'Farland, 1830. 23 p. CtHT; CtY; DLC; MB; MBAt; MWA; MdHi; Nh; NjR; BrMus.   1716

Hale, Nathan.
An epitome of universal geography; or, A description of the various countries of the globe... Boston, Richardson, Lord & Holbrook, 1830. 404 p. CtHC; ICU; IU; LShC; MB; MBAt; MDeeP; MH; MHi; MWA; MiU; MoSHi; NN; OO; TxU-T.   1717

[Hale, Salma] 1787-1866.
... History of the United States... Keene, N.H., J. & J. W. Prentiss, 1830. 298, 24 p. At head of title: Premium history.   CtHT-W; MBAt; MH; NhD.   1718

[----] ---- To which is added Questions, adapted to the use of schools... New-York, Collins and Hannay, 1830. 298, 24 p. At head of title: Premium history.   DLC; ICU; IU; IaHA; KyBgW; MeBa; MiD-B; NIC; NcAS; NjR; OClWHi.   1719

Hale, Sarah Josepha (Buell), 1788-1879.
Good little boy's book.   The well-behaved little attentive little boy... Edited by Mrs. S. J. Hale. New-York, E. Dunigan [183-?] 62 (i.e. 60) p. NN.   1720

---- Poems for our children...

Part first. Boston, Marsh, Capen & Lyon [Waitt & Dow, pr.] 1830. 24 p. CSmH; ICU; MB; MBAt; MH; MWA; NN; NNC.   1721

---- Sketches of American character. 2d ed. Boston, Putnam and Hunt and Carter & Hendee, 1830. 287 p. DLC; IU; MB; MnH; NPV; PHi; PU; RPB.   1722

---- ---- 3d ed. Boston, Putnam & Hunt, Carter & Hendee, 1830. 287 p. CU; MnHi; RPB.   1723

---- The three baskets; or How Henry, Richard, and Charles were occupied while papa was away. New-York, E. Dunigan [183-?] 62 p. NN.   1724

Hall, Anna Maria (Fielding), Mrs. S. C. Hall," 1800-1881.
     Chronicles of a school room. Boston, Cottons & Barnard, 1830. 249 p. CtY; DLC; MBAt; MH; NNU; TxU.   1725

Hall, Gordon.
     The conversion of the world, or The claims of six hundred millions, and the ability and duty of the churches. New York, American Tract Society [183-?] 20 p. OSW.   1726

Hall, James, 1793-1868.
     An oration delivered at Vandalia, July 4, 1830. Vandalia, Ill., Pr. by Blackwell and Hall, 1830. 15 p. ICHi; MH; PPAmP.   1727

Hall, Marshall, 1790-1857.
     Researches principally relative to the morbid and curative effects of loss of blood... Philadelphia, E. L. Carey and A. Hart; Thomas Kite, pr., 1830. 173 p. CtY; IU-M; IaU; LNOP; MBCo; MdBM; MdUM; MiDW-M; MoSW-M; NBMS; NBuU-M; NNNAM; NbU-M; NhD; NjR; OCGHM; PP; PPC; RPM.   1728

Hall, O. A.
     A brief oratorical treatise on astronomy and natural philosophy. 3d ed. Hartford, Hammer & Phelps, prs., 1830. 23 p. NN.
                                            1729
---- New Haven, H. Howe, 1830. 24 p. CtY.   1730

Hall, Robert, 1764-1831.
     The Works of the Rev. Robert Hall, A.M., Minister of Broadmead and Chapel, Bristol, England. 1st complete ed., with a brief memoir of the author, in two volumes. New York, Pub. by G. & C. & H. Carvill, Flagg and Gould, prs., Andover, 1830. 2 vols. CtHC; CtHT; CtY; DLC; IU; KyBgW; LNB; MH-AH; MeB; NRU; NcMHi; OMC; PLT; RP.
                                            1731

Hall, Samuel R., 1795-1877.
     Lectures on school-keeping. 2d ed. Boston, Pub. by Richardson, Lord & Holbrook, 1830. xi, [13], 136, [11] p. CtHT-W; DLC; IEG; LNHT; MBAt; MH; MWA; MdBE; MeB; MeHi; NCH; NNU; OMC; OO; BrMus.   1732

Hall, Silas.
     Discourse before the Baptist Church in Abington. Boston, 1830. Sabin 29847.   1733

Hallworth, T.
     Scripture history: with additions from the books of the Maccabees and Josephus, on a plan by which the recollection of events is facilitated, and that of dates rendered easy. 3d ed., enl. and much improved. Boston, Strong and Crittenden, 1830. 220 p. DLC; ICMcC; MoS.   1734

Halsey, J. F.
     An appeal to patriots, philanthropists and Christians in behalf of the temperance of reform, delivered in the First Presbyterian Church at the anniversary of the

Allegheny County Temperance Society, Jan. 1, 1830. Pittsburgh,
Pub. by Newcomb, 1830. 16,
[1] p. PPPrHi; PPi.   1735

Halsey, Luther, 1794-1880.
   The character of the Christian ministry adapted to this
country and age. A lecture, delivered Nov. 1, 1830, at the
opening of the winter session of
the Western Theological Seminary
of the Presbyterian Church...
Pub. by request. Pittsburgh, Pr.
by D. & M. Maclean, 1830. 32 p.
NAuT; NRAB; NcD; NjP; OClWHi;
PLT; PPi.   1736

Halstead, Oliver.
   A full and accurate account of
the new method of curing dyspep-
sia, discovered and practiced by
O. Halstead. With some obser-
vation on diseases of the diges-
tive organs. New York, O. Hal-
stead [Browns, prs.] 1830. 155 p.
CSt-L; CtY; DLC; IU-M; InU-M;
KyLxT; MBCo; MdBM; MdUM;
MiDW-M; MoSMed; NBMS; NBuU-
M; NbU-M; NjP; NjR; OCGHM;
PPC; PPL; PU.   1737

Halsted, William.
   A digested index to the decisions of the Superior courts of
the state of New Jersey. Trenton, Pr. by Joseph Justice,
1830. 392 p. Nj; NjN; NjP;
NjR; NjT; PU-L.   1738

Hambden. See Johnston, Josiah
Stoddard.

[Hamilton, Alexander] 1757-1804.
   ...Appeal to American Chris-
tians, on the practice of war.
By Pacificus [pseud.] Pub. by
the Executive committee of the
American Peace Society. New-
York, Pr. by M'Elrath and
Bangs, 1830. CSfCW; CSmH;
CtY; DLC; MH; NN; NNC; NjR;
OC; BrMus.   1739

[Hamilton, James]
   An argument in support of the
claims of James Hamilton,
Pierce Butler, James Villier,
Dennis Laronde, Jumonville de
Villier, and others, and in reply
to an argument, in support of
the claims of Joseph C. Cabell,
and others. [1830] 38 p. PPL.
                                   1740

Hamilton, Luther.
   Reasons for the Unitarian be-
lief, plainly stated in nine lectures. Boston, Bowles & Dearborn, 1830. 137 p. CBPac; MB;
MBAU; MH; MWA; NCaS; NbOU.
                                   1741

---- 'Worship God.' A sermon
preached at the dedication of the
church of the First Congregational Society in Taunton, Mass.
October 7, 1830... Pub. by
request. Boston, Pub. by
Gray & Bowen [I. R. Butts, pr.]
1830. 16 p. CtHT-W; DLC; MB;
MBAt; MH-AH; MHi; MWA;
RPB; BrMus.   1742

Hamilton, William S.
   Courier Extra. Monday morning July 26, 1830. William S.
Hamilton to his fellow citizens
and old friends in Sangamo County... Bdsd. IHi.   1743

Hamilton College. Clinton, N. Y.
   Catalogue of the corporation,
officers and students... Clinton,
Dec. 1, 1830-1. [Utica, 1830]
17 p. NCH; OCHP.   1744

Hamline, Leonidas Lent, 1797-
1865.
   An address delivered in Zanesville, Ohio, at the request of a
committee of the Zanesville and
Putnam Colonization Society, on
the 5th July, 1830. Zanesville,
Pr. by Peters & Pelham, 1830.
15 p. DLC.   1745

Hampden almanac & housewife's
companion for 1831. By Isaac

Bickerstaff, Jun. Hartford, H. Burr, Jr. [1830] 12 1. CtHi; CtY; InU; MWA. 1746

---- ---- Springfield, Hampden Whig [1830] Drake 3983. 1747

Hampshire Bible Society.
The fourteenth annual report of the directors of the Hampshire Bible Society, presented at the annual meeting October 13, 1830. Amherst, J. S. and C. Adams, prs., 1830. 8 p. MA. 1748

Hance, William.
An address and lectures, delivered before the Botanic Society in Columbus, Ohio. 2d ed. Pub. by Horton Howard. Columbus, O., Pr. by Charles Scott, 1830. 42 p. DLC; NcDaD; OC; OClWHi; PPC. 1749

---- An appeal to the citizens of Ohio; showing the unconstitutionality, injustice, and impolicy of the medical law. Columbus, Pr. by Charles Scott, 1830. 20 p. DNLM; R; WHi. 1750

Hancock, Thomas, 1783-1849.
The principles of peace exemplified in the conduct of the Society of Friends in Ireland, during the rebellion of the year 1798; with preliminary and concluding observations... From the London 2d rev. and enl. ed. Providence, H. H. Brown, pr., 1830. 215 p. Ct; CtMW; InRE; MiD; NcD; NjMD; PSC-Hi; RPB. 1751

Hancock House, Boston.
Hancock House, Beacon Street, Boston. [Boston, 183-?] (Lithograph) MB. 1752

Handel and Haydn Society, Boston.
Boston Handel and Haydn Society. Collection of church music; being a selection of the most approved psalm and hymn tunes, anthems, sentences, chants, &c. Together with many beautiful extracts from the works of Haydn, Mozart etc. harmonized for three and four voices with a figured base for the organ and piano forte. Edited by Lowell Mason. 9th ed. with additions and improvements. Boston, Richardson, Lord & Holbrook, 1830. 358 p. CtHT-W; ICN; MB; MBC; MH; MHi; MnS; MeBaT; RPB. 1753

Hanna, John Smith.
A lecture on mechanics: in which a principle of self-motion is advocated... Washington, D. C., Pr. by Gales & Seaton, 1830. 24 p. DeGE; MdBL. 1754

Hanning, John.
A mirror calculated to the meredian of a pure Democratic republic, and inscribed with esteem and great respect, to the American ladies, for their perusal. Harrisburg, Montgomery & Dexter, 1830. 12 p. OClWHi; PHi. 1755

The hapless lovers. See Place, Mrs. Perry.

The happy watchman. See More, Hannah. 1756

Hare, Robert, 1781-1858.
Essays on electricity. Being a portion of his compendium of the course of chemical instruction in the medical department of the University of Pennsylvania. Published in advance for the use of students. Philadelphia, 1830. 23 p. PPC. 1757

[----] A vindication of the Cherokee claims, addressed to the town meeting in Philadelphia, on the 11th of January, 1830. [Philadelphia? 1830?] 8 p. CSmH;

DLC; ICN; LNHT; MHi; MWA;
MdHi; PHi; PPAmP; PPL; PU;
RPB; WHi; BrMus.   1758

Harper, Joseph M.
   Mr. Harper's report to the
Legislature of the state of New-
Hampshire on the culture of silk.
[Concord, N.H., 1830] 32 p.
DeGE.   1759

Harris, John, 1802-1856.
   Mammon; or Covetousness,
the sin of the Christian Church.
New York, Pub. by the Ameri-
can Tract Society [183-?] 29 p.
WHi.   1760

Harris, Thaddeus Mason, 1768-
1842.
   Memorials of the First church
in Dorchester, from its settlement in New England to the end
of the second century. In two
discourses, delivered July 4,
1830... Boston, From the office
of the Daily Advertiser; W. L.
Lewis, pr., 1830. 67 p.
CBPac; CSmH; CtY; DLC; ICN;
MB; MBAt; MH-AH; MHi; MWA;
MdBJ; MiD-B; NBLiHi; NNUT;
NhHi; OClWHi; PHi; RPB; WHi;
BrMus.   1761

Harris, William Andrew, 1830-.
   Original and only builder of
the Harris Corliss Engine. Providence, 1830. 40 p. RHi.   1762

Harrison, William Henry, pres.
U.S., 1773-1841.
   Remarks of General Harrison,
late envoy extraordinary and
minister plenipotentiary of the
United States to the Republic of
Colombia, on certain charges
made against him by that government. To which is added, an
unofficial letter, from General
Harrison to General Bolivar, on
the affairs of Colombia; with
notes, explanatory of his views
of the present state of that coun-

try. Washington, Pr. by Gales
& Seaton, 1830. 69 p. DLC;
PPL.   1763

Harrod, John J., comp.
   The academical reader, comprising selections from the most
admired authors, designed to
promote the love of virtue, piety,
and patriotism... Comp. by John
J. Harrod. Baltimore, John J.
Harrod, pub., Wm. Wooddy, pr.,
1830. 323, [1] p. DLC; PPL;
TNJ.   1764

---- The introduction to The academical reader; comprising a
great variety of pleasing and instructive pieces, from various
authors... By John J. Harrod...
Baltimore, J. J. Harrod, 1830.
168 p. DHEW; DLC; MdBE;
MdHi.   1765

---- The new and most complete
collection of camp, social, and
prayer meeting hymns and spiritual songs, now in use. Compiled by John J. Harrod. 2d ed.
Baltimore, Pub. by J. H. Harrod. Wm. Wooddy, pr., 1830.
318 p. DLC; MB.   1766

Harry Winter; the shipwrecked
sailor boy. To which is added
The oak at home. New York,
Pr. by Mahlon Day, 1830. 12 l.
PP.   1767

Hart, Cyrus Wadsworth.
   Colloquy on the immortality
of the soul, with an essay on
prudence. To which is added, a
love touch. Steubenville, Pr. by
James Wilson, 1830. 48 p.
OCHP; OClWHi; PPPrHi.   1768

Hart, Joseph C.
   A modern atlas of fourteen
maps, drawn and engraved to illustrate Hart's Geographical exercises. 7th ed., rev. and corr.
New York, R. Lockwood, 1830.

14 maps. DLC; NIC.   1769

Hartford County Union, Board of
Managers.
New England Sunday school
hymn book. Prepared by the
board of managers of the Hart-
ford County Union. Hartford,
Ct., Pub. by D. F. Robinson &
Co., 1830. 110 p. Ct; CtSoP;
MBNMHi; NHC-S.   1770

Hartford Female Seminary.
Regulations of the Hartford
Female Seminary together with a
catalogue of the officers, teach-
ers and pupils, of the same, for
the two terms ending Oct. 26,
1830. Hartford, Hudson and
Skinner, pr., 1830. 8 p. PHi.
                            1771
Harvard University.
A catalogue of the library of
Harvard University in Cambridge,
Massachusetts... Cambridge, E.
W. Metcalf and company, 1830-
31. 3 v. in 4. CSmH; CU; CtHT-
W; CtSoP; CtY; DLC; GU; ICN;
IU; LNHT; MB; MBAt; MH; MHi;
MdBJ; MiU; MnU; MoS; NBLiHi;
NCH; NIC; NN; NcD; NjP;
OClWHi; OO; PPL; ScU; TU; WHi;
BrMus.   1772

---- A catalogue of the officers
and students of Harvard University, for the academical year
1830-31. Cambridge, Hilliard
and Brown, 1830. 31 p. KHi;
MH; MS; MeB; MeHi; MiD-B;
NjR.   1773

---- Catalogus senatus academici,
et eorum qui munera et officia
gesserunt... in universitate Har-
vardiana... Cantabrigiae, Typis
E. W. Metcalf et soc., acade-
miae typographorum, 1830. 11,
71, [3] 28 p. DLC; MH; MdHi;
MeHi; MiD-B; NNNAM; NjP;
PPL.   1774

---- The fourth annual report of
the president of Harvard University to the overseers on the state
of the university, for the academical year 1828-9. Cambridge,
E. W. Metcalf and co., Printer
to the university, 1830. 16,
xlvi p. MH.   1775

---- Harvard University, Cambridge. Order of performances
for exhibition Monday, July 12,
1830. Cambridge, Pr. by E. W.
Metcalf & Co., 1830. 3 p. DLC.
                            1776
---- ---- Order of performances
for exhibition, Tuesday, May 4,
1830. Cambridge, Pr. by E. W.
Metcalf and Company, 1830. 3 p.
MB.   1777

---- ---- Order of performances
for exhibition, Tuesday, October
19, 1830. Cambridge, Pr. by E.
W. Metcalf and Company, 1830.
3 p. MB.   1778

---- Illustrissimo Levi Lincoln,
Armigero, LL. D. Gubernatori;
Honoratissimo Thomae-Lindall
Winthrop, Armigero... Caeterisque Universitatis Harvardinae
curatoribus... Exercitationes
hasce juvenes in artibus initiati
... Habita in Comitiis Universitatis Cantabrigiae Massachu-
settensis, Die Augusti XXV,
Anno Salutis MDCCCXXX. Re-
rumque publicarum foederatarum
Americae Summae Potestatis LV.
Excudebant E. W. Metcalf et Soc.
3 p. DLC.   1779

---- Report of the President of
Harvard University, submitting
for consideration a general plan
of studies, conformably to a vote
of the Board of Overseers of that
seminary, passed February 4,
1830. Cambridge, Pr. by E. W.
Metcalf and Company, 1830. 16
p., 5 bdsds. CSt; CtHT; CtY;
DLC; KHi; M; MB; MBAt; MH;

MHi; NN; RPB; BrMus.   1780

Harvey, Joseph, 1787-1873.
An inquiry concerning the obligations of believers to the visible church. New Haven, Nathan Whiting, 1830. 248 p. CtHC; CtHi; CtSoP; CtY; MA; NRAB; NbCrD; OClWHi; OMC; VtMiM.
1781

Hassler, Ferdinand Rudolph, 1770-1843.
Logarithmic and trigonometric tables; to seven places of decimals, in a pocket form. In which the errors of former tables are corrected. By F. R. Hassler... New York, C. & G. & H. Carvill, 1830. 10, [314] p. CtY; DLC; GU; KWiU; MB; NCH; NIC; NjR; PPAmP.   1782

---- Tablas logaritmicas y trigonometricas para las siete decimales, corregidas. Por F. R. Hassler... Nueva-York, C. y G. y H. Carvill, 1830. 10, [314] p. CtY; DLC; KHi.   1783

Haviland, John, 1792-1852.
The practical builders' assistant; for the use of carpenters, masons, plasterers, cabinetmakers and carvers, with working drawings selected from... examples, from the antique: together with... original designs, with their plans, elevations and sections... 150 engravings. By John Haviland... 2d ed. Baltimore, F. Lucas, jr. [1830?] 4 v. CtY; DLC; ICJ; MiD.   1784

Hawes, Joel, 1789-1867.
Lectures to young men, on the formation of character, &c. Originally addressed to the young men of Hartford and New Haven, and published at their request. 4th ed. With an additional lecture on reading. Stereotyped by A. Chandler. Hartford, Cooke & co., 1830. 172 p. CtHT-W;

DLC; GDC; LNHT; MB; MiD-B; NSchU; OClW; PU.   1785

---- A tribute to the memory of the Pilgrims, and a vindication of the Congregational Churches of New England... Hartford, Cooke and Co., and Packard and Butler, G. F. Olmsted, pr., Hartford, 1830. vi, [2], 226 p. CBPac; CU; Ct; CtHC; CtHT; CtHT-W; CtMW; CtSoP; CtY; FOA; ICMe; ICN; ICU; IaGG; KyBC; M; MA; MB; MBAt; MBC; MDeeP; MH; MWA; MdBE; MdBJ; MeBat; MeHi; MiD-B; NB; NBLiHi; NNS; NcD; NbCrD; NbHi; NhP; NjR; OClW; OClWHi; OHi; OO; PHi; PPPrHi; RHi; RP; RPB; TU; VtU; WBB; WHi.   1786

Hay, E. E. Rt, Rev. Bishop
The sincere Christian instructed in the faith of Christ, from the written word... 2d American ed. Eugene Cummiskey, Cummiskey's Catholic Library, No. 2. [183-?] 408 p. MB.   1787

The haymakers. Philadelphia, American Sunday School Union, [1830?] 16 p. DLC; BrMus.   1788

Hayne, Robert Young, 1791-1839.
Defence of the South!! General Hayne, in reply to Mr. Webster. Charleston, S. C., Pub. by A. E. Miller, 1830. 20 p. DLC; MBAt; MHi; MiD-B; NHi; PPL; RP; ScC.   1789

---- Remarks of Mr. Hayne, of South Carolina against the Pension Bill. Delivered in the Senate of the United States, May 1830. Washington, Pr. by Duff Green, 1830. 13 p. MWA. 1790

---- Second speech of Mr.

Hayne, of South Carolina: in reply to Mr. Webster; the resolution offered by Mr. Foot, relative to the public lands, being under consideration. Delivered in the Senate, January 27, 1830. Washington, Pr. by Gales & Seaton, 1830. 32 p. CSmH. 1791

---- ---- Washington, Gales and Seaton, 1830. 20 p. CLU; NHi. 1792

---- ---- Washington, Pr. by D. Green, 1830. 15 p. DLC; MWA; NHi; NN. 1793

---- The several speeches made during the debate in the Senate of the United States, on Mr. Foot's resolution, proposing an inquiry into the expediency of abolishing the office of surveyor general of public lands, and to suspend further surveys, &c. By General Hayne of South Carolina and Mr. Webster of Massachusetts. Charleston, A. E. Miller, 1830. 112 p. DLC; ICU; NcD; OMC; ScHi; ScU. 1794

---- Speech of Mr. Hayne, of South Carolina, in the Senate of the United States, January 21, 1830, on Mr. Foot's resolution, proposing an inquiry into the expediency of abolishing the office of Surveyor General of Public Lands, and for discontinuing further surveys, until those already in market shall have been disposed of. [Washington? 1830] 20 p. CSmH. 1795

---- Speech of Mr. Hayne, of South Carolina, on Mr. Foot's resolution, proposing an inquiry into the expediency of abolishing the office of surveyor general of public lands, and for discontinuing further surveys, &c. Delivered in the Senate of the United States, January 21, 1830. Washington, Pr. by Duff Green, 1830.

42 p. DLC; MWA. 1796

---- Speeches of Messrs. Hayne and Webster, in the United States Senate, on the resolution of Mr. Foot. [Boston?] Pr. by Richardson, Lord & Holbrook and Beals & Homer [1830?] 40 p. NcU; OClWHi. 1797

---- ---- [Washington, 1830] 16 p. PPL. 1798

---- Speeches of the Hon. Robert Y. Hayne, and the Hon. Daniel Webster, delivered in the Senate of the United States, Jan. 21 and 26, 1830. With a sketch of the preceding debate on the resolution of Mr. Foot, respecting the sale &c., of public lands. Boston, Pub. by Carter & Hendee [Pr. by Isaac R. Butts] 1830. 136 p. CSmH; CtY; MB; MH; MWA; MiD-B; MoS; NIC; NNUT; NcU; Nh; OO; PHi; PPL; RPB; Sc; ScC. 1799

Haynes, Lemuel, 1753-1833.
Universal salvation, a very ancient doctrine; with some account of the life & character of its author. A sermon at Rutland, West parish in the year 1805. Princeton, N. J., Pr. by Hugh Madden, 1830. 8 p. CtHC. 1800

Hays, Isaac, 1796-1879.
Description of a fragment of the head of a new fossil animal, discovered in a marl pit near Moorestown, New Jersey. [Philadelphia, 1830] p. [471]-477. Extracted from Transactions of American Philosophical Society, Vol. VIII. DLC; PPAN. 1801

Hazard's Register.
New-Years address of Hazard's Register of Pennsylvania. [Philadelphia] Pr. by T. W. Ustick [1830] Bdsd. PPL. 1802

Hazen, Edward.
Das deutsche sinnbildliche A B C büchlein, oder erstes buch für kinder. Besonders eingerichtet um den unterricht der jugend leicht und angenehm zu machen. Von E. Hazen ... Philadelphia, Denny und Walker, 1830. 36 p. P. 1803

---- The speller and definer or Class book No. 2. Designed to answer the purpose of a spelling book. Stereotyped by J. Howe, Philadelphia. Pub. by M'Elrath & Bangs, New York; D. F. Robinson & Co., Hartford, Conn.; Denny & Walker & David Clark, Philadelphia; Armstrong & Plaskitt & Cushing & Sons, Baltimore. 1830. 215 p. MDeeP. 1804

---- The symbolical primer; or, Class book no. 1. Part the first. By E. Hazen. New York, Pub. by M'Elrath, Bangs & co. [c1830] 44 p. CtHi; DLC; MH; MiD-B; NN; NNC; OClWHi. 1805

---- ---- Part the second. New York, Pub. by McElrath & Bangs; D. F. Robinson & Co., Hartford, Con.; Denny & Walker, and David Clark, Philadelphia; Armstrong & Plaskitt, and Cushing & Sons, Baltimore [1830] 72 p. KU. 1806

Heber, Reginald, bp. of Calcutta, 1783-1826.
The life of Reginald Heber, D.D., lord bishop of Calcutta. By his widow. With selections from his correspondence, unpublished poems, and private papers; together with a journal of his tour in Norway, Sweden, Russia, Hungary, and Germany, and a history of the Cossaks. In two volumes. New-York, Protestant Episcopal Press, 1830. 2 v. CSmH; CtHT; CtY; DLC; GEU; GHi; ICU; InNd; KyLoP; MBAt; MBC; MWA; MdBJ; MiD-B; MnS; NBuDD; NCH; NN; NNUT; NcU; NjR; OCl; PPi; RPB; ScU; TU; Vi; VtU. 1807

---- Poems. By the late Rt. Rev. Reginald Heber... Hingham [Mass.] C. and E. B. Gill, M. Pratt, pr., 1830. 192 p. CSmH. 1808

Hedge, Levi.
Elements of logick; or, A summary of the general principles and different modes of reasoning. Boston, Hilliard, Gray & Co., 1830. 178 p. CtHT-W; MeBaT; NNF; OMC. 1809

The Heidelberg Catechism. Translated from the German. Hagerstown, Md., Pr. by Gruber and May, 1830. 54 p. PLERC-Hi; PLT. 1810

---- The Heidelberg catechism, or Method of instruction in the Christian religion. Trans. from the German. Philadelphia, Leimer, 1830. PPPrHi. 1811

[Helmuth, Justus Henry Christian] 1745-1825.
Kurze andachten einer gottsuchenden seele, auf alle tage der woche und andere umstande eingerichtet 9. aufl. Germantaun, Gedruckt bey Michael Billmeyer, 1830. 26 p. Integral part of Evangelical Lutheran ministerium of Pennsylvania and adjacent states. Erbauliche liedersammlung... 9. aufl. Germantaun, 1830. PPL; RPB. 1812

A help to the Gospels. See American Sunday School Union.

Hemphill, Joseph, 1770-1842.
Mr. Hemphill's speech on the bill to construct a national road from Buffalo, passing by the seat of the general government, to New Orleans. Delivered in the House

of Representatives, U.S., 23d March, 1830. [Washington, D.C., W. Greer, pr., 1830?] 23 p. DLC; MWA; PPL. 1813

Hendricks, William.
Washington City, May 13, 1830. Dear Sir: Heretofore, it has been my practice, at the close of every session, to address a letter to the people of the state... William Hendricks. 2 p. DLC. 1814

Henkel, David.
David Henkel against the Unitarians. A treatise on the person and incarnation of Jesus Christ, in which some of the principal arguments of the Unitarians are examined. Pub. by order of Evangelical Lutheran Tennessee Synod. New-Market, Pr. in S. Henkel's office, 1830. 119 p. NcD; PPAmP; PPLT; ScCoT; Vi; ViU; ViW. 1815

---- A treatise, or a few fragments on regeneration, by David Henkel; pastor of the Evangelical Lutheran Church, residing in Lincoln County, N.C. New-Market, Va., Pr. in S. Henkel's office, 1830. 39 p. NcD; ViU. 1816

Hennen, John, 1779-1828.
Principles of military surgery; comprising observations on the arrangement, police and practice of hospitals, and on the history, treatment, and anomalies of variola and syphilis... 1st American from the 3d London ed. With life of the author, by his son, Dr. John Hennen. Philadelphia, Carey & Lea [Griggs & Dickinson, prs.] 1830. xviii, 452 p. ArU-M; CSt; CtMW; DLC; GU-M; KyU; LU; MBCo; MdUM; MnU; MoSW; NBuU-M; NN; NNNAM; Nh; NjR; OC; OCGHM; TNJ; ViU. 1817

Henry, John R.

Utility and importance of the Louisville & Portland Canal around the falls of the Ohio River. Philadelphia, Charles Alexander, pr., 1830. 15 p. PPi. 1818

Henry, Matthew, 1662-1714.
The Christian's daily walk with God. From the works of the Rev. Matthew Henry. New York, John P. Haven, 1830. 96 p. MWA. 1819

---- Communicant's companion; or, Instructions and helps for the right receiving of the Lord's Supper. Shippensburg, Galbraith, [Stereotyped, H. Simmons & co.] 1830. [ix], 224 p. GMiW; MoS; NjP; OO; PHi; ViU. 1820

---- An exposition of the Old and New Testament: wherein each chapter is summed up in its contents; the sacred text inserted at large, in distinct paragraphs; each paragraph reduced to its proper heads; the sense given, and largely illustrated; with practical remarks and observations: By Matthew Henry... New York, J. P. Haven, 1830. 6 v. MB; NNUT. 1821

---- The life of the Rev. Philip Henry. By his son, Rev. Matthew Henry... Rev. and enl. New York, John P. Haven, 1830. 238 p. ICU; MHi; PPiPT. 1822

---- ... The parable of the prodigal son... [New York, American Tract Society, 183-?] 8 p. DLC. 1823

---- The pleasantness of a religious life. Boston, Pub. by Peirce and Williams. Philadelphia, Towar, J. & D. M. Hogan, 1830. 167 p. GDC; MBC. 1824

Henry, Robert R.
Letter to the New-York Cham-

ber of Commerce on "Discretionary power," showing "it cannot be entrusted to any one without danger of abuse," consequently the necessity and propriety of their prompt interference to have that "dangerous power" taken by law from the Inspector General of Pot and Pearl ashes, his Deputies, and all other Inspectors... New-York, Pr. for the Author, 1830. 124 p. DLC; MWA; NN; ScU.   1825

Hermann. See Letters addressed to the editor.

Hertz, Daniel, comp.
  Poetischer himmels-weg, oder kleine, geistliche lieder-sammlung, zum gebrauch des "offentlichen und häuslichen Gottesdienstes, und erbauung aller Gott liebenden seelen jeder confession. Zusammengetragen von Daniel Hertz... Zweyte auflage. Libanon, [Penn.] Gedruckt für den Verfasser, bey J. Hartman, 1830. xi, 286, 8 p. CSmH; MiU-C; P; PHi; PPL; PPPrHi.   1826

Hervé, J.
  ... A discourse on the history and importance of the philosophy of the human mind. Delivered at Miss Mackenzie's academy; as introductory to a course of logick and moral philosophy. By J. Hervé. Richmond, Pr. by Samuel Shepherd & Co., 1830. 24 p. ICN; MB; PPAmP; PPC; RP; Vi; ViU.   1827

Hervey, James, 1714-1758.
  Meditations and contemplations by the Rev. James Hervey, A.M. ...In two volumes. New York, S. & D. A. Forbes, prs., 1830. 2 vols. MB; MdW; NN; NjR; PU.
                                      1828
---- ---- Philadelphia, Pub. by M'Carty & Davis, 1830. 2 v. MdW; MoS; NNG.   1829

Hervey, William, missionary to India.
  Christians made rich through the poverty of Christ; a sermon delivered in Holden, March 7, 1830. Worcester, Spooner & Church, prs., 1830. 23 p. CtSoP; ICN; MB; BrMus.   1830

[Hewett, D.]
  The writing master; a new comprehensive system of penmanship. ...New York, J. Conner, 1830. [4] p. MH.   1831

Hicks, Edward, 1780-1849.
  Sermon delivered at Friends' Meeting, Rose Street, on First Day Morning, 11th mo. 21st, 1830. By Edward Hicks. New York, Isaac T. Hopper, T. B. Town and Co., prs., 1830. PSC-Hi. (not located, 1971) 1832

Hicks, Elias, 1748-1830.
  The last letter of Elias Hicks; written to Hugh Judge of Ohio... To which is prefixed some notice of his life, ministry, last sickness, and death. [Pub. by Isaac T. Hopper, New York, and M.T. C. Gould, Philadelphia] [1830?] 4 p. PHi; PPL.   1833

---- Six queries proposed to Elias Hicks, in a letter from a friend, in New York, with E. H.'s answers. New York, William A. Mercein, pr., 1830. 8 p. CSmH; CtY; DLC; ICMe; MH; MWA; MdHi; NN; NcD; NjR; PHC; PSC-Hi; WHi; BrMus.   1834

High School Society of New York.
  Charter, by-laws and rules and regulations of the High Schools in the city of New York. New York, Pr. by William A. Mercein, 1830. 19 p. DLC. 1835

Hildreth, Hosea, 1782-1835.
  Duties and rights of a Congregational minister. A sermon and

statement, with notes... Salem, Foote and Brown, prs., 1830. 24 p. CtHC; MH-AH; MHi; MWA; NjPT; NjR; OMC; PPL; RPB.
1836

[----] Lives of the Evangelists and Apostles of the New Testament. For the use of Sunday schools and families. Cambridge, Pub. by Hilliard and Brown [E. W. Metcalf and company], 1830. 119 p. MB; MBC; MH-AH.
1837

---- A view of the United States, for the use of schools and families... Boston, Carter & Hendee; Baltimore, C. Carter, 1830. 162 p. MB; MH.
1838

Hill, Stephen Prescott.
... Theatrical amusements. A premium tract... Philadelphia, Pub. by The Baptist General Tract Society... [183-?] CSmH.
1839

Hill, William, 1769-1852.
A sermon upon the subject of confirmation... Preached in Winchester, at the First Presbyterian Church, June 27th, 1830. Winchester, Pr. by Samuel H. Davis, 1830. 21 p. PPLT; PPPrHi; ViU.
1840

Hill, William W.
A discourse delivered in the Baptist Church at Raleigh, during the session of the Legislature, on Monday evening, Nov. 30, 1829, in explanation of the views, and in defence of the principles of the Associated Methodists. Raleigh, Lawrence and Lemay, 1830. 12 p. NcU.
1841

[Hillhouse, James]
Propositions for amending the constitution of the United States, providing for the election of president and vice-president, and guarding against the undue exercise of executive influence, patronage and power. Washington, Pr. by Gales & Seaton, 1830. 40 p. CSmH; DLC; MWA; PPL.
1842

The hills. Revised by the Committee of Publication. Philadelphia, American Sunday School Union. ...1830. 16 p. CtHi.
1843

[Hinckley, Mary]
The Seymour Family: or, Domestic Scenes. ... Boston, Leonard C. Bowles, 1830. 4-244 p. (nos. on outer edge of page); 48-288 p. (nos. on inner edge of page). ViU.
1844

---- Sequel to the Seymour Family or Domestic scenes... Boston, Leonard C. Bowles, 1830. 230 p. MB; MBAt; MH; OMC; PU; ViU.
1845

Hind, John, 1796-1866.
Elements of algebra; designed for use of students in the university. 2d ed. Cambridge, Pr. by J. Smith, 1830. ix, 530 p. MB; OO.
1846

Hinds, John, pseud. See Badcock, John.

Hinton, John Howard, 1791-1873, ed.
The history and topography; of the United States: ed. by John Howard Hinton, A. M. Assisted by several literary gentlemen in America and England... London, R. Fenner, Sears & co.; Philadelphia, T. Wardle, & I. T. Hinton, 1830-32. 2 v. CSmH; ViU.
1847

Hints addressed to the farmers of Essex. Salem, Pr. by W. & S. B. Ives, 1830. 22 p. DLC.
1848

Hints for the representatives of the country. [Cap. title: Pennsylvania Rail-Way... Philadelphia, 1830] 24 p. NN; PPL.
1849

Hints on education. New York, Tract Association, 1830. (Tract No. 17). PSC-Hi.   1850

Hints respecting Divine worship. [New York, 183-?] (Protestant Episcopal Tract Society, no. 93) 4 p. DLC.   1851

Hints to aid. See American Sunday School Union.

Hirsch, Meier.
A collection of arithmetical and algebraic problems and formulae. Boston, Carter, Hendee and Babcock, 1830. xii, 342 p. LNHT.   1852

Historical and Philosophical Society of Ohio.
Circular. [Columbus, O. ? 183-?] 8 p. CSmH.   1853

The history of a pocket prayer book. See Dorr, Benjamin.

The history of Ann Lively. See American Tract Society. New York.

History of Anna Emery. See American Tract Society. New York.

The history of Edwin Judd. Philadelphia, American Sunday School Union [1830?] 36 p. NN; BrMus.
                                    1854
The history of George Hicks. By a Sunday school teacher. Revised by the Committee of Publication. Philadelphia, American Sunday School Union, 1830. BrMus.
                                    1855
... The history of honest Roger; founded on fact. By a clergyman. New-York, Pub. by the American Tract Society [183-?] 36 p. (Series iv, no. 3). NN.   1856

The history of insects... New York, Pub. by Samuel Wood &

sons [1830?] 28 p. CSmH.   1857

The history of J. W. , a poor boy. Philadelphia, American Sunday School Union [1830?] BrMus.
                                    1858
A history of New York. See Irving, Washington.

The history of Peter Thomson. See American Tract Society. New York.

History of the Covenanters. See Sime, William.

The history of the great plague in London. See Defoe, Daniel.

A history of the most distinguished martyrs, in various ages and countries of the world; embracing accounts of their sufferings and death, with other interesting particulars. Compiled from the most authentic documents. Philadelphia, William Stavely, 1830. 528 p. GDC; ViU.
                                    1859
History of the New Testament. An outline of the principle events recorded in the New Testament. New Haven, Durrie & Peck, 1830. 124 p. MH-AH.   1860

... History of the outrage committed upon the family of Elder George Witherell at Hartford, New York, on the night of September 27, 1830. 25-40 p. Anti-Masonic Pamphlets. No. 3. NN; PPFM.   1861

A history of the proceedings and extraordinary measures of the Legislature of Maine, for the year 1830. With several opinions of the Justices of the Supreme Court on the questions submitted to their decision by the Senate and the Governor. Portland, Me., 1830. 120 p. CSmH; M; MB; MHi; Me;

MeHi; MeU; MnU; OCLaw; OClWHi. 1862

A history of the unexampled sufferings of an Italian lady, (The Dutchess of C____:)... Written by herself. Watertown [N. Y.] Pub. by Knowlton & Rice, 1830. 72 p. CSmH. 1863

History of the United States. See Hale, Salma.

The history of Thomas Brown. Revised by the Committee of publication of the American Sunday School Union. Philadelphia, American Sunday School Union, [183-?] 16 p. (iv series, no. 403) DLC. 1864

Hitchcock, Edward, 1793-1864.
Dyspepsy forestalled & resisted: or, Lectures on diet, regimen, & employment; delivered to the students of Amherst College; spring term, 1830. Amherst, J. S. & C. Adams and co.; New York, J. Leavitt; [etc., etc.] 1830. 360 p. DLC; GDC; MB; MBC; MDeeP; MH; MeB; NIC; Nh; OO; PPC; TU. 1865

---- An essay on alcoholic & narcotic substances, as articles of common use. Addressed particularly to students. Pub. under the direction of the American Temperance Society. It being the essay to which a premium was awarded. Amherst [Mass.] J. S. & C. Adams and Co.; New York, J. Leavitt; [etc., etc.] 1830. 48 p. CU; Ct; DLC; DNLM; MB; MH-AH; MHi; MWA; NN; NNNAM; NbU; NjR; OO; PPL; PPPrHi. 1866

---- ---- 2d ed. Amherst, Pub. by J. S. & C. Adams; Jonathan Leavitt, New York; Peirce and Williams, Boston, 1830. 36 p. Ct; DLC; In; MA; MB; MH; MWA; NIC; NN; NjR; PPL. 1867

Hitchcock & Stafford's annual almanac and directory calendar for 1831. [New Haven, Hitchcock & Stafford, 1830] Bdsd. Drake 990. 1868

Hobart, John Henry, 1775-1830.
The candidate for confirmation instructed; ... Sermon... and an address after confirmation, with prayers. By John Henry Hobart, D.D. ...3d ed. New York, Stereotyped by Jas. Conner, Pr. at the Protestant Episcopal Press, 1830. 56 p. MWA. 1869

---- Catechism number three. The church catechism enlarged, explained, & proved from scripture, in a catechism drawn up, with alterations & additions, from various approved catechisms. New York, General Protestant Episcopal Sunday School Union, [183-?] 1 p. l., 105 p. CtHT. 1870

---- The old paths. A sermon, preached in the season of Lent. Stereotyped by James Conner. New-York, Protestant Episcopal Tract Society [1830] 12 p. NNG; PPL. 1871

---- The reciprocal duties of minister and people. A sermon preached in St. Luke's Church, Rochester... August 29, 1830, at the institution of the Rev. Henry J. Whitehouse, A.M. into the rectorship of said church... New York, Pub. by T. & J. Swords; Edward J. Swords, pr. 1830. 22 p. CtY; InID; MH; NGH; NN; NNG; PPL; WHi. 1872

Hobby, William.
Exposition of a part of the frauds, corruptions and improprieties committed in the pay department of the army of the United States since the year 1816... 2d ed. Washington City, 1830. 32 p. LNHT. 1873

Hobson, Samuel J.
　An essay on the history, preparation & therapeutic uses of iodine. Philadelphia, 1830. 60, [1] p. DLC; MBCo; MWA; NNNAM; PHi; PPC; PU. 1874

Der Hoch-Deutsche Americanische Calender auf 1831. Von Carl Friederich Egelmann. Germantaun, M. Billmeyer [1830] 18 l. CLU; CtY; DLC; InU; MH; MWA; P; PHi; PPL; PPeSchw; WHi.
1875
Hodgson, William Brown.
　A catalogue of Arabic, Turkish and Persian manuscripts. The private collection... Washington, 1830. 10 p. CtY; PPAmP.
1876
Hofland, Barbara (Wreaks) Hoole.
　The history of a clergyman's widow, and her young family. By Mrs. Hofland... New York, W. B. Gilley, 1830. 180 p. DLC.
1876a
---- The history of a merchant's widow and her young family. New York, W. B. Gilley, 1830. 178 p. MB; NN. 1877

---- Little Manuel. The captive boy. A true story. By Mrs. Hofland. Boston, B. F. Edmands [183-] CtY; ICN; MiD-B. 1878

---- The stolen bay. A story, founded on facts. By Mrs. Hofland... New-York, W. B. Gilley, 1830. 154 p. GAT; NN. 1879

Hoit, Samuel, d. 1835?
　Stop the Slanderers! $150 Reward, for the delivery to me, on this side of the Sabin, the editor of the Port Gibson Correspondent, Mississippi. Samuel Hoit. San Felipe de Austin, Texas, June 26, 1830. 4-page folder printed on page [1]. TxU. 1880

Holbach, Paul Thierry, baron de.
　Good sense; or, Natural ideas opposed to supernatural, (being a translation from the "Bon sens du Curé Meslier,") By Baron Holbach... Re-published from the English edition... 2d ed. New York, Pub. by Wright and Owen, 1830. v, 140 p. RPB. 1881

Holbrook, Josiah, 1789-1854.
　Apparatus for schools, academies and lyceums... Boston, Carter, Hendee & Babcock [183-] Bdsd. MB. 1882

---- Circular. (An advertisement of Holbrook's Scientific Toys.) [Boston, Mass., 1830] BrMus.
1883
---- Easy lessons in geometry, intended for infant and primary schools: but useful in academies, lyceums and families... 3d ed. Boston, Pub. by Carter & Hendee, 1830. 36 p. DLC; MH; NNC; TxU-T. 1884

[----] Geometry [Diagrams.] [Boston, Peirce and Williams, 1830] Bdsd. (To accompany his "Easy lessons in Geometry") MH.
1885
---- Scientific tracts, designed for instruction and entertainment adapted to schools, lyceums, and families. Conducted by Josiah Holbrook and others. Boston, Carter, Hendee, and Babcock. Pr. by I. R. Butts, 1830. Vol. I 26-48 p. ViU. 1886

---- ---- Boston, Boston Classic Press; I. R. Butts. Pub. by Carter and Hendee, 1830. 580 p. CtHT; IEG; KyDC; MBC; MNBedf; MWA; OC; VtU. 1887

[Holbrook, Silas Pinckney] 1796-1835.
　Sketches, by a traveller... Boston, Pub. by Carter & Hendee, 1830. 2 l., 315 p. CSmH; DLC; IU; KyLx; MB; MiD; NBLiHi; OMC; OrU; PHi; PPL;

PU.   1888

Holford, George Peter.
The destruction of Jerusalem.
An absolute and irresistible proof
of the divine origin of Christianity: including a narrative of the
calamities which befell the Jews
... Stereotype ed. Exeter, N. H.,
Pub. by Leonard Jackson, 1830.
89 p. MWA.   1889

Holland, John.
Memoirs of the life and ministry of the Rev. John Summer-
field, A. M. 2d ed. New York,
Pr. for Jonathan Leavitt; Boston,
Crocker & Brewster. By William A. Mercein (Gen. agent for
the work), 1830. 360 p. CtHT;
KMK; NCH.   1890

---- ---- 3d ed. New York,
Pr. for McElrath and Bangs by
William A. Mercein, 1830. 360
p. Ct; ICU; IEG; KyLoS; ViRUT.
                                    1891
---- ---- 4th ed. New York,
Pub. by McElrath & Bangs, Pr.
by William A. Mercein, 1830.
360 p. MH; MWA.   1892

---- ---- 5th ed. New-York,
Pr. and pub. by M'Elrath &
Bangs, 1830. 360 p. TNJ.   1893

Holland Land Company.
An address to the landholders
& inhabitants of the Holland Purchase, on the subject of the Holland Land Company's title, and
remonstrating against the proceedings of a county convention,
held at Buffalo, 11th Feb. 1830.
Buffalo, Pr. by Day, Follett &
Haskins, 1830. 16 p. NBuHi;
NN.   1894

Hollatz, David, d. 1771.
Die Evangelische Gnaden
Ordnung, wie eine Seele von der
Cigenen Gerechtigkeit und Fröm-
migkeit herunter... Voin David

Hollazen. ... Erste verbesserte
Amerikanische, von der fünsten
Europäischen Auflage. Libanon,
(Penns.) Gedruckt fur H. Krob,
bey J. Hartman, 1830. xviii,
197 p. P; PLT; PPL; PU.   1895

Holman, Jonas Welch, 1805-
1873.
The faith once delivered to the
Saints or, Apostolic doctrine and
order, defended by Scriptures.
To which is added a short account of the life... of the author
... Philadelphia, Pub. by the
author, 1830. 144 p. MWA.   1896

Holmes, John, 1773-1843.
Speech of Mr. Holmes, of
Maine. Delivered in the Senate
of the United States, February
18, 1830, on the debate which
arose upon Mr. Foot's resolution relative to the public lands.
Washington, Pr. and pub. at the
office of the National journal,
1830. 24 p. DLC; MWA.   1897

---- Supplement to the Baltimore
Chronicle and Marylander. Speech
of Mr. Holmes, of Maine, in the
Senate of the United States, on
his resolutions, calling upon the
president of the United States for
the reasons of his removing
from office, and filling the vacancies thus created, in the recess of the Senate. In Senate
United States - April 28, 1830.
24 p. MdHi; PPL.   1898

---- Speech of Mr. Holmes of
Maine, in the Senate of the United
States, on his resolutions calling
upon the President of the United
States for the reasons of his removing from office and filling
the vacancies this created in the
recess of the Senate. Brunswick,
Me., Pr. at the Free Press Office, 1830. 40 p. CtY; MeHi.
                                    1899
---- ---- Washington, Pr. and

pub. at the Office of the National Journal, 1830. 28 p. PPL.
1900

Holmes, Sylvester.
Two sermons, occasioned by the death of Josiah H. Coggeshall, Esq. who died Oct. 24, 1817. and Maj. John Coggeshall, who died July 19, 1830. By S. Holmes. New-Bedford, S. S. Smith, pr., 1830. 46 p. MBC; MH; MNBedf; RPB.
1901

Holt, Bifield, 1785-1830.
History of the Church of Christ, from the creation to the present time... Portland, Shirley and Hyde, 1830. 143 p. Williamson 4648.
1902

Holyoke, Edward Augustus, 1728-1829.
An ethical essay, or An attempt to enumerate the several duties to God, our Saviour, our neighbor and ourselves. To which is added an appendix. With a biographical memoir, by John Brazer. [Salem] Pr. by Foote & Brown, prs., Gazette Office, 1830. xxviii, 183 p. CSmH; CU; DLC; MB; MBNEH; MH-AH; MWA; PPAmP; RPAt; WHi.
1903

Home, Henry, Lord Kames.
Elements of criticism... Complete in one volume. New York, Pub. by Collins & Hannay, W. E. Dean, pr., 1830. 476 p. CU; CtHT; CtY; IaDmD; LNHT; NRU; TxU; ViU.
1904

Home industry, the most direct road to national prosperity. [183-?] 1 p. DLC.
1905

Home, sweet home. See Bishop, Henry Rowley.

Homer.
The hymns of Homer, translated into verse from the original Greek: with notes, critical and explanatory. To which is prefixed, an inquiry into the life of Homer. By Columbus C. Conwell, M.D. Philadelphia, Pr. by Mifflin & Parry, 1830. 127 p. CSf; ICU; MdHi; NBLiHi; PPL; PU.
1906

[Hook, James] 1746-1827.
The celebrated dance in Tekeli, arranged as a rondo for the piano forte by Mr. Holst. 2d ed. ... Philadelphia, Pub. by G. E. Blake [183-?] 4 p. CSmH.
1907

Hooker, Edward William, 1794-1875.
A discourse on preaching the word; delivered in the chapel of the Theological Seminary, Andover, Mass. and published at the request of the students: with notes ... Andover, Pub. by Mark Newman, Flagg & Gould, prs., 1830. 40 p. CBPac; CoU; Ct; CtHT-W; CtY; DLC; ICN; MB; MBAt; MBC; MH; MHi; MiD-B; MoSpD; NNC; NNUT; NjPT; NjR; PPPrHi; WHi; BrMus.
1908

Hooker, Worthington.
Oration delivered before the Norwich Lyceum and Mechanics' Institute, on the 5th of July, 1830 ... Norwich, Pr. by J. Dunham, 1830. 20 p. CtHi; CtY.
1909

Hooper, Robert.
Examinations in anatomy, physiology, practice of physic, surgery, chemistry, obstetrics, materia medica, and pharmacy; For the use of students. New-York, Pub. by Collins and Co. [W. E. Dean, pr.] 1830. [2], 182 p. CtY; DLC; PPL; ViRA.
1910

Hooper, William.
Discipline of the heart, to be connected with the culture of the mind; a discourse on education, delivered to the students of college, at Chapel Hill, N.C., Aug.

22, 1830, and pub. by their request. By William Hooper. New York, Sleight & Robinson, 1830. 24 p. CtY; NcU. 1911

Hopkins, Caleb.
An easy instructor in the most useful knowledge. Containing a first book, spelling book & dictionary... New York, J. & J. Harper, 1830. 2 v. in 1. DLC. 1912

Hopkins, Ezekiel.
An exposition of the Ten Commandments. By Rev. Ezekiel Hopkins. New-York, American Tract Society, [183-?] 442 p. CBCDS. 1913

Hopkins, Hiram B.
Renunciation of Free Masonry by Hiram B. Hopkins, Esq., deputy sheriff of Lockport, N.Y. Boston, J. Marsh, 1830. 12 p. CtY; MH; MHi; MWA; WHi; BrMus. 1914

Hopkins, William Fenn.
Gunpowder by Lieut. Hopkins, prof. of chemistry, U.S.M.A. West Point, N.Y. West Point, N.Y., [183-?] 12 p. NWM. 1915

Hopkinson, Joseph, 1770-1842.
Eulogium in commemoration of the Hon. Bushrod Washington, late one of the chief justices of the Supreme Court of the United States. Philadelphia, T.S. Manning, pr., 1830. 32 p. CtHT; DLC; MBC; MH-L; MiD-B; NN; PHi; PPAmP; PPL; PU; RNR; RPB; ScCC; TxU. 1916

---- Extract of a letter from Judge Hopkinson of Philadelphia, to a gentleman in England... Philadelphia, Pub. by Robert Desilver, 1830. 8 p. MdW; MiD-B; NjR; PPL; PPPrHi. 1917

Hopkinton Academy.
A catalogue of the officers, instructers and students of Hopkinton Academy, for 1830. Concord, Pr. by Luther Roby, 1830. 8 p. MA; MBC; Nh. 1918

Horatius Flaccus, Quintus.
Q. Horatii Flacci poëmata... Novi Eboraci. Impensis G. & C. & H. Carvill [Typis Gulielmi E. Dean] 1830. [xi], xcv, 343, 612, xxii p. CtY; PPL. 1919

Horner, J.M.
A letter addressed to the Baptist denomination in general and the members of those churches composing the New York, Warwick, Hudson River, and Danbury Associations, in particular... J.M. Horner [183-?] 3 p. DLC. 1920

Horner, William Edmonds, 1793-1853.
A treatise on special and general anatomy...2d ed., rev. and corr. Philadelphia, Carey and Lea [Griggs & Dickinson, pr.] 1830. 2 v. ArU-M; CU; DNLM; GU; KyBgW; LNOP; MdBL; MeB; MnU; MoSU-M; MsU; NcC; Nh; OCGHM; OU; PPC; RPM; ViRMC. 1921

Hosack, David.
Address delivered at the first anniversary of the New York City Temperance Society...May 11, 1830. [New York, John P. Haven, 1830] 24 p. DLC; In; MBC; OCGHM; PLT; PPL (Caption title) 1922

---- Dr. Hosack's address delivered before the New York City Temperance Society, May 11, 1830... Stereotype ed. New York, Pub. by John P. Haven, 1830. 24 p. CtY; DLC; MWA; OClWHi. 1923

The house that Jack built. To the labouring class of the community of Baltimore... [Signed] A friend to the laboring man. [Baltimore, 183-] 1 p. DLC. 1924

The house the rogues built.
[New York, 183-?]   Bdsd.   MB.
                                   1925
How, Samuel Blanchard, 1790-
1868.
    An address, delivered by the
Rev. S. B. How, at his inaugura-
tion as principal of Dickinson
College, in Carlisle, Pa., on
Tuesday, March 30, 1830. Car-
lisle, Pa., Pr. at the Herald of-
fice, 1830. 23 p. MB; MBAt;
MBC; MH-AH; NNUT; PHi;
PPPrHi.   1926

---- An address on intemperance,
delivered before the Temperance
Society of Cumberland County,
Pennsylvania... Carlisle, Pr. by
George Fleming, 1830. 15 p.
NNUT; NjR; PHi; PPPrHi.   1927

[Howard, H. R.]
    ...Pictorial life and adven-
tures of John A. Murrell, The
great western land pirate. By the
editor of the New York National
Police Gazette. Philadelphia, T.
B. Peterson & brothers [183-?]
At head of title: "Murrell!
"Hare!" and "Turpin" series!
MH.   1928

Howard and Napoleon.   By the
author of: "The Sword, or
Christmas presents." Portsmouth,
John W. Shepard, 1830. 104 p.
NhHi.   1929

Howe, J. & Co.
    Specimen of printing types,
and ornaments, from the letter-
foundry of J. Howe & Co. Philadelphia, 1830. DLC; MWA; NNC.
                                   1930

[Howe, Jemima] 1755-1792.
    Narrative of the captivity of
... Watertown, Pub. by Knowlton & Rice, 1830. 16 p. Cover
title only. Goodspeed's Cat. 308,
Jan. 1939. No. 134.   1931

Howe, John, 1630-1705.
    Select practical works of Rev.
John Howe and Dr. William
Bates. Collected and arranged,
with biographical sketches, by
James Marsh.   Burlington,
Chauncey Goodrich; New York,
G. & C. & H. Carvill, 1830.
xvi, 550 p. CtHC; MA; MH; MiU;
NcMHi; NhD; PWW; VtU.   1932

[Howitt, Mary (Botham)] 1799-
1888.
    Peter Parley's fable of The
spider and fly. Boston, Carter
and Hendee, 1830. 13 p. DLC.
                                   1933
Howitt, William.
    George Fox and his first dis-
ciples; or The Society of Friends
as it was and as it is. [Phila-
delphia, 183-?] 38 p. MB; MH.
                                   1934
[Howland, Mrs.]
    The infant school manual, or,
Teacher's assistant. ...Prepared
for the use of teachers. 2d ed.,
rev. imp. and enl.   Boston,
Pub. by Carter and Hendee. Baltimore, Charles Carter, 1830.
viii, 13-314 p. CtHT-W; NNC;
RHi.   1935

[----] ---- Worcester, Dorr and
Howland, 1830. viii, [13]-292 p.
DLC.   1936

Howland, John, 1757-1854.
    Address delivered before the
Providence Association of Mechanicks and Manufacturers, on
the occasion of opening Mechanicks' Hall, January 10, A.D.
1825. By John Howland, esq.,
president of the association. Pub.
by the association.   Providence,
H. H. Brown, pr., 1830. 12 p.
DLC; DeGE; RHi; RNHi; RPB.
                                   1937
Hoyle, Edmund, 1672-1769.
    Hoyle's improved edition of
the rules for playing fashionable
games: ... carefully revised

from the last London ed. with
several additions. New York,
Pub. by W. C. Borradaile, 1830.
288 p. CSmH; MH; MWA; NN;
NjP; OCA.   1938

Huchings' improved almanack for
1831. By David Young. New-
York, John C. Totten [1830] 18 1.
MWA; MnU; NBLiHi; NHi.   1939

Huching's revived almanack for
1831. By David Young. New-
York, John C. Totten [1830] 18 1.
MB; MWA; NN.   1940

[Hudson, Charles]
A summary view of the evi-
dences of divine revelation ex-
hibited in the form of a cate-
chism. Designed for the use of
Sabbath schools. Boston, Marsh,
Capen & Lyon, and Carter &
Hendee [etc., etc.] 1830. 54 p.
M; MH; MH-AH; MHi; MWA.
1941
Hudson, David.
Letters addressed to the Anti-
Masonic committee, appointed to
correspond with Masons, at the
Anti-Masonic Convention held in
Ravenna, April 23rd 1830... To-
gether with an address adopted
by the Masonic convention...
June 24th, 1830. Ravenna, Pr.
at the office of the Western
Courier, 1830. 24 p. OClWHi.
1942
Hughs, Thomas.
The universal class-book: be-
ing a selection of pieces, in
prose and verse. Philadelphia,
U. Hunt; Louisville, Ken., Mor-
ton & co., 1830. 300 p. DLC;
InRE; MB; PPAmP.   1943

Huidekoper, Harm, Jan. 1776-
1854.
A letter on the Unitarianism
of the first three centuries of the
Christian era by Oberlin [pseud.]
[Meadville, Pa., T. Atkinson,
1830] 14 p. CBPac; IEG; MB;

MH; MH-AH; MoS; PPAmP; VtU.
1944
Hull, J. H.
English grammar, by lectures;
comprehending the principles and
rules of syntactical parsing on a
new and highly improved system
...6th ed. Saratoga Springs, G.
M. Davison, 1830. 144 p. CtHT-
W; InU; MH; MPB; OMC.   1945

Humane Society of the Common-
wealth of Massachusetts.
Circular, signed by Charles
Lowell, John Heard, Jr., Geo.
Hayward [1830] 1 p. MHi.   1946

The Humorists own book: A cabinet of original and selected anecdotes... New York, Leavitt & Allen [183-?] 284 p. MB. (Missing
1971)   1947

Humphrey, Heman, 1779-1861.
Indian rights & our duties. An
address delivered at Amherst, Hart-
ford, etc. December, 1829. Am-
herst, J.S. & C. Adams & co.; S.
Butler & Son, Northampton, New
York, J. Leavitt; [etc., etc.] 1830.
24 p. CSmH; Ct; DLC; ICN; ICU;
KU; MB; MBC; MDeeP; MH-AH;
MWA; MdBJ; NN; NjPT; NjR; OO;
PHi; PPL.   1948

---- ---- 2d ed. Amherst, J.S.
& C. Adams and co.; New York,
J. Leavitt [etc., etc.] 1830. 24
p. CtHT-W; CtY; DLC; MH;
MWA; NN; WHi.   1949

---- The kingdom of Christ. A
sermon printed before the annual
convention of the Congregational
ministers of Massachusetts, in
Boston, May 29, 1830. Boston,
Pub. by Peirce and Williams,
1830. 36 p. CoU; ICN; MB;
MBC; MH-AH; MWA; MeB; NN;
NcU; RPB; WHi.   1950

Der Hundertjahrige Calender von
1799 bis 1899. Baltimore, Jo-

hann T. Hanzsche, 1830. 48 l.
MWA; MdBE; <u>PPL</u>.   1951

[Hunt, Freeman] 1804-1858.
   American anecdotes: original
and select. By an American.
Boston, Putnam & Hunt, 1830.
2 v. CSmH; DLC; ICN; ICU;
MB; MBNEH; MH; MWA; MnHi;
MoS; NN; PHi; PP; PU; RPB;
Vi; WHi; BrMus.   1952

Hunter, Charles G.
   Sir, On the evening of the 10th
inst. I received a letter from
Mr. Charles H. Duryee, request-
ing me to come immediately to
Philadelphia... [Philadelphia,
1830] [3] p. <u>PPL</u>.   1953

Huntington, Daniel.
   Religion, and the triumphs of
faith: poems, by Rev. Daniel
Huntington. Boston, Perkins &
Marvin, 1830. 40 p. MBC; MH-
AH; BrMus.   1954

Huntington, Eleazer.
   The American penman. Comprising the art of writing plain
and ornamental. Designed as a
standard work for the use of
schools. Hartford, Conn., Pub.
by Henry Benton, 1830. 20 pl.
CtHi.   1955

Huntington, Jabez Williams.
   Speech of Mr. Huntington, on
the bill to provide for the re-
moval of the Indians west of the
Mississippi, delivered in...May
18, 1830. 28 p. MA; MWA.
                                      1956
Hutching's almanack for 1831.
By David Young. New-York, Dan-
iel D. Smith [1830] 18 l. NHi;
NN.   1957

Hutchings Improved Almanack for
the year of our Lord, 1831. By
David Young, philom. New York,
J. C. Totten [1830] 18 l. MWA.
                                      1958

Hutchings (Revived) almanac for
1831. New-York, N. B. Holmes
[1830] Drake 7095.   1959

Hutchins' improved almanac and
ephemeris for 1831. Albany,
Tracy Doolittle [1830] 18 l. MWA.
                                      1960
---- By David Young. New-
York, Caleb Bartlett [1830] 18 l.
MWA; NBLiHi.   1961

---- New-York, Caleb Bartlett
[1830] 18 l. Ct; MH; MWA; NHi;
NN; NjMo; NjR; OO.   1962

---- New-York, N. B. Holmes
[1830] 18 l. CtHi.   1963

---- Newburgh, Sneden & Hath-
away [1830] 18 l. DLC.   1964

Hutchins' improved almanac for
1831. By David Young. New-
York, C. Brown [1830] 18 l. NN.
                                      1965
Hyde, Alvan.
   Essay on the state of infants.
New York, Cornelius Davis,
1830. 12 p. CBPac; CtY; MBC;
MNBedf; MWΛ; OClW; PLT.
                                      1966
---- An example from the Holy
Scriptures, improved to aid the
cause of temperance: A sermon
delivered at Lee, Massachusetts,
November 15, 1829. Sanbornton
[N. H.] David N. Moulton, pr.,
1830. 21 p. MHi.   1967

Hyde, Jabez Backus, b. 1774.
   Mr. Hyde's protest against the
proceedings of the Buffalo Pres-
bytery, and the Synod of Genes-
see... Warren, Pa., Pr. by
Purviance, 1830. 19 p. PPPrHi.
                                      1968
Hymns for infant schools. New
York, Pr. and sold by Mahlon
Day [183-?] 23 p. RPB.   1969

Hymns for little children. Wendell, Metcalf, 1830. 18 p.

Cover title: Hymns for children.
MA; MWA. 1970

I

I am an infidel. See American
Tract Society.

I am no hypocrite. See American Tract Society.

Ill temper a bad play fellow. To
which is added conversations on
rewards and punishments... New-
Haven, S. Babcock, publisher...
S. Babcock & co., Charleston,
Sidney's press, 1830. 23 p.
CtHi; MH. 1971

Illinois.
... An address, delivered by
Ninian Edwards, governor of the
state of Illinois, to both houses of
the legislature, December 7, 1830.
Printed by order of the legislature. Vandalia, Pr. by R. Blackwell, public printer, 1830. 37 p.
At head of title: Illinois intelli-
gencer-extra. CSmH; DLC; ICN.
1972
---- A bill for an act to amend
an act entitled "An act relative
to criminal jurisprudence..."
[1830?] 7 p. I-Ar. 1973

---- ... List of lands entered on
the books of the auditor of public
accounts, for the state of Illinois,
subject to taxation for the several
years set forth (with interest and
costs) and upon which the taxes
have not been paid... [Vandalia,
October 2, 1830] 31 p. At head
of title: Illinois Intelligencer--
Extra. I-Ar; IHi. 1974

Illinois Gazette Extra. See: To
the Hon. Thomas H. Benton.

Illustration of Shakespeare. Two
hundred and thirty vignette engravings, from designs by Thurs-

ton. Philadelphia, 1830. 37 p.
MB; MH. 1975

Impartial Humane Society, Baltimore.
Acts incorporating the Impartial Humane Society of the city of
Baltimore; also, the by-laws for
the regulation of said society.
Baltimore, Pr. by Thomas Murphy, 1830. 14 p. PPL. 1976

Improvements in Massachusetts.
To the citizens in favor of a rail
road from Boston to Vermont.
Boston, John H. Eastburn, pr.,
[1830?] Bdsd. MWA; NN (photostat copy). 1977

In Jesu Namen. Kleine Religiöse
Aufsätze. No. 51. [Philadelphia,
Gedruckt bey Conrad Zentler,
1830] 24 p. PHi. 1978

Indian melodies. See Schoolcraft,
James.

The Indian question. [Albany,...
1830] (Albany Argus Extra. Friday, June 19, 1830). 1979

Indian relations... New York,
1830. NN. 1980

Indiana.
Journal of the House of Representatives of the state of Indiana;
being the fourteenth session of
the General Assembly; begun and
held at Indianapolis, in said state,
on Monday the seventh day of December, A.D. 1829. Indianapolis,
Smith and Bolton, state prs.,
1829 [i.e. 1830] 552, 15, 4 p.
In; InU. 1981

---- Journal of the Senate of the
state of Indiana; being the fourteenth session of the General Assembly; begun and held at Indianapolis, in said state, on Monday
the seventh day of December,
A.D. 1829. Indianapolis, Smith

and Bolton, state prs. 1829 [i. e. 1830] 436, 15 p. In.   1982

---- Laws of the state of Indiana, passed and published at the fourteenth session of the General Assembly, held at Indianapolis, on the first Monday in December, one thousand eight hundred and twenty-nine. By authority. Indianapolis, Ind., Smith and Bolton, state prs., 1830. 205 p. In; In-SC; InHi; InU; N.   1983

---- Message of His Excellency James Brown Ray; delivered in person, to both houses of the General Assembly of the state of Indiana, on Tuesday, the seventh of December, 1830. Indianapolis, A. F. Morrison, pr. to the Senate [1830] 24 p. CSmH.   1984

---- Reports of cases argued and determined in the supreme court of judicature of the state of Indiana. With tables of the cases and principal matters. By Isaac Blackford, A. M. one of the judges of the court. Vol. I. Containing the cases from May term, 1817, being the first term of the court, to May term, 1826, both inclusive. Indianapolis, Pr. by Douglass and Maguire, 1830. xiv, 488 p. DLC; In-SC; InU; M.   1985

The Indiana Almanack, for the year of our Lord 1831... By Jeremiah Smith. Indianapolis, Ind., Pub. by G. Smith, N. Bolton and J. Smith. George Smith, pr. [1830] [24?] p. InHi (incomplete. Missing [p. 23-24.]) 1986

Indigent Widow's and Single Women's Society.
     The thirteenth annual report for the year 1829, of the managers of the Indigent Widows' and Single Women's Society... Philadelphia, Pr. by Order of the Society, Lydia R. Bailey,

pr., 1830. 8 p. PPL.   1987

Infant lessons. By the author of "Helen and Maria" &c. Boston, Leonard C. Bowles, and Wait, Greene & Co. 1830. 46 p. MH.   1988

Infant school grammar. See Bethune, Mrs. Joanna (Graham).

The infant school manual. See Howland, Mrs.

Infant School Society of Philadelphia.
     Constitution of the Infant School Society of the city of Philadelphia. [Philadelphia, ca. 1830] [1] p. PPL.   1989

Infant School Society of the Northern Liberties and Kensington.
     Second annual report of the board of managers of the Infant School Society of the Northern Liberties and Kensington. [Philadelphia, 1830] 4 p. PPL. 1990

The infant's grammar. Baltimore, Pub. by F. Lucas Jr. [183?] 12 l. RPB.   1991

Infidelity: comprising Jenyn's Internal evidence, Leslie's method, Lyttleton's Conversion of Paul, Watson's reply to Gibbon and Paine, A notice of Hume on miracles, and An extract from West on the resurrection. New York, American Tract Society [183-?] 576 p. CSmH; DLC.   1992

Ingersoll, Charles M.
     Conversations on English grammar, explaining the principles and rules of the language; illustrated by appropriate exercises, adapted to the use of schools... 8th ed. Portland, Shirley and Hyde, 1830. 251 p. CU; CtMW; MH; MeHi; NNC; WU.   1993

Ingersoll, George Goldthwait,

1796-1863.

A discourse delivered before the legislature of Vermont, on the day of general election, October 14, 1830. Pub. at the request of the Legislature. Burlington, Chauncey Goodrich, 1830. 46, [1] p. CSmH; CtHC; CtHT; DLC; ICN; MA; MBAt; MBC; MH-AH; MHi; NN; NjR; OCHP; VtHi; VtU; BrMus.   1994

Ingraham, Joseph Wentworth, 1799-1848.

Letters to Sunday scholars, on the geography, &c. of the places mentioned in, or connected with, the account of the nativity of our Saviour and the season of Advent. New York, Protestant Episcopal Sunday School Union depository [183-?] MH.   1995

An inquiry into the necessity and general principles of reorganization in the United States... By an observer. Albany, 1830. BrMus.   1996

Insect architecture. See Rennie, James.

The insolvent register for the last five years; being a complete list of applicants advertised in the city and county of Philadelphia for the benefit of the insolvent law of the state of Pennsylvania. Alphabetically arranged. For the use of merchants and traders generally. Philadelphia, 1830. 60 p. PHi.   1997

Instructions for the aeolina or mund harmonica, with a selection of popular melodies expressly arranged for the instrument ... New York, Bourne, 1830. 16 p. NN.   1998

Instructions to town committees respecting the registry law. [183-?] 1 p. DLC.   1999

Intercourse with the Greek government on the subject of education in Greece. From the Missionary Herald for February, 1830. [Boston? 1830?] 8 p. DLC.   2000

Invincible reasons, which should forever attach a Roman Catholic to his religion, and engage all Protestants to embrace the same. Translated from the French. Boston, Pub. by William Smith for the editor of "The Jesuit." 1830. 28 p. DGU; PPCCH.
                                  2001
An invitation to prayer. [New-York, New-York Protestant Episcopal Tract Society, 183-?] 4 p. MH.   2002

Ipswich Female Seminary, Ipswich, Mass.

Catalogue of the officers and members of Ipswich Female Seminary, 1830. Newburyport, Pr. at the Herald Office, [1830] 8 p. M.   2003

Ireland, William Henry, ed.

The Napoleon anecdotes; illustrating the mental energies of the late emperor of France; and the characters and actions of his contemporary statesmen and warriors. Boston, Wells & Lily, 1830. 3 vols. CtHT; DLC; MB; MBAt; MDeeP; MH; MoSU; NjR; PPL; RPB.   2004

Iriarte, Don Tomas De.

Fabulas literarias de Don Tomas De Iriarte... Nueva ediciones, anadidas las variantes de otras ediciones, y nueve fabulas postumas del misno autor. Cambrigia, por Hilliard y Brown, libreros de la universidad [Cambrigia: En la imprenta de E. N. Metcalf y Companero impresores de la universidad] 1830. [2], 115 p. IEG; KHi; MeLB.   2005

Irma. See Kennicott, James H.

Irving, Christopher, d. 1856.
A catechism of astronomy:
containing the motions, magni-
tudes, periods, distances and other phenomena of the heavenly
bodies... 4th American ed., rev.
and corr. by John Griscom...
New York, Pub. by Collins and
Hannay, 1830. 99 p. NSmB; NjR.
                                    2006
---- A catechism of the history
of England... New York, 1830.
100 p. DLC.   2007

Irving, John Treat, 1778-1838.
A discourse on the advantages
of classical learning, with a
sketch of the character of the
late William Samuel Johnson, delivered before the Association of
the Alumni of Columbia College,
at their anniversary, 5th May,
1830... New-York, G. & C. & H.
Carvill [Ludwig & Tolefree, prs.]
1830. 35 p. CtHi; CtY; MB;
MBAt; MH; NIC; NNC; NjPT;
PPL; RPB; BrMus.   2008

[Irving, Washington] 1783-1859.
Bracebridge Hall; or, The humorists. A medley, by Geoffrey
Crayon, Gent. ...4th ed. Philadelphia, Carey & Lea, 1830. 2
vols. MB; NN.   2009

[----] The devil and Tom Walker:
together with Deacon Grubb and
the Old Nick. Woodstock, Vt.,
R. & A. Colton, 1830. 32 p.
CtY; DLC.   2010

[----] A history of New York
from the beginning of the world
to the end of the Dutch dynasty
...By Diedrich Knickerbocker...
7th ed. Philadelphia, Carey &
Lea, 1830. 2 v.   NN.   2011

---- The life and voyages of
Christopher Columbus. New
York, G. & C. & H. Carvill,

1830. 252, [4] p. CtHC; IEN;
MWA; BrMus.   2012

[----] The sketch-book of Geoffrey Crayon, Gent... In two volumes. 7th American ed. Philadelphia, Carey & Lea, 1830. 2
vols. NIC; BrMus.   2013

Ismar, F. A.
The school of industry, at
New-Harmony, state of Indiana,
and Madame Maria Duclos Fre-
tageot; a letter to Mr. William
Maclure. By F. A. Ismar. [New
Harmony?] Pr. for the author,
1830. 18 p. NNC.   2014

Ives, Elam, 1802-1864.
American psalmody: A col-
lection of sacred music... By E.
Ives, Jun. and D. Dutton, Jun.
2nd ed., greatly enl. with alterations and improvements. Hartford, Pub. by H. & F. J. Huntington, Boston - Crocker & Brewster, New York, J. Leavitt;
Philadelphia, Towar, J. & D.M.
Hogan, 1830. [Cover dated 1831]
368 p. CtHT-W; CtMW; ICN; MB;
NNUT; NbU; PPL; ViRVal. 2015

J

Jack the Piper, or The pleasant
pastime of the fryar and the boy.
2d ed. Boston, 1830. 11 p.
MH.   2016

Jackson, Daniel. See Mitchell,
Isaac.

Jackson, Halliday, 1771-1835.
Civilization of the Indian na-
tives; or, A brief view of the
friendly conduct of William Penn
towards them in the early settlement of Pennsylvania... Philadelphia, Marcus T. C. Gould; New
York, Isaac T. Hopper, 1830.
120 p. CSmH; DLC; ICN; KHi;
MBAt; MH-AH; MnU; OHi; PHC;

PPL (impf.); PSC-Hi; PU;
BrMus.   2017

---- Sketch of the manners, customs, religion and government of
the Seneca Indians in 1800. Philadelphia, M. T. C. Gould, 1830.
34 p. MH; PSC-Hi; BrMus. 2018

Jackson, Henry.
Sovereignty of the divine gov-
ernment; a discourse in the First
Baptist meeting house, Charles-
ton, Mass., Nov. 1829. Boston,
William Collier, 1830. 36 p. M;
RPB.   2019

[Jackson, Isaac W.]
Remarks on Professor Silli-
man's Elements of chemistry.
New York, Pr. for the author,
1830. 24 p. CtHT-W; MB; NN;
NNNAM; NbU; NjR; PPL; BrMus.
                                 2020

Jackson, Samuel.
Introductory lecture to the institutes of medicine. Philadelphia, W. Sharpless, 1830. 35 p.
DLC; NBM; PHi; ScCC.   2021

Jacobs, Friedrich, 1764-1847.
The Latin reader... Partly
translated from the German and
partly drawn from other sources,
by John D. Ogilley... New York,
Collins & Hannay, Collins & co.,
and White Gallaher & White, 1830.
238 p. DLC; KyDC; LNHT; MH;
NNNAM; Nh.   2022

---- ---- Part second. Chiefly
from the 4th German ed. of F.
Jacobs and F. W. Doering. Bos-
ton, Hilliard, Gray, Little and
Wilkins, 1830. iv, 148 p. CtHT-
W; MH; OSW.   2023

---- ---- First part, from the
5th German ed. Stereotype ed.
Boston, Hilliard, Gray, Little and
Wilkins. Stereotyped at the Boston Type and Stereotype Foundry,
1830. 233 p. NNG.   2024

[James, George Payne Rains-
ford]
Darnley, or The field of the
cloth of gold, by the author of
"Richelieu." New York, J. &
J. Harper, 1830. 2 vols. MBL;
MH; NCH; NN; NRU.   2025

[----] De l'Orme. By the author
of "Richelieu," and "Darnley."
New York, J. & J. Harper, 1830.
2 v. in 1. CtHT; IU; MB; MH;
NCH; WHi.   2026

James, John Angell, 1785-1859.
Christian charity explained, or
The influence of religion upon
temper. Stated; in an exposition
of the thirteenth chapter of the
first Epistle to the Corinthians.
2d ed. New York, J. Leavitt;
Boston, Crocker and Brewster,
1830. 288 p. ICMcC; KyLoP;
MBC; MH; MWA.   2027

---- The Christian father's present, to his children... 6th American ed. Boston, Pub. by Leonard W. Kimball, 1830. 2 v.
MB; MdBE.   2028

---- Christian fellowship, or,
The church members guide...
Edited by J. O. Choules... 3d
American ed. From the 4th Lon-
don ed. Corr. and improved by
the author. Boston, Lincoln & Ed-
mands, 1830. CtY; IaDmD; MBC;
MWA; NjP; TxHR.   2029

---- The family monitor, or A
help to domestic happiness. From
the 3d London ed., corr. and enl.
Boston, Pub. by Crocker and
Brewster; New York, Jonathan
Leavitt, 1830. 205 p. CtY;
KyBgW; KyLoS; MB; MBC; MWA;
MeB; MiU; NR; NbHi; NhD; OClW;
PU; RPB; USlC; WHi.   2030

Jameson, Robert.
Narrative of discovery and ad-
venture in Africa, from the earli-

est ages to the present time: with illustrations of the geology, mineralogy, and zoology. New York, J. & J. Harper, 1830. 359 p. KyLo; NjR; TxU. 2031

Jane and her teachers; or, The Sunday School of Ellington. Philadelphia, American Sunday School Union [1830?] BrMus. 2032

Jaudon, Daniel, 1767-1826.
The English orthographical exposition. Being a compendious selection of the most useful words in the English language, alphabetically arranged... by Daniel Jaudon, Thomas Watson & Stephen Addington. 15th ed. Philadelphia, Towar, J. & D. M. Hogan; Pittsburg - Hogan & Co. Stereotyped by J. Howe. [Cover dated 1832] 223 p. PP; PHi. 2033

[----] A short system of polite learning, being an epitome of the arts and sciences, designed for the use of schools. By an eminent writer of Philadelphia. 9th American ed., imp. Philadelphia, Pub. by McCarty & Davis, Stereotyped by J. Howe, 1830. 198 p. MoSpD; NbHi; PHi; PSC-Hi; PU. 2034

Jay, William, 1769-1853.
The Christian contemplated in a course of lectures. Delivered in Argyle Chapel, Bath... 2d American from the last London ed. Boston, Pub. by Lincoln & Edmands. Sold also by Crocker & Brewster, Boston. J. Leavitt & J. P. Haven, N. York: at the Tract Depository; Philadelphia, by Armstrong & Plaskett, J. Jewett and Cushing & Sons. Baltimore, and by Booksellers generally, 1830. xviii, 432 p. GDC; ICU; InCW; MH; OC; OO; PHi. 2035
---- ---- 2d American ed. Philadelphia, Pr. and pub. by William Stavely, 1830. 278 p. KyBC; NN; NSyU; NbOU. 2036

No entry. 2037

---- Exercises for the closet: For every day in the year. Boston, Crocker & Brewster, and Peirce & Parker; New York, Jonathan Leavitt [Peirce & Parker, prs.] 1830. 2 vols. CBPac; CtHC; CtMW; ICMcC; MH; OO. 2038

[Jeffers, William N.]
An address to the people of the county of Salem. [Salem, 1830] 12 p. PPL. 2039

Jefferson, Thomas, 1743-1826.
Memoir, correspondence, and miscellanies, from the papers of Thomas Jefferson. Ed. by Thos. Jefferson Randolph. ...2d [Amer.] ed. Boston, Gray and Bowen; New York, G. & C. & H. Carvill, 1830. 4 v. AB; CSmH; CtSoP; CtY; DLC; GDC; GU; IaHA; ICU; KyLx; MB; MBAt; MdBJ; ScC; TNJ; TxU; ViU; WHi. 2040

Jefferson College. Canonsburg, Pa.
Catalogue of the officers and students of Jefferson College, Canonsburg. August, 1830. Pittsburgh, Pr. by D. & M. Maclean, [1830] [16] p. MHi; PWW. 2041

---- Washington, Mississippi.
Catalogue of the officers and students of Jefferson College, Washington, state of Mississippi. Natchez, Pr. by Andrew Marschalk, 1830. 12 p. CtY; DNA; MHi; NN; NjP; PPAmP. 2042

Jefferson County, O.
Proceedings of a public meeting, holden in Jefferson county,

Ohio, on the subject of the canal policy. [Steubenville?] 1830. 30 p. NN.   2043

Jefferson, Mo.
Audi[tor M]issouri, City of Jefferson, 30th December, 1830. [2] p. MoKcU.   2044

Jenkins, Charles, 1786-1831.
Three sermons on the obligations, duties, and blessings of the Sabbath. To which are added remarks on the report made to the House of Representatives of the United States, March 1830, on Sabbath mails. Portland, Pub. by Shirley, Hyde, and Co., 1830. 116, [1] p. Ct; MBC; MeHi.
                    2045

Jenkins, Henry, 1810-.
Lessons for infant Sabbath Schools: with a plan for conducting an infant class. Worcester, Pub. by Dorr and Howland [E. & G. Merriam, prs.] 1830. 108 p. DLC; OMC.   2046

Jenkins, Joseph.
An address delivered before the Grand Lodge of Massachusetts at the installation of officers, December 28, 1829. By Joseph Jenkins, G. M. Boston, Peirce & Williams, 1830. 24 p. CBPac; DLC; IaCrM; MB; MBAt; MBC; MH; MHi; MWA; MdHi; NCH; NGH; NNFM; NjR; PHi; RPB; WHi; BrMus.   2047

---- Grand Lodge, of the most ancient and honorable Fraternity of Free and Accepted Masons of the commonwealth of Massachusetts. Boston, Press of the Masonic Mirror. Moore & Sevey, 1830. 15 p. MWA; NNFM; OCM.
                    2048

Jenks, Benjamin.
Prayers and offices of devotion; for families, and for particular persons, upon most occasions. New-York, Pub. by G.

G. Sickles, 1830. 336 p. ViAl.
                    2049

Jennings, R. L.
An address delivered before the First Society of Free Enquirers in Boston, on Sunday, July 4, 1830. Boston, Hooton & Teprell, prs., 1830. 17 p. DLC; MB; MiD-B; NIC; RPB.   2050

Jeremy, George.
A treatise on the equity jurisdiction of the high court of chancery. 1st American, from the last London ed. Philadelphia, Robert H. Small [Russell & Martien, prs.] 1830. lxxii, 603 p. CSmH; In-SC; Ky; MH-L; Me-LR; MoU; NIC; NNC; OCLaw; PPB; PU; W.   2051

[Jerrold, Douglas]
The drunkard's fate, or Fifteen years of a drunkard's life; a melo drama in three acts. New-York, E. B. Clayton, 1830. 52 p. (At head of title: - Clayton's edition.) MH.   2052

Jess, Zachariah.
A key to the American tutor's assistant... Philadelphia, 1830. 215 p. DAU.   2053

Jessy and Kate; or Industry and idleness. An instructive story. For children and youth. New-Haven, S. Babcock, publisher; Charleston, S. Babcock & co., Sidney's press, 1830. 23 p. CtHi; CtY.   2054

Jesus the child's best teacher. Revised for the Committee of Publication. Philadelphia, American Sunday School Union, 1830. BrMus.   2055

[Jewett, Isaac Appleton]
Prize essay. A brief history and defence of the drama. [1830] [3], 69 p. PPL.   2056

Jim Crow. Baltimore, Pub. by
Geo. Willig, Junr. [183-?] [2] p.
CSmH.   2057

Joerres, Lewis.
  The little companion. Rule of
pure proportion, or Improvements
of common arithmetic, a new
method of calculation, performed
by Lewis Joerres. Philadelphia,
Pr. for the Author, 1830. 35 p.
PPL; PRHi.   2058

Johlson, Joseph, 1777-1851.
  Instruction in the Mosaic Re-
ligion. Translated from the Ger-
man of J. Johlson, by Isaac
Leeser. Philadelphia, Pr. by
Adam Waldie, 5590 [1830]. viii,
139 [2] p. CSmH;DLC; KyBC;
MdBC; MdBE; PHi; PPDrop;
PPL; PU; BrMus.   2059

Johnny Q. ! (i. e. John Quincy
Adams) A new song, to be sung
on Election Day. [New-York?
1830?] BrMus.   2060

Johns, Kensey.
  Speech of Kensey Johns, Jr. of
Delaware on the Indian Bill, in
...May--1830. Washington, Pr.
and pub. at the office of the Na-
tional Journal, 1830. 16 p. MWA.
                              2061
[Johnson, Richard] 1573-1659?
  The seven champions of Chris-
tendom. New York, S. King,
1830. 48 p. MH; PP.   2062

Johnson, Richard Mentor.
  Johnson's report on Sunday
Mails. In Congress, March 4,
1830. Published by Henry Bowen,
Boston [1830] Bdsd. MHi; PHi;
PPPrHi.   2063

Johnson, Samuel, 1709-1784.
  Johnson's dictionary of the
English language in miniature, to
which are added, an alphabetical
account of the heathen deities, and
a copious chronological table of

remarkable events, discoveries
and inventions in Europe, by the
Rev. Joseph Hamilton, M. A. ...
1st Albany from the last English
ed. Pub. by Wm. Disturnell,
Albany, 1830. 295 p. CtY; NUtHi.
                              2064
---- Dictionary, improved by
Todd abridged for the use of
schools. With the addition of
Walker's pronunciation, an abstract of his Principles of English pronunciation with questions,
a vocabulary of Greek, Latin and
Scripture proper names, and an
appendix of Americanisms. Boston, Carter and Hendee, 1830.
MH.   2065

---- Johnson's English dictionary,
as improved by Todd, and
abridged by Chalmers; with
Walker's pronouncing dictionary,
combined. To which is added,
Walker's Key to the classical
pronunciation of Greek, Latin,
and Scripture proper names.
Boston, Pub. by Perkins and Marvin, and Hilliard, Gray, Little &
Wilkins, 1830. 1156 p. GDC;
IU; KyLoF; KyU; MdBL; WBB.
                              2066
Johnson, Walter Rogers, 1794-
1852.
  Observations on the Electrical
Characters of Caoutchouc, or
Gum Elastic; with some applications of which they are suscept-
ible. By Walter R. Johnson,
M. A. N. S. P. Professor of Mechanics and Natural Philosophy in
the Franklin Institute. (Read Ap-
ril 20, 1830) 8 p. MH; MWA;
PP.   2067

---- Remarks on the duties of
the several states, in regard to
public education... Philadelphia,
Pr. for the author, by William
Sharpless, 1830. 8 p. CtY; DLC;
MH; OClWHi; PPL; PPi; RPB.
                              2068
Johnston, David Claypole, 1797-

1865.

Scraps for the year 1830. Designed and etched by D. C. Johnston. Boston, 1830. MBAt; PP. 2069

---- A splendid procession of free masons. Just published; drawn & engd. by Gebalibus Crackfordi, M.D., LL.D. &c. [Boston? 1830?] Bdsd. MB. 2070

Johnston, Josiah Stoddard.

The removing power. Extracts from Mr. Johnston's speech on Mr. Foot's resolution in the Senate. [1830] 12 p. PPL. 2071

---- Speech (in continuation) of Mr. Josiah S. Johnston, of Louisiana: the resolution of Mr. Foot, ... April 2, 1830. Washington, Pr. by Gales & Seaton, 1830. [43], 76 p. MWA. 2072

---- Speech of Mr. Johnston, of Louisiana, on the power of a state to annul the laws of the Union: The resolution of Mr. Foot, of Connecticut, relative to public lands, being under consideration. ... April 2, 1830. Washington, Pr. by Gales & Seaton, 1830. 22 p. PPL. 2073

---- ---- March 30, 1830. Washington, Pr. by Gales & Seaton, 1830. 40 p. MWA; PPL. 2074

[----] Strictures on Mr. Lee's exposition of evidence on the sugar duty, in behalf of the committee appointed by the free trade convention. [Signed Hambden] [1830] 18 p. PPL. 2075

Jones, Elizabeth C.

Infantine ditties... Providence, Cory, Marshall and Hammond, 1830. 24 p. DLC. 2076

Jones, James.

Practical forms of writs,

processes, &c. selected from the most approved precedents and adapted to the laws of ... Illinois... Galena [Ill.] Pr. and pub. by the author, 1830. 164 p., 1 l., 52, 10 p. CSmH; DLC; ICHi; ICN; IHi; NRAB. 2077

Jones, John Paul, 1747-1792.

Life and correspondence of John Paul Jones, including his narrative of the campaign of the Liman. From original letters and manuscripts in the possession of Miss Janette Taylor. Stereotyped by A. Chandler. New York [D. Fanshaw, pr.] 1830. 555 p. CSmH; Ct; CtHT; CtY; DLC; DeGE; DeWi; ICN; Ia; KHi; LNHT; MB; MHi; MMeT; MnHi; MoS; NBLiHi; NN; NcU; NjR; OClWHi; PPPrHi; PU; RPB; TN; ViU; VtU; WHi; BrMus. 2078

Jones, John Richter, 1803-1863.

An address delivered at a town-meeting of the Anti-masonic citizens of Philadelphia, Oct. 5th, 1830. Philadelphia, Clarke, 1830. 15 p. IaCrM; MB; PP; PPAmP; WHi. 2079

Jones, Samuel T.

Specifications of two patents for a new railroad car, denominated the pendulous rail-road car, and for a mode... of adapting rail-way cars... to run on ordinary roads... and also of enabling carts... to run securely upon rail-roads. Granted to Samuel T. Jones, of Philadelphia, on the 22d day of February, 1830. To which are appended remarks by the editor of the Journal of the Franklin Institute... Philadelphia, 1830. [2], 8 p. "From the Journal of the Franklin Institute, for March and April 1830." DeGE; MWA; NbO; PPAmP; PPL. 2080

Jones, Thomas.

The practical dyer containing

a collection of choice receipts
for producing all the most common and permanent colours on
cotton, woolen silk, and linen...
New York, Pr. for the publisher,
1830. 24 p. MWA.   2081

Jones, Thomas P.
    Charge addressed to the grad-
uates in medicine, at the commencement of the Medical Department of the Columbian College, D.C. March 10, 1830.
Washington, Gales & Seaton,
1830. 12 p. PPL.   2082

No entry.   2083

Josephus, Flavius.
    The works of Flavius Joscphus,
the learned and authentic Jewish
historian and celebrated warrior.
With three dissertations concerning Jesus Christ, John the Baptist, James the Just, God's command to Abraham, etc., and explanatory notes and observations.
Trans. by William Whiston. Stereotype ed. Baltimore, Armstrong & Berry [183-?] 648 p.
CtMW; CtY; GEU-T; MB; MdBE;
MdBS; MoS; NRU; NbL; Nh; OC;
PU; TN.   2084

Journal of the convention, holden
at Windsor, Vermont, September
29-30, for the purpose of taking
into consideration subjects connected with the improvements of
the navigation of the Connecticut
River. Published by order of the
convention. Windsor, Pr. by

Simeon Ide, 1830. 19 p. DLC;
MH; MiD; Nh; Vt; VtU.   2085

Judson, Roswell, 1769-1835.
    Two epistles of free stricture
on the American dictionary of
Mr. Webster, on the Hebrew
grammar and Hebrew chrestom-
athy of Mr. Stuart, and on the
manual Hebrew lexicon of Mr.
Gibbs... 2nd rev. ed. New
Haven, Herald office, 1830. 67,
[1] p. CSmH; CtHT-W; CtY;
MBAt; MH-AH; NN; NjN; OCl;
TxU; ScHi.   2086

Juicio imparcial sobre los acontecimientos de Mexico, en 1828
y 1829. See Zavala, Lorenzo de.

Julia changed; or, The true se-
cret of a happy Christmas.
Philadelphia, American Sunday
School Union [1830?] BrMus.
                             2087

Junius, pseud.
    The letters of Junius. ...Bos-
ton, Reed [Pr. by J.H.A. Frost,
Boston] 1830. 2 v. DLC; KyLxT;
KyU; LNB; MH; MdBP; MiD-B;
NIC; NRU; OCl; OO; ScU; THi;
WHi.   2088

Justice, pseud. See Reply to
Censor.

The juvenile almanac; or, series
of monthly emblems [for 1831]
New-York, Mahlon Day [1830]
12 1. NIC.   2089

Juvenile anecdotes; or A present
for a good child. New-Haven,
S. Babcock, publisher...S. Babcock & Co., Charleston. Sidney's
press, 1830. 23 p. CtHi; MH.
                             2090
The juvenile cabinet: no. 152 -
Memory; no. 153 - Children of
the Hartz Mountains; no. 155 -
The Pilgrims. Philadelphia, The
American Sunday School Union,
1830. 36 p. OO; BrMus.   2091

Juvenile casket. With engravings. Worcester, Pub. by J. Grout, Jr. [183-?] 24 p. CtY; NN.   2092

Juvenile poems. Wendell, Mass. J. Metcalf, 1830. 18 p. MA; MNF; MWA.   2093

K

Kames, Henry Home, Lord, 1696-1782.
   Elements of criticism. New York, Collins & Hannay, 1830. 476 p. CU; CtY; DLC; KyU; LNHT; NjP; ViU.   2094

Kanawha Co., Va. Manufacturers of Salt.
   Memorial of the manufacturers of salt in Kanawha county, Virginia: Praying for a restoration of the duty on imported salt. Addressed to the Senate and House of Representatives of the United States. Kanawha C. H. Virginia, Pr. at the office of the Kanawha Banner, 1830. 19, 7 p. CSmH; DLC; MB; ScU; WHi.   2095

Kelley, Hall Jackson, 1790-1874.
   A geographical sketch of that part of North America, called Oregon... Boston, Pr. and pub. by J. Howe, 1830. 80 p. CSmH; CtY; DLC; ICN; LNHT; MBAt; MBC; MH; NBLiHi; NN; NhHi; OMC; OrHi; PHi; WHi; BrMus.   2096

Kellogg, Ezra B.
   War contrary to the gospel. A sermon, preached before the Peace Society of Windham County, February 4, 1830... Pub. by request. Providence, H. H. Brown, pr., 1830. 32 p. Ct; CtY; MB; MBAt; MBC; MH; MHi; MWA; MeB; MiD-B; NNC; RHi; RP; RPB; BrMus.   2097

Kemble, Charles, 1775-1854.

The point of honor; a play, in three acts. Taken from the French. By Charles Kemble. Baltimore, Pr. and pub. by J. Robinson, Circulating library and Dramatic repository, 1830. 48 p. DLC; KU; MH; MWA.   2098

Kendall, James, 1769-1859.
   A sermon delivered at the ordination of Hersey Bradford Goodwin as colleague pastor with Ezra Ripley, D.D. of the Congregational Church and Society in Concord, Mass. Concord, Pub. at the Gazette Office [I. R. Butts, pr.] 1830. 38 p. CSmH; ICU; MB; MBAt; MBC; MCon; MH; MHi; MWA; MiD-B; MnHi; NN; OClWHi; RPB; BrMus.   2099

[Kennedy, John Pendleton] 1795-1870.
   A review of Mr. Cambreleng's report from the Committee of Commerce, in the House of Representatives, at the first session of the Twenty first Congress. By Mephistopheles. Baltimore, Pr. by Wm. Ogden Niles, 1830. 72 p. CSmH; CtY; DLC; DeGE; ICU; IU; KyDC; LNHT; MB; MH; MHi; MdHi; MiD-B; NIC; NN; NNC; NcD; Nh; PHi; PPAmP; PPL; PU; RPB; Vi; WHi.   2100

[Kenney, Lucy]
   Alexander the great, or, The learned camel. [Washington, D.C., 1830?] 12 p. CSmH; DLC.   2101

[Kennicott, James H.]
   ...Irma; or, The prediction, a tragedy in five acts. New York, E. B. Clayton, 1830. 56 p. (At head of title: Clayton's edition.) CSmH; ICU; MH; NN; NcU; WM.   2102

Kenrick, John.
   Complete course of exercises in Latin syntax; adapted to Zumpt's grammar. New York, G. & C. & H. Carvill, 1830. vii,

200 p. LShC; MB; MH; MdBS;
MoS; NGH; ViU.   2103

Kentucky.
    Acts passed at the first ses-
sion of the thirty-eighth General
Assembly for the commonwealth
of Kentucky, begun and held in
the town of Frankfort, on Monday
the seventh day of December, in
the year of our Lord one thousand eight hundred and twenty-
nine... Frankfort, J. G. Dana
and A. G. Hodges, public prs.,
1830. 312 p. KyBgW; KyHi;
KyU; MiD-B; NNLI; Nb; NcAS;
Nj; Nv; RPL; T; W.   2104

---- Journal of the House of
Representatives of the commonwealth of Kentucky begun and
held in the town of Frankfort, on
Monday the seventh day of December in the year of Our Lord
1829... Frankfort, Pr. by A. G.
Meriwether, pr. for the State,
1829 [i. e. 1830] 350 p. InU; Ky;
KyU.   2105

---- Journal of the Senate of the
commonwealth of Kentucky, begun
and held in the town of Frankfort, on Monday the seventh day
of December, in the year of our
Lord 1829... Frankfort, Pr. by
A. G. Meriwether, pr. for the
state, 1829 [i. e. 1830] 317 p.
Ky; KyLo; NdHi; TNJ.   2106

---- Report of the Committee on
Education, of the House of Representatives of Kentucky, on so
much of the governor's message
as relates to schools and seminaries of learning. 2d ed. --2000
copies. Lexington, Ky., Pr. by
Joseph G. Norwood, 1830. 52 p.
CtY; DLC; ICU; KyDC; MBC;
MH; MHi; NbU; NcD; NjR; OO;
PHi; PPL; PU; ScCC.   2107

---- Reports of cases at com-

mon law and in equity, argued
and decided in the Court of Appeals of the commonwealth of
Kentucky. By Thomas B. Munroe.
Vol. VII.   Commencing with the
14th day of April 1828. Frankfort, Pr. by Albert G. Hodges,
1830. vi, 2-738 p. KyBgW;
KyLxT; KyU-L; MdBB; N-L.
                                 2108
---- Resolutions of the General
Assembly of Kentucky upon the
American system of tariff, and
in answer to certain proceedings
of the legislatures of South-Carolina, and other states, concerning the powers of the general
government in relation to the
tariff, and internal improvements.
Frankfort, K., Dana and Hodges,
1830. 23 p.   MWA; BrMus. 2109

Kentucky Colonization Society.
    First annual report of the
Kentucky Colonization Society,
Auxiliary to the American Soci-
ety for Colonizing the Free
People of Colour in the U. States.
Frankfort, J. H. Holeman, pr.,
1830. 16 p. KyDC.   2110

Kentucky Reporter, Lexington,
Ky.
    Address of the carrier of the
Kentucky Reporter. New-Year's
day, 1830. [Lexington, Ky.,
1830] 12 p. DLC.   2111

Kerr, Alexander.
    Brief memorials of four chil-
dren.   Boston, Peirce & Williams, 1830. 67 p. DLC; MH.
                                 2112
Key, Francis Scott, 1779-1843.
    Daniel Murray, late Lieutenant
in the American Navy. From a
letter of the Hon. Francis S.
Key, United States attorney of
the District of Columbia. [New
York, American Tract Society,
183-?] 4 p. (American Tract
Society, New York [Publications.
Separates)] No. 441) CSmH. 2113

A key to knowledge; or, Things in common use, simply and shortly explained in a series of dialogues. Written by a Mother. A new edition. Baltimore, Pub. by Mordecai Stewart, R. J. Matchett, pr. [183-?] 132 p. MdHi. 2114

Key to the first step in teaching children to read according to the lesson system of education. 1st American from 3d Edinburgh ed. New-York, J. Leavitt [etc., etc.] 1830. MH. 2115

Kidwell, Jonathan.
A series of strictures on the subject of future and endless punishment: being the substance of the arguments used in a public debate held at Indianapolis, Jan. 21, 1830, on that subject, between the Rev. E. Ray and the publisher. Cincinnati, Pr. by S. Tizzard, 1830. 74 p. OCHP; OClWHi; PPPrHi. 2116

Kilbourn, John.
A geography of the state of Ohio. Designed for common schools. Columbus, O., E. Glover, 1830. 72 p. DLC; O. 2117

Kilpin, Samuel, 1774-1830.
Memoir of Rev. Samuel Kilpin, of Exeter, England; with some extracts from his correspondence. To which is added his narrative of Samuel Wyke Kilpin, his only surviving child, who died at the age of thirteen. New York, Pub. by the American Tract Society, D. Fanshaw, pr. [183-?] 156 p. ViU. 2118

Kimball, Daniel.
Address delivered before the Needham Temperance Society by Daniel Kimball... Dedham, H. & H. W. Mann, prs., 1830. [3], 16 p. DLC; MBAt; MBC; MH; NN; RPB; BrMus. 2119

King, D. C.
New and rich goods cheap!!! D. C. King, having lately supplied his store in Groton... opposite the first parish meeting house. Lowell, Journal press... [1830?] Bdsd. MHi. 2120

King, Job, 1778- .
Life, death and confession of Capt. Job King. [Providence, 183-?] 7 p. MB. 2121

King, Jonas.
Extracts of a letter from Jonas King, missionary to western Asia, addressed to his friends in Syria, just before his departure from that country, as published in the Missionary Herald, for May, 1828. Baltimore, 1830. 10 p. PPL. 2122

King Andrew the first, "Born to Command." [n. p., 183-] Bdsd. DLC. 2123

[Kingsley, James Luce] 1778-1852, comp.
Extracts for translation. Used by the students of Yale College. New Haven, Pr. by H. Howe, 1830. 72 p. CtY; MH. 2124

Kippis, Andrew, 1725-1795.
A narrative of the voyages round the world, performed by Captain James Cook. ... Boston, Pub. by N. H. Whitaker, 1830. 2 v. in 1. CSfCP; CtMW; LNX; MdHi; NNC; OMC; WHi. 2125

Kirkham, Samuel.
English grammar in familiar lectures. ... New York, Robert B. Collins. Stereotyped ed. [1830] 228 p. ViU. 2126

---- ---- 11th ed., enl. and improved. Stereotyped by Wm. Hagar & Co., New York. New York, Pub. by the author, Marshall, Dean & Co., prs., Rochester, 1830. 228 p. P.   2127

---- ---- 16th ed. , enl. and
improved. New York, Stereotyped by Wm. Hagar & Co. , Pr.
and pub. by M'Elrath & Bangs,
1830. 228 p. PLFM.   2128

---- ---- 17th ed. , enl. and improved. Stereotyped by Wm. Hagar & Co. , New York. Cincinnati, Morgan & Sanxay, prs. ,
1830. 228 p. KyLxT; OC; OO;
P; PLFM.   2129

---- ---- To which are added,
an appendix, and a key to the
exercises; designed for the use
of schools and private learners.
Stereotyped by Wm. Hagar & Co. ,
New York. 18th ed. , enl. and
improved. Cincinnati, Morgan &
Sanxay, 1830. 228 p. OC; OO;
P.   2130

---- ---- 20th ed. , enl. and imp.
New York, M'Elrath & Bangs,
1830. MH.   2131

---- ---- 21st ed. , enl. and imp.
New York, 1830. 228 p. CtY;
MH; NSyU.   2132

Kirtland, Dorance, 1770-1840.
    A treatise on the practice in
Surrogates' Courts in the state of
New York; with a historical view
of the origin of the probate of
wills, granting letters of administration, and the office of surrogate, in this state, and under the
British Government. And the
amendments passed fifty-third
session. Albany, William & A.
Gould & Co. ; New York, Gould,
Banks & Co. [Chauncey Goodrich, pr. , Burlington, Vt.] 1830.
vi, 213 p. CtY; K; MiD-B;
NBuG; NN; NNU; NRAL; VtU; WU.
                          2133
Kitchiner, William, 1775-1827.
    ... The cook's oracle; and
Housekeeper's manual. Contain-

ing receipts for cookery, and directions for carving... With a
complete system of cookery for
Catholic families... being the result of actual experiments instituted in the kitchen of William
Kitchiner, M.D. Adapted to the
American public by a medical
gentleman. From the last London ed. New-York, J. & J.
Harper, 1830. 432 p. CtY; IU;
IaU; KU; LNT; MBC; NRHi; NcA-
S; NcU; ViU; WHi.   2134

Kite's town and country almanac
for 1831. By William Collom.
Philadelphia, Thomas Kite [1830]
18 1. CLU; CtY; MWA; N; NjR;
PHi; PP.   2135

Kittredge, Jonathan, 1793-1864.
    An address, delivered before
the Temperance Society of Plymouth, N. H. July 4, 1829. Boston, Pub. by Peirce & Williams,
1830. 24 p. CSmH; MB; MBC;
MH-AH; MWA; NNC; Nh; OO;
BrMus.   2136

Kleines Gesangbuch. Allentown,
Penn. , Blumer, 1830. KyDC.
                          2137
Knapp, Samuel Lorenzo, 1783-
1838.
    An address delivered before
the New-England Society, on the
22d of December, 1829. New-
York, Pr. and sold by G. F.
Hopkins & Son, 1830. 22 p. CtY;
ICN; IaCrM.   2138

[----] Sketches of public characters. Drawn from the living
and the dead... By Ignatius Loyola Robertson (pseud.) New
York, Pub. by E. Bliss, and
sold by G. & C. & H. Carvill
[etc.], G. L. Austin & Co. , prs. ,
1830. 259, [1] p. CSmH; CtHT-
W; CtY; DLC; ICN; LNHT; MBAt;
MHi; MiD; MnM; NIC; NNC; NNS;
NUtHi; NcD; NjR; P; PLFM;
PPL; PU; RPB; TxU; WHi;

BrMus. 2139

Kneeland, Abner.
A review of the evidences of Christianity, in a series of lectures, delivered in Broadway Hall New York, August, 1829... 2d ed. New York, Pub. at Tammany Hall. Also, at the office of the Free Enquirer, and by the author, 1830. 204 p. DLC; ICMe; IEG. 2140

Knickerbocker's almanac for 1831. By David Young. New York, Caleb Bartlett [1830] 12 l. MB; MWA. 2141

---- ---- New-York, C. Brown [1830] 18 l. InU; MWA; N. 2142

Knowles, James Davis, 1798-1838.
Life of Mrs. Ann H. Judson, late missionary to Burmah; with an account of the American Baptist mission to that empire. Prepared for the American Sunday School Union; by James D. Knowles... Revised by the committee of publication. Philadelphia, American Sunday School Union, 1830. 266 p. CtHT-W; CtY; DLC; KyBgW; NbOM; NjP; OO; PHi; PPL; PPeSchw; RHi; ScCliTO; BrMus. 2143

Knowles, James Sheridan.
Appendix to rudiments of gesture; consisting of a debate on the character of Julius Caesar. ...Designed for practical exercises in declamation. [1], 1 [i.e. 50] p. PPL. 2144

[Knowles, Jonathan]
A statement of facts, relative to the building of the meeting house, for the Methodist Society, in Lowell. Pr. for the author, 1830. 8 p. MBC. 2145

Knoxville Female Academy, Knoxville, Tennessee.
Catalogue of the trustees, instructors and students of the Knoxville Female Academy. Summer Session, 1830. Knoxville, T., Pr. by F. S. Heiskell, 1830. 12 p. TU (Not located) 2146

Koch, Christophe Guillaume de, 1737-1813.
Tableau des revolutions de l'Europe... Hartford, 1830. ViU. 2147

Kozeluch, Leopold, 1754-1818, arranger.
John Anderson my jo, a Scotch air sung by Sinclair. Arranged by Kozeluch. Boston, Pub. by C. Bradlee [183-?] 3 p. CSmH. 2148

Kuhn, Joseph L.
Correspondence between Captain Joseph L. Kuhn, of the U. S. Marines, and the officers of the government. Washington, Pr. by Peter Force, 1830. 64 p. CtY; DLC. 2149

L

Labarraque, Antoine Germain, 1777-1850.
Method of using the chloride of soda, either for dressing ill-conditioned sores or as a means of disinfecting animal substances. New Haven, H. Howe, 1830. 7 p. Ct; CtHT-W; CtY; DLC; DNLM; MBAt; MHi; MWA; MeB; PPAN; ScC. 2150

Lacock, Abner, 1770-1837.
Letter from Abner Lacock... to the Hon. David Scott, esq., president of the board of canal commissioners, of Pennsylvania ...Pittsburgh, "Statesman" print, 1830. 1 p. l., 31 p. DLC; PPL. 2151

The ladder of learning; to be as-
cended early in the morning. New
Haven, S. Babcock, Sidney's
press, 1830. 17 p. CtHi; DLC.
                                2152

A lady, pseud.   See The child's
diadem.

A lady, pseud.   See Pinckney,
Maria Henrietta.

A lady, pseud.   See Stringer,
Mrs.

A lady, pseud.   See Wirt, Mrs.
Elizabeth W. G.

A lady of New Hampshire.   See
Conversations on the Burman
mission.

A lady of Philadelphia.   See Leslie, Eliza.

A lady of Philadelphia, pseud.
See Reflections and tales.

Laennec, René Théophile Hya-
cinthe, 1781-1826.
   A treatise on the diseases of
the chest and on mediate auscul-
tation.   Translated from the lat-
est French ed., with notes and a
sketch of the author's life, by
John Forbes... From the 3d rev.
London ed., with additional notes.
New York, S. Wood & sons [etc.]
[R. & G. S. Wood, pr.] Phila-
delphia, J. Grigg [etc.] 1830.
xxviii, 736 p. GEU-M; GU-M;
IU; IaU; KyLxT; LNOP; MBCo;
MdBM; MeB; MoSMed; MsU;
NNNAM; Nh; OCU-M; PU; RPM;
TNJ; ViU.   2153

Lafitte; or, The Baratarian chief.
A tale.   To which is added: The
sea voyage, by Richard Penn
Smith.   Hamilton, Williams, Or-
ton & Co., 1830. 117 p. CSmH;
CtY; MBAt.   2154

Lamb, J.

The dog.   Burlington, C.
Goodrich, 1830. 16 p. MB. 2155

[Lamb, Jonathan]
   The American primer; or,
First book for primary schools.
Burlington, C. Goodrich, 1830.
36 p. CtSoP; DLC; NN; VtU.
                                2156
[----] Gospel sonnets, or poems
on various religious subjects in
three parts; designed principally
for youth.   Written by a layman.
Burlington, Pr. for the author,
1830. 174 p. ICN; IU; RPB;
WHi.   2157

[----] Reflections on war, by a
Layman.   Published by the Minot Peace Society.   Portland,
Shirley, Hyde & Co., prs.,
1830.   12, [2] p. Ct; RPB. 2158

The lamb.   New York, M. Day,
pr. [1830] Bdsd. PPL.   2159

Landon, Letitia Elizabeth.
   The Venetian bracelet, The
lost pleiad.   A history of the
lyre.   Boston, Cottons & Barnard, 1830. viii, 236 p. MBL;
MnU; RP; RPA; RPB.   2160

Landrum, Abner.
   The Edgefield hive, containing
original essays and selections on
various subjects. Pottersville,
S. C., 1830.   NN Imprints catalogue.   2161

Lane Theological Seminary, Cincinnati.
   Annual report of the trustees,
with a Catalogue... January,
1830. Cincinnati, 1830.   Sabin
38861.   2162

Larkin, N. I.
   Elementary geometry, both
linear, plane, and solid. Boston,
Pub. by Perkins & Marvin, 1830.
64 p. MH; NNC.   2163

Larkins, Edward.
An original essay on the knowl-
edge and foreknowledge of God.
Philadelphia, Pr. by Samuel
Neall & Co., 1830. 40, [2] p.
PHi.   2164

The lark's nest. Philadelphia,
American Sunday School Union,
[1830?] BrMus.   2165

The late duel. See Drake, R.
Dillon.

[Lathrop, John Hiram]
An address to the people of
the United States on the subject
of the Anti-Masonic excitement,
or new party. By a citizen of
New York. Albany, Pr. by J. B.
Van Steenbergh, 1830. 31 p.
IaCrM; MA; MB; MBC; MiD-B;
N; PU.   2166

[Lathrop, John Hiram]
An address to the people of
the United States on the subject
of the Anti-Masonic excitement,
or new party. By a citizen of
the United States. Rochester, Pr.
by Tuttle & Sherman, 1830. 18 p.
NRHi.   2167

Latimer, Thomas, comp.
Moral and religious gleamings
or interesting stories. Philadelphia, William Stavley, 1830.
InU.   2168

Latrobe, John Hazelhurst Bone-
val.
The eulogium of Ephriam
Barker, late member of Phoenix
R. A. Chapter, no. 7. ...deliv-
ered at the request of Phoenix
Royal Arch Chapter...November,
A. L. 2830. ...Baltimore, Pr.
by J. Robinson, 1830. 16 p.
IaCrM.   2169

Lavater, Johann Caspar, 1741-
1801.
Aphorisms on man. Tr. from

the original manuscript of the
Rev. John Caspar Lavater; citi-
zen of Zuric... 1st American ed.
Lancaster, Pr. and sold by W.
Albright, 1830. 140 [2] p.
CSmH; DLC; MWA; NN; P; PPL;
PU.   2170

[Law, Thomas] 1756-1834.
An address to the Columbian
Institute, on the question, "What
ought to be the circulating medi-
um of a nation?" ... Washington,
Pr. by Gales & Seaton, 1830.
39 p. DLC; DeGE; LNHT; MB;
PPL; BrMus.   2171

Law, William.
Humble, earnest, and affec-
tionate address to the clergy...
To which is prefixed a short ac-
count of the author. Exeter,
N. H., Stereotyped by James &
Sawyer, for the publishers, 1830.
192 p. CtHi; MBC; OO; RP.
                              2172

---- A third letter to Dr. Hoadley, Bishop of Bangor; being a
reply to his representation of the
committee of convocation. Philadelphia, Pr. by Jesper Harding,
1830. 132 p. CBCDS; CtHT;
LNB; MdHi; MeBaT; MoS; NNG;
NjR; RNR.   2173

---- Two letters to Dr. B.
Hoadley, Bishop of Bangor, in
defence of Episcopacy. Philadel-
phia, Pr. and pub. by Jasper
Harding, 1830. 92 p. CBCDS;
CtHT; ICU; MdHi; MeBaT; MoS;
NN; NNG; NjR; RNR.   2174

Lawrence, John.
The horse in all his varieties
and uses; his breeding, rearing
and management, whether in labour or rest; with rules occa-
sionally interspersed, for his
preservation from disease. Philadelphia, E. L. Carey & A. Hart
[etc.] 1830. [2], 238 p. [12] p.
ads. CSmH; MDeeP; MH; MeBaT;

NBM; NIC; OClW; P; <u>PPL</u>; TNJ;
ViU.   2175

[Lawrence, Joshua]
The North-Carolina Whig's
apology, for the Kehukee Association. Tarborough, Pr. at the
Office of the "North-Carolina
Free Press," 1830. 56 p. NcU.
                                  2176
---- A patriotic discourse delivered by the Rev. Joshua Lawrence, at the old church in Tarborough, North Carolina, on Sunday, the Fourth of July, 1830.
n. p. 1830.   23 p. NCH; WHi;
BrMus.   2177

Lawrence & Lemay's North Carolina almanack for 1831. By Dr.
Hudson M. Cave.   Raleigh, Lawrence & Lemay [1830] 18 1. MH;
MWA; NcD.   2178

[Lawson, James]
Tales and sketches, by a cos-
mopolite.   New-York, Elam Bliss
[Thos. Snowden, pr.] 1830. 4 1.,
[5], 256 p. CSmH; ICU; MH;
MWA; NCH; NN; NNS; RPB;
BrMus.   2179

The lawyers' common-place book,
with an alphabetical index of most
of the heads which occur in general reading and practice. Boston,
Hilliard, Gray, Little and Wilkins, 1830.   3 ledger type vols.
with printed title page and index;
all other pages blank, to be filled
in by the lawyer. GU.   2180

A layman, pseud.   See Chandler,
A.

A layman, pseud.   See Lamb,
Jonathan.

Lea, Pryor.
Circular of Mr. Lea to his
constituents of the Second congressional district of Tennessee.
Knoxville, Tenn., Pr. by F. S.

Heiskell, 1830. 16 p. T.   2181

---- Speech of Mr. Prior Lea,
of Tennessee on the bill proposing to construct a national road
from Buffalo to New Orleans...
Washington, Pr. by D. Green,
1830. 15 p. DLC; ICU; NN. 2182

Leavitt, Dudley.
The teacher's assistant, and
scholar's mathematical directory
... Concord, Pub. by Marsh
Capen and Lyon, 1830. 109, [7]
p. CtHT-W; Nh; NhHi; RPB;
BrMus.   2183

Leavitt, Joshua, 1794-1873.
The Christian lyre... Stereo-
typed by A. Chandler. New
York, Pub. by J. Leavitt, at the
Theological Bookstore; Sleight &
Robinson, prs., 1830. [4], 213,
[7] p. MBC; MeBaT.   2184

---- ... Easy lessons in reading,
for the use of the younger classes
in common schools.   3rd ed.
Watertown, N. Y., Pub. by Knowlton & Rice, 1830. 156 p. CtHT-
W; DLC.   2185

---- ---- Keene, N. H., Pub.
by J. & J. W. Prentiss [Stereo-
typed by T. H. Carter & Co.,
Boston] 1830.   156 p. MPB.
                                  2186
---- Seamen's devotional assistant and mariners' hymns.   Prepared under direction of the American Seamen's Friend Society.
Stereotyped by A. Chandler. Pub.
by the Society at their office.
New York, Sleight & Robinson,
pr., 1830.   512 p. CtY; ICN;
MH-AH; MWA; MeBaT; NNUT;
RNHi.   2187

Leavitt's.   The improved farmer's and scholar's almanack for
1831.   By Dudley Leavitt. Concord, Horatio Hill & Co.; Hill
and Barton, prs. [1830] 12 1.

DLC; MB; MBAt; MHi; MWA;
NBLiHi; NhHi.   2188

---- Issue with 24 l. CLU; ICU;
InU; MBC; MWA; MdBJ; MiD-B;
MnU; N; NHi; NcD; NhHi; OClWHi;
WHi.   2189

[Lee, Mrs. Hanna Farnham
(Sawyer)]
    Grace Seymour... New York,
Elam Bliss, 1830. 2 v. in 1.
CSmH; CtHT; IU; PU.   2190

Lee, Henry.
    Oration on the great Washing-
ton. [Boston, 1830] MH.   2191

Lee, Thomas Jones, 1785-1835.
    The national class book; a se-
lection of exercises in reading,
for the higher classes in common
schools. Hallowell [Me.] Glazier,
Masters & co., 1830. 288 p.
DLC.   2192

---- The primary class book; a
selection of easy lessons in reading for the younger classes in
common schools... 4th ed. Hallowell, Pr. and pub. by Glazier,
Masters and Co., 1830. 179 p.
OOxM.   2193

---- A spelling-book, containing
the rudiments of the English language. With appropriate reading
lessons. Boston (Mass.), 1830.
BrMus.   2194

Legendre, Andrieu Marie, 1752-
1833.
    Elements of geometry...
Translated from the French for
use of university students at
Cambridge, New England. By
John Farrar... Boston, Hillard,
Gray, Little, & Wilkins, 1830.
xvi, 224 p. CoG; KMK; MH;
OCX.   2195

---- ---- Trans. from the
French by David Brewester. 2d

ed. New-York, White, Gallaher
& White; Collins & Hannay; and
J. Ryan, 1830. 316 p. (Revised
and altered for the use of the
Military Academy at West Point.)
CtB; CtMW; InU; MH; MdHi;
NCH; NNC.   2196

Le Guire, Amos.
    A juvenile poem, entitled The
Heliad; or, Christ, the Light of
the world... Cooperstown, [N.Y.]
Pr. by H. & E. Phinney, 1830.
60 p. CSmH; N; RPB.   2197

Lehigh Coal and Navigation Co.
    Report of the board of man-
agers... Philadelphia, Pr. by
Timothy A. Conrad, 1830. 16 p.
DBRE; DIC; DLC; IU; MH; MWA;
MiU-T; NN; P; PPAmP.   2198

Leib, James R.
    Lecture on the nature and ob-
jects of the modern philosophy.
Delivered Saturday, November
20, 1830, before the members of
the Franklin Institute. Philadelphia, Clark & Raser, prs.,
1830. 16 p. MB; MBAt; MH;
PPL.   2199

---- Lecture on scientific education... December 18, 1830, before the ... Franklin Institute...
Philadelphia, Clark & Raser,
prs., 1830. 16 p. MBAt.   2200

[Leigh, Benjamin Watkins] 1781-
1849.
    The letters of Algernon Syd-
ney, in defence of civil liberty
and against the encroachments of
military despotism, written by
an eminent citizen of Virginia,
and first published in the Richmond Enquirer in 1818-19. To
which are added, in an appendix,
the remarks of Mr. Ritchie as
referred to by the author of "Algernon Sydney" in page 30 of
this pamphlet. With an introduction by the present publisher.

Richmond, Pr. and pub. by T. W.
White, 1830. viii, 65 p. CSmH;
CtHT-W; CtY; DLC; ICU; IaU;
MBAt; MBC; MH; MdHi; MeBaT;
NIC; NbU; NjR; OClWHi; OkHi;
PHi; PPL; RPB; ScU; TN; TxU;
Vi; ViU.   2201

Leland, John, 1754-1841.
    Short sayings on times, men,
measures and religion, exhibited
in an address, delivered at Che-
shire, July 5, 1830. By John Leland... Pittsfield [Mass.] Pr. by
Phinehas Allen and son [1830?]
24 p. CSmH.   2202

Lempster, N. H. Congregational
Church.
    Confession of faith, adopted by
the Congregational Church in
Lempster, N. H. October 29,
1829. Concord, Statesman Office; Asa M'Farland, pr., 1830.
11 p. MBC.   2203

Leonard, Levi Washburn, 1790?-
1864.
    The literary and scientific
class book. Keene, N. H., J. &
J. W. Prentiss, 1830. 318 p.
MH.   2204

---- Sequel to Easy lessons. A
selection of reading lessons.
Keene, N. H., Pub. by J. and J.
W. Prentiss, 1830. 214 p. CSmH;
CtHT-W; CtHi; MWA; MiU; NN;
Nh; NhHi.   2205

Le Ray de Chaumont, James
Donatien, 1760-1840.
    Address delivered before the
Jefferson County Agricultural Society, at the annual cattle show,
28th September, 1830. [Water-
town? N. Y.] 1830. 28 p. Ct;
DLC; MB; MiD-B; NN; PPAmP.
                                  2206
Leroy, Louis.
    Curative medicine, or purga-
tion, directed against the cause
of diseases, discovered by Doc-

tor Leroy, of Paris. Translated
from the 12th ed. by Gabriel
Paul of St. Louis... St. Louis,
Pub. by G. Paul from the Repub-
lican Press, 1830. 169 p. DLC;
NN.   2207

Leslie, Charles.
    A short and easy method with
the Deists... New York, New
York Protestant Episcopal Tract
Society [No. 36] Pr. at the Protestant Episcopal Press, 1830.
40 p. MBD; MH; NNUT; PPL.
                                  2208
---- ---- Philadelphia, Pr. and
pub. by J. Harding, 1830. 107
p. CBCDS; CtHT; ICU; IEG;
MdHi; MeBaT; MoS; NNG; NjR;
PPL (Lacks last p.); RNR.   2209

---- Subjects of divine revelation in A letter to a converted
deist... New York, New York
Protestant Episcopal Tract Society, 1830. 23 p. NNG.   2210

[Leslie, Eliza] 1787-1858.
    ... Seventy-five receipts for
pastry, cakes, and sweetmeats.
By a lady of Philadelphia. 2d
ed. Boston, Munroe and Francis, etc., etc., 1830. [10], [7]-
104 p. At head of title: Third
edition. With an appendix. MH.
                                  2211
Lessons without books. See
Sedgwick, Catherine Maria.

Lester, Ebenezer A.
    Lester's pendulum steam en-
gine. Boston, August 2, 1830.
16 p. MH; MH-BA; MWA. 2212

Letamendi, Augustin de.
    Introduction to the French lan-
guage, with classical, analytical,
and synthetical elucidations...
Columbia, Pr. for the author by
S. J. McMorris, 1830. 130 p.
PU; ScU.   2213

A letter from a young woman to

a member of the Religious Society of Friends, with his reply.
Philadelphia, Pub. by John Townsend, John Richards, pr., 1830.
8 p. PHC; PPL; PSC-Hi.   2214

A letter on the Unitarianism.
See Huidekoper, Harm.

Letter to Rev. John N. Maffet,
by a member of the Zettetick
Society. Portsmouth, N.H., January, 1830. 11 p. NhHi.   2215

Letter to the editor of the Courier and Enquirer, in reply to an
article... on the college question. [New York, 1830] 4 p.
CtHT; MB; PPAmP.   2216

Letters addressed to Martin Van
Buren... See Corrector, pseud.

Letters addressed to the editor
of the Banner of the Constitution.
Charleston [T. Town, pr.]
January 16, 1830. 11 p.
NN; PPAmP.   2217

Letters of a Catholic in answer
to the "Protestant." New York,
Pr. by J. McLoughlin, 1830.
62 p. DGU; NRSB; PPCCH. 2218

The letters of Algernon Sydney.
See Leigh, Benjamin Watkins.

Letters of Christian sympathy to
mourners. Baltimore, Pub. by
John Midwinter, R. J. Matchett,
pr., 1830. 142, [2] p. MdHi;
PPL; PRHi; PSC.   2219

Letters on Methodism: or some
remarks on the spirit, doctrines,
disciplines, management, and
general influence of the Methodist Episcopal Church in the
United States of America. Pub.
by Lewis Merriam, 1830. 46 p.
Ct; MBC; MiU.   2220

Letters to George M'Duffie.

See Brutus, pseud.

Leverett, Frederick Percival,
1803-1836.
...The new Latin tutor; or
Exercises in etymology, syntax
and prosody; compiled chiefly
from the best English works.
Boston, Hillard, Gray, Little and
Wilkins, 1830. 350 p. [Stereotype
ed.] CLSU; CtHT-W; DLC; KHi;
LNB; MH; MHi; NN; NNC; TxU-
T.   2221

Levizac, Jean Pons Victor Le-
coutz de, d. 1813.
A theoretical and practical
grammar of the French tongue;
in which the present usage is
displayed, agreeably to the decisions of the French academy.
Rev. and cor. by Mr. Stephen
Pasquier... 7th American ed.,
with Voltairian orthography, according to the dictionary of the
French Academy. [Stereotyped
by A. Chandler] New York, W.
E. Dean, Collins & co. [etc.]
1830. x, 444 p. CtY; KyU; MH;
MiDU; TxU-T; ViU.   2222

Lewis, Matthew Gregory, 1775-
1818.
Ambrosio; or, The monk. A
romance. New York, J. A.
Clussman, 1830. 3 v. in 2. DLC;
PEL.   2223

---- ... Timour the Tartar; a
grand romantic melodrama, in
two acts. New-York, E. B.
Clayton [Clayton & Van Norden,
prs.] 1830. 40 p. (Clayton's
ed.) MH; NCH.   2224

Lewis, Samuel, of Philadelphia.
The state of New York
[New York, 183-] Folded map.
MB.   2225

Lewis, Thomas.
Little Jane, a memoir of Jane
E. J. Taylor. 1st American

from the 4th London ed. New
York, Jonathan Leavitt; Boston,
Crocker and Brewster, 1830. 94
p. MWA.   2226

Lexington. See Wetmore, Prosper Montgomery.

Lexington and Ohio Rail Road
Company.
    An act to incorporate the Lex-
ington and Ohio Rail Road Company, n. p. [1830] 11 p. DBRE;
MiU-T; NN.   2227

Lexington, Ky. Eclectic Insti-
tute.
    Prospectus of the Rev. Mr.
Peers's school, to be known
hereafter by the name of the Ec-
lectic Institute and conducted by
Rev. O. Peers, Mr. H. Hulbert
Eaton, and Mr. Henry A. Gris-
wold. Lexington, Ky., Pr. by
Joseph G. Norwood, 1830. 20 p.
CSmH; ICU; KyLo; KyU; MH;
MHi; MoSM; PU.   2228

Lhomond, Charles François,
1727-1794.
    Elements of French grammar
... Trans. from the French, with
notes, and such illustrations as
were thought necessary for the
American pupil. For the use of
schools. By an instructor. Portland, Samuel Colman; Brunswick,
Griffin's Press, 1830. viii, [3]-
108 p. CSmH; CtMW; DLC; IEG;
MB; MBAt; MH; MeHi; NBuU;
NNC.   2229

---- French exercises selected
chiefly from Wanostrocht and
adapted to the elements of French
grammar by M. Lhomond... By
an Instructer [sic] Portland,
Samuel Colman; Brunswick, Griffin's Press, 1830. viii, 102 p.
CSmH; CtY; MB; MH; NBuU;
NNC.   2230

---- ... Viri illustres urbis

Romae, a Romulo ad Augustum.
... Edito Novi-Eboraci, emendata
et stereotypa. To which is added
a dictionary... By James Hardie.
New-York, Georg Long, 1830.
vii, 136, [108] p. At head of
title: [Stereotype Edition] ViU.
                           2231
---- Viri Romae; with introduc-
tory exercises... By Frederic
P. Leverett and Thomas G.
Bradford. Boston, Hilliard, Gray,
Little, and Wilkins, 1830. 2,
209 [1] p. DLC; ICMcC; MB;
MH; NNC; OMC; RNR.   2232

Liability of Stockholders in manufacturing corporations: reasons
for repealing the laws of Massachusetts which render the members of manufacturing companies
personally liable for their debts.
Boston, 1830. 12 p. MHi.   2233

The life of Africaner, a Namac-
qua chief, of South Africa. Revised by the committee of publication. Philadelphia, American
Sunday School Union [1830?] 35
p. ICN.   2234

The life of Archbishop Leighton,
with brief extracts from his writings. New York, American
Tract Society, 1830. Christian
biography No. 2. 60 p. CtW;
MBC; WHi.   2235

The life of John Frederic Oberlin, pastor of Waldbach, in the
Ban de La Roche. Compiled for
the American Sunday School Union, and revised by the Committee of publication. Philadelphia,
American Sunday School Union,
1830. 140 p. CtHC; CtY; DLC;
GDC; ICN; KWiU; LU; MB; MBC;
MH; MMeTHi; OClWHi; OO; PHC;
PHi; PU; ViRUT.   2236

The life of Saint Patrick, Apostle
of Ireland. To which is added
the celebrated hymn, composed

above twelve hundred years since, by his disciple, St. Fiech; comprehending A Compendious History of his Life. Baltimore, Pub. by Fielding Lucas, Jun'r [183-?] 192 p. MdW. 2237

Life of Sir William Wallace. See Carrick, John D.

The life of the Rev. C. F. Swartz, missionary of Trichinopoly & Tanjore in India. New York, American Tract Society, 1830. 60 p. CtW; NhHi. 2238

The life of the Rev. John Wesley, A. M. abridged from authentic sources by a friend of Sabbath schools. New York, Pub. by J. Emory and B. Waugh, for the Methodist Episcopal Church, at the Conference office. J. Collard, pr., 1830. 104 p. CtW; NjMD. 2239

The life of the Rev. Thomas Coke... Abridged from authentic sources. By a Friend of the Sabbath Schools. Pub. by J. Emory and B. Waugh, for the Methodist Episcopal Church. New York, J. Collord, pr., 1830. 88 p. CtMW; IEG; NcD. 2240

[Lillo, George]
[George Barnwell] [New York, Pub. by D. Longworth, 183-?] 64 p. Imperfect all material before p. [7] wanting. CSmH. 2241

The lily, a holiday present, with steel embellishments. New York, E. Sands [1830] 232 p. DLC; MB; MH. 2242

[Lincoln, Solomon] 1804-1881.
Sketch of Nantasket: (now called Hull,) in the county of Plymouth. First pub. in the Hingham gazette. Hingham [Mass.] Gazette press, 1830. 16 p. DLC; MH. 2243

Lincoln Academy, Wiscasset, Me.
Laws of Lincoln Academy. Wiscasset, Citizen's Press [A. Herrick, pr.] 1830. 8 p. MeHi. 2244

Lindl, Ignaz, 1774-1834.
Der Kern des Christenthums, nebst einer Abhandlung über die Sünde wider den heiligen Geist, in Predigten vorgetragen. Harrisburg (Pa.), Gustav S. Peters, 1830. 108, 58 p. MH; P; PHi; PLT. 2245

Linn, William.
An oration delivered in the Presbyterian meeting-house, in the village of Ithaca, at the celebration of the fifty-fourth anniversary of American independence, July 5, 1830. Ithaca, Mack, 1830. 11 p. NCH. 2246

List and dates of appointment of the Spanish governors of Louisiana between 1769 and 1800... [New Orleans, 1830] 11 p. PPL. 2247

Little, Peter.
To the freemen of Baltimore City and County... Peter Little [183-] 1 p. DLC. 2248

The little child's book. Boston and New York, C. S. Francis and Co. [1830] MH; RPB. 2249

---- New York, Blakeman & Mason, [c 1830] 64 p. DLC. 2250

Little Edward. (A story.) Philadelphia, American Sunday School Union [1830?] BrMus. 2251

Little Lucy and her lamb. See My father, a poem.

The little philosopher. See Abbott, Jacob.

Little poems for little readers. Worcester, Pub. by J. Grout, Jr. [183-] 16 p. NN. 2252

The little present for a good
child. Wendell, Mass. , J. Metcalf, 1830. 17 p. MHa.   2253

Little Schuylkill Navigation, Rail
Road and Coal Company.
    The act, and supplements
thereto, authorising the incorporation of the Little Schuylkill Navigation, Rail Road and Coal Company. Reading, Douglass W.
Hyde, 1830. 33 p. MB; MWA.
                                       2254
The little songster for good children. Bouckville [N. Y.] Sta-
tioner's company [183-?] 16 p.
RPB.   2255

The little story book...Revised
by the Committee of Publication.
Philadelphia, American Sunday
School Union [1830?] BrMus.
                                       2256
Little Susan and her lamb. New-
York, Pr. by Mahlon Day, 1830.
17 p. CtHi.   2257

---- Boston, Wait, Greene and
Co. [c1830] 6 p. DLC; PP. 2258

Lives of remarkable youth of
both sexes. Philadelphia, E.
Littell, 1830. 222 p. MB; MBC;
MH; MWA; NjP; PU.   2259

Lives of the Evangelists. See
Hildreth, Hosea.

Livingston, Edward, 1764-1836.
    Speech of Mr. Livingston, of
Louisiana, on Mr. Foot's resolution, proposing an inquiry into
the expediency of abolishing the
office of Surveyor general of
public lands, and for discontinuing further surveys, &c. Delivered in the Senate of the United
States, Feb. 29, 1830. Charleston, Pr. by J. S. Burges, 1830.
24 p. CSmH; ICU; MH; MHi;
MWA; MiU; PPAmP; PU; ScC.
                                       2260
---- ---- Washington, Pr. by

Duff Green, 1830. 58 p. DLC;
MH; PPL.   2261

Lobstein, Johann Friedrich Daniel, 1777-1835.
    A treatise upon the semeiol-
ogy of the eye, for the use of
physicians; and the countenance,
for criminal jurisprudence...
New York, C. S. Francis. Philadelphia, Towar & Hogan, [etc. ,
etc.] J. Seymour, pr. , 1830.
175, [5] p. CSt-L; DNLM; ICJ;
MBCo; MiU; NBM; NIC-V;
NbU-M; OCGHM; PPL; PU.
                                       2262
Locke, John, 1632-1704.
    ...Some thoughts concerning
education, by John Locke: and
a Treatise of education, by John
Milton... Boston, Pub. by Gray
& Bowen [Samuel N. Dickinson,
pr.] 1830. 15, viii, [1], 317 p.
The library of education. CtHC;
DLC; ICU; KWiU; MH; MdBJ;
MdW; MeB; MoS; NPV; OMC;
PPDrop; PPF; PPL; PU.   2263

Lockhart, John Gibson.
    The history of Napoleon Bona-
parte. New York, Pub. and pr.
by J. & J. Harper, 1830. 2 vols.
(Harper's stereotype ed.) DLC;
MDeeP; MHi; MdBP; NN; NNS;
NjR; RPB; TN.   2264

London: a descriptive poem.
New York, Pub. by Samuel Wood
and sons [1830?] MB.   2265

Long, Stephen Harriman, 1784-
1864.
    Description of the Jackson
bridge, together with directions
to builders of wooden or frame
bridges. Patented March, 1830.
Baltimore, Pr. by Sands & Neilson, 1830. 24 p. DBRE; DLC;
MdHi; MiU-T; NIC; NN; PPAmP.
                                       2266
---- Narrative of the proceed-
ings of the board of engineers,
of the Baltimore and Ohio Rail-

Road Company, from its organization to its dissolution, together with an exposition of facts, illustrative of the conduct of sundry individuals. Baltimore, Pr. by Bailey & Francis, 1830. 2 v. 189, 95 p. CSt; CtY; DBRE; DLC; MH; MWA; MiU-T; N; NN; NNC; PPL.   2267

Long Island and Farmer's almanack for 1831. New York, David Felt [1830] MWA.   2268

Long Island Bible Society.
    The fifteenth annual report of the Long Island Bible Society, Brooklyn, Sept. 15, 1830. Brooklyn, A. Spooner, 1830. 26 p. NBLiHi.   2269

Long Island Sound Harbour Company.
    An act to incorporate the Long Island Sound Harbour Company, passed April 16, 1830. New York, Pr. at the office of the New-York Amulet, 1830. 12 p. NN.   2270

[Longfellow, Henry Wadsworth], ed.
    French exercises: Selected chiefly from Wanostrocht... Portland [Maine] Samuel Colman, 1830. 102 p. CSmH.   2271

[----] Manuel de proverbes dramatiques... Portland, Samuel Colman; Brunswick, Griffin's press, 1830. 2 p. l., [3]-188 (i. e. 288) p. CSmH; DLC; ICU; MB; MH; NNC; NjP; PPL; PU; TxU.   2272

Longworth's American almanac, New-York register, and city directory for the fifty-fifth year of American independence... New York, Pub. by Thomas Longworth [J. Seymour, pr.] 1830. 1 v., various pagings. NNS; RNHi.   2273

A looker-on. See To the members of the Legislature.

Loomis' calendar, or the New-York and Vermont almanack for 1831. Albany, G. J. Loomis [1830] 12 l. CtHi; MWA; MnU; N; NHi; NT.   2274

De l'Orme. See James, George Payne Rainsford.

The lost children. Providence, Cory, Marshall and Hammond [1830] 15 p. RPB.   2275

The lost heir. See Power, Tyrone.

...The lost opportunity; or, Some account of Robert Careless. Baltimore, Pub. by the Protestant Episcopal Female Tract Society, John D. Toy, pr., 1830. 8 p. Series of tracts. No. 75. PPL.   2276

The lottery ticket. See Beazley, Samuel.

A loud call to the living!!! A short account of three men that were killed by lightning at Suffield, May 20, viz. Samuel Remington, James Bagg, Jonathan Bagg [Cuts] [Three columns of verse] [183-?] 1 p. DLC. 2277

Louisa's tenderness. See Berquin, Arnaud.

Louisiana.
    Acts passed at the second session of the ninth legislature of the state of Louisiana, begun and held in Donaldsonville, on Monday [Jan. 4, 1830]...Donaldsonville, C. W. Duhy, state pr., 1830. 156 p. IU; LNHT; LU.   2278

---- Answer of the central committee of the sugar planters of the state of Louisiana, to the cir-

cular of the hon. S.D. Ingham,
secretary of the treasury, dated
1st. July 1830. [New Orleans?
1830?] 7 p. MB.　　　　2279

---- Directions taken from an
act passed in the state of Louisiana providing for the inspection of beef and pork in the city
of New Orleans. [183-?] 1 p.
DLC.　　　　2280

---- Journal de la chambre des
representans de l'état de la Louisiane, neuvieme législature,
seconde session. Tenue a Donaldsonville, le quatrieme jour
du mois de janvier, A.D. mil
huit cent trente. Donaldsonville, C. W. Duhy, imprimeur de
l'état, 1830. 111 p. LU.　2281

---- Journal du senat de l'état
de la Louisiane, neuvième législature, seconde session, tenue à
Donaldsonville. Donaldsonville,
La., C. W. Duhy, imprimeur de
l'état, 1830. 68 p. LNHT.　2282

---- Journal of the House of
Representatives of the state of
Louisiana, Ninth legislature second session begun and held in
the town of Donaldsonville, on
the fourth day of January A.D.
eighteen hundred and thirty. Donaldsonville, C. W. Duhy, state
pr., 1830. 112 p. DLC.　　2283

---- Journal of the Senate of the
state of Louisiana, ninth Legislature, second session, begun and
held in the town of Donaldsonville, on the fourth day of January, 1830. Donaldsonville, La.,
C.W. Duhy, state pr., 1830. 68
p. LNHT.　　　　2284

The Louisiana almanack for 1831.
By Elijah Middlebrook. New-
Orleans, Benjamin Levy [1830]
18 l. AU.　　　　2285

Louisville, Ky.
An account of the Louisville
city school, together with the
ordinances of the city council and
the regulations of the board of
trustees, for the government of
the institution. Louisville, Pr.
by Norwood & Palmer, 1830.
24 p. KyLo; MHi; OCHP; PPL.
　　　　2286
Louisville and Portland Canal
Company.
Fifth annual report of the president and directors of the Louisville and Portland Canal Company.
[Louisville, 1830] Pr. on pages
1 and 2 of a 4-page fold. WHi.
　　　　2287
Lovechild, Mary.
Studies and stories by Mary
Lovechild. Boston, Pub. by Carter, Hendee, and Babcock [Cam-
bridge, E. W. Metcalf & Co.]
1830. [4], 86 p. MB.　　2288

[Lowe, R.]
Sacred to the memory of the
illustrious Champion of liberty
General George Washington...
[New York] John I. Donlevy, engr.
[183-?] Bdsd. CSmH.　　2289

Lowell, Charles.
The wisdom and goodness of
God in the appointment of men,
and not angels, to the Christian
ministry. A sermon, preached
in Berlin, at the ordination of
Mr. Robert Folger Wallcut, February 10, 1830. Boston, Pub.
by Leonard C. Bowles, 1830.
32 p. CtHC; CtSoP; ICMe; MBAt;
MBC; MH; MHi; MWA; MiD-B;
NNG; NjPT; PHi; RPB; BrMus.
　　　　2290
Lowell, Mass.
Report of a joint committee
of the city council on the public
schools and school houses in
Lowell. [183-?] 8 p. M.　2291

Lowville Academy.
Catalogue of the trustees and

students... for the year 1830, ending on the 15th of September. [Lowville? 1830] [2] p. NN. 2292

Lucas, Fielding, Jr., 1781-1854, comp.
A new and elegant general atlas, containing maps of each of the United States. Baltimore [183-?] 3 p., 31 maps. MB. 2293

Luis de Grenada.
The memorial of a Christian life. By the Rev. F. Lewis de Granada. Revised edition. Baltimore, Pub. by F. Lucas, Jr. [183-?] 264 p. MdW. 2294

Lumpkin, Wilson, 1783-1870.
Speech of Mr. Wilson Lumpkin, of Georgia, on the bill providing for the removal of the Indians. Delivered in the House of Representatives of the United States, May, 1830. Washington, Pr. by Duff Green, 1830. 19 p. DLC; GU-De. 2295

Lunt, George.
A lecture delivered before the Newburyport Lyceum, October 15, 1830. ...Newburyport, Pr. by W. & J. Gilman, 1830. 16 p. CtSoP; MBAt; MBC; MiD-B; MNe; RPB. 2296

Luther, Martin, 1483-1546.
A selection of the most celebrated sermons of Martin Luther, minister of the gospel and principal leader in the Protestant reformation. (Never before published in the United States.) To which is prefixed, a biographical history of his life. New York, S. & D. A. Forbes, prs., 1830. 204 p. CtHC; MeBaT; NBF; TxDaM. 2297

Lyman, Huntington.
An address delivered before the Temperance Society of Franklinville, at their annual meeting in Sept., 1830. New York, Henry C. Sleight, 1830. 15 p. MBAt; MBC; MiD-B; PPPrHi; WHi. 2298

Lynch, James.
[Campaign document. Tuscaloosa, 1830] 1 p. DLC. 2299

Lynchburg, Va.
Report of the watering committee to the common council of the corporation of Lynchburg, relative to the water works. Lynchburg, Fletcher, 1830. 12 p. NN; NcD. 2300

Lynn, a poem. See Mudge, Enoch.

[Lytton, Edward George Earl Lytton Bulwer-Lytton, 1st baron] 1803-1873.
Falkland... by the author of "Pelham" ... Philadelphia, Carey & Lea, 1830. 192 p. CSmH; CtHT; LNHT; NGH; PHi. 2301

[----]---- New York, Pr. by J. and J. Harper, 1830. (At head of title: Harper's stereotype ed.) 117 p. CtHT-W; MB; NIC. 2302

[----] Paul Clifford: By the author of "Pelham," "The Disowned" "Devereux;" In two volumes. New York, Pr. by J. & J. Harper, 1830. 2 vols. MB; NRU; TNJ. 2303

M

McAllister, A.
A dissertation on the medical properties and injurious effects of the habitual use of tobacco... Utica, Press of W. Williams, 1830. 24 p. DLC; NCH; NN; NNNAM; NUt. 2304

M'Calla, William Latta, 1788-1859.
A correct narrative of the

proceedings of the Presbytery of
Philadelphia, relative to the re-
ception and installation of Mr.
Albert Barnes: with three letters
in answer to one, relative to the
aforesaid proceedings. Philadelphia, Russell & Martien, 1830.
40 p. GDC; MH-AH; NcMHi;
NjP; NjPT; NjR; OCHP; PHi.
                                    2305
M'Carter's country almanac for
1831. By David Young. Charleston, J. J. M'Carter [1830] 18 l.
MWA.   2306

[McClung, John Alexander] 1804-
1859.
    Camden; a tale of the South...
Philadelphia, Carey & Lea, 1830.
2 v. CSmH; CtY; DLC; MnU;
PU; ScU; Vi; BrMus.   2307

M'Corkle, S. M.
    Thoughts on the Millenium,
with a comment on the Revela-
tions; also a few remarks on
church government. Nashville,
Pr. at the Republican and Gazette
Office, 1830. 82 p. 2 l. NN.
                                    2308
Macculloch, John, 1773-1835.
    An essay on the remittent &
intermittent diseases, including, generically, marsh fever &
neuralgia... Philadelphia, Carey
& Lea, 1830. 474 p. ArU-M;
CSt-L; IC; ICJ; KyLxT; LNOP;
LNT-M; MBCo; MdBM; MeB;
NNNAM; NjR; OCGHM; PPC.
                                    2309
[MacDill, David]
    An address occasioned by the
opposition which originated in
Cincinnati, Ohio, against the attempt to stop the Sabbath mails;
delivered in the Associate Reformed Church in Hamilton, on
the last Sabbath in December
1829. Newburgh, C. U. Cush-
man, 1830. 16 p. MH; NCH;
PLT.   2310

McDowell, Joseph Nash.

An introductory lecture, on
the causes obstructing the progress of medical science... Published at the request of his
class. Cincinnati, Williamson &
Wood, prs., 1830. 19 p. CSmH;
OCHP; OClWHi.   2311

---- A valedictory address, delivered by appointment, before
the Medical and Philosophical Society of Ohio, at the close of its
winter session, February 27,
1830. Cincinnati, March, 1830.
ICU; OCHP.   2312

McDuffie, George, 1790-1851.
    Mr. McDuffie's speeches
against the prohibitory system;
delivered in the House of Representatives, in April & May,
1830. [Washington, 1830] 72 p.
CSmH.   2313

---- National and state rights,
considered by the Hon. George
M'Duffie, under the signature of
One of the people, in reply to
the "Trio," with the advertisement prefixed to it, generally
attributed to Major James Hamilton, jr. when published in
1821. Charleston, W. S. Blain,
1830. 40 p. CU; DLC; MBAt;
MH; MHi; NB; PHi; PU; ScU.
                                    2314
---- The reply of the Honourable
George McDuffie on the prohibitory system. [Charleston? 1830]
28 p. (t. p. wanting) ICU.   2315

---- Speech of Mr. M'Duffie
against the prohibitory system in
the House of Representatives,
April, 1830. Columbia, Pr. at
the office of the "Southern Times"
1830. 68 p. N; ScU.   2316

---- Speech of Mr. McDuffie, of
South Carolina, against the prohibitory system... April, 1830.
Washington, Pr. by Duff Green,
1830. 29 p. NcU.   2317

---- The speech (of the Hon. George McDuffie) on the tariff, delivered in the House of Representatives, April 26, 1830. [Charleston? S. C., 1830] 31 p. (t. p. wanting) ICU.   2318

M'Elroy, Joseph.
A sermon, delivered Jan. 10, 1830, in the Scotch Presbyterian Church in Cedar street, New York, on the occasion of the death of Rev. John M. Mason... New York [Sleight & Robinson, prs.] 36 p. DLC; ICMcC; MB; MBC; MiU-C; NjPT; NjR; PHi.
        2319

M'Farlane, Alexander.
An essay on the use of ardent spirits, as an article of common drink and traffic. Carlisle, Pr. by George Fleming, 1830. 48 p. NN; NNUT; OOxM; PPiPT. 2320

MacFarlane, Charles, 1799-1858.
The Armenians. A tale of Constantinople. Philadelphia, Carey and Lea [E. & G. Merriam, pr.] 1830. 2 v. DLC; MB; PU; RPA; ViAl.   2321

MacGowan, John, 1726-1780.
The life of Joseph, the son of Israel, in eight books. From a late London edition. Woodstock, Vt., Pub. by Colton & Smith; Rufus Colton, pr., 1830. 163 p. DLC; PU.   2322

[McHenry, James] 1785-1845.
The betrothed of Wyoming. An historical tale...3d ed. Philadelphia, Sold by the principal booksellers; and in New York, Boston, Baltimore and Washington, 1830. 231 p. CSmH; CtHT-W; DLC; ICN; MB; MH; MWA; MiD-B; NN; NjP; OClWHi; P; PHi; PPL; PU; VtU.   2323

---- Feelings of Age, to which is added the Star of Love; poems ...2d ed. Philadelphia, Banks

& brother, 1830. PPAmP; RPB; BrMus.   2324

---- The pleasures of friendship, and other poems. 4th American ed. Philadelphia, John Grigg, J. Harding, pr., 1830. vi p., 2 l., [13]-200 p. MH; MdBJ; RPB.   2325

---- ---- 5th American ed. Philadelphia, J. Grigg, 1830. 1 p. l., [v]-vi p., 2 l., 13-200 p. DLC; MH; PHi; TxU.   2326

McIlvaine, Charles Pettit.
The temple of God; or The holy Catholic church and communion of saints, in its nature, structure and unity. Philadelphia, Protestant Episcopal Book Society, 1830. 143 p. PPPrHi. 2327

McKeen, Silas, 1791-1877.
The triumph of Christ's enemies no cause of discouragement; a sermon delivered at Winthrop, June 21, 1830 on the evening previous to the meeting of the general conference of Maine... Portland, Pr. by Shirley, Hyde & Co., 1830. [3]-26 p. CSmH; CtHC; CtY; DLC; MBAt; MBC; MeBaT; MeLB; RPB.   2328

---- The watchman's report. A sermon delivered in Bradford, Vt. on Thanksgiving day, December 3, 1829... Haverhill, N.H., Post press, Henry F. Evans---printer, January, 1830. 18 p. CSmH; MBAt; MBC; NhHi; NjR.   2329

[Mackenzie, Alexander Slidell] 1803-1848.
A year in Spain. By a young American...2d ed. New York, Pub. by G. & C. & H. Carvill, Hilliard, Gray and Co., Boston, 1830. 2 v. GEU; InGrD; LNHT; MWH; Md; MeU; NRHi; NRU; NWM; Nh; NjPT; O; OO; PPL;

Vi.   2330

Mackenzie, Colin.
Mackenzie's five thousand re-
ceipts; in all the useful and do-
mestic arts; constituting a com-
plete practical library relative to
agriculture, bees, bleaching...
A new American, from the latest
London ed. By an American
physician. Philadelphia, J. Kay,
Jun.; Pittsburgh, J. I. Kay &
Co., 1830. 456 p. ICJ; MB;
NjP; NjR; OC; OHi.   2331

---- ---- Adapted to the convenience, necessities and means
of the western states. Published
by Taylor Webster. At the Telegraph office. Hamilton, Ohio,
1830. 312 p., 2 l. ICHi; InR.
                              2332
Mackintosh, Sir James, 1765-
1832.
The history of England. ...
Philadelphia, Carey & Lea [Ster-
eotyped by J. Howe] 1830-33. 3
v. CtHT; CtY; DLC; MH; MdBP;
MiD; MoSpD; NN; NNUT; NcA-S;
Nh; NjP; O; PPL; RNR; ViU.
                              2333
M'Knight, John.
An address delivered May 16,
1830, at the consecration of the
new church in St. Thomas.
Chambersburg, Pa., Pr. by J.
Pritts [1830?] 15 p. OCHP; PHi.
                              2334
Mackray, William.
Effect of the reformation upon
civil society. By William Mack-
ray... New York, John P. Haven
[etc., etc.] 1830. 143, 48 p.
NNUT; OO.   2335

Maclaurin, Robert.
The pious shepherd; or Life
and character of James Wait.
Boston, Pub. by James Loring,
1830. 108 p. LNB.   2336

McLellan, Isaac, 1806-1899.
The fall of the Indian, with

other poems. By Isaac McLellan,
jun. ...Boston, Carter and Hen-
dee, 1830. 99 p. CSmH; CtHC;
CtHT-W; DLC; IU; MB; MDeeP;
MH; MiD; MnU; NBLiHi; NCH;
NNC; PU; RPB; TxU; WHi;
BrMus.   2337

MacLeod, Donald.
The orator's text book: Containing a variety of passages in
prose and verse, selected as exercises in reading and recitation;
also a debate ... to which is
prefixed an introduction, containing Mr. Knowles's Abstract of
Walker's system. Washington
City, Pub. by Pishey Thompson;
Rothwell & Ustick, prs., 1830.
xi, 300 p. CSmH; CtHT-W; DLC;
MB; MH; MdBS; OOxM.   2338

MacMahon, Bernard, 1775?-1816.
American gardener's calender;
adapted to the climates and seasons of the United States. 8th ed.
imp. Philadelphia, A. M'Mahon,
1830. 618 p. MH.   2339

MacMillan, John, 1752-1833.
A sermon: Sin abounding and
grace superabounding. Pitts-
burgh, Pub. by request. Pr. by
D. & M. Maclean, 1830. 23 p.
PWW.   2340

McMurray, William.
A sermon occasioned by the
death of Col. Henry Rutgers,
preached in the church in Market
Street, February 28th, 1830.
New York, Rutgers Press, 1830.
40 p. MBC.   2341

M'Naughton, James, 1796-1874.
A discourse delivered at the
anniversary meeting of the Kappa
Alpha Phi Society of the College
of Physicians and Surgeons of the
Western District. Albany, Pr.
by Websters and Skinners, 1830.
23 p. DLC; MB; N; NBuU-M;

NNNAM; NjR; OCHP; <u>PPL</u>. 2342

---- An enquiry into the present
system of medical education, in
the state of New-York... By an
observer. Albany, Pr. by Websters and Skinners, 1830. 16 p.
MH; N; NN; NNC; NNNAM; NjR;
WHi; BrMus.   2343

McNeill, William Gibbs.
    To the stockholders of the
Baltimore and Ohio Rail-Road
Company. [Baltimore, 1830]
36 p. DBRE.   2344

[McNemar, Richard]
    A revision and confirmation of
the social compact of the United
Society called Shakers, at Pleasant Hill, Kentucky... Published by
order of the church. Harrods-
burg, Ky., Pr. by Randall and
Jones, 1830. 12 p. CSmH; DLC;
ICN; NN; OClWHi.   2345

McPherson, Richard W.
    To the citizens of Charles
County. Fellow countrymen: Circumstances beyond my control
have delayed until this late period
any notice, from me, of a publication signed by Daniel Jenifer of
24th Nov. last. ...December 18,
1830. 2 p. DLC.   2346

Macquin, Ange Denis, 1756-1823.
    Description of the picture
"Christ rejected by the Jews..."
Boston, F. S. Hill, 1830. 15 p.
MB; NN.   2347

---- ---- Now exhibiting at the
Hall of Independence. By A. D.
M'Quinn... Philadelphia, Pr. by
Garden and Thompson, 1830. 16
p. <u>DLC</u>; KyDC; MBAt; MDeeP;
MH; MHi; MWA; MdBJ; MdHi;
MiD-B; P; <u>PPL</u>; ScU; WHi;
BrMus.   2348

Madden, Richard Robert, 1798-

1886.
    The Mussulman. ...Philadel-
phia, Carey & Lea [Griggs &
Dickinson, prs.] 1830. 2 v.
MBAt; MDeeP; MH; NGH; NNS;
<u>PPL</u>; RPA; ViU.   2349

---- Travels in Turkey, Egypt,
Nubia and Palestine, in 1824,
1825, 1826 and 1827. Philadel-
phia, Carey & Lea [Griggs &
Dickinson, prs.] 1830. 2 vols.
CtHT-W; GHi; KyHi; MB; MWA;
MdAS; NNS; P; <u>PPL</u>; PU; RPA;
TNJ.   2350

Maffitt, John Newland, 1794-1850.
    Christmas sermon, on the
subject of primitive Christianity,
delivered in the Methodist Church
in John street, Dec. 25, 1830.
New York, Pub. by H. R. Piercy
& co., prs., 1830. 15 p. MB.
                                 2351
---- A plea for Africa. A sermon delivered at Bennet street
church, in behalf of the American Colonization Society, July 4,
1830... Boston, Putnam & Hunt,
1830. 14 p. CSmH.   2352

---- ---- Boston, E. W. Critten-
den, 1830. 14 p. DLC; MBAt;
MWA; MdBJ; OO; PHi; PPPrHi;
RP.   2353

Magdalen Society.
    Report of the managers of the
Magdalen Society, for 1829.
[Philadelphia, 1830] 12 p. PPAmP;
<u>PPL</u>.   2354

MaGendie, François, 1783-1855.
    Formulary for the preparation
and employment of several new
remedies... Trans. from the 6th
ed. of the Formulaire of Mr.
Magendie... New York, Repr. by
J. J. Harper for F. & N. G.
Carnes, 1830. 145, 18 p. MBCo;
MiDW-M; NIC-M; NRAM; ViRA.
                                 2355
Magie, David, 1795-1865.

Debts; the substance of three sermons, delivered in the Second Presbyterian Church, Elizabethtown... Elizabeth-Town, Pr. by Sanderson & Brookfield, 1830. 32 p. CSmH; IU; MB; MH-AH; N; NCH; NjP; NjR; WHi.   2356

The mail robbers. Report of the trials of Michael Mellon, the Lancaster mail robber: And George Wilson and James Porter alias May, the Reading Mail Robbers... Taken in short hand by John Mortimer. Philadelphia, Pub. by J. Mortimer, 1830. 2 l., 160 p. KyDC; MBAt; MH-L; MoU; N-L; NNLI; PHi; PP; PPAmP; PPL.   2357

Maine.
An abstract of the laws and regulations relating to the Cumberland and Oxford Canal. Portland, Pr. by Thomas Todd, 1830. 18, [2] p. MeHi.   2358

---- The annual report of the warden of the state prison, and documents accompanying the same. Portland, Day & Fraser, prs. to the state, 1830. 10 p. Me-LR; MeHi.   2359

---- Documents accompanying the Governor's message, relating to the road from Baring to Houlton. Portland, Day & Fraser, prs. to the state, 1830. 16 p. Me-LR; MeHi.   2360

---- Laws of the state of Maine, to which are prefixed the Constitution of the United States and of said state, with an appendix. Hallowell, Glazier, Masters & Co., 1830. iii, [1], 682, xcv, [1] p. MeAu; Mi-L; Nj.   2361

---- Letter from the treasurer of the state to the president of the Senate, and the speaker of the House of Representatives, trans-

mitting his annual report on the state of finances, Dec. 31, 1830. Portland, Day & Fraser, prs. to the state, 1830. 32 p. MeHi.   2362

---- Message of the governor of Maine, to both branches of the Legislature, February 10, 1830. Printed by order of the House. Portland, Day & Fraser, prs. to the state, 1830. 18 p. MeHi; Mid-D.   2363

---- Opinions of the Justices of the Supreme Judicial Court, in answer to questions propounded by the Hon. Nathan Cutler, late acting Governor, and by the Council. Portland, Day & Fraser, prs. to the state, 1830. 8 p. MeB; MeHi.   2364

---- Private acts of the state of Maine, passed by the tenth Legislature at its session held in January, 1830. Published agreeably to the Resolve of the 28th of June, 1820. Portland, Day & Fraser, prs. to the state, 1830. [4], [1225]-1267, [8] p. Me-LR; MeBa; MeU; Mo.   2365

---- Private and special acts of the state of Maine, passed by the tenth Legislature, at its session, commencing January 6th, 1830. Published agreeably to the Resolve of the 28th of June, 1820. Portland, Day & Fraser, prs. to the state, 1830. [4], [113]-207, [6] p. In-SC; Me-LR; MeU; Nb.   2366

---- Public laws of the state of Maine, passed January session, 1830. Hallowell, Pr. by Glazier, Masters & Co., 1830. 223-250, iv p. R.   2367

---- Report of the bank commissioners, November 2, 1830. 7 p. MeHi.   2368

---- Report of the Committee of elections, and statement of the minority of said committee, in the case of Andrew Roberts, claiming to hold a seat in the House of Representatives, as a member from the town of Waterborough. Portland, Day & Fraser, prs., 1830. 10 p. MH; Me-LR; MeHi.   2369

---- Report of the committee of elections, in the case of Joseph C. Small, claiming to hold a seat in the House of Representatives, as a member from the district composed of the towns of Unity, Burnham & Troy. Portland, Day & Fraser, prs. to the state, 1830. 7 p. Me-LR; MeHi. 2370

---- Report of the committee on the affairs of the state prison. Portland, Day & Fraser, prs. to the state, 1830. 24 p. Me-LR; MeHi.   2371

---- Report of the Land Agent, with the accompanying documents. Portland, Day & Fraser, prs. to the State, 1830. 12 p. MeHi.
2372

---- Reports of the agents appointed to open the Canada Road. Portland, Day & Fraser, prs. to the state, 1830. 8 p. Me-LR; MeHi.   2373

---- Resolves of the tenth Legislature of the state of Maine, passed at that session, which commenced on the sixth day of January, and ended on the nineteenth day of March one thousand eight hundred and thirty. Published agreeably to the Resolve of the 28th June, 1820. Portland, Day and Fraser, prs. to the state, 1830. [6], 89-146, [7] p. IaU-L; In-SC; MeU; Mi-L; Mo; Ms; Nb; Nj.   2374

---- Rules and orders to be ob-

served in the House of Representatives of the state of Maine, during the continuance of the tenth Legislature, 1830. Portland, Day & Fraser, prs. to the state, 1830. 24 p. Me-LR; MeHi. 2375

---- Rules and orders to be observed in the Senate of the state of Maine, during the continuance of the tenth Legislature, 1830. Portland, Day & Fraser, prs. to the state, 1830. 20 p. Me-LR.
2376
The Maine farmer's almanac for 1831. By Daniel Robinson. Hallowell, Glazier, Masters & Co. [1830] 24 l. MBAt; MH; MWA (2 varieties); MeB; MeHi.   2377

---- ---- Portland, Shirley, Hyde & Co. [1830] 24 l. MWA.
2378
The Maine register, and United States calendar for 1831. Portland, Shirley, Hyde and Company; Hallowell, Glazier, Masters and Company [1830] 122, [2] p. DLC; MHi; MWA; MeBa; MeHi; MeU; N; Nh.   2379

Mair, John.
Mair's introduction to Latin syntax. From the Edinburgh stereotype edition. Rev. and cor. by A. R. Carson... To which is added, copious exercises upon the declinable parts of speech... By David Patterson... New-York, Collins & Hannay, and Collins & Co., 1830. viii, 248 p. CtHT; CtHT-W; DLC; MiU; MoS; OCl; PHi.   2380

---- ---- New York, W. E. Dean, 1830. 248 p. IaHi.   2381

Maistre, Joseph Marie de.
Letters on the Spanish Inquisition. A rare work, and the best which has ever appeared on the subject. ... Translated from the French with additional Notes and

Illustrations. By T. J. O'Flaherty, S. E. C. Boston, Massachusetts. Boston, Wm. Smith, pr., 1830. xx, 164 p. DGU; DLC; MB; MdW; MdBS; NN.   2382

Malcolm, Howard, 1799-1879.
   A dictionary of important names, objects, and terms, found in the Holy Scriptures... Boston, Pub. by Lincoln and Edmands, Sold by Crocker & Brewster [etc.] 1830. 176 p. CtHT-W; DLC; MBC; MDeeP; NhD; RNHi; ViRU; VtU.   2383

---- ---- 2d ed. Boston, Pub. by Lincoln and Edmands, Sold by Crocker & Brewster [etc.] 1830. 240 p. PPL.   2384

Malte-Brun, Conrad, 1775-1826.
   A new general atlas, exhibiting the five great divisions of the globe, Europe, Asia, Africa, America and Oceanica. Drawn and engraved particularly to illustrate the Universal Geography by M. Malte Brun. Philadelphia, J. Grigg, 1830. 40 maps. CSmH; GU; MH; PU.   2385

The manual for invalids. See Graham, Thomas John.

The manual of St. Augustin, revised and corrected. Baltimore, Pub. by F. Lucas, Junr. [183-?] 94 p. DGU.   2386

Manuel de proverbes dramatiques See Longfellow, Henry Wadsworth.

Map of New York, Pennsylvania and New Jersey published by Ebenezer Hutchinson. Woodstock, Vt., 1830. Entered according to act of Congress, the 4th day of May, 1830, by John G. Darby of the state of Vermont. VtHi.
          2387
Maps from the British school geography. See Edmands, B. F.

[Marcet, Jane (Haldimand)] 1769-1858.
   Conversations on chemistry; in which the elements of that science are familiarly explained... 12th American, from the last London ed. with additions and corrections. To which are now added, explanations of the text ...by J. L. Comstock...together with a new and extensive series of questions by J. L. Blake. Hartford, Pub. by Cooke and Packard and Butler, 1830. 348 p. KU.   2388

[----] Conversations on natural philosophy, in which the elements of that science are familiarly explained. Philadelphia, John Grigg, L. Johnson, Pr., 1830. 220, 8 p. CtSoP; GDC; KyLo; MH; MdW; NjR; PU; RPA.   2389

---- Conversations on vegetable physiology; comprehending the elements of botany, with their applications to agriculture. By the author of "Conversations on chemistry," and "Natural philosophy." Adapted to the use of schools by Rev. J. L. Blake. Boston, Crocker & Brewster; New York, J. Leavitt, 1830. 372 p. CSt; IU; MB; MBHo; MH; NNC; OClW; PPC; PU-Penn; TxU-T.   2390

---- ---- New York, Pr. for G. & C. & H. Carvill by Sleight and Robinson, 1830. xii, 354 p. CtMW; KyLx; LNHT; MB; MdHi; MnHi; NNNAM; NRU; NjR; OClWHi; PU.   2391

March, Alden.
   A lecture on the expediency of establishing a medical college and hospital in the city of Albany. Delivered January 11, 1830; introductory to a course on anatomy and operative surgery. Albany, L. G. Hoffman, 1830. 20 p. DNLM; N; NN; NNNAM.   2392

A mariner's sketches. See
Ames, Nathaniel.

Marks, David, Jr.
Poetical sketches... Rochester,
Pr. for the author, by E. Peck
& Co., 1830. 30 p. NN has
photostat of t. p.   2393

[Marks, Richard]
Macarius, or Memoirs of a
naval officer. Boston, Peirce and
Williams, 1830. 53+ p. MH.
                              2394

Marselus, Nicholas I.
The good old way, a sermon
in the Middle Dutch Church in
Nassau Street, New York, April
18, 1830. New York, William
A. Mercein, 1830. 32 p. MB;
NjR; PPPrHi; RPB.   2395

Marsh, Christopher Columbus,
b. 1806.
The science of double-entry
book-keeping, simplified by the
introduction of an infallible rule
for dr. and cr. calculated to in-
sure a complete knowledge of the
theory and practice of accounts.
By C. C. Marsh, accountant...
Philadelphia, Towar, J. & D. M.
Hogan, Wm. Brown, pr., 1830.
v. p. DLC; NWM; P; PP; PPL.
                              2396

Marsh, James, 1794-1842, ed.
Select practical theology of the
seventeenth century...In five
volumes. ... New York, G. &
C. & H. Carvill. Burlington,
Chauncey Goodrich, 1830. 5 vols.
CtHC; ICU; KyBC; MB; MBC;
MoSpD; NSyU; OMC; VtU.   2397

Marsh, John, 1788-1868.
Putnam and the wolf; or, The
monster destroyed. An address,
delivered at Pomfret, Con., October 28, 1829, before the Windham Co. Temperance Society.
By Rev. John Marsh... Published
by request of the Society. (2d ed.)
Hartford [Conn.] D. F. Robin-

son & Co., Peter B. Gleason &
Co., prs. 1830. 24 p. MB; MH-
AH; MWA; NjR; ScC.   2398

Marshall, Elihu F.
A spelling book of the English
language; or, The American tutor's assistant. Intended particularly for the use of 'Common
schools,' the pronounciation being adapted to the much improved
principles of J. Walker. Stereotyped ed. Bellows Falls, James
I. Cutler & Co., Pr. by Cook &
Taylor, 1830. 156 p. CtHT-W;
MH; MWA; NH; NNC; NjR; VtU.
                              2399
---- ---- Wells River, I. White,
1830. 156 p. MH.   2400

Marshall, Humphrey.
The letter of a private student,
or, An examination of the "Evidences of Christianity" as exhibited and argued, at Cincinnati,
April, 1829; by the Rev. Alexander Campbell, in a debate with
Mr. Robert Owen... Frankfort,
Ky., Pr. by J. H. Holeman,
1830. iv, 60 p. ICU.   2401

Marshall, [Rev.] and Rev. Newton.
Manifesto of the teachers of
Spring Ridge Academy, containing
their doctrines and views in relation to education, tuition and
school discipline. Read before
the board of visitors, and a number of ladies and gentlemen assembled to witness the examination of the students. December
16, 1830. Raymond, Miss., Pr.
by S. T. King, [1830] [16] p.
TxU.   2402

Martin, George W.
To those who claim reservations under the Treaty of Dancing Rabbit Creek. [n. p., n. d. --
Natchez? 1830?] 2 p. MsWJ (2
copies, reported in July, 1937,
as seen there by Mr. J. A Mc

Millen, of LU; but could not be found there in June, 1943, for more detailed description.) 2403

[Martin, Joseph Plumb] 1760-1850.
A narrative of some of the adventures, dangers and sufferings of a revolutionary soldier; interspersed with anecdotes of incidents that occurred within his own observation. Written by himself... Hallowell [Me.] Pr. by Glazier, Masters & co., 1830. 213 p. DLC; MdHi; MeHi; MiU-C; NN; OClWHi; PHi; PPL; WHi.   2404

Martin, William Dobbin.
Speech of Mr. Martin, of South Carorina [!] on a motion to allow a drawback on cotton bagging... Washington, Pr. by Duff Green, 1830. 15 p. CSmH. 2405

Martinet, Louis, 1795-1875.
Manual of pathology; containing the symptoms, diagnosis, and morbid characters of diseases... By L. Martinet... Trans. with notes and additions, by Jones Quain... 2d American ed. Philadelphia, Carey and Lea [Brookfield, Mass., E. & G. Merriam, prs.] 1830. 275 p. CSt-L; KyLJM; MBCo; MdBM; MdUM; MoSMed; NBMS; OClM; PPC; PPF; ViU.   2406

---- Manual of therapeutics. By L. Martinet, D.M.P. Translated with alterations and additions, by Robert Norton, M.D. ...New York, C. S. Francis [Clayton & Van Norden, prs.] 1830. 278, [2] p. CSt-L; DLC; DNLM; MBCo; MWA; MoSMed; RPM.
                                    2407

Mary and Archie Graham. (A tale) Philadelphia, American Sunday School Union, 1830. BrMus.   2408

Mary and her sister; to which is

added A story about the creation. Designed for young people. By the Author of Helen and Maria. New-Haven, S. Babcock, Publisher, ...Charleston, S. Babcock & Co.   Sidney's Press, 1830. 23 p. CtHi.   2409

Mary and Thomas; or, A mother's present. New-Haven, S. Babcock, Sidney's Press, 1830. 17 p. CtHi; DLC.   2410

Maryland.
Acts of the General Assembly of Maryland, relating to the poor of Baltimore city and county; together with the by-laws of the trustees for the poor of Baltimore city and county. Baltimore, John D. Toy, pr., 1830. 56 p. MdHi; PPL.   2411

---- The annual report of the Treasurer of the Western Shore, for December session, 1830. To the General Assembly of Maryland.   In pursuance of an act of the Legislature, passed at December session, 1824, entitled, An act relating to the treasurers of the Western and Eastern Shores. Annapolis, Pr. by Jeremiah Hughes, 1830. 38 p. MdHi.
                                    2412
---- Communication from the executive department, enclosing the report and memorial of the president and directors of the Chesapeake and Ohio Canal Company, and a communication from the executive of Georgia, relative to the election of president and vice president, to the Legislature of Maryland. February 1st, 1830. Annapolis, Pr. by J. Hughes, 1830. 10 p. MdHi.   2413

---- Communication from the executive department, to the Legislature of Maryland, enclosing a communication from the principal of the Pennsylvania Institution for the Deaf and Dumb. Annapolis, Jeremiah Hughes, pr., 1830. 7 p. MdHi.   2414

---- Communication from the Treasurer for the Western Shore, enclosing a Statement of such returns as had been made to him in pursuance of the Resolution No. 77, of December Session 1827, prepared and presented in obedience to said Resolution. Annapolis, Pr. by J. Hughes, 1830. [4] p. MdHi.   2415

---- Communication from the Treasurer of the Western Shore to the House of delegates, in obedience to their order of the 18th Ult. enclosing statements from the several banks. Annapolis, J. Hughes, pr., 1830. 4 p. MdHi.   2416

---- Communication of the Treasurer of the W. Shore, enclosing a report from the managers of the Washington Monument. January 12th, 1830. Annapolis, J. Hughes, pr., 1830. 6 p. MdHi.   2417

---- (Document No. 1) Accompanying the executive communication of the 29th December 1830. Correspondence between the clerk of the council, and the Secretary at War, relative to the survey of the Pocomoke, Annapolis. Pr. by Jonas Green, Dec. 1830. 5 p. MdHi.   2418

---- (Document No. 2) Accompanying the executive communication of the 29th December 1830 Communication from the governor of Connecticut covering a report of the legislature of that state, on the subject of the constitution of the United States. Annapolis, Pr. by Jonas Green, Dec. 1830. 5 p. MdHi.   2419

---- (Document No. 3) Accompanying the executive communication of the 29th December 1830 Communication from Robert Hunter of New York, upon the subject of a memorial to congress, in relation to revolutionary soldiers. Annapolis, Pr. by Jonas Green, Dec. 1830. 8 p. MdHi.   2420

---- (Document No. 4) Accompanying the executive communication of the 29th December, 1830. Circular from the Rhode-Island Historical Society. Annapolis, Pr. by Jonas Green, 1830. 5 p. MdHi.   2421

---- (Document No. 4) Accompanying the executive communication of the 29th December 1830. Communication from the Governor of Virginia, relative to the Chessapeake [sic] and Ohio canal. Annapolis, Pr. by Jonas Green, Dec. 1830. 7 p. MdHi.   2422

---- (Document No. 5) Accompanying the executive communication of the 29th December, 1830. Communication from the Governor of Louisiana approving of the tariff of 1828. Annapolis, Pr. by Jonas Green, Dec. 1830. 4 p. MdHi.   2423

---- (Document No. 5) Accompanying the executive message of the 31st December 1829. Report of arms and accoutrements, of the Twelth [sic] brigade, M. M. Annapolis, Jeremiah Hughes, pr. 1830. 4 p. MdHi.   2424

---- (Document No. 6) Accompanying the executive communication of the 29th December, 1830. List of the deaf and dumb in the Pennsylvania institution. Annapolis, Pr. by Jonas Green, Dec. 1830. [iv] p. MdHi.   2425

---- (Document No. 8) Accompanying the executive communication of the 29th December, 1830. Report and resolutions of the General Assembly of Kentucky upon the American system. Annapolis, Pr. by Jonas Green, Dec. 1830. 18 p. MdHi.   2426

---- (Document No. 9) Accompanying the executive communication of the 29th December 1830. Governor of Ohio, answering the resolution of the state of Pennsylvania, relative to the tariff. Annapolis, Pr. by Jonas Green, Dec. 1830. 4 p. MdHi.   2427

---- (Document No. 10) Accompanying the executive communication of the 29th December, 1830. Communication from the Governor of Delaware, approving of the tariff. Annapolis, Pr. by Jonas Green, Dec. 1830. 4 p. MdHi.   2428

---- (Document No. 10) Accompanying the executive message of the 31st December 1829. Letter from George Winchester, Esq. President of the Baltimore and Susquehanna Rail Road Company, Annapolis, Jeremiah Hughes, pr. 1830. 6 p. MdHi.   2429

---- (Document No. 11) Accompanying the executive communication of the 29th December 1830. Report of the directors of the Maryland Penitentiary. Annapolis, Pr. by Jonas Green, Dec. 1830. 1 p. MdHi.   2430

---- (Document No. 11) Accompanying the executive communication of the 29th December 1830. Report of the directors of the Maryland penitentiary. Annapolis, Pr. by Jonas Green, Dec. 1830. 9, [ii] p. MdHi.   2431

---- Journal of the proceedings of the House of Delegates of... Maryland, at a session... begun ...December...28th...1829 [to March 1st, 1830] Published by authority. Annapolis, Pr. by J. Hughes, 1829 [i. e. 1830] 600 [i. e. 598]   MdBB; MdHi.   2432

---- Journal of the proceedings of the Senate of... Maryland, at a session... begun... December ...28th...1829 [to March 1st, 1830] Published by authority. Annapolis, Pr. by J. Hughes, 1829 [i. e. 1830] 59 p. MdHi.
                                2433

---- [Laws made and passed] by the General Assembly of the state of Maryland, at a session ...begun... on the last Monday of December...A. D. 1829... Annapolis, Pr. by Jeremiah Hughes, 1830. 1 v. various pagings. (t. p. defective) Ia-L.   2434

---- A list of the delegates to the General Assembly of Maryland, declared and returned to have been duly elected on the first Monday of October, A. D. 1830... Prepared from the official returns by Gideon Pearce, clerk of the House of Delegates of Maryland. Annapolis, Pr. by J. Green, 1830. 6, [ii] p. MdHi.
                                2435

---- Message from the executive, to the General Assembly of Maryland. December session, 1830. Annapolis, Pr. by Jeremiah Hughes, 1830. 15 p. MdHi.
                                2436

---- (Mr. McPherson.) Report of the select committee, on the communication relative to the tariff, the Colonization Society, and of the method of electing president and vice president. Annapolis, Pr. by J. Hughes, 1830. 7 p. MdHi.   2437

---- [Mr. Teackle.] Report of the committee appointed by the House of Delegates, in conjunction with a like committee on the part of the Senate, to visit and inspect the seminary of the primary school, in the city of Annapolis. Pr. by order of the House of Delegates. Annapolis, Jeremiah Hughes, pr., 1830. 56 p. DLC; MdBE; MdHi.   2438

---- ---- Report of the select committee, to which was referred the memorials and petitions of great numbers of citizens of different counties, praying the establishment of a financial institution under the style of the Bank of the State of Maryland. Annapolis, Pr. by J. Green, Dec. 1830. 48 p. CSmH; CtHT-W; DLC; MB; MBC; MdHi; PPL; ScU.   2439

---- Report of Mr. Teackle, chairman of the select committee upon the memorials of sundry citizens of different counties praying the establishment of a state's bank to be founded upon the invested money in the treasury for the supply of revenue and the general convenience of the people made in the House of Delegates of the General Assembly of Maryland, at December session, 1829. Annapolis, Pr. by J. Hughes, 1830. 15 p. DLC; PHi.   2440

---- Report of the adjutant general, to the governor, Communicated to the General Assembly, January 3d, 1830. Annapolis, Pr. by J. Hughes, 1830. 7 p. MdBP; MdHi.   2441

---- Report of the commissioners on the survey of the Pocomoke river, &c. Annapolis, Pr. by J. Hughes, 1830. 7 p. MdHi.   2442

---- Report of the committee of claims on the account of the Treasurer of the Eastern Shore of Maryland. January 3, 1830. Annapolis, Pr. by J. Hughes, 1830. 4 p. MdHi.   2443

---- Report of the committee of claims on the accounts of the Treasurer of the Western Shore of Maryland. January 8, 1830. Annapolis, Pr. by J. Hughes, 1830. 8 p. MdHi.   2444

---- Report of the committee of ways and means, to the House of Delegates, January 29, 1830. Annapolis, J. Hughes, pr., 1830. 12 p. MdHi.   2445

---- Report of the directors of the Maryland penitentiary, made to the executive and communicated by his excellency, Governor Carroll, to the legislature, at December session, 1830. Baltimore, Pr. by Lucas and Deaver, 1830. 20 p. MdHi.   2446

---- Report of the joint committee, appointed on the subject of St. John's College. [Annapolis? 183-] 5 p. DLC; MdHi.   2447

---- Report of the Treasurer for the Western Shore, to the General Assembly, concerning the Union bank of Maryland, In obedience to an order of the last House of Delegates, passed 6th of March, 1829. Annapolis, Pr. by J. Hughes, 1830. 5 p. MdHi.   2448

---- Report of the Treasurer of the Western Shore, of the avails of certain revenue, for the last ten years. January 12th, 1830. Annapolis, Pr. by J. Hughes, 1830. 4 p. MdHi.   2449

---- Reports of cases argued and determined in the Court of appeals of Maryland. By Richard

W. Gill, attorney at law, and
John Johnson, clerk of the Court
of appeals. Containing cases in
1829-[1842] Baltimore, Pub. by
Fielding Lucas, jr., Lucas and
Deaver, pr. 1830-[1845] 12 v.
CLSU; CU-Law; Ia; KyU-L;
MWCL; MdBB; MdBE; MiD-B;
MoU; NNLI; Ni; OClW; OrSC;
P; PU-L; RPL; Sc-SC; TU-L;
TxSC; U; Vi-L; BrMus.   2450

Maryland Jockey Club.
    [Rules] "At a meeting of sub-
scribers for the purpose of
forming a Jockey Club..." [Bal-
timore, 1830] 6 p. MdBP.   2451

Maryland Savings Institution,
Baltimore.
    Charter and by-laws of the
Maryland Savings Institution. Incorporated 1827. Baltimore, Pr.
by Lucas and Deaver, 1830. 20
p. MdHi.   2452

Maryland University.
    Address of the Trustees of the
University of Maryland to the
public. With laws. 1830. [Bal-
timore, 1830] 22 p. DLC; MB;
NIC; PHi; PPAmP.   2453

---- Memorial of the trustees of
the University of Maryland, and
the trustees of Baltimore College,
to the Legislature of Maryland.
Baltimore, John D. Toy, 1830.
31 p. DLC; MdBE; MdBP; MdHi;
NNG; PHi; BrMus.   2454

Mary's book of hymns, containing hymns for very young children. Concord, N.H., Pub. by
R. H. Sherburne & Co., 1830.
16 p. MH; NhHi; RPB.   2455

Mason, Benjamin.
    The doctrine of particular and
unconditional election, as advanced by Samuel Martin... By
Benjamin Mason, late of Chester
County, Penna. Philadelphia,

Marcus T. C. Gould, New York,
Isaac T. Hopper, 1830. 103, 16
p. PHC; PHi; PSC-Hi.   2456

Mason, Henry.
    Poetry, a poem delivered be-
fore the Franklin Debating Society, in Chauncy Hall, January
17, 1830, being the celebration
of their 7th anniversary. Boston,
Pr. for the Society by Isaac R.
Butts, 1830. 9 p. CSmH; MB;
MH; NCH.   2457

Mason, James A.
    A shaver for John Chettle; or,
A vindication of the doctrine of
the real presence. Boston, Pub.
by William Smith, for the editors of "The Jesuit." 1830. iv,
72 p.   DGU; MChB; MWH. 2458

Mason, Lowell, 1792-1872.
    Juvenile Psalmist; or, The
child's introduction to sacred music. 2d ed.   Boston, Richardson, Lord & Holbrook, 1830.
32 p. KU; MBC; MH.   2459

Mason, Richard.
    The gentleman's new pocket
farrier, comprising a general description of the noble and useful
animal, the horse; together with
the quickest and simplest mode
of fattening... Also, a concise
account of the diseases to which
the horse is subject, with such
remedies as long experience has
proved to be effectual. By Richard Mason... 5th ed., with additions.   To which is added a
prize essay on mules... Richmond, Pr. by P. Cottom, 1830.
388 p. CtHT-W; DLC; OClW;
ViU.   2460

Mason, Thomas, 1769-1851.
    A discourse delivered at
Northfield, Mass. Sabbath day,
Feb. 28, 1830. By Thomas Mason... on occasion of the close of
his ministerial labors in that

place. Submitted to the requests, and published by the friends of the author. Greenfield, Mass., Phelps & Ingersoll, prs., 1830. 11, [1] p. CSmH; MDeeP; MHi; RPB; ViU.   2461

The Masonic character. See Moore, Charles Whitlock.

Masonic principles. See Slade, William.

Massachusetts.
   An act defining the general powers and duties of manufacturing corporations. Passed February 23, 1830. [Boston, 1830] 13 p. MHi.   2462

---- An act to establish the Boston, Providence and Taunton Rail Road Corporation [Boston, 1830] 11 p. DLC; M; MB; MBAt; MH; NNC; PPL.   2463

---- An act to establish the Massachusetts Rail Road Corporation. [Boston, 1830] 11 p. (House document no. 56.) M; MB; MBAt; MH; MWA; NNC; PPL.   2464

---- ...An act to establish the Massachusetts Rail Road Corporations. [Boston, 1830] 21 p. (House document no. 4) M; MB; MBAt; MH; MWA; NN; NNC; P PL.   2465

---- An act to incorporate the Franklin Railroad Company [Boston, 1830] 17 p. (House doc. No. 35.) M; MB; MBAt; MH-BA; MWA; NN; NNC.   2466

---- By His Excellency Levi Lincoln, a proclamation: With the advice of the executive council, I appoint the annual fast...to be observed on Thursday, the eighth day of April next... [Boston, 1 March, 1830] Bdsd. MHi.   2467

---- Circular. Sir, The government of the United States having directed a survey and examination of Connecticut River, and also of the Farmington and the Hampshire and Hampden Canals, it has become desirable to ascertain as far as may be, the quantity of goods...to be transported to and from the town of ____ annually... Northampton, Mass., September 22d, 1830. Bdsd. M.
                                               2468
---- Commonwealth of Massachusetts. Head Quarters, Boston, September 6th, 1830. General orders... By His Excellency' command, William H. Sumner, Adjutant General. 1 p. DLC.   2469

---- Laws of the commonwealth for the government of the Massachusetts State Prison, with the rules and regulations of the Board of Inspectors, and details of the police and discipline, adopted by the warden, on the completion of the new prison, October 1829. Charlestown, Press of the Bunker-Hill Aurora, 1830. 112 p. M; MB; MBAt; MH; MHi; MWA; NN; OCLaw; OClWHi; BrMus.   2470

---- Laws of the Commonwealth of Massachusetts, passed by the General Court, at their session, which commenced on Wednesday, the sixth of January, and ended on Saturday, the thirteenth of March, one thousand eight hundred and thirty. Published agreeably to a resolve of the 16th January 1812. Boston, Dutton & Wentworth, prs. to the state, 1830. 295-486, xi p. IaU-L; MH-L; MdBB; Mo; Nj; R; Wa-L.
                                               2471
---- Laws of the Commonwealth of Massachusetts, passed by the General Court, at their session, which commenced on Wednesday, the twenty-sixth of May, and

ended on Monday, the seventh of
June, one thousand eight hundred
and thirty. Published agreeably to
a resolve of the 16th January
1812. Boston, Dutton & Wentworth, prs. to the state. 1830.
489-520, iii p. IaU-L; MH-L; Mo;
Nj; R; Wa-L.   2472

---- Message of His Excellency
Levi Lincoln, Communicated to
the two branches of the Legislature, January 6, 1830. Boston,
Dutton and Wentworth, prs., 1830.
40 p. M; MB; MBAt; MH; MHi;
MWA; NNC.   2473

---- Proclamation: Thanksgiving,
December 2, 1830. Bdsd. MHi.
                               2474
---- The proprietors of Charles
River Bridge in equity vs. the
proprietors of the Warren Bridge.
[Boston, 1830?] 206 p. MH; MHi.
                               2475
---- [Report of the committee of
both houses on the plan to con-
struct a rail road from the city
of Boston to the town of Lowell,
together with an act to establish
the Boston and Lowell Railroad
Corporation. n.p. (1830)] 21 p.
(Senate. 1829/30, session 2,
document no. 21.) DBRE; M;
MB; MBAt; MH; MWA; MiU-T;
PPL.   2476

---- Report of the Directors of
Internal Improvement on the sub-
ject of rail roads. Transmitted
to the legislature, January ses-
sion, 1830. Boston, Dutton &
Wentworth, prs., 1830. 61 p.
DBRE; IU; MeH; NIC; NN; NNC;
NRU; PPL; RPB.   2477

---- Report of the select committee of the House of Representatives... on legalizing the study of
anatomy. Boston, Dutton &
Wentworth, 1830. 118 p. IU-M;
OC.   2478

---- Resolves of the General
Court of the Commonwealth of
Massachusetts, passed at their
[May & June] session... Boston,
Dutton and Wentworth, prs. to
the state, 1830. 430, iii p.
IaU-L; MHa; Nb; R.   2479

---- Rules and orders to be observed in the Senate of the commonwealth of Massachusetts, for
the year 1830-31. Pub. by order
of the Senate. Boston, Dutton &
Wentworth, state prs., 1830. 34
p. MWHi.   2480

---- Speech of His Excellency
Levi Lincoln, delivered to the
two branches of the Legislature,
in convention, May 29, 1830.
Boston, Dutton and Wentworth,
prs., 1830. 20 p. DLC; MA;
MBC; MH; MHi; MiD-B; PU.
                               2481
---- [Statements of sundry expenditures for surveying railways
and canals, since June session,
1824, including all monies paid
as incident thereto.] January
25th, 1830. [Boston, Dutton &
Wentworth, 1830] 8 p. (House
document no. 14.) M; MB; MBAt;
MH; MWA; NN.   2482

---- Tax for the year 1830...
An act to apportion and assess a
tax of seventy five thousand dol-
lars. [Boston, 1830] 20 p. MB.
                               2483
Massachusetts. Ancient and Hon-
orable Artillery Company.
    Rules and regulations of the
Ancient and Honorable Artillery
Company, with the charter. Re-
vised August, 1830. Boston, John
H. Eastburn, pr., 1830. 29 p.
NCH.   2484

Massachusetts Anti-Slavery Society.
    [Commission for agents] [n.p.
1830] 1 p. DLC.   2485

Massachusetts Bible Society.

Twenty first annual report of the Massachusetts Bible Society, Boston, T. R. Marvin, printer, 1830. 15 p. MBD; MNe.　　2486

Massachusetts Charitable Mechanic Association, Boston.

Order of services at the eighth triennial festival of the Massachusetts Charitable Mechanic Association, on Thursday, October 7, 1830. at the Federal Street Baptist Meeting-House. [Boston, 1830] Bdsd. MB.　2487

Massachusetts Episcopal Missionary Society.

Report of the board of directors of the Massachusetts Episcopal Missionary Society: read at the annual meeting of the Society in St. Paul's Church, Boston, Wednesday evening June 16, 1830 together with the second semi-annual report of the city missionary, and the treasurer's statement. Boston, Putnam & Hunt, 1830. 30 p. MB; MBD; MHi; MWA.　　2488

---- To the Protestant Episcopalians of the city of Boston. January 30 [183-?] 4 p. MHi.
　　2489

Massachusetts General Hospital.

By-laws of the Massachusetts General Hospital; with the rules and regulations... Boston, 1830. 28 p. MHi; BrMus.　　2490

Massachusetts Journal.

Address of the carriers of the Massachusetts Journal, January 1, 1830. [Boston, 1830] Bdsd. MB.　　2491

Massachusetts Missionary Society.

Thirty-first annual report of the Massachusetts Missionary Society, presented by the executive committee at the anniversary meeting in Boston, May 25, 1830.

Boston, Pr. by Crocker & Brewster, 1830. 39, [2] p. ICN; MA; NjR; WHi.　　2492

The Massachusetts register and United States calendar for 1831. Boston, James Loring [1830] 126 1. CtHT-W; ICN; InU; MB; MH; MWA; MdBJ; MeB; MeHi; MiD-B; MnU; MoSpD; NBLiHi; NCH; NN; Nh; OClWHi; RPB.
　　2493

Massachusetts Sabbath School Union.

Fifth annual report of the Massachusetts Sabbath School Union, Presented at the annual meeting May 27, 1830. Boston, T. R. Marvin, pr., 1830. 40 p. CSmH; MBC; MWA; MiD-B; NRAB; WHi.　　2494

Mathews, Charles.

...The wolf and lamb, a popular farce, in one act... Philadelphia, Frederick Turner [ca 1830] 28 p. RPB.　　2495

Mathews, John Hubbersty, b. 1796.

A treatise on the doctrine of presumption and presumptive evidence, as affecting the title to real and personal property. ... With notes and references to American cases, by Benjamin Rand. New York, Pub. by Gould, Banks and Co. and by Wm. and A. Gould and co. Albany [E. & G. Merriam, prs., Brookfield, Mass.] 1830. [v]-xxxv, [1], 508 p. DLC; Ky; MH-L; PPB; PU.　　2496

Mathies, James.

Rochester, A satire; and other miscellaneous poems... Rochester, 1830. 130 p. PU.　2497

[Maxwell, William Hamilton] 1792-1850.

Stories of Waterloo; and other tales... New York, J. & J.

Harper, 1830. 2 v. LU; NCH.
2498

Maxwell, Wright and Company,
Rio de Janeiro.
Commercial formalities of
Rio de Janeiro... Baltimore, Pr.
by Benjamin Edes, 1830. 77 p.
1 l. DeGE; DLC; PPL.   2499

May, Samuel J.
...On prejudice. Pr. for the
American Unitarian Association.
Boston, Gray and Bowen...[Pr.
by I. R. Butts] 1830. 16 p. 1st
series. No. 41. CBPac; CtHC;
MB; MBAt; MMeT-Hi; MeLB.
2500

Mayhew, Experience.
Narratives of the lives of pi-
ous Indian women who lived on
Martha's Vineyard more than one
hundred years since... Boston,
J. Loring, 1830. 108 p. DLC;
ICN; MBAt; MBC; NRU; OClWHi;
TNJ.   2501

Mayhew, Jonathan, 1720-1766.
Two objections to the right
and duty of free inquiry and private judgement answered. 2d ed.
Pr. for American Unitarian Society. Boston, Gray & Bowen
[183-?] 10 p. DLC.   2502

Maynard, Lyman.
The doctrine of a future pro-
bation, defended in two dialogues
between an inquirer and a minister. By Lyman Maynard...
Southbridge [Mass.] Office of the
Register, J. Snow, pr., 1830.
46 p. CSmH.   2503

Mead, Asa, 1792-1831.
Christians should unite to dis-
seminate the principles of peace:
a sermon delivered before the
Hartford County Peace Society at
their semi-annual meeting in
East Windsor, Sept. 30, 1830.
Hartford, Pr. by Philemon Canfield, 1830. 18 p. CSmH; Ct;

CtHC; MBAt; MBC; MeB;
OClWHi; VtU.   2504

Mead, Mathew, 1630?-1699.
Der Beynahe ein Christ en-
deckt: Oder, Der irrige Re-
ligions-Bekenner, geprüft und
verworfen. Der wesentliche In-
halt von Sieben Predigten, zuerst
gepredigt zu Sanct Sepulchre's in
London, in Jahr 1661, von Mathew Mead...Aus dem Englischen
übersetzt, und herausgegeben von
Daniel Weiser. Selins-grove,
Pennsylvanien, Amos Stroh, 1830.
xxxvi, 192 p., 4 l. CSmH; MH;
MWA; P; PHi; PP; PPG; PPL.
2505

---- ---- Harrisburg, Johann
Weinbrenner, 1830. 153 p.
Bound with this is: Auszüge von
einer Abhandlung... MiU-C; NN;
P; PHi.   2506

Mecarius. See Marks, Richard.

Mechanics' Saving Fund Society.
Baltimore.
Charter and by-laws of the
Mechanics' Saving Fund Society
of Baltimore. Baltimore, Pr.
by William Wooddy, 1830. 23 p.
MdHi.   2507

Medary, Jacob, and Campbell,
Hiram.
Proposals for publishing by
subscription a weekly newspaper
in the city of Cincinnati to be
called the Western Temperance
Advocate and Weekly Review.
[Batavia? 1830] Bdsd. O.   2508

Medical College of Ohio. Cincinnati.
A catalogue of the officers and
students in the Medical College
of Ohio, during the session of
1829-30. Cincinnati, Pr. for the
class, 1830. 8 p. DNLM; MHi;
OCHP; PPC.   2509

Medical Society of New Jersey.

The law incorporating Medical societies, and the bylaws, rules and regulations, with the table of fees and rates for charging of the Medical Society of New Jersey. New Brunswick, N. J., Rutgers Press, Terhune & Letson, prs., 1830. 56 p. NjR.
2510

Medical Society of South Carolina.
The members of the Medical Society of South Carolina, residing in Charleston, to its inhabitants. [Charleston, 1830] 8 p. NNNAM.
2511

Medical Society of the City and County of N. Y.
Memorial ... to the honorable the Legislature, remonstrating against a repeal, of the statute, regulating the practice of physic and surgery, in the state of New-York. New-York, Joseph C. Spear, printer, 1830. 8 p. DNLM; MH; NN; NNNAM; PPL.
2512

Medical Society of the County of New York.
Report of the committee appointed to draft a circular. New-York School of Medicine. [New York, 183-?] 1 l. NNNAM.
2513

Medical Society of the State of New York.
Transactions of... for the year 1830... Albany, Pr. by Websters and Skinners, 1830. 66 p. N; NNNAM; NjR.
2514

Meeke, Mary.
The birth-day present: or Pleasing tales of amusement and instruction... New York, King, 1830. 24 p. MB.
2515

Meeker, Eli.
Sermons on philosophical evangelical and practical subjects designed for the use of various de-

nominations of Christians. New York, Stereotyped by James Conner [Sleight & Robinson, prs.] 1830. 424 p. CSmH; CtHC; ICMcC; ICU; MBC; MH; NjN; OO; TNJ.
2516

Meeting of various denominations of Christians, held in Lenox, Madison County, N. Y.
Proceedings... March 11, 1830. 23 p. NN.
2517

Mellen, Grenville, 1799-1841.
The age of print: A poem delivered before the Phi Beta Kappa Society at Cambridge, 26 August, 1830. Boston, Pub. by Carter and Hendee, 1830. 40 p. CSmH; CtHT-W; DLC; ICU; MB; MBAt; MH; MHi; MeHi; MiD-B; MnHi; NIC; OClW; RPB; TxU; BrMus.
2518

---- Ode, by Grenville Mellen, esq. Sung at the meeting of the C. C. Temperance Society at North Yarmouth, April 28, 1830. [Portland, Shirley, Hyde & Co., 1830] 2 p. CtY.
2519

Mellen, Prentiss, 1764-1840.
Charge of Chief Justice Mellen, 1830. 11 p. Cover title. On verso of cover: Shirley, Hyde & Co. have for sale a great variety of the most tracts and books on the subject of Temperance... Pages 3 and 4 cover contain: Ode, by Grenville Mellen, esq. Sung at the meeting of the Cumberland County Temperance Society, at North Yarmouth, April 28, 1830. CtHC; MHi.
2520

Melvill, Henry, 1798-1871.
Bible thoughts. Selected from his published discourses. New-York, American Tract Society, D. Fanshaw, pr., [183-?] 354 p. (Christian library, 19.) MH; ViU.
2521

Member of the Zettetick Society.
See Letter to Rev. John N. Maffet.

[Memminger, Christopher Gustavus] 1803-1888.
  The book of nullification, by a spectator of the past. Charleston, 1830. 31 p. CSmH; DLC; MHi; NcD; PU; ScC.   2522

Memoir of A. E. Starr, of Connecticut. Philadelphia, American Sunday School Union [1830?] BrMus.   2523

Memoir of Anna Louisa Campbell. See G., G. E.

Memoir of Clementine Cuvier, daughter of Baron Cuvier; with reflections... New York, American Tract Society [183-] 96 p. DLC; MB.   2524

Memoir of Hannah Ripley, a Sabbath Scholar. A narration of facts. Boston, From the press of True & Greene [Written by E. P. (Parsons) Jr. and H. J. H. (Henry J. Howland)] 1830. 15, [1] p. KU; MWA.   2525

Memoir of Joanna Turner as exemplified in her life, death and spiritual experience. With a recommendatory preface... by the Rev. D. Bogue, D. D. 2d American ed. Baltimore, Midwinter, 1830. 257 p. PPPrHi.   2526

Memoir of Jude Caine who died in Liverpool Feb. 3, 1829. Philadelphia, American Sunday School Union, 1830. 18 p. NhHi.   2527

A memoir of Mary Jane Graham. Philadelphia, Pub. by the Tract Association of Friends [1830] (No. 45.) 12 p. PPL.   2528

Memoir of Mrs. Eleanor Emerson, accompanied with Dr. Wor-

cester's sermon, occasioned by her death. With an appendix... 3d ed. Boston, L. W. Kimball, 1830. 154 p. NNUT; Nh; RPB.
                                       2529
Memoir of ...William Ward, one of the Serampore missionaries. Revised by the Committee of Publication. Philadelphia, American Sunday School Union [1830?] BrMus.   2530

Memoirs of a New England village choir. See Gilman, Samuel.

Memoirs of Augustus Hermann Francke. See Brown, Rezeau.

Memoirs of David Brainerd... Philadelphia, American Sunday School Union, 1830. 141 p. PPPrHi; BrMus.   2531

Memoirs of Henry Obookiah, a native of Owhyhee, and a member of the Foreign Mission School; who died at Cornwall, Conn. Feb. 17, 1818, aged 26 years. Revised by the Committee of publication. Philadelphia, American Sunday School Union, 1830. 126 p. MHa; OO; PPAmP; RPB.   2532

The memoirs of John Amiralle. See Southwick, John B.

Memoirs of John Frederic Oberlin. See Atkins, Sarah.

Memoirs of Luther & Calvin, the great reformers of the Christian religion. New Haven, Nathan Whiting [183-?] 72 p. CtY. 2533

Memoirs of P. J. Spener compiled from the German. Revised by the Committee of Publication. Philadelphia, American Sunday School Union [1830?] BrMus.
                                       2534
Memoirs of Sergeant D., his daughter, and the orphan Mary.

Revised by the Committee of Publication. Philadelphia, American Sunday School Union, 1830. BrMus.   2535

Memoirs of the Gloucester Fox Hunting Club. See Milnor, William.

Memoirs of the life of the Right Honourable George Canning. See Therry, Sir Roger.

A memorial for Sunday School girls. Philadelphia, American Sunday School Union, 1830. BrMus.   2536

Mengous, Petros.
    Narrative of a Greek Soldier: ... detailing events of the late war in Greece ... By Petrose Mengous. New York, Pr. and pub. by Elliott and Palmer, 1830. 256 p. CtHT-W; LNHT; MBAt; MS; MWH; MiD; NUt; Nh; NjP; BrMus.   2537

Mephistopheles, pseud. See Kennedy, John Pendleton.

Mercer, Jesse.
    The cluster of Spiritual songs, divine hymns, and sacred poems ... 5th ed. corr. Published for the Proprietor. For sale by J. J. Woodard. Philadelphia, Collins & Hannay, New York, 1830. 540 p. DLC; MeBaT.   2538

---- Ten letters, addressed to the Rev. Cyrus White, in reference to his scriptural view of the atonement, by his friend and fellow labourer in the Gospel of Christ, Jesse Mercer. Washington, Wilkes County, Ga., Pr. at the news office, 1830. 46, [2] p. G.   2539

Merchants' Exchange Reading Room, N. Y.
    Circular... New-York, 28th April, 1830. 4 p. folder printed on 1st page only. NN.   2540

Mérimée, Prosper, 1803-1870.
    1572 a chronicle of the times of Charles IX. translated from the French of Prosper Merimée ... New York, G. & C. & H. Carvill, 1830. 286 p. DLC; DeWi; MBL; NcD.   2541

[Merriam, George] 1803-1880.
    The child's guide: comprising familiar lessons, designed to aid in correct reading, spelling, defining, thinking, and acting. Brookfield, Mass., E. and G. Merriam, 1830. 178 p. DLC.
                                   2542

Merrick, Pliny.
    A letter on speculative Free Masonry, by Pliny Merrick, Esq., being his answer to Gen. Nathan Heard and Col. Gardner Burbank upon their application for his views upon that subject. 2d ed. Worcester, Pub. by Dorr and Howland, Morrill and Grout, prs., 1830. 20 p. MB; MWA; PHi.   2543

Methodist Episcopal Church.
    A collection of hymns adapted to the use of the Methodist Episcopal Church, including the whole collection of the Rev. John Wesley, M. A. ... New York, Pub. for the use of the Methodist Episcopal Church in the United States. Hoyt, pr., 1830. 7, 230, 8 p. MBAt; NNUT; NcD.
                                   2544
---- ---- New York, Pub. for the use of the Methodist Episcopal Church in the United States of America; Hoyt, pr., 1830. 544 p. DLC.   2545

---- Minutes of the annual conferences of the Methodist Episcopal Church, for the year 1830. New-York, Pub. by J. Emory and B. Waugh, for the Methodist

Episcopal Church, J. Collord,
pr., 1830. 42 p. PPL; PPPrHi.
2546
---- ---- Cincinnati, Pub. by
Charles Holliday for the Method-
ist Episcopal Church. Press of
Morgan & Sanxay, 1830. 36 p.
ISB.   2547

---- A review of some of the
leading doctrines of the Methodist
Episcopal Church... New Haven,
Baldwin & Treadway, 1830. 24 p.
MBC.   2548

A Methodist preacher. See An
apology for uniting.

Methodist Protestant Church.
    Constitution and discipline of
the Methodist Protestant Church.
Baltimore, Pub. for the Book
committee of the Methodist Protestant Church by John J. Harrod.
Wm. Wooddy, pr., 1830. 159,
[1] p. DLC; IEG; MH; MdBE;
MdBS; OClWHi.   2549

---- Constitution of the Methodist Protestant Church: Adopted
by a general convention of minis-
teral and lay delegates, from the
associated Methodist Churches,
held in Baltimore, November,
1830. To which is prefixed by the
publisher, a summary declaration
of rights explanatory of the reasons and principles of government.
Baltimore, J. J. Harrod, 1830.
31 p. KyDC; KyLx; MH; MdBE;
MdBP; MdHi.   2550

Miami University, Oxford.
    Catalogue of the officers of Mi-
ami University, Oxford, Ohio.
July, 1830. Pub. by W. W. Bishop [Oxford? 1830] 16 p. OOxM.
2551
---- Oratorical Club.
    The champions of the Oratori-
cal Club. [Oxford?] 1830. Kyle
311.   2552

Michigan (Territory)   ·
    Acts passed at the first ses-
sion of the fourth legislative
council of the Territory of Michigan. Begun and held at the Council chamber, in the City of Detroit on Tuesday the eleventh day
of May... Pontiac, Pr. by Thomas
Simpson, 1830. 64 p. C-L; DLC;
MH-L; Mi; MiD-B; MiU; NNB; Nb;
OCLaw; RPL; WHi; WaU-L. 2553

---- Discours du Gouverneur.
Concitoyens du conseil legisla-
tiff... Lew Cass. Detroit, le 12
de Mai, 1830. Bdsd. MiD-B.
2554

---- Journal of the legislative
council of the territory of Michigan, being the first session of
the fourth council. Begun and
held at the city of Detroit, May
11, 1830. Monroe, Pr. by Edw.
D. Ellis, 1830. 148 p. DLC; M;
MiD-B; MiGr; MiU; MnHi; NN;
WHi.   2555

Michigan register, and farmers'
calendar for 1831. Detroit, Geo.
L. Whitney [1830] 14 l. MiD-B.
2556
Middlebrook's almanac for 1831.
By Elijah Middlebrook. Bridgeport, Stanley Lockwood [1830] 12
l. MWA.   2557
---- ---- Middletown, D. D. Par-
melee [1830] 12 l. NHi; NNA.
2558
---- ---- New Haven, S. Babcock [1830] 14 l. Ct; CtHi; CtY;
InU; MWA (2 varieties); NN.
2559
---- ---- New Haven, S. Babcock; Hartford, D. F. Robinson
& Co. [1830] 12 l. CtY.   2560

Middlebrook's almanack for 1831.
By Elijah Middlebrook. Bridgeport,
J. B. & L. Baldwin [1830] 12 l. Ct;
CtB; CtHi; CtY; MWA.   2561

Middlebury Female Seminary.
Middlebury, Vermont.
Catalogue of the officers and
members of Middlebury Female
Seminary, 1830. Middlebury, Pr.
by Ovid Miner, 1830. 8 p. MH;
VtMiS. 2562

Middlesex Auxiliary Society for
the Education of Pious Youth for
the Ministry of God.
Annual report of the directors
of the Middlesex Auxiliary Society for the Education of Pious
Youth for the Ministry of God.
Presented June 8, 1830. Boston,
Pr. by Jonathan Howe, 1830.
12 p. MBC; MWA. 2563

Middlesex Canal.
Regulation relative to the navigation... Boston, Mechanicks
Magazine, 1830. 18 p. MH-BA.
2564

Miles, Solomon P.
Mathematical tables, comprising logarithms of numbers, logarithmic sines, tangents, and se-
cants, natural sines, meridional
ports, difference of latitude, and
departure astronomical refrac-
tions. & etc. Boston, Carter &
Hendee, 1830. 10, 78 p. MB;
MH; NNe; NWM; OMC; PPi; PU;
BrMus. 2565

The Military Academy at West
Point, unmasked; or Corruption
and military despotism exposed.
By Americanus. Washington,
1830. 28 p. Sabin 48952. 2566

Miller, David.
The practical horse farrier,
containing a treatise on the different diseases of horses, and
the cures for the same. Hamilton, Ohio, Pr. for the publisher, by E. Shaeffer, 1830. 128,
[3] p. OClWHi. 2567

Miller, James William, d. 1829.
Poems and sketches... Boston,

Carter & Hendee, 1830. 1 p. l.,
165 p. CSmH; DLC; ICU; MB;
MH; NNC; NbU; BrMus. 2568

Miller, Robert.
The dying confession...
Whitesboro, 1830. NN imprint
catalogue. 2569

Miller, Samuel, 1769-1850.
The importance of mature
preparatory study for the minis-
try: an introductory lecture, de-
livered at the opening of the
summer session of the Theologi-
cal Seminary at Princeton, New
Jersey, June 3, 1829... Andover
[Mass.] Pub. and for sale by
Mark Newman, Flagg & Gould,
prs., 1830. 30 p. CSmH; CtHC;
DLC; ICN; MBAt; MBC; MH;
MdBJ; MeB; MiD-B; NCH; NjP;
NjR; PHi; PPPrHi; TxU. 2570

---- Letters concerning the constitution and order of the Christian
ministry: addressed to the members of the Presbyterian church
in the city of New York. To
which is prefixed, a letter on the
present aspect and bearing of the
Episcopal controversy. 2d ed.
Philadelphia, Towar & Hogan,
1830. 485 p. CBPac; CtHC;
CtHT; GDC; IEG; KyLoP; LNB;
MBC; MeBaT; MiU; NCH; NcU;
Nh; NjP; NjR; OMC; PPPrHi;
RNR; BrMus. 2571

---- The utility and importance
of creeds and confessions addressed particularly to candidates for the ministry. Philadelphia, Presbyterian board of publication [c1830] 119 p. CtHC.
2572
Miller's planters' and merchants'
almanac for 1831. By Joshua
Sharp. Charleston, A. E. Miller
[1830] 24 l. ScC; ScHi. 2573

---- ---- Charleston, A. E. Miller [1830] (2d ed.) Drake

13278.   2574

---- ---- Charleston, A. E. Miller [1830] (3d ed.) 24 l. MWA; Sc.   2575

Milmon, Henry Hart, 1791-1868.
The history of the Jews, from the earliest period to the present time. By Rev. H. H. Milmon... In three volumes. New York, Pub. by J. & J. Harper [etc.] 1830. 3 vols. C; MH-AH; MdBLC; MdW; NBuDD; NNS; NRU; NcU; NjR; P; RP; ScCC; ViR; TNJ.   2576

Milner, Henry M.
...Masaniello; or, The dumb girl of Portici: a musical drama, in three acts. New-York, R. H. Elton, publisher, 1830. 47 p. MB; MH; MWA.   2577

[Milnor, William, jr.] 1769-1848.
An authentic historical memoir of the Schuylkill Fishing Company of the state in Schuylkill... By a member. Philadelphia, Pub. by. Judah Dobson, 1830. viii, 127 p. DLC; MB; MBAt; MH; PHi; PP; PPAmP; PPL; PU; RNR; WHi.   2578

[----] Memoirs of the Gloucester fox hunting club, near Philadelphia. Philadelphia, Pub. by Judah Dobson, 1830. 56 [1] p. (Issued with An authentic historical memoir of the Schuylkill Fishing Company.) DLC; MH; PHi; PP; PPL.   2579

Milton, John.
Paradise lost; a poem in twelve books... By John Milton. New York, H. R. Piercy [1830?] 283 p. NjP.   2580

---- ---- New York, S. & D. A. Forbes, 1830. 316 p. ICU. 2581

---- ---- Philadelphia, Pub. by L. Johnson, 1830. 3 l., 306 p. IU; MoS.   2582

---- Milton's poetical works... Together with the life of the author... New York, C. Wells [183-] 3 p. l. [5]-321, 232 p. DLC.   2583

Miniature almanack for 1831. Boston, Richardson, Lord & Holbrook [1830] 14 l. MHi; MWA; NN; WHi.   2584

---- Issue with 20 l. CLU; MWA; MnU; WHi.   2585

Miniature almanack, for the year of our Lord 1831. ..."Much in a little." Hartford, Pub. by H. & F. J. Huntington [1830?] unpaged. CtHi.   2586

The minstrel boy, containing a collection of the most fashionable and delightful songs. Philadelphia, Pub. and for sale, wholesale only, by Freeman Scott, 1830. 144 p. PPL.   2587

[The minstrel's cabinet; a new collection of the most popular, sentimental, comic patriotic, and naval songs... New-York, D. Mallory, 183-?] 2 v. RPB.
                        2588
Missionary Society of Connecticut.
The trustees of the Missionary Society of Connecticut to the benevolent and patriotic in every part of the state. [Hartford, P. B. Gleason & Co., prs., 1830] 4 p. CtSoP.   2589

Mississippi.
Auditor's office, Jackson, November 22, 1830. To the honorable the General Assembly of the state of Mississippi. In obedience to a resolution of the General Assembly, passed No-

vember 16, 1830, requiring the auditor of public accounts and the treasurer to lay before the General Assembly, on Monday the 22nd inst. their respective reports as auditor and treasurer... [Jackson, Pr. by Peter Isler, 1830] Bdsd. Ms-Ar. 2590

---- Journal of the House of Representatives, of the state of Mississippi, at their thirteenth session, held in the town of Jackson. Pub. by authority. Jackson, Pr. by Peter Isler, 1830. 295 p. DLC; M; Ms; Ms-Ar; MsU; MsWJ; NN; OClW; WHi. 2591

---- Journal of the House of Representatives, of the state of Mississippi, at their fourteenth session, held in the town of Jackson. Pub. by authority. Jackson, Pr. by Peter Isler, 1830. 262 p. CSmH; DLC; M; Ms; Ms-Ar; MsU; MsW; NN; OClW; WHi. 2592

---- Journal of the Senate of the state of Mississippi. At their thirteenth session, held in the town of Jackson. Pub. by authority. Jackson, Miss., Peter Isler, state pr., A.D. 1830. 182 p., MsU; MsWJ. 2593

---- Journal of the Senate of the state of Mississippi, at their fourteenth session, held in the town of Jackson. Pub. by authority. Jackson, Pr. by Peter Isler, 1830. 206 p. CSmH; DLC; M; Ms; MsU; MsWJ; NN; WHi. 2594

---- Laws of the state of Mississippi, passed at the thirteenth session of the General Assembly, held in the town of Jackson. Pub. by authority. Jackson, Peter Isler, state pr., 1830. 206, viii, [14] p. DLC; Ia; In-SC; M; MH-L; MdBB; Mi-L; MiU-L; Ms; Ms-Ar; MsU; MsWJ; NN; NNB; NNC-L; NNLI; OCLaw; RPL. 2595

---- Laws of the state of Mississippi, passed at the fourteenth session of the General Assembly, held in the town of Jackson. Pub. by authority. Jackson, Peter Isler, state pr., 1830. 146, xviii p. C-L; DLC; ICLaw; Ia; In-SC; M; MH-L; Mi-L; MiU-L; Mo; Ms; Ms-Ar; MsU; NNB; NNC-L; NNLI; Nb; Nj; Nv; O-SC; OCLaw; RPL. 2596

---- Official documents, transmitted to the Senate of the state of Mississippi, and printed by authority thereof. [Jackson, Pr. by Peter Isler, 1830] Bdsd. CSmH. 2597

---- Secretary of state's office, Jackson, November 24, 1830. The Honorable A.M. Scott, Lieutenant Governor and President of the Senate. Sir:-- Agreeably to a Resolution of the honorable body, over which you preside, of the 23d instant--I herewith have the honor to hand you an abstract of the census of the state ... [Jackson, 1830] Bdsd. Ms-Ar. 2598

---- Treasurer's report. Treasurer's office, Jackson, Nov. 22, 1830. To the Honorable the General Assembly of the state of Mississippi. Gentlemen:--Pursuant to the provisions of an act of the General Assembly, entitled An act concerning the appointment and duties of Treasurer and Auditor of Public Accounts passed the 18th June, 1822, and of Sundry acts amendatory thereto:... [Jackson, Pr. by Peter Isler, 1830] Bdsd. Ms-Ar. 2599

Missouri.

The decisions of the Supreme Court of the state of Missouri, from 1828 to 1830. Published in compliance with an act of the General Assembly of the state of

Missouri, entitled, "An Act to provide for the publication and distribution of thf [sic] decisions of the Supreme Court of this State." Approved, January first, in the year of our Lord one thousand eight hundred and twenty seven. John C. Edwards, Secretary of State. City of Jefferson, Calvin Gunn, pr., 1830. viii, 239, 2, 12 p. P.   2600

Mitchell, Alexander.
Universalism, and the editors of the Sentinel and Star in the West exposed.... Also, Dr. Franklin's motion for prayers in the national convention, and his letter to Thomas Paine, about his Age of Reason; is appended. Eaton, O., Pr. by E. Edmonson, 1830. 40 p. PPPrHi.   2601

Mitchell, Alfred.
Sermon, delivered in the Second Congregational Church in Norwich: on the second Sabbath in July, 1829... Norwich, Pr. by J. Dunham, 1830. 32 p. CtHi.   2602

[Mitchell, Isaac]
Alonzo and Melissa: or the unfeeling father. An American tale... by Daniel Jackson, Jr. [pseud.] Philadelphia, Abel Brown, 1830. 256 p. DLC; MB; MH; ViU.   2603

Mitchell, John Kearsley, 1798-1858.
On the penetrativeness of fluids... Extracted from the American Journal of the Medical Sciences, for November, 1830. Philadelphia, Pr. by Joseph R. A. Skerrett, 1830. 34 p. PHi; PPL.   2604

Mitchell, Mary.
A short account of the early part of the life of Mary Mitchell, written by herself. With selections from some other of her writings and two testimonies of monthly-meetings of Friends on Rhode-Island and Nantucket, concerning her. New York, Pr. by R. & G. S. Wood, 1830. InRE; MBC; MH; MiD-B; NPV; OClWHi; RNHi.   2605

Mitford, Mary Russell, 1787-1855.
Our village: Sketches of rural character and scenery. New York, E. Bliss [J. Seymour, pr.] 1830. 2 l., [13]-275 p. PU.   2606

Mix, Silas.
An oration, delivered at the national celebration, at New-Haven, Con., July 3, 1830. Published by request. New-Haven, Pr. by Charles Adams [1830?] 20 p. Ct; CtHi; DLC; MH; PPL.   2607

The modern traveller. A popular description, geographical, historical and topographical, of the various countries of the Globe. In ten volumes. Boston, Pub. by Wells & Lilly, and Thomas Wardel, Philadelphia, 1830-31. 10 vols. MB; MC; MH-AH; MWA; Mi; NGH; NNS; NcU; OClWHi; P; PU; RP; TNJ.   2608

Mohawk and Hudson Railroad Company.
An act to incorporate the Mohawk and Hudson Rail Road Company, passed April 17, 1826. And an act to amend the act to incorporate the Mohawk and Hudson Rail Road Company, passed April 17, 1826. Passed March 28, 1828. New York, Ludwig & Tolefree, 1830. 12 p. DBRE.   2609

The monitor: containing reasons against desertion in husband or wife. Also principles for receiving and paying money. To which is added some considerations on temperate societies.

Concord, Pr. by Henry E. Moore, 1830. 22 p. NhHi. 2610

Monson Academy.
Catalogue of the trustees, instructors and students of Monson Academy, during the year ending August 18th, 1830. Springfield, A. G. Tannatt, pr., 1830. 8 p. MMonsA. 2611

Montefiore, Joshua, 1762-1843.
Synopsis of mercantile laws, with an appendix; ... A new edition, revised, corrected and enlarged, with reference to the alterations effected by the revised statutes of the state of New York. New York, G. & C. H. Carvill [H. R. Piercy, pr.] 1830. xvii, [168], 335, [3] p. CU-Law; KWiU; LNB; LU; MH-L; MiU; MoU; Ms; NNC-L; NNLI; NRAL; OCLaw; UU. 2612

Montgomery, George Washington, 1804-1841.
Novelas espanolas. El serrano de las Alpujarras; y El cuadro misterioso. Brunswick, imprenta de Griffin, se halla de venta en la libraria de Colman, Portland, 1830. 80 p. CSmH; DLC; NBuU. 2613

Montgomery, Henry.
The importance and method of early religious education. Pr. for the American Unitarian Association. Boston, Gray & Bowen [I. R. Butts, pr.] 1830. 48 p. ICMe; M; MBAt; MHi; MMeT-Hi; MeB; OClWHi. 2614

Montgomery, Robert, 1807-1855.
The omnipresence of the diety. A poem by Robert Montgomery. New-York, Pub. by A. Sherman, agent, 1830. 144 p. NNU; TxU. 2615

[Moore, Charles Whitlock]
To the ingenious and candid. The Masonic character and correspondence of General Washington. By the editor of the Masonic Mirror. Boston, Moore and Sevey, 1830. 18 p. CSmH; MB; MH; MWA. 2616

Moore, Gabriel T.
To the freemen of Stokes County. [2] p. Bdsd. NcU. 2617

Moore, Henry, 1751-1844.
The life of Mrs. Mary Fletcher, consort and relict of the Rev. John Fletcher, Vicar of Madeley, Salop. Compiled from her journal and other authentic documents. By Henry Moore... New York, Pub. by J. Emory and B. Waugh for the Methodist Episcopal Church. J. Collord, pr., 1830. 391 p. CtW; NcD. 2618

Moore, Humphrey, d. 1871.
A discourse, to encourage abstinence from distilled spirits. Delivered in Milford, N. H. November, 1829; and afterward in several neighboring towns, by Humphrey Moore... Amherst, Pr. by R. Boylston, at the Cabinet press, February, 1830. 16 p. CSmH. 2619

Moore, Thomas.
The poetical works of Thomas Moore, including his melodies, ballads, etc. Complete in one volume. Philadelphia, Pub. by J. Crissy and J. Grigg. Stereotyped by J. Johnson, 1830. 419 p. KyBB; RPAt; WvU. 2620

Moravians.
The church litany of the United Brethren... New Echota [Ga.], Pr. for the United Brethren, Jno. F. Wheeler, pr., 1830. 12 p. MB. 2621

[More, Hannah] 1745-1833.
The happy waterman; or Honesty the best policy... New York, Pr. and sold by Mahlon Day,

1830. 23 p. N.   2622

---- ... The history of Tom White, the post boy. By Hannah More. Published by the "Episcopal Female Tract Society of Philadelphia," for the "Society of the Protestant Episcopal Church for the Advancement of Christianity in Pennsylvania." Philadelphia, Pr. by William Stavely, 1830. 12 p. (Religious tracts, No. 71) PPL.   2623

---- The pilgrims, an allegory... Philadelphia, American Sunday School Union [1830?] 1 p. l., [5]-36 p. (No. 919. IX series.) CSmH.   2624

---- Practical piety or the influence of the religion of the heart in the conduct of the life. New York, T. & J. Swords, 1830. 264 p. MH; OMC.   2625

---- The shepherd of Salisbury Plain. By Hannah More. New ed. Revised by the Committee of Publication. Philadelphia, Pub. by the American Sunday School Union [1830] 70 p. MeBa; PPL; PSC-Hi; BrMus.   2626

---- ---- New York, American Tract Society [183-?] 28 p. MnS.   2627

[----] ... 'Tis all for the best. New York, Pub. by the American Tract Society, D. Fanshaw, pr., [183-?] 16 p. CSmH.   2628

---- ... The valley of tears; a vision, or, Bear ye one another's burthens. By Hannah More. Published by the "Episcopal Female Tract Society of Philadelphia," for the "Society of the Protestant Episcopal Church for the Advancement of Christianity in Pennsylvania." Philadelphia, Pr. by William Stavely, 1830. 8 p. (Religious tracts - no. 78.)

PPL.   2629

---- The works of Hannah More. With a sketch of her life... Philadelphia, Pub. by J. J. Woodward, 1830. 2 v. FTU; GEU; GU; MB; MdBS-P; MoS; NCH; NNUT; NbOP; Nj; OCHP; RPA; TNJ; ViU.   2630

Morgan, Sydney Owenson, Lady.
    France in 1829-30. By Lady Morgan... in two volumes. New-York, Pr. by J. & J. Harper; Sold by Collins and Hannay [etc.] 1830. 2 vols. CSmH; GEU; ICU; KHi; KyLx; LNHT; MeBa; NCH; NNC; NcD; NjR; PPL; VtU; WU.   2631

Morgan, William, 1774-ca. 1826.
    The mysteries of free masonry; containing all the degrees of the order conferred in a master's lodge, as written by Captain William Morgan... Rev. and cor. to correspond with the most approved forms [and] ceremonies in the various lodges of Free masons throughout the United States. By George R. Crafts... New York, Wilson and Company [183-?] 112 p. CSmH.   2632

The morning ride. Philadelphia, American Sunday School Union [1830?] BrMus.   2633

Morris, Bethuel F., and Ray, James M.
    Addresses, delivered at the Sunday school celebration of the fifty-fourth anniversary of American independence, in Indianapolis, on Saturday, the 3d of July, 1830. By Hon. B. F. Morris, and James M. Ray, esq. Indianapolis, Ind., Pr. by Douglass & Maguire, 1830. 20 p. In; PPPrHi.   2634

Morris, John Williams.
    Memoirs of the life and writings of the Rev. Andrew Fuller,

late pastor of the Baptist Church at Kettering, and first secretary to the Baptist Missionary Society. 1st American from the last London ed. Edited by Rufus Babcock, jun. Boston, Pub. by Lincoln & Edmands, 1830. 320 p. CtHC; GMM; ICMcC; MB; MBC; MH-AH; MoSpD; NNUT; NcD; RPB; ViAl; VtU.   2635

[Morrison, John B.]
An original tale; Isabella of Brooke; contrasting the manners and customs of Pennsylvania and Virginia, with the polished refinements of the present age. (By a Pennsylvanian) Pittsburgh, Pub. by the author, 1830. 118 p. CtY; MWA; PPi; PPiU; TxU.
2636

Morrison, Thomas.
Morrison's new map of the Huson river, with a description of the adjoining country... Pub. and sold by Thomas Morrison, Philadelphia. Elliott's public printing office [1830] 1 p. DLC.
2637

---- The traveller's companion. Morrison's North River traveller's companion, containing a map of the Hudson or North river, with a description of the adjoining country... Also a table showing the distance of the principal towns in the United States from each other; the length of the principal railroads and canals, finished or in progress, in the United States. Philadelphia, [Thomas Morrison, 183-?] folded map. DBRE; MB.   2638

Morsman, Oliver.
A history of Breed's (commonly called) Bunker's Hill Battle... Sackets Harbor (N.Y.), T. W. Haskell, 1830. 17 p. MH; MMal.
2639
Morton, Daniel Oliver, 1788-1852, comp.

Memoir of the Rev. Levi Parsons, first missionary to Palestine from the United States, containing sketches of his early life and education, his missionary labours in this country, in Asia Minor and Judea, with an account of his last sickness and death. 2d ed. Compiled and prepared by the Rev. Daniel O. Morton. Burlington, Pub. by Chauncey Goodrich [etc., etc.] 1830. 408 p. DLC; GEU; ICU; MH; MnSM; NN; NjPT; OClW; OO; RPB.   2640

Morton, Samuel George, 1799-1851.
Notice of the Academy of Natural Sciences of Philadelphia. By a member. Philadelphia, 1830. 11 p. [Extracted from the Am. Journal of Science and Arts, no. 1, vol. 1a.] DLC.   2641

---- Synopsis of the organic remains of the Ferruginous sand formation of the United States; with Geological Remarks. ["Extracted from the American Journal of Science and Arts, No. 2, Vol. 17."] 31 p. PPL.   2642

Morton, Thomas, 1764?-1838.
The children in the wood, an opera, in two acts... Pr. from the acting copy. Cumberland's ed. ...as now performed at the London & New York theatres. New York, Clayton & Van Norden, 1830. 36 p. MH; NCH.
2643

No entry.   2644

Moses, Myer.
The commercial directory and a digest of the laws of the United

States relating to commerce...
Tables of calculation applicable
to manufactures of imported wool
or cotton. New York, Ludwig
& Tolefree, 1830. 280 p. DeGE;
Ia; MB; MH-L; NNC-L; NUtHi;
WHi.   2645

---- Full annals of the revolution
in France 1830. To which is
added a full account of the celebration of said revolution in the
city of New York on the 25th of
November, 1830. Being the forty-
seventh anniversary of an event
that restored our citizens to their
homes and to the enjoyment of
their rights and liberties. New
York, Pr. by J. & J. Harper
[etc.] 1830. 255, 151 p. CSfCW;
DLC; GAGT; MBC; MH; NCH;
NjP; NjR; RPB; BrMus.   2646

Most important testimony ad-
duced on the trial of John Francis Knapp and Joseph Jenkins
Knapp, jr., for the murder of
Capt. Joseph White of Salem...
April 6, 1830. Providence, 1830.
36 p. RPB.   2647

A Mother, pseud.   See Adams,
Catherine (Lyman).

The mother's gift. New-York, Pr.
and sold by Mahlon Day [183-?]
8 p. RPB.   2648

Moultrie, James, 1793-1869.
    An eulogium on Stephen Elliott,
M.D. and LL.D. professor of nat-
ural history, and botany in the
Medical College of S.C. Deliv-
ered by appointment of the facul-
ty, and the philosophical society,
at the opening of the college on
8th November, 1830. Charleston,
Pr. by A.E. Miller, 1830. 46 p.
MB; MBAt; MH; NNBG; NcD;
PPAmP; RPB; ScC; ScHi; ScU.
                                        2649
Mount Auburn Cemetery.

The picturesque pocket companion, and visitors guide, through
Mount Auburn: illustrated with
upwards of sixty engravings on
wood. Boston [183-?] 252 p.
MHi.   2650

Mount Carbon Railroad Company.
    Act of incorporation and by-
laws of the Mount Carbon Rail
Road Company. Philadelphia, Pr.
for the company by Thomas
Town, 1830. 24 p. DBRE; DeGE;
ICU; IU; MH; MWA; MiU-T; NN;
PHi; PPL.   2651

Mount Vernon Female School.
Boston.
    First annual catalogue... From
June 1829, to June 1830. Boston, T.R. Marvin, pr., 1830.
12 p. MH.   2652

[Mudge, Enoch] 1776-1850
    Lynn, a poem. Lynn, C.F.
Summers, 1830. 27 p. DLC.
                                        2653
Muenscher, Wilhelm, 1766-1814.
    Elements of dogmatic history
... Trans. from the 2d ed. ...
by James Murdock. New Haven,
Pub. by A.H. Maltby [Baldwin
and Treadway, pr.] 1830. 203 p.
CtHC; CtY; ICU; MB; MH; OO;
PPL.   2654

Mulkey, William.
    A syllabical spelling book...
To which is added, a hieroglyph-
ical arrangement of the alphabet
... Baltimore, Pub. by Armstrong & Plaskitt, and Plaskitt
& co., 1830. [2], 166 p. NNC.
                                        2655
---- ---- Washington, 1830.
144 p. NNC.   2656

Mumford, John I.
    Albany, 18th Jan. 1830. To
the members of the Legislature
of the state of New-York. I received on Saturday, an address
to the members of the Legisla-

ture, dated 13th inst., signed
James Watson Webb... [Albany,
1830] Bdsd. NN.   2657

Murder of Joseph White. The
following lines were written on
the death of Mr. Joseph White,
of Salem, who was found murdered in his bed on the morning
of the 7th April, 1830, aged 82.
Sold wholesale and retail, corner of Merchant's Row & Market
Square, Boston [1830] Bdsd.
MHi.   2658

Murray, Lindley, 1745-1826.
Abridgement of Murray's Eng-
lish grammar... Albany, 1830.
MH.   2659

---- ---- Bellows Falls, J. I.
Cutler and Co., 1830. 108 p.
MH.   2660

---- ---- Boston, Lincoln & Edmands, 1830. MH.   2661

---- ---- From the latest London ed., corr. by Mr. Murray
himself. Stereotyped by T. Wool-
son, Claremont N.H. Concord,
N.H., Pub. by Marsh, Capen &
Lyon, 1830. 100 p. At head of
title: Murray's abridgment - Revised ed. NNC.   2662

---- ---- Peekskill, N.Y., Pr.
by S. Marks & son, 1830. 107 p.
CSmH.   2663

---- The English reader; or,
Pieces in prose and poetry, se-
lected from the best writers...
Baltimore, Pub. by Armstrong
& Plaskitt, 1830. 252 p. MdHi.
                          2664

---- ---- Boston, Lincoln &
Edmands, 1830. 264 p. IEdS;
MdW.   2665

---- ---- Stereotyped by A.
Chandler, New-York. Cleaveland, Pr. and pub. by R. Pew

& Co., 1830. 258 p. OClWHi
(incomplete).   2666

---- ---- Stereotyped by A.
Chandler, New York. Hallowell,
Pub. by Calvin Spaulding [1830]
258 p. MBE.   2667

---- ---- Providence, J. Hutchens, 1830. MH.   2668

---- The English reader, or Pieces
in prose and verse. Albany, Pub.
and sold by G. L. Loomis, 1830.
250p. MH; MPB.   2669

---- ---- Newark, N. J., Benjamin Olds, 1830. 252 p. CtMW;
NN; PP.   2670

---- ---- Pr. and pub. by William Williams, Utica, 1830.
252 p. DLC; MWA; MWHi; NUt;
OCl.   2671

---- Introduction to the English
reader; or, A selection of pieces,
in prose and poetry; calculated
to improve the younger classes
of learners in reading... with an
appendix by Israel Alger. Boston, Lincoln and Edmands, 1830.
168 p. MH; PU-Penn.   2672

---- ---- Georgetown, D.C.,
Samuel S. Rind, 1830. xii, 153
p. DLC; DWP.   2673

---- ---- Philadelphia, J. M'-
Dowell, 1830. 167 p. ICU; PHi;
PU-Penn.   2674

---- Key to the exercises adapted to Murray's English grammar,
calculated to enable private learners to become their own instructers, in grammar and composition. By Lindley Murray. Stereotyped from the last English edition, by H. & H. Wallis, New-
York. New-York, Pub. by Collins & Hannay, 1830. viii, 168 p.
AzU; NNC.   2675

---- Murray's system of English grammar, improved and adapted to the present mode of instruction in this branch of science. By Enoch Pond. 3d ed. Worcester, Pub. by Dorr and Howland, 1830. 66 p. MFiHi; NjN; BrMus.   2676

Musical Fund Society of Philadelphia.
  The twenty-second concert will take place at their hall, in Locust Street, on Thursday, Nov. 18th, 1830. [Philadelphia, 1830] Bdsd. PPL.   2677

The musical man's companion; or, A new collection of love, masonic, sea and other songs. Paris, (Me.), Pub. at the Oxford bookstore, Asa Barton, pr., [1830?] 69 p. RPB.   2678

My father, a poem. New-York, Mahlon Day [183-?] Title on cover: Little Lucy and her lamb. 8 p. RPB.   2679

My grandfather Gregory. Rev. by the Committee of Publication. Philadelphia, American Sunday School Union, 1830. 144 p. PHi.
                                  2680
---- Another ed. [1830] 144 p. PHi.   2681

My mother. A poem. See Gilbert, Ann Taylor.

My sister. See Elliott, Mary (Belson).

Myers, Peter D., comp.
  The Zion songster: a collection of hymns and spiritual songs, generally sung at camp and prayer meetings, and in revivals of religion. Compiled by Peter D. Myers. New York, P. D. Myers, 1830. 352 p. NNG.   2682

---- ---- 3d ed., enl. and imp. New York, Pub. by the compiler, 1830. 352 p. ICN; RPB.   2683

N

Narrative of Emily Graham. Philadelphia, American Sunday School Union [1830?] BrMus.
                                  2684
A narrative of some of the adventures. See Martin, Joseph Plumb.

Narrative of the loss of the Kent by fire in the Bay of Biscay on the first of March 1825, in a letter to a friend by a passenger. Boston, Perkins & Marvin, 1830. 68 p. MB; PU.
                                  2685
National and domestic customs of the Jews, with a large and valuable map of Palestine; etc. Prepared by a Friend of youth. New York, Jonathan Leavitt, 1830. CtHC; MH; OMC.   2686

The National calendar and gentleman's almanac for 1831. Baltimore, Henry Vicary; William Wooddy, pr. [1830] 18 l. PP.
                                  2687
The national calendar for 1831. By Peter Force. Washington City, Peter Force [1830] 174 l. CtY; DLC; DWP; GU; InU; NBLiHi; NjP; OClWHi.   2688

---- ---- Washington City, Peter Force [1830] (2d ed.) 186 l. MBAt.   2689

National circular. Addressed to the head of each family in the United States. [New York, W. A. Hallock [183-] 12 p. Ct; DLC; MH; WHi; BrMus.   2690

National Journal, Washington, D. C.
  New Year's address of the carriers of the National Journal. Friday January 1, 1830. [Wash-

ington, D. C., 1830] 1 p. DLC.
2691

National Republican Party. Kentucky. Convention, 1830.
Proceedings of the National Republican Convention held at Frankfort, Kentucky, on Thursday, December 9, 1830. 19 p. MB. 2692

---- Maryland.
Address of the convention of National Republicans, at Baltimore, to the Voters of Maryland. [Baltimore, 1830] Sabin 45050.
2693

Natural history of enthusiasm. See Taylor, Isaac.

Natural history of insects. See Rennie, James.

Nature and philosophy. Adapted from the French. By a citizen of Richmond. (Va.) as now performed at the New-York theatres. New-York, R. Hobbs, publisher, 1830. 33 p. ICU; MB; MH; RPB; Vi. 2694

The nautical almanack and ephemeris, for the year 1831. New York, Repub. by John H. Wheeler, Mission & Utley, 1830. 75, [1] p. MWA. 2695

The naval monument. See Bowen, Abel.

[Neal, John] 1793-1876.
Authorship, a tale. By a New Englander over-sea. Boston, Gray and Bowen, 1830. iv, 267 p. CSmH; CtHT-W; CtY; DLC; ICN; IU; LNHT; MB; MH; MWA; MeHi; MnU; NIC; NN; NjP; PP; PU; RPB; ViU. 2696

---- Our country. An address delivered before the alumni of Waterville-College, July 29, 1830. Portland, S. Colman [Todd, pr.] 1830. 36 p. CSmH; CtY; MH;

MWA; MdHi; NN; NNC; NjP; OClWHi; RPB; WHi. 2697

Neapolitan captive. Interesting narrative of the captivity and sufferings of Miss Viletta Laranda, A native of Naples... Communicated by an officer of respectable rank in the Army, to his friend in Paris. 3d ed. New York, Pub. by Charles C. Henderson, 1830. 36 p. MBAU. 2698

Neele, Henry, 1798-1828.
The tales of the late Henry Neele... Blanche of Bourbon. The garter. The magician's visitor. The comet. The houri. The poet's dream. Hamilton [N. Y.] Pub. by Williams, Orton & co., at the University press, 1830. 156 p. CSmH. 2699

The "Negro Pew" being an inquiry concerning the propriety of distinction in the house of God, on account of color. Boston [183-?] 108 p. MHi. 2700

Nelson, E.
The use of ardent spirits in a professing Christian a great sin. A discourse delivered before the Temperance Society in Woburn, December 14, 1829... Boston, Peirce and Williams, 1830. 12 p. MBC; MH; MWA; MiD-B; BrMus. 2701

Nepos, Cornelius.
Cornelius Nepos De Vita Excellentium Imperatorum. Accedunt Notae Anglicae atque index historicus et geographicus. Bostoniae, Hilliard, Gray, Little et Wilkins, 1830. iv, 192 p. ICMcC; ICU; KWiU; MB; MH; MeBa; MnSH; NNC; OClW; PLFM; PPL. 2702

Neu Jahrs-Wunsch Des Herumträgers des Unabhängigen Republikaners. Zum 1sten Januar

1830. ALT.   2703

Der Neue, Americanische Land-
wirthschafts-Calender auf 1831.
Von Carl Friedrich Egelmann.
Reading, Johann Ritter u. Comp.
[1830] 18 l. InU; MWA; P;
PPAmP; PPL; PPeSchw; PR;
PRHi.   2704

Der neue Nord-Americanische
Stadt und Land Calender Auf das
Jahr... 1831. Hagerstaun, Pr.
by J. Gruber [1830] Seidensticker p. 245.   2705

Der neue Pennsylvanische Stadt-
und Land-Calender a 1831. Allentown, Heinrich Ebner [1830]
Drake 11735.   2706

Neuer Gemeinnüzige Pennsylvan-
ischer Calender auf 1831. Lancaster, Johann Baer [1830]
Drake 11736.   2707

Nevin, John W.
    A summary of Biblical antiqui-
ties... By John W. Nevin... Revised and corr. by the author for
the American Sunday School Union.
Philadelphia, American Sunday
School Union, 1830. 2 v. CtY;
MoSpD; NIC; BrMus.   2708

New Bedford Courier.
    The carriers of the New-Bed-
ford Courier, to their patrons.
January 1, 1830. [New Bed-
ford, Mass.] Pr. by the New
Bedford Courier [1830] Bdsd.
MNBedf.   2709

New Bedford, Mass.
    Report of the selectmen. Ex-
penditures for the town of New-
Bedford, paid by the selectmen,
during the year ending March 22,
1830. New Bedford [Mass.] B.
T. Congdon, pr., 1830. Bdsd.
MNBedf.   2710

---- Friends' Academy.

A catalogue of the trustees,
instructers, and pupils of
Friends' Academy, New-Bedford,
Mass.   For the year ending July
1st, 1830. New-Bedford, S. S.
Smith [1830] 16 p. M; MB; MH;
MNBedf; MWA.   2711

New Bedford Young Men's Temperance Society.
    Constitution of the... adopted
July 183- and their address to
the public. New Bedford [183-]
24 p. MHi.   2712

New Brunswick (N. J.), Almanack
for 1831. By Joshua Sharp. Philadelphia, Griggs & Dickinson, for
Joseph C. Griggs, New Brunswick, (N. J.) [1830] 18 l. NBLiHi;
NjHi; NjR.   2713

New Castle and Frenchtown Railroad Company.
    Acts passed by the legislatures
of Maryland and Delaware, authorising the construction of a
railroad from French-Town to
New-Castle. n. p. [1830?] 23 p.
CSt; DBRE; NNC.   2714

The New England almanac &
Methodist register for 1831. By
Aaron Lummus. Boston, John
Putnam [1830] 30 l. DLC; MBAt;
MHi; MWA; MiD-B; PHi.   2715

---- ---- Boston, Putnam &
Hunt [1830] 28 l. MB; MWA;
MnU; N; NHi.   2716

The New-England almanack, and
farmers' friend for 1831. By
Nathan Daboll. New-London,
Samuel Green [1830] 16 l. CLU;
Ct; CtHT-W; CtHi; CtW; CtY;
DLC; InU; MB; MH; MWA; N;
NB; NNC; OClWHi; WHi.   2717

The New England Anti-Masonic
almanac for 1831. By Edward
Giddings. Boston, John Marsh &
Co. [1830] 24 l. CLU; CtHi;

IaCrM; InU; MA; MB; MH; MHi; MWA; MnU; NIC; OClWHi; PPFM. 2718

---- ---- Boston, John Marsh & Co.; Philadelphia, S. W. Tobey [1830] 24 l. MBAt; N; NBLiHi; NHi.   2719

No entry   2720

The New England farmer's almanac for 1831. By Thomas G. Fessenden. Boston, Carter & Hendee; I. R. Butts, pr. [1830] 20 l. CLU; CtY; DLC; InU; MBAt; MBC; MH; MHi; MWA; MeHi; MiD-B; MnU; N; NHi; NN; NhHi; OClWHi; RPB; WHi. 2721

---- Issue with 24 l. Ct; KyHi; NjP; NjR; OC.   2722

---- By Truman Abell. Windsor, Simeon Ide [etc.] [1830] 24 l. DLC; InU; MWA; N; NhHi; NjR; OClWHi; Vt; VtHi.   2723

The New England Gazetteer; containing descriptions of all the states, counties and towns in New England... By John Hayward. 13th ed. Concord, N. H. [183-?] 514 p. MHi.   2724

New England Palladium.
   Address, to the patrons of the New-England Palladium, respectfully presented by the carriers, on the commencement of the new-year... Boston, January 1, 1830. [Boston, 1830] Bdsd. MB   2725

The New England primer; containing the Assembly's catechism; the account of the burning of John Rogers; a dialogue between Christ, a youth, and the devil; and various other useful and instructive matter. Adorned with cuts. With a historical introduction, by Rev. H. Humphrey...

Worcester, S. A. Howland [183-?] 64 p. Ct; DLC; MH; MiU-C; OClWHi; RPB.   2726

New England primer, for the more easy attaining the true reading of English. New Haven, S. Babcock, 1830. 66 p. Md.
                                2727

New England primer, improved ... To which is added, the Episcopal and the Assembly of divines' catechisms. New-Haven, Pub. by S. Babcock [1830?] 71, [1] p. CSmH.   2728

---- New and improved edition. New-York, Pub. for the booksellers. M. Day, pr., [183-] 71 p. CtHi.   2729

---- An easy and pleasant guide to the art of reading: to which is added, the Assembly's Shorter catechism. Philadelphia, Pub. and sold by F. Scott [1830?] 36 p. DLC; OClWHi.   2730

---- Boston, Massachusetts Sabbath School Society [183-?] 64 p. MH; WHi.   2731

---- To which is added, the Shorter catechism of the Westminster Assembly of Divines. Pittsburgh, Pub. by John H. Mellor [1830?] 48 p. CtSoP; MWA; NN.   2732

---- Pittsburgh, Pub. by Luke Loomis & Co. [1830?] 47 p. CtHT-W; CtSoP; DLC; MHi; MWA; NN; OClWHi.   2733

New England Society of Charleston, S. C.
   Rules of the New England Society of Charleston, S. C. Founded Jan. 6, 1819. To which is added a list of officers and members. Revised, Charleston, Pr. at the Office of the Courier, 1830. 25 p. DLC; IU.   2734

The New-England Sunday school hymn book. Prepared by the Board of managers of the Hartford County Union. Hartford, Pub. by D. F. Robinson & Co., 1830. 110 p. RPB.   2735

A New Englander over-sea, pseud. See Neal, John.

The new grist mill at Saccarappa [Maine] near the South West end of Long Bridge is now in operation...July, 1830. Bdsd. MeHi.
                                2736
New Hampshire.
    Journal of the honorable Senate of the state of New-Hampshire, at their session holden at the capitol in Concord, commencing Wednesday, June 2, 1830. Pub. by authority. Sandbornton, Pr. by N. Howland, 1830. 109 p. IaHi; Mi.   2737

---- Journal of the House of Representatives of the state of New-Hampshire, at their session, holden at the capitol in Concord, commencing Wednesday, June 2, 1830. Published by authority. Sandburton, Pr. by N. Howland, for the state, 1830. 228 p. MHi; Mi.   2738

---- The laws of the state of New-Hampshire; with the constitutions of the United States and of the state prefixed. Pub. by authority. Hopkinton, I. Long, jr., Luther Roby, pr.] 1830. vii, 623 p. Ar-SC; C; CSt; CU-Law; CtMW; DLC; IU; IaU-L; In-SC; Ky; M; MBU-L; MdBB; Mi-L; NNC-L; NNLI; Nb; Nj; Nv; OClW; R; TU; W; WaU.
                                2739
---- Reports of cases argued and determined in the Superior court of Judicature of the state of New Hampshire, from January term in the county of Merrimack, in the year 1827 to May

term, in the county of Grafton, in the year 1829, both inclusive. Vol. IV.   Chester, Currier, French and Brown, 1830. 590 p. Az; FU-L; G; IU-Law; Ia; In-SC; KyU-L; L; LU-L; MBU-L; MdBB; MdUL; MiD-B; Ms; NNIA; NNLI; Nc-S; Nd-L; NdU-L; Nv; U; WvW.   2740

The New-Hampshire annual register, and United States calendar for 1831. By John Farmer. Concord, Horatio Hill and Co.; Hill and Barton, prs. [1830] 72 l. CtY; ICN; InU; KyU; MB; MHi; MWA; MdBP; MiD-B; NHi; Nh; NhHi.   2741

New Hampshire Bible Society.
    The nineteenth report of the New Hampshire Bible Society, presented at the annual meeting of the Society, holden at Portsmouth, September 8, 1830. Concord, Pr. by Fisk & Chase, 1830. 40 p. DLC.   2742

New Hampshire Medical Society, Centre District.
    By-laws.   Concord, 1830. 16 p. NhHi.   2743

New Hampshire Missionary Society.
    Twenty-ninth annual report. Missionary Society...Holden at Portsmouth.   Concord, Pr. by Asa M'Farland, 1830. 31 p. MB; MiD-B.   2744

New Hampshire Savings Bank.
    Act of incorporation and by-laws of the New-Hampshire Savings Bank in Concord. Concord, Pr. at the N. H. Journal office, 1830. 16 p. MB; MBC; MiD-B; NhHi.   2745

New Hampshire Society for the Promotion of Temperance.
    First annual report of the New-Hampshire Society for the

Promotion of Temperance, read before the Society, June 2, 1830, together with the address of Rev. President Lord, upon the same occasion. Concord, Pr. by Asa M'Farland, 1830. 16 p. MH; PPL. 2746

New Haven (Conn.) Gymnasium.
Catalogue... February, 1830. 8 p. CtY. 2747

New Haven County Medical Society.
A report on the expediency of repealing that section of the medical laws of this state which excludes irregular practitioners from the benefits of law in collection of fees. New Haven, 1830. 16 p. MHi. 2748

New Haven Young Ladies Institute.
Catalogue of the instructors and pupils in the New Haven Young Ladies Institute during its first year, November, 1830. New Haven, 1830. 12 p. Ct; MB; MH; MiD. 2749

New Ipswich Academy.
Catalogue of New-Ipswich Academy for the term ending August 1830 with a statement of the plan of instruction. Amherst, N.H., Pr. by R. Boylston, 1830. 11 p. NhHi. 2750

New Jersey.
Acts of the fifty-fourth General Assembly of the state of New Jersey. At a session begun at Trenton, on the twenty-seventh day of October, one thousand eight hundred and twenty-nine: being the first sitting... Trenton, Joseph Justice, pr., 1829 [1830] 10 p. In-SC; Nb; Nj; T; W. 2751

---- ---- Acts--Being the second sitting. Trenton, Pr. by Joseph Justice, 1830. [11]-142 p.

PPL. 2752

---- Journal of the proceedings of the Legislative-council of the state of New Jersey, convened at Trenton... being the first sitting of the fifty-fourth and fifty-fifth sessions. Bridgeton, N.J.: Samuel S. Sibley, 1830-31. 2 v. NN; Nj. 2753

---- Minutes of the proceedings of the Legislative council of the state of New Jersey, sitting as a high Court of impeachment, at the city of Trenton, in the year ... one thousand eight hundred and thirty... [Bridgeton, N.J.] 1830. 26 p. (Part of no. 2753?) DLC. 2754

---- Rules and orders of the interior court of common pleas for the county of Bergen. Paterson, D. Burnett, pr., 1830. 16 p. NjR. 2755

---- Votes and proceedings of the fifty-fourth and fifty-fifth General Assemblies of the state of New Jersey, at sessions begun at Trenton... being the first sittings. Trenton, N.J., Joseph Justice, 1830-31. 2 v. Nj; NjR. 2756

New-Jersey almanac for 1831. By David Young. Salem, Elijah Brooks [1830] 18 l. MWA; NHi. 2757
---- Trenton, George Sherman [1830] 18 l. CtY; DLC; MBC; MWA; NHi; NjR; NjT; PHi. 2758

New-Jersey almanack for 1831. By David Young. Elizabeth-Town, Thomas O. Sayre [1830] 18 l. CtY; MWA; NjHi; NjR. 2759

---- ---- Newark, Benjamin Olds, [1830] 18 l. CLU; CtY; DLC; MWA; NjHi; NjR. 2760

New Jersey Missionary Society.
A statement of the proceedings

of the Princeton corresponding executive committee of the New Jersey Missionary Society. Princeton, Hugh Madden, pr., 1830. 20 p. NCH; NjP; NjR; PPPrHi.   2761

New Jerusalem Church. General Convention.
    Journal of proceedings of the twelfth General Convention Receivers of the Doctrines of the New Jerusalem in the United States. Held at the Temple of the Second New Jerusalem Church of Philadelphia, June 3d, 4th, & 5th, 1830. Philadelphia, Clark & Raser, 1830. 20, [2] p. OClWHi.   2762
New model of Christian missions. See Taylor, Isaac.

The New-Orleans directory & register by John Adems Paxton ... New-Orleans, Pr. for the author, A. T. Penniman & Co., prs., 1830. [312] p. LNHT.   2763
New Red Lion Vigilance Association.
    District list. [Philadelphia? ca. 1830] Bdsd. DeGE.   2764

New riddle book. New York, Pr. and sold by Mahlon Day, 1830. 18 p. MHi.   2765

New Salem Academy.
    Catalogue of the trustees, instructers, and students of New Salem Academy, October 1830. Wendell, J. Metcalf [1830] Bdsd. MB; MH.   2766

The new Sunday school hymn book. Prepared for the American Sunday School Union, and revised by the Committee of Publication. Philadelphia, American Sunday School Union [1830?] iv, 159, [1] p. NBuG.   2767

The new universal letter writer, containing a course of interesting letters. 8th ed., imp. Philadelphia, Towar & D. M. Hogan, 1830. 228 p. MWA; MoSHi; NSyHi; NhHi.   2768

New Year's address. [three columns of verse] Wilton, Jan. 1st, 1830. 1 p. DLC.   2769

New York (City)
    Annual report of the comptroller with the accounts of the corporation of the city of New-York... New-York, Pr. by P. Van Pelt, 1830. 15 p. NjR.   2770
---- A digest of all the laws and ordinances made and established by the mayor, aldermen & commonalty, of the city of New York, in common council convened, up to first of January, 1830; in which the plain and full meaning and operative parts of the ordinances are preserved. By a student at law. ...New York, Pr. and pub. by S. Gould, 1830. 125, 8 p. MH-L; NNC; NNLI; Nh.   2771

---- Fourth annual report of the governors of the Almshouse, New York, for the year 1830. New York, Charles Shields, pr., 1830. NjR.   2772

---- In Common council, September 20, 1830. The following report was received from the commissioners of the Alms-House, and directed to be printed for the use of the members. J. Morton, Clerk. [New York, 1830] 19 p. MB; ScU.   2773

---- Names and places of abode of the members of the Common Council, and of the officers who hold appointments under them. New-York, Pr. by Peter Van Pelt, 1830. 20 p. NBLiHi.   2774

New York (State)

An abstract of the most important alterations, of general interest, introduced by the Revised statutes; the principal part of which originally appeared in numbers published in the Ontario messenger; collected and examined by the author of those numbers, with the addition of notes, marginal references, forms of conveyances, &c., and an index. Canandaigua, Pr. by Day and Morse, at the office of the Ontario messenger, 1830. 2 p. l., 137 p. CSmH.   2775

---- ... Annual report of the commissioners of the canal fund of the state of New-York. ... Albany, Pr. by Croswell and Van Benthuysen, 1830. 31 p. MCM; MiD-B.   2776

---- Annual report of the Superintendent of Common Schools in the state of New York. [Presented Jan. 16th 1830] Republished by the Pennsylvania Society for the Promotion of Public Schools. Philadelphia, Mifflin & Parry, prs., March 18, 1830. 1 l., 14 p. PPL.   2777

---- Annual report of the trustees of the State Library. In Senate, February 19, 1830. No. 190. [Senate document no. 190?] 34 p. MB.   2778

---- Copy of the Register of Canal Boats, as appears from the book of registry, of those boats in the Comptroller's Office, on the 1st day of January 1830. [1830] 30 p. N.   2779

---- In Chancery, before the Chancellor. Daniel D. Campbell, complainant, vs. Joseph C. Yates, defendant. Albany, Pr. by Packard and Van Benthuysen, 1830. 82 p. MB; NjR.   2780

---- Journal of the Assembly of the state of New-York, at their fifty-third session, begun and held at the capitol, in the city of Albany, the 5th day of January, 1830. Albany, Pr. by E. Croswell, pr. to the state, 1830. 907 p. MB; NNLI; BrMus. 2781

---- Journal of the Senate of the state of New-York, at their fifty-third session, begun and held at the capitol, in the city of Albany, the 5th day of January, 1830. Albany, Pr. by E. Croswell, pr. to the state, 1830. 411 p. MB; NNLI; BrMus.   2782

---- Laws of the state of New York, passed at the fifty-third session of the legislature, begun and held at the city of Albany, the fifth day of January, 1830. Albany, Pr. by E. Croswell, pr. to the state, for Wm. Gould & Co., Albany, 1830. 483 p. ArSC; Az; C; CoU; IaU-L; In-SC; L; MH-L; Mi-L; N; NNLI; NNU; Nb; Nj; R; RPL; TxU-L; W; Wa-L.   2783

---- Legislative documents of the Senate and Assembly of the state of New York, fifty-third session 1830. Albany, Pr. by E. Croswell, pr. to the state, 1830. 3 v. ICU; NNLI; WHi; BrMus.   2784

---- Manual of the system practised in the primary departments of the New-York Public Schools. Prepared by S. W. Seton. New York, Pr. by Mahlon Day, 1830. 84 p. PPL.   2785

---- ... Memorial of the Professors of Rutgers Medical Faculty (Manhattan College) in the city of New York, in refutation of an attack upon them by the College of Physicians and Surgeons in the city of New-York. [Albany, 1830] 5, [1] p. (No.

297. In Senate, Mar. 19, 1830)
NjR.   2786

---- Notes on the revised stat-
utes of the state of New York.
Pointing out the principal altera-
tions made by them in the com-
mon and statute law.   Albany
(N.Y.), Pr. by Websters and
Skinners, 1830. 232 p. C; Ct;
ICLaw; IaU-L; MH-L; MdBB;
NNLI; WaU; BrMus.   2787

---- Report of the Superintendent
of Common Schools, in relation
to the Central Asylum and the
New-York Institution for the Instruction of the Deaf and Dumb.
Made to the Senate, March 3,
1830. Albany, Pr. by Croswell
and Van Benthuysen, 1830. [ii],
36 p. NbU; R; RPB.   2788

---- Reports of cases argued and
determined in the Court of Chan-
cery of the state of New York.
By Alonzo C. Paige. New York,
Pub. by Gould & Banks; and by
William Gould & Co. Albany,
G. M. Davison, Pr., Saratoga
Springs, 1830 [-49] 11 v. DLC;
FTU; Md; MiDu-L; NCH; NNC-L;
NNLT; NjR; OClW; PP; PPB;
PU; RPL; W.   2789

---- The revised fifty dollar act,
being title IV. chapter II. of
part III. of the revised statutes
of the state of New-York, entitled 'Of courts held by justices
of the peace,' which took effect
January 1, 1830. Rochester
[N.Y.] Pr. and pub. by E. Peck
& co., Sold also by William Williams, Utica... 1830. 68 p.
CSmH.   2790

---- Revised statute relating to
common schools being title II of
chapter XV. passed at the extra
session of the Legislature of the
state of New York, Dec. 3, 1827.
Albany, 1830. 40 p. N (not loc.

1971).   2791

---- Rules and orders of the
Court of common pleas for the
county of Columbia, made and
published by the judges of the
said court, November term, 1830.
Hudson, Pr. and pub. by B. Wilbur, 1830. 26 p. CSmH.   2792

---- Rules and orders of the
court of common pleas of Suffolk
county. Adopted May 25, 1830.
Sag-Harbour, Pr. at the Watchman office, 1830. 18 p. NSmB.
                          2793

---- Rules and orders of the
Supreme court of the state of
New-York, revised and established by the court, pursuant to
the directions of the Revised
statutes, and adapted to the provisions thereof. With precedents of bills of costs, and of
pleadings &c. in the actions of
ejectment approved by the judges.
Albany, William Gould & co.
[B.D. Packard & Co., prs.]
1830. vii, 51 p. MH-L; N;
NNLI.   2794

---- Selections from the revised
statutes of the state of New York:
containing all the laws of the
state relative to slaves, and the
law relative to the offence of kid-
napping; which several laws commenced and took effect January
1, 1830. Together with extracts
from the laws of the United
States, respecting slaves. New
York, Vanderpool & Cole, 1830.
44 p. ICN; MB; MH; PPL. 2795

---- Statutes regulating the practice of physic and surgery in the
state of New-York; together with
a system of medical ethics. Also by-laws of the Medical Society of the county of Washington
...with the names of officers and
members... Salem, N.Y., Pr.
by Dodd & Stevenson, 1830.

48 p. NNNAM. 2796

New-York almanack for 1831. By David Young. New York, John C. Totten [1830] 18 l. MWA; NHi; NjR. 2797

---- ---- [Newark] Benjamin Olds [1830] 18 l. MWA; NjR. 2798

New York and Erie Railroad Company.
A letter to the public, in relation to the New York and Erie Railroad Co. ...New York, W. G. Boggs, pr. [183?] 8 p. CSt. 2799

The New-York annual register for the year of our Lord 1830. By Edwin Williams. New-York, Pub. by J. Leavitt, and sold by Collins & Hannay; Collins & Co.; Samuel Wood & sons. Pr. by J. Seymour [1830] vi, 348 p. CSt; CtHT-W; IU; IaHi; LNHT; MB; MiU-C; NBLiHi; NCH; NN; NNA; OHi; PHi; PPAmP; PU; BrMus. 2800

The New York Anti-Masonic almanac for 1831. New York, United States Anti-Masonic Book Store [1830] 18 l. NHi; NjHi; NjR. 2801

New York Asylum for Lying-in Women.
Seventh annual report of the managers... March 13, 1830. New York, J. Post's office, 1830. 20 p. OClWHi. 2802

New York. Bank for Savings.
Eleventh report of the Bank for Savings, in the city of New York... New York, Thomas Snowden, pr., 1830. 9, [1] p. PPL; PHi. 2803

New York City Temperance Society.
Address to the inhabitants of New York. New York, 1830. MWA. 2804

---- First annual report of the New York City Temperance Society, presented May 11, 1830. New York, Pr. by Sleight & Robinson, 1830. 51, [4], 24 p. MBC; MH; PPL; PPPrHi; WHi. 2805

New York City Tract Society.
Third annual report of the New York City Tract Society, auxiliary to the American Tract Society; with the eighth annual report of the Female Branch of the New York City Tract Society. Presented February 3, 1830... New-York, Pr. for the Society, by D. Fanshaw, 1830. 6 l., 7-26 p., 2 l. MiD-B. 2806

New York. College of Physicians and Surgeons.
Memorial of the trustees of the College of Physicians and Surgeons of the City of New-York, in reply to the "Memorial of the professors of Rutgers' Medical Factulty." New-York, Pr. by J. & J. Harper, 1830. 24 p. MH; NNNAM; NjR; OC; PPL; WHi. 2807

The New-York cries, in rhyme. Copyright secured. New York, Pr. and sold by Mahlon Day, 1830. 17, [1] p. MHi. 2808

New York Dispensary.
The annual report of the Board of Trustees of the New-York Dispensary, January, 1830. New York, Pr. at the Protestant Episcopal Press, 1830. 12 p. DLC; MBCo; MiD-B; NNG; PHi. 2809

---- The charter and by-laws of the New-York Dispensary, instituted 1790... New York, Pr. by Mahlon Day, 1830. 21 p. MiD. 2810

New York Female Association.
Address and constitution of the New York Female Association, to aid in giving support and instruction to the indigent

deaf and dumb. New York, Pr.
by E. Conrad, 1830. 16 p. <u>PHi</u>.
2811

New York General Theological
Seminary of the Protestant Episcopal Church.

Proceedings of the board of
trustees of the General Theological Seminary of the Protestant
Episcopal Church in the United
States. At a stated meeting,
held August 5th, and 6th, 1829;
and at their annual meeting, held
from the 27th to the 29th of July,
1830, in the city of New York.
Pub. by order of the trustees.
New-York, Pr. at the Protestant
Episcopal Press, 1830. 28 p.
InID.   2812

New York Hospital.
Report of the governors of the
New-York Hospital, to the honor-
able, the House of Assembly of
the state of New-York. March
19, 1830. New York, Pr. by
Mahlon Day, 1830. 16 p.
NNNAM.   2813

New York Institution for the Instruction of the Deaf and Dumb.
Eleventh annual report of the
directors of the New York Institution for the Instruction of the
Deaf and Dumb, to the legislature of the state of New York;
...to which is added, the address of the Rev. Dr. Milnor...
New-York, Pr. by E. Conrad,
1830. 38 p. NbU.   2814

New York Life Insurance and
Trust Company. Charters.
An act to incorporate the New-
York Life Insurance and Trust
Company. Passed March 9, 1830.
[New York, Clayton & Van Nor-
den, prs., 1830] 7 p. DLC; MB.
2815

---- Rates and proposals of the
New-York Life Insurance and

Trust Company, no. 30 Wall-
street, for insurance on lives,
granting annuities, receiving
money in trust, and the management of trust estates. Act of incorporation passed March 9, 1830.
New-York, Clayton & Van Norden, prs., 1830. 39, [1] p.
CSmH; DLC.   2816

---- ---- New York, Clayton &
Van Norden, prs., 1830. 33 [1]
p. CSmH; Ct; DLC; MH; NCH;
NN; NNC; PHi; PPAmP; <u>PPL</u>.
2817

New York Lyceum of Natural
History.
Index to the library of the Ly-
ceum of Natural History, of New
York. [New York] Pr. for the
Society by J. Seymour [1830]
72 p. DLC; DNLM; MBAt; MHi;
NNC; PHi; PPAmP; <u>PPL</u>; TNJ.
2818

New York. Mercantile Library
Association.
Catalogue of the books belong-
ing to the Mercantile Library
Association of the city of New-
York: to which are prefixed,
the Constitution, and the rules
and regulations of the same.
New-York, Pr. by J. & J.
Harper, 1830. 160 p. NBu; NN.
2819

The New York preceptor; or,
Third book. New York, Pub. by
Samuel Wood & Sons, and Samuel S. Wood & Co. Baltimore
[1830] 68 p. <u>PPL</u>.   2820

The New York primer; or, Second book... New York, Samuel
S. and William Wood [1830?]
32 p. OClWHi.   2821

New York Protestant Episcopal
Missionary Society.
The fourteenth annual report
of the board of managers of the
New York Protestant Episcopal
Missionary Society. Adopted by
the Society at the anniversary

meeting, held in October 1830.
With an appendix. New York, Pr.
at the Protestant Episcopal Press,
1830. 40 p. NNG; NjR.   2822

New York. Protestant Episcopal
Press.
   The second annual report of
the board of trustees of the New
York Protestant Episcopal Press.
Read before the Society, in St.
John's Chapel, October 7, 1830.
New York, Pr. at the office of
the Society, 1830. 14 p. MBD;
MHi; NNG; PPL.   2823

New-York Protestant Episcopal
Sunday School Society.
   The thirteenth annual report
of the board of managers of the
New York Protestant Episcopal
Sunday School Society, instituted
in 1817. New-York, Pr. by T.
and J. Swords, 1830. 20 p.
NNG.   2824

New York Protestant Episcopal
Tract Society.
   The twenty-first annual report
of the board of trustees of the
New-York Protestant Episcopal
Tract Society. Read before the
Society, in St. John's Chapel,
October 7, 1830. New-York, Pr.
at the Protestant Episcopal Press,
1830. 15, [1] p. CtHT; MHi;
MiD-B; NNG.   2825

New York State Colonization Society.
   African colonization. Proceedings of the New-York State Colonization Society, on its first anniversary; together with an Address to the public, from the
managers thereof: Albany, Pr.
by Websters and Skinners, 1830.
27 p. CtHC; ICN; MB; NCH;
NUtHi; NbU.   2826

New York State Society for the
Promotion of Temperance.
   First annual report of the New-

York State Society for the Promotion of Temperance. Presented by the Executive Committee, January 19, 1830. Albany,
Pr. for the Society, by Packard
and Van Benthuysen, 1830. 48 p.
IU; KyDC; KyLx; MBC; MHi;
MdHi; MiD-B; N; NN; Nh; NjR;
OCHP; PPPrHi; RPB; ScCC; WHi.
                              2827

---- Temperance tracts for the
people. 1st ser., no. 8-9. [Al-
bany] Pub. by the New York State
Temperance Society [183-?] 2
nos. Contents.--No. 8 Farmers
and temperance.--no. 9. Drink-
ing usages. CSmH.   2828

New York. University.
   Annual report of the Regents
of the University of the state of
New York. Made to the Legis-
lature, February 27, 1830. Al-
bany, Pr. by Crosswell and Van
Benthuysen, 1830. 6 p. MH;
NNM; NbU.   2829

---- Instructions from the Regents of the University, to the
several academies subject to
their visitation; prescribing the
requisites and forms of academ-
ic reports, &c. Albany, Pr. by
E. Croswell, pr. to the state,
1830. 24 p. NbU.   2830

New York. Working men.
   The proceedings of a meeting
of mechanics and other working
men held at Military Hall,
Wooster Street, New York, on
Tuesday evening, Dec. 29, 1829.
Including the address, resolu-
tions, and plan of organization
for the city and county of New
York, prepared by a Conference
Committee of several wards and
adopted by the meeting. New
York, 1830. 23 p. DeGE; ICU;
MH-BA; PPL.   2831

---- Proceedings of the General
Executive Committee of the Me-

chanics and other Workingmen of
... New York, June 21st, 1830.
New York, 1830. 16 p. Sabin
54054.   2832

New York. Workingmen's State
Convention.
    The Auburn Free Press Extra.
Auburn, Saturday, August 28,
1830. Proceedings of the Workingmen's State Convention, in the
town of Salina, Wednesday August
25, 1830. Auburn, Pr. by Henry
Oliphant, 1830. 11 p. DLC;
NAuHi.   2833

---- Williams (Ezekiel). Independent nomination! "At a meeting of working-men and other
persons favorable to political
principle, held pursuant to public
notice at the Capitol, on Friday
evening, October 22, 1830..."
NN.   2834

New York Young Men's Society
for the Promotion of Temperance.
    Address. [New York, 1830]
[J. Post, pr.] 8 p. PPL.   2835

---- An address to the young
men of the United States, on the
subject of temperance. By the
New-York Young Men's Society
for the Promotion of Temperance. Pub. under the direction
of the Board of managers. New
York, Jonathan Leavitt, 1830.
22 p. CBPac; CtHC; ICU; NN;
OO; ScCC.   2836

The New Zealanders.   See Craik,
George Lillie.

Newcastle and Frenchtown Rail
Road Company.
    An act to authorize the New-
Castle and French-Town Turnpike Company to make a rail
road from French-Town, on Elk
River, to the Delaware line, in
a direction towards New-Castle.

[Dover? n.p., 1830?] [21] p.
CSt.   2837

Newcomb, R. E.
    An address delivered before
the Franklin County Temperance
Society at Buckland, October 20,
1830... Greenfield, Mass.,
Phelps & Ingersoll, prs., 1830.
16 p. MDeeP; BrMus.   2838

Newhall, Ebenezar.
    Religious patriotism; or, At-
tachment to Jerusalem, a sermon
delivered at the dedication of the
new meeting house erected for the
Congregational Church and First
Society in Oxford, Mass. Nov.
3, 1829. Boston, T. R. Marvin,
1830. 16 p. CBPac; MB; MBAt;
MBC; MH-AH; MWA; MiD-B;
RPB; BrMus.   2839

Newman, Robert.
    A new view of the solar sys-
tem and the motion of matter.
Winchester, Samuel H. Davis,
1830. 200 p. Winchester Republican, December 3, 1830.
Not located.   2840

Newman, Samuel Phillips, 1796-
1842.
    A lecture on a practical meth-
od of teaching rhetoric, delivered
in the Representatives' Hall,
Boston, August 19, 1830... Boston, Hilliard, Gray, Little &
Wilkins, 1830. 22 p. CtHT; MB;
MeB; PPL.   2841

Newport, N. H.
    "By-laws of the town of New-
port in relation to the extinguish-
ment of fires.   Duties of fire-
wards &c. as adopted by the vote
of the town at the annual meeting
in March 1830.   Agreeably to
the statute in such case made
and provided." Bdsd. NhNep.
                                    2842
Newport, R.I. James Hammond's
Circulating Library.

Catalogue of James Hammond's circulating library, No. 106 Thames Street, Newport, R.I. 4000 vols. [Newport] James Atkinson, pr., 1830. 71 p. Hammett's Bibliography of Newport.
2843

Newport Artillery Company.
The charter and regulations of the Artillery Company, of the town of Newport, in the state of Rhode-Island. Incorporated 1741. Newport, Pr. by William Read, 1830. 24 p. PPL. 2844

Newton, John.
...The life of the Rev. John Newton, Rector of St. Mary Woolnoth, London. An authentic narrative written by himself... New-York, Pub. by the American Tract Society, 1830. 116 p. (Christian Biography. No. I.) MiD-B; NRHi; WHi. 2845

Newton, Mass. First Congregational Church.
The Confession of Faith and Covenant of the First Congregational Church in Newton. As revived and adopted, Nov. 1829. Boston, E. K. Allen, 1830. 8 p. MBC. 2846

Newton Theological Institution.
Report of the professors of the Newton Theological Institution, to the trustees, Sept. 9, 1830. With other papers exhibiting its objects and its present state... Boston, Lincoln & Edmands, 1830. 22 p. MBD; MHi; NNUT. 2847

The Newtonian reflector, or New-England almanac for 1831. By Anson Allen. Hartford, H. Burr, Jun. [1830] 12 1. Ct; CtHi; CtY; DLC; InU; MB; MHi; MWA; MiD-B; N; NN; WHi. 2848

Nicholson, Peter.
The carpenter's new guide: being a complete book of lines for carpentry and joinery treating fully on practical geometry... Philadelphia, John Grigg; Wm. Brown, pr., 1830. 127 p. InTR; Md; NjR. 2849

Nicklin, (P. H.) & T. Johnson.
Catalogue of ancient & modern law books, for sale by P. H. Nicklin & T. Johnson, Law-Booksellers, No. 175. Chestnut Street, Philadelphia, 1830. 15, [1] p. PPL. 2850

Nina, an Icelandic tale. By a mother, author of "Always Happy," &c., &c. Boston, Munroe and Francis, etc., etc. [183-?] 99, 8 p. MH. 2851

Noble, Samuel.
An appeal in behalf of the views of the eternal world and state and the doctrines of faith and life... Boston, Pub. by Adonis Howard, 1830. iv, 246 p. CtMW; MH; MWA; MiU; PU; RPA; ScC. 2852

Norcross, C. T.
Sacred songs; being a collection of hymns for the use of Christian denominations. Hallowell, Glazier, Masters & Co., 1830. 192 p. MeHi. 2853

[Normanby, Constantine Henry Phipps] 1st Marquis of, 1797-1868.
The English at home. By the author of "The English in Italy," and "The English in France." New York, Pr. by J. & J. Harper; sold by Collins & Hannay, Collins and Co., G. & C. & H. Carvill [etc.] 1830. 2 vols. PU; TNJ; WU. 2854

Norman's Columbia County almanack for 1831. By Edwin E. Prentiss. Hudson, Norman's [1830] 12 1. MWA. 2855

Norristown new and much improved musical teacher; or, Repository of sacred harmony, psalms, hymns & spiritual songs ... Norristown, Pa., Sower [c1830] 144 p. PU. 2856

The North American calandar [sic] or The Columbian almanac for 1831. Wilmington, R. Porter & Son [1830] 18 1. DLC; InU; MWA; N; NHi. 2857

North Carolina.
Acts passed by the General Assembly, of the state of North Carolina, at the session of 1829-30. Raleigh, Pr. by Lawrence & Lemay, prs. to the state, 1830. 98 p. Ar-SC; IaU-L; In-SC; MdBB; Ms; Nb; NcU; Nj; Nv; OClW; W. 2858

---- Debate on the bill for establishing a bank of the state, in the Senate and House of Commons of North Carolina in December, 1829. Raleigh, Pr. by J. Gales & Son, 1830. 90 p. ICU; NcD; NcU. 2859

---- Journals of the Senate & House of Commons of the General Assembly of the state of North Carolina, at the session of 1829-30. Raleigh, Pr. by Lawrence & Lemay, prs. to the state, 1830. 283 p. NcU. 2860

---- Report... [General Assembly. Committee on Education, December 20, 1830] Raleigh, Lawrence & Lemay, 1830. 4 p. NcSal. 2861

---- Report [General Assembly. Committee on Finance. November 30th, 1830] Raleigh, Lawrence & Lemay, 1830. 4 p. NcSal. 2862

---- ---- December 30th, 1830] Raleigh, Lawrence & Lemay,

1830. 4 p. NcSal. 2863

---- ... Report of the Board for Int'l Improvements. 1830. Raleigh, Pr. by Lawrence & Lemay, prs. to the state, 1830. 35 p. NcU. 2864

---- Report of the Committee on the University. Raleigh, Pr. by Lawrence & Lemay, prs. to the state, 1830. 4 p. (at top of pg. Number 18. A.D. 1830) NcU. 2865

---- Report on incorporating the Mecklenburg Gold Mining Company. Raleigh, Pr. by Lawrence & Lemay, prs. to the state, 1830. 8 p. [At top of pg.: Number 15. A.D. 1830] NcU. 2866

---- Report on the erection of a new county out of a portion of the counties of Burke and Buncombe. Raleigh, Pr. by Lawrence & Lemay, prs. to the state, 1830. 4 p. [At top of pg.: Number 9. A.D. 1830] NcU. 2867

---- Report on the establishment of a mint in the state of North Carolina. Raleigh, Pr. by Lawrence & Lemay, prs. to the state, 1830. 8 p. [At top of pg.: Number 20. A.D. 1830] NcU. 2868

---- Report relative to the removal of free persons of color. [Raleigh, 1830] 1 1. (General Assembly. Joint Select Committee on the Propriety of Establishing a Fund to be Appropriated to the Removal of Free Persons of Color from this State.) NcSal. 2869

---- Rules of order for the government of the General Assembly of North Carolina; to which are prefixed the constitutions of North Carolina and of the United States. Raleigh, Pr. by Lawrence & Lemay, prs. to the state, 1830. 45 p. NcU. 2870

---- A statement of the revenue of North Carolina. [Raleigh] 1830. Bdsd. NcU.   2871

---- Statements of the several banks in North Carolina, transmitted to the General Assembly pursuant to a resolution of that body of the 12th Dec. 1829. Raleigh, Lawrence and Lemay, 1830. 8 p. NcU.   2872

---- Treasurer's report. [Raleigh, 1830] 18 p. NcU.   2873

---- University.
Catalogue of the faculty and students of the University of North-Carolina. November, 1830. Hillsborough, Pr. by Dennis Heartt, 1830. 12 p. NcU.
2874
---- Memorial of the trustees of the University of North Carolina. Raleigh, Pr. by Lawrence & Lemay, prs. to the state, 1830. 12 p. [At top of pg.: Number 5. A.D. 1830] NcU.   2875

---- Raleigh, 28th June, 1830. Sir:--We are required by a solemn resolution of the trustees of the University...to urge the attendance of every member of the Board...on the 19th day of July next... [Raleigh, 1830] [1] p. NcU.   2876

The North-Carolina Whig's apology. See Lawrence, Joshua.

Northern Baptist Education Society.
Act of incorporation, constitution and by-laws, of the Northern Baptist Education Society. Boston, Lincoln & Edmands, 1830. 20 p. DLC; MB; MH; MiD-B.
2877
The Northern traveller. See Dwight, Theodore.

North-western Journal.

Circular. North-western Journal. The publication of the journal was commenced in this city on the 20th of November: twelve numbers have been printed ... The present circular is issued to meet a demand from several quarters for copies of the original prospectus, of which none remain... William Ward, editor. George L. Whitney, proprietor. Detroit, February 1830. Pr. on p. 1 of 4-page folder. WHi.   2878

Norwich Sabbath School Union.
Sixth annual report of the Norwich Sabbath School Union auxiliary to the Connecticut Sabbath School Union. Presented at the annual meeting, April 19th, 1830. Norwich, Pr. by J. Dunham, 1830. 23 p. CtHi.   2879

Notes on the sayings and doings of Dr. Lacey and his three friends; as partly set forth in their celebrated report, with its numerous affidavits and other appendages. By Philo Corrector, Esq. M.N.A. &c. ...Albany, Pr. for the public, 1830. 55 p. N; NN.   2880

Notice! An oration on the subject of temperance will be delivered this afternoon, Wednesday, at 2 o'clock in the Chapel of Yale College. The young men and citizens of New Haven generally, are respectfully invited to attend, November 24, 1830. [New Haven, 1830] 1 l. CtY.
2881
Nott, Samuel, Jun., 1788-1869.
The freedom of the mind, demanded of American freemen; being lectures to the Lyceum, on the improvement of the people. Boston, Pub. by Crocker & Brewster. New York, J. Leavitt, 1830. 131 p. Ct; CtHC; CtHT; LNHT; MBC; MH; MWA;

OClW; OMC; PPL; RPA.   2882

Nucleus Club, Maine.
Constitution, rules and orders,
by-laws and library regulations
of Nucleus Club, instituted April
7, 1820. Brunswick, Griffin's
press, 1830. 22 p. CSmH; MH.
                             2883

Nugent, Thomas.
A new pocket dictionary of the
French and English language in
two parts. I. French and English.
II. English and French... 5th
American from last London ed.
By Thomas Nugent, LL. D. and
J. Ouiseau, A. M. Philadelphia,
R. W. Pomeroy; Stereotyped by
J. Harding, 1830. 452 p. CtHC;
CtHT; DLC; MB; MH; MdBL;
NjP; OHi.   2884

Nursery lessons, designed for
children eight or ten years old.
Philadelphia, American Sunday
School Union, [1830?] BrMus.
                             2885

Nuttall, Thomas, 1786-1859.
An introduction to systematic
and physiological botany... 2d ed.
Cambridge, Pub. by Hilliard &
Brown [E. W. Metcalf & Co.,
prs.] 1830. xi, 362 p. ArU; CSt;
CtHT-W; DLC; DeWi; GEU; In;
KU; MB; MBC; MBHo; MH; MiD;
MnU; MtU; OClW; OU; PP; RP;
ScC; WyU.   2886

O

Oberlin, pseud.   See Huidekoper,
Harm.

Obi.   See Earle, William, Jr.

Observations on the road from
Baltimore to Philadelphia. [Phil-
adelphia? 1830] 12 p. PPL.
                             2887
An observer, pseud.   See An inquiry into the necessity and general principles of reorganization

of the United States.

An observer, pseud.   See Mc-
Naughton, James.

Odiorne, James Creighton, 1802-
1879.
Opinions on speculative mason-
ry, relative to its origin, nature,
and tendency... Boston, Perkins
and Marvin, 1830. viii, 280 p.
CSmH; GDC; GU; ICMcC; ICU;
IaCrM; MBAt; MBC; MH; MHi;
MoSM; MdHi; MiU; MoSpD; NIC;
NNC; NNS; NNUT; NhD; NhHi;
OCM; OO; PHi; PPL; RPA; ScU;
TNJ; VtU; BrMus.   2888

An offering of sympathy to parents bereaved of their children.
See Parkman, Francis.

Official documents, &c. in relation to the United States. [Steu-
benville, O., Pr. by Jas. Wilson, 1830?] 60 p. CSmH. 2889

Ogden, David Longworth, 1792-
1863.
Two discourses, the first, on
the misapplication of religious
names; and the second, on the
misrepresentation of benevolent
actions; delivered in Berlin,
Worthington Society, June 13,
1830. Hartford, Hudson & Skinner, prs., 1830. 49 p. CSmH;
Ct; CtHT-W; CtSoP; IU; MBC;
MiD-B.   2890

[Ogle, Alexander, Jr.]
Truth's proofs that Masonic
oaths do not impose any obliga-
tions. Norwich, Pr. by L. Hunt-
ington Young, 1830. 24 p. CtHi.
                             2891
Ohio.
An act, to incorporate the
town of Sandusky, in the county
of Huron; with the amendments.
Sandusky, Pr. by D. & J. K.
Campbell, 1830. 14 p. MiD-B;
OClWHi.   2892

---- Acts of a general nature, passed at the first session of the twenty-eighth General Assembly of the state of Ohio, begun and held in the town of Columbus, Dec. 7, 1829, and the twenty-eighth year of said state. Vol. XXVIII. Pub. by authority. Columbus, Pr. by Olmsted and Bailhache, 1830. 69 p. C-L; Ct; CtY-L; DLC; ICU-L; MH-L; MdBB; MiU-L; NN; Nb; Nv; OCHP; PPB; WaU.
2893

---- Acts of a local nature, passed at the first session of the twenty-eighth General Assembly of the state of Ohio, begun and held in the town of Columbus, December 7, 1829, and the twenty-eighth year of said state. Vol. XXVIII. Columbus, Pr. by Olmsted & Bailhache, 1830. 232 p. ICU-L; IU; MH-L; MdBB; NN; NNLI; OCLaw; RPL.   2894

---- Cases decided in the Supreme Court of Ohio, at a special session, in Columbus, December, 1829. Reported in conformity with the act of assembly. By Charles Hammond, attorney at law. Vol. IV. Cincinnati, Pub. by Lodge, L'Hommedieu and Hammond, 1830-31. 558, [2] p. CtY-L; DLC; MH-L; MdBB; NNB; OCLaw.   2895

---- Journal of the House of Representatives of the state of Ohio: being the first session of the twenty-eighth General Assembly, begun and held in the town of Columbus, in the county of Franklin, Monday, December 7, 1829. and in the twenty-eighth year of said state. Pub. by authority. Columbus, Olmsted & Bailhache, state prs., 1829 [i. e. 1830] 60 3 p. DLC.   2896

---- Journal of the Senate of the state of Ohio: being the first session of the twenty-eighth General Assembly begun and held in the town of Columbus in the county of Franklin; Monday, December 7, 1829, and in the twenty-sixth [?] year of said state. Columbus, Olmsted & Bailhache, state prs., 1829 [i. e. 1830] 460 p. DLC; MH; NN; OHi; WHi.   2897

An old-fashioned churchman. See A full-length portrait.

[Oliver, Henry Kemble] 1800-1885.
An elementary treatise on the construction and use of the mathematical instruments usually put into portable cases. Boston, Perkins & Marvin, 1830. 68 p. DLC; DeGE; KyDC; MH; NNG; NcU; BrMus.   2898

Olmstead, Denison, 1791-1859.
Introduction to natural philosophy: designed as a textbook for the use of the students in Yale College. New Haven, H. Howe, 1830. 2 v. CtW; MH; MeB; OMC.
2899

---- Observations on the meteoric shower of November 1827. From the American Journal of Science and Arts. New Haven, H. Howe, 1830. MHi.   2900

Olney, Jesse, 1798-1872.
The National preceptor: ... 2d ed. ...Hartford, Pub. by Goodwin & Co. and D. F. Robinson & Co., 1830 [c1829?] CSmH; MH.   2901

---- A practical system of modern geography, or A view of the present state of the world. 4th ed. Hartford, D. F. Robinson & Co., 1830. 268 p. CtHT-W; DLC; MDeeP; MH.   2902

---- ---- 5th ed. Hartford, D. F. Robinson & co., 1830. 268 p. MH; NbHi.   2903

---- ---- 6th ed. Hartford, D.
F. Robinson & co., 1830. 283 p.
CSt; Ct; DLC; MH; N; TxU-T.
2904

On the duty of morning and eve-
ning devotion. New-York, New
York Protestant Episcopal Tract
Society, 1830. 36 p. NNG. 2905

...On the use of tobacco. [Pub.
by J. Emory and B. Waugh, for
the Tract Society of the Methodist Episcopal Church, J. Collard,
pr., 1830] 20 p. No. 127. PPL.
2906

On worship, ministry, and
prayer. Philadelphia, To be had
of Thomas Kite, 1830. 16 p.
PHC. 2907

Onderdonk, Benjamin Tredwell,
bp. 1791-1861.
A sermon, preached in Trinity Church, New York, at the
funeral of the Right Reverend
John Henry Hobart... on Thursday
evening, September 16th, 1830.
...New York, Pr. at the Protestant Episcopal Press, 1830.
87 p. CtHT; CtMW; MB; MWA;
MiD-B; NGH; NNC; NNS; NNUT;
PHi; PPL; RPB; WHi; BrMus.
2908

[Onderdonk, Henry Ustick] 1789-
1858.
Episcopacy tested by Scripture.
From the Protestant Episcopalian
for November and December, 1830.
[Philadelphia, 1830?] 28 p. PPL.
2909

---- Man saved by mercy: a
discourse, delivered in St. Paul's
Church, Baltimore, in the evening of 21st October, 1830, by
the Right Rev. Henry U. Onderdonk... Baltimore, Pr. by Joseph Robinson, 1830. 20 p.
CSmH; CtHT; MWA; MdHi; MiD-
B; NGH; NNG; PPL; PPPrHi;
RPB. 2910

One hundred Scriptural arguments
for the Unitarian Faith. 5th ed.

Boston, Pr. for American Unitarian Association. Gray & Bow-
en, [I. R. Butts, pr.] 1830. 16
p. (American Unitarian Association, No. 2). DLC; ICMe;
KyDC; MB; MH; MHi; MMeT-Hi;
BrMus. 2911

One of the people. See Address
to the clergy of all ranks.

Oneida Institute of Science and
Industry, Whitestown, N. Y.
Second report of the Trustees
of the Oneida Institute of Science
and Industry. Whitestown, March
20, 1830. Utica, Press of William Williams, 1830. 28 p. MB.
2912

The only son; or, The history of
J. Ross and his mother... Revised by the Committee of Publication. Philadelphia, American Sunday School Union [1830]
BrMus. 2913

Opie, Amelia (Alderson), 1769-
1853.
Illustrations of lying, in all
its branches. By Amelia Opie.
From the 2d London ed. Hartford, S. Andrus, 1830. 283 p.
CtMW; PU. 2914

The Oregon country. See American Society for Encouraging the
Settlement of the Oregon Territory.

Original poems for infant minds.
See Gilbert, Mrs. Ann (Taylor).

Original poems, with imitations
of Horace. By an Albanian. Albany, Nicholson, pr. [1830?] 46,
4 p. DLC. 2915

An original tale; Isabella of
Brooke. See Morrison, John B.

Osborn, V. R.
A discourse on the spirit of
the times, delivered in the Meth-

odist meeting house, at Manchester, Con., February 1830. Hartford, Pr. at the Times Office, 1830. 24 p. Ct; CtHT; CtHi.   2916

Otis Harrison Gray. An address ... See Boston, An address.

Otis, Harrison Gray, 1765-1848.
    Mr. Otis's speech to the citizens of Boston, on the evening preceding the late election, of member[s] of Congress. Boston, J. H. Eastburn, 1830. 27 p. CSmH; CtHC; MB; MBAt; MBC; MH; MHi; Mi; OCHP; PPL; BrMus.   2917

---- Another edition. "...member to Congress." Boston, J. H. Eastburn, 1830. 27 p. PPL.   2918

Outlines of the life of General Lafayette: with an account of the French revolution of 1830, until the choice of Louis Philip as king. Tappan, N.Y., W. Broadwell and co., 1830. iv, [3]-250 p. CSmH; PHi; VtU.   2919

Owen, Robert Dale, 1801-1877.
    Letters addressed to William Gibbons, of Wilmington, Del. in reply to "An exposition of modern scepticism"; together with An address to the Society of Friends, and a letter to Eli Hilles, Benj. Ferris and others. [First pub. in the F. Enquirer.] Philadelphia, Pr. for J. A. M'-Clintock, 1830. 24 p. DeWi; PHC; PPL; PSC-Hi; WHi.   2920

---- Popular tracts, no. 1-14. New York, Pub. at the office of the Free Enquirer, 1830. 14 pts. in 1 vol. ICU; In; InGrD; InHi; InU; LNHT; MB; MH; MiD-B; O; BrMus.   2921

---- Popular Tracts. No. 1. Containing A tale of Old England.

"Darby and Susan." New York, Pub. at the office of the Free Enquirer, 1830. 18 p. In; PPL.   2922

---- No. 2. Truth and Error. [From the New Harmony Gazette-now the Free Enquirer.] [New York, Pub. at the office of the Free Enquirer, 1830] (In Owen's Popular Tracts, no. 2) In; PPL.   2923

---- Popular tracts. No. 3. Containing An address to the industrious classes; a sketch of a system of national education by Francis Wright, and an address to the conductors of the New York Periodical Press, by Robert Dale Owen. New York, Office of the Free Enquirer, 1830. 12 p. DLC; In; PPL.   2924

---- No. 4. Prossimo's Experience. [Extracted from the Free Enquirer 1830] (Owen's Popular tracts) 12 p. PPL.   2925

---- No. 5. Cause of the people. By Robert Dale Owen. [Extracted from the Free Enquirer] [New York, Pub. at the office of the Free Enquirer, 1830] (In Owen's Popular Tracts, no. 5) 12 p. In; PPL.   2926

---- Popular Tracts. No. 6. Containing a sermon on loyalty; a remonstrance to God; and a sermon on Free Enquiry. New York, Office of the Free Enquirer, 1830. (In Owen's Popular Tracts, no. 6.) 24 p. In; PPL.   2927

---- Popular Tracts. No. 7. Containing effects of missionary labours; by Robert Dale Owen. And Religious revivals; by John Neale. New York, Office of the Free Enquirer, 1830. (In Owen's Popular Tracts, no. 7) 1 l., 10 p.

In; MH; PPL.					2928

---- No. 8.	Fables.	By Francis Wright [Extracted from the Free Enquirer] [New York, Office of the Free Enquirer, 1830] (Owen's Popular Tracts, no. 8) 18 p. DLC; In; NN; PPL.		2929

---- No. 9.	The French Revolution. [Extracted from the Free Enquirer] [New York, Office of the Free Enquirer, 1830] (In Owen's Popular Tracts, no. 9) 8 p. In; PPL.				2930

---- Popular Tracts. No. 10. Containing situations by Robert Dale Owen.	New York Office of the Free Enquirer, 1830.	16 p. In; PPL.					2931

---- No. 11.	Wealth and misery.	By Robert Dale Owen. [Extracted from the New Harmony Gazette] [New York, Office of the Enquirer, 1830] (In Owen's Popular Tracts, no. 11)	16 p. In; PPL.					2932

---- No. 12.	Galileo and the Inquisition.	By Robert Dale Owen.	[Extracted from the Free Enquirer.] [New York, Office of the Free Enquirer, 1830] (In Owen's Popular Tracts, no. 12.) 8 p. In;	PPL.				2933

---- No. 13.	A tract and a warning.	By Robert Dale Owen. [Extracted from the Free Enquirer] [New York, Office of the Enquirer, 1830] (In Owen's Popular Tracts, no. 13)	4 p. In.				2934

---- No. 14.	The new book of Chronicles.	(As rendered from the original Hebrew, by a learned Rabbi.) [New York, Office of the Enquirer, 1830] (In Owen's Popular Tracts, No. 14)	24 p. PPL.				2935

---- Reply to a report of the New York Typographical Society. [New York, 1830]	12 p. NN.					2936

The Oxonians.	See Beazley, Samuel.

P

Pacificus, pseud.	See Hamilton, Alexander.

Page, Cary Selden, b. 1806?	Speech, delivered before the Literary club of Alexa.	1830. Alexandria, Pr. by S. Snowden, 1830.	14 p.	DLC.		2937

Paine, Elijah.	The practice in civil actions and proceedings at law in the state of New York in the Supreme Court and other courts of the state, and also in the courts of the United States.	New York, G. & C. & H. Carvill [Sleight & Robinson, prs.]	1830.	2 vols.	CSt; CU; MH-L; MdBB; NIC-L; NNLI; NNU; NjP; NjR; PU; VtU; W; BrMus.		2938

Paine, Thomas, 1737-1809.	The theological works of Thomas Paine.	To which are added the profession of faith of a Savoyard vicar, by J. J. Rousseau; and other miscellaneous pieces.	New York, W. Carver, 1830.	xiv, [7]-424 p.	CSmH. ICMcC; MB; MMeT-Hi; WHi.		2939

Paley, William, 1743-1805.	The principles of moral and political philosophy by William Paley, D.D.	In two volumes. Exeter, N.H., Pub. by John C. Gerrish, 1830.	2 v.	CtHT-W.		2940

Palfrey, John Gorham, 1796-

1881.
The prospects and claims of pure Christianity. Boston, Gray & Bowen, 1830. [I. R. Butts, pr.] (American Unitarian Association. 1st series, No. 42). 36 p. CBPac; CtHC; ICMe; MB; MBAU; MH-AH; MMeT-Hi; MNBedf; MeBaT. 2941

---- A sermon preached in the church in Brattle Square, Boston, August 1, 1830, the Lord's day after the decease of the Honourable Isaac Parker, chief justice of Massachusetts. Boston, Nathan Hale and Gray & Bowen [W. L. Lewis, pr.] 1830. 1 p. l., 32 p. CSmH; CtHC; ICN; IaHi; KWiU; MB; MBAt; MH-AH; MHi; MeHi; MiD-B; NBLiHi; NNG; Nh; NjR; PHi; PPAmP; RPB; WHi; BrMus. 2942

[----] The young child's prayer book. Pt. I. Boston, Gray and Bowen, 1830. MH. 2943

[----] The youth's prayer book. Boston, Gray and Bowen, 1830. 55 p. MB; MH-AH; PPPrHi. 2944

Palmer's New-England almanac for 1831. New-Haven, Durrie & Peck [1830] Ct; CtHi; CtY; MWA; N. 2945

Parker, Edward Lutwyche, 1785-1850.
A sermon delivered at the funeral of the Rev. Amasa A. Hayes; pastor of the Presbyterian Church in Londonderry: October 26, 1830. Dunstable, N. H., Thayer & Wiggin, prs. 1830. 16 p. CSmH; Nh; NhHi; RPB. 2946

Parker, Joel.
An address delivered before the Association in Keene, for the Promotion of Temperance, August 5, 1829. Keene, N. H., Pub. by Geo. Tilden, 1830. 22 p.

MB; MBAt; MBC; MWA; MiD-B; BrMus. 2947

---- Lectures on Universalism by Joel Parker. Rochester, N. Y., Pr. by Elisha Loomis, 1830. 126 p. CSmH; MoSpD; NN. 2948

Parker, Jonathan T., comp.
The American legendary: consisting of original and select tales. Series I, Volume I. Rutland, Pr. by E. Maxham, 1830. 298, [2] p. CSmH; CtY; MWA; MnHi; PU. 2949

Parker's miniature almanack for 1831. Boston, Amos B. Parker; Booton & Teprell, prs. [1830] 16 l. MHi; MWA; NN. 2950

Parkes, Mrs. William.
Domestic duties; or, Instructions to young married ladies, on the management of their households, and the regulation of their conduct in the various relations and duties of married life. 3rd American from the 3rd London ed., with notes and alterations adapted to the American reader. New York, Pr. by J. & J. Harper, 1830. 400 p. ICU; MNBedf. 2951

Parkhurst, John.
The primitive style of missions. A sermon, preached at Tyngsboro before the Middlesex Baptist Missionary Society, at their sixth anniversary, on the second Wednesday in June, 1830. Lowell, From the Office of the Lowell Journal, 1830. 12 p. MBC; BrMus. 2952

Parkhurst, John L.
First lessons in reading and spelling on the inductive method of instruction. Boston, Crocker & Brewster, 1830. 92, [1] p. DLC; OO. 2953

[Parkman, Francis] 1788-1852 comp.

An offering of sympathy to parents bereaved of their children, and to others under affliction; being a collection from manuscripts and letters not before published. Boston, Pr. and pub. by Samuel N. Dickinson, 1830. 1 l., xvii, 224 p. CBPac; CtHC; KWS; MB; MH; MoSpD; PPL; RPB. 2954

---- The providence of God displayed in the revolutions of the world. A sermon preached in the New-North Church... Sept. XIX. Occasioned by the recent revolutions in the government of France. Boston, Pr. by Samuel N. Dickinson, 1830. 18 p. CSmH; CtSoP; ICMe; LNHT; MBAU; MBAt; MH-AH; MHi; MeHi; MiD-B; NhHi; PHi; BrMus. 2955

Parley, Peter, pseud. See Goodrich, Samuel Griswold.

Parlor lectures on scripture history. See Adams, Catherine (Lyman).

Parsons, Usher.

On the comparative influence of vegetable and animal decomposition as a cause of fever... Philadelphia, Pr. by Joseph R. A. Skerrett, 1830. 36 p. CtHT-W; DLC; MB; MBAt; MeB; NNNAM; PPPrHi; RHi; RPB; BrMus. 2956

A pastor's address to the young people of his charge, on the rite of confirmation. Published under the direction of the Society for the Promotion of Christian Knowledge in the Diocese of Connecticut. Hartford, H. & F. J. Huntington, 1830. 19 p. CSmH; CtHT; DLC; NNG. 2957

Patty Parsons and the plum-cake.

Philadelphia, American Sunday School Union [1830?] BrMus. 2958

Paul, Joseph M., firm, Philadelphia.

Mills at Eayrestown, for sale or to let... [Philadelphia] Pr. by J. Rakestraw [ca. 1830] Bdsd. DeGE. 2959

Paul Clifford. See Lytton, Edward George Earle Lytton Bulwer-Lytton.

Paul Pry's almanac for 1831. By David Young. New-York, C. Brown [1830] 18 l. CSmH; DLC; MWA; NBLiHi; NN; RWe. 2960

[Paulding, James Kirke] 1778-1860.

Chronicles of the city of Gotham, from the papers of a retired common councilman. Containing: The azure hose. The politician. The dumb girl. Ed. by the author of "The backwoodsman" [etc.] New York, G. & C. & H. Carvill [Sleight & Robinson, prs.] 1830. 270 p. CSmH; CtHT-W; CtY; DLC; ICU; Ia; MB; MH; MWA; MdBP; MiD-B; NCH; NN; NNS; NjP; PPL; PU; RPB; ScU; TNJ; TxU; WU; BrMus. 2961

[Peabody, Augustus, ed. and comp.]

The child's song book, for the use of schools and families; being a selection of favourite airs, with hymns and moral songs, suitable for infant instruction. Boston, Pub. by Richardson, Lord & Holbrook, 1830. 104 p. CtHT-W; DLC; MB; MBC; MH; MoS; NN; PPL; WHi. 2962

[Peabody, Nathaniel]

First lessons in grammar, on the plan of Pestalozzi. By a teacher in Boston. Boston, Carter & Hendee, 1830. 60 p.

MB; MBAt; NNC; PU; BrMus.
2963
Peabody, Oliver William Bourn,
1799-1848.
An address delivered before
the Peace Society, of Exeter,
N.H. at their annual meeting,
April 1830. Exeter, Pub. by
Francis Grant, for the Society.
C. Norris, pr., 1830. 16 p.
CSmH; Ct; CtSoP; ICMe; MB;
MBAt; MeB; MeHi; NNC; NhHi;
PPL; BrMus.   2964

Peace in believing. See Story,
Robert.

Peake, Richard Brinsley, 1792-
1847.
"Master's rival;" or, A day
at Boulogne; a farce... New York,
R. H. Elton, 1830. 52 p. DeGE;
MH; MWA; PPL.   2965

The pearl; or, Affection's gift.
A Christmas and New Year's
present. Philadelphia, Thomas
T. Ash [Adam Waldie, pr.]
1830. 220 p.   DLC; KU; MB;
PP; ViU; WU.   2966

Pearson, Hugh Nicholas, 1777-
1856.
Memoirs of the life and writ-
ings of the Rev. Claudius Buchan-
an... in some parts abridged and
in others, enlarged. New York,
American Tract Society [183-?]
(Christian Library, 16.) MH.
2967
Pearson, John.
November trade sale. Card.
The subscriber respectfully gives
notice to the trade, that his sec-
ond fall sale to booksellers...
will be held... the 4th and 5th
November next... John Pearson,
New York Long Room, 169
Broadway. New-York, September
9, 1830... [New York, 1830]
Bdsd. MB.   2968

Peck, Alfred.

Freedom from sin: a sermon
delivered at the funeral of Benj.
Brink, Jr., Dec. 30, 1830. By
Rev. Alfred Peck, of Sheshe-
quin, Pa. [1830] 8 p. PHi. 2969

[Peirce, Cyrus, 1790-1860]
An address to the inhabitants
of Nantucket on education and
free schools.   Providence [183?]
24 p. MHi.   2970

Peirson, Abel Lawrence, 1794-
1853.
Address on temperance, delivered in Salem Jan. 14, 1830.
Boston, Perkins & Marvin, 1830.
32 p. MB; MBC; MHi; BrMus.
2971
Peixotto, Daniel L. M.
Anniversary discourse pronounced before the Society for the
Education of Orphan Children and
the Relief of Indigent Persons of
the Jewish Persuasion. New
York, J. Seymour, 1830. 47 p.
MB; PPAmP; PPDrop.   2972

Pelby, William.
Letters on the Tremont the-
atre, respectfully addressed to
the primitive subscribers, its
friends and patrons, by William
Pelby... Boston, Press of J. H.
Eastburn, 1830. 44 p. DLC; MB;
MH; MHi; PPAmP; PU.   2973

Pelham's primer; or, Mother's
spelling book. For children at a
very early age. New-Haven, S.
Babcock. Sidney's Press, 1830.
36 p. CtHi; NN.   2974

Pemberton, Christopher Robert,
1765-1822.
A practical treatise on various diseases of the abdominal
viscera. With notes by John
Hayes, M.D. ...Richmond, Pr.
by Peter Cottom, and for sale at
his book store, 1830. xi, 196 p.
CU; DNLM; MB; NNNAM; NcWsW;
Vi.   2975

Penington, Isaac.
Brief extracts from the works
of Isaac Penington. Philadelphia,
Pr. by Joseph Rakestraw, 1830.
72 p. InRE; NNUT; PPL; PSC-
Hi.   2976

Penn, William, pseud. See
Evarts, Jeremiah.

Penney, Joseph, 1793-1860.
The house of mirth. A discourse preached in the First
Presbyterian Church in Rochester, December 20, 1829. Rochester, Pr. by E. Peck & Co.,
1830. 20 p. CSmH; NRHi. 2977

Pennsylvania.
Act of Assembly of Pennsylvania incorporating the Wallen-
paupack Improvement Company
with the report of Henry G. Sargent, esq. civil engineer. In relation to the proposed route, to
open the coal-region of the Lack-
awannock Valley to the New York
market. Easton, Pa., Josiah P.
Hetrich, pr., 1830. 21 p. PU.
                                   2978
---- An act to authorize a loan
to defray the expenses of the
Pennsylvania Canal & Railroad.
Harrisburg, 1830. 8 p. DBRE;
MB; PHi.   2979

---- Acts of the Legislature of
Pennsylvania, relating to the
Schuylkill Navigation Company.
Philadelphia, Pr. by J. Kay,
1830. 43 p. DLC; DeGE; NNC;
PHi.   2980

---- Bericht der Canal Commis-
säre von Pennsylvanien, betreffend die Pennsylvanischen Canäle
und Riegelstraszen... Gelesen im
Hause der Representaten, Dec.
22, 1830. Harrisburg, Gedruckt
bey Jacob Baab, 1830. 54 p.
PPL.   2981

---- Bericht von der Committee

über Mittel und Wege, betreffend
die Finanzen der Republik... Ge-
selen im Hause der Representan-
ten, Februar 22, 1830. Harrisburg, Gedruckt von Jacob Baab,
1830. 12 p. PPL.   2982

---- Cases adjudged in the courts
of Pennsylvania, before and since
the Revolution. By A. J. Dallas.
3d ed. Notes by Thomas I. Wharton. Philadelphia, P. H. Nicklin
and T. Johnson. Thomas Kite,
pr., 1830. Vol. 1: xii, 538 p.
Id-L; Wy.   2983

---- The Constitution of the
United States of America. The
Constitution of the commonwealth
of Pennsylvania. And rules for
the government of the House of
Representatives of the said com-
monwealth. Harrisburg, Welsh
& Miller, 1830. 60 p. P; PHi.
                                   2984
---- In the Supreme Court for
the Eastern District of Pennsyl-
vania, of March term, 1828.
George M'Callmont vs. Henry
Whitaker. [Philadelphia, 1830]
44, [1] p. PPL.   2985

---- Journal of the fortieth House
of Representatives... [Nov. 3,
1829-Apr. 7, 1830] Vol. 1. Harrisburg, Pr. by Welsh & Miller,
1830. 912, 12, [2], 49 p.
CSmH.   2986

---- ---- Vol. 2. Containing
messages, reports and documents.
Harrisburg, Welsh & Miller,
1830. 770, 8 p. Mi.   2987

---- Journal of the Senate...
which commenced... on the third
day of November, 1829... Vol. 2.
Containing the appendix. Harrisburg, Pr. by Welsh & Miller, 1830.
491, 4 p., 1 l. CSmH; CtHT.
                                   2988
---- Laws of the General Assembly of the state of Pennsylvania,

passed at the session of 1829-30.
In the fifty-fourth year of inde-
pendence. Pub. by authority.
Harrisburg, James Cameron,
1830. 14, 412, 33 p. IaU-L; Ky;
L; MdBB; Mi-L; Mo; Ms; NNLI;
Nb; Nj; Nv; P; R; RPL; T; TxU-
L; W.   2989

---- Report of a committee of
the House of Representatives,
appointed upon the application of
James Clarke, Acting Commissioner on the Juniata Division of
the Pennsylvania Canal, to investigate his official conduct in
relation to certain charges set
forth against him in a petition
which had been presented...
March 23, 1830. Harrisburg,
Welsh and Miller, 1830. 14 p.
DLC; P; PHi; PPi.   2990

---- Report of the canal commissioners of Pennsylvania, relative to the Pennsylvania canals
and rail-road. Read in the House
of Representatives, Dec. 22,
1830. Harrisburg, Pr. by Henry
Welsh, 1830. 48 p. DLC; MBAt;
MWA; NN; P; PPL.   2991

---- ---- Read in the Senate,
Dec. 23, 1830. Harrisburg, Pr.
by Henry Welsh, 1830. 48 p.
MB; MH-BA; MWA; MiU-T; PPF.
                               2992
---- Report of the Committee of
Ways and Means, relative to the
finances of the Commonwealth...
February 22, 1830. Harrisburg,
1830. 11 p. MHi.   2993

---- Report of the State Treasurer, shewing the receipts and expenditures at the Treasury of
Pennsylvania, from the first day
of December, 1829, to the thir-
tieth November, 1830, inclusive.
Harrisburg, Pr. by Henry Welsh,
1830. 351 p. PPL.   2994

---- Report on the finances of

the Commonwealth of Pennsylvania, for the year 1830. Made
to the Legislature, by the Auditor General, agreeably to law.
Harrisburg, Pr. by Hugh Hamilton & Son, 1830. 42 p. PPL.
                               2995
---- A report on the state of
education in Pennsylvania. Accompanied with two bills for the
establishment of a general system of public instruction; and
other proceedings, adopted by a
town meeting of working men and
others, friendly to to [!] that
object. Held in the County
Court House, Feb. 11, 1830.
Also, an address on the moral
and political importance of general education...by the Rev. M.
M. Carll. Philadelphia, Pub. by
order of the Meeting, Garden &
Thompson, prs., 1830. iv, 32 p.
MH; PPAmP; PPL; PU.   2996

---- Rules of the courts of common pleas, orphans' court, and
quarter sessions, within the 15th
judicial district of Pennsylvania:
adopted in Nov'r--1830. West-
Chester, From the Record-press
[1830] 28 p. CSmH; PHi.   2997

---- Twelfth annual report of the
controllers of the public schools
of the first school district of the
state of Pennsylvania. With their
accounts. Philadelphia, Pr. by
order of the board of control,
by Garden & Thompson, 1830.
16 p. OClWHi; PPL.   2998

Pennsylvania almanac for 1831.
By John Ward. Philadelphia,
M'Carty & Davis [1830] 18 l.
CtY; InU; MWA; N; NjR; PDoBHi;
PHi; PLF.   2999

Pennsylvania. Citizens.
  Memorial to the Senate and
House of Representatives of the
commonwealth of Pennsylvania in
General Assembly met. [n. p.,

183-?] Bdsd. CSmH.   3000

Pennsylvania Colonization Society.
Report of the board of man-
agers of the Pennsylvania Coloni-
zation Society, with an appendix.
Philadelphia, Pr. for the Society
by Thomas Kite, 1830. 48 p.
CtHT; DLC; IU; M; MH; MdHi;
OClWHi; P; PPL; WHi.   3001

Pennsylvania Historical Society.
Memoirs of the Historical So-
ciety of Pennsylvania. Vol. II.
Part II. ... Philadelphia, E.
Littell [Adam Waldie, pr.] 1830.
221 p. MB; MNBedf; MeHi; NNA;
R.   3002

Pennsylvania Hospital.
State of the accounts of the
Pennsylvania Hospital... for the
year ending 4th month, 24th,
1830. Bdsd. PPL.   3003

Pennsylvania Institution for the
Deaf and Dumb, Philadelphia.
Tenth annual report to the
Legislature... together with documents illustrative of the useful-
ness of that establishment. Philadelphia, Pr. for the board of
managers by Thomas Kite, 1830.
31 [1] p. CSmH; KyD; MB; MHi;
MnHi; OClW; PPL; RPB.   3004

Pennsylvania. Manual Labour
Academy.
Second annual report of the
board of trustees of the Manual
Labour Academy of Pennsylvania.
November 9, 1830. Philadelphia,
Pr. by Wm. F. Geddes, 1830.
15 p. PPL; PPPrHi.   3005

Pennsylvania Rail-way. See
Hints for the representatives of
the country.

Pennsylvania Silk Society.
Address of the Pennsylvania
Silk Society to the public. [Phil-
adelphia, Jan. 1, 1830] 4 p.

DeGE; MWA; PPAmP; PU. 3006

Pennsylvania Society for Discouraging the Use of Ardent Spirits.
Report. Of the Board of Managers of "The Pennsylvania Society for Discouraging the Use
of Ardent Spirits." Read... May
26th, 1830. [Philadelphia] 1830.
8 p. PU.   3007

Pennsylvania. University.
Catalogue of the officers and
students of the University of
Pennsylvania. Philadelphia,
Jan., 1830. 24 p. MdHi; P;
PPL; PU.   3008

---- University of Pennsylvania.
Report of the Committee of Ways
and Means on the capital, engagements and responsibilities of the
University, made October 5th,
1830. Philadelphia, Pr. by Joseph R. A. Skerrett, 1830. 8 p.
PPL.   3009

Der Pennsylvanische Anti-Frei-
maurer Calender au 1831. Lancaster, Samuel Wagner [1830]
Drake 11741.   3010

The penny primer. New York,
Pr. and sold by Mahlon Day,
[c 1830] 4 l. PP.   3011

The people's doctors. See
Drake, Daniel.

The people's friend, pseud.
See Drake, Daniel.

Performances at the ordination
of Hersey Bradford Goodwin, as
colleague pastor with Rev. Ezra
Ripley, D.D., in Concord, Mass.
on Wednesday, February 17th,
1830. [Concord, Mass., Pr. by
Herman Atwill, 1830] 4 p.
CSmH; MB.   3012

Perkins, Ephraim.
Proposals, by Ephraim Per-

kins, of Trenton, Oneida Co.,
N. Y. for publishing in pamphlet
form, a letter addressed to the
Oneida Presbytery...Dated Sep-
tember 13th, 1830. 1 p. DLC.
                                        3013
Perkins, Samuel, 1767-1850.
   Historical sketches of the
United States, from the peace of
1815 to 1830. New York, Pub.
by S. Converse [Sleight & Robin-
son, prs.] 1830. 444 p. CSmH;
CoU; CtHT-W; ICN; IaU; LNHT;
MB; MHi; MdHi; MiD-B; MnHi;
NCH; NN; NjP; OClWHi; RPB;
WHi; BrMus.   3014

Perrin, Jean Baptiste, fl. 1786.
   Fables amusantes, avec une
table générale et particuliére des
mots et de leur signification en
anglais selon l'ordre des fables,
pour en rendre la traduction plus
facile à l'écolier. Par M. Perrin. Edition revue et corrigée
par un Maitre de langue française.
Stéréotype de A. Chandler. Philadelphia, R. W. Pomeroy, 1830.
180 p. DLC; ViU.   3015

---- The elements of French and
English conversation. Rev. and
corrected by C. Preudhomme.
Philadelphia, Pub. by R. W. Pom-
eroy, 1830. 216 p. CtHT-W.
                                        3016
Pestalozzi, Johann Heinrich,
1746-1827.
   Letters of Pestalozzi on the
education of infancy. Addressed
to mothers. Boston, Pub. by Car-
ter and Hendee [Pr. by I. R.
Butts] 1830. viii, 51 p. DLC;
GHi; ICU; IaHi; KyBC; MH; MHi;
MeBaT; NNU; NcU; Nh; OCl;
OMC; OO; RP; TNJ.   3017

Peter Parley's fable of the spider
and fly. See Howitt, Mrs. Mary
(Botham).

Peter Prim's profitable present
to the little misses and masters

of the United States... Philadelphia, Morgan & sons [1830?] 8 l.
DLC.   3018

Petersburg Railroad Company.
   Petersburg Rail Road Law.
An act to incorporate the Peters-
burg Rail Road Company. (Passed
February 10th, 1830.) ...[Peters-
burg, Pescud, pr., 1830] 16 p.
Vi.   3019

Peyre-Ferry, Pierre?
   Hymne patriotique, composé
pour la célébration de la révolu-
tion de juillet 1830, et chanté au
banquet des Français à Philadel-
phie le 30 septembre 1830, par
Peyre Ferry [Philadelphia, Pub-
lié par le Comité d'arrangement,
1830] [4] p. DeGE.   3020

The phantasmagoria of New-York,
a poetical burlesque upon a certain libellous pamphlet, written
by a committee of notorious fa-
natics, entitled the Magdalen report. New York, Pr. for the
publisher, [1830] 12 p. PPL.
                                        3021
The pharmacopoeia of the United
States of America, by the authority of "The General convention for
the formation of the American
pharmacopoeia," held in 1830.
2d ed., from the 1st ed., pub.
in 1820, with additions and corrections. New York, S. Converse [D. Fanshaw, pr.] 1830.
176 p. CSt-L; CU-M; DLC; ICJ;
ICU; MBCo; MdBM; MiU; NBuU;
NcD; OkU; ScU; TxU; ViRMC;
WaU.   3022

Phelps, Dudley, d. 1849.
   An address, delivered January
24, 1830, in the Second Baptist
meetinghouse in Haverhill, preparatory to the organization of the
East-Haverhill Temperance Society. Haverhill, Pr. by A. W.
Thayer, 1830. 23 p. CSmH; DLC;
MB; NHC-S.   3023

Phelps, Eliakim.
An address delivered before
the Geneva Abstinence Society on
Sabbath evening. Geneva, James
Bogert, 1830. 24 p. NGH.   3024

Phelps, Humphrey.
Map of the state of New York,
with the latest improvements...
New York, Pub. by Humphrey
Phelps... 1830. CSmH; MB;
MH-BA.   3025

Philadelphia.
A digest of the acts of Assem-
bly, and the ordinances of the
commissioners and inhabitants of
the incorporated district of the
Northern Liberties... By John
Miles. Philadelphia, Pr. by
Joseph Rakestraw, 1830. 220 p.
Ct; MH-L; PHi; PPL; PU.   3026

---- Report of the Watering com-
mittee of the Select and Common
Councils of Philadelphia, relative
to the termination of the Colum-
bia and Philadelphia Rail road.
Philadelphia, Pr. by Lydia R.
Bailey, 1830. 18 p. CSmH; DLC;
DeGE; MH; MHi; P; PHi;
PPAmP; PPF; PPL; PU.   3027

---- Report of the Watering committee, to the Select and Common
Councils. Read February 11,
1830.   Pub. by order of the councils.   Philadelphia, Pr. by Lydia
R. Bailey, 1830. 30 p. CtY;
DBRE; DLC; ICJ; MH; MHi;
MiU-T; NN; NNC; PPAmP; THi.
                             3028
---- Statement of the expenditures of the city commissioners
for year 1829.   Philadelphia,
1830. 43 p. MHi.   3029

Philadelphia almanack for 1831.
By Joseph Cramer. Philadelphia,
Uriah Hunt; W. Pilkington & Co.,
prs. [1830] 18 l. DLC; NBLiHi;
PHi; PPL.   3030

Philadelphia. Apprentices' Library Company.
Catalogue of books, belonging
to the Apprentices' Library Company of Philadelphia, Instituted
in 1820.   Philadelphia, Pr. for
the Apprentices' Library, 1830.
88 p. PPL.   3031

---- Citizens.
To the Honourable the Senate
and House of Representatives of
the State of Pennsylvania.   The
memorial of the subscribers,
citizens of the city and county of
Philadelphia, Respectfully sheweth that imprisonment for debt is
a discreditable remnant of a bar-
barous system of ancient times...
Philadelphia, March 12, 1830.
1 p. DLC.   3032

---- To the Senate and House of
Representatives of the commonwealth of Pennsylvania, the memorial of the subscribers, citizens of the city and Liberties of
Philadelphia.   Philadelphia, Nov.
29, 1830. Bdsd. PPL.   3033

Philadelphia. College of Pharmacy.
The charter, and laws, of the
Philadelphia College of Pharmacy.
To which is added a list of the
officers and members. Philadelphia, Pr. by Timothy A. Conrad,
1830. 12 p. PPL.   3034

---- First Unitarian Church.
Ticket of invitation and admission to a concert of sacred music, to be given in the First Unitarian Church, on Friday Evening, May 28, 1830. [4] p. PPL.
                             3035
---- General Theatrical Fund.
Rules and regulations of the
General Theatrical Fund, established in Philadelphia, December
21, 1829.   Philadelphia, Pr. by
C. Alexander, 1830. 11 p. MH;
NjR; PPL.   3036

---- German Reformed Congregation.

Charter of the German Reformed otherwise called the Calvinist Congregation in the city of Philadelphia, in the province of Pennsylvania. [Philadelphia, 1830] 8 p. (Issued with its Proceedings?) PHi. 3037

---- Proceedings of the Corporation of the German Reformed Congregation, of Philadelphia relating to the discharge of their minister. Philadelphia, Pr. at No. 8, Go-Forth Alley, 1830. 24 p. PHi. 3038

---- House of Refuge.

The second annual report of the House of Refuge of Philadelphia, With an appendix. Philadelphia, Jesper Harding, pr., 1830. 32 p. DLC; MH-AH; PPL. 3039

Philadelphia in 1830-1: or, A brief account of the various institutions and public objects in this metropolis. Forming a complete guide for strangers and a useful compendium for the inhabitants. Philadelphia, E. L. Carey and A. Hart, 1830. 284, [2] p. DLC; IU; MH; MiU; NNUT; ViU; BrMus. 3040

---- Philadelphia, E. L. Carey and A. Hart, Pr. by James Kay, Jun. & Co., 1830. 288 p. DLC; PPL. 3041

Philadelphia. Law Academy.

Constitution and by-laws of the Law Academy of Philadelphia. Adopted November 10, 1830. Philadelphia, Pr. by Mifflin & Parry, 1830. 12 p. PU. 3042

---- Maclarian Lyceum.

Report of the transactions of the Maclarian Lyceum of the Arts and Sciences of Philadelphia, from its commencement in 1826 to January, 1830. Submitted by

John T. Sharpless... Philadelphia, J. Richards, pr., 1830. 11, [1] p. PHi; PPL. 3043

---- Orphan Society.

Fifteenth annual report of the Philadelphia Orphan Society, read at the anniversary meeting, January 5, 1830. Philadelphia, Pr. by Lydia R. Bailey, 1830. 13, [5] p. PPL. 3044

---- St. James's Church.

Charter and by-laws of St. James's Church, in the city of Philadelphia. Philadelphia, Pr. by Mifflin & Parry, 1830. 28 p. MiD-B; NNG; PHi; PPAmP; PPL. 3045

---- St. Paul's Church.

Report of the vestry of St. Paul's Church to the congregation at their meeting March 1st 1830, in reference to improvements in the church together with statements of the present state of affairs of the church. Philadelphia, Pr. by William Stavely, 1830. 8 p. PHi. 3046

Philadelphia. Second New Jerusalem Church.

Order of worship, for the use of the Second New Jerusalem Church of Philadelphia. Philadelphia, Pr. and pub. by Thomas S. Manning, 1830. 108, 224, [ccxxv]-ccxxxii p. PPL. 3047

---- Second Presbyterian Church.

By-laws of the trustees of the Second Presbyterian Church in the city of Philadelphia. Adopted October 7th, 1830... Philadelphia, J. W. Allen, prs., 1830. 12 p. CSmH; WHi. 3048

---- Charter of the Second Presbyterian Church of the city of Philadelphia; together with the Act of the Legislature of Pennsylvania, re-establishing & confirming the same. Also the Supplements thereto. Philadelphia, Pr. by J. W. Allen, 1830. 22 p. CSmH; PHi; PPPrHi.   3049

Philadelphia Society for Alleviating the Miseries of Public Prisons.
Constitution of the Philadelphia Society for Alleviating the Miseries of Public Prisons. Philadelphia, Jesper Harding, pr., 1830. 10 p. CU; M; MHi; PPL.
3050
Philadelphia Society for Bettering the Condition of the Poor.
Circular of appeal. Philadelphia, Oct. 25, 1830. 1 p. PHi.   3051

---- First annual report of the Philadelphia Society for Bettering the Condition of the Poor. Philadelphia, Wm. Stavely, pr., 1830. 11 p. PHi; PPAmP; PPPrHi. 3052

Philadelphia. Society for the Establishment and Support of Charity Schools.
Annual report of the board of managers of the Philadelphia Society for the Establishment and Support of Charity Schools...
Philadelphia, Pub. by order of the Society, Garden and Thompson, prs., 1830. 11 p. PPL.
3053
---- United Churches of Christ Church, St. Peter's and St. James's.
Annual return of marriages, baptisms, & burials of the Episcopal Churches in Philadelphia. ... From December 25, 1829 to December 25, 1830. [Philadelphia, 1830] Bdsd. PPL.   3054

---- Working Men's Beneficial Society.
Constitution and by-laws, of the Working Men's Beneficial Society, of the city and county of Philadelphia. Philadelphia, J.

Coates, Jr., pr., 1830. 25 p. PPL.   3055

Philalethes, pseud.
An exposition of the principles of the Roman Catholic religion; with remarks on its influence in the United States. By Philalethes. Hartford, Pr. for the Author, 1830. 24 p. CtSoP; MWA; MeBaT; NCH; NjR; PHi; PPL; PPPrHi.
3056
Philandros.
An astonishing affair! The Rev. Samuel Arnold cast and tried for his cruelty, though his cause was advocated in a masterly manner by the Right Hon. Joseph Almon Clark Pray, ... By Philandros, [pseud.] Concord, Pr. by Luther Roby, 1830. 168 p. CSmH (108 p.); CtHT-W; CtY; IU; MB; MBAt; MBC; MH; MWA; MiD-B; MoU; NhD; NhHi.
3057
Phillips, Daniel.
Extracts from the writings of Daniel Phillips and Wm. Penn; to which are added some remarks and observations, shewing the analogy between George Keith, and the opposers of Elias Hicks. New-York, 1830. 16 p. MH.
3058
Phillips, Sir Richard.
The French phrase book; or Key to French conversation, containing the chief idioms of the French language. 3d ed. Boston, Hilliard, Gray, Little & Wilkins, 1830. 96 p. MB; MH.   3059

[Phillips, Stephen Clarendon]
Practical infidelity briefly considered in reference to the present times. Printed for the American Unitarian Association. Boston, Gray and Bowen, [I. R. Butts, pr.] 1830. 20 p. (American Unitarian Association, Tracts, 1st ser., Vol. III, No. 37.) CBPac; ICMe; MB; MBAU; MCon; MH-AH; MHi; MeB.   3060

Phillips Exeter Academy.

Catalogue of the officers and students of Phillips Exeter Academy, 1829-30. Exeter, Charles Norris, pr., 1830. 12 p. NhExP.
3061

Philo Cor-rector, pseud. See Notes on the sayings.

Phinney, Elias.

Address delivered before the Middlesex Society of Husbandmen and Manufacturers. At their annual festival, October 7, 1830. Charlestown, Pr. by William W. Wheildon, 1830. 28 p. PPL.
3062

Phinney's calendar, or Western almanac for 1831. By Edwin E. Prentiss. Cooperstown, H. & E. Phinney [1830] 18 l. CLU; CtHi; DLC; FSpHi; InU; MH; MWA; MnU; NCooHi; NHi; NN; NRMA; NUtHi; OClWHi; PHi; WHi. 3063

---- ---- Oxford, George Hunt [1830] 18 l. Drake 7111.   3064

Phoebus, John H., comp.

Chants, adapted to the service of the Protestant Episcopal Church in the United States. ... New-Haven, Pub. by Durrie and Peck. Baldwin & Treadway, pr., 1830. 23 p. Ct; CtHi; CtY; IEG; MB; VtMiS.   3065

A physician, pseud. See Graham, Thomas John.

A physician, pseud. See A solemn warning to drunkards.

Picard, Louis Benoit, 1769-1828.

Oeuvres choisies de L. B. Picard... New York, Philadelphia [etc.] C. De Behr, 1830. vii, 292 p. DLC; Ia; ViU; BrMus.
3066

Pickering, David, 1788-1859.

Lectures in defence of divine revelation, delivered at the Universalist Chapel, in Providence, R.I., Providence, Pub. by Samuel W. Wheeler; Cranston and Knowles, prs., 1830. 216 p. DLC; MBC; MMeT-Hi; MWA; R; RHi; RP; RPB.   3067

Pickering, Ellen, d. 1843.

The poor cousin. A novel. By Ellen Pickering... Philadelphia, T. P. Peterson [1830?] 116 p. DLC; LNHT.   3068

[Pickering, Henry] 1781-1838.

Poems. By an American ... Boston, Carter and Hendee, 1830. vi p., 1 l., [5]-84 p. DLC; MB; MHi; RPB; TxU; BrMus.   3069

Pickering, Octavius, 1791-1868.

Case of the Proprietors of Charles River Bridge against the proprietors of Warren Bridge, argued and determined in the supreme Judicial Court of Mass. By Octavius Pickering... Boston, Hilliard, Gray, Little & Wilkins, 1830. 203 p. DLC; M; MBS; MH; MiD-B.   3070

Picket, Albert.

The essentials of English grammar: Being the second part of the Juvenile Spelling Book: Containing obvious definitions and rules for speaking and writing correctly. By A. & J. W. Picket, principals of the Cincinnati Female Institution, authors of the American School Class Books, &c. Stereotyped by Oliver Wells & Co. Cincinnati, Pub. by E. H. Flint. G. T. Williamson, pr., 1830. 234 p. ODW.   3071

Picket, Albert.

The juvenile instructer, or American school class book, no. 2, being a natural grammar & reader... New York, C. Bartlett, 1830. 214 p. OO.   3072

[----] [Juvenile spelling book... rev. ed. New York, 1830] t.p.

missing. CtHT-W. 3073

---- The new juvenile expositor,
or Rational reader, and key to
the Juvenile spelling book: comprising the definitions of all the
syllabic words in that work...be-
ing American school class book
no. 4. By A. & J. W. Picket...
Cincinnati, E. H. Flint, 1830.
384 p. DLC; OCHP. 3074

---- Picket's juvenile or universal primer, being a first book
for young children: introductory
to the Juvenile Spelling-book. A
new edition, revised. ...New-
York, C. Bartlett, 1830. 48 p.
NN. 3075

Pictorial life. See Howard, H.
R.

The picture alphabet No. 7. A
B C. Concord, Pub. by Hoag &
Atwood, 1830. 16 p. NhHi. 3076

The picture alphabet; or, A B C
in rhyme. New Haven, S. Babcock [1830?] 8 p. CtY; DLC.
3077

The picture book; or A gift for
Charles. New-Haven, S. Babcock, Sidney's press, 1830. 1 p.
l., [4]-17 p. (Babcock's New-
Haven no. 1 toy books. New series, 2d edition, book 14) CtHi;
CtY. 3078

Picture riddler. Boston, Pr. by
Munroe & Francis [183-?] NN.
3079

Pictures of animals. Wendell,
J. Metcalf, 1830. 18 p. MWA.
3080

Pictures of animals for children.
Boston, Munroe & Francis
[183-?] 26 colored plates. MH.
3081

Pictures of birds and beasts.
Wendell, J. Metcalf, 1830. 18 p.
MNF. 3082

Pierce, E.
An address... before the
Greene County Medical Society...
By E. Pierce, M.D. ...Catskill,
Pr. by Faxon & Elliott, 1830.
8 p. NNNAM. 3083

Pierce, Erasmus J.
Circular. During the few
leisure hours that the dull winter
has afforded me, I committed to
paper, a part of the thoughts and
reflections that obtruded on my
mind... [Articles on The Navy
and Education] Philadelphia,
March 6, 1830. 1 p. DLC. 3084

Pierce, John, 1773-1849.
Discourse delivered at Dor-
chester on 17 June, 1830, to
commemorate the completion of
the second century from its set-
tlement by our Pilgrim fathers.
Boston, From the office of the
Daily Advertiser, W. L. Lewis,
pr., 1830. 36 p. CSmH; CtSoP;
ICN; MB; MBAt; MBC; MH; MHi;
MWA; MdBJ; MeBaT; MiD-B;
NBLiHi; NNUT; Nh; OO; PHi;
RPB; WHi. 3085

Pierpont, John, 1785-1866, comp.
The American first class book;
or, Exercises in reading and
recitation; selected principally
from modern authors of Great
Britain and America...By John
Pierpont. Boston, Hilliard,
Gray, Little and Wilkins, 1830.
480 p. CLSU; MB; MH; NRU;
NjR; OCY; RPB. 3086

---- ... Introduction to the na-
tional reader; a selection of easy
lessons. ... By John Pierpont
... Boston, Pub. by Richardson,
Lord & Holbrook, 1830. 168 p.
(At head of title: Pierpont's in-
troduction.) CSt; CtY; MB; MH;
MNS. 3087

---- The young reader: to go

with the spelling book. By John
Pierpont... Boston, Richardson,
Lord, and Holbrook, 1830. 162 p.
DLC; MH. 3088

Pike, John Gregory, 1784-1854.
A guide for young disciples of
the Holy Savior in their way to
immortality, forming a sequel to
Persuasives to early piety. New-
York, American Tract Society
[183-?] 465 p. (Evangelical family library, 11.) MH; ViU. 3089

---- Persuasives to early piety,
interspersed with suitable prayers.
J. G. Pike. New York, American Tract Society [183-?] (Evangelical family library, no. 10)
ICT; KyBgW; LU; MH; MoS; OMC;
ViU; BrMus. 3090

Pike, Stephen.
Pike's system of arithmetick
abridged: designed to facilitate
the study of the science of numbers comprehending the most per-
spicuous and accurate rules, illustrated by useful examples, to
which are added Appropriate questions, for the examination of
scholars; and a short system of
book-keeping. By Dudly Leavitt;
Stereotyped by Perkins and Chase,
Concord, N.H., H. Hill & Co.,
1830. 228 p. CtHT-W; DAU; MH;
BrMus. 3091

---- The teachers' assistant, or
A system of practical arithmetic; wherein the several rules of
that useful science, are illustrated by a variety of examples,
a large portion of which are in
federal money. The whole designed to abridge the labour of
teachers, and to facilitate the instruction of youth. A new ed.,
with corrections and additions by
the Author. Compiled by Stephen
Pike. Philadelphia, Pub. and
sold by M'Carty & Davis; Stereotyped by L. Johnson... Philadel-

phia, 1830. 198 p. MiDSH; PAlt.
3092
The Pilgrim fathers; or, The
lives of some of the first settlers of New England. Designed
for Sabbath School Libraries.
Portland, Pub. by Shirley, Hyde
& Co., 1830. 123 p. DLC; ICU;
MB; MH; MHi; MiD-B; NhHi.
3093
[Pinckney, Maria Henrietta]
The quintessence of long
speeches, arranged as a political catechism; by a lady for her
god-daughter. Charleston, Pr.
by A. E. Miller, 1830. 24 p.
DLC; ICU; MB; MH; NHi; NN;
ScC; ScHi. 3094

Pinkham, Rebekah P.
A narrative of the life of Miss
Lucy Cole of Sedgwick, Maine...
By Rebekah P. Pinkham... Bos-
ton, Pub. by James Loring, 1830.
108 p. DLC; MeHi. 3095

Pittsburgh Cabinet Makers.
The Pittsburgh cabinet makers'
book of prices. Pittsburgh, Jos.
Snowden, pr., 1830. 91, [1] p.
Not loc. 3096

Pittsburgh. Citizens.
At a meeting of the citizens of
Pittsburgh, held in the court-
house, on the 30th January, 1830,
to take into consideration the
present situation of the Cherokees, and other tribes of Indians,
it was, on motion of W. M. Irwin, esq. [Signed by several cit-
zens.] [1830] 1 p. folded leaf-
let. Not loc. 3097

Place, Mrs. Perry.
The orphan; or, A brief memoir of Mrs. Place. Written by
herself. [Portland?] Pr. for the
author, 1830. 19 p. MH. 3098

---- The hapless lovers; or,
Sheckem and Dinah. A pathetic
memoir for the use of children.

Designed to allure them to a love
of Sacred Scriptures. By the author of The orphan. Portland,
Pr. for the author, 1830. 21 p.
M.   3099

A plain and serious address to
parents, on the subject of Sunday
Schools. New-York, Protestant
Episcopal Tract Society, 1830.
8 p. NNG.   3100

A plain man's defence of the
church service; being a dialogue
between Steady and Candid about
going to church... Stereotyped by
James Conner, New York. New
York, Protestant Episcopal Tract
Society, Pr. at the Protestant
Episcopal Press, 1830. 12 p.
MBD; NNG.   3101

Plainfield Academy, Plainfield,
Conn.
    Catalogue of the trustees, in-
structors, and students... for the
year ending Aug. 1830. Brooklyn [Conn.] Holbrook & Webber,
prs., 1830. CSmH.   3102

A plan of the town of Charlottesville... [Charlottesville, ca.
1830] Bdsd. ViU (photostat)
                                3103
Planche, James Robinson, 1796-
1880.
    The brigand; a romantic dra-
ma, in two acts. Baltimore, J.
Robinson, 1830. MH.   3104

---- The Vampire; or, The bride
of the isles. A romantic melo-
drama, in two acts: preceded by
an introductory vision... Baltimore, Pr. and pub. by J. Robinson, Circulating Library and Dramatic Repository, 1830. 41 p.
CSmH; MH; MWA.   3105

Planter's almanac for 1831, calculated for the meridian of Mobile. Mobile, Pub. by Odiorne
and Smith, 1830. Title from ad-

vertisement in Mobile Commer-
cial Register, Nov. 20, 1830.
                                3106
Playfair, John.
    Elements of geometry: ... By
John Playfair, F. R. S. ... From
the last London ed., enl. New-
York, Pub. by Collins & Hannay,
Collins & co., O. A. Roorbach,
White, Gallaher & White, and G.
& C. & H. Carvill. W. E. Dean,
pr., 1830. 333 p.   GMiW; MH;
NNC; PLFM; TNJ.   3107

Plea for the Indians; the following document was written as a
memorial to be signed by citizens of Hartford, Connecticut...
to the Senate and House of Representatives in Congress assembled. [Boston, 1830] 16 p.
WHi.   3108

Pleasant stories; for good little
girls. New Haven, S. Babcock;
Sidney's Press, 1830. [18] p.
CtHi; CtY.   3109

A pleasing toy, for girl or boy.
Wendell, J. Metcalf, 1830. 18 p.
MNF.   3110

Plough, A. L.
    Dear Sir: Men are liable to
be imposed upon by unfounded
pretensions, until they are in-
formed as to the nature and extent of the knowledge which a
professional man ought to possess.
...[testimonials to Plough's abili-
ties as dentist--latest dated 1830]
[New York, 1830] 14 p. PPL.
                                3111
Plutarchus.
    Plutarchs' Lives, translated
from the original Greek; with
notes, critical and historical; and
a life of Plutarch. A new ed. ...
Baltimore, Pub. by William and
Joseph Neal, 1830. xx, 748 p.
GAU; PPL.   3112

---- ---- By John Langhorne and

William Langhorne carefully corrected and printed from the last London ed. Philadelphia, James Crissy, 1830. 4 vols. CtMW; ICMcC; IU; MiD; NNG; NcAS; OClW.　　　　　　　　　　3113

Plymouth, N. H. , Congregational Church.

Articles of faith and government, and covenant, adapted by the Congregational Church, in Plymouth, 1830... Concord, N. H. , Pr. by Hoag and Atwood, 1830. 8 p. ICN.　　　　　3114

Pocket Companion: or, Every man his own lawyer: by a Gentleman of the Bar. Laid down in so plain a manner, that the farmer, mechanic, apprentice, or school boy, can draw any instrument of writing, without the assistance of an attorney. Prefaced with several pages of scrip: etc. Stereotyped by L. Johnson. Philadelphia, M'Carty & Davis, 1830. 108 p. DeGE; MH-L; OCLaw; PPeSchw.　　　　　　　　　3115

The pocket lawyer, or, Self-conveyancer: containing all the most useful forms, rendered so plain, that every man can draw any instrument of writing, without the assistance of an attorney. In a method entirely new. 3d ed. Pittsburgh, Robert Patterson, 1830. 107 p. IaU; IaU-L.　3116

Poems. See Pickering, Henry.

Poesias de un Jóvan Americána. Boston [1830?] BrMus.　　3117

The poetic gift. Wendell, Mass. , J. Metcalf, pr. , 1830. 8 p. KU.　　　　　　　　　　　3118
The poetical works of Rogers, Campbell, J. Montgomery, Lamb, and Kirke White. Complete in one volume. Philadelphia, Carey & Lea, 1830. 5 p. l. , 98, viii,

66, viii, 195, v, 29, xxiii, 56 p. (also paged consecutively, 496 p.) KyDC; MH; MeB.　　　　3119

Poetry for schools. See Robbins, Eliza.　　　　　　　　　　3120

Poinsett, Joel Roberts, 1779-1851.

Observaciones sobre las instrucciones que dió el Presidente de los Estados Unidos... a los representantes de aquella República en el Congreso de Panama en 1826; sobre la conducta del Sr. Poinsett... y sobre nuestras relaciones con la América Española en general, con una copia de las Instrucciones. Filadelfia, Imprenta de Guillermo Stavely, 1830. iv, 59 p. BrMus.　　　3121

Pollock, Robert, 1798-1827.

The course of time. A poem. ...7th Amer. ed. Boston, L. W. Kimball & Carter & Hendee [etc. , etc.] 1830. xxxii, 240 p. IaDmD; MH; MoS; NNF; OClWHi.　　　　　　　　　　3122
---- ---- New-York, Charles Wells [1830] xiv, [13]-328, x p. MoSU.　　　　　　　　　3123

---- ---- New York, Edward Kearny [ca 1830] xiv, [13]-328, x p. RPB.　　　　　　　3124

---- ---- Philadelphia, L. A. Key, and sold by Turner & Hughes, Raleigh, N. C. , 1830. 248, [4] p. of advs. DGU; OCl. 　　　　　　　　　　3125
---- ---- Watervliet, N. Y. , Pub. by A. & C. A. Warren, 1830. xxvi, 221 p. CSmH; NBuG; NN. 　　　　　　　　　　3126
---- Ralph Gemmell, or The banks of the Irvine; a Scottish tale illustrating the happy reconciliation of a family and the power of religions truth. 2d Boston ed. Boston, J. Loring, [183-?] MH.　　　　　　　　　　3127

Pontchartrain Rail Road Company.
An act to incorporate the Pont-
chartrain Rail Road Company.
Published by order of the board of
directors. New Orleans, Pr. by
Atherton T. Penniman & Co. for
Thomas Stroud and Co., 1830. 16
p. MB.   3128

Poor Richard's almanack for 1831.
Rochester, Marshall, Dean, & Co.
[1830] 12 l. MBAt; MWA; N;
NBuHi; NN; NRMA; NRU; WHi.
                                3129
Poor Richard's revised almanac
for 1831. New York, Christian
Brown [1830] 18 l. MWA; NBLiHi;
NN.   3130

Poor Will's almanac for 1831. By
William Collom. Philadelphia,
Joseph Rakestraw [1830] 18 l.
CtY; PDoBHi.   3131

Poor Will's pocket almanack for
1831. Philadelphia, Kimber &
Sharpless [1830] 24 l. InU; MWA;
MnU; NjR; PHi.   3132

Pope, Alexander, 1688-1744.
    The poetical works of Alex-
ander Pope, esq., to which is
prefixed the life of the author by
Dr. Johnson. Philadelphia, Pub.
by J. J. Woodward; Stereotyped
by L. Johnson, 1830. 484 p.
AMob; CtHC; GEU; KWiU; LNT;
MH; MWH; MdBE; MeBaT; MoS;
NPV; NjMD; NjP; OClW; OHi;
PPL; PU; ScU; TNJ; TxU; ViU;
BrMus.   3133

A popular description, geographical, historical and topographical
of Mexico and Guatemala. Boston,
Wells & Lilly, and Thomas
Wardle, Philadelphia, 1830. 2
vols. in 1. (Also issued as vols.
vi and vii of Modern Traveller.)
MWA.   3134

Porter, Anna Maria, 1780-1832.
    The barony...New York, Pr.

by J. & J. Harper, 1830. 2 v.
KU; RPB.   3135

---- The Hungarian brothers. By
Miss Porter. New York, S. &
D. A. Forbes, prs., 1830. 2 v.
CtHT; NIC.   3136

Porter, Arthur L.
    The chemistry of the arts; be-
ing a practical display of the arts
and manufactures which depend on
chemical principles... By Arthur
L. Porter... Philadelphia, Carey
& Lea, 1830. 2 vols. CU; DeGE;
ICU; KyLxT; LNT; MB; MH; MiU;
NCH; NNC; NNNAM; NRU; PPi;
RPB; TU; WHi.   3137

Porter, Ebenezer, 1772-1834.
    Analysis of the principles of
rhetorical delivery as applied to
reading and speaking... 3d ed.
By E. Porter. Andover, Flagg &
Gould; New York, J. Leavitt,
1830. xvi, [13]-404 p. GU-M;
IEN; MB; MH; MoSpD; NIC; NN;
NjP.   3138

Porteus, Beilby.
    A summary of the principal
evidences for the truth, and divine origin, of the Christian Revelation. By Beilby Porteus, D.D.
New York, New York Protestant
Episcopal Tract Society, 1830.
44 p. MBD; NNG.   3139

The Portland directory, containing names of the inhabitants, their
occupations, places of business,
and dwelling houses. With lists of
the streets, lanes and wharves,
the town officers, public offices
and banks. Portland, S. Colman
[Todd & Holden, prs.] 1830. 86,
[10] p. MH.   3140

Portland, Maine.
    Report of the School Commit-
tee of Portland, March 30, 1829.
Portland, 1830. Sabin 64378.
                                3141

Portsmouth, N. H.
Report of the committee on
the subject of erecting an addition to the alms-house, and also
the report of the committee on
the accounts of the selectmen,
overseers of the poor and school
committee, at the annual town
meeting of the inhabitants of
Portsmouth, held by adjournment,
April 15, 1830. Portsmouth, Pr.
by Gideon Beck, 1830. 15 p.
NhD; NhHi.   3142

---- Report of the school committee of the town of Portsmouth,
March 25, 1830. [Portsmouth,
1830] 7 p. NhD.   3143

---- North Parish Library.
North Parish Library, 1830.
At the commencement of this
year, the Directors Report;...
50 volumes have been added
since the printing of the last annual catalogue, a list of which
is annexed. [1] p., (i. e., p. 15
only, to be added to earlier cata-
logs) MBC.   3144

Post, Henry A. V.
A visit to Greece and Con-
stantinople, in the year 1827-8.
By Henry A. V. Post... New
York, Sleight & Robinson, prs.
Sold by G. & C. and H. Carvill
[etc.] Philadelphia, Carey and
Hart, 1830. vi, 367 p. CSt;
CtHT; GMiM; ICJ; IaU; MH;
MdBE; MnU; NCH; NRU; PPL;
RPB; WHi.   3145

Potter, Alonzo.
A sermon, delivered in Christ
Church, Hartford, before the Connecticut Church Scholarship Society, August 5, 1829, published
by request of the board of directors. Boston, Putnam & Hunt,
1830. 22 p. CtHT; MBAt; MBC;
MiD-B; NGH; NNG; NcU; NjR;
PPL; RPB.   3146

Potter, Robert.
Mr. Potter's appeal to the
citizens of Nash, Franklin, Warren and Granville [1830?] 1 p.
DLC.   3147

Powel, Mr.
Mr. Powel's stock of improved
Durham short horned cattle, imported, or bred by him, will be
offered for sale, on Wednesday
the 16th of June next, at 10 o'-
clock, at Powelton, on the Schuylkill, opposite to Philadelphia.
May 25, 1830. 16 p. PHi; PPL.
                                    3148

[Powel, John Hare] 1786-1856.
Remarks on the termination of
the Pennsylvania Rail-Way. Philadelphia? 1830? 16 p. DBRE;
MH-BA; P; PPAmP; PPL.   3149

Powell, J.
Buffalo house. The subscriber
informs his friends and the publick, that he has taken the stand
lately occupied by Mr. O. C.
Church, known by the name of
the Buffalo House, and situated
nearly in the centre of the village. E. Powell, Jr. Buffalo,
May 1, 1830. Buffalo, Day, Follett & Haskins, prs., 1830.
Bdsd. NBuHi.   3150

Power, John.
The Catholic Christian's guide
to Heaven; or, A manual of spiritual exercises for Catholics;
with the evening office of the
church, in Latin and English, and
a selection of pious hymns. New
York, Pub. by James Ryan [J.
Seymour, pr.] 1830. iv, 226 p.
DGU.   3151

[Power, Tyrone] 1797-1841. (i. e.
William Grattan Tyrone)
The lost heir... and The pre-
diction. In two volumes. New
York, Pr. by J. & J. Harper,
Sold by Collins & Hannay, Col-
lins & Co. [etc.] 1830.

2 v. NCH.   3152

Powers, Grant.
An address delivered on the
centennial celebration, to the
people of Hollis, N. H. , September 15th, 1830...Dunstable,
N. H. , Thayer & Wiggin, 1830.
35 p. CSmH; MDeeP; MH; MoSpD;
NBLiHi; NhD; NhHi; OClWHi;
RPB; WHi; BrMus.   3153

Practical infidelity. See Phillips, Stephen Clarendon.

Practical reading lessons on the
three great duties, which man
owes to his maker - his fellow
beings - and himself. Baltimore,
Pr. and pub. by Lucas & Deaver,
1830.   252 p. CtHi; MdBJ; MdBS-
P; PPL.   3154

---- Philadelphia, E. L. Carey
& A. Hart, 1830. 250 p. MB;
MWA; NjR.   3155

A practical view of the common
causes of inefficiency in the
Christian ministry of the Congregational and Presbyterian Churches of the United States. By a
Baconian Biblist. Philadelphia,
Pr. and pub. by William Stavely,
1830. 40 p. CSmH; CtHi; MB
(attributed to A. S. Colton); NNUT;
PHi; PPPrHi.   3156

Pratt, Thomas.
The Columbian monitor; showing the influence of education and
its importance, particularly in
the United States. By Thomas
Pratt... Harrisburg [Pa.] Montgomery and Dexter, prs. , 1830.
4 p. l. , [iii]-vii, [9]-269, [1] p.
DLC; NNC; PLFM; PPiHi;
TxDaH.   3157

Pray, George.
Defence and justification of the
conduct of Mr. George Pray, a
member of the First Church of

Christ in Weymouth, Mass. , in
consequence of being called on
by the church to account for having recently absented himself
from the Communion table. Boston, 1830. 12 p. MH.   3158

Prayer delivered at Tammany
hall, New-York, at a late "revival" meeting there held. [New
York, 183-?] Bdsd. CSmH. 3159

Prayers for children. Boston
[1830?] BrMus.   3160

Preble, Jedidiah, 1765-1847.
Birth, parentage, life and ex-
perience of Jedidiah Preble, 3d.
Written by himself. Portland, J.
and W. E. Edwards, 1830. 216 p.
DLC; MeHi.   3161

Prentice, Charles.
Sermon, delivered September
20, 1829, at the twenty-fifth anniversary of his ordination. To
which is added, a brief narrative
of a revival of religion. Litchfield, Pr. by Henry Adams, 1830.
32 p. C; CtHi; MBC; RPB;
BrMus.   3162

Prentiss, Joseph.
A discourse, delivered before
the Grand Chapter of the state of
New York, at its annual commu-
nication at Albany, on Feb. 2,
1830... Albany, Pr. by Websters
& Skinners, 1830. 12 p. IaCrM;
MBFM; N; NNFM; OC.   3163

Presbyterian Church in the U. S. A.
Minutes of the General Assem-
bly of the Presbyterian Church in
the United States of America:
With an appendix, A. D. 1830.
Vol. VII. Philadelphia, Pub. by
the stated clerk of the Assembly.
Pr. by William F. Geddes, and
L. R. Bailey, 1830. 152 p. InU;
KyLoP; PPL; TxDaM; WHi. 3164

---- Psalms and hymns adapted

to public worship, and approved by the General Assembly of the Presbyterian Church in the United States of America. Philadelphia, Solomon Allen, 1830. 666 p. NNG. 3165

---- ---- Philadelphia, Presbyterian board of publication [1830] 254, 481, 82 p. OU. 3166

---- Board of Missions.
The fourteenth annual report of the Board of Missions of the General Assembly of the Presbyterian Church in the United States. Laid before that body in May 1830. Philadelphia, Clark & Raser, prs., 1830. 47, [1] p. PPL. 3167

---- Presbytery of Carlisle.
Pastoral letter of the Presbytery of Carlisle to the churches under its care. Chambersburg, Pa., Herald Office, 1830. 7 p. PPPrHi. 3168

---- Presbytery of Chillicothe.
Two letters on the subject of slavery, from the Presbytery of Chillicothe to the churches under their care. Hillsborough, Pr. by Whetstone & Buxton, Cincinnati, 1830. 50 p. CSmH; NN; TxU. 3169

---- Presbytery of Philadelphia.
Sketch of the debate and proceedings of the presbytery of Philadelphia, in regard to the installation of the Rev. Albert Barnes in that First Presbyterian Church in Philadelphia. June, 1830. New York, Sleight & Robinson, 1830. 35 p. NNG; PHi. 3170

---- A true and complete narrative of all the proceedings of the Philadelphia Presbytery and of the Philadelphia Synod, in relation to the case of the Rev. Albert Barnes. Philadelphia, Pr. by Russell & Martien, 1830.

48 p. PHi. 3171

Presbyterian Church in the U.S.A. Synod of Indiana.
Annual abstract of the proceedings of the synod of Indiana. Convened at Madison, on Thursday, October 21, 1830. This paper is periodical, and the postage in the state is by law one and a half cents. Madison, N. Bollton [sic], pr., 1830. 19 p. In; NN; OCHP; PPPrHi. 3172

---- Synod of Philadelphia.
Minutes of the Synod of Philadelphia, at their sessions held in Lancaster, October, 1830. 21 p. PPPrHi. 3173

A present to children... Baltimore, Samuel S. Wood & Co. [c 1830] 16 l. MB; PP. 3174

Pressly, John T.
Parental duty: a sermon, delivered in Hopewell, Newton County, Georgia. By John T. Pressly. Pub. at the particular request of the congregation. Augusta, W. Lawson, 1830. 22 p. GDC. 3175

Price, William.
Address delivered by William Price, Esq. before the Alumni Association of Dickinson College, at their annual meeting in Carlisle, Pa. September 21st, 1830. Carlisle, Pr. by Ann C. Phillips & son, 1830. 21 p. DLC; MH; P; PHi; PPAmP; PPPrHi. 3176

Price, William Robert, 1795-1869.
A treatise on the vine; embracing its history from the earliest ages to the present day, with descriptions of above two hundred foreign, and eighty American varieties... New York, Pub. by T. & J. Swords, G. & C. & H. Carvill [etc.], 1830.

355 p. CSmH; CtHT-W; DLC; DeGE; GU; IU; KyBgW; LNB; MBHo; MH; MdBS; MdU; NHi; NIC; NbU; NcU; NjR; OH; PPL; RPB; BrMus. 3177

---- ---- Charleston, Pub. by Joseph Simmons [J. Seymour, pr.] 1830. 352 p. MeU. 3178

Princeton Theological Seminary.
Catalogue of the officers and students of the Theological Seminary. Princeton, N. J., Hugh Madden, pr., 1830. 7 p. M; MB; Nh; NjP; NjR. 3179

Princeton University.
Catalogus collegii Neo-Caesariensis. Rerumpublicarum foederatarum Americae summae potestatis, anno LV. Princetoniae, typis G. D'Hart, 1830. 47 p. MBC; MH; MdHi; TNJ. 3180

The principles of anti-masonry. See Arch, Royal.

Prindle's almanac for 1831. By Charles Prindle. New-Haven, A. H. Maltby [1830] 12 l. Ct; CtB; CtHi; CtY; DLC; InU; MB; MWA; N; NHi. 3181

Printers' ode. Written for the celebration of the French revolution, in the City of Washington, October 28, 1830. 1 p. DLC. 3182

Prison Discipline Society.
Fifth annual report of the board of managers of the Prison Discipline Society, Boston, 1830. Stereotyped at the Boston Type and Stereotype Foundry. [Boston, Perkins & Marvin, 1830] 96 p. [also numbered [331]-426] KyDC; MdHi; MeHi; MiD; NbHi; PPL; ScU. 3183

---- First, second, third, and fourth annual reports of the Prison Discipline Society, 1826 to 1829. [Boston, 1830] 48, 100, 85, 96 p. [Also numbered inclusively 330 p.] PPL. 3184

The prize; or, The story of George Benson and Wm. Sandford... Philadelphia, American Sunday School Union [1830?] 32 p. BrMus. 3185

Proceedings of a meeting of Physicians and Surgeons, held at the Shakspeare Hotel, New-York, 13th February, 1830. Bdsd. NjR. 3186

Professor Hale and Dartmouth College. See Alumnus.

The progressive reader, or Juvenile monitor. Carefully selected from the most approved writers. Designed for the younger classes of children in primary schools ... Concord [N. H.] Hoag & Atwood, 1830. 216 p. DGU; DLC. 3187

The prompter. See Webster, Noah.

Proofs of the supreme divinity of the Lord Jesus Christ, and of the doctrine of the divine trinity, plainly deduced from the Holy Scriptures. (From a London ed.) Philadelphia, Pub. by D. Harrington, Martin & Boden, prs., 1830. 24 p. DLC; PPPrHi. 3188

Proposals for forming a Society of Education. [Boston? 1830?] 4 p. PPL. 3189

Proposition for an anthracite coal steam power boat and barge company... See Sullivan, John Langdon.

Propositions for amending the constitution. See Hillhouse, James.

Protestant Episcopal Church in the U. S. A.

The book of common prayer
etc., ...Stereotyped by D. & G.
Bruce. New York, Pub. by New
York Protestant Episcopal Press,
1830. 478 p. NN.   3190

---- ---- New York, Pr. at the
Protestant Episcopal Press, 1830.
8, 480, [116] p.   3191

---- ---- New-York, Pub. from
the stereotype plates of the auxiliary New-York Bible and Common Prayer Book Society, and
to be had at their depository,
Protestant Episcopal Press buildings, Pr. at the Protestant Episcopal Press, 1830. xx, 37-394,
3-56 p. IaPeC; NNG.   3192

---- ---- Stereotyped by D. &
G. Bruce, New-York. New
York, Pub. by Caleb Bartlett,
1830. 459, 78 p. CSmH; MnHi.
                                3193
---- ---- Philadelphia, Samuel
F. Bradford, 1830. 381 p. LU;
NNG; PU; RPB.   3194

---- Hymns of the Protestant
Episcopal Church... Hartford,
S. Andrus, 1830. 124 p. NN;
NNG.   3195

---- Hymns of the Protestant
Episcopal Church in the United
States of America, set forth in
General Conventions... Stereo-
typed, by James Conner... New
York, Pub. by the New-York
Protestant Episcopal Press, 1830.
117 p. CBPac; CtHi; LNHT; LU;
MBD; MHi; MiU-C; WHi.   3196

---- ---- Stereotyped by William
Hagar & Co., New York. New
York, Pr. and pub. by Caleb
Bartlett, 1830. 43, [11] p. PPL.
                                3197
---- ---- Stereotyped by L.
Johnson, Philadelphia. Philadel-
phia, Pub. by Wm. Stavely,
1830. 50 p. NNG.   3198

---- Music of the church. A
collection of psalms, hymns, and
chant tunes, adapted to the worship of the Protestant Episcopal
Church in the United States.
3d octavo ed. New York, Pr.
by Peter C. Smith; Pub. by
Samuel F. Bradford, Philadelphia, 1830. xxxi, 238 p. CtHT;
CtHT-W.   3199

---- Alabama (Diocese)
Journal of the proceedings of
the second annual convention of
the clergy and laity of the Protestant Episcopal Church, in the
diocese of Alabama, held in Mobile, Monday, January 25, 1830.
[Mobile? 1830] 5 p. ABCA.
                                3200

---- Connecticut (Diocese)
Journal of the proceedings of
the annual convention of the Prot-
estant Episcopal Church, in the
Diocese of Connecticut: Held in
St. Paul's Chapel, New Haven,
Wednesday, June 2d, and Thurs-
day, June 3d, A.D. 1830. Mid-
dletown, Pr. by W[illiam] D.
Starr, 1830. 63 p. CtHC.   3201

---- Georgia (Diocese)
Journal of the proceedings of
the eighth annual convention of
the Protestant Episcopal Church
in the diocese of Georgia... Savannah, W. T. Williams, 1830.
20 p. NN.   3202

---- Maine (Diocese)
Abstract of the journals of the
conventions of the Protestant
Episcopal Church in the state of
Maine, from its organization in
the year 1820, to the end of 1829.
Portland, Day & Frazer, prs.,
1830. 16 p. MB; MHi.   3203

---- Maryland (Diocese)
Journal of a convention of the
Protestant Episcopal Church of
Maryland, held in St. Paul's
Church, Baltimore, June 9th,

10th, 11th, and 12th, 1830. Baltimore, J. Robinson, 1830. 48 p.
NNG.   3204

---- Massachusetts (Diocese)
Journal of the proceedings of
the annual convention of the
Protestant Episcopal Church in
the Commonwealth of Massachusetts, held in Trinity Church,
Boston, June 16, 17, 1830. Cambridge, E. W. Metcalf & co.,
1830. 52 p. MBD; WHi.   3205

---- New Jersey (Diocese)
Journal of the proceedings of
the forty-seventh annual convention of the Protestant Episcopal
Church, in the state of New Jersey...held in Trinity Church at
Swedesborough... New Brunswick,
Pr. by Terhune & Letson, 1830.
56 p. NjR; PPL.   3206

---- New York (Diocese)
Journal of the proceedings of
the forty-fifth convention of the
Protestant Episcopal Church in
the state of New-York: Held in
Trinity Church, in the city of
New-York, on Thursday, October
7, Friday, October 8, and Saturday, October 9. A. D. 1830. to
which is prefixed a list of the
clergy of the Diocese of New-
York. New-York, Pr. at the
Protestant Episcopal Press, 1830.
78, [2] p. IEG; MBD.   3207

---- North Carolina (Diocese)
Journal of the proceedings of
the 14th annual convention of the
Protestant Episcopal Church in
the state of North Carolina, hold-
en in St. James's Church, Wilmington, on Thursday May 20th,
Friday May 21st, Saturday May
22d, and Monday May 24th, 1830.
Fayetteville, Pr. by Edward J.
Hale, 1830. NcU.   3208

---- Ohio (Diocese)
Journal of the proceedings of

the thirteenth annual convention
of the Protestant Episcopal
Church in the diocese of Ohio:
held at Gambier, September 8th,
9th, & 10th, 1830. Acland
Press, Gambier, O.; George W.
Myers, pr., 1830. 35, [1] p.
CSmH; MBD; NN; OCHP.   3209

---- Pennsylvania (Diocese)
Journal of the proceedings of
the forty-sixth convention of the
Protestant Episcopal Church in
the state of Pennsylvania, held
in St. Peter's Church, in the
city of Philadelphia, on Tuesday,
May 18th, Wednesday, May 19th,
and Thursday, May 20th, 1830.
Philadelphia, Pub. by order of
the convention. Jesper Harding,
pr., 1830. 64 p. MBD; PPL.
                              3210
---- South Carolina (Diocese)
Journal of the proceedings of
the forty-second annual conven-
tion of the Protestant Episcopal
Church in the diocese of South
Carolina; held at St. Michael's
Church, Charleston, on the 17th,
18th and 19th of February, 1830.
Charleston, Pr. by A. E. Miller,
1830. 52 p. MBC; NN; NNG.
                              3211
---- Tennessee (Diocese)
Journal of the proceedings of
the second convention of the
clergy and laity of the Protestant
Episcopal Church in the state of
Tennessee, held in the Masonic
Hall at Franklin, on Thursday,
July 1--Friday, July 2--and Sat-
urday, July 3, 1830. Nashville,
Pub. by order of the convention.
Hunt, Tardiff, & Co., prs.,
1830. 16 p. ICN; NN.   3212

---- Vermont (Diocese)
Journal of the proceedings of
the convention of the Protestant
Episcopal Church in the state of
Vermont, 1830. Woodstock, Pr.
by David Watson, 1830. 12 p.
MB; MHi.   3213

---- Virginia (Diocese)
Journal of the proceedings of
a convention of the Protestant
Episcopal Church of the diocese
of Virginia, which assembled in
the town of Winchester, on
Thursday the 20th day of May,
1830. Richmond, Pr. by John
Warrock, 1830. 38 p. CSmH; ViU.
                                    3214

The Protestant's abridger and an-
notator, by F. Valera. (Controversial notes upon a periodical
entitled: "The Protestant.")
No. 1-3. New York, 1830.
BrMus.   3215

Providence
A list of persons assessed in
the Town Tax of thirty-five thousand dollars, voted by the freemen of Providence, June, 1830.
With the amount of valuation and
tax of each. Providence, Pr. and
pub. by Hutchens & Weeden, 1830.
40 p. RHi.   3216

Providence Association for the
Promotion of Temperance.
Quarterly report of the committee. No. 1, July, 1830. Providence, Hutchens & Weeden,
1830. 22, ii p. NN; PPPrHi;
RPB.   3217

Providence Association of Firemen for Mutual Assistance.
Constitution [of the Providence
Association of Firemen for Mutual Assistance.] Providence,
1830. 8 p. RP; RPB.   3218

Providence Association of Mechanics and Manufacturers.
Explanation of the engraved
certificate of membership, issued April, 1830. [Providence,
1830] Bdsd. RP.   3219

The Providence directory; containing names of the inhabitants,
their occupations, places of business, and dwelling-houses; with

lists of the streets, lanes,
wharves, etc. Also, banks, insurance offices, and other public institutions; being a desider-
atum to almost every man in
business. The whole carefully
collected and arranged. Providence, Pub. by H. H. Brown,
1830. [iii], 150, 5 p. CSmH;
MBNEH; MWHi; RHi.   3220

Provident Society for Employing
the Poor.
Sixth annual report of the
Provident Society for Employing
the Poor. Philadelphia, Pr. by
Martin & Boden, 1830. 8 p.
PPL.   3221

Public dinner. See Adams
County, Mississippi. Citizens.

Public School Society of New
York.
Twenty fifth annual report of
the trustees of the Public School
Society of New-York. New-
York, Pr. by Mahlon Day, 1830.
20 p. MiD; PPL.   3222

[Publicola] pseud.
Thirteen essays on the policy
of manufacturing in this country.
From the New York Morning
Herald. Philadelphia, Pr. by
Clark & Raser, 1830. 1 p. l.,
30 p. Signed: Publicola. At-
tributed to Mathew Carey by Sab-
in, Bibl. Amer., and Halkett &
Laing. DeGE; KU; MB.   3223

Pugsley, Charles.
[Investigation of charges of
Dr. Charles Pugsley vs. Dr.
Samuel Hogg & Dr. Walker be-
fore Nashville Medical Society
1830. Nashville, 1830] 12 p.
(Title page wanting on the T copy.
The above title is taken from a
typed sheet pasted on the cover.)
T.   3224

---- To the public. (Nashville,

May 4th 1830.) [Statement regarding investigation before the Nashville Medical Society of charges made against Pugsley by Dr. Samuel Hogg] 12 p. (t. p. lacking) T.   3225

The pulpit assistant.   See Anderson, James.

Purblind, Pen, pseud.
Trial of Sanballet, on an indictment for extracting from offal-barrel, before the categorical court of pawing pleas, in session at Growlville... [Boston? ca. 1830] 16 p. DLC.   3226

Putnam, Samuel.
The introduction to the analytical reader. Consisting of easy and interesting lessons in reading... To which are added a few simple questions on the rudiments of grammar, by the inductive method. By Samuel Putnam... 2d ed. Boston, Perkins & Marvin, 1830. 142 p. DLC; MH.   3227

Putnam and the wolf; The fool's pence; The poor man's house repaired; and Jamie. New York, American Tract Society [183-] 94 p. The Society's publications, nos. 240, 308, 313, 346. Each story has special half t. -p. and separate paging, as well as continuous paging. CSmH.   3228

Puzzlewell, Peter.
Riddles and charades, by Peter Puzzlewell, esq. Cooperstown, Pr. and sold by H. & E. Phinney, 1830. 28 p. NUt.   3229

Q

A quarrel settled in a pleasant manner. New-Haven, S. Babcock; Sidney's Press, 1830. 17 p. CtHi; CtY.   3230

Queens County, N. Y.
Rules & orders of the Court of Common Pleas of the County of Queens [adopted June 1st, 1830] Hempstead, [L.I.], Pr. and pub. by Le Fevre and Hutchinson, 1830. 23 p. NBLiHi.   3231

Questions and answers suitable for children. Philadelphia, Pr. by Thomas Kite, 1830. 18 p. PHi.   3232

Questions for the examination of scholars in Tytler's Elements of general history. By an experienced teacher. Concord, N. H., Pub. by Horatio Hill & Co., 1830. 44, [2] p. (With Tylter's Elements). PPL.   3233

Quincy, Josiah.
An address to the citizens of Boston, on the XVIIth of September MDCCCXXX... The close of the second century from the first settlement of the city. Boston, J. H. Eastburn, Pr. to the city, 1830. 68 p. CSmH; CtHT-W; CtSoP; DLC; ICU; KU; LNHT; MB; MBAt; MH; MHi; MWA; MiD-B; MdHi; MeB; NNC; NNUT; Nh; NjR; OClWHi; PPL; PPPrHi; RPB; WHi; BrMus.   3234

---- Extracts from an address to the citizens of Boston, on the 200th anniversary of the founding of the city Sept. 17, 1830. Boston, Beacon Press, Thomas Todd, [1830] 4 p. RPB.   3235

The quintessence, being a selection from the American and foreign annuals for 1830. Sandbornton, Pub. by Howland and Moulton, 1830. 142 p. ICU; NhHi.   3236

The quintessence of long speeches. See Pinckney, Maria Henrietta.

R

Rafinesque, Constantine Samuel, 1783-1840.

... American manual of the grape vines and the art of making wine: including an account of 62 species of vines, with nearly 300 varieties. An account of the principal wines, American and foreign. Properties and uses of wines and grapes. Cultivation of vines in America; and the art to make good wines. With 8 figures. By C. S. Rafinesque... Philadelphia, Pr. for the author, 1830. 1 p. l., [5]-64 p., 1 l. At head of title: Eight figures... CtHT-W; DLC; KU; MBHo; MH; NYBT; OCLloyd; PHi; PPL (lacking title); VtU; WHi; BrMus. 3237

Raguet, Condy, 1784-1842.

The currency. Albany, 1830. MB. 3238

---- Of the principles of banking. [Albany? 1830] 6 p. DLC; MB. 3239

The rail-road almanac for 1831. By Charles F. Egelmann. Baltimore, James Lovegrove; R. J. Matchett, pr. [1830] 18 l. MdBE; ViRVal. 3240

Rail road line from New York to Buffalo... New York [183-?]. Bdsd. (Receipt blank for passage) NN. 3241

Randolph, Mrs. Mary.

The Virginia house-wife; or, Methodical cook. 4th ed., with amendments and additions. Washington, P. Thompson, 1830. 186 p. DLC; LNHT; NcD; NcU; OHi; Vi; ViU. 3242

Randolph, Thomson.

The practical teacher; being an easy and rational introduction to arithmetic... 3d ed. carefully rev. and cor. Baltimore, Armstrong & Plaskitt and Plaskitt & Co., 1830. 172 p. MdHi; PU. 3243

Rankin, John, 1793-1886.

A sermon on the divinity of the Saviour, by John Rankin, pastor of the Presbyterian Church of Ripley, Brown County, Ohio, and author of letters on slavery. West Union, David Murray, Jr., pr., 1830. 23 p. OCHP; OClWHi; PPPrHi. 3244

Ratier, Felix Severin, 1797-1866.

A practical formulary of the Parisian hospitals; exhibiting the prescriptions employed by the physicians and surgeons of those establishments... Trans. from the 3d ed. of the French... by R. D. M'Lellan... New York, C. S. Francis; Boston, Munroe & Francis [Clayton & Van Norden, pr.] 1830. 262, [2] p. MBCo; MoSMed; NRU-M; PPL; PU; ViU. 3245

Ravenscroft, John Stark.

A sermon, preached on Sunday, December 20, 1829, at the consecration of Christ Church, Raleigh, N. C. New-York, Protestant Episcopal Press, 1830. 16 p. NNG; NcU. 3246

---- The works of the Right Reverend John Stark Ravenscroft ... containing his sermons, charges, and controversial tracts; to which is prefixed, A memoir of his life... In two volumes... New York, Protestant Episcopal press, 1830. 2 vols. AB; CBCDS; CtHT; ICU; LNHT; MBD; MiD; NIC; NNS; NcD; NcU; NhD; WHi; BrMus. 3247

Rayment, Rev. B.

Piety exemplified: With appropriate illustrations from historical and other sources; Interspersed with familiar reflections, adapted to the capacity of youth.

By the Rev. B. Rayment. Baltimore, Pub. by Fielding Lucas, Jr. Sands & Neilson, prs. [183-?] 269 p. MdBS; MdW.   3248

Read, John Meredith, 1797-1874.
Remarks of John M. Read, one of the deputation from the general town meeting of the citizens of the city of Philadelphia, held January 16, 1830, relative to the termination of the Columbia and Philadelphia Rail Road; before the committee on inland navigation and internal improvement of the House of Representatives, at Harrisburg, on Wednesday the 17th February, 1830. Philadelphia, Pr. by Lydia R. Bailey, 1830. 24 p. DBRE; DLC; DeGE; ICU; MB; MH-BA; MiD-B; MnHi; NN; OClWHi; PHi; PPAmP; PPL.   3249

Reader's almanac for the middle, southern and western states for 1831. By Nathan Bassett. Baltimore, John J. Harrod; William Wooddy, pr. [1830] 18 l. MdBE.   3250

Reasons, assigned by the Church in North Wrentham for withdrawing from their masonic brethren and others and being formed into a distinct and separate church... Published by vote of the Church. Boston, T. R. Marvin, pr., 1830. 32 p. CBPac; DLC; IaCrM; MB; MH; MHi; NNUT; OClWHi; PPFM.   3251

Reasons for repealing the laws of Massachusetts, which render the members of manufacturing companies personally liable for their debts. Boston, Dutton and Wentworth, prs., 1830. 12 p. CSmH; M; MB; MH-BA; MHi; OCLaw.   3252

[Redfield, William C.] 1789-1857.
Sketch of the geographical rout [!] of a great rail-way, by which it is proposed to connect the canals and navigable waters of New York, Pennsylvania, Ohio, Indiana, Illinois, Michigan, Missouri, and the adjacent states and territories... 2d ed., with additions. New York, G. and C. and H. Carvill, 1830. 48 p. CU-B; CtY; DBRE; DLC; DeGE; ICN; MB; MBAt; MH; MHi; MiU-T; MnHi; N; NIC; NN; OClWHi; PPF; PPL; PU; BrMus.   3253

Reed, Ephraim, comp.
Musical monitor, 6th ed., corr., enl. & greatly improved. Ithaca, Mack & Andrus, 1830. 254, [2] p. DLC; ICN; NIC; OClWHi.   3254

Reed, John.
The Christian labourer. A sermon, preached in Christ Church, Poughkeepsie, September 26th, 1830, on occasion of the death of the Right Reverend John Henry Hobart, D.D., bishop of the Protestant Episcopal Church in the state of New-York. New-York, Pr. at the Protestant Episcopal Press, 1830. 16 p. NNG; NjR.   3255

---- A Pennsylvania Blackstone, being a modification of the Commentaries of Sir William Blackstone, so altered as to present an elementary exposition of the laws of Pennsylvania, common and statute, with a short notice of the judiciary of the United States. In two volumes. Carlisle, Pr. by George Fleming for the author, 1830. 2 vols. NN.   3256

Reflections and tales. By a lady of Philadelphia. Philadelphia, Pub. by the authoress, John Richards, pr., 1830. 108 p. DLC; MWA; PPL.   3257

Reflections on the state of affairs in the South. First published in the National Intelligencer.

[Washington? 1830?] 14 p. <u>PU</u>; <u>ViU</u>.
3258
Reflections on war. See Lamb,
Jonathan.

Reformation melodies, new selection; hymns and spiritual
songs... Portsmouth, N. H., Pub.
and sold by Robert Foster, 1830.
94, [2] p. WHi.   3259

Reformed Church in America.
The acts and proceedings of
the General Synod of the Reformed Dutch Church in North
America at New Brunswick, June
1830. New York, Vanderpool
and Cole, prs., 1830. [3], 228-
304 p.   NcMHi; NjR.   3260

---- Board of Education.
Second annual report of the
Executive Committee of the Board
of Education...presented at the
annual meeting held June, 1830.
New York, Rutgers Press, 1830.
(Not loc.)   3261

Reformed Church in the United
States.
Hochdeutsche Reformirte Kir-
chen - ordnung in den Vereinigten
Staaten von Nord-America; von
den Classical-versammlungen
genehmigt, und von der im Jahr
1828 zu Mifflinburg gehaltenen,
Synode angenommen. Sunnytaun,
Pa., Enos Benner, 1830. 25 p.
CSmH; PLERCHi; PLFM;
PPPrHi.   3262

---- Verhandlungen einer Synode
der Hochdeutschen Reformirten
Kirche, in den Ver. Staaten von
Nord America. Gehalten zu Hägerstaun, Md. am 26sten September, 1830. York, Penns. Gedruckt bey D. May und B. Flory,
1830. 33 p. DLC; <u>PPL.</u>   3263

Reformed Society of Israelites.
Charleston, S. C.
The sabbath service and mis-

cellaneous prayers, adopted by
the Reformed Society of Israelites. Founded in Charleston,
South Carolina, November 21,
1825. Charleston, Pr. by J. S.
Burges, 1830. [8]-68 p. NN. 3264

Refuge in the City of Boston.
Annual report of the directors
of the Penitent Females' Refuge.
Read at the annual meeting, January, 1830. Boston, T. R. Marvin, pr., 1830. 12 p. MH; <u>NjR.</u>
3265
Refutation of the calumnies on
the character of Thomas Paine.
Providence, 1830. BrMus. 3266

Reichel, Charles F.
The happy nation. A sermon
preached on July 4th, 1830, at
the Moravian Church at Lancaster, by the Rev. Charles F.
Reichel... [Lancaster, Pa.] Pr.
by William Albright [1830] 13 p.
N; PHi.   3267

Reid, W. W.
An address delivered before
the Monroe County Temperance
Society at the village of Brock-
port, April 20, 1830. By W. W.
Reid. Published at the request
of the Society. Rochester, Pr.
by E. Peck & Company, 1830.
24 p. NRHi.   3268

The reign of reform. See Bots-
ford, Mrs. Margaret.

Relations between the Cherokees
and the government of the United
States. [1830] 15 p. <u>PPL.</u>
3269
Religion and its image. See
Cameron, Lucy Lyttleton (Butt).

Remarks and correspondence on
the use of cotton canvass as pref-
erable to hemp, for the sails of
ships of war, or merchant vessels, supported by the testimony
of naval officers, ship owners,

captains, &c. Baltimore, Sands & Neilson, 1830. 27 p. MH.
3270

Remarks, &c. The executive committee of the New-York Magdalen Society have put a finishing stroke to their iniquity... [New York? 1830?] 14 p. PPL. 3271

Remarks on physical education. See Channing, William Ellery.

Remarks on Professor Silliman's Elements. See Jackson, Isaac W.

Remarks on the doctrine of the influence of the Holy Spirit. Philadelphia, Pub. by the Tract Association of Friends, [1830] 8 p. (No. 15) PPL. 3272

Remarks on the public lands. See Everett, Edward.

Remarks on the termination of the Pennsylvania rail way. See Powel, John Hare.

Remarks upon a plan for the total abolition of slavery in the U. S. By a citizen of New York. New York [1830?] BrMus. 3273

[Remonstrance to granting the petition of John F. Loring, and others, for a railroad from Boston to Lowell. Boston, 1830] 12 p. DLC; MH-BA. 3274

The removal of the Indians. An article from the American Monthly Magazine. An examination of an article in the North American Review; and an exhibition of the advancement of the Southern tribes, in civilization and Christianity. ... Published by Peirce & Williams, Boston. 1830. 1 p., 1, 72 p. CBPac; CSmH; CtHC; MB; MBC; MH; MWA; MdHi; MeBaT; MiD-B; NIC; OCHP; OClWHi; OHi; PHC; PPAmP;

PPL; T; TxU; WHi; BrMus. 3275

[Rennie, James] 1787-1867.
.... Insect architecture. Boston, Lilly & Wait, [etc.] 1830. xii, 420 p. The Library of Entertaining Knowledge. Vol. 4. CtHT; GU; KyDC; MB; MH-Z; MNBedf; MeB; MiD-U; NRU; NhD; Nj; PPL; RP; WU. 3276

[----] A natural history of insects. Illustrated with anecdotes and numerous engravings... Boston, Pub. by Carter & Hendee. Baltimore, Charles Carter. [Boston, Waitt & Dow's, pr.,] 1830. 107 p. MHa; NNC; RPA. 3277

[----] ---- First series. New-York, Pr. by J. & J. Harper, 1830. 292 p. At head of title: Harper's Stereotype Edition. ICU; MdHi; MeBa; NBU; NIC; NhD; P; THi; WU-A. 3278

Rennie, John.
A sermon, preached in the Second Presbyterian Church, Charleston, January 24, 1830, on the death of the Rev. William Ashmead... Columbia, Pr. by M. Morris and Wilson, 1830. 26 p. MB; NHi; NjR. 3279

Renwick, James, 1790-1863.
Treatise on the steam engine ... New-York, G. & C. & H. Carvill [Ludwig & Telefree, prs.] 1830. 328 p. CSmH; CtHT; CtY; DBRE; DLC; ICJ; LNHT; MH-BA; NGH; NIC; NN; NjP; OCl; P; PPF; PPL; RNR; Vi; BrMus. 3280

A reply to "A narrative of the proceedings..." See Vethake, Henry.

Reply to a report of the New York Typographical Society. See Owen, Robert Dale.

Reply to Censor, or, An appeal

to the good sense of the people
of South Carolina. (By Justice
(pseud.).) Columbia, S. C., Pr.
at the Times and Gazette office,
[183-?] 16 p. MH.   3281

A reply to the disquisition of a
member of the Philadelphia Theological Debating Society, on the
text What think ye of Christ? ...
Norfolk, Pr. by T. G. Broughton,
1830. CSmH.   3282

The report of a meeting of work-
ingmen in the city of Wheeling,
Va., on forming a settlement in
the state of Illinois. [Wheeling,
Oct. 4, 1830] 12 p. DLC; MdBP;
OClWHi; PHi; Wv-Ar; WvU. 3283

Report of the case of John Dodge,
executor of the last will and testament of Unite Dodge, deceased,
vs. Thomas H. Perkins, Decided
at the March term of the Supreme judicial court of Massachusetts, Boston, County of Suffolk.
Present the whole court. Boston,
Pr. by F. Ingraham, 1830. 85, L
(i. e. 50) p. CSmH; MBAt; MH-L.
                          3284
Report of the case of Timothy
Upham against Hill and Barton,
publishers of the New-Hampshire
Patriot, for alleged libels...
Dover [N. H.] Pub. by Geo. W.
Ela...1830. 159, [1] p. CSmH.
                          3285
A report of the evidence and
points of law arising in the trial
of John Francis Knapp, for the
murder of Joseph White, Esquire
before the Supreme judicial court
of the commonwealth of Massachusetts: Together with the charge
of his honor Chief Justice Parker,
to the grand jury, at the opening
of the court. Salem, Pub. by W.
& S. B. Ives, 1830. 74, 72 p.
DLC; ICN; MB; MBC; MH; MHi;
MoU; N; NNC; Nh; PP; Vi. 3286

Report of the trial of Daniel H.

Corey, on an indictment for the
murder of Mrs. Matilda Nash,
at the term of the Superior
court of judicature, holden at
Keene, ... on the first Tuesday of
October, A. D. 1830...Newport,
French & Brown, 1830. 80 p.
MB; Nh; NhHi; BrMus.   3287

Report of the trial of Edward
Williams, for the murder of his
wife; before the Honorable Isaac
Darlington, President Judge, and
his Associate Judges Pearce and
Sharp, in the Court of Oyer and
Terminer held at the Borough of
West Chester, in and for the
County of Chester, in the fif-
teenth Judicial district of Penn-
sylvania, at November term, 1830.
West Chester, Pub. by Hamnum
& Hemphill, Dec. A. D. 1830.
67, [1] p. MB; MH-L; PP; PPB.
                          3288
Report on the coal formation of
the valleys of Wyoming and Lack-
awana. With miscellaneous re-
marks and communications. New
Haven, H. Howe, 1830. 29 p.
CtY; PHi.   3289

Reports and documents relative to
the termination of the Pennsylvania Rail Road. Philadelphia,
1830. 30 p. DLC; PHi.   3290

Repplogel, George.
A book comprising a new system for the preservation of bees.
Discovered through a series of
practical experience. Greensburgh, Pa., Pr. for the Author,
1830. 24 p. PHi.   3291

Representation of the unrighteous
judgment against Christ, as it
has been discovered hewn on
stone--Done at Jerusalem, the 3d
day of April, in the year of our
Lord 34. Harrisburg, Pr. and
for sale by G. S. Peters [1830]
Bdsd. PPL.   3292

A respectful appeal. See Berean.

Review of an article in the North American [Review] for January 1830, on the present relations of the Indians. [n. p. , 1830?] 24 p. WHi; BrMus.   3293

A review of Dr. Woods' letters to Dr. Taylor, on the permission of sin. Together with remarks on Dr. Bellamy's treatise, on the same subject. First published in the Quarterly Christian Spectator for September, 1830. New-Haven, Baldwin & Treadway, prs. , 1830. CtHi; DLC; MA; PPL.   3294

Review of high church and Arminian principles, first published in the Christian Spectator for 1830. Hartford, Pub. by D. F. Robinson and co. New-Haven, Baldwin & Treadway, prs. , 1830. 24 p. CtHC; CtHT; CtY; ICMe.   3295

A review of Mr. Cambreleng's report. See Kennedy, John Pendleton.

A review of the constitution of Maine. By an elector. [n. p.] October 1830. 24 p. OClWHi; PPL.   3296

Review of the evidence of the pretended general conspiracy. 3d ed. Philadelphia, H. C. Carey & I. Lea, 1830. 24 p. MWA; MdBS.   3297

A revision and confirmation. See McNemar, Richard.

Rhode Island.
    At the General Assembly of the state of Rhode Island and Providence Plantations, begun and holden [by adjournment] at Providence, on the second Monday of January, in the year of our Lord, One thousand eight hundred and thirty, and of independence, the fifty-fourth. Present: His Excellency James Fenner, Governor, His Honor Charles Collins, Lieut. Governor. Providence, William Simons, Jr. , pr. , 1830. 71 p. C; Ia; MdBB; Mi; W.   3298

---- At the General Assembly of the state or Rhode-Island and Providence Plantations, begun and holden at Newport, within and for said State, on the first Wednesday of May, in the year of our Lord, One thousand eight hundred and thirty, and of independence, the fifty-fourth. Present: His Excellency James Fenner, Governor, His Honor Charles Collins, Lieut. Governor. Providence, William Simmons, Jr. , pr. , 1830. 59 p. C; Ia; Mi; W.   3299

---- At the General Assembly of the state of Rhode Island and Providence Plantations, begun and holden [by adjournment] at Newport, within and for said state on the third Monday of June, in the year of our Lord, One thousand eight hundred and thirty, and of independence, [the] fifty-fourth. Present His Excellency James Fenner, Governor, His Honor Charles Collins, Lieut. Governor. Providence, William Simmons, Jr. , pr. , 1830. 53 p. C; Ia; Mi; W.   3300

---- At the General Assembly of the state of Rhode Island and Providence Plantations, begun and holden at Providence, within and for said state, on the last Monday of October, in the year of our Lord, One thousand eight hundred and thirty, and of independence, the fifty-fifth. Present: His Excellency James Fenner, Governor, His Honor Charles Collins, Lieut. Governor. Providence, William Simmons, pr. , 1830. 76 p. C; Ia; MdBB; Mi; Nb.   3301

Rhode-Island almanack for 1831. By Isaac Bickerstaff. Providence,

H. H. Brown [1830] 12 1. CLU;
CU; Ct; DLC; ICN; ICU; InU;
MB; MBC; MH; MWA (2 varie-
ties); N; NHi; NjR; OMC; RHi;
RP; RPA; RPB; RU; WHi.   3302

Rhode Island Historical Society.
    Circular. Providence, R. I.
Nov. 1, 1830. At an adjourned
meeting of the Board of Trustees
of the Rhode Island Historical Society, holden October 25, 1830,
the subject of the early history
of our Country being under consideration and the Board being
deeply impressed with the importance of procuring every authentic paper and document relative
thereto... 1 p. DLC.   3303

The Rhode-Island register and
United States calendar for 1831.
Providence, H. H. Brown [1830]
24 1. MWA; NN; RHi; RPB;
WHi.   3304

Rhode Island Sunday School Union.
    The fifth report of the Rhode-
Island Sunday School Union, read
at their annual meeting, held in
Providence, on Wednesday evening, April 7, 1830. Published
by the board of managers. Providence, H. H. Brown, pr., 1830.
24 p. DLC; RHi; RP.   3305

Rice, Harvey.
    Oration, delivered on the fifty-
fourth anniversary of American
independence. By H. Rice, Esq.
At Cleaveland, Ohio, A. D. 1830.
July 1830. [Cleaveland] T. J. M'-
Lain, pr. [1830] 27 p. OClWHi.
                            3306
Richardson, John Smythe, 1777-
1850.
    The argument of the Hon. J.
S. Richardson in reply to Chancellor Harper, and in opposition
to nullification and convention
delivered before the large assem-
blage of people near Columbia,
on the 20th September 1830.

Columbia, Pr. at the "Times
and Gazette" office, 1830. 12 p.
NHi; ScU.   3307

---- To the people. An address
in five numbers, originally published in the Camden Journal by
"Jefferson." Republished by permission of the author the Hon.
J. S. Richardson, together with
his speech delivered at the States-
burg dinner, in opposition to dis-
union, convention and nullification. Charleston, Pr. at the office of the Irishman and Southern
Democrat, 1830. 40 p. A-Ar;
MHi; MWA; NHi; PU; ScC; ScHi;
ScU.   3308

Richardson, Joseph, 1778-1871.
    Speech of Mr. Richardson, of
Massachusetts House of Representatives - March 30, 1830.
... [Washington, 1830] CSmH.
                            3309
Richardson, Samuel.
    The history of Pamela; or
Virtue rewarded. A narrative,
which has its foundation in truth,
adapted to inculcate in the minds
of both sexes, the principles of
virtue and religion. 1st American from the last London edition.
New York, Pub. by W. C. Borradaile, 1830. 108 p. CtY; DLC;
MB.   3310

Richland School.
    Catalogue of the officers and
students of the Richland School
at Rice Creek Springs, Richland
District, S. C., December 1,
1830. Columbia, S. C., Pr. at
the "Times & Gazette" office,
1830. 10 p. MHi; ScCC.   3311

Richmond, Legh, 1772-1827.
    Annals of the poor: Contain-
ing the Dairyman's Daughter,
The Negro servant, and Young
Cottager, etc., etc. ...A new
ed., with sketch of author, by
the Rev. John Ayre, A. M.

Philadelphia, Pub. by William
Stavely, 1830. 226 p. NN; NNG.
                                3312
Richmond Society for the Promotion of Temperance.
    First annual report, January
3, 1830.   Richmond, Pr. by F.
W. White, 1830. 15 p. NN; Vi.
                                3313
Richmond, Va.   Union Theological
Seminary.
    Catalogue of the professors
and students of the Union Theological Seminary of the Presbyterian Church, Prince Edward
County, Virginia.   Richmond, Pr.
by J. Macfarlan, 1830. 6 p.
KyDC; MH; NcMHi; PPPrHi;
ViR.   3314

Rickman, William.
    [No. 1.] Thoughts on education, including the draft of a constitution for a contemplated society to be called the United
States Education Improvement Society. Baltimore, Pub. by Wm.
Rickman, and Sold by John J.
Harrod and Henry Vicary. Wm.
Wooddy, pr., 1830. 24 p. PPL.
                                3315
Rights of the Indians.   [Meeting
in Boston, Jan. 21, 1830, to consider the present relations between the government of the United
States and the Indians. Cherokees.] [Boston, 1830] 16 p.
DLC; ICN; MB; MH; MHi; MWA;
MdHi; MnHi; NN; PHi; PPL;
WHi; BrMus.   3316

Rights of the States.   A reply to,
--and review of an opinion, of
the Hon'ble William Wirt, (herewith re-published) entitled, Rights
of the Indians, upon the question
"Has the State of Georgia a right
to extend her laws over the Cherokees within the Cherokee Territory?" ... Wm. A. Chisholm, pr.
1830. 35 p. MB; MH-L; NNB. 3317

The ringleader.   A tale for boys.

Philadelphia, American Sunday
School Union [1830?] BrMus.
                                3318
Rippon, John, 1751-1836.
    A selection of hymns, from
the best authors, including a great
number of originals: intended to
be an appendix to Dr. Watts's
Psalms and hymns by John
Rippon, D.D. 8th American,
from the 18th London ed., with
enl., Philadelphia, Pub. by David Clark, 1830. unp. hymns
number 1-588 and [719]-1306,
continuing the numbering of Watts
with which this is bound. ViRU.
                                3319
The rise of the West.   See
Schoolcraft, Henry Rowe.

The rivals.   See Griffin, Gerald.

Riverhead Temperance Society.
    Address of the Board of managers, of the Riverhead Temperance Society. Brooklyn, Pr. by
A. Spooner, 1830. 12 p. NBLiHi.
                                3320
Roane, Samuel Calhoun.
    The Arkansas justice: Being
a compilation of the statute laws
now in force in the Territory of
Arkansas, relating to the duties
of justices of the peace. To
which are added the necessary
forms and precedents, by Sam C.
Roane, Esq., attorney at law.
Little Rock, Pr. and pub. by Wm.
E. Woodruff, 1830. viii, 57,
xxvi, [2] p. ArU; MH-L.   3321

Roanoke Navigation Company.
    Report of the Roanoke Navigation Company, 1830. Raleigh, Pr.
by Lawrence & Lemay, prs. to
the state, 1830. 4 p. (At head of
title: Number 6. A.D. 1830) NcU.
                                3322
Robbins, Asher, 1757-1845.
    Speech of Mr. Robbins, of
Rhode Island, in the Senate
United States, May 20, 1830, on
Mr. Foot's resolution respecting

a survey of the public lands.
Washington, Pr. and pub. at the
Office of the National Journal,
1830. 11 p. CtHT-W; PPL.
3323
[Robbins, Eliza] 1786-1853.
American popular lessons,
chiefly selected from the writings
of Mrs. Barbauld, Miss Edgeworth, and other approved writers. Revised and corr. by the
author. New York, Pub. by R.
Lockwood [W. B. Van Brunt, pr.]
1830. 249 p. PPL.   3324

[----] Elements of mythology:
or Classical fables of Greeks,
Romans... Syrian, Hindu, Scan-
dinavian... American... comparing
polytheism with true religion.
Philadelphia, Towar, J. & D.M.
Hogan; Pittsburgh, Hogan & Co.,
1830. 348 p. CSt; CtY; DLC;
MB; MH; MdU; MnHi; MsU; NCH;
NR; NhHi; OMC; PHi; PV. 3325

[----] Poetry for schools; de-
signed for reading and recitation
... 2d ed. rev. and corr. New
York, White, Gallaher, and
White, 1830. 348 p. CtHT-W;
DLC; NNUT.   3326

[----] Sequel to American popular lessons intended for the use
of schools: By the author of
American popular lessons...
New-York, Pub. by Collins and
Hannay, 1830. 376 p. CtHT-W.
3327
[----] Tales from American history; containing the principal
facts in the life of Christopher
Columbus. For the use of young
persons, and schools. By the
author of American popular lessons... New-York, Pub. by Wm.
Burgess, Juvenile emporium,
1830. 238, 14 p. CtHT-W; DLC;
MH; MWA; MdBE; MiD-B; NCH;
NN; OClWHi; TNJ; BrMus. 3328

[----] ---- New York, Harper

& Brothers, pub. [c 1830] 3 v.
MiD-B.   3329

Robbins, Forman C.
An address to the friends of
James Cresson, Jun., and others. By Forman C. Robbins.
Philadelphia, 1830. 20 p. NjR.
3330
Robbins, Royal, 1787-1861.
Outlines of ancient history,
on a new plan. Embracing biographical notices of illustrious
persons, and general views of
geography, population, politics,
religion, military and naval affairs, arts, literature, manners,
customs, and society of ancient
nations. Hartford, E. Hopkins,
1830. 228 p. DLC.   3331

---- Outlines of modern history,
on a new plan. Embracing biographical notices of illustrious
persons and general views of the
geography, population, politics,
religion, and society of modern
nations. ...Hartford, Pub. by
Edward Hopkins, 1830. 396 p.
CtHi; DLC.   3332

Robert and Louisa, or Diligence
rewarded, written for the American Sunday School Union, to
which is now added, an account
of Mary L---- and a sketch of
the life and conversion of Lydia.
... Philadelphia, American Sunday School Union, 1830. [7]-66 p.
ViRVB; BrMus.   3333

Robert Dale Owen unmasked by
his own pen; showing his unquali-
fied approbation of a most ob-
scenely indelicate book entitled
"What is love; or, Every woman's
book." ... New York, Charles N.
Baldwin, 1830. 14 p. NjR. 3334

Robertson, Ignatius Loyola, pseud.
See Knapp, Samuel Lorenzo.

Robertson, William, 1731-1793.

...The history of the reign of the Emperor Charles V. with a view of the progress of society in Europe; from the subversion of the Roman empire, to the beginning of the sixteenth century. New York, J. & J. Harper, 1830. 610 p. CtHT; IU; MB; MWA; MoS; P; TNJ; ViU. 3335

Robinson, Samuel.
A course of fifteen lectures on medical botany, denominated Thomson's new theory of medical practice; in which the various theories that have preceded it are reviewed and compared. Delivered in Cincinnati, Ohio, by Samuel Robinson... With introductory remarks by the proprietor. Boston, Pr. by Jonathan Howe, 1830. 192 p. DLC; MBCo; MdAS; NBMS; NNNAM; NRU-M; PPC; PPL; TxU. 3336

---- ---- 2d ed. Columbus, Pub. by Horton Howard. Charles Scott, pr., 1830. 162 p. DLC; DNLM; MBCo; MnU; NNNAM; OClWHi. 3337

Rogers, Ammi, 1770-1852.
Memoirs of the Rev. Ammi Rogers, A.M., a clergyman of the Episcopal Church... Also an index to the Holy Bible; and a concise view of the authority, doctrine, and worship in the Protestant Episcopal Church. Composed, compiled, and written by the said Ammi Rogers. 3d ed., with additions, omissions and alterations. Middlebury, Pr. by J. W. Copeland, 1830. 268 p. CSmH; Ct; DLC; ICN; IU; IaU; MB; MDeeP; MH; NNG; NcWsW; Nh; OCHP; RHi; Vt; VtHi. 3338

Rogers, Henry, d. 1837.
Directions for a family medicine chest, put up and sold by Henry Rogers, chemist and druggist, Charleston, Kanawha county, Virginia. [Laidly & Co., prs., 1830?] 9 p. Norona 695. 3339

Rogers, Hester Anne.
An account of the experience of Mrs. Rogers, written by herself. Also, spiritual letters, illustrating and enforcing holiness of heart. Selections translated from her manuscript journals. New York, S. & D.A. Forbes, 1830. 234 p. CtMW; MBNMHi; NR. 3340

Rollin, Charles.
The ancient history of the Egyptians, Carthaginians, Assyrians, Babylonians, Medes and Persians, Macedonians, and Grecians. Translated from the French... From the latest London edition... New York, Pr. & pub. by George Long, 1830. 4 v. ABS; ArU; C; GU; IU; KyDC; MBC; MoS; NN; NcD; Nh; PPL; TNJ; TxH; ViU. 3341

Rollin, Charles.
Ancient history of the Egyptians, Grecians... Hartford, Conn., Andrus & Judd [183-?] 7 v. NN. 3342

Roorbach, Orville Augustus, 1803-1861.
A catalogue of historical, scientific, law, medical, chemical, biographical, theological, juvenile, novels, school, classical, and miscellaneous books, for sale at O. A. Roorbach's. Charleston, 1830. 47 p. NN. 3343

Root, David.
A sermon delivered at the dedication of the new church edifice, of the Second Presbyterian Society, Cincinnati, May 20, 1830. Cincinnati, Pr. at the Office of the Christian Journal, by Robinson & Fairbank, 1830. 20 p. IEG; NjN; OCHP; OClWHi; PPPrHi. 3344

Rose, John.
The United States' arithmeti-
cian: or The science of arithmetic simplified. Adapted to the
commerce of the United States...
Bridgeton, N. J., The proprietor,
1830. ix, [3], 240 p. DLC. 3345

[Rosenmueller, Ernst F. C.]
Views of interesting places in
the Holy Land (after the original
sketches of L. Mayers); with a
brief sketch of ...events associated with them in the sacred
scriptures, and of their modern
appearance and situation. Philadelphia [1830?] DLC; BrMus.
3346

Ross, Arthur Amasa, 1791-1864.
Address before the Society for
the Promotion of Temperance in
Centerville. Providence, H. H.
Brown, pr., 1830. 16 p. MBC;
RHi; RPE.   3347

Ross, Frederick A.
A sermon, on intemperance,
delivered in the First Presbyter-
ian Church, in Knoxville, Tenn.
on the evening of the twelfth of
October, 1829; by Rev. Frederick
A. Ross; and pub. at the request
of the young gentlemen of that
town. Pr. at the "Calvinistic
Magazine" Office, Rogersville,
Tenn., 1830. 16 p. CSmH;
PPPrHi; T.   3348

[Rossini, Gioacchino Antonio]
1792-1868.
Il Turco in Italia waltz for the
piano forte arranged by Wm. Taylor. [New York? 183-?] [2] p.
CSmH.   3349

Rothbaust, John, comp.
The Franklin harmony and easy
instructor in vocal music; selected from the most eminent and
approved authors in that science,
for the use of Christian churches
of every denomination, singing
schools and private societies. Eng-

lish and German church tunes.
2d improved ed. Chambersburg,
Pa., Pr. by Henry Ruby [1830]
195 p. ICN; P; PP.   3350

The roving bachelor; Tom Hal-
lard; Betsey Baker, etc. Philadelphia, 1830. MH.   3351

Rowan, John, 1773-1843.
Speech of Mr. Rowan, of Kentucky, on Mr. Foot's resolution,
relating to the public lands, in
reply to Mr. Webster, of Massachusetts. Delivered in the Senate
United States, February 4th,
1830. Washington, Pr. by Way
and Gideon, 1830. 41 p. DLC;
PPL.   3352

Rowson, Susanna (Haswell), 1762-
1824.
Charlotte Temple... A tale of
truth by Mrs. Rowson. Pub. by
Fisher & Brother. Boston, Philadelphia, New York, Baltimore.
[183-?] 165 p. MHi.   3353

---- ---- New York, G. G.
Sickels, 1830. 138 p. MnU; NN.
3354

Roxbury, Mass.
Order of exercises, at the celebration of the completion of two
centuries, since the settlement of
the town of Roxbury. At the Rev.
Dr. Porter's meeting house, in
said town. Oct. 8, 1830. [Boston]
Charles P. Emmons, pr. [1830]
Bdsd. MB; MHi.   3355

---- First Church.
Order of services at the ordination of Mr. George Putnam, as
colleague pastor with the Rev.
Eliphalet Porter, D.D. over the
First Church and Religious Society in Roxbury, July 7, 1830.
Boston, Beals & Homer, prs.
[1830] Bdsd. MB; MHi.   3356

A Royal Arch Mason, pseud. See
A defence of the institution.

Royall, Anne (Newport), 1769-
1854.

Letters from Alabama on various subjects: to which is added,
an appendix, containing remarks
on sundry members of the 20th &
21st Congress, and other high
characters, &c. &c. at the seat
of government. In one volume.
By Anne Royall... Washington,
1830. 232, 6 p. DLC; ICN;
MoSM; NNC; OCHP; PPL; Vi.
                                    3357
---- Mrs. Royall's southern
tour; or Second series of the
Black book... Washington, 1830-
1831. 3 vols. CSmH; DGU; DLC;
ICN; MH; MHi; MWA; P; ScU;
TU; ViL.   3358

Rudd, John Churchill, 1779-1848.
The last illness and death of
...J. H. Hobart... Bishop of the
Protestant Episcopal Church in
the state of New York. From the
[Auburn] Gospel Messenger, Sep-
tember 13, 1830. [New York?
1830?] BrMus.   3359

---- A series of discourses addressed to young men, on the
principles and duties by which
their conduct should be regulated.
Auburn, Pr. at the Gospel Messenger Office, by Philo B. Barnum, 1830. 120 p. CSmH; CtY;
NAuT.   3360

---- Tribute to departed excel-
lence. An address upon the life
and character of the Right Reverend John Henry Hobart, D.D.,
bishop of the Protestant Episcopal Church in the state of New-
York, delivered in St. Peter's
Church, Auburn, Sunday P.M.,
September 19, 1830. Auburn, Pr.
at the Gospel Messenger Office,
by Philo B. Barnum, 1830. 16 p.
CSmH; CtY; DLC; N; NAuT; NIC;
NN; PHi.   3361

The ruinous consequences of

gambling. [New York, American
Tract Society, 183-?] 16 p. ([Am-
erican Tract Society. Publications. (Separates)] no. 22)
CSmH.   3362

Rules of pronunciation in reading
Latin. New Haven, A. H. Malt-
by, 1830. 7 p. Ct.   3363

The Runaway. Written for the
American Sunday School Union
and revised by the Committee of
Publication. Philadelphia, American Sunday School Union [183-?]
13 p. MB.   3364

Rush, Benjamin, 1745-1813.
The effects of ardent spirits
upon the human body and mind.
New York, Pub. by the American
Tract Society [1830?] 1 l., 8 p.
1 l. (At head of title: No. 25.)
NNNAM.   3365

---- Medical inquiries and obser-
vations upon the diseases of the
mind. 4th ed. Philadelphia, John
Grigg, 1830. 365 p. CSt; DNLM;
GU; KU; LNL; MBCo; MdBE;
NNC-M; NNNAM; NcAS; NjP; P;
PPC; PU; TxU-M.   3366

Rush, Richard, 1780-1859.
Interesting correspondence.
Correspondence between the com-
manders and owners of the Philadelphia and Providence regular
line of packets, and the Hon.
Richard Rush... [Providence?]
1830. 18 p. RHi; RPB.   3367

---- ---- Letter from Mr. Richard Rush on the policy of the
American system, in answer to
the following... Washington, Pr.
at the office of the National Journal, 1830. 8 p. DLC; DeGE;
PPL.   3368

---- Letter and accompanying
documents from the Hon. Richard
Rush to Joseph Gales, esq.,

mayor of the city of Washington; respecting the loan of a million and a half of dollars, negotiated by the former, in Europe, for the said city and the towns of Georgetown and Alexandria, under the authority of an act of Congress of the United States, passed on the 24th of May, 1828. Pub. by order of the Corporation of the city of Washington. Washington, Pr. by P. Force, 1830. 171 p. DLC.   3369

Russell, Jonathan, 1771-1832.
An oration, pronounced July 4, 1800, at the Baptist meeting house in Providence; it being the anniversary of American independence. Watertown, N.Y., Pr. by W. Woodward, 1830. 20 p. CSmH; CtHT-W; DLC; MB; MH; MHi; NBuG; RHi; BrMus.   3370

Russell, William, 1798-1873
...The history of Modern Europe: with a view of the progress of society from the rise of the modern kingdoms to the Peace of Paris, in 1763. By William Russell, LL.D. And a continuation of the history to the present time. By William Jones, esq. With annotations by an American. New York, Pub. by J. & J. Harper, Sold by Collins and Hannay [etc.] 1830. 3v. (Harper's stereotype ed.) MB; NN; OClW; OO; PPL; TNJ.   3371

---- A lecture on the infant school system of education, and the extent to which it may be advantageously applied to all primary schools, delivered... August 21, 1830, before the convention which formed the American Institute of Instruction. Boston, Hilliard, Gray, Little, & Wilkins, 1830. 27 p. CtHT-W; DLC; PPAmP; PPL.   3372

---- Lessons in enunciation; comprising a course of elementary exercises, and a statement of common errors in articulation, with the rules of correct usage in pronouncing... Boston, Richardson, Lord & Holbrook [Stereotyped by Lyman Thurston & Co.] 1830. (81p.) CtHT-W; DLC; MB; MH; MeLB; NN; NNUT; OMC; PPL; RP; BrMus.   3373

---- On associations of teachers: An address delivered at a meeting held in Dorchester, on Wednesday, 8th of September, for the purpose of forming an Association of teachers, for Norfolk county... Boston, Pub. by Samuel N. Dickinson, 1830. 16 p. DLC.   3374

---- Rudiments of gesture, comprising illustrations of common faults in attitude and action... Boston, Pub. by Carter and Hendee, Baltimore, Charles Carter [Pr. by I.R. Butts] 1830. viii, 48 p. DLC; MB; LNHT; MH; NNC; PPL; PU-Penn.   3375

Rusticus, Nicholas.
Pride or A touch at the times, a satirical poem, addressed to all genuine reformers in this glorious age of anti-ism. By Nicholas Rusticus, Esquire, I. Qr Nui. ...Boston, Pub. by John Marsh & Co. Condon, pr., 1830. 16 p. DLC; MB; MBAt; MH; NNFM; NNP; PPFM; PPL; BrMus.   3376

Ruter, Martin, 1785-1838, comp.
The martyrs, or A history of persecution, from the commencement of Christianity to the present time: including an account of the trials, tortures, and triumphant deaths of many who have suffered martyrdom. Compiled from the works of Fox and others. By Martin Ruter, S.T.D. president of Augusta College. Cincinnati, Pub. by E. Deming.

Pr. at the Chronicle office, 1830. 561, [3] p. DLC; LNT; NN; NNUT; NPV; OClWHi.   3377

---- ---- Cincinnati, Pub. by R. Robbins. Pr. at the Chronicle office, 1830. 561, [3] p. DLC; MeLB; MsCliM; NN; NPV; OAU.   3378

Rutgers Medical College, New York.

    Geneva College - Rutgers Medical Faculty. Catalogue of the officers and students, for the session of 1829-30. And graduates of the preceding sessions. Published by the class. New-York, C. S. Van Winkle, pr., 1830. 8 p. NNNAM; NjR; OCHP.   3379

Rutgers University.

    The statutes of Rutgers College, in the city of New-Brunswick, N. J. July, 1830. Rutgers Press, Pr. by Terhune & Letson, New Brunswick, 1830. 15 p. PPPrHi.   3380

S

S., J. and C., C.

    History of the French revolution of 1830, with all the anecdotes relating to it. Philadelphia, 1830. 214 p. MH; MWA; NcD; P; PHi; PLFM; ViU.   3381

S., J. W.

    Wild achievements, and romantic voyages, of Captain John Francis Knapp... while commander of the ship General Endicott ... By his supercargo. Boston, Pub. for the author, 1830. 28 p. MB; MSaP.   3382

Sabbath miscellany. See Amicus, Sabbati.

Saco, José Antonio, 1797-1879.

    Impugnacion por D. José Antonio Saco, a un folleto recien

impreso en la Habana, e impropriamente titulado Contestacion al numero setimo del Mensagero semanal de Nueva-York. [Parte segunda] Nueva-York, Impresa por G. F. Bunce, 1830. 2 p. l., [3]-88 p. MB.   3383

---- Memoria sobre caminos, en la isla de Cuba. Por don Jose Antonio Saco. Nueva-York, Impr. por G. F. Bunce, 1830. iv, [1], [5]-96 p. CU-B; DLC; MB; MH; PPL.   3384

Sacred to the memory. See Lowe, R.

St. Andrew's Society. Charleston.

    Rules of the Saint Andrew's Society of the city of Charleston, S. C. Charleston, 1830. 46 p. Sabin 12087.   3385

St. George's Society.

    The constitution and by-laws of the St. George's Society... New York, Edward Grattan, pr., 1830. 27 p. NjR.   3386

St. Louis.

    Ordinanaces of the city of St. Louis; passed since the publication of the revised Code of Ordinances in 1828; Revised, arranged, and published chronologically; Pursuant to a resolution of the Board of Aldermen, of 7th May, 1830. Saint Louis, Pr. by Charles & Paschall, 1830. 78 p. MH-L.   3387

Salem, Mass.

    Annual report of the receipts and expenditures to March 8, 1830. [Salem, 1830] 2 p. MHi.   3388

---- Regulations for the public schools of the town of Salem. Salem, Pr. by Foote and Brown,

1830. 16 p. M; MB; MH. 3389

Salem Mechanic Library.
Catalogue of the Salem Mechanic Library with the rules and by-laws: instituted August 1820. Salem, 1830. 31 p. MHi. 3390

Sallustius Crispus, C.
C. Crispi Sallustii de Catilinae Conjuratione Belloque Jugurthino historiae. Animadversionibus illustravit Carlus Anthon,... Edito Secunda. Novi Eboraci, Sumtibus G. et. C. et. H. Carvill, 1830. xi, 386 p. MH; NN. 3391

[Saluces, Mme. de]
Foscarini: or, The Patrician of Venice. In two volumes. New York, Pr. by J. & J. Harper, 1830. 2 v. NRU. 3392

Eine Sammlung von geistlichen lieblichen liedern, aus verschiedenen gesangbücher gesammelt zum gebrauch des deffentlichen und privat wahren gottesdienstes ... Harrisburg, Gedruckt bey Jacob Baab, 1830. 391 p. DLC; PHi. 3393

Sanders, Francis Williams, 1769-1831.
An essay on uses and trusts and on the nature and operation of conveyances at common law, and of those which derive their effect from the statute of uses. 1st American from the 4th London ed. rev., cor. and considerably enl. Philadelphia, R. H. Small, 1830. 2 v. in 1. C; IU; IaHi; MdBB; MiU-L; Ms; NN; NcD; NcU; NhD; OCLaw; PPB; PU-L; ViU; WU-L. 3394

Sandford, Peter P., 1781-1857.
The Christian sabbath: or, The universal and perpetual obligation of the Sabbath, and the divine authority of its change from the seventh to the first day

of the week, under the Christian Dispensation: Being a Discourse on Matt. XII. 8. New-York, Pr. by J. and J. Harper, 1830. 32 p. CSmH; MWA; PPPrHi. 3395

The Sanfords, or, Home scenes ... New-York, E. Bliss, 1830. 2 v. DLC; MH. 3396

Sangerfield Meeting. Waterville, N. Y.
Proceedings of the Sangerfield Meeting, held at the Presbyterian Meeting House in the village of Waterville, January 14, 1830. With the address of Elder Nathan N. Whiting, on the subject of speculative Free Masonry. Utica, Press of William Williams, 1830. 16 p. IC; IaCrM; MB; NN. 3397

Santangelo, Orazio Donato Gideon de Attellis, b. 1774.
Santangelo's reply to the editors of the Redactor,... New York, Pr. for the author, 1830. 27, [1] p. DLC. 3398

Sargent, John, 1780-1833.
A memoir of Rev. Henry Martyn, B. D. late fellow of St. John's College, Cambridge, and the chaplain to the Honourable East India Company. From the 10th London ed., corr. and enl. New York, American Tract Society [1830?] 444 p. CSmH; CtHT; MH. 3399

Sargent, Lucius Manlius, 1786-1867.
My mother's gold ring. Boston, Damrell & Moore [183-] 12 p. (Temperance tales no. 1) CSmH. 3400

Say, Jean-Baptiste.
A treatise on political economy; or The production, distribution and consumption of wealth ...

Translated from the 4th ed. of the
French, by C. R. Prinsep, M. A.
with notes by the translator. 4th
American ed. Containing a trans-
lation of the introduction, and
additional notes by Clement C.
Biddle.   Philadelphia, John Grigg,
[Wm. Brown, pr.] 1830. 15, [1],
lvii, 455p.   CtHT; DLC; IaU;
KyLou; LU; MB; MH; MdBS-P;
MiU; MoU; NN; NcU; OO; PHC;
PPL; PU-L; ViU; WU; Wv.   3401

Say, Thomas.
   American conchology, or De-
scriptions of the shells of North
America, illustrated by colored
figures from original drawings
executed from nature by Thomas
Say... New-Harmony, Indiana.
Pr. at the School Press, 1830.
[33] p.   CU; DLC; In; InHi; InU;
MH.   3402

Scenes and incidents of domestic
and foreign travel, with sketches
in natural history, and poetical
selections.   Philadelphia, T.
Wardle [183-?] 338 p. DLC; MH;
MoS; OSW; TxU; WHi.   3403

Schenck, Peter H.
   Frauds on the revenue; ad-
dressed to the people of the United
States, and to their Representa-
tives in Congress. New York, Pr.
by J. M. Danforth, 1830. 13 p.
DLC; DeGE; IU; NN; BrMus.
                                 3404
Schimmelpennick, Mary.
Anne (Galton), 1778-1856.
   Manuel of La Mère Agnès, or
A gift from an Abbess to her
Nuns. A specimen of "La Re-
ligieuse Parfaite et imparfaite,"
of la Mere Agnes de St. Paul
Arnaud, Abbess of Port Royal.
By M. A. Schimmelpenninck[!]
Philadelphia, Pr. & pub. by
Thomas Kite, 1830. 60 p. PHi.
                                 3405
Schmucker, Samuel Simon, 1779-
1873.

A plea for the sabbath school
system, delivered Feb. 2, 1830
at the anniversary of the Gettys-
burg, Pa., Sunday School...
Gettysburg, Pa., Pr. by H. C.
Neinstedt, 1830. 32 p. CSmH;
ICA; ICMcC; MBC; MWA; MiU;
N; NcU; NjR; OSW; PPLT;
PPPrHi; TxDaM.   3406

School Convention of Franklin
County, Mass.
   The Franklin primer, or Lessons in spelling and reading,
adapted to the understanding of
children; composed and published
by a committee, appointed for the
purpose by the School convention
of Franklin county, May 25, 1826.
9th ed. Greenfield, Mass., Pub.
and sold wholesale and retail,
by A. Phelps, 1830. 54 p. (Imprint on cover: Bellows Falls,
Vt., Pub. by James I. Cutler &
co., 1832.) CSmH; DLC (cover
imp. dated 1831); MWA.   3407

The school of good manners...
New York, Samuel Wood & sons;
Baltimore, Samuel S. Wood &
Co. [c 1830] 46 p. CtY.   3408

Schoolcraft, Henry Rowe.
   A discourse, delivered on the
anniversary of the Historical So-
ciety of Michigan, June 4, 1830.
Pub. by request. Detroit, Pr.
by Geo. L. Whitney, 1830. 44 p.
CSmH; Ct; IGK; MB; MH; MHi;
MiD-B; MiU; NHi; NN; OClWHi;
PPAmP; PPL; WHi.   3409

[----] The rise of the West; or,
A prospect of the Mississippi
Valley. By H. R. S. A retrospect;
or, The ages of Michigan. By H.
W. Detroit, Pr. by Geo. L.
Whitney, 1830. 36 p. Mi.   3410

[Schoolcraft, James]
   Indian melodies... New York,
Elam Bliss [J. Seymour, pr.]
1830. 52 p. NN.   3411

Schroeder, John Frederick,
1800-1857.

The great man in Israel: A
discourse on the character of the
Right Reverend John Henry Ho-
bart, D. D. delivered in Trinity
Church, and St. Paul's and St.
John's Chapels, in the city of
New-York, September A. D.
MDCCCXXX. New-York, Pr. at
the Protestant Episcopal Press,
[Wm. Van Norden, pr.] 1830.
28 p. MBAt; MBNEH; MH; MiD-
B; NGH; NNC; NjP; NjR; PPAmP;
WHi; BrMus.   3412

---- ---- 2d ed. New-York, Pr.
at the Protestant Episcopal
Press [Wm. Van Norden, pr.]
1830. 27, [1] p. CSmH; CtHT;
MB; PHi.   3413

---- Plea for the industrious
poor and strangers, in sickness.
An address delivered at the opening of an edifice erected by the
trustees of the New York dispensary, January 11, 1830...
New York, Protestant Episcopal
press, 1830. [5], 28 p. DLC;
KyLx; MB; MBD; MH; MiD-B;
MnHi; NBMS; NjR; PHi; BrMus.
                                     3414
---- ---- 2d ed. New York, Pr.
by Wm. Van Norden, 1830. 28 p.
NNG; PPPrHi.   3415

Schuylkill Navigation Company.

Report of the president and
managers... to the stockholders.
January 4, 1830. Philadelphia,
Pr. by James Kay, jun. & co.,
[1830] 12 p. DBRE; DIC; DLC;
ICJ; MH-BA; MWA; MiU-T; NN;
OClWHi; PPAmP.   3416

Scott, John, 1777-1834.

Memoir of the Rev. Thomas
Scott, rector of Aston, Sandford,
Bucks.; abridged from his Life
compiled by his son. Approved by
the Publishing Committee of the
Kennebec Co. Sunday School

Union. Augusta, P. A. Brinsmade, 1830. 236 p. DLC.   3417

---- ---- Augusta, Me., Pub.
by P. A. Brinsmade at the Depository of Kennebec Sunday
School Union, Easton & Severance, prs., Augusta, 1830. 239
p. MB; MeHi.   3418

Scott, John Morin.

An address delivered to the
Law Academy of Philadelphia, at
the opening of the session, in
September 1830. Published by the
academy. Philadelphia, Pr. by
Mifflin & Parry, 1830. 16 p.
DLC; MH-L; MWA; MiD-B; NBuG;
NjP; PHi; PPAmP; PPL; PPPrHi.
                                     3419
Scott, Orange, 1800-1847, comp.

The new and improved camp
meeting hymn book: being a
choice selection of hymns from
the most approved authors. Designed to aid in the public and
private devotions of Christians.
By Orange Scott... Pub. by the
compiler. Brookfield [Mass.]
E. and G. Merriam, prs., 1830.
192 p. DLC; IEG; RPB.   3420

Scott, Sir Walter, 1771-1832.

... Letters on demonology and
witchcraft. Addressed to J. G.
Lockhart, esq. by Sir Walter
Scott, bart. New York, Pr. by
J. & J. Harper, Sold by Collins
and Hannay [etc.] 1830. 338 p.
At head of title: Harper's Stereo-
type edition. PPL.   3421

---- Tales of a grandfather; being stories taken from Scottish
history. ... Third series. Philadelphia, Carey and Lea, 1830.
2 v. in 1. PPL.   3422

The Scottish farmer... Philadel-
phia, American Sunday School
Union, 1830. 143 p. NNU-W;
BrMus.   3423

Scougal, Henry, 1650-1678.
    The works of the Rev. Henry
Scougal, together with his funer-
al sermon by the Rev. Dr. Gair-
den; and an account of his life,
and writings. Philadelphia, J.
Kay, jr. & bro.; Pittsburgh, J.
I. Kay [183-] 272 p. DLC;
NNUT.   3424

The scrap table for MDCCCXXXI.
Boston, Carter, Hendee & Bab-
cock, 1830. 184 p. CSmH;
CtHT-W; CtY; MB; MH; NBLiHi;
NN; PU; BrMus.   3425

The Scripture directory to baptism. See Chandler, A.

Scripture history, or Interesting
narratives recorded in the lives
of the prophets & apostles, compiled from the Old and New Testaments for the instruction of
youth. By a clergyman. Embellished with twelve colored engravings. Published by J. & B.
Turnbull, Steubenville, 1830. 24
p. OrCS.   3426

Scripture history, short sketches
of characters from the Old Testament... New York, Pr. and sold
by Mahlon Day at the New Juvenile
book store, 1830. 18 p. DLC.
                               3427
Scripture illustrations: explanatory of numerous texts... 2d series. Philadelphia, American
Sunday School Union [183-?]
CSmH.   3428

Scripture natural history of quadrupeds. See Althans, Henry.

Scripture sketch for young mas-
ters. New Haven, S. Babcock,
Sidney's Press, 1830. [18] p.
CtHi.   3429

[Scupoli, Lorenzo] 1530-1610.
    The spiritual combat: to
which is added, the peace of the

soul, and, the happiness of the
heart, which dies to itself, in
order to live to God... Baltimore, Pub. by Fielding Lucas,
Jr. [ca 1830] 288 p. RPB.
                               3430
Seabury, Samuel.
    On Christian unity. A sermon,
by Samuel Seabury, D.D. [New-
York, Protestant Episcopal Tract
Soc., Pr. at the Protestant Episcopal Press, No. 44, 1830] 8 p.
DLC; ICU; NN; PPL.   3431

Sears, James H.
    A standard spelling book. New
Haven, Durrie & Peck, 1830.
144 p. MB.   3432

Second trial of John Francis
Knapp by a new jury, recom-
menced at Salem, August 14,
1830, for the murder of Capt.
Joseph White, before the Supreme
judicial court of the commonwealth of Massachusetts, at a
special session, commenced at
Salem, July 20, 1830. Reported
for the publishers. Boston, Dutton & Wentworth, 1830. 28 p.
DLC; DNLM; MBC; MH-L; NIC-
A.   3433

Secondary lessons. See Willard,
Samuel.

[Sedgwick, Catharine Maria]
    Clarence; or, A tale of our
own times. By the author of
"Hope Leslie," &c., &c. Phila-
delphia, Carey & Lea [Sleight &
Robinson, prs., New York] 1830.
2 v. CLU; CSmH; CtHT; CtY;
DLC; ICU; IaCrM; MB; MBAt;
MWA; NN; NNC; NNS; NRU; NcU;
PPL; PU; RPA; RPB; TxU; WaU.
                               3434
[----] Lessons without books.
By the author of 'The beatitudes'
...Boston, Pub. by L. C.
Bowles [Waitt & Dow's pr.] 1830.
2 vols. MB; TNJ.   3435

[----] Stories of the Spanish conquests in America. Designed for the use of children. By the author of 'The beatitudes,' and 'Lessons without books.' ... Boston, L. C. Bowles [Waitt & Dows, pr.] 1830. 3 v. ArBaA; CU-B; DLC; MB.   3436

[Sedgwick, Susan Ann Livingston (Ridley)] 1789-1867.
The young emigrants. A tale designed for young persons. By the author of Morals of pleasure ... Boston, Pub. by Carter and Hendee [Pr. by I. R. Butts] 1830. 240 p. CSmH; ICU; MB; MBAt; MWH; OClWHi; PPL.   3437

Sedgwick, Theodore.
An address delivered before the Berkshire Agricultural Society, October 7, 1830. Pittsfield, Pr. by Phinehas Allen and son, November, 1830. 20 p. DLC; MBC; MH; MPiB; PPAmP.   3438

Sega, Giacomo.
An essay on the practice of dueling, as it exists in modern society, occasioned by the late lamentable occurence near Philadelphia. By James Sega, LL. D. Trans. from the Italian, by the author... Philadelphia, 1830. 1 p. l., 45 p. DLC; ICU; MBAt; MBC; MH; MiD-B; OCLaw; PHi; PPAmP; RPB; BrMus.   3439

---- What is true civilization; or Means to suppress the practice of duelling, to prevent, or to punish, crimes, and to abolish the punishment of death. Boston, William Smith, pr., 1830. 8, [iii]-xiv, 243 [1] p. DLC; LNHT; MH; MeBa; NN; PPL; RPB; ScU.   3440

Select hymns for youth... New-York, Pr. and sold by Mahlon Day, at the New Juvenile bookstore, 1830. 23 p. DLC.   3441

A selection of hymns. See Dabney, Jonathan Peele.

Self-Examining Society.
A new society, called the Self-Examining Society. ... The constitution... [n. p., 183-?] Bdsd. CSmH.   3442

Sellers, Joseph.
The sun in the East, against the Sentinel and Star in the West. By Joseph Sellers, Sen. [n. p., 1830?] 40 p. O.   3443

The separation. See Bury, Lady Charlotte (Campbell).

Sequel to the Seymour family. See Hinckley, Mary.

Sergeant, John, 1779-1852.
Discourse... before the trustees, faculty, and students of Rutgers College at New Brunswick, N. J. ...   Rutgers Press, Terhune & Letson, prs., 1830. 34 p. NjR.   3444

Sergeant, Thomas.
Constitutional law. ... 2d ed., with additions and improvements. Philadelphia, Pr. by Thomas Kite, Pub. by P. H. Nicklin & T. Johnson, 1830. xi, 440 p. Ia; LNT-L; LU; MH; Md; Me; MiU; NCH; NIC-L; NNLI; NhD; NjP; NjR; OCLaw; RPL; Tx-SC; U; W; BrMus.   3445

A series of letters. See Baptist, Edward.

A sermon upon goats. [Signed: Boston U. Magazine, 1830] Bdsd. PPL.   3446

Sermons preached in St. Paul's Church, Baltimore, on the occasion of the consecration of the Right Rev. William M. Stone, D. D. Bishop of Maryland. Baltimore, Pr. by Joseph Robinson,

1830. 72 p. PPL.   3447

Seton, Samuel Worthington.
The abecedarian, for infant
schools; comprising the comparative and analytical alphabet; exhibiting a classification and analysis of the letters, illustrated
by various analogies... New
York, Pr. by J. B. Requa, 1830.
52 p. IaU; BrMus.   3448

The seven champions of Christendom. See Johnson, Richard.

Seventy-five receipts for pastry.
See Leslie, Eliza.

Severance, Moses.
The American manual; or New
English reader: consisting of
exercises in reading and speak-
ing, both in prose and poetry;
selected from the best writers...
Waterloo, N. Y., Pr. by C.
Sentil, 1830. 364p. OCl.   3449

Sewall, Thomas, 1786-1845.
An address delivered before
the Washington City Temperance
Society, November 15, 1830.
Published by the Society. Wash-
ington, Wm. Greer, pr., 1830.
24 p. CSmH; MBAt; MBC; MH;
MWA; MdBS-P; NjR; OO; PHi;
PPAmP; RPB; VtU; WHi; BrMus.
          3450
---- Address on the effects of
intemperance on the intellectual,
moral, and physical powers.
Originally delivered before the
Washington City Temperance
Society. New York, American
Tract Society [183?] 4, 20 p.
DLC; PPC.   3451

---- ... The effects of intemperance on the moral, intellectual, and physical powers, including the predisposition to disease and death. New-York,
American Tract Society [183-?]
24 p. CSmH; DLC.   3452

---- An eulogy on Dr. Godman,
being an introductory lecture, de-
livered November 1, 1830. Wash-
ington, Pr. by W. Greer, 1830.
24 p. DLC; IEN-M; MB; MBAt;
MBCo; MdHi; MiD-B; NNC;
NNNAM; PHi; PPC; RPB; BrMus.
          3453
---- ---- New York, American
Tract Society [1830] 20 p. DNLM.
          3454
---- ---- New York, American
Tract Society, 1830. 16 p.
DNLM.   3455

---- ... Memoir of Dr. John D.
Godman... Pub. by the Ameri-
can Tract Society, New York
[1830?] 24 p. No. 370. PPL.
          3456
The Seymour family. See
Hinckley, Mary.

Shakers.
A brief exposition of the es-
tablished principles and regula-
tions of the United society called
Shakers... Albany [N. Y.] Pr. by
Packard & Van Benthuysen, 1830.
23 p. DLC; MH; NNUT; OCHP;
OClWHi; PPL.   3457

Shakespeare, William, 1564-1616.
...Julius Caesar; a tragedy
in five acts. New York, E. B.
Clayton, 1830. 71 p. (Cumberland's ed.) MH; PU.   3458

---- The plays of William
Shakespeare. Accurately printed
from the text of the corrected
copy left by the late George
Steevens, Esq. With glossarial
notes, and a sketch of the life
of Shakespeare... Philadelphia,
Pub. by M'Carty and Davis,
1830. 8 v. CtY; MoSU.   3459

Shaler, Charles.
Address delivered at the consecration and dedication of the
new Masonic hall in the city of
Pittsburgh, July 26, 1830.

15 p. OClWHi.   3460

Shand, Peter J., 1800-1886.
An oration delivered before
the Revolution and Cincinnati Societies of Charleston, S. C. Fifth
of July, 1830 (the Fourth falling
on Sunday). By Peter J. Shand,
a Member of the Revolution Society. Charleston, Pr. by A. E.
Miller, 1830. 20 p. MB; MHi;
MWA; ScC.   3461

Sharp, Daniel.
Reflections against the Bap-
tists refuted. A sermon, deliv-
ered at the dedication of the
Baptist Meeting House in New
Bedford, October 22, 1829...
Boston, Pr. by Lincoln & Ed-
mands [1830?] 24 p. RPB. 3462

Shaw, Benjamin, comp.
A new selection of hymns and
spiritual songs, designed for
prayer, conference and camp-
meetings. Woodstock, Pr. by
David Watson, 1830. 160 p. OC;
Vt.   3463

Sheldon English & Classical
School. Southampton, Mass.
The annual catalogue, of the
officers and students of the Shel-
don English & Classical School,
Southampton, Mass. November,
1830.   Northampton, T. W.
Shepard, pr., 1830. 12 p. MH;
MWA.   3464

The Shepherd and his Flock.
Philadelphia, American Sunday
School Union [1830] DLC;
BrMus.   3465

Sherman, Eleazer, b. 1795.
Narrative of Eleazer Sherman,
giving an account of his life, experience, call to the ministry of
the gospel and travels as such to
the present time. Providence,
H. H. Brown, pr., 1830. 2 v. in
1. CSmH; ICN; M; RHi.   3466

Sherman, John.
A description of Trenton Falls,
Oneida County, New York. By
John Sherman.   Utica, Press of
William Williams, 1830. 18 p.
NN; NNA; NUt.   3467

Sherwood, Adiel, 1791-1879.
Knowledge necessary and desirable for a minister of the
Gospel, a discourse delivered
before the Baptist convention of
Georgia, April 18, 1830.   Pub.
by request of the convention and
congregation.   Milledgeville, Camak & Ragland, prs., 1830.
18 p. DLC; NRAB.   3468

Sherwood, Mary Martha (Butt),
1775-1851.
The children of the Hartz
Mountains; or The little Beggars
...Revised by the Committee of
Publication. Philadelphia, Amer-
ican Sunday School Union [1830?]
36 p. DLC; ICU; MH.   3469

---- Easy questions... New-
Haven, S. Babcock; Sidney's
Press, 1830. [18] p. CtHi. 3470

---- The errand boy... Revised
by the Committee of Publication.
Philadelphia, American Sunday
School Union, 1830. BrMus.
                             3471
---- The happy choice; or, The
potters' common...Revised by
Committee of Publication. Phila-
delphia, American Sunday School
Union, 1830. 69 p. CtY; BrMus.
                             3472
---- The improved boy... New-
Haven, S. Babcock; Sidney's
press, 1830. 1 p. l., [4]-17 p.
CtHi; CtY.   3473

---- Little Henry and his bearer.
New York, American Tract Society [183-?] 40 p. ([Tract] No.
107). MnS.   3474

---- ---- 4th ed. Andover,

Mass., Flagg & Gould [183-?]
32 p. (American Tract Society,
Publications no. 107). CtY;
MB.   3475

---- Little Robert and the owl.
Wendell, J. Metcalf, 1830. 22 p.
MWA.   3476

---- ... Primer; or First book
for children. New-Haven, S.
Babcock, Publisher... Charleston,
S. Babcock & Co., Sidney's
press, 1830. 23 p. CtHi.   3477

---- The Shepherd of the Pyre-
nees... Revised by the Committee of Publication. Philadelphia,
American Sunday School Union
[1830?] 54 p. MiDW; NNC;
BrMus.   3478

Shewen, William, 1631?-1695.
   A small treatise concerning
evil thoughts and imaginations,
and concerning good thoughts and
heavenly meditations... By W. S.
Philadelphia, Marcus T. C.
Gould; New York, Isaac T. Hop-
per, 1830. p. 106-132 in his
The true Christian's faith. PSC-
Hi.   3479

---- The true Christian's faith
and experience briefly declared.
By William Shewen... (London)
Pr. 1684-5. Philadelphia, Repr.
and pub. by M. T. C. Gould; Jesper Harding, pr., 1830. 136 p.
MB; PSC; PSC-Hi.   3480

Shillitoe, Thomas, 1754-1836.
   Extracts from an address to
the Society of Friends. Philadelphia, Pub. by the Tract Association of Friends [1830?] 12 p.
No. 64. PPL.   3481

Shipherd, John Jay, 1802-1844.
   The Bible class book; designed
for youth's and adults in Sabbath
schools and Bible classes. Middlebury, Vermont Sabbath School

Union; Pr. by O. & J. Miner,
1830. 24 p. VtHi; VtMiS.   3482

---- The Sabbath school guide;
or, A selection of interesting and
profitable scripture lessons, illustrated and applied by questions
and answers. Designed as a permanent system of Sabbath school
instruction. No. IV. Burlington,
Chauncey Goodrich; Pr. by Ovid
Miner, 1830. 64 p. MH; VtHi;
VtMiS; VtU.   3483

Shoreham, Vermont. Newton
Academy.
   Catalogue of the trustees and
students of Newton Academy,
Shoreham, Vt. for the year ending Aug. 1830. Brandon, Telegraph Office, 1830. 8 p. VtMiM.
                             3484

A short account of the happy
death of Mrs. Frances Lambeth.
Greensborough, Wm. Swaim, pr.,
1830. 8 p. NcU.   3485

A short system of polite learning. See Jaudon, Daniel.

The Shoshonee Valley. See
Flint, Timothy.

Sich a gitting up stairs sung by
Mr. Bob Farrel. The original
Zip Coon. Baltimore, Pub. by
G. Willig Jr. [183-?] [3] p.
CSmH.   3486

Sigston, James.
   Memoir of the life and ministry of Mr. William Bramwell,
lately an itinerant Methodist
preacher, with extracts from his
interesting and extensive correspondence. 2d American ed.
New York, Pub. by J. Emory,
for Methodist Episcopal Church,
1830. 249 p. NcD.   3487

---- ---- 3d American ed. New
York, Pub. by J. Emory and B.
Waugh, for the Methodist Episco-

pal Church [J. Collard, pr.]
1830. 249 p. CtMW; NNG; NcD.
3488

Silliman, Benjamin, 1799-1864.
Elements of chemistry. Arranged in the order of lectures
given in Yale College. New Haven,
H. Howe, 1830. 2 v. CtY; Ia-HA;
KyT; MH; MPiB; OCU; OMC.
3489

[Sime, William]
History of the Covenanters in
Scotland. By the author of the
History of the reformation, etc.
...Philadelphia, Presbyterian
board of publication, [1830] 2 v.
IU; NNUT.   3490

Simons, Thomas Young, 1797-
1857.
The annual address to the
graduates of the Medical College
of South Carolina, delivered
March 23, 1830, after conferring
the degree of Doctor of Medicine.
Charleston, A. F. Cunningham,
1830. 13 p. DLC; MB; NBM;
NcD.   3491

Sinclair, William.
Catholic emancipation in England and Ireland, vindicated and
recommended, on the principles
of universal freedom, civil and
religious, As in this happy and
prosperous republic: A discourse. Baltimore, Pr. by Matchett & Wood, 1830. 40 p. DGU;
MdHi.   3492

Sir, A printed paper... See
Drake, R. Dillon.

Sir, It is with the greatest reluctance... See Griffith, H.
Wharton.

Sir, The following statement was
prepared. See Westcott, Hampton.

Six essays on public education.
From the New York Daily Senti-

nel. New York, Pub. at the office of the Daily Sentinel, 1830.
22 p. NNC; PPL; RPB.   3493

Sketch of Nantasket. See Lincoln, Solomon.

Sketch of the character and manners of all nations. Embellished
with a representative cut of each
people. Concord, N. H., Pub. by
R. H. Sherburne & Co., 1830.
35 p. DLC; NhHi; OCHP. 3494

Sketch of the geographical rout[!]
See Redfield, William C.

A sketch of the life and character of William Penn. Philadelphia, Tract Association of Friends
[1830?] 32 p. (Tract Assoc. of
Friends. Tract no. 73) DLC;
PPL.   3495

A sketch of the life of Stephen H.
Bradley, from the age of five to
twenty-four years; including his
remarkable experience of the
power of the Holy Spirit, on the
second evening of November,
1829... Madison, Conn., 1830.
12 p. CtHi; CtY; MiD-B.   3496

Sketch of the peace cause. See
American Peace Society.

Sketches. See Holbrook, Silas
Pinckney.

Sketches from the Bible. Philadelphia, American Sunday School
Union, 1830. 67 p. BrMus. 3497

Sketches of public character.
See Knapp, Samuel Lorenzo.

Skillman, John B.
Skillman's New-York Police
Reports. Illustrated with engrav-
ings. Written in 1828-29. New-
York, Pr. by Ludwig & Tolefree,
1830. 151 p. CLSU; Ct; CtHT;
MH; MdHi; NIC; NNU; OCLaw;

PP; PPL; WaU. 3498

Skinner, Otis Ainsworth.
A sermon delivered in the Universalist Meeting House in Woburn, Mass., Wednesday evening, January 13, 1830, in reply to Dr. Beecher's sermon against Universalism, delivered in the Congregational Meeting House in said town, Thursday evening, January 7, 1830... Boston, Pr. at the Trumpet office, 1830. 22 p. ICMe; M; MB; MMeT-Hi; MWA; NNUT; PPL; BrMus. 3499

Skinner, Roger Sherman.
The New-York State register, for the year of our Lord 1830... New York, Pr. for the author by Clayton & Van Norden, 1830. 408 p. Ct; DLC; MB; MBC; MBNEH; MH; Mi; NIC; NR; NRHi; NUtHi; OClWHi; P; BrMus. 3500

Skinner, Thomas Harvey, 1791-1871.
Human depravity; or, Man a fallen being, a sermon delivered in the Murray Street Church, on the evening of March 21, 1830. New York, Henry C. Sleight, Pr. by Sleight & Robinson, 1830. 34 p. MH-AH; NCH; PPL. 3501

Skinner, Warren.
Essays on the coming of Christ. Boston, G. W. Bazin, 1830. 173 p. MH. 3502

---- Four sermons, Delivered at Cavendish, Vt., on the doctrine of endless misery. Woodstock, Pr. by E. Avery, September, 1830. 96 p. MDeeP; MMeT-Hi; OC; OClWHi. 3503

[Slade, William, 1786-1859]
Masonic penalties. Castleton, [Vt.] Pr. by H. H. Houghton [1830] 52 p. CSmH; DLC; IaCrM; NN; PHi; PPFM; RPB;

BrMus. 3504

---- A memorial to the Legislature of Vermont, for the repeal of acts incorporating the Grand Lodge and Grand Chapter of Vermont. Presented October 23, 1830. [Montpelier? 1830] 14 p. DLC; DNLM; MB; MBFM; VtHi; VtU. 3505

[Slaughter, James]
To the Public. [Conc. his successful treatment of disease.] [Philadelphia, Oct. 25, 1830] 24 p. PPL. 3506

Smelt, Caroline E.
Extracts from the memoirs of Caroline E. Smelt. Philadelphia, To be had of Thomas Kite, 1830. 16 p. NjR; PHC. 3507

Smiley, Thomas Tucker, d. 1879.
An easy introduction to the study of geography... 7th ed., imp. Philadelphia, Pr. for the author, and for sale at J. Grigg's ...Jesper Harding, pr., 1830. iv, 11-256 p. MH; NNC. 3508

---- The new federal calculator, or Scholar's assistant... For the use of schools and counting houses. Philadelphia, Pub. and for sale by J. Grigg; and for sale by booksellers and country merchants generally in the Southern and Western states [Stereotyped by J. Howe] 1830. 180 p. KHi; MiU; NNC; OClWHi; PLFM; ViU. 3509

Smith, Mr. See Featherstonhaugh, George William.

Smith, Edward.
Bible election explained, in a sermon on Romans, XI, 5. Hagerstown, Md., J. Maxwell, pr., 1830. 40 p. NcU; PHi. 3510

Smith, Elisha.

The botanic physician: being a compendium of the practice of physic, upon botanical principles. By Elisha Smith. New York, Murphy & Bingham, prs., 1830. viii, 624 p. <u>DLC</u>; ICJ; IEN-M; NNNAM. 3511

Smith, George.
A short treatise upon the most essential and leading points of Wesleyan or Primitive Methodism; being designed as a reply to those persons in our church who have very charitably represented the author as alienated from, and using his influence against Methodists. Poultney, Pr. by L. J. Reynolds, 1830. 34 p. DLC; NN; NjMD. 3512

[Smith, George W.]
A view and description of the Eastern Penitentiary of Pennsylvania. Philadelphia, Pub. for the Philadelphia Society for Alleviating the Miseries of Public Prisons, by C. G. Childs, engraver, 1830. 8 p. DNLM; KyLxT; MH-L; NNC; O; OClW; OClWHi; PHC; PHi; <u>PPL</u> (two variant issues); WHi; BrMus. 3513

[Smith, Horatio] 1779-1849.
Walter Colyton; a tale of 1688. By the author of "Brambletge House," etc., etc. New York, Pr. by J. & J. Harper; Sold by Collins & Hannay; Collins & Co., G. & C. & H. Carvill, O. A. Roorbach, White, Gallaher and White, A. T. Goodrich, W. B. Gilley, R. Bliss, C. S. Francis, G. C. Morgan, M. Bancroft, W. Burgess, N. B. Holmes, McElrath and Bangs, J. Leavitt, G. W. Blucker and J. P. Havens; Albany, O. Steel, and Little & Cummings, 1830. 2 v. CtY; MH; NcU; NjP; OMC; RPA. 3514

Smith, Hugh, 1795-1849.
The Christian taught of God.

A sermon, delivered in St. Paul's Church, Augusta, (Geo.) on Sunday morning, November 8, 1829, in respect to the memory of Mrs. Priscilla Jones. Worcester, Pr. by S. H. Colton and co., 1830. 20 p. CtY; MH; MWA; MWHi; NN. 3515

Smith, John.
Narrative of the shipwreck and sufferings of the crew and passengers of the English brig Neptune, which was wrecked in a violent snow storm on the 12th of January, 1830, on her passage from Bristol [Eng.] to Quebec. By John Smith... New York, Pub. by J. Smith, 1830. 36 p. DLC; ICHi; MH; MHi; NCH; NhHi; OClWHi; PHi; <u>PPL;</u> RPB; WHi. 3516

Smith, John, 1766-1831.
A sermon, delivered in Winthrop, June 12, 1830, before the Maine Missionary Society, at their twenty-third anniversary. Portland, Shirley, Hyde and Co., 1830. 39, [1] p. MBC; MH-AH; MWA; MeBa; MeBaT; MiD-B; PPPrHi. 3517

Smith, John Rubens.
Prospectus of J. R. Smith's Drawing and Perspective Academy, Philadelphia. [Philadelphia, January 13, 1830] 8 p. <u>PHi.</u> 3518

Smith, Joseph.
See The Book of Morman.

Smith, Nathan Ryno.
Surgical anatomy of the arteries, with plates and illustrations ... Baltimore, J. D. Toy & W. R. Lucas [J. D. Toy, pr.] 1830. 104 p., 3 l., [iii]-iv p. IU-M; MBCo; MdHi; MoSMed; PPC. 3519

Smith, R. Barnwell.
Speech at the great state rights' meeting in Columbia, on the 20th

of September, 1830. Columbia,
1830. 7 p. PPAmP.   3520

Smith, Reuben, 1789-1860.
   Africa given to Christ: a sermon preached before the Vermont
Colonization Society, at Montpelier, Oct. 20, 1830. Published
by the board of directors. Burlington, Chauncey Goodrich [Uni-
versity Press, C. Goodrich, pr.]
1830. 16 p. DLC; ICN; MBC;
MH-AH; NN; OCHP; VtU; BrMus.
                           3521
Smith, Richard Penn, 1799-1854.
   The deformed; or, Woman's
trial, a play in five acts...
Philadelphia ed. C. Alexander,
pr., 1830. 87 p. DLC; ICU; MB;
MH; NjP; PPL; PU; RPB.   3522

---- The disowned; or, The
prodigals, a play, in three acts.
By Richard Penn Smith...Phila-
delphia, C. Alexander, pr.,
1830. 67 p. DLC; ICU; MB; MH;
MiD; PHi; PPL; PU; RPB. 3523

Smith, Roswell Chamberlain,
1797-1875.
   Intellectual and practical grammar, in a series of inductive
questions, connected with exercises in composition. Part I [-II]
Boston, Pub. by Perkins & Marvin [T. R. Marvin, pr.] 1830. 123,
82 p. CtHT-W; DLC; MB; MDeeP;
MH; NCH; NIC; NNC; RHi; RPB.
                           3524
---- Practical and mental arithmetic. Boston, Richardson, Lord
& Holbrook, 1830. MH.   3525

[Smith, Seba]
   Letters of J. Downing, Major,
Downingville Militia, second bri-
gade, to his old friend Mr.
Dwight, of the New York Daily
Advertiser. New York, J. & J.
Harper, 1830. 318 p. NcD. 3526

Smith, Sheldon.
   An oration pronounced at the

Working Men's Celebration of the
54th anniversary of American Independence, at Buffalo, N. Y.
Buffalo, N. Y., Pr. by Horace
Steele, at the office of The Working Men's Bulletin. 1830. 12 p.
NBuHi.   3527

Smith, Southwood.
   A treatise on fever. Philadel-
phia, Carey & Lea, publishers,
I. Ashmead & Co., prs. 1830.
x, 448, 8 p. CSt-L; DNLM; GU-
M; ICU-R; KyLxT; MdBJ; MeB;
NIC; NNC; NRAM; NjR; OC; P;
PPC; TNJ; VtU.   3528

Smith, William, 1728-1793.
   The history of the late prov-
ince of New-York, from its dis-
covery, to the appointment of
Governor Colden, in 1762. By
the Hon. William Smith... New
York.   Pub. under the direction
of the New-York Historical So-
ciety, Grattan, pr., 1830. 2 v.
CU; Ct; DLC; DeGE; IU; In;
LNHT; M; MBAt; Me; NNC;
NNG; NjP; PPAmP; RPB; ScC.
                           3529

Smith, William, 1762-1840.
   Speech of Mr. Smith of South
Carolina: The resolution of Mr.
Foot of Connecticut, relative to
the Public Lands, being under
consideration. Delivered in the
Senate, February 25, 1830.
Washington, Pr. by Gales & Sea-
ton, 1830. 55 p. PPL; ScU.
                           3530

Smith, Worthington.
   The guilt of being accessary to
intemperance. A sermon. St.
Albans, Pr. by J. Spooner, 1830.
15 p. MH; BrMus.   3531

Smythe, Elizabeth Anne.
   The adventures of Orphan
Henry; or, The sure road to
wealth and happiness... By Eliz-
beth Anne Smythe. Boston, Pub.
by Munroe & Francis [1830] 64,
[3] p. PPL.   3532

Smyth, William, 1797-1868.
Elements of algebra. Portland, Shirley & Hyde; Brunswick, Griffin, pr., 1830. 264 p. DLC; ICU; MH. 3533

[Snelling, William Joseph] 1804-1848.
Tales of the Northwest; or Sketches of Indian life and character. By a resident beyond the frontier. Boston, Hilliard, Gray, Little, and Wilkins [Pr. by I. R. Butts] 1830. viii, 288 p. CSmH; CtY; DLC; ICN; LU; MBAt; MH; MWA; MnU; O; OC; PPL; WHi; WaU; BrMus. 3534

[----] Tales of travels west of the Mississippi by Solomon Bell ... Boston, Gray & Bowen, 1830. xvi, 162 p. CSmH; DLC; ICN; IHi; LU; MB; MBAt; MH; NN; OClWHi; OMC; Vi; WHi. 3535

Snodgrass, William D.
The victorious Christian awaiting his crown: a discourse, January 3, 1830, occasioned by the death of Rev. John M. Mason... New York, John P. Haven; Sleight & Robinson, prs., 1830. 37 p. DLC; MBAt; MBC; MH; NjR; PHi; PPPrHi; RPB. 3536

Snow, Charles Henry.
A geography of Boston, county of Suffolk and the adjacent towns. Boston, Pr. by Carter & Hendee, 1830. 162p. CtSoP; ICN; M; MB; MBC; MH; MiD-B; NNC; NhHi; RP; TxU; WHi. 3537

The snow drop. Philadelphia, American Sunday School Union, [1830?] 16 p. MB; BrMus. 3538

Social and camp-meeting songs for the pious... 18th ed. Baltimore, Pub. by Armstrong & Plaskitt...and John Plaskitt & Co., 1830. 215, [1] p. MoS. 3539

Society for Improving the Condition and Elevating the Character of Industrious Females. [Philadelphia? 1830?] 4 p. PPL. 3540

Society for the Encouragement of Faithful Domestics, Philadelphia.
...Address to the public of the Society for the Encouragement of Faithful Domestics. [Philadelphia, 1830] 12 p. (At head of title: Philadelphia, July 20, 1830.) DeGE; PPL; PU. 3541

---- First report of the board of managers of the Society for the Encouragement of Faithful Domestics. Philadelphia, Pr. by Mifflin & Parry, 1830. 8 p. DeGE; MdHi; PPL. 3542

Society for the Promotion of Christian Knowledge, Piety and Charity.
A plain and serious address on the subject of the Christian religion, urging the practice of it in a candid and charitable spirit. ... Boston, Gray & Bowen [I. R. Butts, pr.] 1830. 36 p. CBPac; ICMe; MB; PPAmP; WHi. 3543

Society for the Reformation of Juvenile Delinquents in the City of New York.
Fifth annual report of the managers of the Society for the Reformation of Juvenile Delinquents in the City and State of New York. New York, Pr. by Mahlon Day, 1830. 44 p. DLC; MH; OClW. 3544

A solemn warning to drunkards, and an appeal to the rising generation, on the important subject of health in body and mind. By a physician. [New York, Pub. by J. Emory and B. Waugh, for the Tract Society of the Methodist Episcopal Church, 1830] 12 p. (Methodist Episcopal Church, Tract Society, no. 90) MnU. 3545

Solitary musings. [Washington?
1830] 19 p. <u>DLC</u>.   3546

Songs of Sion; or, Maine collec-
tion of sacred music. Charles-
ton, Me., Hinkley & Norcross;
Hallowell, Glazier, Masters &
Co., prs., 1830. 150, [2] p.
RPB.   3547

The songster's magazine. A
choice collection of the most approved patriotic, comic sentimental, amatory and naval songs,
both ancient and modern... Cincinnati, Pub. by John H. Wood.
Wood & Stratton, prs., [1830?]
[156] p. DLC.   3548

South Carolina.
Acts and resolutions of the
General Assembly of the state of
South Carolina, passed in Decem-
ber, 1829. Columbia, D. & J.
M. Faust, 1830. 44, 99, [10] p.
IaU-L; In-SC; MdBB; Nb; Nj;
OCLaw; W.   3549

---- A digest of the laws of the
United States & the state of
South-Carolina, now in force, relating to the militia; with an appendix, containing the patrol laws;
the laws for the government of
slaves & free persons of colour;
the decisions of the Constitutional
court & court of appeal of South
Carolina thereon; and an abstract
from the rules and regulations of
the United States Army. By
Thomas D. Condy, Lieutenant
Colonel, 17th Regiment, South
Carolina Militia. Charleston, A.
E. Miller, 1830. 196 p. Ct; MB;
MH; MH-L; NN; ScC; ScU. 3550

---- Reports of cases argued and
determined in the Court of Appeals of South Carolina. Vol. IV.
Containing law opinions in 1826,
1827 and 1828. Columbia, S. C.
Pr. by David W. Sims, state and
U. S. pr., 1830. [8], 595 p.

LNL-L; MWC-L; MdBB; MdU-
L.   3551

---- Abbeville district, Citizens.
Preamble and resolutions,
adopted at the great anti-tariff
meeting, of the people of Abbeville district on Thursday, 25th
Sept. 1828. Columbia, S. C.:
Pr. by David W. Sims, 1830.
28 p. ICN; ScU.   3552

South Massachusetts Education
Society.
First annual report of the
South Massachusetts Education
Society; together with the Consti-
tution. June 9, 1830. New-Bed-
ford, S. S. Smith, 1830. 15 p.
MH; NN.   3553

Southard, Samuel Lewis, 1787-
1842.
Address delivered before the
Newark Mechanics' Association,
July 5, 1830. Newark, Pr. by
W. Tuttle & Co., 1830. 27 p.
CSmH; DLC; IU; MB; MdHi; NjN;
NjR; P; PHi; PPAmP; <u>PPL</u>;
PPPrHi; WHi.   3554

A southern traveler's visit to
New England. Boston, Lincoln
& Edmunds, 1830. 16 p. NHi;
NjP; RPB.   3555

A Southerner, pseud. See Duke,
Seymour R.

Southey, Robert.
The life of Nelson. New
York, Pr. by J. & J. Harper
[etc.] 1830. 309 p. CL; CtB;
LNHT; MdBP; MiU; NGH;
NN; NhD; RPB; VtU.   3556 ·

Southgate, Horatio, 1781-1867.
The Probate manual, containing forms adapted to the practice
of Probate Courts in the state of
Maine. Also, the laws establishing probate courts, regulating
wills, the descent, distribution,

division, and sale of estates.
Portland, Pr. by Thomas Todd,
1830. 264, [39] p. MeHi.   3557

Southmayd, Daniel S.
    The sure advancement of gos-
pel truth: A sermon, preached
on the day, of the annual thanksgiving, November 26, 1829. Boston, Pr. by Peirce & Williams,
1830. 24 p. DLC; MB; MBC;
MH-AH; MWA; NN; NNUT; RPB;
BrMus.   3558

[Southwick, John B.]
    The memoirs of John Amir-
alle, a native of the Isle of Scio,
Greece: containing an account of
his voyages and remarkable adventures. By a citizen of Albany.
Albany, Pr. for the proprietor.
1830. 71, [1] p. NHi.   3559

Southworth, Constant.
    The lamp-lighter's address...
January 1, 1830. C. Southworth.
[Boston, 1830] Bdsd. MB.   3560

Spalding, Horace.
    The Biblical manual: contain-
ing brief illustrations of various
scripture tables, necessary for a
clear understanding of the sacred
writings... Boston, James Loring's [c1830]   70, [1] p.
MBNMHi; NRAB; OClWHi.   3561

A spectator of the past, pseud.
See Memminger, Christopher
Gustavus.

Speeches on the passage of the
bill for the removal of the Indi-
ans, delivered in the Congress
of the United States, April and
May, 1830. Boston, Pub. by
Perkins and Marvin. New York,
Jonathan Leavitt, 1830. viii, 304
p. CSt; CtHT-W; GDC; ICN; In;
KHi; LU; MBAt; MdBJ; MeHi;
MiD-B; MoSpD; NN; NcD; NjP;
OHi; OkU; PPL; RPA; Tx; ViU;
BrMus.   3562

Spencer, J.
    Parting advice; A farewell
sermon, preached to the Protes-
tant Episcopal Congregation of
St. John's Church, Carlisle: by
Rev. J. Spencer, D.D. on Sun-
day, April 11, 1830. Baltimore,
Richard J. Matchett, 1830. 31 p.
NNG.   3563

Spicer, Tobias, b. 1788.
    An attempt to explain some
part of the seventh chapter of St.
Paul's Epistle to the Romans.
Vergennes [Vt.] Pr. by Gama-
liel Small, 1830. 24 p. CSmH;
MBC; NN; VtMiS; VtU.   3564

---- A vindication of the char-
acter of the Apostle Paul. By
Tobias Spicer, Minister of the
Gospel. Vergennes [Vt.], Pr.
by Gamaliel Small, 1830. 24 p.
MB; MBC; VtMiS.   3565

The spirit of the Annuals for
MDCCCXXX. Philadelphia, E.
Littell & Bro., Sold also by J.
Grigg, Philadelphia; G. & C. &
H. Carvill, New York; E. J.
Coale, Baltimore; P. Thompson,
Washington; Carter & Hendee,
Boston; C. D. Bradford & Co.,
Cincinnati; Ariel Works, Rich-
mond; E. Thayer, Charleston,
1830. 432 p. CtY; LNHT; TxU.
                            3566
The spiritual combat. See Scu-
poli, Lorenzo.

The spiritual mirror; or, Look-
ing-glass: exhibiting the human
heart as being either the temple
of God, or habitation of devils...
Translated into the German language, from which it is now
translated, by Peter Bauder,
Newburyport, Pub. by Charles
Whipple, 1830. 80 p. MH; NN.
                            3567
Sprague, Charles, 1791-1875.
    An ode: pronounced before
the inhabitants of Boston, Sep-

tember, the seventeenth, 1830,
at the Centennial celebration of
the settlement of the city. Bos-
ton, John H. Eastburn, city pr.,
1830. 22 p. CSmH; CtHT-W;
DLC; ICN; ICU; MB; MBAt; MBC;
MH-AH; MHi; MMeT; MeHi; MnU;
NIC; NNC; NhHi; NjR; OClWHi;
OMC; PHi; PPAmP; PPL; PU;
RPB; TxU; WHi; BrMus.   3568

Sprague, Peleg, 1793-1880.
Speech of Mr. Sprague, of
Maine: delivered in the Senate
of the United States, February
3d, 1830, in the debate which
arose upon Mr. Foot's resolution
relative to the public lands.
Washington, Pr. by P. Force,
1830. 23 p. CSmH; DLC.   3569

---- Speech of Mr. Sprague, of
Maine: delivered in the Senate
of the United States, 16th April,
1830, in reply to Messrs. White,
McKinley and Forsyth, upon the
subject of the removal of the Indians. Washington, Pub. at the
office of the National Journal,
Peter Force, pr., 1830. 36 p.
CSmH.   3570

Sprague, William Buell, 1795-
1876.
A discourse delivered at
Castleton May 27, 1830, at the
opening of the Vermont Classical
Seminary. ...Albany, Pr. by
Packard & Van Benthuysen, 1830.
27, [1] p. ICU; MB; MH; MHi;
NIC; NN; NbU; RPB; VtU;
BrMus.   3571

---- Lectures to young people.
...With an introductory address,
by Samuel Miller, D.D., professor in the Theological Seminary
at Princeton. New York, Pub.
by John P. Haven; Albany, Pr.
by Packard & Van Benthuysen,
1830. xxii, 288 p. In; MPiB;
VtU; BrMus.   3572

---- A sermon, addressed to the
Second Congregational Society, in
Greenwich, Connecticut, Septem-
ber 1, 1830, at the installation
of the Reverend Joel Mann, as
their pastor. Albany, Packard
& Van Benthuysen, 1830. 26 p.
CU; CtMW; MBAt; MWA; MiD-B;
NN; RPB; BrMus.   3573

---- A sermon addressed to the
Second Presbyterian Congrega-
tion in Albany, on the Fourth of
July, 1830... Albany, Pr. by
Packard and Van Benthuysen,
1830. 17 p. ICMe; MB; MHi;
MWA; MiD-B; N; NN; OClWHi;
PHi; BrMus.   3574

Spratt, George.
The foolishness of preaching
Gods instituted means of salvation. A sermon, preached by
appointment before the New Jersey Baptist Association, convened at Cape May, W. N.J.,
September 7, 1830. Bridgeton,
(W. N.J.) Pr. by Franklin Ferguson, 1830. 16 p. NRAB. 3575

Spring, Gardiner, 1785-1873.
Discourses delivered in Mur-
ray Street Church on Sabbath
evenings, during the months of
March, April and May, 1830, by
Dr. Spring, Dr. Cox, Dr. Skin-
ner, Dr. DeWitt, Dr. Miller, Dr.
Sprague, Dr. Griffin and six
others. New York, Henry C.
Sleight, Clinton Hall. Pr. by
Sleight & Robinson, 1830. 501 p.
CtHC; ICMcC; ICU; IU; KyLoP;
MB; MBC; MH; MeBaT; MiD; NN;
NbOP; NjP; OMC; PPLT; ViRUT;
VtU; BrMus.   3576

---- Moses on Nebo or Death
a duty. A sermon occasioned
by the death of the Rev. Joseph
S. Christmas... Preached... on
the evening of the sabbath after
his interment. New York, Pub.
by John P. Haven [J. Seymour,

pr.] 1830. 47 p. CSmH; DLC;
ICN; MB; MBC; MH; MiD-B;
MnHi; NIC; NjR; OClWHi;
PPPrHi; RPB; ViRUT; BrMus.
3577

Sproat, Granville Temple.
The pilgrim's song: or Origi-
nal hymns for public and private
use. Taunton, Pr. by Edmund
Anthony, 1830. 90 p. CSmH;
DLC; MB; MBC; MH; NHi; PU;
RPB. 3578

Sproat, Nancy.
Village poems. By Mrs. N.
Sproat. New-York, S. Wood &
sons [1830?] 63, [1] p. DLC;
ICU; IU; BrMus. 3579

Squire, Patrick, pseud?
Late news from the Infernal
Regions, together with A variety
of miscellaneous articles, from
the pen of Patrick Squire, By his
Confidential Agent and Publisher,
William Provence. Fayetteville,
T. , Pr. for the publisher, by E.
and J. B. Hill [1830] 15, [1] p.
CSmH. 3580

Stabler, Edward.
Two letters from Edward Stabler, late of Alexandria. [2nd.
letter dated: 1st Mo. 17th, 1830]
4 p. PPL. 3581

The stage, canal, and steamboat
register for 1830. Utica, Pr.
and pub. by William Williams,
[1830] 16 p. CSmH; NBu. 3582

Stanley, Jesse.
Practical arithmetic rendered
easy by familiar rules and examples, and specially adapted to
the commerce and currency of
the U.S. ... Philadelphia, Thos.
Kite, 1830. 2 v. ICU. 3583

The Stanwood family. See Dean,
Christopher C.

A star of Virginia. See G. , G.

E. Memoir of Anna Louisa Campbell.

Starke, W. W.
Speech of W. W. Starke of
Abbeville, on codifying the laws,
delivered in the House of Repre-
sentatives, in December, 1828.
Columbia, S. C. , David W. Sims,
State and U. S. pr. , 1830. 23 p.
CSmH. 3584

Starkie, Thomas, 1782-1849.
A practical treatise on the
law of evidence, and digest of
proofs, in civil and criminal proceedings. By Thomas Starkie...
With reference to American decisions by Theron Metcalf and
Edward D. Ingraham. 3d American ed. Philadelphia, P. H.
Nicklin and T. Johnson, law
booksellers, 1830. 3 vols. CU;
CtHT; IU-L; Ia; KyLxT; NcD;
OCLaw; PP; TU; TxU-L; ViU.
3585

Starkweather, J.
The advice of Gamaliel. Il-
lustrated and enforced. A ser-
mon. Boston, Pr. by T. R.
Marvin, 1830. 22 p. MBC; MH-
AH; MNe; MWA. 3586

Stärr, John.
Ueber den Zustand der Seele
nach dem ode bis zur Auferweck-
ung ihres Körpers. Nach den
Ansichten der verschiedensten
Völker und Seeten bis zur Auf-
klärung der Bibel. Von John
Stärr. Orwigsburg, Penns.
Gedruckt bey Thoma und May,
1830. 36 p. PPL. 3587

State of the application to Congress. See Gilpin, Joshua.

State register, of Connecticut
for 1831. Hartford, H. & F. J.
Huntington; P. B. Gleason & Co.
prs. [1830] 77 l. CtHi; CtY;
MHi; MWA. 3588

State Rights Party. Charleston,
S. C.
    Proceedings and the resolution
and address adopted by the State
Rights Party in Charleston at a
meeting held at the Carolina coffee house, on Thursday evening,
9th Sept., 1830. [Charleston]
A. E. Miller [1830] 14 p. CSmH;
MB; NHi; PPAmP; ScHi; ScU.
                                    3589
---- Proceedings of the State
Rights celebration at Charleston,
S. C., July 1st, 1830. Containing
the speeches of the Hon. Wm.
Drayton & Hon. R. Y. Hayne,
who were the invited guests; also
of Langdon Cheves, James Hamilton, jr. and Robert J. Turnbull,
esqrs. and the remarks of His
Honor the intendant, H. L. Pinckney, to which is added the volun-
teer toasts given on the occasion.
Charleston, Pr. by A. E. Miller,
1830. 56 p. AB; CSmH; CU; CtY;
DLC; MHi; NN; NcD; OCHP; RP;
ScC; ScHi; ScU.   3590

A statement of facts, relative to
the building of the meeting
house. See Knowles, Jonathan.

A statement ot the Indian relations; with a reply to the article
in the sixty-sixth number of the
North American Review, on the
removal of the Indians. New
York, Clayton & Van Norden,
prs., 1830. 21 p. CSmH; DLC;
ICU; MdHi; NIC; NbHi; OClWHi;
PHi; PPAmP; PPL.   3591

A statistical chart of the United
States, with the distances and
population of the principal towns,
according to the census of 1830
... Hartford, Conn., Folsom &
Hurlbut, prs. [1830] 1 p. DLC.
                                    3592
---- New-Haven, Conn., Bald-
win & Treadway, prs. [183-?]
Bdsd. CSmH.   3593

---- [Washington, D. C.] C. L.
Adams [1830] 1 p. DLC; RPB.
                                    3594
Stearns, Charles, 1753-1826.
    The ladies' philosophy of love,
in four cantos. Woodstock,
1830. 49 p. VtU.   3595

Stearns, John Glazier.
    Calvinism and Arminianism
compared and tested by the scriptures. Utica, From the press
of Bennett & Bright, 1830. 166 p.
ICU; N; NRAB; NUt.   3596

Steele, J.
    The substance of an address
delivered by Rev. J. Steele, in
the Associated Reformed Synod
of the West at their meeting in
Steubenville, on the evening of
October 16th, 1829, on the question of making the holding of
slaves a term of communion in
the church. Washington, Guern-
sey Co., O., Pr. by Hamilton
Robb, 1830. 43, [1] p. CSmH;
OClWHi; OO; PPPrHi; TxU; WHi.
                                    3597
Steele, John B.
    The signs of the millennium;
a sermon at the anniversary of
the missionary society... New
York, Rutgers Press, William
A. Mercein, pr., 1830. 22 p.
NjR.   3598

Steele, Oliver, 1800-1861.
    A catalogue of theological,
medical, classical, miscellaneous and school books, for sale
by Oliver Steele, nos. 433 &
437 South Market-street, Albany.
[Albany] G. J. Loomis, 1830.
4, 85, [1] p. CSmH; MiU-C.
                                    3599
Steele's Albany almanack for
1831. Albany, Oliver Steele
[1830] 12 l. MWA; N; NCooHi;
NHi; NN; NSchU.   3600

Sterndale, Mary.
    Delia's birthday (and other in-

teresting stories). Boston, Munroe & Francis [183-] MB.   3601

Sterne, Laurence.
The works of Laurence Sterne, in one volume: with a life of the author, written by himself. Philadelphia, Pub. by Henry Adams, and sold by John Grigg. Stereotyped by J. Howe, 1830. [2], 416 p. CtHT; ICU; KyDC; MdAS; MdBL; NBu; NRAB; OCh; PP; TNJ; ViL.   3602

Stetson, Caleb, 1793-1870.
A sermon preached before the Ancient and Honorable Artillery Company, June 7, 1830, on the celebration of the 192d anniversary. Cambridge, E. W. Metcalf & Co., 1830. 19 p. M; MH-AH; MHi; NCH; NhHi; OMC; PU; BrMus.   3603

Stewart, Alvan, 1790-1849.
Prize address, by Alvan Stuart [!] esq., Utica, N.Y. for the New-York Temperance Society. [n.p., 183-?] 24 p. CSmH.   3604

Stockman, John R.
To the voters of Hardin and Meade Counties... Your fellow-citizens John R. Stockman. July 14th, 1830. 3 p. DLC.   3605

Stockton, Joseph, 1779-1832.
The western calculator; or, A new compendious system of practical arithmetic; containing the elementary principles and rules of calculation, in whole, mixed, and decimal numbers. Arranged, defined, and illustrated in a plain and natural order, and adapted to the use of schools, throughout the western country, and the present commerce of the United States. In eight parts. By J. Stockton, A.M. 6th ed. Pittsburgh, Pr. and pub. by Johnston & Stockton, 1830. 203, [1] p. CSmH.   3606

Stoddard's diary; or Columbia almanack for 1831. By Edwin E. Prentiss. Hudson, A. Stoddard [1830] 12 l. MWA; NHi; PHi.   3607

The stolen fruit; An interesting story. New-Haven, S. Babcock. Sidney's Press, 1830. 17 p. CtHi.   3608

Stone, Thomas Treadwell, 1801-1895.
Sketches of Oxford county... Portland [Me.] Shirley & Hyde, 1830. 111, [1] p. DLC; MH; MeHi; NBLiHi; OClWHi; WHi.   3609

Stories of the Spanish conquests in America. See Sedgwick, Catherine Maria.

Stories of Waterloo. See Maxwell, William Hamilton.

Storrs, Henry Randolph, 1787-1837.
....Speech of Mr. Storrs, of New York, in committee of the whole house, on the bill for the removal of the Indians west of the Mississippi. Utica, Pr. and pub. by Northway & Porter, 1830. 53 p. GDC; GU; IC; IU; KHi; MB; MBC; MeB; N; NCH; NN; WHi.   3610

[Story, Robert]
Peace in believing: A memoir of Isabella Campbell of Rosneath, Dumbartonshire, Scotland. With a preliminary essay, by an American clergyman... From the last English edition. New York, Jonathan Leavitt; Boston, Crocker & Brewster [G. L. Austin & Co., prs.] 1830. 307 p. MB; MeB; PP; PPL; VtU.   3611

The story of a revolutionary patriot; or the singular adventures of General Putnam. For the children of the United States.

New Haven, A. H. Maltby, 1830.
67 p. MH; MWA; WHi.   3612

The story of Alice Green. See
Goodrich, Samuel Griswald.

The story of little Benjamin; or
Confess your faults. Concord,
N. H. , R. H. Sherburne & Co. ,
1830. 16 p. NhHi.   3613

Stout, Z. Barton.
    An address, delivered before
the Domestic Horticultural Society of the western part of New
York, at its annual meeting, in
Geneva, Sept. 28, 1830. By Z.
Barton Stout. (Published at the
request of the society.) Canandaigua, Pr. by Morse & Harvey,
1830. 15, [1] p. CSmH;
NCanHi; PPAmP.   3614

Stow, Alexander W.
    An address delivered April 17,
1830, before the Young Men's
Temperance Society of Rochester,
Alexander W. Stow, Esq. Rochester, Pr. by Tuttle & Sherman, 1830. 32 p. Copy in library of Admiral Franklin Han-
ford, Scottsville, N. Y.   3615

Stow, Baron, 1801-1869.
    An address, delivered before
the Epping Temperance Society,
November 9, 1830. Portsmouth,
N. H. , Pr. by Miller & Brewster,
1830. 16 p. Nh.   3616

---- An address, delivered before
the Portsmouth Temperance Society, October 25, 1830. By
Baron Stow... Portsmouth, N. H. ,
Pr. by Miller & Brewster, 1830.
16 p. DLC; MBC.   3617

---- An address delivered before
the Temperance Society of South-
Berwick, Me. , Nov. 26, 1829.
... 2d ed. Portsmouth, N. H. ,
Pub. by Miller & Brewster, 1830.
24 p. MBC; Nh; OO.   3618

The stranger's guide. See Tanner, Henry Schenck.

The stray lamb. New York,
Mahlon Day [c 1830] 8 p. ICU;
PP.   3619

---- J. Metcalf, Wendell, 1830.
8 p. MA.   3620

Street, Alfred Billings.
    An oration, delivered in Mon-
ticello, July 5th, 1830, by Alfred B. Street. Monticello, Pr.
by Frederick A. De Voe, 1830.
12 p. N; RPB.   3621

Streeter, Russell.
    The crafty designs of the
orthodox clergy exposed, through
the carelessness of one of their
agents. Together with a solemn
appeal to all lovers of civil and
religious liberty. Woodstock,
Pr. by E. Avery, 1830. 16 p.
MMeT-Hi.   3622

Strictures on Mr. Lee's exposition. See Johnston, Josiah
Stoddard.

Strictures on seceding Masons.
See Boston Masonic Mirror.

[Stringer, Mrs.]
    The chain of affection; a mor-
al poem; and other pieces, by a
Lady [Mrs. Stringer] Privately
printed, Richmond [1830?]
BrMus.   3623

Strong, Titus.
    Young scholars manual, or
Companion to the spelling book,
consisting of easy lessons in the
several branches of early education. Intended for the use of
schools... 8th ed. Greenfield,
Mass. , Pub. by A. Phelps. Also
for sale by... Goodwin & co. ,
Hartford, 1830. 93 p. CtHi;
BrMus.   3624

Stuart, Moses, 1780-1852.

Course of Hebrew study adapted to the use of beginners. ... Vol. II. Andover, Pr. and pub. by Flagg & Gould. Also by Crocker and Brewster, Boston, and Jonathan Leavitt, New York. 1830. 204 p. CtHT-W; GDC; MBAt; MWA; NN; ViRU; BrMus. 3625

---- Essay on the prize-question, whether the use of distilled liquors, or traffic in them, is compatible, at the present time, with making a profession of Christianity? New York, Pub. by John P. Haven. Boston, Perkins & Marvin; Philadelphia, Towar, J. & D. M. Hogan & co.; Pittsburg, Hogan & co. Flagg & Gould, prs., Andover, 1830. 70 p. CSmH; CtHC; ICN; In-Hi; MBC; MB; MBC; MH-AH; MeBaT; MnHi; NIC; NNS; NNUT; NjR; PPL; PPPrHi; RPB; TxH; BrMus. 3626

---- Exegetical essays on several words relating to future punishment. Andover, Pr. at the Codman Press by Flagg & Gould, for Perkins & Marvin, 1830. 156 p. CBPac; CtHC; GDC; ICU; MB; MBAt; MDeeP; NGH; NNUT; NhD; OClW; OKU; RPB; TxH; VtU. 3627

---- A letter to William E. Channing, D.D. on the subject of religious liberty. Boston, Perkins & Marvin, 1830. 52 p. CBPac; CtHC; ICN; MA; MB; MBAt; MBC; MHi; MMeT; MWA; MeB; MiD-B; MoSpD; NN; NjR; OClWHi; PHC; RPB; VtU; WHi. 3628

---- ---- 2d ed. Boston, Perkins & Marvin, 1830. 52 p. CtHT-W; DLC; MB; MBAt; MH-AH; MHi; MWA; NHi; NNUT; NbCrD; NjR; PPL; RHi; RPB; BrMus. 3629

---- ---- 3d ed. Boston, Per-

kins and Marvin, 1830. 52 p. CBPac; CtHT-W; CtY; MBAt; MH; MHi; MWA; MeHi; NN; OClWHi; PHi; PPAmP; PPPrHi; RNR; BrMus. 3630

The substance of a letter, said to be from a Committee of Devils to a Gentleman, and his answer to said Committee. Wilmington, O., Pr. by W.H.P. Denny [1830] 48 p. CSmH; DLC. 3631

Sullivan, John Langdon, 1777-1865.

A description of a sub-marine aqueduct, to supply New-York with water from New-Jersey: connected with a commercial canal, and rail-way, for the direct western trade of this city. New-York, G. & C. & H. Carvill [Ludwig & Tolefree, prs.] 1830. 29 p. MiU-T; NN; NNE; PPL; ScU; WHi. 3632

---- Practical principles of railways, proper for the climate of the United States, and adapted to the use of the Winans rail-way carriage. [1830] 20 p. DBRE; DLC; NN. 3633

---- Profits of rail roads in the United States considered; with a description of the compound leverage carriage, and explanations of its increase of effect of power. Also, an inquiry into the proper method of building railroads, in reference to the climate of the middle and northern states. With some remarks on the partial application of the United States revenue to internal improvements. By J. L. Sullivan ... New York, Pr. by Clayton & Van Norden, 1830. 20 p. CSt. 3634

[----] Proposition for an anthracite coal steam power boat and barge company, for passengers on the North River. [New York]

Pr. by Clayton & Van Norden, [1830] 12 p. DLC; WHi.   3635

Sullivan, Thomas Russell.
A discourse at the dedication of the Congregational Meeting-house, April 28, 1830. Keene, J. & J. W. Prentiss, prs., 1830. 25 p. CtHT; CtY; MB; MH-AH; MiD-B; NhHi; PPAmP; RPB; BrMus.   3636

Sullivan, William, 1774-1839.
A discourse delivered before the Pilgrim Society, at Plymouth, on the twenty-second day of December, 1829. Boston, Carter and Hendee [Pr. by Isaac R. Butts] 1830. 60 p. CtSoP; DLC; ICU; MB; MBAt; MH-AH; MHi; MiD-B; NIC; NjN; NjR; OCLaw; PHi; PPL; RPB; ScCC; BrMus.
3637
---- The political class book; intended to instruct the higher classes in schools, in the origin, nature and use of political power ... With an appendix upon studies of practical men; with notices of books suited to their use. By George B. Emerson. Boston, Richardson, Lord & Holbrook, 1830. xxi, 148 p. CSt; CtY; DLC; ICMe; MB; MH; MWA; MoS; NGH; NNC; OHi; OMC; PWW.
3638
A summary view. See Hudson, Charles.

Sumner, John Bird.
Apostical preaching considered in an examination of St. Paul's epistles. ...1st American ed. New-York, Pub. by the New-York Protestant Episcopal Press, 1830. 236, [7] p. CBCDS; CtHT; MH-AH; OC; WM.   3639

The Sun Anti-Masonic almanac for 1831. By Wm. Collom. Philadelphia, J. Clarke [1830] 18 l. InU; MWA; N; NIC; NNFM; NjR; P; PP; PPFM; PPeSchw.   3640

The Sunday Scholar's baptism. New York, General Protestant Episcopal Sunday School Union, Pr. at the Protestant Episcopal Press, 1830. 16 p. PHi.   3641

The Sunday School children. (A story.) Revised by the Committee of Publication. Philadelphia, American Sunday School Union [1830?] 30 p. DLC; BrMus.
3642
Sunday School Teacher's convention. [Philadelphia, 1830] 7, [1] p. PPL.   3643

Sunday mails; or, Inquiries into the origin, institution and proper mode of observance, of the first day of the week, or Christian Sabbath. Philadelphia, Pub. for the benefit of Sunday Mails, 1830. 36 p. CU; MH; MHi; PHi; PPL; PPPrHi.   3644

Sutherland, Joel B.
A manual of legislative practice and order of business in deliberative bodies. 2d ed. Philadelphia, Pr. by P. Hay & Co., 1830. v, [2], 245, [1], 144 p. CU; ICU; MB; MHi; Nj; P; PHi; PLFM; PU; TxU; BrMus.   3645

Swan, William.
Memoir of the late Mrs. Paterson, wife of the Rev. Dr. Paterson, St. Petersburg; Containing extracts from her diary and correspondence. By the Rev. William Swan, Missionary at Selinginsk. From the 3d Edinburgh ed. Boston, Pub. by Perkins & Marvin, 1830. xii, [9]-212 p. Ct; GDC; NNUT; PPiW; ViRUT.   3646

Swedenborg, Emanuel, 1688-1772.
A brief exposition of the doctrine of the New Church which is meant by the New Jerusalem in the Apocalypse. Trans. from

the Latin of Emanuel Swedenborg
originally published in Amster-
dam in the year 1769... Boston,
A. Howard, 1830. iv, 92 p. CU;
CtMW; MB; MH; MdBP; NCH;
Nh; RPA; WHi.   3647

---- The Decaloque explained,
as to its external and internal
sense. [Boston, 183-?] 40 p.
(Boston Society of the New Jerusalem. New Jerusalem tracts,
7). MH.   3648

---- New Jerusalem tracts. Vol.
1 By Emanuel Swedenborg. Boston, A. Howard, 1830. 92 p.
CtMW; MB; NjP; RPB; WHi.
                            3649

Sweetser, William, 1797-1875.
   An address delivered before
the Chittenden County Temperance
Society, August 26, 1830. Pub-
lished by request of the Society.
Burlington, Pr. by Chauncey
Goodrich, 1830. 19 p. M; MH;
MMeT; VtHi; VtU; BrMus. 3650

---- An address, delivered
March 24, 1830, before a meeting of the young men of Burlington; assembled for the purpose
of forming a Temperance Society. Published by request of
the Society. Burlington, Chauncey Goodrich, 1830. 12 p. MH;
NN.   3651

Swigert, Jacob, 1793-1869.
   The Kentucky justice comprising the office and authority of
justices of the peace, constables,
jailers, coroners and escheators.
in the state of Kentucky, whether
arising under the common or
statute law of the state, or the
laws of the United States...2d
ed. Frankfort, Ky., Jacob H.
Holeman, 1830. viii, 2-309 p.
In; KyLoF.   3652

Swords's pocket almanack,
Churchman's calendar for 1831.

New-York, T. & J. Swords;
Edward J. Swords, pr. [1830]
50 l. MHi; MWA; N; NHi; NNG;
NNS; NjR; PHi; PP; PPL;
BrMus.   3653

Sydney, pseud.
   Sydney, on retrocession. To
the Congress of the United
States. [Washington, 183-?] 15
p. DLC; MB; ScU.   3654

A syllabus of plane trigonometry;
containing as much of the science as is requisite to under-
stand the more advanced parts
of mathematics, together with a
full account of the method of
forming trigonometrical tables.
Cambridge, Pr. for W. T.
Grant, 1830. 2 p. l., ii, 64 p.,
1 l. CtY.   3655

A system of school geography.
See Goodrich, Samuel Griswold.

T

...A table of logarithms, of
logarithmic sines, and a tra-
verse table. New York, J. &
J. Harper, 1830. 91 p. (At
head of title: Harper's stereo-
type edition.) NN; OClW; OMC.
                            3656
Tafel, John Frederick Immanu-
el.
   Letter to the Rev. Manning
B. Roche, of the New Jerusalem
Church, by John Frederick Im-
manuel Tafel, D.D., Librarian
of the University of Tubingen.
Philadelphia, Thomas S. Man-
ning, pr., 1830. 15 p. MB.
                            3657
Die Täglichen Loosungen und
Lehrtexte der Brüdergemeine
für das Jahr 1831. Allentown,
Gedruckt bey Heinrich Ebner und
Comp. 1830. 121, [1] p. MA;
WHi.   3658

Talbot, Mary Elizabeth.
  Rurality. Original desultory
tales. Providence, Marshall &
Hammond, prs., 1830. 196 p.
CSmH; CtY; DLC; ICU; MB; MH;
MnU; NNC; NcD; NcU; NjP; PU;
RHi; RP; RPB.   3659

Tales and sketches. See Lawson, James.

Tales from American history.
See Robbins, Eliza.

Tales of the Northwest. See
Snelling, William Joseph.

Tales of travels west. See
Snelling, William Joseph.

The Tame pheasant or Benevo-
lence rewarded. New York, S.
King [183-?] 20 p. PPeSchw.
                                 3660
Tanner, Henry Schenck, pub.,
1786-1858.
  Index to the new plan of Philadelphia and adjoining districts
with references to find the streets
public buildings, etc. Philadelphia, Pub. by H. S. Tanner,
Mifflin and Parry, 1830. 44 p.
DLC; PP; PPAmP (44, 16 p.);
PPL; PU.   3661

---- [Map of the] United States
of America: by H. S. Tanner,
1830. 2d ed. [Philadelphia, Henry S. Tanner, 1830] NN.   3662

---- Memoir on the recent surveys, observations, and internal
improvements, in the United
States, with brief notices of the
new counties, towns, villages,
canals and rail-roads, never be-
for delineated. By H. S. Tanner.
Intended to accompany his new
map of the United States. 2d ed.
Philadelphia, Pub. by the author,
1830. [2], 108, [8] p. CSmH;
CtY; DBRE; DLC; ICJ; IHi;
MBAt; MH; MWA; NN; NcD; NjP;

P; PPL; PU; TxU.   3663

[----] A plan of Philadelphia,
or The stranger's guide to the
public buildings, places of
amusement... Philadelphia, Carey
and Hart; Pr. by James Kay,
Jun. & Co., 1830. CSmH.   3664

---- Plan of Pittsburg and adjacent country surveyed by Wm.
Darby. Pittsburg, Pub. by R.
Patterson, and W. Darby; Philadelphia, Engraved by H. S. Tanner [1830] map. PPAmP. 3665

[----] The strangers' guide to
the public buildings, places of
amusement, streets lanes...
steam-boat landings, stage offices, etc., etc. of the city of
Philadelphia and adjoining districts... 2d ed. Philadelphia,
Pub. by H. S. Tanner, Mifflin
and Parry, prs., 1830. 38, 16
p. "A list of maps, charts, and
geographical works, recently published, and for sale by H. S.
Tanner..." 16 p. at end. DeGE;
PHi; PPL.   3666

---- Traveller's pocket map of
Ohio with its canals, roads, &
distances. [Philadelphia, H. S.
Tanner, c 1830] OO.   3667

---- "The traveller's pocket map
of Pennsylvania." Philadelphia
[Henry S. Tanner, c 1830]
DBRE; DLC; MB; MH.   3668

---- The travellers pocket map
of Tennessee with its roads and
distances from place to place
along the stage and steamboat
routes. Philadelphia, H. S. Tanner [c 1830] NNF.   3669

Tanner, John, 1780?-1847.
  A narrative of the captivity
and adventures of John Tanner,
(U. S. interpreter at the Saut [!]
de Ste. Marie,) during thirty

years residence among the Indians in the interior of North America, Prepared for the press by Edwin James. New York, G. & C. & H. Carvill, 1830. 426 p. CSmH; DLC; ICN; KU; KyU; MB; Md; MnHi; NN; NcD; NjP; PHi; PPL; ScU; ViU; VtU; WHi. 3670

The tariff: its true character and effects, practically illustrated. Charleston, Pr. by A. E. Miller, 1830. 2 l., 52 p. CtY; DLC; MHi; MdBJ; NN; PPAmP; PU; ScU. 3671

[Taylor, Isaac] 1787-1865.
Natural history of enthusiasm ... Boston, Pub. by Crocker & Brewster; New York, J. Leavitt, 1830. 302 p. CBPac; CtHT; FTa; ICU; KyLoP; LNHT; MB; MH; MWA; MdBP; MoSpD; NN; NNUT; NjR; OC; P; TN. 3672

[----] New model of Christian missions to popish, Mahometan, and pagan nations, explained in four letters to a friend. ...New York, Leavitt; Boston, Crocker & Brewster, 1830. 152 p. LNHT; MBC; MeB; NCH; NIC; NSyU; NjMD; OMC; RPA. 3673

---- Scenes in America, for the amusement and instruction of little tarry-at-home travellers. Hartford, Pub. by Silas Andrus, 1830. 117 p. MB; NBuG; NhHi. 3674

---- Scenes in Asia, for the amusement and instruction of little tarry-at-home travellers. Hartford, Silas Andrus; New York, Stereotyped by James Conner, 1830. vi, [4], 7-124 p. CtHi; MNF; MPB; MdBL; NBLiHi. 3675

Taylor, Jane, 1783-1824.
The contributions of Q. Q. to a periodical work: with some pieces not before published by the late Jane Taylor. Philadel-

phia, Thomas Kite, 1830. 2 vols. MH; PHi. 3676

---- A day's pleasure: to which are added Reflections on a day's pleasure, and Busy idleness. New-York, Pr. and sold by Mahlon Day, at the new juvenile book-store, 1830. 47 p. MB. 3677

---- ... "I can do without it." By Miss Jane Taylor, Published by the "Episcopal Female Tract Society of Philadelphia," for the "Society of the Protestant Episcopal Church for the Advancement of Christianity in Pennsylvania." [Philadelphia, William Stavely, pr., 1830?] 4 p. Religious tracts, - No. 73. PPL. 3678

---- Lucy's wishes; or The folly of idle thoughts by Jane Taylor. New-York, Pr. and sold by Mahlon Day, 1830. 18 p. MH. 3679

Taylor, John.
History of Clear Creek Church; and Campbellism exposed. Frankfort [Ky.] Pr. by A. G. Hodges, 1830. 60 p. ICU; NGH; PPPrHi. 3680

Taylor, Nathaniel William, 1786-1858.
Review of Dr. Tyler's strictures on the means of regeneration. New Haven, Baldwin & Treadway, 1830. 56 p. CU; Ct; ICU; IU; MA; MBC; NCH; OClW. 3681

Taylor, Thomas, 1758-1835.
Jacob wrestling with God and prevailing; or A treatise concerning the necessity and efficacy of faith in prayer... 1st American ed. Published by James M'-Greger. Harrisburg [Pa.] Pr. by Francis Wyeth, 1830. 138 p. CSmH; DLC; MdBB; P; PHi. 3682

A teacher. See Conversations on common things.

A teacher of little children in
Philadelphia. See Ely, John.

Teale, Thomas Pridgin, 1801?-
1867.
    A treatise on neuralgic dis-
eases, dependent upon irritation
of the spinal marrow and gang-
lia of the sympathetic nerve. ...
Concord, Pub. by Horatio Hill &
co., [1830?] iv, 120 p. DLC;
MiU; MoU; NcD; ViU.   3683

---- ---- Philadelphia, E. L.
Carey and A. Hart; Thomas Kite,
pr., 1830. iv, 120 p. ArU-M;
CSt-L; CU; DLC; DNLM; ICJ;
IU; KyLxT; MH; MoSU-M; NN;
NNNAM; NhD; OCGHM; OClM;
OU; PP; PPC; PU; RPM.   3684

Tekatoka.
    To "Standing Bear," alias Gen.
Samuel Houston. Sir: [Little
Rock, 1830] Bdsd. National Un-
ion Catalog: Hargrett.   3685

Temperance almanack for 1831.
Rochester, Pr. and pub. by E.
Peck & Co. [1830] 18 l. NR;
NRMA.   3686

---- Rochester, Pr. and sold by
E. Peck & Co. [1830] 12 l.
Drake 7118.   3687

Temperance Society of Fishkill-
Landing.
    First annual report of the
board of managers of the Temperance Society of Fishkill-Land-
ing. Presented at the Annual
meeting, August 10, 1830. [Par-
menter and Spalding, prs., New-
burgh] 8 p. NN.   3688

Temperance Society of Virginia.
    The third annual report of the
Virginia Society for the Promotion of Temperance. [Richmond?
1830?] 20 p. Vi.   3689

Templi carmina. See Brown,

Bartholomew.

The Ten Commandments. Philadelphia, American Sunday School
Union [183-?] 16 p. NN; BrMus.
                             3690
... Ten dialogues on the effects
of ardent spirits. New York,
Pub. by The American Tract Society, [183-?] 32 p. NN.   3691

Tennessee.
    Acts passed at the stated ses-
sion of the eighteenth General
Assembly of the state of Tennes-
see, 1829. Printed by authority.
Allen A. Hall & Frederick S.
Heiskell, prs. to the state.
Nashville, Pr. at the Office of
the Republican and Gazette,
1829 [i. e. 1830] viii, 147,
xxxix, xv, 308, L p., [1] p. er-
rata. DLC; IaU-L; In-SC; MH-
L; Mi-L; Mo; Ms; NN; NNB; Nj;
Nv; OCLaw; RPL; T; TKL; TU.
                             3692
---- Journal of the House of
Representatives, of the state of
Tennessee, at the eighteenth Gen-
eral Assembly, held at Nashville,
F. S. Heiskell & A. A. Hall, prs.
to the state. "Knoxville Regis-
ter" Office, F. S. Heiskell, pr.,
1829 [i. e. 1830] 836 p. 4 charts.
DLC; TKL.   3693

---- Journal of the Senate of the
state of Tennessee, at the eighteenth General Assembly, held
at Nashville. F.S. Heiskell & A.
A. Hall, prs. to the state.
"Knoxville Register" Office, F.
S. Heiskell, pr., 1829 [i. e.
1830] 692, [2] p. 4 charts. DLC;
NN; T; TKL.   3694

Tennessee State Medical Association.
    Transactions of the Medical
Society of the state of Tennessee, for the year 1830. Printed
by order of the Society. Nashville, Pr. at the Republican &

Gazette Office, 1830. 23 p.
DNLM; T.   3695

Terentius Afer, Publius.
    P. Terenti Carthaginiensis
Afri Andria. Notulis Aglicis il-
lustravit Cranmore Wallace, in
usum Juventutis Academicae.
Boston, Richardson, Lord, et
Holbrook, 1830. 80 p. MH; PPL;
PU.   3696

The testimony of truth. [Con-
cerning Odd Fellows of Pennsyl-
vania] Philadelphia, 1830. 12+ p.
PHi.   3697

Thacher, Moses, 1795-1878.
    An address, delivered before
the Anti-Masonic convention of
delegates, for Plymouth county,
assembled at Halifax, Mass. Dec.
9, 1829. Boston, John Marsh
& Co., 1830. 18, [2] p. MB;
MWA; MoSU; NIC; PPFM; PPL.
                                   3698
---- Masonic oaths neither mor-
ally nor legally binding. An ad-
dress, delivered at Weymouth,
South Parish, June 21, at Wor-
cester, July 5, on the fifty-
fourth anniversary of American
Independence; and at Reading,
July 12, 1830. Boston, Pub. by
Peirce & Williams, [1830] 30 p.
CSmH; CtSoP; DLC; MB; MHi;
MeBaT; PHi; PPFM; WHi;
BrMus.   3699

---- Masonic oaths neither mor-
ally nor legally binding. An address, delivered at Weymouth,
South Parish, June 21, at Worcester, July 5, on the fifty-
fourth anniversary of American
Independence, and at Reading,
July 12, 1830. Worcester,
Mass., Dorr & Howland, 1830.
30 p. IaCrM; MBC; MWA;
MWHi.   3700

Thacher, Tyler.
    Perfectionism examined (in a

sermon). New York [1830?]
BrMus.   3701

The thatcher's wife: or, An account of M. C. Philadelphia,
American Sunday School Union,
[1830?] BrMus.   3702

Thayer, G. F.
    A lecture on the spelling of
words, and a rational method of
teaching their meaning. Deliv-
ered in the Representatives' Hall,
Boston, August 21, 1830, before
the convention which formed the
American Institute of Instruction.
Boston, Hilliard, Gray, Little
& Wilkins, prs., 1830. 19 p.
MeB.   3703

Thayer, Nathaniel, 1769-1840.
    A discourse, delivered Janu-
ary 27, 1830, at the ordination
of the Rev. Christopher T.
Thayer, to the pastoral care of
the First Parish in Beverly.
Salem, Foote & Brown, 1830.
36 p. MBAU; MBC; MH-AH;
MeBaT; MiD-B; NCH; NjR; OO;
PHi; PPPrHi; RPB; BrMus. 3704

[Therry, Sir Roger] 1800-1874.
    Memoirs of the life of the
Right Honourable George Canning
... New-York, A. Sherman [etc.]
1830. 2 v. CSmH; KyLx; MH;
MeBa; NGH; NjR; PU.   3705

Thiersch, D. Friedrich.
    Greek tables; or A method of
teaching the Greek paradigm, in
a more simple and fundamental
manner... To which is added an
essay on the dialects, from
Buttmann's grammar. Translated
by R. B. Patton,... 2d ed., rev.
and enl. New York, G. & C. &
H. Carvill, 1830. 92 p. CtHT-
W; IaB; InGrD; LU; MH; NjR;
VtU.   3706

Thirteen essays. See Publicola.

Thirteen sermons on crimes of
an enormous nature and the
crimes of public men. ... To
which is added an address to the
working people. Philadelphia,
Pub. by W. A. Leary [183-?]
MB.   3707

Thomas A. Kempis, 1380-1471.
    An extract of the Christian's
pattern: or, A treatise on the
imitation of Christ, written in
Latin by Thomas A. Kempis. By
Rev. John Wesley, A. M. New
York, Pub. by J. Emory & B.
Waugh, for the Methodist Episcopal Church, at the conference
office, J. Collard, pr., 1830.
160 p. MiDSH.   3708

---- The imitation of Christ. In
three books. By Thomas A Kem-
pis, rendered into English from
the original Latin, by John Payne.
With an introductory essay, by
Thomas Chalmers, of Glasgow.
A new ed., Edited by Howard
Malcolm. Boston, Pub. by Lin-
coln & Edmands, 1830. 228 p.
CtY; ICMcC; ICN; MB; MWA;
MiD-B.   3709

---- Der Kleine Kempis, oder
kurze Sprüche und Gebethlein, aus
denen Meistens unbekannten werk-
lein des Thomae a Kempis. Harrisburg (Pa.), Bey Gustav S.
Peters, 1830. 256 p. PHi; PPL.
                                 3710
Thomas, Abel Charles, 1807-
1880.
    A lecture on capital punishment.
Delivered in the First Universalist Church, Philadelphia, on the
evening of June 20, 1830. Philadelphia, [M. Sharpless, pr.]
1830. 4-24 p. MMeT; MMeT-
Hi; MWA; PHi; PPL; PU.   3711

Thomas, Edward.
    On the necessity of promoting
the knowledge and practice of
Christianity. A sermon,

preached before the Protestant
Episcopal Society for the Ad-
vancement of Christianity, in
South Carolina, on its twentieth
anniversary, in St. Phillip's
Charleston, February 16th, 1830.
Charleston, Pr. by Archibald E.
Miller, 1830. 16 p. CSmH; NNG;
ScC.   3712

[Thomas, William]
    Address to the voters of Mor-
gan County. [Jacksonville?
1830] 4 p. IHi.   3713

Thomas and Ellen; or, The Bible
the best book. Philadelphia,
American Sunday School Union,
[1830?] BrMus.   3714

Thomason, John.
    A historical sketch of the
Thomasonian system of the practice of medicine on botanical
principles as originated by Samuel Thomson... Albany, Pr. by
B. D. Packard & Co., 1830.
NN; NNNAM; NhHi.   3715

Thompson, James, 1700-1748.
    The seasons, by James Thomp-
son, to which is prefixed the life
of the author, by P. Murdock,
D. D. F. R. S. New-York, S. & D.
A. Forbes, prs., 1830. v. p.
MB; MH; NN.   3716

Thompson, Otis, 1776-1859.
    A sermon, preached at the fu-
neral of Mr. Joseph Smith, who
died suddenly, on the 17th of
June, 1830 in the seventy-second
year of his age. Providence, Wm.
Marshall & Co., prs. [1830] 12 p.
CSmH; RPB; BrMus.   3717

Thompson, Pishey, bookseller,
Washington, D. C.
    Catalogue of books: a great
proportion of which are for sale,
at very low prices, by Pishey
Thompson, Washington city...
Philadelphia, J. Grigg, 1830.

39, [1] p. DLC; KyDC.   3718

---- Catalogue of books on sale, by Pishey Thompson... Washington city... Georgetown, D. C., Pr. by Benjamin Homans, 1830. 88 p. DLC; KyDC.   3719

Thomson, James.
Address directed to the citizens of the United States of America, on behalf of the new nations lately subject to the Spanish government. (Signed, James Thomson.) New York, D. Fanshaw, 1830. 23 p. MBAt; NN.
3720

Thornton, John.
The fruits of the spirit, being a comprehensive view of the principal graces which adorn the Christian character. ...1st American from the 4th London ed. Portland, Shirley, Hyde & Co., 1830. 274 p. GDC; MH-AH; OCL.   3721

Thoughts on reason and revelation, particularly the revelation on the scriptures. Philadelphia, To be had of Thomas Kite, 1830. 12 p. InRE.   3722

Thoughts on vital religion. 2d ed. ... Boston, Gray and Bowen [Pr. by I. R. Butts] 1830. 16 p. 1st series, No. 38. American Unitarian Association. CBPac; ICMe; MBAU; MH-AH; MHi; MMeT-Hi; MNF; MeB; MeLB; N; Nh; ViU.
3723
Three letters to the editor of the American Quarterly Review. See White, William.

Tillinghast, John L.
A general collection of forms and precedents, ...in civil actions at law; adapted to the revised statutes of the state of New York. By John L. Tillinghast, counsellor at law. Albany, Pub. by William Gould and Co., 1830.

801 p.   C; IU-Law; In-SC; MH-L; Ms; N-L; NNLI; NbU-L; OClW; RPL.   3724

The timely remembrancer; or, A warning from heaven to all vile sinners upon earth... New York, Pr. at Greenwich printing office, 1830. 8 p. NjR.   3725

Timothy, pseud.   See Fifty-five reasons.

'Tis all for the best.   See More, Hannah.

Tiverton, R. I.   Calvinistic Congregational Church.
Articles of faith and form of covenant, adopted by the Calvinistic Congregational Church in Tiverton, A. D. 1829, with scripture proofs and illustrations. To which are added, Rules of practice, to be observed in the discipline of the church. Published by order of the church, for the use of its members. Jonathan King, pastor of said church. New-Bedford, Stephen S. Smith, 1830. 12 p. RPB.   3726

To the citizens of Nashville. To redress a grievance of a personal chastisement, which I felt it my duty to inflict on Nathaniel Dick of New Orleans, on Tuesday last, he has appealed to your "justice and magnanimity." ... Nashville, November 16th, 1830. Bdsd. DLC.   3727

... To the Hon. Thos. H. Benton, Senator from the state of Missouri. (Illinois Gazette Extra. Vol. X. Shawneetown, Ill. November 22, 1830.) Bdsd. I-Ar.
3728
To the independent yeomanry of the Jackson party. [New York? 183-?] 8 p. NNC.   3729

To the ingenious and candid. See
Moore, Charles Whitlock.

To the members of the General
Assembly of Rhode Island.
[1830] 24 p. RHi.   3730

To the members of the Legislature... A Looker-on. Albany,
March 31, 1830. The currency
... 2 l., 3 p. NN   3731

---- Albany, April 1st, 1830.
History of banking in Pennsylvania... 2 l., 4 p. NN.   3732

To the people. No. 4. [Philadel-
phia? 183-?] Signed Homo. 6 p.
PU.   3733

To the public. See Slaughter,
James.

To the Rev. Mr. Moore, in Hallowell. (A letter, signed "Block-
head," in defense of Universalism.) [Boston? 1830?] 8 p.
BrMus.   3734

To the voters of St. Mary's
County. See Dorsey, John Larkin.

To the voters of the First ward.
Fellow-citizens, You will all
agree with me, that any man who
stands convicted by a jury of his
countrymen of fraud, deserves
not their suffrage for the mean-
est office in their gift. - Therefore, examine your tickets carefully before you vote to-day...
[Washington] Monday, June 7th,
1830. 1 p. DLC.   3735

To the working men of Washington. Fellow-citizens, This day
assert your rights as freemen,
in the election of a chief magis-
trate of the City... [Signed] A
mechanic. June 7th, 1830. 1 p.
DLC.   3736

To those commencing a religious
life. [New York, American
Tract Society, 183-?] 8 p. (American Tract Society, New York
[Publications. (Separates)] no.
262). CSmH.   3737

Todd, Charles W.
   An apology for leaving the
Presbyterian, and joining with
the Protestant Episcopal Church;
in a letter addressed to Union
Presbytery of East Tennessee.
...together with a brief view of
the evidence which induced a
change in his sentiments relative to church government. Knoxville, T., Pr. by F. S. Heiskell, 1830. 36 p. PPPrHi. 3738

The token; a Christmas and New
Year's present. Ed. by S. G.
Goodrich... Boston, Gray and
Bowen, 1831 [i.e. 1830] 320 p.
NNC.   3739

Tom Steady. See American
Tract Society. New York.

Tommy Wellwood. See American Tract Society. New York.

Toplady, Augustus.
   The doctrine of absolute pre-
destination stated and asserted
with a preliminary discourse on
the divine attributes... Philadelphia, L. A. Key, 1830. 216 p.
NjR; PPPrHi; PPiW; ScU;
TxAuPT.   3740

Torrey, Jesse.
   The moral instructor, and
guide to virtue: being a compendium of moral philosophy.
In 8 parts... 25th ed. Philadelphia, Pub. and sold by John
Grigg, and sold by booksellers
and country merchants generally.
Stereotyped by J. Howe, 1830.
300 p. NCH; PLFM; PSC-Hi; TNJ.
                                3741
Torrey, Jesse.

A pleasing companion for little girls and boys: blending instruction with amusement. Being a selection of interesting stories, dialogues, fables and poetry... 2d ed. rev. New York, Isaac T. Hopper. Philadelphia, M. T. C. Gould, Stereotyped by L. Johnson, 1830. 142 p. NN; PSC-Hi. 3742

---- ---- 25th ed. Philadelphia, Pub. and sold by John Grigg, and sold by Booksellers and Country Merchants generally. Stereotyped by L. Johnson, 1830. 2 vols. PRHi. 3743

Toulmin, G. H.
The eternity of the universe. Philadelphia, Pr. for the Publisher, J. Coates, Jr., pr., 1830. 113 p. MB. 3744

The tourist. See Vandewater, Robert J.

Tower, Reuben.
An appeal to the people of the state of New-York, in favor of the construction of the Chenango Canal, with statements and documents, to prove the claim of that part of the state for this improvement; and arguments on the subject of the supply of water, cost of construction, and revenue. By Col. R. Tower. Utica, Dauby & Maynard, prs., 1830. 32 p. CSmH; CtY; DLC; ICJ; IU; M; MB; MBC; N; NBu; NCH; NN; NUt; NbU; RPB; WHi; BrMus. 3745

Town and country almanc for 1831. By Nathan Bassett. Baltimore, Cushing & Sons; William Wooddy, pr. [1830] 18 l. DLC. 3746

Townley, James, 1714-1778.
...High life below stairs; a farce, in two acts. New-York, E. B. Clayton, 1830. Clayton's ed. MH. 3747

Tracy, Joseph, 1793?-1874.
Christian liberty. A sermon, at the ordination of the Rev. Daniel Wild, as Pastor of the Congregational Church in Brookfield, Vt., July 1, 1830. Pub. by request of the Church and Society, and of the Ordaining Council. Windsor, Pr. at the Chronicle Press, by John C. Allen, 1830. [3]-16 p. CtHC; ICN; MBC; MiD-B; NN; RPB; Vt; VtMiM; VtU. 3748

Transylvania University.
Transylvania Journal of Medicine... Extra. A catalogue of the officers and students of Transylvania University, Lexington, Kentucky. January, 1830. Lexington, Kentucky, Pr. by J. G. Norwood, Short Street, 1830. 16 p. DLC; KyLxT; KyU; MBAt; MBC; MH; MHi; MWA; N; NN; PPAmP. 3749

A traveller, pseud. See Holbrook, Silas Pinckey.

The traveller's directory: exhibiting the distances on the principal land and water thoroughfares of the state of New-York: and showing the reciprocal and relative distances of each place from the chief towns on three routes between Albany and Buffalo. Rochester, Marshall, Dean & co., 1830. 12 p. DLC. 3750

Trenck, Friedrich, freiherr von der, 1726-1794.
The life, adventures and uncommon escapes of Frederick baron Trenck, the Prussian. Written by himself. Sandborton [N. H.] Howland and Moulton, 1830. 62 p. CtY. 3751

The trial and conviction of John Francis Knapp for the murder of Joseph White, Esq. of Salem on the sixth of April 1830. Boston,

Pub. by Charles Ellms, 1830.
35, [1] p. DLC; RNHi.   3752

Trial: Commonwealth vs. J. T.
Buckingham, on an indictment for
libel, 1822. 4th ed. Boston, J.
T. Buckingham; E. W. Metcalf &
co., prs., 1830. 56 p. MB;
MBAt; MH; NjR; PHi.   3753

The trial in the case of the Commonwealth, versus John Francis
Knapp, for the murder of Joseph
White, esq. of Salem, Mass. at
a special session of the S. J.
court, holden at Salem on the
third Tuesday in July, 1830.
[n.p., 1830?] 1 p. l., [5]-36 p.
DLC; MBC; PHi.   3754

Trial of Anti-Christ. See Gregory, William.

The trial of Colonel Charles L.
Harrison, accused of having
robbed the branch bank of the
Commonwealth of Kentucky, at
Louisville, of 25,000 dollars, on
the night of the 17th September,
1829. [By] a member of the bar.
Cincinnati, Pr. for the Reporter,
at the Chronicle office, 1830.
83 p. CtY-L.   3755

Trial of George Crowninshield,
J. J. Knapp, jun. and John Fran-
cis Knapp for the murder of
Capt. Joseph White, of Salem, on
the night of the sixth of April,
1830. Report by John W. Whit-
man, esq. Boston, Beals and
Homer [etc.] 1830. 104 p. CtY;
MB; MBNEH; MH-L; N-L; PPB;
RPB.   3756

Trial of John Francis Knapp as
principal in the second degree
for the murder of Capt. Joseph
White, before the Supreme judicial court of the commonwealth
of Massachusetts, at a special
session, commenced at Salem,
July 30, 1830. Reported for the

publishers. Boston, Dutton and
Wentworth, 1830. 60 p. Ct; DLC;
ICN; MB; MBNEH; MH; MNBedf;
Mi-L; N-L; NIC-A; NhHi; NjR;
PP.   3757

... Trial of John Francis Knapp
for the murder of Joseph White.
Boston, 1830. Boston Courier,
supplement. Aug. 14, 1830.
MBAt.   3758

Trial of Sanballet. See Purblind,
Pen.

Trials of Capt. Joseph J. Knapp,
jr. and George Crowninshield,
Esq. for the murder of Capt.
Joseph White, of Salem, on the
night of the sixth of April, 1830.
Boston, C. Ellms, 1830. 32 p.
ICN; MH.   3759

The tricolor: devoted to the
politics, literature, &c. of Conti-
nental Europe. Nos. 1 to IV inclusive... Containing a full account of the late Revolution in
France... by Robert Greenhow.
New York, Pr. by Ludwig &
Tolefree, 1830. 1 l., 65, [1] p.
DLC.   3760

The triple cord; or, Three plain
reasons why no Roman Catholic
can conform to the Protestant
Church. Boston, Pub. by Wm.
Smith, for the Editors of "The
Jesuit." 1830. 12 p. DGU. 3761

Triumph of liberal principles
over legal intolerance, as evi-
denced in Hudson City by the judicial authorites of Columbia
County, N.Y., on 15th April,
1830, by a Citizen. Hudson,
1830. 17 p. "From NN imprint.
catal., but not in NN."   3762

Troubat, Francis Joseph, 1802-
1868.
     A digest of the acts of Assem-
bly of Pennsylvania, passed in

the sessions of 1824-5, 1825-6, 1826-7, 1827-8, and 1828-9, with an appendix containing the acts passed in 1829-30. With notes of Judicial decisions. 2d ed. Philadelphia, Robert H. Small, pr., 1830. 308, 47 p. Ia; NNLI; WaU.   3763

---- A digest of the acts of Assembly of Pennsylvania, passed in the session of 1829-30. With notes of judicial decisions by Francis J. Troubat & William W. Haley, Philadelphia, R. H. Small, 1830. 47, [1] p. DLC; NNC.
                                  3764

The Troy directory, for 1830. Troy, Pr. and pub. by Tuttle & Gregory, 1830. 72 p. DLC; MWA; NT.   3765

A true and complete narrative. See Engles, William Morrison.

A true and faithful account of the most material circumstances attending the mysterious disappearance of Samuel Field and Francis C. Jenkerson, generally believed to have been murdered. Together with an account of the discovery of the bodies, as detailed in the examination before Justices Aplin, Staples and Patten, of Joseph Antoine, Johan Fransoeis Wohlfahrt and Joanna Susan Wohlfahrt, who were suspected of the murder of these unfortunate boys. Providence, Pr. and sold wholesale and retail by H. H. Brown, 1830. 36 p. DLC; MH; MH-L; NN; RHi; RNHi; RPB; BrMus.   3766

True piety. See David, J. B., bp.

True Reformed Dutch Church in the U.S.A.
    The acts and proceedings of the General Synod of the True Reformed Dutch Church, in the United States of America, At Owasco, June 1830. New-York, Pr. by M'Elrath & Bangs, 1830. 13 p. NSchHi.   3767

True Republican Society of Philadelphia.
    Constitution and by-laws of the True Republican Society, of the City & Liberties of Philadelphia. Philadelphia, Pr. for the Society, 1830. 36 p. PHi.   3768

Trueba y Cosio, Joaquin Telesforo, 1799?-1835.
    The romance of history. Spain. Subjects. The Gothic king, The cavern of Covadonga. By Don T. De Trueba... Watertown, Knowlton & Rice, 1830. 87 p. DLC; NjR.   3769

---- ---- New York, Pr. by J. & J. Harper, Sold by Collins & Hannay [etc.] 1830. 2 vols. CtHT; DLC; GDC; MdBP; NcG; PPL; RPB; TNJ; VtU.   3770

Trumbull, Henry.
    History of the discovery of America, of the landing of our forefathers, at Plymouth, and of their most remarkable engagements with the Indians in New England... Boston, Pub. by George Clark, 1830. 256 p. CoD; CtMW; DLC; DeWi; IU; MB; MHi; MdHi; MoSM; NN; NcU; NhHi; OClWHi; OHi; PU; T; TxDaM.
                                  3771

Truth advocated: in letters addressed to the Presbyterians. By Vindex. Baltimore, Pr. for the publisher, 1830. 180 p. CSmH; GDC; MdHi; PPPrHi.   3772

The truth stated and illustrated respecting the views, feelings and conduct of the persecuted minister, who was indicted and arrested for the correction of his adopted son. By Philandros. Concord, 1830. Sabin 97266. 3773

Truth's proofs. See Ogle, Alexander Jr.

Tucker, Mark, 1795-1875.
A plea for entire abstinence. A discourse, delivered in Troy ...January 17, before the Troy Temperance Society, and in Lansingburgh...January 24, 1830. Published by request. Troy, N.Y., Tuttle and Gregory, prs., 1830. 24 p. CSmH; PPL. 3774

---- ---- 2d ed. Boston, Richardson, Lord & Holbrook, 1830. 24 p. CBPac; ICU; MWA; NN; OO. 3775

Tucker, William.
The family dyer and scourer; being a complete treatise on the arts of dyeing and cleaning every article of dress, bed and window furniture, silks, bonnets... From the 4th London ed. Philadelphia, E. L. Carey and A. Hart, Sold by J. Grigg [etc.] [1830?] [2], 180 p. DLC; OClWHi; PPL; RPi. 3776

Tuckerman, Joseph, 1778-1840.
Prize essay. An essay on the wages paid to females for their labour; in the form of a letter, from a gentleman in Boston to his friend in Philadelphia... Philadelphia, For sale by Carey & Hart... Boston, by Carter & Hendee [etc., etc.,] 1830. 58 p. CSmH; ICU; MB; MBAt; MBC; MH; MHi; MWA; MiD; NN; PHi; PPL; ScC; BrMus. 3777

---- A letter addressed to the Hon. Harrison Gray Otis, Mayor of Boston, respecting the house of correction, and the common jail, in Boston. Boston, Pub. by Carter and Hendee [I. R. Butts, pr.] 1830. 36 p. DLC; ICU; MB; MBAU; MBAt; MHi; MWA; NN; PPL; BrMus. 3778

---- Mr. Tuckerman's first semi annual report of the fourth year of his service as a minister at large in Boston, May, 1830. Boston, Gray & Bowen [Pr. by I. R. Butts] 1830. 28 p. CSmH; DLC; ICU; MH-AH; MHi; MWA. 3779

---- Mr. Tuckerman's second semi annual report of the fourth year of his service as a minister at large in Boston. Boston, Gray and Bowen [Pr. by I. R. Butts] 1830. 35 p. OO; PPL. 3780

Il Turco in Italia. See Rossini, Gioacchino Antonio.

Turner, Edward.
Elements of chemistry, including the recent discoveries and doctrines of the science. By Edward Turner. With notes by Franklin Bache. 3d American from the 2d London ed. Philadelphia, James Kay, 1830. xix, [14]-580 p. PMA. 3781

Tuscarora and Cold Run Tunnel and Railroad Company.
An act to incorporate the Tuscarora and Cold Run Tunnel and Railroad Company. Approved April 6, 1830. Pottsville [Pa.], Pr. by Benjamin Bannan, 1830. 15 p. CSmH; DBRE; MWA; PHi; PPM. 3782

[Tuttle, Sarah]
Conversations on the Choctaw Mission. By the author of Conversations on the Bombay Mission. Rev. by the publishing committee... Boston, Pr. by T. R. Marvin, for the Massachusetts Sabbath School Union, 1830. 2 v. in 1. CSmH; CtHT-W; DLC; GDC; GU; ICMcC; ICN; MBC; MH-AH; MWA; MdBE; MoSpD; NN; NNUT; OCHP; OMC; PU; ViRUT. 3783

Twelve letters to young men, on the sentiments of Miss Frances Wright, and Robert Dale Owen ... Philadelphia, Thomas Kite, pr., 1830. 48 p. N; NN; NjR; BrMus.   3784

The two arrows; or Frank and Charley. New Haven, S. Babcock. Sidney's Press, 1830. [18] p. CtHi.   3785

The two friends; or, Religion the best guide for youth. Revised by the Committee of Publication. Philadelphia, American Sunday School Union, 1830. 72 p. DLC; BrMus.   3786

Tyler, Bennet, 1783-1858.
    Persuasives to immediate repentance. Portland, Me., [1830?] Williamson: 9980.   3787

---- A vindication of the strictures on the review of Dr. Spring's dissertation on the means of regeneration in the Christian Spectator for 1829, in reply to the Reviewer and Evangelus Pacificus. Portland, Shirley & Hyde, 1830. 63 p. CSmH; CU; Ct; IU; IaU; MA; MBC; MH; MWA; MeBaT; MeHi; MoSpD; NCH; OO; PPL; PPPrHi.   3788

Tyng, Stephen Higginson.
    The importance of uniting manual labour with intellectual attainments, in a preparation for the ministry. A discourse... Philadelphia, Pr. by William Stavely, 1830. 32 p. CSmH; CtHT; DLC; NNG; NjR; PHi; PPL; PPPrHi; ScU.   3789

Tyrone, William Grattan. See Power, Tyrone.

Tyson, Job Roberts, 1803-1858.
    An address, delivered at the request of the board of managers of the Apprentices' Library Com-

pany of Philadelphia, in the Hall of The Franklin Institute, on the 26th March, 1830. Philadelphia, Pr. by John Young, 1830. 16 p. CSmH; MWA; MdHi; PHi; PPAmP; PPL; PPPrHi; PSC; PU; BrMus.   3790

Tytler, Alexander Fraser. See Woodhouslee, Alexander Fraser Tytler.

U

Uncle Sam's almanack for 1831. Philadelphia, Denny & Walker [1830] 18 l. CLU; CtY; MWA; NjR; PHi; PPiU.   3791

Union Bank of Maryland, Baltimore.
    Proceedings at a meeting of the stockholders of the Union Bank of Maryland, June, 1830. Baltimore, John D. Toy, pr., 1830. 15 p. MdHi.   3792

---- Proceedings of the stockholders of the Union Bank of Maryland, in general meeting in June and July, 1830. Baltimore, John D. Toy, pr., 1830. 2p. l., 68 p. MdBP; MdHi; PHi; PPL.
                                   3793
The union Bible dictionary, for the use of schools, Bible classes and families. Prepared for the American Sunday-School Union, and revised by the committee of publication. Philadelphia, American Sunday-School Union, New York, Boston, Louisville, Ky., St. Louis, 1830. 648 p. NUtHi.
                                   3794
Union Canal Company.
    Annual report of the managers of the Union Canal Co. of Pennsylvania to the stockholders, November 16, 1830. Philadelphia, Pr. by Lydia R. Bailey, 1830. 12 p. PPi.   3795

Union College.
Catalogue of the senior class, in Union College, 1829-30. Schenectady, S. S. Riggs, pr., 1830. 7 p. NSchU.   3796

---- Adelphic Society.
Catalogue of the members of the Adelphic Society, instituted in Union College, in 1797. [Union Press, Wilson & Wood, Schenectady, ca. 1830] Imprint on verso of t. -p. contains names of members of the class of 1830; hence date ca. 1830. NSchU.
3797
The unique; or Biography of many distinguished characters; with fine portraits. illus. with anecdotes. 3d ed. imp. Boston, Charles H. Peabody, 1830. 254 p. ICN; MB; MH; MWA; MiU; MnU; NjR; PPL; PSC-Hi; RPB; BrMus.
3798
United States.
Aaron Reynolds. Feb. 4, 1830. Mr. Chilton, from the Committee on Military Pensions, to which was referred the case of Aaron Reynolds, Made the following report: Washington, Duff Green, 1830. 1 p. (Rep. No. 153) DLC; NjR.   3799

---- Aaron Snow. Feb. 9, 1830. Mr. Wingate, from the Committee on Revolutionary Claims, to which had been referred the case of Aaron Snow, made the following report: Washington, Duff Green, 1830. 1 p. (Rep. No. 171) DLC; NjR.   3800

---- Abstract of infantry tactics; including exercises and manoeuvres of light-infantry and riflemen; for the use of the militia of the United States... Boston, Hilliard, Gray, Little and Wilkins, 1830. 138 p. CU; CtHT-W; DLC; ICU; KyHi; LNHT; MB; MH; MHi; MdHi; MeHi; MiD; NIC; NcD; NhHi; NjP; NjR; OClWHi; PHi;

ScU; THi; TxU; Vi; ViU.   3801

---- Accountability of public agents abroad, &c. (To accompany bill H. R. No. 398) March 30, 1830. Printed by order of the House of Representatives. Washington, Pr. by Duff Green, 1830. 9 p. (Doc. No. 85) DLC; NjR.   3802

---- An act declaratory of the several acts to provide for certain persons engaged in the land and naval service of the United States in the Revolutionary war. March 23, 1830. Received. [Washington, 1830] 3 p. (H. R. 248). DNA.   3803

---- An act for the better organization of the Militia of the District of Columbia. April 10, 1830. Read twice, and referred to the Committee on the Militia. [Washington, 1830] 23 p. (H. R. 235) DNA.   3804

---- An act for the more effectual collection of the impost duties. May 13, 1830. Read, and passed to a second reading. [Washington, 1830] 7 p. (H. R. 164) DNA.   3805

---- An act for the punishment of crimes in the District of Columbia. December 30, 1830. Received. December 31, 1830. Read twice, and referred to the Committee on the District of Columbia. [Washington, 1830] 8 p. (H. R. 339) DNA.   3806

---- An act for the re-appropriation of certain unexpended balances of former appropriations. April 2, 1830. Received. [Washington, 1830] 3 p. (H. R. 365) DNA.   3807

---- An act for the relief of Alexander Claxton. March 22,

1830. Received. [Washington, 1830] 2 p. (H.R. 84) DNA. 3808

---- An act for the relief of Captain Daniel McDuff. February 23, 1830. Received. February 24, 1830, Read, and passed to a second reading. [Washington, 1830] 1 p. (H.R. 81) DNA. 3809

No entry.   3810

---- An act for the relief of certain officers and soldiers of the Virginia State line during the Revolutionary war. May 13, 1830. Read, and the consideration thereof postponed until Tuesday next. Mr. Potter, from the Committee on the Public Lands, to which was referred the bill from the Senate, entitled "An act for the relief of certain officers and soldiers of the Virginia State line during the Revolutionary war," reported the same without amendment. [Washington, 1830] 1 p. (S. 134) DNA.   3811

---- ---- May 26, 1830. Ordered to be engrossed, as amended by the House of Representatives and read for the third time to-morrow. [Washington, 1830] 5 p. (S. 130) DNA.   3812

---- An act for the relief of certain persons engaged in the land and naval service of the United States in the Revolutionary war. March 23, 1830. Received. [Washington, 1830] 3 p. (H.R. 311) DNA.   3813

---- An act for the relief of Ephraim Whitaker. April 6, 1830. Read twice, and referred to the Committee on Pensions. [Washington, 1830] 1 p. (H.R. 157) DNA.   3814

---- An act for the relief of Gregoire Sarpy, or his legal representatives. March 23, 1830. Read and committed to a Committee of the Whole House to-morrow. Mr. Test, from the Committee on Private Land Claims, to which was referred the bill from the Senate, entitled "An act for the relief of Gregoire Sarpy, or his legal representatives," reported the same without amendment. [Washington, 1830] 1 p. (S. 70) DNA.   3815

---- An act for the relief of John Glass. March 29, 1830. Received. March 31, Read, and passed to a second reading. [Washington, 1830] 1 p. (H.R. 120) DNA.   3816

---- An act for the relief of John H. Wendal, a Captain in the Revolutionary War. March 22, 1830. Received. [Washington, 1830] 1 p. (H.R. 160) DNA.
                                 3817

---- An act for the relief of Stephen Olney. March 22, 1830. Received. [Washington, 1830] 1 p. (H.R. 74) DNA.   3818

---- An act for the relief of sundry owners of vessels sunk for the defence of Baltimore. May 3, 1830. Read twice, and referred to the Committee on Commerce. [Washington, 1830] 2 p. (H.R. 191) DNA.   3819

---- An act for the relief of sundry Revolutionary and other officers and soldiers, and for other purposes. February 17, 1830. Read, and passed to a second reading. February 18, 1830, Read second time, and referred to the Committee on Pensions. [Washington, 1830] 8 p. (H.R. 72) DNA.   3820

---- An act for the relief of the representatives of John P. Cox. January 4, 1830. Re-printed by order of the House of Representatives. [Washington, 1830] 1 p. (S. 25) DNA.   3821

---- An act for the relief of the widows and orphans of the Officers, Seamen, and Marines, of the sloop of war Hornet. February 19, 1830. Read twice, and referred to the Committee on Naval Affairs. [Washington, 1830] 1 p. (H. R. 218) DNA. 3822

---- An act for the relief of the widows and orphans of the officers, seamen, and marines of the United States' schooner Wild Cat. May 24, 1830. Printed by order of the House of Representatives. [Washington, 1830] 2 p. (S. 158) DNA.   3823

---- An act making appropriations for building light-houses, light-boats, beacons, and monuments, placing buoys, and for improving harbors and directing surveys. April 7, 1830. Received. [Washington, 1830] 12 p. (H. R. 304) DNA.   3824

---- ---- May 14, 1830. Printed as proposed to be amended by the Senate. Referred to the Committee on Commerce. [Washington, 1830] 16 p. (H. R. 304) DNA.   3825

---- ---- December 14, 1830. Ordered to be printed by the House of Representatives, [Washington, 1830] 15 p. (H. R. 304) DNA.   3826

---- An act making appropriations for certain fortifications for the year one thousand eight hundred and thirty. February 12, 1830. Read twice, and referred to the Committee on Finance. [Washington, 1830] 1 p. (H. R. 110) DNA.   3827

---- An act making appropriations for examinations and surveys, and also for certain works of internal improvement. April 2, 1830. Received. [Washington, 1830] 2 p. (H. R. 279) DNA.   3828

---- An act making appropriations for the improvement of certain harbors, and for removing obstructions at the mouths of certain rivers, for the year one thousand eight hundred and thirty. March 31, 1830. Read twice, and referred to the Committee on Commerce. [Washington, 1830] 3 p. (H. R. 242) DNA. 3829

---- An act making appropriations for the Indian Department, for the year one thousand eight hundred and thirty. February 12, 1830. Read twice, and referred to the Committee on Indian Affairs. [Washington, 1830] 2 p. (H. R. 162) DNA.   3830

---- An act making appropriations for the Military Service for the year one thousand eight hundred and thirty. February 26, 1830. Received. [Washington, 1830] 3 p. (S. 144) DNA.   3831

---- An act making appropriations for the Naval service for the year one thousand eight hundred and thirty. February 26, 1830. Received. [Washington, 1830] 5 p. (H. R. 129) DNA.   3832

---- An act making appropriations for the support of government for the year one thousand eight hundred and thirty. February 15, 1830, Received. February 16, 1830, Read, and passed to a second reading. [Washington, 1830] 15 p. (H. R. 102) DNA. 3833

---- An act making appropriations to carry into effect the treaty of Butte des Mortes. April 7, 1830. Received. [Washington, 1830] 1 p. (H. R. 369) DNA. 3834

---- An act relating to the Orphans' Courts in the District of Columbia. May 13, 1830. Read twice, and referred to the Committee on the District of Columbia. [Washington, 1830] 1 p. (H. R. 443) DNA. 3835

---- An act to alter the bridge and draws across the Potomac, from Washington City to Alexandria. Feb. 2, 1830. Mr. Powers, from the Committee for the District of Columbia, to which was referred the bill from the Senate, entitled "An act to alter the Bridge and Draw across the Potomac, from Washington City to Alexandria," reported the same with amendments. [Washington, 1830] 4 p. (S. 40) DNA. 3836

---- An act to amend an act, entitled "An act to extend the time for locating Virginia Military Land Warrants, and returning surveys thereon to the General Land Office," approved the twentieth day of May, one thousand eight hundred and twenty-six. January 33, 1830. Received. January 28, Read, and passed to second reading. February 4, Read second time, and referred to Committee on Public Lands. [Washington, 1830] 2 p. (H. R. 17) DNA. 3837

---- An act to amend the charter of Georgetown. May 13, 1830.

Read twice, and referred to the Committee on the District of Columbia. [Washington, 1830] 2 p. (H. R. 233) DNA. 3838

---- An act to authorize the appointment of a Marshal for the Northern District of the state of Alabama. Mr. Wickliffe, from the Committee on the Judiciary, to which was referred the bill from the Senate, entitled "An act to authorize the appointment of a Marshal for the Northern District of the State of Alabama," reported the same with an amendment. [Washington, 1830] 2 p. (S. 66) DNA. 3839

---- An act to authorize the Commissioners of the Sinking Fund to redeem the public debt of the United States. March 18, 1830. Printed by order of the House of Representatives. [Washington, 1830] 2 p. (S. 45) DNA. 3840

---- An act to authorize mounting and equipment of a part of the army of the United States. April 1, 1830. Read and committed to the Committee of the Whole House on the state of the Union. Printed by order of the House of Representatives. Mr. Drayton, from the Committee on Military Affairs, to which was referred the bill from the Senate, entitled An act to authorize the mounting and equipment of a part of the army of the United States, reported the same without amendment. [Washington, 1830] 1 p. (S. 119) DNA. 3841

---- An act to confirm certain claims to lands in the District of Jackson Court House, in the state of Mississippi. May 17, 1830. Re-printed by order of the House of Representatives. [Washington, 1830] 4 p. (S. 126) DNA. 3842

---- An act to establish a uniform rule for the computation of the mileage of members of Congress, and for other purposes. January 4, 1830. Read, and passed to a second reading. [Washington, 1830] 2 p. (H. R. 19) DNA.   3843

---- An act to grant pre-emption rights to settlers on the Public Lands. January 25, 1830. Read twice, and committed to the Committee of the Whole House to which is committed the bill H. R. [No. 49] to dispose of reverted and relinquished lands.. Mr. Isacks, from the Committee on Public Lands, to which was referred the bill from the Senate, entitled "An act to grant pre-emption rights to settlers on the public lands," reported the same, with amendments. [Washington, 1830] 3 p. (S. 19) DNA.   3844

---- An act to grant to the state of Alabama certain lands for the purpose of improving the navigation of the Coosa river, and to connect its waters with those of the Tennessee river by a canal. April 12, 1830. Read, and committed to the Committee of the Whole House on the state of the Union. Mr. Blair, from the Committee on Internal Improvements, to which was referred the bill from the Senate, entitled "An act to grant to the State of Alabama certain lands for the purpose of improving the navigation of the Coosa river, and to connect its waters with those of the Tennessee river by a canal," reported the same with amendments. [Washington, 1830] 3 p. (S. 92) DNA.   3845

---- An act to incorporate the Alexandria Canal Company. May 13, 1830. Read, and passed to a second reading. [Washington,

1830] 19 p. (H. R. 184) DNA.
                                3846
---- An act to incorporate the Alexandria Canal Company. [n. p., 1830] 12 p. DLC.   3847

---- An act to provide for an exchange of lands with the Indians residing in any of the states or territories, and for their removal west of the river Mississippi. April 26, 1830. Read twice, and committed to the Committee of the Whole House on the state of the Union. Pr. by order of the House of Representatives. [Washington, 1830] 4 p. (S. 102) DNA.   3848

---- An act to provide for taking the fifth Census or enumeration of the inhabitants of the United States. February 9, 1830. Received. February 10, 1830. Read, and passed to a second reading. February 12, 1830. Read a second time, and referred to the Committee on the Judiciary. [Washington, 1830] 15 p. (H. R. 116) DNA.   3849

---- An act to provide for the appointment of Commissioners to digest, prepare, and report to Congress at the next Session thereof, a code of statute law, civil and criminal, for the District of Columbia. April 23, 1830. Received. [Washington, 1830] 2 p. (H. R. 372) DNA.   3850

---- An act to provide for the final settlement of land claims in Florida. May 3, 1830. Read twice, and referred to the Committee on Public Lands. [Washington, 1830] 4 p. (H. R. 206) DNA.   3851

---- An act to provide for the legal adjudication and settlement of the claims to land therein mentioned. April 16, 1830. Committed to a Committee of the Whole House to-morrow. Printed by order of the House of Representatives. [Washington, 1830] 4 p. (S. 21) DNA. 3852

---- An act to reduce the price of a portion of the public lands heretofore in market, and to grant a preference to actual settlers. May 10, 1830. Postponed to Monday, 17th instant. Mr. Isacks, from the Committee on the Public Lands, to which was referred the bill from the Senate of the following title, reported the same without amendment. [Washington, 1830] 3 p. (S. 5) DNA. 3853

---- An act to regulate and fix the compensation of the clerks in the Department of State. February 12, 1830. Read Twice, and referred to the Committee on Foreign Relations. [Washington, 1830] 2 p. (H. R. 143) DNA. 3854

---- An act to relinquish the reversionary interest of the United States in certain Indian reservations in the State of Alabama. April 9, 1830. Received. April 10, 1830. Read twice, and referred to the Committee on Public Lands. [Washington, 1830] 2 p. (H. R. 97) DNA. 3855

---- ---- [Washington, 1830] 2 p. (H. R. 97) DNA. variant prtg. of no. 3855. 3856

---- An act to re-organize the Navy of the United States. May 24, 1830. Printed by order of the House of Representatives. [Washington, 1830] 3 p. (S. 120) DNA. 3857

---- Acts of Virginia--Chesapeake and Ohio Canal. Message from the President of the United States transmitting two acts of the legislature of Virginia, respecting the Chesapeake and the Ohio Canal Company. March 9, 1830. Referred to the Committee on Internal Improvement. April 24, 1830. Bill reported, No. 441. Washington [Pr. by Duff Green] 1830. 4 p. (Doc. no. 94) DLC; NjR. 3858

---- Additional clerks in the Post Office Department. Jan. 26, 1830. Mr. Johnson, of Kentucky, from the Committee on the Post Office and Post Roads, made the following report: Washington, Duff Green, 1830. 5 p. (Rep. No. 122) DLC; NjR. 3859

---- Additional land - Fort Washington. Feb 4, 1830. Mr. Drayton, from the Committee on Military Affairs, to which the subject had been referred, made the following report: Washington, Duff Green, 1830. 1 p. (Rep. No. 151) DLC; NjR. 3860

---- Adjutant General Jones. Letter from the Secretary of War transmitting a copy of the proceedings of the General court martial in the case of Adjutant General Roger Jones. May 14, 1830. Read, and laid upon the table. Washington [Pr. by Duff Green] 1830. 58 p. (Doc. No. 104) DLC; NjR. 3861

---- Alabama. Memorial of sundry holders of certificates of Purchase, and relinquishers of Public lands. Dec. 23, 1830. Printed by order of the House of Representatives. Washington, Duff Green, 1830. 2 p. (Rep. No. 9) DLC; NjR. 3862

---- Alexander Boyd. Jan. 11, 1830. Mr. Gurley, from the Committee on Private Land Claims, to which was referred the case of Alexander Boyd, made the following report: Washington,

1830. 2 p. (Rep. No. 68) DLC; NjR. 3863

---- Alexander Claxton. Jan. 7, 1830. Mr. Miller, from the Committee on Naval Affairs, made the following report: Washington, Duff Green, 1830. 2 p. (Rep. No. 61) DLC; NjR. 3864

---- Alexander Fridge. Jan. 13, 1830. Mr. Gurley, from the Committee on Private Land Claims, made the following report: Washington, Duff Green, 1830. 1 p. (Rep. No. 76) DLC; NjR. 3865

---- Alexander Love. Jan. 27, 1830. Mr. Gurley, from the Committee on Private Land Claims, made the following report: Washington, Duff Green, 1830. 1 p. (Rep. No. 125) DLC; NjR. 3866

---- Alfred Conkling. April 3, 1830. Read, and laid upon the table. Mr. Wickliffe, from the Committee on the Judiciary, to which had been referred the petition of Martha Bradstreet, complaining of the official conduct of Alfred Conkling, District Judge of the United States for the Northern District of New York, made the following report. Washington, Duff Green, 1830. 1 p. (Rep. No. 342) DLC; NjR. 3867

---- ---- April 8, 1830. Read, and laid upon the table. Washington, Duff Green, 1830. 11 p. (Rep. No. 343) DLC; NjR. 3868

---- Allowance to jurors - Courts, U.S. Jan. 4, 1830. Read, and laid upon the table. Mr. Buchanan, from the Committee on the Judiciary, to which the subject had been referred, made the following report: Washington, Duff Green, 1830. 1 p. (Rep. No. 49)

DLC; NjR. 3869

---- Alter organization marine corps. Report, in part, upon so much of the President's Message, referred to the Military Committee, as relates to the expediency of merging the Marines in the United States' Artillery or Infantry. Feb. 5, 1830. Mr. Drayton, from the Committee on Military Affairs, made the following report: Washington, Duff Green, 1830. 1 p. (Rep. No. 158) DLC; NjR. 3870

---- Amend the rules. Feb. 23, 1830. Read, and laid upon the table. Feb. 24, 1830. Considered and postponed until Monday, 1st March. Washington, Duff Green, 1830. 1 p. (Res. No. 7) DLC; NjR. 3871

---- Amendment. Jan. 5, 1830. Read, and committed to the Committee of the Whole House to which the said bill is committed. Mr. Wickliffe submitted the following, which, when the bill [No. 37] establishing Circuit Courts, and abridging the jurisdiction of the District Courts in the Districts of Indiana, Illinois, Missouri, Mississippi, the Eastern District of Louisiana, and the Southern District of Alabama, shall be taken up for consideration, he will move as an amendment. [Washington, 1830] 3 p. (H. R. 37) DNA. 3872

---- Amendment. Jan. 19, 1830. Read, and committed to the Committee of the Whole House to which the said bill is committed. Mr. Spencer, of New York, submitted the following, which, when the bill [No. 37] establishing Circuit Courts, and abridging the jurisdiction of the District Courts in the Districts of Indiana, Illinois, Missouri, Mississippi, the

Eastern District of Louisiana, and the Southern District of Alabama, shall be taken up for consideration, he will move as an amendment. [Washington, 1830] 5 p. (H.R. 37) DNA. 3873

---- Amendment. Jan. 20, 1830. Committed to the Committee of the Whole House to which the said bill is committed. Mr. Everett, of Vermont, submitted the following, as an amendment to the bill (37) establishing Circuit Courts, and abridging the jurisdiction of District Courts in the Districts of Indiana, Illinois, &c. &c. [Washington, 1830] 2 p. (H.R. 37) DNA. 3874

---- Amendment. Jan. 22, 1830. Read, and committed to the Committee of the Whole House to which the said bill is committed. Mr. Carson submitted the following, which when the "Bill to construct a national road from Buffalo, in the State of New York, passing by the Seat of the General Government, in the District of Columbia, to New Orleans, in the State of Louisiana," shall be taken up for consideration, he will move as an amendment. [Washington, 1830] 1 p. (H.R. 86) DNA. 3875

---- Amendment. Feb. 22, 1830. Printed by order of the House of Representatives. Mr. Crawford, of Pennsylvania, submitted the following as an amendment to the "bill (H.R. No. 37) establishing Circuit Courts, and abridging the jurisdiction of the District Courts in the districts of Indiana, Illinois, Missouri, Mississippi, the Eastern district of Louisiana, and the Southern district of Alabama." [Washington, 1830] 6 p. (H.R. 37) DNA. 3876

---- Amendment. Feb. 27, 1830.

Committed to the Committee of the Whole House to which the said bill is committed. Mr. Craig submitted the following, which, when the bill (No. 86) to construct a national road from Buffalo, in the state of New York, passing by the seat of the general government, in the District of Columbia, to New Orleans, in the state of Louisiana, shall be taken up for consideration, he will move as an amendment to the same: [Washington, 1830] 1 p. (H.R. 86) DNA. 3877

---- Amendment. Mar. 12, 1830. Printed by order of the House of Representatives. An additional section proposed as an amendment to bill No. 119, by the Committee on the Post Office and Post Roads. [Washington, 1830] 1 p. (H.R. 119) DNA. 3878

---- Amendment. Mar. 16, 1830. Read, and committed to the Committee of the Whole House to which the said bill is committed. Mr. Lea submitted the following, which, when the bill to construct a national road from Buffalo, in the State of New York, passing by the Seat of the General Government, in the District of Columbia, to New Orleans in the State of Louisiana, shall be taken up for consideration, he will move as an amendment thereto: [Washington, 1830] 3 p (H.R. 86) DNA. 3879

---- Amendment. Mar. 18, 1830. Read, and committed to the Committee of the Whole House on the state of the Union to which the said bill is committed. Mr. Martin submitted the following, which, when the bill (H.R. No. 367) appropriating the nett proceeds of the public lands to the use of the several States and Territories, shall be taken up for consideration, he will move as an amendment thereto: [Washington, 1830] 1 p. (H. R. 367) DNA.

3880

---- Amendment. Apr. 13, 1830. Printed by order of the House of Representatives. Mr. Barringer submitted the following as an amendment to the bill (H. R. No. 185) to amend "An act authorizing the State of Tennessee to issue grants, and forfeit rights to certain grants therein described, and to settle the claims to the vacant and unappropriated lands within the state, passed April eighteenth, one thousand eight hundred and six. [Washington, 1830] 2 p. (H. R. 185) DNA.

3881

---- Amendment. Apr. 22, 1830. Read and committed to the Committee of the Whole House on the state of the Union to which the said bill is committed. Mr. Russel submitted the following which, when the bill (H. R. No. 171) granting to the state of Ohio, upon certain conditions, all the lands of the United States within that state, shall be taken up for consideration, he will move as an amendment thereto: [Washington, 1830] 2 p. (H. R. 171) DNA.

3882

---- Amendment. Apr. 24, 1830. Mr. Benton offered the following as an amendment, to be added to the bill requiring vessels in the bays and rivers of the United States to display a light in the night time. [Washington, 1830] 2 p. (S. 128) DNA.   3883

---- Amendment. Apr. 24, 1830. Read, and committed to the Committee of the Whole House to which the said bill is committed. Mr. Whittlesey submitted the following, which, when the bill (H. R. 191) for the relief of sundry owners of vessels sunk for the defence of Baltimore," shall be

taken up for consideration, he will move as an amendment of the same. [Washington, 1830] 2 p. (H. R. 191) DNA.   3884

---- Amendment. Apr. 24, 1830. The Committee on the Judiciary, to whom were referred the "bill to re-organize the establishment of the Attorney General, and erect it into an Executive Department, and the resolution of the fifteenth instant on the subject," report the following amendment to the said bill. [Washington, 1830] 4 p. (S. 87) DNA.   3885

---- Amendment. May 3, 1830. Read and committed to the Committee of the Whole House to which the said bill (No. 270,) is committed. Mr. Sevier, submitted the following as an amendment to the bill (H. R. No. 270) to authorize the selection of certain school lands in the Territory of Arkansas. [Washington, 1830] 1 p. (H. R. 270) DNA.

3886

---- Amendment. May 6, 1830. Read twice, and committed to the Committee of the Whole House to which the said bill is committed. Mr. Scott submitted the following as an amendment of the bill (H. R. No. 164) to amend "An act in alteration of the several acts imposing duties on imports:" [Washington, 1830] 1 p. (H. R. 164) DNA.   3887

---- Amendment. May 13, 1830. Mr. Chilton submitted the following, which, when the bill from the Senate (No. 134) of the following title, shall be taken up for consideration, he will move as an amendment: An act extending the provisions of the Revolutionary pension law. [Washington, 1830] 2 p. (S. 134) DNA. 3888

---- Amendment. May 15, 1830.

Mr. Earll submitted the following, as an amendment to the bill from the Senate, (No. 102) to provide for an exchange of lands with the Indians residing in any of the States or Territories, and for their removal West of the river Mississippi. [Washington, 1830] 1 p. (S. 102) DNA. 3889

---- Amendment. May 17, 1830. Printed by order of the House of Representatives. Mr. Doddridge, submitted the following as an amendment to the bill from the Senate, of the following title: An act for the relief of certain officers and soldiers of the Virginia State line, during the Revolutionary war. [Washington, 1830] 4 p. (S. 130) DNA. 3890

---- Amendment. May 22, 1830. Read, and committed to the Committee of the Whole House, to which the said bill is committed. Mr. Pettis submitted the following; which, when the bill from the Senate (No. 34) entitled An act to cause the Northern and Western boundary lines of the State of Missouri to be better marked and established, and to divide certain land adjoining said boundary among the half breed Indians of the Sac and Fox tribes, shall be taken up for consideration, he will move as an amendment thereof. [Washington, 1830] 2 p. (S. 34) DNA. 3891

---- Amendment. May 22, 1830. The following amendment of the House of Representatives to the Senate bill, (No. 129) was read, laid on the table, and ordered to be printed: [Washington, 1830] 2 p. (S. 129) DNA. 3892

---- Amendment to be proposed by Mr. Vinton to the bill from the Senate (No. 5) to reduce the price of the public lands heretofore in market, and to grant a preference to actual settlers. May 10, 1830. Ordered to be printed. [Washington, 1830] 2 p. (S. 5) DNA. 3893

---- Amendments. Mar. 18, 1830. The Committee on Public Lands, to whom were referred the following amendments, proposed by the House of Representatives to the bill of the Senate, entitled "An act for the relief of the Purchaser of Public Lands," reported the same with the following amendments thereto. [Washington, 1830] 6 p. (S. 28) DNA. 3894

---- Amendments proposed to the "bill to provide for an exchange of lands with the Indians residing in any of the States or Territories, and for their removal West of the river Mississippi." Apr. 9, 1830. Ordered to be printed. [Washington, 1830] 2 p. (S. 102) DNA. 3895

---- American canvass, cables, and cordage. In the House of Representatives, April 22, 1830. Mr. Spencer, of New York, from the Committee on Agriculture, reported the following resolution: Washington [Pr. by Duff Green] 1830. 26 p. (Rep. No. 381) DLC; NjR. 3896

---- Amos Binney. May 24, 1830. Read, and referred to the Committee of the Whole House to which is committed the bill H. R. No. 441, confirming certain acts of the Legislature of Virginia, relating to the Chesapeake and Ohio Canal Company. Washington, Duff Green, 1830. 36 p. (Rep. No. 412) DLC; NjR. 3897

---- Amos Edwards - sureties of. Dec. 30, 1830. Mr. Daniel, from the Committee on the Judiciary, to which had been referred the case of the sureties of Amos Edwards, made the following report: Washington, Duff Green, 1830. 3 p. (Rep. No. 13) DLC; NjR.   3898

---- Amount of postage for one year prior to 31st March, 1829. Letter from the Postmaster General, transmitting a statement of the amount of postages accruing in the United States for one year prior to 31st March, 1829. Feb. 11, 1830. Read, and laid upon the table. Washington, Pr. by Duff Green, 1830. 83 p. (Doc. No. 61) DLC; NjR.   3899

---- Andrew H. Richardson. May 3, 1830. Mr. Whittlesey, from the Committee of Claims, made the following report. Washington, Duff Green, 1830. 2 p. (Rep. No. 389) DLC; NjR.   3900

---- Andrew Jackson President of the United States of America, to all and singular to whom these presents shall come, greeting: Whereas a treaty between the United States of America, and the Mingoes, chiefs, captains and warriors, of the Choctaw nation, was entered into at Dancing Rabbit creek, on the twenty-seventh day of September in the year of our Lord one thousand and eight hundred and thirty... [Washington, D.C., 1830] 7 p. DLC.
                                3901

---- ---- Articles of agreement between the United States of America and the band of Delaware Indians, upon the Sandusky river, in the state of Ohio... entered into on the third day of August, eighteen hundred and twenty-nine, at Little Sandusky, in the state of Ohio, by John M'Elvain, commissioner on the part of the United States, and certain chiefs on the part of the band of Dela-

ware Indians... [Washington, 1830] 1 l. DLC; MB.   3902

---- Ann Brashears. Jan. 20, 1830. Mr. Test, from the Committee on Private Land Claims, made the following report. Washington, Duff Green, 1830. 2 p. (Rep. No. 101) DLC; NjR. 3903

---- Ann D. Baylor. Feb. 26, 1830. Mr. Burges, from the Committee on Revolutionary Claims, to which was referred the case of Ann D. Baylor, made the following report: Washington, Pr. by Duff Green, 1830. 1 p. (Rep. No. 237) DLC; NjR. 3904

---- ---- Dec. 21, 1830. Mr. Dickinson, from the Committee on Revolutionary Claims to which had been referred the petition of Ann D. Baylor, made the following report: Washington, Duff Green, 1830. 1 p. (Rep. No. 5) DLC; NjR.   3905

---- Annual report--Navy pension fund. Feb. 15, 1830. Printed by order of the House of Representatives. Washington, Pr. by Duff Green, 1830. 63 p. (Doc. No. 63) DLC; NjR.   3906

---- Annual report, of the commissioners of the Sinking Fund. Feb. 8, 1830. Read, and laid upon the table. Washington, Pr. by Duff Green, 1830. 13 p. (Doc. No. 53) DLC; NjR.   3907

---- Annual report of the Secretary of the Senate, showing the expenditure from the contingent fund, &c. Dec. 8, 1830. Referred to the Committee on the Contingent Fund, and ordered to be printed. Washington, Duff Green, 1830. 4 p. (Doc. No. 2) DLC; PU.   3908

---- Anthony Foreman and John

G. Ross. April 16, 1830. Mr. Whittlesey, from the Committee of Claims, made the following report: Washington, Duff Green, 1830. 3 p. (Rep. No. 367) DLC; NjR. 3909

---- Antoine Dequindre, et al. March 3, 1830. Mr. Whittlesey, from the Committee of Claims, to which was referred the case of Antoine Dequindre, et al. made the following report: Washington, Pr. by Duff Green, 1830. 4 p. (Rep. No. 268) DLC; NjR. 3910

---- Appeals and writs of error courts United States, in Florida. Jan. 4, 1830. Read, and laid upon the table. Mr. Buchanan, from the Committee on the Judiciary, to which the subject had been referred, made the following report: Washington, Duff Green, 1830. 1 p. (Rep. No. 50) DLC; NjR. 3911

---- Appropriations--first session twenty-first Congress. Statement of appropriations made during the first session of the twenty-first Congress of the United States of America; specifying the amount and object of each. May 31, 1830. Washington, Pr. by order of the House of Representatives. Washington, Pr. by Duff Green, 1830. 23 p. (Doc. No. 122) DLC; NjR. 3912

---- Appropriations for examinations and surveys, &c. Message from the President of the United States approving of the act making "appropriations for examinations and surveys, and also for certain works of internal improvement." May 31, 1830. Read, and laid upon the table. Washington, [Pr. by Duff Green] 1830. 1 p. (Doc. No. 123) DLC; NjR. 3913

---- Appropriations--War Department, &c. for 1829. Letter from the Secretary of War, transmitting a statement of appropriations from the War Department for the year 1829, the expenditure of the same, &c. &c. Mar. 15, 1830. Read, and laid upon the table. Washington, Pr. by Duff Green, 1830. 17 p. (Doc. No. 78) DLC; NjR. 3914

---- Ardent spirits--Army and Navy. Letter from the Secretary of War, in reply to a resolution of the House of Representatives of the 28th ultimo, in relation to allowing to the soldiers and seamen of the United States an equipment in money, in lieu of the present allowance for ardent spirits. Jan. 14, 1830. Read, and laid upon the table. Washington, Pr. by Duff Green, 1830. (Doc. No. 22) DLC; NjR. 3915

---- Ardent spirits---Midshipmen. Letter from the Secretary of the Navy, transmitting opinions of surgeons of the Navy, in relation to allowing to the Midshipmen of the Navy of the United States, ardent spirits as a part of their ration. Jan. 14, 1830. Read, and laid upon the table. Washington, Pr. by Duff Green, 1830. 22 p. (Doc. No. 23) DLC; NjR. 3916

---- Ardent spirits to soldiers. Feb. 8, 1830. Mr. Drayton, from the Committee on Military Affairs, made the following report: Washington, Duff Green, 1830. 2 p. (Rep. No. 166) DLC; NjR. 3917

---- Argument of the counsel for the United States in the Supreme Court, in the cases of the United States, vs. George I. F. Clark, John and Antonio Huertes, Joseph M. Hernandez, et al. [1830] 20 p. PPL. 3918

---- Ariel Ensign. April 29, 1830. Mr. Crane, from the Committee of Claims, to which was referred the case of Ariel Ensign, made the following report: Washington, Duff Green, 1830. 2 p. (Rep. No. 386) DLC; NjR.   3919

---- Arming and organizing the Militia of the U.S. March 3, 1830. Laid before the House by the Chairman of the Committee on the Militia, and committed to the Committee of the Whole House to which is committed the Bill H.R. No. 168. Washington, Pr. by Duff Green, 1830. 17 p. (Doc. No. 72) DLC; NjR.   3920

---- Armories and arms. Letter from the Secretary of War, transmitting a statement of expenditures at the United States' armories, and the arms manufactured therein, during the year 1829. March 26, 1830. Read, and laid upon the table. Washington, Pr. by Duff Green, 1830. 7 p. (Doc. No. 84) DLC; NjR.
3921

---- Articles, diminished importation of. Letter from the Secretary of the Treasury transmitting the information required by a resolution of the House of Representatives of the 30th January, 1829, in relation to articles upon which imposts are laid so high as to diminish or lessen the importance thereof, &c. January 29, 1830. Read, and laid upon the table. Washington, [Pr. by Duff Green] 1830. 13 p. (Doc. No. 119) DLC; DeGE; NjR.   3922

---- Assays - gold coins - mint of the United States. Letter from the Secretary of the Treasury, transmitting a report of assays, made at the Mint of the United States, of foreign gold coins,

during the year 1829. Feb. 8, 1830. Read, and laid upon the table. Washington, Pr. by Duff Green, 1830. 2 p. (Doc. No. 52) DLC; NjR.   3923

---- Assignees of Comfort Sands. Letter from the Secretary of the Treasury in reply to a resolution of the House of Representatives in relation to the claim of the assignees of Comfort Sands, et al. May 25, 1830. Read, and laid upon the table. Washington, [Pr. by Duff Green] 1830. 2 p. (Doc. No. 108) DLC; NjR. 3924

---- Assistant Secretary of State. (To accompany bill H.R. 438) Letter from the Secretary of State to the chairman of the Committee on Foreign Affairs, in relation to the appointment of an Assistant Secretary of State. April 23, 1830. Laid before the House by the Chairman of the Committee on Foreign Affairs, and ordered to be printed. Washington, [Pr. by Duff Green] 1830. 16 p. (Rep. No. 380) DLC; NjR.   3925

---- Attorney General of the U.S. and Attorney of the U.S. for the territory of Arkansas. Letter from the Attorney General of the United States, transmitting copies of correspondence between the Attorney of the United States for the territory of Arkansas, and the Attorney General of the United States, relative to cases decided by the Superior Court of the territory of Arkansas, &c. &c. Feb. 1, 1830. Read, and laid upon the table. Washington, Pr. by Duff Green, 1830. 12 p. (Doc. No. 45) DLC; NjR.   3926

---- B. H. Reeves, G. O. Sibley, and Thomas Mather. May 26, 1830. Read, and committed to the Committee of the Whole House to-morrow. Mr. Whittlesey, from the Committee of Claims, to which was referred the claim of B. H. Reeves, G. O. Sibley, and Thomas Mather, made the following report: Washington, Duff Green, 1830. 14 p. (Rep. No. 416) DLC; NjR. 3927

---- Balances on the books of the fourth auditor. Letter from the Comptroller of the Treasury transmitting an abstract of balances on the books of the fourth auditor which appear to have been due more than three years prior to the 30th September, 1830. December 24, 1830. Read, and laid upon the table. Washington, Pr. by Duff Green, 1830. 32 p. (Doc. No. 17) DLC; NjR. 3928

---- Balances on the books of the revenue. Letter from the Comptroller of the Treasury, transmitting a list of the register, of balances standing on the books of the revenue, which have remained unsettled by collectors of the customs, and others, more than three years, prior to the 30th Sept. last. Feb. 11, 1830. Read, and laid upon the table. Washington, Pr. by Duff Green, 1830. 5 p. (Doc. No. 60) DLC; NjR. 3929

---- Balances on the books of the treasury. Letter from the Comptroller of the Treasury transmitting a list of balances on the books of the register and of the second and third auditors; a list of officers who have not rendered their accounts within the year; and an abstract of money advanced prior to 3d March, 1809, unaccounted for. December 13, 1830. Read, and laid upon the table. Washington, Pr. by Duff Green, 1830. 187 p. (Doc. No. 4) DLC; NjR. 3930

---- Baldwin M. Leland. December 28, 1829. Read, and laid upon the table. February 15, 1830. Committed to a Committee of the Whole House to-morrow. Mr. McIntire, from the Committee of Claims, made the following report: Washington, Pr. by Duff Green, 1830. 3 p. (Rep. No. 203) DLC; NjR. 3931

---- Baltimore and Ohio Rail Road Company. February 19, 1830. Mr. Hemphill, from the Committee on Internal Improvements, to which had been referred the memorial of the Baltimore and Ohio Rail Road Company, made the following report: Washington, Pr. by Duff Green, 1830. 1 p. (Rep. No. 211) DLC; NjR. 3932

---- Bank of Chillicothe. Jan. 4, 1830. Mr. Whittlesey, from the Committee of Claims, made the following report: Washington, Duff Green, 1830. 3 p. (Rep. No. 45) DLC; NjR. 3933

---- Bank of Missouri. Letter from the Secretary of the Treasury transmitting the information required by a resolution of the House of Representatives, in relation to the claim of the United States on the Bank of Missouri, &c. &c. May 26, 1830. Read, and laid upon the table. Washington [Pr. by Duff Green] 1830. 2 p. (Doc. No. 111) DLC; NjR. 3934

---- Bank of the United States. April 13, 1830. Read, and laid upon the table. Mr. McDuffie, from the Committee of Ways and Means, to which the subject had been referred, made the following report: Washington, Duff Green, 1830. 42 p. (Rep. No. 358) DLC; DeGE; NjR. 3935

---- ---- [Washington, 1830]

31 p. DeGE.   3936

---- Banks in the District of
Columbia. Jan. 22, 1830. Read,
and laid upon the table. Washington, Pr. by Duff Green, 1830.
10 p. (Doc. No. 33) DLC; NjR.
                                                 3937

---- Bartholomew Delapierre.
May 3, 1830. Mr. Chilton, from
the Committee on Military Pensions, made the following report: Washington, Duff Green,
1830. 1 p. (Rep. No. 391) DLC;
NjR.   3938

---- Benjamin Gibbs. Mr.
Goodenow, from the Committee
on Revolutionary Claims, made
the following report: Washington, Duff Green, 1830. 1 p. (Rep.
No. 168) DLC; NjR.   3939

---- Benjamin Homans, Jan. 13,
1830. Mr. Whittlesey, from the
Committee of Claims, to which
was referred the case of Benjamin Homans, made the following
report: Washington, Duff Green,
1830. 1 p. (Rep. No. 74) DLC;
NjR.   3940

---- Benjamin Pendleton. May
31, 1830. Mr. Campbell P.
White, from the Committee on
Naval Affairs, made the following report: Washington, Duff
Green, 1830. 2 p. (Rep. No.
418) DLC; NjR.   3941

---- Benjamin Wells. February
26, 1830. Mr. Burges, from
the Committee on Revolutionary
Claims, to which was referred
the case of Benjamin Wells,
made the following report:
Washington, Pr. by Duff Green,
1830. 4 p. (Rep. No. 241) DLC;
NjR.   3942

---- Bernard Kelley. Dec. 17,
1830. Mr. Johnson, of Kentucky,
from the Committee on the Post

Office and Post Roads, made the
following report: Washington,
Duff Green, 1830. 4 p. (Rep. No.
2) DLC; NjR.   3943

---- A bill allowing the duties
on foreign merchandise imported
into Louisville, Pittsburg, Cincinnati, St. Louis, and Nashville,
to be secured and paid at those
places. December 29, 1829...
December 30. Read second time,
and referred to Committee on
Commerce. Jan. 5, 1830. Reported with an amendment...
[Washington, 1830] 3 p. (S. 26)
DNA.   3944

---- A bill allowing the duties
on foreign merchandise imported
into Pittsburg, Cincinnati, Louisville, St. Louis, Nashville, and
Natchez, to be secured and paid
at those places. December 28,
1830. Read twice, and committed to the Committee of the
Whole House on the state of the
Union. Mr. Cambreleng, from
the Committee on Commerce,
reported the following bill:
[Washington, 1830] 5 p. (H. R.
520) DNA.   3945

---- A bill altering the time of
holding Circuit and District
Courts in the state of Ohio.
April 6, 1830. Mr. Rowan, from
the Committee on the Judiciary,
reported the following bill; which
was read, and passed to a second reading: [Washington, 1830]
1 p. (S. 170) DNA.   3946

---- A bill amendatory of the
act for the continuation of the
Cumberland road. May 24, 1830.
Read twice, and committed to the
Committee of the Whole House
on the state of the Union. Mr.
Vinton, from the Committee on
Internal Improvements, reported
the following bill: [Washington,
1830] 2 p. (H. R. 483)

DNA. 3947

---- A bill amending and supplementary to the act to aid the state of Ohio in extending the Miami canal from Dayton to Lake Erie, and to grant a quantity of land to said State, to aid in the construction of the canals authorized by law, and for making donations of land to certain persons in Arkansas Territory. February 8, 1830. Mr. Barton, from the Committee on Public Lands, reported the following bill; which was read, and passed to a second reading: [Washington, 1830] 2 p. (S. 84) DNA. 3948

---- A bill appropriating the nett proceeds of the public lands to the use of the several states and territories. March 18, 1830. Read twice, and committed to the Committee of the Whole House on the state of the Union. Mr. Hunt, from the select committee to which the subject had been referred, reported the following bill: [Washington, 1830] 1 p. (H. R. 367) DNA. 3949

---- A bill authorizing a subscription of stock in the Baltimore and Ohio Railroad Company. February 19, 1830. Read twice, and committed to the Committee of the Whole House on the state of the Union. Mr. Hemphill, from the Committee on Internal Improvements, reported the following bill: [Washington, 1830] 2 p. (H. R. 264) DNA. 3950

---- ---- March 12, 1830. Mr. Hendricks, from the Committee on Roads and Canals, reported the following bill; which was read, and passed to a second reading. [Washington, 1830] 2 p. (S. 133) DNA. 3951

---- A bill authorizing a sub-scription of stock in the Delaware and Hudson Canal Company. April 16, 1830. Read twice, and committed to the Committee of the Whole House on the state of the Union. Mr. Hemphill, from the Committee on Internal Improvements, reported the following bill: [Washington, 1830] 2 p. (H. R. 429) DNA. 3952

---- A bill authorizing a subscription of stock in the Maysville, Washington, Paris, and Lexington Turnpike Road Company. February 24, 1830. Read twice, and committed to the Committee of the Whole House on the state of the Union. Mr. Letcher, from the Committee on Internal Improvements, reported the following bill: [Washington, 1830] 1 p. (H. R. 285) DNA. 3953

---- A bill authorizing a subscription of stock to the Morris Canal and Banking Company. April 16, 1830. Read twice, and committed to a Committee of the Whole House to-morrow. Mr. Hemphill, from the Committee on Internal Improvements, reported the following bill: [Washington, 1830] 2 p. (H. R. 427) DNA. 3954

---- A bill authorizing a subscription to the stock of the South Carolina Canal and Rail Road Company. February 19, 1830. Read twice, and committed to the Committee of the Whole House on the state of the Union. Mr. Hemphill, from the Committee on Internal Improvements, reported the following bill: [Washington, 1830] 3 p. (H. R. 265) DNA. 3955

---- A bill authorizing additional clerks for the General Post Office Department, and for other purposes. January 26, 1830. Read twice, and committed to a Committee of the Whole House to-morrow. Mr. Johnson, of Kentucky, from the Committee on the Post Office and Post Roads, reported the following bill: [Washington, 1830] 1 p. (H. R. 153) DNA.   3956

---- A bill authorizing paymasters to employ citizens to aid them in the discharge of their duties in certain cases. January 28, 1830. Read twice, and ordered to be engrossed and read the third time to-morrow. Mr. Drayton, from the Committee on Military Affairs, reported the following bill: [Washington, 1830] 1 p. (H. R. 172) DNA.
3957

---- A bill authorizing the appointment of an Assistant Secretary of State. April 23, 1830. Read twice, and committed to the Committee of the Whole House on the state of the Union. Mr. Archer, from the Committee on Foreign Affairs, reported the following bill: [Washington, 1830] 2 p. (H. R. 438) DNA.   3958

---- A bill authorizing the appointment of another Brigadier General for the territory of Arkansas. January 26, 1830. Read twice, and ordered to be engrossed, and read the third time to-morrow. Mr. Clark, of Kentucky, from the Committee on the Territories, to which the subject had been referred, reported the following bill: [Washington, 1830] 1 p. (H. R. 159) DNA.
3959

---- A bill authorizing the county of Allen to purchase a portion of the reservation including Fort Wayne. March 22, 1830. Mr. Kane, from the Committee on Public Lands, reported the following bill; which was read, and passed to a second reading. [Washington, 1830] 1 p. (S. 141)

DNA.   3960

---- A bill authorizing the Fourth Auditor to examine into, and report upon certain claims of Gates Hoit, against the United States. February 20, 1830. Read twice, and committed to a Committee of the Whole House to-morrow. Mr. Drayton, from the Committee on Military Affairs, reported the following bill: [Washington, 1830] 1 p. (H. R. 268) DNA.
3961

---- A bill authorizing the Legislature of the territory of Arkansas to lease the Salt Springs, in said territory, and for other purposes. February 12, 1830. Read twice, and committed to a Committee of the Whole House to-morrow. Mr. Irvin, from the Committee on the Public Lands, reported the following bill: [Washington, 1830] 2 p. (H. R. 241) DNA.   3962

---- A bill authorizing the name of Aaron Reynolds to be placed on the pension roll. February 4, 1830. Read twice, and committed to a Committee of the Whole House to-morrow. Mr. Chilton, from the Committee on Military Pensions, reported the following bill: [Washington, 1830] 1 p. (H. R. 195) DNA.   3963

---- A bill authorizing the payment of a sum of money to the officers and crews of Gun Boats No. 149, and No. 154. February 12, 1830. Read twice, and committed to a Committee of the Whole House to-morrow. Mr. C. P. White, from the Committee on Naval Affairs, reported the following bill: [Washington, 1830] 1 p. (H. R. 239) DNA.   3964

---- A bill authorizing the Secretary of State to issue a patent to John Powell. December 27,

1830. Read twice, and ordered to be engrossed, and read the third time on Wednesday next. Mr. Buchanan, from the Committee on the Judiciary, reported the following bill: [Washington, 1830] 1 p. (H. R. 515) DNA.   3965

---- A bill authorizing the Secretary of the Treasury to refund a sum of money, now in the Treasury; to Charles Henry Hall. March 9, 1830. Read twice, and committed to the Committee of the Whole House on the state of the Union. Mr. McDuffie, from the Committee of Ways and Means, reported the following bill: [Washington, 1830] 1 p. (H. R. 335) DNA.   3966

---- A bill authorizing the transportation of merchandise, with the benefit of drawback, between the Atlantic Ocean and the Northern Lakes. April 2, 1830. Read twice, and committed to the Committee of the Whole House on the state of the Union. Mr. Cambreleng, from the Committee on Commerce, reported the following bill: [Washington, 1830] 2 p. (H. R. 402) DNA.   3967

---- A bill changing the residence of the collector in the district of Burlington, in the state of New Jersey. February 5, 1830. Mr. Woodbury, from the Committee on Commerce, reported the following bill; which was read, and passed to a second reading. [Washington, 1830] 1 p. (S. 82) DNA.   3968

---- A bill concerning judgments in the Courts of the United States within the state of New York. March 8, 1830. Read twice, and ordered to be engrossed and read the third time to-morrow. Mr. Storrs, of New York, from the Committee on the Judiciary, to

which the subject had been referred, reported the following bill: [Washington, 1830] 3 p. (H. R. 331) DNA.   3969

---- A bill concerning slavery in the District of Columbia. April 19, 1830. Read twice, and committed to a Committee of the Whole House on Thursday next. Mr. Washington, from the Committee for the District of Columbia, reported the following bill: [Washington, 1830] 4 p. (H. R. 433) DNA.   3970

---- A bill concerning the heirs of Robert Fulton, deceased. March 3, 1830. Read twice, and committed to a Committee of the Whole House to-morrow. Mr. White, from the Select Committee to which was referred the case of the heirs of Robert Fulton, reported the following bill: [Washington, 1830] 1 p. (H. R. 320) DNA.   3971

---- A bill concerning the town and village commons in Missouri. April 1, 1830. Mr. Barton, from the Committee on Public Lands, reported the following bill; which was read, and passed to a second reading: [Washington, 1830] 1 p. (S. 163) DNA.   3972

---- A bill confirming certain acts of the Legislature of the state of Virginia, relating to the Chesapeake and Ohio Canal Company. April 24, 1830. Read twice, and committed to the Committee of the Whole House on the state of the Union. Mr. Craig, of Virginia, from the Committee on Internal Improvements, to which the subject had been referred, reported the following bill: [Washington, 1830] 1 p. (H. R. 441) DNA.   3973

---- A bill confirming the claims

of James Porlier, and others, to certain lands therein named. January 15, 1830. Read twice, and committed to a Committee of the Whole House to-morrow. Mr. Hunt, from the Committee on the Public Lands, reported the following bill: [Washington, 1830] 3 p. (H. R. 114) DNA. 3974

---- A bill confirming to Joshua Kennedy, his claim to a tract of land in the city of Mobile. March 25, 1830. Read twice, and committed to a Committee of the Whole House to-morrow. Mr. Pettis, from the Committee on Private Land Claims, reported the following bill: [Washington, 1830] 2 p. (H. R. 384) DNA. 3975

---- A bill declaratory of the several acts to provide for certain persons engaged in the land and naval service of the United States in the Revolutionary War. February 15, 1830. Read twice, and committed to the Committee of the Whole House on the state of the Union. Mr. Bates, from the Committee on Military Pensions, reported the following bill: [Washington, 1830] 2 p. (H. R. 248) DNA. 3976

---- A bill declaratory of the several acts to provide for certain persons engaged in the Land and Naval service of the United States, in the Revolutionary War. February 26, 1830. Mr. Foot, from the Committee on Pensions, reported the following bill; which was read, and passed to a second reading: [Washington, 1830] 2 p. (S. 113) DNA. 3977

---- A bill establishing Circuit Courts, and abridging the jurisdiction of the District Courts in the Districts of Indiana, Illinois, Missouri, Mississippi, the Eastern District of Louisiana, and the Southern District of Alabama. Amendment proposed by Mr. Strong. January 14, 1830. Committed to the Committee of the Whole House to which the said bill is committed. [Washington, 1830] 2 p. (H. R. 37) DNA. 3978

---- A bill establishing Circuit Courts, and abridging the jurisdiction of the District Courts in the Districts of Indiana, Illinois, Missouri, Mississippi, the Eastern District of Louisiana, and the Southern District of Alabama. Amendment proposed by Mr. Strong. February 12, 1830. [Washington, 1830] 5 p. (H. R. 37) DNA. 3979

---- A bill establishing the territorial government of Huron. January 6, 1830. Read twice, and committed to a Committee of the Whole House to-morrow. Mr. Clark, from the Committee on the Territories, reported the following bill: [Washington, 1830] 11 p. (H. R. 76) DNA. 3980

---- A bill explanatory of an act, entitled "An act to reduce and fix the Military Peace Establishment of the United States," passed March second, one thousand eight hundred and twenty-one. January 18, 1830. Read twice, and committed to a Committee of the Whole House to-morrow. Mr. Vance, from the Committee on Military Affairs, reported the following bill: [Washington, 1830] 1 p. (H. R. 118) DNA. 3981

---- A bill explanatory of an act to compensate Registers and Receivers of the Land Offices for extra services rendered under the provisions of the act of the second March, one thousand eight hundred and twenty-one. February 12, 1830. Read twice, and committed to a Committee of the Whole House to-morrow. Mr. Irvin, from the Committee on the Public Lands, reported the following bill: [Washington, 1830] 1 p. (H. R. 240) DNA.   3982

---- A bill extending further the right of debenture to the port of Key West, and altering the limits of the district of Key West. March 4, 1830. Mr. Woodbury, from the Committee on Commerce, reported the following bill; which was read, and passed to a second reading. [Washington, 1830] 2 p. (S. 118) DNA.   3983

---- A bill extending the privilege of debenture to merchandise transported by land, or by land and water. April 3, 1830. Read twice, and committed to the Committee of the Whole House on the state of the Union. Mr. Cambreleng, from the Committee on Commerce, reported the following bill. [Washington, 1830] 1 p. (H. R. 401) DNA.   3984

---- A bill extending the provision of the Revolutionary pension law. March 13, 1830. Read twice, and committed to the Committee of the Whole House on the state of the Union. Mr. Chilton, from the Committee on Military Pensions, reported the following bill: [Washington, 1830] 1 p. (H. R. 347) DNA.   3985

---- A bill extending the provisions of the pension laws of the United States. February 15, 1830. Read, and committed to the Committee of the Whole House on the state of the Union, to which the above mentioned bill is committed. Mr. Chilton, submitted the following, which, when the "bill (H. R. No. 248) declaratory of the several acts to provide for certain persons engaged in the

land and naval service of the United States in the Revolutionary War," shall be taken up for consideration, he will move as an amendment: [Washington, 1830] 2 p. (H. R. 248) DNA.   3986

---- A bill fixing the ratio of apportionment of members of the House of Representatives among the states, after the expiration of the Twenty Second Congress. January 27, 1830. Read twice, and committed to a Committee of the Whole House on the state of the Union. Mr. Storrs, from the Select Committee to which was referred so much of the President's Message as relates to the Fifth Census, &c. &c. reported the following bill: [Washington, 1830] 1 p. (H. R. 167) DNA.   3987

---- A bill for adjusting the claims of the state of South Carolina against the United States. January 6, 1830. Mr. Benton, from the Committee on Military Affairs, reported the following bill; which was read, and passed to a second reading: [Washington, 1830] 3 p. (S. 39) DNA.   3988

---- A bill for ascertaining the latitude of the southerly bend, or extreme of Lake Michigan, and of certain other points, for the purpose, thereafter, of fixing the true Northern boundary lines of the states of Ohio and Illinois. January 29, 1830. Read twice, and committed to the Committee of the Whole House on the state of the Union. Mr. Clark, from the Committee on the Territories, to whom the subject had been referred, reported the following bill: [Washington, 1830] 3 p. (H. R. 181) DNA.   3989

---- A bill for authorizing a patent to be issued to Moses Shaw.

March 26, 1830. Read, and postponed until Monday next.   Mr.
Storrs, from the Committee on
the Judiciary, reported the following bill: [Washington, 1830]
1 p. (H. R. 393)   DNA.
                               3990
---- A bill for closing certain
accounts, and making appropriations for arrearages in the Indian Department.   May 21, 1830.
Read twice, and committed to
the Committee of the Whole
House on the state of the Union.
Mr. Verplanck, from the Committee of Ways and Means, reported the following bill: [Wash-
ington, 1830]   3 p.   (H. R. 480)
DNA.   3991

---- A bill for further extending
the powers of the Judges of the
Superior Court of the territory of
Arkansas, under the act of the
twenty-sixth day of May, one
thousand eight hundred and twenty-four, and for other purposes.
January 14, 1830. Read twice,
and committed to a Committee of
the Whole House on the state of
the Union. Mr. Storrs, of New
York, from the Committee on the
Judiciary, to which the subject
had been referred, reported the
following bill: [Washington,
1830] 4 p. (H. R. 112) DNA.
                               3992
---- A bill for improving the
avenue leading from the Capitol
to the Executive Offices. February 10, 1830. Read twice, and
committed to a Committee of the
Whole House to-morrow. Mr.
Powers, from the Committee for
the District of Columbia, reported the following bill: [Washing-
ton, 1830] 1 p. (H. R. 224) DNA.
                               3993
---- A bill for promoting the
growth and manufacture of silk.
March 8, 1830. Read twice, and
committed to the Committee of
the Whole House on the state of

the Union.   Mr. Spencer, of New
York, from the Committee on
Agriculture, reported the following bill: [Washington, 1830] 8
p. (H. R. 345) DNA.   3994

---- A bill for re-organizing the
Courts of Justice in the District
of Columbia.   March 24, 1830.
Read twice, and committed to the
Committee of the Whole House
on the state of the Union. Mr.
Powers, from the Committee for
the District of Columbia, reported the following bill: [Wash-
ington, 1830] 29 p. (H. R. 382)
DNA.   3995

---- A bill for the adjustment
and settlement of the claims of
the state of South Carolina against
the United States.   January 11,
1830. Read twice, and committed to a Committee of the Whole
House to-morrow. Mr. Drayton,
from the Committee on Military
Affairs, reported the following
bill: [Washington, 1830] 3 p.
(H. R. 91) DNA.   3996

---- A bill for the benefit of
Charles Brown, a soldier of the
Revolutionary War. January 18,
1830. Read twice, and commit-
ted to a Committee of the Whole
House to-morrow. Mr. Chilton,
from the Committee on Military
Pensions, reported the following
bill: [Washington, 1830] 1 p.
(H. R. 128) DNA.   3997

---- A bill for the benefit of
Daniel McDuff.   April 10, 1830.
Mr. McKinley, from the Committee on Public Lands, reported
the following bill; which was read
twice, and ordered to be engrossed: [Washington, 1830] 2 p.
(S. 176) DNA.   3998

---- A bill for the benefit of
John Berryhill, on account of
military services. May 3, 1830.

Read twice, and committed to a Committee of the Whole House to-morrow. Mr. Chilton, from the Committee on Military Pensions, reported the following bill: [Washington, 1830] 1 p. (H.R. 453) DNA. 3999

---- A bill for the benefit of John Boone. May 3, 1830. Read twice, and committed to a Committee of the Whole House to-morrow. Mr. Chilton, from the Committee on Military Pensions, reported the following bill: [Washington, 1830] 1 p. (H.R. 451) DNA. 4000

---- A bill for the benefit of Saint Vincent's Female Orphan Asylum of the City of Washington, under the direction of the "Sisters of Charity." April 17, 1830. Mr. Chambers, from the Committee on the District of Columbia, reported the following bill; which was read, and passed to a second reading: [Washington, 1830] 1 p. (S. 181) DNA. 4001

---- A bill for the benefit of schools in Lawrence county, Mississippi. April 5, 1830. Mr. Ellis, from the Committee on Public Lands, reported the following bill; which was read, and passed to a second reading: [Washington, 1830] 1 p. (S. 165) DNA. 4002

---- A bill for the benefit of the Columbian College of the District of Columbia. March 12, 1830. Read twice, and committed to a Committee of the Whole House to-morrow. Mr. Varnum, from the Committee for the District of Columbia, reported the following bill: [Washington, 1830] 1 p. (H.R. 344) DNA. 4003

---- A bill for the benefit of the creditors of Bennet and Morte.

February 22, 1830. Mr. Johnson, from the Committee on Finance, reported the following bill; which was read, and passed to a second reading: [Washington, 1830] 1 p. (S. 104) DNA. 4004

---- A bill for the benefit of the New York Institution for the instruction of the Deaf and Dumb. January 18, 1830. Mr. Barton, from the Committee on Public Lands, reported the following bill; which was read, and passed to a second reading: [Washington, 1830] 1 p. (S. 62) DNA. 4005

---- ---- April 5, 1830. [Washington, 1830] 2 p. (S. 62) DNA. 4006

---- A bill for the benefit of the Pennsylvania Institution for the instruction of the Deaf and Dumb. February 22, 1830. Mr. Barton, from the Committee on the Public Lands, reported the following bill; which was read, and passed to a second reading. [Washington, 1830] 1 p. (S. 101) DNA. 4007

---- A bill for the better organization of the Militia of the District of Columbia. February 11, 1830. Read twice, and committed to the Committee of the Whole House on the state of the Union. Mr. Thompson, of Georgia, from the Committee on the Militia, reported the following bill. [Washington, 1830] 29p. (H.R. 235) DNA. 4008

---- A bill for the continuation of the Cumberland Road, in the States of Ohio, Indiana, and Illinois. February 22, 1830. Mr. Hendricks, from the Committee on Roads and Canals, reported the following bill; which was read, and passed to a second reading: [Washington, 1830] 2 p. (S. 100) DNA. 4009

---- ---- March 2, 1830. Read
twice, and committed to a Committee of the Whole House to-
morrow. Mr. Vinton, from the
Committee on Internal Improvements, reported the following
bill: [Washington, 1830] 2 p.
(H. R. 315) DNA.   4010

---- A bill for the distribution
of certain books therein mentioned.   May 17, 1830. Read
twice, and ordered to be engrossed, and read the third time
to-morrow. Mr. Everett, from
the Committee on the Library,
reported the following bill.
[Washington, 1830] 3 p. (H. R.
471) DNA.   4011

---- A bill for the encouragement of Augusta College, in Kentucky. January 13, 1830. Mr.
Kane, from the Committee on
Public Lands, reported the following bill; which was read, and
passed to a second reading:
[Washington, 1830] 1 p. (S. 57)
DNA.   4012

---- A bill for the erection of a
National Armory upon the Western waters. January 4, 1830.
Read twice, and committed to a
Committee of the Whole House
to-morrow. Mr. Drayton, from
the Committee on Military Affairs, reported the following bill:
[Washington, 1830] 1 p. (H. R.
63) DNA.   4013

---- A bill for the further regulation of vessels bound up James'
River, in the state of Virginia.
January 19, 1830. Read twice,
and ordered to be engrossed, and
read the third time to-morrow.
Mr. Cambreleng, from the Committee on Commerce, to which
the subject had been referred,
reported the following bill: [Wash-
ington, 1830] 1 p. (H. R. 132)
DNA.   4014

---- A bill for the gradual increase of the Corps of Engineers,
and for other purposes. January
4, 1830. Read twice, and committed to a Committee of the
Whole House to-morrow. Mr.
Drayton, from the Committee on
Military Affairs, reported the
following bill: [Washington,
1830] 2 p. (H. R. 56) DNA. 4015

---- A bill for the improvement
of the lands of the United States
in the state of Louisiana. January 12, 1830. Mr. Livingston,
from the Committee on Public
Lands, reported the following
bill; which was read, and passed
to a second reading: [Washing-
ton, 1830] 2 p. (S. 53) DNA.
                                  4016
---- A bill for the improvement
of the Mail Road between Louisville and St. Louis.   January 20,
1830.   Mr. Hendricks, from the
Committee on Roads and Canals,
reported the following bill; which
was read, and passed to a second reading: [Washington, 1830]
1 p. (S. 68) DNA.   4017

---- A bill for the more effectual collection of the impost duties. May 5, 1830. Laid before
the House by Mr. Buchanan, and
ordered to be printed. [Wash-
ington, 1830] 5 p. (H. R. 164)
DNA.   4018

---- A bill for the organization
of the Topographical Engineers.
January 4, 1830. Read twice,
and committed to a Committee
of the Whole House to-morrow.
Mr. Drayton, from the Committee on Military Affairs, reported
the following bill: [Washington,
1830] 1 p. (H. R. 57) DNA. 4019

---- A bill for the payment of
certain mounted volunteers of the
Territory of Arkansas whilst in
the service of the United States.

April 9, 1830. Read twice, and committed to the Committee of the Whole House on the state of the Union. Mr. Drayton, from the Committee on Military Affairs, reported the following bill: [Washington, 1830] 1 p. (H. R. 415) DNA.					4020

---- A bill for the payment of the unsatisfied claims of the Militia of the state of Georgia, for services rendered in the years 1792, 1793, and 1794. January 4, 1830, Read twice, and committed to a Committee of the Whole House to-morrow. Mr. Drayton, from the Committee on Military Affairs, reported the following bill: [Washington, 1830] 1 p. (H. R. 64) DNA.					4021

---- A bill for the preservation and repair of the Cumberland Road. February 25, 1830. Read twice, and committed to the Committee of the Whole House on the state of the Union. Mr. Letcher, from the Committee on Internal Improvements, reported the following bill: [Washington, 1830] 3 p. (H. R. 292) DNA.					4022

---- A bill for the punishment of crimes in the District of Columbia. March 11, 1830. Read twice, and committed to the Committee of the Whole House on the state of the Union. Mr. Powers, from the Committee for the District of Columbia, reported the following bill: [Washington, 1830] 7 p. (H. R. 339) DNA.					4023

---- ---- April 27, 1830. Taken up and considered by the House, amended, and postponed until Thursday next, and ordered to be printed as amended. [Washington, 1830] 8 p. (H. R. 339) DNA.					4024

---- A bill for the re-appropriation of certain unexpended balances of former appropriations. March 18, 1830. Read twice, and committed to the Committee of the Whole House on the state of the Union. Mr. Verplanck, from the Committee of Ways and Means, reported the following bill: [Washington, 1830] 3 p. (H. R. 365) DNA.					4025

---- A bill for the regulation of the Navy Pension Fund. April 9, 1830. Mr. Hayne, from the Committee on Naval Affairs, reported the following bill; which was read, and passed to a second meeting: [Washington, 1830] 3 p. (S. 175) DNA.					4026

---- A bill for the regulation of the pay and emoluments of officers in the Army of the United States. January 4, 1830. Read twice, and committed to a Committee of the Whole House to-morrow. Mr. Drayton, from the Committee on Military Affairs, reported the following bill: [Washington, 1830] 1 p. (H. R. 59) DNA.					4027

---- A bill for the relief of Aaron Snow. February 9, 1830. Read twice, and committed to a Committee of the Whole House to-morrow. Mr. Wingate, from the Committee on Revolutionary Claims, reported the following bill: [Washington, 1830] 2 p. (H. R. 216) DNA.					4028

---- A bill for the relief of Abel Allen. May 8, 1830. Read twice, and ordered to be engrossed, and read the third time to-morrow. Mr. Ford, from the Committee on Military Pensions, reported the following bill: [Washington, 1830] 1 p. (H. R. 464) DNA.					4029

---- A bill for the relief of Abraham Brownson. April 6, 1830. Mr. Chase, from the Committee on Pensions, reported the following bill; which was read, and passed to a second reading. [Washington, 1830] 1 p. (S. 169) DNA. 4030

---- A bill for the relief of Alexander Claxton. January 7, 1830. Read twice, and committed to a Committee of the Whole House to-morrow. Mr. Miller, from the Committee on Naval Affairs, reported the following bill: [Washington, 1830] 2 p. (H. R. 84) DNA. 4031

---- A bill for the relief of Alexander Fridge. January 13, 1830. Read twice, and committed to a Committee of the Whole House to-morrow. Mr. Gurley, from the Committee on Private Land Claims, reported the following bill: [Washington, 1830] 1 p. (H. R. 108) DNA. 4032

---- A bill for the relief of Alexander Love. January 27, 1830. Read twice, and committed to a Committee of the Whole House to-morrow. Mr. Gurley, from the Committee on Private Land Claims, reported the following bill: [Washington, 1830] 1 p. (H. R. 165) DNA. 4033

---- A bill for the relief of Alexander Oswald Brodie, of New York. February 5, 1830. Read twice, and committed to a Committee of the Whole House to-morrow. Mr. Cambreleng, from the Committee on Commerce, reported the following bill: [Washington, 1830] 1 p. (H. R. 204) DNA. 4034

---- A bill for the relief of Andrew H. Richardson, executor of Valentine Richardson. May 3, 1830. Read twice, and committed to a Committee of the Whole House to-morrow. Mr. Whittle-

sey, from the Committee of Claims, reported the following bill: [Washington, 1830] 1 p. (H. R. 450) DNA. 4035

---- A bill for the relief of Ann Brashears, of Mississippi. January 20, 1830. Read twice, and committed to a Committee of the Whole House to-morrow. Mr. Test, from the Committee on Private Land Claims, reported the following bill: [Washington, 1830] 2 p. (H. R. 139) DNA. 4036

---- A bill for the relief of Ann D. Baylor. February 26, 1830. Read twice, and committed to a Committee of the Whole House to-morrow. Mr. Burges, from the Committee on Revolutionary Claims, reported the following bill: [Washington, 1830] 2 p. (H. R. 296) DNA. 4037

---- A bill for the relief of Anthony M. Minter and John Brantley. Mar. 10, 1830. Mr. McKinley, from the Committee on Public Lands, reported the following bill; which was read, and passed to a second reading: [Washington, 1830] 1 p. (S. 127) DNA. 4038

---- A bill for the relief of Antoine Dequindre, Richard Smith, and others, Michigan Volunteers. March 3, 1830. Read twice, and committed to a Committee of the Whole House to-morrow. Mr. Whittlesey, from the Committee of Claims, reported the following bill: [Washington, 1830] 2 p. (H. R. 318) DNA. 4039

---- A bill for the relief of Ariel Ensign. April 29, 1830. Read twice, and committed to the Committee of the Whole House to which is committed the bill (No. 342) for the relief of Sylvester Havens. Mr. Crane, from the

Committee of Claims, reported the following bill: [Washington, 1830] 1 p. (H.R. 447) DNA.

4040

---- A bill for the relief of Barnard Kelley. December 17, 1830. Read twice, and committed to a Committee of the Whole House this day. Mr. Johnson, of Kentucky, from the Committee on the Post Office and Post Roads, reported the following bill: [Washington, 1830] 2 p. (H.R. 501) DNA.   4041

---- A bill for the relief of Bartholomew Delapierre, of the city of New York. May 3, 1830. Read twice, and committed to a Committee of the Whole House to-morrow. Mr. Chilton, from the Committee on Military Pensions, reported the following bill: [Washington, 1830] 1 p. (H.R. 452) DNA.   4042

---- A bill for the relief of Benedict Joseph Flaget. March 29, 1830. Read twice, and committed to the Committee of the Whole House to which is committed bill (No. 300) to remit the duties upon certain articles imported for the use of the Theological Seminary and Kenyon College, in Ohio. Mr. Verplanck, from the Committee of Ways and Means, reported the following bill: [Washington, 1830] 1 p. (H.R. 396) DNA.   4043

---- A bill for the relief of Benjamin Gibbs. February 8, 1830. Read twice, and committed to a Committee of the Whole House to-morrow. Mr. Goodenow, from the Committee on Revolutionary Claims, reported the following bill: [Washington, 1830] 1 p. (H.R. 214) DNA.   4044

---- A bill for the relief of Benjamin Homans. January 13, 1830.

Read twice, and committed to a Committee of the Whole House to-morrow. Mr. Whittlesey, from the Committee of Claims, reported the following bill: [Washington, 1830] 1 p. (H.R. 106) DNA.   4045

---- A bill for the relief of Benjamin Pendleton. May 31, 1830. Read twice, and committed to a Committee of the Whole House to-morrow. Mr. Campbell P. White, from the Committee on Naval Affairs, reported the following bill: [Washington, 1830] 1 p. (H.R. 498) DNA.   4046

---- A bill for the relief of Benjamin Wells. February 25, 1830. Read twice, and committed to a Committee of the Whole House to-morrow. Mr. Burges, from the Committee on Revolutionary Claims, reported the following bill: [Washington, 1830] 2 p. (H.R. 297) DNA.

4047

---- A bill for the relief of Beverly Chew, the heirs of William Emerson, deceased, and the heirs of Edwin Lorraine, deceased. Feb. 16, 1830, Read, and passed to a second reading. February 17, 1830, Read second time, and referred to the Committee on the Judiciary. February 19, 1830. Reported without amendment. [Washington, 1830] 2 p. (S. 96) DNA.   4048

---- A bill for the relief of Caleb Stark. March 29, 1830. Mr. Bell, from the Committee of Claims, reported the following bill; which was read, and passed to a second reading: [Washington, 1830] 1 p. (S. 157) DNA.

4049

---- A bill for the relief of Captain Daniel McDuff. January 6, 1830. Read twice, and committed to a Committee of the Whole House to-morrow. Mr. Clay, from the Select Committee, to which had been referred the petition of Daniel McDuff, reported the following bill: [Washington, 1830] 1 p. (H. R. 81) DNA. 4050

---- A bill for the relief of Captain John Woods. January 15, 1830. Read twice, and committed to a Committee of the Whole House to morrow. Mr. Clay, from the Committee on the Public Lands, reported the following bill: [Washington, 1830] 2 p. (H. R. 117) DNA.   4051

---- A bill for the relief of Captain Thomas Paine. February 24, 1830. Read twice, and committed to a Committee of the Whole House to-morrow. Mr. Overton, from the Committee of Ways and Means, reported the following bill: [Washington, 1830] 1 p. (H. R. 283) DNA.   4052

---- A bill for the relief of certain importers of cloths. May 4, 1830. Read twice, and committed to a Committee of the Whole House tomorrow. Mr. Verplanck, from the Committee of Ways and Means, reported the following bill: [Washington, 1830] 2 p. (H. R. 457) DNA.   4053

---- A bill for the relief of certain inhabitants of East Florida. February 9, 1830. Read twice, and committed to the Committee of the Whole House on the state of the Union. Mr. Archer, from the Committee on Foreign Affairs, reported the following bill: [Washington, 1830] 2 p. (H. R. 221) DNA.   4054

---- A bill for the relief of certain insolvent debtors of the United States. March 9, 1830. Read twice, and committed to the Committee of the Whole House on the state of the Union. Mr. Buchanan, from the Committee on the Judiciary, reported the fol-

lowing bill: [Washington, 1830] 6 p. (H. R. 336) DNA.   4055

---- A bill for the relief of certain officers and soldiers of the Revolution, their heirs, or legal representatives. March 22, 1830. Read twice, and committed to a Committee of the Whole House to-morrow. Mr. Potter, from the Committee on Public Lands, reported the following bill: [Washington, 1830] 2 p. (H. R. 370) DNA.   4056

---- A bill for the relief of certain officers and soldiers of the Virginia State line during the Revolutionary war. March 17, 1830. Mr. Barton, from the Committee on Public Lands, reported the following bill; which was read, and passed to a second reading: [Washington, 1830] 1 p. (S. 134) DNA.   4057

---- A bill for the relief of certain persons engaged in the Land and Naval service of the United States, in the Revolutionary war. March 2, 1830. Read twice, and committed to a Committee of the Whole House to-morrow. Mr. Burges, from the Committee on Revolutionary Claims, reported the following bill: [Washington, 1830] 3 p. (H. R. 311) DNA.
4058

---- A bill for the relief of Charles Cassedy. May 7, 1830. Read twice, and committed to a Committee of the Whole House to-morrow. Mr. Whittlesey, from the Committee of Claims, reported the following bill: [Washington, 1830] 1 p. (H. R. 460) DNA.   4059

---- A bill for the relief of Charles Collins. January 29, 1830. Read twice, and committed to a Committee of the Whole House to-morrow. Mr. Verplanck, from the Committee of Ways and Means, reported the following bill: [Washington, 1830] 1 p. (H. R. 182) DNA.   4060

---- A bill for the relief of Charles Wilkes, Junior. March 17, 1830. Read twice, and committed to the Committee of the Whole House to which is committed the bill (No. 84,) for the relief of Alexander Claxton. Mr. White, from the Committee on Naval Affairs, reported the following bill: [Washington, 1830] 2 p. (H. R. 360) DNA.   4061

---- A bill for the relief of Coleman Fisher. March 16, 1830. Read twice, and committed to a Committee of the Whole House to-morrow. Mr. Test, from the Committee on Private Land Claims, reported the following bill: [Washington, 1830] 2 p. (H. R. 355) DNA.   4062

---- A bill for the relief of Collin McLachlan. February 15, 1830. Read twice, and committed to a Committee of the Whole House to-morrow. Mr. Young, from the Committee on Revolutionary Claims, reported the following bill: [Washington, 1830] 1 p. (H. R. 249) DNA.   4063

---- A bill for the relief of Crosby Arey. April 3, 1830. Read twice, and committed to a Committee of the Whole House to-morrow. Mr. Harvey, from the Committee on Commerce, reported the following bill: [Washington, 1830] 1 p. (H. R. 405) DNA.   4064

---- A bill for the relief of Daniel Goodwin, executor of Benjamin Goodwin, deceased. March 19, 1830. Read twice, and committed to a Committee of the Whole House to-morrow. Mr.

Dickinson, from the Committee on Revolutionary Claims, reported the following bill: [Washington, 1830] 1 p. (H. R. 371) DNA.   4065

---- A bill for the relief of Daniel Jackson and Lucius M. Higgins, of Newbern in North Carolina. December 31, 1830. Read twice, and committed to a Committee of the Whole House to-morrow. Mr. Loyall, from the Committee on Commerce, reported the following bill: [Washington, 1830] 1 p. (H. R. 529) DNA.   4066

---- A bill for the relief of Daniel Johnson. March 26, 1830. Read twice, and committed to a Committee of the Whole House to-morrow. Mr. Drayton, from the Committee on Military Affairs, reported the following bill: [Washington, 1830] 1 p. (H. R. 388) DNA.   4067

---- A bill for the relief of Daniel Steenrod and Daniel Loomis. March 6, 1830. Mr. Ruggles, from the Committee of Claims, reported the following bill; which was read, and passed to a second reading. [Washington, 1830] 1 p. (S. 122) DNA.   4068

---- A bill for the relief of David Beard. February 25, 1830. Mr. Smith, of Maryland, from the Committee on Finance, reported the following bill; which was read, and passed to a second reading: [Washington, 1830] 1 p. (S. 112) DNA.   4069

---- A bill for the relief of David Brooks. April 9, 1830. Read twice, and committed to a Committee of the Whole House to-morrow. Mr. Bockee, from the Committee on Military Pensions, reported the following bill: [Washington, 1830] 1 p. (H. R.

417) DNA.   4070

---- A bill for the relief of David Guard. April 30, 1830. Mr. Barton, from the Committee on Public Lands, reported the following bill; which was read, and passed to a second reading: [Washington, 1830] 1 p. (S. 185) DNA.   4071

---- A bill for the relief of David Kennard. May 14, 1830. Read twice, and committed to a Committee of the Whole House to-morrow. Mr. Bockee, from the Committee on Military Pensions, reported the following bill: [Washington, 1830] 1 p. (H. R. 468) DNA.   4072

---- A bill for the relief of David Rogers and Sons. January 26, 1830. Read twice, and committed to a Committee of the Whole House to-morrow. Mr. Ingersoll, from the Committee of Ways and Means, reported the following bill: [Washington, 1830] 1 p. (H. R. 154) DNA.   4073

---- A bill for the relief of Don Carlos Dehault Delassus. February 25, 1830. Read twice, and referred to Committee of Claims. March 12, Committee of Claims discharged, and referred to Committee on Foreign Relations. March 31, Reported without amendment, with a special report. [Washington, 1830] 1 p. (S. 111) DNA.   4074

---- A bill for the relief of Dorothy Wells. February 15, 1830. Read twice, and committed to a Committee of the Whole House to-morrow. Mr. Test, from the Committee on Private Land Claims, reported the following bill: [Washington, 1830] 2 p. (H. R. 252) DNA.   4075

---- A bill for the relief of Ebenezer Rollins. April 2, 1830. Mr. Silsbee, from the Committee on Finance, reported the following bill; which was read, and passed to a second reading: [Washington, 1830] 2 p. (S. 164) DNA.   4076

---- A bill for the relief of Eber Hubbard. March 12, 1830. Read twice, and committed to a Committee of the Whole House to-morrow. Mr. Whittlesey, from the Committee of Claims, reported the following bill: [Washington, 1830] 1 p. (H. R. 341) DNA.   4077

---- A bill for the relief of Edmund Brooke. February 26, 1830. Read twice, and committed to a Committee of the Whole House to-morrow. Mr. Burges, from the Committee on Revolutionary Claims, reported the following bill: [Washington, 1830] 2 p. (H. R. 295) DNA.   4078

---- A bill for the relief of Edward Lee. February 22, 1830. Read twice, and committed to a Committee of the Whole House to-morrow. Mr. Whittlesey, from the Committee of Claims, reported the following bill: [Washington, 1830] 1 p. (H. R. 269) DNA.   4079

---- A bill for the relief of Eleanor Courts, widow of Richard Henly Courts, deceased. February 26, 1830. Read twice, and committed to a Committee of the Whole House to-morrow. Mr. Goodenow, from the Committee on Revolutionary Claims, reported the following bill: [Washington, 1830] 2 p. (H. R. 302) DNA.   4080

---- A bill for the relief of Eliakim Crosby. March 3, 1830. Read twice, and committed to a

Committee of the Whole House to-morrow. Mr. Pettis, from the Committee on the Public Lands, reported the following bill: [Washington, 1830] 1 p. (H. R. 319) DNA.   4081

---- A bill for the relief of Elisha Ives. February 1, 1830. Read twice, and committed to a Committee of the Whole House to-morrow. Mr. Whittlesey, from the Committee of Claims, reported the following bill: [Washington, 1830] 1 p. (H. R. 186) DNA.   4082

---- A bill for the relief of Elisha Tracy. February 2, 1830. Mr. Ruggles, from the Committee of Claims, reported the following bill; which was read, and passed to a second reading: [Washington, 1830] 1 p. (S. 77) DNA.   4083

---- A bill for the relief of Elizabeth Dandridge. February 10, 1830. Read twice, and committed to the Committee of the Whole House to which is committed the bill (No. 173) for the relief of the representatives of Thomas Blackwell. Mr. Young, from the Committee on Revolutionary Claims, reported the following bill: [Washington, 1830] 1 p. (H. R. 229) DNA.   4084

---- A bill for the relief of Elizabeth Scott, assignee of Alexander Scott, junior. April 23, 1830. Mr. King, from the Committee on Finance, reported the following bill; which was read, and passed to a second reading: [Washington, 1830] 1 p. (S. 182) DNA.   4085

---- A bill for the relief of Elizabeth Williams. February 11, 1830. Read twice, and committed to a Committee of the Whole

House to-morrow. Mr. Whittlesey, from the Committee of Claims, reported the following bill: [Washington, 1830] 1 p. (H. R. 230) DNA.   4086

---- A bill for the relief of Enoch Hoyt and Joseph Moss, soldiers of the Revolution. April 26, 1830. Read twice, and committed to a Committee of the Whole House to-morrow. Mr. Forward, from the Committee on Military Pensions, reported the following bill: [Washington, 1830] 1 p. (H. R. 445) DNA.   4087

---- A bill for the relief of Ephraim F. Gilbert. February 24, 1830. Read twice, and committed to a Committee of the Whole House to-morrow. Mr. McIntire, from the Committee of Claims, reported the following bill: [Washington, 1830] 2 p. (H. R. 282) DNA.   4088

---- A bill for the relief of Ephraim Whitaker. January 26, 1830. Read twice, and committed to a Committee of the Whole House to-morrow. Mr. Bockee, from the Committee on Military Pensions reported the following bill: [Washington, 1830] 1 p. (H. R. 157) DNA.   4089

---- A bill for the relief of Eugene Borell, of Louisiana. February 15, 1830. Read twice, and committed to a Committee of the Whole House to-morrow. Mr. Test, from the Committee on Private Land Claims, reported the following bill: [Washington, 1830] 2 p. (H. R. 253) DNA.   4090

---- A bill for the relief of Ezekiel Woodworth. April 6, 1830. Mr. Chase, from the Committee on Pensions, reported the following bill; which was read, and passed to a second reading:

[Washington, 1830] 1 p. (S. 167) DNA. 4091

---- A bill for the relief of Fielding L. White. February 1, 1830. Read twice, and committed to a Committee of the Whole House to-morrow. Mr. Johnson, of Kentucky, from the Committee on the Post Office and Post Roads, reported the following bill: [Washington, 1830] 1 p. (H. R. 188) DNA. 4092

---- A bill for the relief of Francis Preston. January 4, 1830. Mr. Barton, from the Committee on Public Lands, reported the following bill; which was read, and passed to a second reading: [Washington, 1830] 1 p. (S. 29) DNA. 4093

---- A bill for the relief of François Isidore Tuillier. January 13, 1830. Read twice, and committed to a Committee of the Whole House to-morrow. Mr. Gurley, from the Committee on Private Land Claims, reported the following bill: [Washington, 1830] 1 p. (H. R. 109) DNA. 4094

---- A bill for the relief of Frederick Raymer. January 4, 1830. Read twice, and committed to a Committee of the Whole House to-morrow. Mr. Burges, from the Committee on Revolutionary Claims, reported the following bill: [Washington, 1830] 1 p. (H. R. 70) DNA. 4095

---- A bill for the relief of General Simon Kenton. April 6, 1830. Read twice, and committed to the Committee of the Whole House to which is commited the bill (H. R. No. 195) authorizing the name of Aaron Reynolds to be placed on the pension roll. Mr. Lecompte, from the Committee on Military Pen-

sions, reported the following bill: [Washington, 1830] 1 p. (H. R. 408) DNA. 4096

---- A bill for the relief of George Banister. April 12, 1830. Mr. Marks, from the Committee on Pensions, reported the following Bill; which was read, and passed to a second reading: [Washington, 1830] 1 p. (S. 178) DNA. 4097

---- A bill for the relief of George Bowen, of South Carolina. April 3, 1830. Read twice, and committed to a Committee of the Whole House to-morrow. Mr. Campbell, from the Committee on the Post Office and Post Roads, reported the following bill: [Washington, 1830] 1 p. (H. R. 403) DNA. 4098

---- A bill for the relief of George E. Tingle. February 17, 1830. Read twice, and committed to a Committee of the Whole House to-morrow. Mr. Clarke, from the Committee on the Territories, reported the following bill: [Washington, 1830] 1 p. (H. R. 256) DNA. 4099

---- A bill for the relief of George Ermatinger. January 29, 1830. Read twice, and committed to a Committee of the Whole House to-morrow. Mr. Whittlesey, from the Committee of Claims, reported the following bill: [Washington, 1830] 1 p. (H. R. 178) DNA. 4100

---- A bill for the relief of George Innes, of New York. February 15, 1830. Read twice, and committed to a Committee of the Whole House to-morrow. Mr. Cambreleng, from the Committee on Commerce, reported the following bill: [Washington, 1830] 1 p. (H. R. 247)

DNA.   4101

---- A bill for the relief of
George Johnston. January 25,
1830. Mr. Rowan, from the Committee on the Judiciary, reported
the following bill; which was read,
and passed to a second reading:
[Washington, 1830] 1 p. (S. 73)
DNA.   4102

---- A bill for the relief of Gregoire Sarpy, or his legal representatives. January 20, 1830.
Mr. Barton, from the Committee
on Private Land Claims, reported the following bill; which was
read, and passed to a second
reading: [Washington, 1830] 1 p.
(S. 70) DNA.   4103

---- A bill for the relief of Henry Becker. March 18, 1830. Mr.
Holmes, from the Committee on
Pensions, reported the following
bill; which was read, and passed
to a second reading: [Washington,
1830] 1 p. (S. 136) DNA. 4104

---- A bill for the relief of Henry H. Tuckerman. February 10,
1830. Read twice, and committed to a Committee of the Whole
House to-morrow. Mr. Dwight,
from the Committee of Ways and
Means, reported the following
bill: [Washington, 1830] 1 p.
(H. R. 222) DNA.   4105

---- A bill for the relief of Henry Kilbourn. March 26, 1830.
Read twice, and ordered to be engrossed, and read the third time
to-morrow. Mr. Crane, from the
Committee of Claims, reported
the following bill: [Washington,
1830] 1 p. (H. R. 389) DNA. 4106

---- A bill for the relief of Henry Williams. January 25, 1830.
Read twice, and committed to a
Committee of the Whole House to-
morrow. Mr. Whittlesey, from

the Committee of Claims, reported the following bill: [Wash-
ington, 1830] 1 p. (H. R. 149)
DNA.   4107

---- A bill for the relief of Hugh
Barnes. January 18, 1830. Mr.
Chase, from the Committee on
Pensions, reported the following
bill; which was read, and passed
to a second reading. [Washington,
1830] 1 p. (S. 64) DNA.   4108

---- A bill for the relief of Ichabod Ward. March 22, 1830. Read
twice, and committed to a Committee of the Whole House to-
morrow. Mr. Young, from the
Committee on Revolutionary
Claims, reported the following
bill: [Washington, 1830] 1 p.
(H. R. 375) DNA.   4109

---- A bill for the relief of Isaac
Pinney. April 8, 1830. Mr.
Chase, from the Committee on
Pensions, reported the following
bill; which was read, and passed
to a second reading: [Washing-
ton, 1830] 1 p. (S. 174) DNA.
                            4110

---- A bill for the relief of Isaiah
Townsend, Peter Dox, and Gerrit
Le Grange, sureties of Gerrit L.
Dox. January 25, 1830. Read
twice, and committed to a Com-
mittee of the Whole House to-
morrow. Mr. Johnson, from the
Committee on the Post Office and
Post Roads, reported the follow-
ing bill: [Washington, 1830] 1 p.
(H. R. 150) DNA.   4111

---- A bill for the relief of J. N.
Cardozo. March 11, 1830. Mr.
Rowan, from the Committee on
the Judiciary, reported the fol-
lowing bill; which was read, and
passed to a second reading:
[Washington, 1830] 1 p. (S. 130)
DNA.   4112

---- A bill for the relief of J. N.

Cardozo. March 17, 1830. Read twice, and committed to a Committee of the Whole House to-morrow. Mr. Overton, from the Committee of Ways and Means, reported the following bill: [Washington, 1830] 1 p. (H.R. 361) DNA.   4113

---- A bill for the relief of J. W. Hollister, et al. January 4, 1830. Read twice, and committed to the Committee of the Whole House to which is committed the bill to remit to George and William Bangs the amount of duties on certain goods destroyed by fire. Mr. Dwight, from the Committee of Ways and Means, reported the following bill: [Washington, 1830] 1 p. (H.R. 67) DNA.   4114

---- A bill for the relief of Jacob Wilderman. January 4, 1830. Read twice, and committed to a Committee of the Whole House to-morrow. Mr. Ramsey, from the Committee of Claims, reported the following bill: [Washington, 1830] 1 p. (H.R. 55) DNA.   4115

---- A bill for the relief of James Abbott. January 6, 1830. Read twice, and committed to a Committee of the Whole House to-morrow. Mr. Whittlesey, from the Committee of Claims, reported the following bill: [Washington, 1830] 1 p. (H.R. 75) DNA.   4116

---- A bill for the relief of James Barnett. January 26, 1830. Read twice, and committed to a Committee of the Whole House to-morrow. Mr. Wingate, from the Committee on Revolutionary Claims, to which was referred the case of James Barnett, reported the following bill: [Washington, 1830] 1 p. (H.R.

161) DNA.   4117

---- A bill for the relief of James Belger. January 18, 1830. Mr. Chase, from the Committee on Pensions, reported the following bill; which was read, and passed to a second reading: [Washington, 1830] 1 p. (S. 63) DNA.   4118

---- A bill for the relief of James Bradford, of Louisiana. March 16, 1830. Read twice, and committed to a Committee of the Whole House to-morrow. Mr. Test, from the Committee on Private Land Claims, reported the following bill: [Washington, 1830] 2 p. (H.R. 356) DNA.
                                     4119

---- A bill for the relief of James Fisk. February 5, 1830. Read twice, and committed to a Committee of the Whole House to-morrow. Mr. Ramsey, from the Committee of Claims, reported the following bill: [Washington, 1830] 1 p. (H.R. 199) DNA.   4120

---- A bill for the relief of James Gibbon. March 2, 1830. Read twice, and committed to a Committee of the Whole House to-morrow. Mr. Burges, from the Committee on Revolutionary Claims, reported the following bill: [Washington, 1830] 1 p. (H.R. 312) DNA.   4121

---- A bill for the relief of James McCarty. February 20, 1830. Read twice, and committed to a Committee of the Whole House to-morrow. Mr. Ramsey, from the Committee of Claims, reported the following bill: [Washington, 1830] 1 p. (H.R. 267) DNA.   4122

---- A bill for the relief of James Monroe. March 6, 1830.

Read twice, and committed to a Committee of the Whole House to-morrow. Mr. Mercer, from the Select Committee to which was referred the Memorial of citizens of Virginia, asking for a revision of the claims of the late President, James Monroe, reported the following bill: [Washington, 1830] 1 p. (H. R. 330) DNA.   4123

---- A bill for the relief of James Schols. February 19, 1830. Read twice, and ordered to be engrossed and read the third time to-morrow. Mr. Buchanan, from the Committee on the Judiciary, reported the following bill: [Washington, 1830] 1 p. (H. R. 261) DNA.   4124

---- A bill for the relief of James Smith. January 8, 1830. Read twice, and committed to a Committee of the Whole House to-morrow. Mr. Whittlesey, from the Committee of Claims, reported the following bill: [Washington, 1830] 1 p. (H. R. 88) DNA.   4125

---- A bill for the relief of James Soyer. March 6, 1830. Read twice, and committed to a Committee of the Whole House to-morrow. Mr. Burges, from the Committee on Revolutionary Claims, reported the following bill: [Washington, 1830] 1 p. (H. R. 327) DNA.   4126

---- A bill for the relief of James Sprague. May 6, 1830. Mr. Barton, from the Committee on Public Lands, reported the following bill; which was read, and passed to a second reading: [Washington, 1830] 1 p. (S. 189) DNA.   4127

---- A bill for the relief of James Thomas, late Quartermaster General of the Army of the United States. February 24, 1830. Mr. Ruggles, from the Committee of Claims, reported the following bill; which was read, and passed to a second reading: [Washington, 1830] 1 p. (S. 109) DNA.   4128

---- A bill for the relief of James W. Brannin, Charles Hughes, and Nathaniel Ford. May 24, 1830. Read twice, and committed to a Committee of the Whole House to-morrow. Mr. Pettis, from the Committee on Private Land Claims, reported the following bill: [Washington, 1830] 2 p. (H. R. 482) DNA.   4129

---- A bill for the relief of James Whitaker. January 29, 1830. Read twice, and committed to a Committee of the Whole House to-morrow. Mr. Buchanan, from the Committee on the Judiciary, reported the following bill: [Washington, 1830] 1 p. (H. R. 180) DNA.   4130

---- A bill for the relief of Jane Muir. March 17, 1830. Read twice, and committed to a Committee of the Whole House to-morrow. Mr. Whittlesey, from the Committee of Claims, reported the following bill: [Washington, 1830] 1 p. (H. R. 358) DNA.   4131

---- A bill for the relief of Jared E. Groce, of the State of Alabama. March 25, 1830. Read twice, and committed to a Committee of the Whole House to-morrow. Mr. Clay, from the Committee on the Public Lands, reported the following bill: [Washington, 1830] 2 p. (H. R. 385) DNA.   4132

---- A bill for the relief of Jasper Parish. February 5, 1830.

Read twice, and committed to a Committee of the Whole House to-morrow. Mr. Whittlesey, from the Committee of Claims, reported the following bill: [Washington, 1830] 1 p. (H. R. 197) DNA. 4133

---- A bill for the relief of Jeremiah Walker, of the State of Louisiana. February 5, 1830. Read twice, and committed to a Committee of the Whole House to-morrow. Mr. Test, of Indiana, from the Committee on Private Land Claims, to which was referred the petition of Jeremiah Walker, reported the following bill: [Washington, 1830] 1 p. (H. R. 205) DNA. 4134

---- A bill for the relief of John Bruce, administrator of Philip Bush. February 27, 1830. Read twice, and committed to a Committee of the Whole House to-morrow. Mr. Bates, from the Committee on Revolutionary Claims, reported the following bill: [Washington, 1830] 2 p. (H. R. 306) DNA. 4135

---- A bill for the relief of John Brunson. February 15, 1830. Mr. Foot, from the Committee of Claims, reported the following bill; which was read, and passed to a second reading: [Washington, 1830] 1 p. (S. 93) DNA. 4136

---- A bill for the relief of John Buhler, of Louisiana. February 15, 1830. Read twice, and committed to a Committee of the Whole House to-morrow. Mr. Test, from the Committee on Private Land Claims, reported the following bill: [Washington, 1830] 2 p. (H. R. 250) DNA. 4137

---- A bill for the relief of John Conard, Marshal of the Eastern District of Pennsylvania. March 22, 1830. Read twice, and committed to a Committee of the Whole House to-morrow. Mr. Buchanan, from the Committee on the Judiciary, reported the following bill: [Washington, 1830] 1 p. (H. R. 379) DNA. 4138

---- A bill for the relief of John Cooper, William Saunders, and William R. Porter. January 11, 1830. Read twice, and committed to a Committee of the Whole House to-morrow. Mr. Bouldin, from the Committee on the Judiciary, reported the following bill: [Washington, 1830] 2 p. (H. R. 100) DNA. 4139

---- A bill for the relief of John Edgar. January 5, 1830. Mr. Burnet, from the Committee on Private Land Claims, reported the following bill; which was read, and passed to a second reading: [Washington, 1830] 1 p. (S. 36) DNA. 4140

---- A bill for the relief of John Edgar, of Illinois. February 18, 1830. Mr. Chambers, from the Committee on Pensions, reported the following bill; which was read, and passed to a second reading: [Washington, 1830] 1 p. (S. 98) DNA. 4141

---- A bill for the relief of John F. Carmichael, of the State of Mississippi. March 3, 1830. Read twice, and referred to the Committee on Public Lands. March 10, 1830. Reported without amendment. [Washington, 1830] 2 p. (S. 116) DNA. 4142

---- A bill for the relief of John F. Girod, of Louisiana. March 2, 1830. Read twice, and committed to a Committee of the Whole House to-morrow. Mr. Nuckolls, from the Committee

on Private Land Claims, reported the following bill: [Washington, 1830] 2 p. (H. R. 314) DNA.
4143

---- A bill for the relief of John F. Ohl. May 14, 1830. Read twice, and committed to a Committee of the Whole House tomorrow. Mr. Gilmore, from the Committee of Ways and Means, reported the following bill: [Washington, 1830] 1 p. (H. R. 469) DNA.
4144

---- A bill for the relief of John Fruge, of Louisiana. March 2, 1830. Read twice, and committed to a Committee of the Whole House to-morrow. Mr. Test, from the Committee on Private Land Claims, reported the following bill: [Washington, 1830] 2 p. (H. R. 316) DNA.
4145

---- A bill for the relief of John Glass. January 18, 1830. Read twice, and committed to a Committee of the whole House to-morrow. Mr. Clay, from the Committee of Claims, reported the following bill: [Washington, 1830] 1 p. (H. R. 120) DNA.
4146

---- A bill for the relief of John H. Thomas, claiming under Antoine Patin. March 30, 1830. Read twice, and committed to a Committee of the Whole House to-morrow. Mr. Pettis, from the Committee on Private Land Claims, reported the following bill: [Washington, 1830] 2 p. (H. R. 397) DNA.
4147

---- A bill for the relief of John H. Wendal, a Captain in the Revolutionary War. January 26, 1830. Read twice, and committed to the Committee of the Whole House to which is committed the bill for the relief of Stephen Olney. Mr. Forward, from the Committee on Military Pensions, reported the following bill: [Washington, 1830] 1 p. (H. R. 160) DNA.
4148

---- A bill for the relief of John Hayner. January 29, 1830. Read twice, and committed to a Committee of the Whole House to-morrow. Mr. Whittlesey, from the Committee of Claims, reported the following bill: [Washington, 1830] 1 p. (H. R. 179) DNA.
4149

---- A bill for the relief of John Heard, Junior, surviving assignee of Amasa Davis, Junior. March 4, 1830. Read twice, and committed to a Committee of the Whole House to-morrow. Mr. Verplanck, from the Committee of Ways and Means, reported the following bill: [Washington, 1830] 1 p. (H. R. 322) DNA.
4150

---- A bill for the relief of John Kaine, John Waggoner, James Spaun, and Abijah Ring. March 26, 1830. Read twice, and committed to a Committee of the Whole House to-morrow. Mr. Forward, from the Committee on Military Pensions, reported the following bill: [Washington, 1830] 1 p. (H. R. 390) DNA.
4151

---- A bill for the relief of John Knight. March 9, 1830. Read twice, and committed to a Committee of the Whole House to-morrow. Mr. Brown, from the Committee on Revolutionary Claims, reported the following bill: [Washington, 1830] 1 p. (H. R. 333) DNA.
4152

---- A bill for the relief of John Lacy. May 24, 1830. Read twice, and committed to a Committee of the Whole House to-morrow. Mr. Miller, from the Committee on Naval Affairs, reported the following bill: [Washington, 1830] 1 p. (H. R. 485) DNA.
4153

---- A bill for the relief of John Lord. February 10, 1830. Read twice, and committed to a Committee of the Whole House to-morrow. Mr. Goodenow, from the Committee on Revolutionary Claims, reported the following bill: [Washington, 1830] 1 p. (H. R. 228) DNA.   4154

---- A bill for the relief of John Moffitt. January 18, 1830. Read twice, and committed to a Committee of the Whole House to-morrow. Mr. Dickinson, from the Committee on Revolutionary Claims, reported the following bill: [Washington, 1830] 1 p. (H. R. 125) DNA.   4155

---- A bill for the relief of John Reily. March 12, 1830. Mr. Barton, from the Committee on Public Lands, reported the following bill; which was read, and passed to a second reading. [Washington, 1830] 1 p. (S. 132) DNA.   4156

---- A bill for the relief of John Riddle. January 18, 1830. Mr. Chase, from the Committee on Pensions, reported the following bill; which was read, and passed to a second reading: [Washington, 1830] 1 p. (S. 65) DNA.
                                  4157
---- A bill for the relief of John Roberts, late Major of infantry in the War of the Revolution. December 21, 1830. Read twice, and committed to a Committee of the Whole House to-morrow. Mr. Dickinson, from the Committee on Revolutionary Claims, reported the following bill: [Washington, 1830] 1 p. (H. R. 505) DNA.
                                  4158
---- A bill for the relief of John Robinson. January 29, 1830. Read twice, and committed to a Committee of the Whole House to-morrow. Mr. Burges, from

the Committee on Revolutionary Claims, to whom was referred the case of John Robinson, reported the following bill: [Washington, 1830] 2 p. (H. R. 175) DNA.   4159

---- A bill for the relief of John Rodgers. December 28, 1830. Read twice, and committed to a Committee of the Whole House to-morrow. Mr. William L. Storrs, from the Committee on Indian Affairs, reported the following bill: [Washington, 1830] 1 p. (H. R. 518) DNA.   4160

---- A bill for the relief of John Sapp. February 15, 1830. Read twice, and committed to a Committee of the Whole House to-morrow. Mr. Whittlesey, from the Committee of Claims, reported the following bill: [Washington, 1830] 1 p. (H. R. 245) DNA.   4161

---- A bill for the relief of John Scott, executor of Charles Yates, deceased. April 16, 1830. Read twice, and committed to a Committee of the Whole House to-morrow. Mr. Burges, from the Committee on Revolutionary Claims, reported the following bill: [Washington, 1830] 1 p. (H. R. 426) DNA.   4162

---- A bill for the relief of John Teel. January 29, 1830. Read twice, and committed to a Committee of the Whole House to-morrow. Mr. Burges, from the Committee on Revolutionary Claims, reported the following bill: [Washington, 1830] 1 p. (H. R. 176) DNA.   4163

---- A bill for the relief of Jonathan Chapman. December 17, 1829. Agreeably to notice given, Mr. Silsbee asked and obtained leave to bring in the following bill; which was read, and passed to a second reading. December 21--Read second time, and referred to Committee on Finance. January 11--Reported without amendment. [Washington, 1830] 2 p. (S. 9) DNA.   4164

---- A bill for the relief of Jonathan Lincoln, administrator of Samuel B. Lincoln, deceased. December 17, 1830. Read twice, and committed to a Committee of the Whole House to-morrow. Mr. Whittlesey, from the Committee of Claims, reported the following bill: [Washington, 1830] 1 p. (H. R. 500) DNA.   4165

---- A bill for the relief of Jonathan Taylor, and the representatives of James Morrison and Charles Wilkins. January 29, 1830. Read twice, and committed to a Committee of the Whole House to-morrow. Mr. Whittlesey, from the Committee of Claims, reported the following bill: [Washington, 1830] 1 p. (H. R. 177) DNA.   4166

---- A bill for the relief of Jonathan Walton and John J. Degraff. April 27, 1830. Read twice, and committed to a Committee of the Whole House to-morrow. Mr. Verplanck, from the Committee of Ways and Means, to which was referred the petition of Jonathan Walton and Company. reported the following bill: [Washington, 1830] 2 p. (H. R. 446) DNA.
4167

---- A bill for the relief of Joseph Chamberlain. April 6, 1830. Mr. Chase, from the Committee on Pensions, reported the following bill; which was read, and passed to a second reading: [Washington, 1830] 1 p. (S. 168) DNA.   4168

---- A bill for the relief of Jos-

eph E. Sprague. January 19, 1830. Mr. Rowan, from the Committee on the Judiciary, reported the following bill; which was read, and passed to a second reading: [Washington, 1830] 1 p. (S. 67) DNA.   4169

---- A bill for the relief of Joseph Eaton, an Assistant Surgeon in the Army of the United States. April 19, 1830. Read twice, and committed to a Committee of the Whole House to-morrow. Mr. Drayton, from the Committee on Military Affairs, reported the following bill: [Washington, 1830] 1 p. (H. R. 430) DNA.   4170

---- A bill for the relief of Joseph Shaw. March 19, 1830. Mr. Chase, from the Committee on Pensions, reported the following bill; which was read, and passed to a second reading: [Washington, 1830] 1 p. (S. 138) DNA.   4171

---- A bill for the relief of Joseph Young. February 5, 1830. Read twice, and committed to a Committee of the Whole House to-morrow. Mr. Young, from the Committee on the Post Office and Post Roads, reported the following bill: [Washington, 1830] 1 p. (H. R. 201) DNA.   4172

---- A bill for the relief of Josiah H. Webb. February 10, 1830. Read twice, and committed to a Committee of the Whole House to-morrow. Mr. Johnson, of Kentucky, from the Committee on the Post Office and Post Roads, reported the following bill: [Washington, 1830] 1 p. (H. R. 225) DNA.   4173

---- A bill for the relief of Jotham Lincoln, administrator of Samuel Bene Lincoln, deceased. February 1, 1830. Read twice, and committed to a Committee of the Whole House to-morrow. Mr. Crane, from the Committee of Claims, to which was referred the case of Jotham Lincoln, administrator of Samuel B. Lincoln, deceased, reported the following bill: [Washington, 1830] 1 p. (H. R. 187) DNA. 4174

---- A bill for the relief of Judah Alden. January 18, 1830. Read twice, and committed to a Committee of the Whole House to-morrow. Mr. Dickinson, from the Committee on Revolutionary Claims, reported the following bill: [Washington, 1830] 1 p. (H. R. 124) DNA. 4175

---- A bill for the relief of Leonard Denison and Elisha Ely. March 26, 1830. Read twice, and committed to a Committee of the Whole House to-morrow. Mr. Whittlesey, from the Committee of Claims, reported the following bill: [Washington, 1830] 1 p. (H. R. 387) DNA. 4176

---- A bill for the relief of Lewis Anderson. December 22, 1830. Read twice, and committed to a Committee of a Whole House to-morrow. Mr. Whittlesey, from the Committee of Claims, reported the following bill: [Washington, 1830] 1 p. (H. R. 506) DNA. 4177

---- A bill for the relief of Lewis Rouse. January 25, 1830. Read twice, and committed to a Committee of the Whole House to-morrow. Mr. McIntire, from the Committee of Claims, reported the following bill: [Washington, 1830] 1 p. (H. R. 151) DNA. 4178

---- A bill for the relief of Lieutenant Colonel Enos Cutler, of the United States' Army. January 20, 1830. Read twice, and committed to a Committee of the Whole House to-morrow. Mr. Drayton, from the Committee on Military Affairs, reported the following bill: [Washington, 1830] 1 p. (H. R. 135) DNA. 4179

---- A bill for the relief of Lucien Harper. March 22, 1830. Mr. Bell, from the Committee of Claims, reported the following bill; which was read, and passed to a second reading. [Washington, 1830] 2 p. (S. 142) DNA. 4180

---- A bill for the relief of Lucy M. Lipscomb. January 14, 1830. Mr. Smith, of Maryland, from the Committee on Finance, reported the following bill; which was read, and passed to a second reading: [Washington, 1830] 1 p. (S. 59) DNA. 4181

---- A bill for the relief of Major M. M. Payne, of the United States' Army. February 8, 1830. Read twice, and committed to a Committee of the Whole House to-morrow. Mr. Drayton, from the Committee on Military Affairs, reported the following bill: [Washington, 1830] 1 p. (H. R. 212) DNA. 4182

---- A bill for the relief of Martha Yeomans, widow of John Yoemans, deceased. February 4, 1830. Read twice, and committed to a Committee of the Whole House to-morrow. Mr. Dickinson, from the Committee on Revolutionary Claims, reported the following bill: [Washington, 1830] 2 p. (H. R. 196) DNA. 4183

---- A bill for the relief of Mary H. Hawkins. February 10, 1830. Read twice, and committed to a Committee of the Whole House to-morrow. Mr. Overton, from the Committee of Ways and Means, reported the following bill: [Washington, 1830] 1 p.

(H. R. 223) DNA.   4184   DNA.   4189

No entry.   4185

---- A bill for the relief of
Mountjoy Bayly. January 12,
1830. Mr. Benton, from the Committee on Military Affairs, reported the following bill; which
was read, and passed to a second reading: [Washington, 1830]
1 p. (S. 52) DNA.   4190

---- A bill for the relief of
Matthias Roll. December 30,
1830. Read twice, and ordered
to be engrossed, and read the
third time to-morrow. Mr.
Sterigere, from the Committee
on Private Land Claims, to
which had been referred the petition of Matthias Roll, reported
the following bill: [Washington,
1830] 1 p. (H. R. 526) DNA.
                                    4186
---- A bill for the relief of Mesheck Browning. February 5,
1830. Read twice, and committed to a Committee of the Whole
House to-morrow. Mr. Whittlesey, from the Committee of
Claims, reported the following
bill: [Washington, 1830] 1 p.
(H. R. 198) DNA.   4187

---- A bill for the relief of Mi-
chael Lewis. January 26, 1830.
Read twice, and committed to the
Committee of the Whole House to
which is committed the bill for
the relief of Alexander Claxton.
Mr. Miller, from the Committee
on Naval Affairs, reported the
following bill: [Washington,
1830] 1 p. (H. R. 156) DNA.
                                    4188
---- A bill for the relief of
Moses Treadwell. April 7, 1830.
Read twice, and committed to a
Committee of the Whole House to-
morrow. Mr. Harvey, from the
Committee on Commerce, reported the following bill: [Washing-
ton, 1830] 1 p. (H. R. 410)

---- A bill for the relief of Nancy Moore. January 6, 1830.
Mr. Kane, from the Committee
on Public Lands, reported the
following bill; which was read,
and passed to a second reading:
[Washington, 1830] 1 p. (S. 38)
DNA.   4191

---- A bill for the relief of Nathaniel Bird. March 11, 1830.
Read twice, and committed to a
Committee of the Whole House
to-morrow. Mr. Burges, from
the Committee on Revolutionary
Claims, reported the following
bill: [Washington, 1830] 2 p.
(H. R. 340) DNA.   4192

---- A bill for the relief of Na-
thaniel Childers. March 29, 1830.
Read twice, and committed to the
Committee of the Whole House
to which is committed the bill
(No. 176) for the relief of John
Test. Mr. Whittlesey, from the
Committee of Claims, reported
the following bill: [Washington,
1830] 2 p. (H. R. 395) DNA.
                                    4193
---- A bill for the relief of Nathaniel Patten. January 6, 1830.
Read twice, and committed to a
Committee of the Whole House
to-morrow. Mr. Johnson, from
the Committee on the Post Office
and Post Roads, reported the following bill: [Washington, 1830]
1 p. (H. R. 80) DNA.   4194

---- A bill for the relief of Oba-
diah Dickerson, and others. May

27, 1830. Read twice, and committed to a Committee of the
Whole House to-morrow. Mr.
Pettis, from the Committee on
Private Land Claims, reported
the following bill: [Washington,
1830] 1 p. (H. R. 494) DNA.
                                    4195
---- A bill for the relief of Patrick Green. April 19, 1830.
Read twice, and committed to a
Committee of the Whole House
to-morrow. Mr. Johnson, from
the Committee on the Post Office
and Post Roads, reported the
following bill: [Washington,
1830] 1 p. (H. R. 432) DNA. 4196

---- A bill for the relief of Payson Perrin. January 6, 1830.
Read, and passed to a second
reading. January 7--Read a second time, and referred to Committee on Finance. January 11--
Reported without amendment.
[Washington, 1830] 1 p. (S. 41)
DNA.   4197

---- A bill for the relief of Percia Tupper, executrix of Samuel
Tupper, deceased. March 22,
1830. Read twice, and committed to a Committee of the Whole
House to-morrow. Mr. Lea,
from the Committee of Claims,
reported the following bill:
[Washington, 1830] 1 p. (H. R.
378) DNA.   4198

---- A bill for the relief of Peter Bargy, jr. Stephen Norton,
and Hiram Wolverton. March 2,
1830. Read twice, and committed to a Committee of the Whole
House to-morrow. Mr. Whittlesey, from the Committee of
Claims, reported the following
bill: [Washington, 1830] 1 p.
(H. R. 307) DNA.   4199

---- A bill for the relief of Peter
Gasney. January 8, 1830. Read
twice, and committed to a Com-

mittee of the Whole House to-
morrow. Mr. Whittlesey, from
the Committee of Claims, to
which was referred the petition
of Peter Gasney, reported the
following bill: [Washington, 1830]
1 p. (H. R. 89) DNA.   4200

---- A bill for the relief of Peter Harmony, of New York.
April 23, 1830. Read twice, and
ordered to be engrossed, and
read the third time to-morrow.
Mr. Cambreleng, from the Committee on Commerce, reported
the following bill: [Washington,
1830] 1 p. (H. R. 436) DNA.
                                    4201
---- A bill for the relief of Peter
Peck. May 19, 1830. Read twice,
and committed to a Committee
of the Whole House to which is
committed the bill for the relief
of John Sapp. Mr. Whittlesey,
from the Committee of Claims,
reported the following bill:
[Washington, 1830] 1 p. (H. R.
475) DNA.   4202

---- A bill for the relief of Philip and Eliphalet Greely. April
26, 1830. Read twice, and committed to a Committee of the
Whole House to-morrow. Mr.
Gilmore, from the Committee of
Ways and Means, reported the
following bill: [Washington, 1830]
1 p. (H. R. 444) DNA.   4203

---- A bill for the relief of
Phineas Sprague, and others.
February 9, 1830. Read twice,
and committed to a Committee of
the Whole House to-morrow. Mr.
Cambreleng, from the Committee
on Commerce, reported the following bill: [Washington, 1830]
1 p. (H. R. 215) DNA.   4204

---- A bill for the relief of Ran-
som Mix. March 18, 1830. Mr.
Foot, from the Committee on
Pensions, reported the following

bill; which was read, and passed to a second reading: [Washington, 1830] 1 p. (S. 137) DNA.
4205

---- A bill for the relief of Richard G. Morriss. March 6, 1830. Read twice, and committed to a Committee of the Whole House to-morrow. Mr. Burges, from the Committee on Revolutionary Claims, reported the following bill: [Washington, 1830] 3 p. (H.R. 328) DNA.   4206

---- A bill for the relief of Richard S. Hackley. March 16, 1830. Read twice, and committed to a Committee of the Whole House to-morrow. Mr. Archer, from the Committee on Foreign Affairs, reported the following bill: [Washington, 1830] 1 p. (H.R. 357) DNA.   4207

---- A bill for the relief of Richard Smith and William Pearse, the second, of Bristol, in Rhode Island. March 15, 1830. Read twice, and committed to a Committee of the Whole House to-morrow. Mr. Cambreleng, from the Committee on Commerce, to which was referred the case of Richard Smith and William Pearse, second, reported the following bill: [Washington, 1830] 1 p. (H.R. 349) DNA.   4208

---- A bill for the relief of Richard W. Steele, a soldier in the late war. March 23, 1830. Read twice, and committed to a Committee of the Whole House to-morrow. Mr. Foster, from the Committee on Private Land Claims, reported the following bill: [Washington, 1830] 1 p. (H.R. 381) DNA.   4209

---- A bill for the relief of Robert A. Forsythe. March 10, 1830. Read twice, and committed to a Committee of the Whole

House to-morrow. Mr. Whittlesey, from the Committee of Claims, reported the following bill: [Washington, 1830] 1 p. (H.R. 337) DNA.   4210

---- A bill for the relief of Robert Eaton. March 18, 1830. Read twice, and committed to a Committee of the Whole House to-morrow. Mr. Gilmore, from the Committee of Ways and Means, reported the following bill: [Washington, 1830] 1 p. (H.R. 364) DNA.   4211

---- A bill for the relief of Robert Kaine, of Buffalo, in the state of New York. March 31, 1830. Read twice, and committed to a Committee of the Whole House to-morrow. Mr. Lent, from the Committee of Claims, reported the following bill: [Washington, 1830] 1 p. (H.R. 400) DNA.   4212

---- A bill for the relief of Robert Smart. April 15, 1830. Read twice, and committed to a Committee of the Whole House to-morrow. Mr. McIntire, from the Committee of Claims, reported the following bill: [Washington, 1830] 1 p. (H.R. 424) DNA.   4213

---- A bill for the relief of Robertson and Barnwall, December 30, 1830. Read twice, and committed to a Committee of the Whole House to-morrow. Mr. Verplanck, from the Committee of Ways and Means, reported the following bill: [Washington, 1830] 1 p. (H.R. 527) DNA.   4214

---- A bill for the relief of Roger Enos. April 5, 1830. Read twice, and committed to the Committee of the Whole House to which is committed the bill (No. 182) for the relief of Charles

Collins. Mr. Verplanck, from the Committee of Ways and Means, reported the following bill: [Washington, 1830] 1 p. (H. R. 406) DNA.   4215

---- A bill for the relief of Samuel Cobun, of Mississippi. February 9, 1830. --Read, and passed to a second reading. February 16. --Read 2d time, and referred to the Committee on Public Lands. March 1. --Reported without amendment. [Washington, 1830] 2 p. (S. 89) DNA.
4216

---- A bill for the relief of Samuel Keep. April 15, 1830. Read twice, and committed to the Committee of the Whole House to which is committed the bill for the relief of Elizabeth Williams. Mr. Crane, from the Committee of Claims, reported the following bill: [Washington, 1830] 1 p. (H. R. 423) DNA.   4217

---- A bill for the relief of Samuel Nowell. March 30, 1830. Mr. Foot, from the Committee on Pensions, reported the following bill; which was read, and passed to a second reading. [Washington, 1830] 1 p. (S. 160) DNA.
4218

---- A bill for the relief of Samuel Sprigg, of Virginia. January 27, 1830. Read twice, and committed to a Committee of the Whole House to-morrow. Mr. Gurley, from the Committee on Private Land Claims, to which was referred the petition of Samuel Sprigg, reported the following bill: [Washington, 1830] 1 p. (H. R. 163) DNA.   4219

---- A bill for the relief of Samuel Ward. February 12, 1830. Mr. Ruggles, from the Committee of Claims, reported the following bill; which was read, and passed to a second reading.

[Washington, 1830] 2 p. (S. 91) DNA.   4220

---- A bill for the relief of Samuel Ward. February 27, 1830. Read twice, and committed to a Committee of the Whole House to-morrow. Mr. Burges, from the Committee on Revolutionary Claims, reported the following bill: [Washington, 1830] 2 p. (H. R. 305) DNA.   4221

---- A bill for the relief of Samuel Watson and George Hoppas, of Ohio. February 25, 1830. Read twice, and committed to a Committee of the Whole House to-morrow. Mr. Test, from the Committee on Private Land Claims, reported the following bill: [Washington, 1830] 2 p. (H. R. 288) DNA.   4222

---- A bill for the relief of Sarah Easton and Dorothy Storer, children and heirs at law of Lieutenant Colonel Robert Hanson Harrison, deceased. January 29, 1830. Read twice, and committed to a Committee of the Whole House to-morrow. Mr. Burges, from the Committee on Revolutionary Claims, reported the following bill: [Washington, 1830] 2 p. (H. R. 174) DNA.   4223

---- A bill for the relief of Simeon C. Whittier. January 18, 1830. Mr. Smith, of Maryland, from the Committee on Finance, reported the following bill; which was read, and passed to a second reading: [Washington, 1830] 2 p. (S. 61) DNA.   4224

---- A bill for the relief of Stephen Hook. February 22, 1830. Read twice, and committed to a Committee of the Whole House to-morrow. Mr. Crane, from the Committee of Claims, reported the following bill:

[Washington, 1830] 1 p. (H. R. 277) DNA.   4225

---- A bill for the relief of Stephen Olney. January 5, 1830. Read twice, and committed to a Committee of the Whole House to-morrow. Mr. Burges, from the Committee on Revolutionary Claims, reported the following bill: [Washington, 1830] 1 p. (H. R. 74) DNA.   4226

---- A bill for the relief of sundry owners of vessels sunk for the defence of Baltimore. February 1, 1830. Read twice, and committed to a Committee of the Whole House to-morrow. Mr. Howard, from the Committee on Commerce, reported the following bill: [Washington, 1830] 1 p. (H. R. 191) DNA.   4227

---- A bill for the relief of sundry Revolutionary and other officers and soldiers, and for other purposes. January 5, 1830. Read twice, and committed to a Committee of the Whole House to-morrow. Mr. Forward, from the Committee on Military Pensions, reported the following bill: [Washington, 1830] 2 p. (H. R. 72) DNA.   4228

---- ---- [Washington, 1830] 8 p. (H. R. 72) DNA.   4229

---- A bill for the relief of Susannah McHugh. February 15, 1830. Read twice, and committed to a Committee of the Whole House to-morrow. Mr. Test, from the Committee on Private Land Claims, reported the following bill: [Washington, 1830] 2 p. (H. R. 251) DNA.   4230

---- A bill for the relief of Sylvester Havens. March 12, 1830. Read twice, and committed to a Committee of the Whole House

to-morrow. Mr. Crane, from the Committee of Claims, reported the following bill: [Washington, 1830] 1 p. (H. R. 342) DNA.   4231

---- A bill for the relief of the bail of Charles Josslyn, late Postmaster at Greene, Chenango County, New York. February 8, 1830. Read twice, and committed to a Committee of the Whole House to-morrow. Mr. Magee, from the Committee on the Post Office and Post Roads, reported the following bill: [Washington, 1830] 1 p. (H. R. 213) DNA.   4232

---- A bill for the relief of the children of Charles Comb or Cohen, and his late wife Margarite, previously Margarite Dozi. February 11, 1830. Read twice, and committed to a Committee of the Whole House to-morrow. Mr. Foster, from the Committee on Private Land Claims, reported the following bill: [Washington, 1830] 2 p. (H. R. 232) DNA.   4233

---- A bill for the relief of the citizens of Shawneetown. February 26, 1830. Read twice, and committed to a Committee of the Whole House to-morrow. Mr. Duncan, from the Committee on the Public Lands, reported the following bill: [Washington, 1830] 2 p. (H. R. 298) DNA. 4234

---- A bill for the relief of the City Council of Charleston, South Carolina. January 20, 1830. Mr. Woodbury, from the Committee on Commerce, reported the following bill; which was read, and passed to a second reading: [Washington, 1830] 2 p. (S. 71) DNA.   4235

---- A bill for the relief of the executors of James Roddey, deceased. February 4, 1830. Mr.

Rowan, from the committee on
the Judiciary, reported the following bill; which was read, and
passed to a second reading:
[Washington, 1830] 1 p. (S. 80)
DNA.   4236

---- A bill for the relief of the
heirs and legal representatives of
Doctor Samuel Kennedy. April
9, 1830. Read twice, and committed to a Committee of the
Whole House to-morrow. Mr.
Fry, from the Committee on
Revolutionary Claims, reported
the following bill: [Washington,
1830] 1 p. (H. R. 413) DNA.
                                4237
---- A bill for the relief of the
heirs and representatives of John
Campbell, late of the City of
New York, deceased. March 5,
1830. Read twice, and committed
to a Committee of the Whole
House to-morrow. Mr. Dickinson,
from the Committee on Revolutionary Claims, reported the following bill: [Washington, 1830]
1 p. (H. R. 323) DNA.   4238

---- A bill for the relief of the
heirs and residuary legatees of
William Carter, late of the State
of Virginia, deceased. March 26,
1830. Read twice, and committed
to a Committee of the Whole
House to-morrow. Mr. Brown,
from the Committee on Revolutionary Claims, reported the following bill: [Washington, 1830]
1 p. (H. R. 391) DNA.   4239

---- A bill for the relief of the
heirs at law of Richard Livingston, a Canadian refugee. February 9, 1830. Read twice, and
committed to a Committee of the
Whole House to-morrow. Mr.
Dickinson, from the Committee
on Revolutionary Claims, reported the following bill: [Washing-
ton, 1830] 1 p. (H. R. 220) DNA.
                                4240

---- A bill for the relief of the
heirs of Alexander Boyd, deceased. January 11, 1830. Read
twice, and committed to a Committee of the Whole House to-
morrow. Mr. Gurley, from the
Committee on Private Land
Claims, reported the following
bill: [Washington, 1830] 1 p.
(H. R. 94) DNA.   4241

---- A bill for the relief of the
heirs of Baptiste Le Gendre.
January 13, 1830. Read twice,
and committed to a Committee
of the Whole House to-morrow.
Mr. Gurley, from the Committee
on Private Land Claims, reported the following bill: [Washing-
ton, 1830] 1 p. (H. R. 107)
DNA.   4242

---- A bill for the relief of the
heirs of Caron de Beaumarchais.
February 19, 1830. Read twice,
and committed to a Committee of
the Whole House to-morrow. Mr.
Archer, from the Committee on
Foreign Affairs, to which had
been referred the case of the
late Caron de Beaumarchais, reported the following bill: [Wash-
ington, 1830] 1 p. (H. R. 262)
DNA.   4243

---- A bill for the relief of the
heirs of Colonel John Ellis, deceased. January 7, 1830. Read
twice, and committed to a Committee of the Whole House to-
morrow. Mr. Gurley, from the
Committee on Private Land
Claims, reported the following
bill: [Washington, 1830] 2 p.
(H. R. 85) DNA.   4244

---- A bill for the relief of the
heirs of Jean Marie Trahaud,
deceased. January 18, 1830.
Read twice, and committed to a
Committee of the Whole House
to-morrow. Mr. Gurley, from
the Committee on Private Land

Claims, reported the following bill: [Washington, 1830] 1 p. (H. R. 123) DNA. 4245

---- A bill for the relief of the heirs of Jeremiah Buckley, deceased. March 19, 1830. Read twice, and committed to a Committee of the Whole House to-morrow. Mr. Baylor, from the Committee on Private Land Claims, reported the following bill: [Washington, 1830] 2 p. (H. R. 374) DNA. 4246

---- A bill for the relief of the heirs of John Tuillier, deceased. January 18, 1830. Read twice, and committed to a Committee of the Whole House to-morrow. Mr. Gurley, from the Committee on Private Land Claims, reported the following bill: [Washington, 1830] 1 p. (H. R. 122) DNA. 4247

---- A bill for the relief of the heirs of John Wilson. March 27, 1830. Read twice, and committed to a Committee of the Whole House to-morrow. Mr. Brown, from the Committee on Revolutionary Claims, reported the following bill: [Washington, 1830] 1 p. (H. R. 394) DNA. 4248

---- A bill for the relief of the heirs of Nicholas Hart, deceased. February 25, 1830. Read twice, and committed to a Committee of the Whole House to-morrow. Mr. Clay, from the Committee on the Public Lands, reported the following bill: [Washington, 1830] 1 p. (H. R. 291) DNA. 4249

---- A bill for the relief of the heirs of William Treadwell. February 5, 1830. Read twice, and committed to a Committee of the Whole House tomorrow. Mr. Burges, from the Committee on Revolutionary Claims, reported the following bill: [Washington,

1830] 1 p. (H. R. 200) DNA. 4250

---- A bill for the relief of the heirs of William Vawters. March 19, 1830. Read twice, and committed to a Committee of the Whole House to-morrow. Mr. Brown, from the Committee on Revolutionary Claims, reported the following bill: [Washington, 1830] 1 p. (H. R. 373) DNA. 4251

---- A bill for the relief of the heirs or legal representatives of Joseph Falconer, deceased. January 18, 1830. Read twice, and committed to a Committee of the Whole House to-morrow. Mr. Dickinson, from the Committee on Revolutionary Claims, reported the following bill: [Washington, 1830] 2 p. (H. R. 126) DNA. 4252

---- A bill for the relief of the heirs or legal representatives of Ulrich Reeser, deceased. January 20, 1830. Read twice, and committed to a Committee of the Whole House to-morrow. Mr. Wingate, from the Committee on Revolutionary Claims, reported the following bill: [Washington, 1830] 1 p. (H. R. 142) DNA. 4253

---- A bill for the relief of the heirs or representatives of widow Dupre. January 13, 1830. Read twice, and committed to a Committee of the Whole House to-morrow. Mr. Whittlesey, from the Committee of Claims, reported the following bill: [Washington, 1830] 1 p. (H. R. 105) DNA. 4254

---- A bill for the relief of the legal representative of John Miller, deceased. April 9, 1830. Read twice, and committed to a Committee of the Whole House to-morrow. Mr. William B. Shepard, from the Committee on the Territories, reported the follow-

ing bill: [Washington, 1830] 1 p.
(H. R. 416) DNA.   4255

---- A bill for the relief of the
legal representatives of Andrew
Nelson, deceased. May 25, 1830.
Read twice, and committed to a
Committee of the Whole House
to-morrow. Mr. C. P. White,
from the Committee on Naval Affairs, reported the following bill:
[Washington, 1830] 1 p. (H. R.
488) DNA.   4256

---- A bill for the relief of the
legal representatives of Colonel
George Baylor. December 21,
1830. Read twice, and committed
to a Committee of the Whole
House to-morrow. Mr. Dickinson, from the Committee on
Revolutionary Claims, reported
the following bill: [Washington,
1830] 1 p. (H. R. 504) DNA.
                                4257

---- A bill for the relief of the
legal representatives of Edward
Moore, deceased. February 5,
1830. Read twice, and committed to a Committee of the Whole
House to-morrow. Mr. Hoffman,
from the Committee on Naval Affairs, reported the following bill:
[Washington, 1830] 1 p. (H. R.
203) DNA.   4258

---- A bill for the relief of the
legal representatives of Edward
Moore, deceased. December 24,
1830. Read twice, and committed
to a Committee of the Whole
House on the 3d of January next.
Mr. Hoffman, from the Committee on Naval Affairs, reported
the following bill: [Washington,
1830] 1 p. (H. R. 512) DNA.
                                4259

---- A bill for the relief of the
legal representatives of General
Moses Hazen, deceased. January 7, 1830. Mr. Bell, from the
Committee of Claims, reported
the following bill; which was read,

and passed to a second reading:
[Washington, 1830] 2 p. (S. 46)
DNA.   4260

---- A bill for the relief of the
legal representatives of James
Davenport, deceased. January
19, 1830. Read twice, and committed to a Committee of the
Whole House to-morrow. Mr.
Forward, from the Committee on
Military Pensions, to which was
referred the case of the representatives of James Davenport,
reported the following bill:
[Washington, 1830] 1 p. (H. R.
133) DNA.   4261

---- A bill for the relief of the
legal representatives of Job Alvord. January 20, 1830. Read
twice, and committed to a Committee of the Whole House to-
morrow. Mr. Goodenow, from
the Committee on Revolutionary
Claims, reported the following
bill: [Washington, 1830] 1 p.
(H. R. 140) DNA.   4262

---- A bill for the relief of the
legal representatives of Joseph
Jeans. April 14, 1830. Read
twice, and committed to the Committee of the Whole House to
which is committed the bill for
the relief of Meshack Browning.
Mr. Whittlesey, from the Committee of Claims, reported the
following bill: [Washington,
1830] 1 p. (H. R. 419) DNA.
                                4263

---- A bill for the relief of the
legal representatives of R. W.
Meade. February 19, 1830. Read
twice, and committed to a Committee of the Whole House to-
morrow. Mr. Archer, from the
Committee on Foreign Affairs,
to which was referred the case
of the heirs of Richard W. Meade,
reported the following bill:
[Washington, 1830] 2 p. (H. R.
263) DNA.   4264

---- A bill for the relief of the legal representatives of Samuel Wagstaff. May 5, 1830. Read twice, and committed to a Committee of the Whole House to-morrow. Mr. Whittlesey, from the Committee of Claims, reported the following bill: [Washington, 1830] 1 p. (H. R. 459) DNA.
                                    4265

---- A bill for the relief of the legal representatives of Simeon Theus, deceased. March 2, 1830. Read twice, and committed to a Committee of the Whole House to-morrow. Mr. Overton, from the Committee of Ways and Means, reported the following bill: [Washington, 1830] 1 p. (H. R. 317) DNA.   4266

---- A bill for the relief of the legal representatives of Simeon Theus, deceased. March 5, 1830. Mr. Rowan, from the Committee on the Judiciary, reported the following bill; which was read, and passed to a second reading: [Washington, 1830] 1 p. (S. 121) DNA.   4267

---- A bill for the relief of the legal representatives of Thomas Gordon, deceased. February 10, 1830. Read twice, and committed to a Committee of the Whole House to-morrow. Mr. Goodenow, from the Committee on Revolutionary Claims, reported the following bill: [Washington, 1830] 1 p. (H. R. 227) DNA.   4268

---- A bill for the relief of the legal representatives of Walter Livingston. January 18, 1830. Read twice, and committed to a Committee of the Whole House to-morrow. Mr. Wingate, from the Committee on Revolutionary Claims, reported the following bill: [Washington, 1830] 1 p. (H. R. 127) DNA.   4269

---- A bill for the relief of the mayor, aldermen, and inhabitants, of the city of New Orleans. May 12, 1830. Mr. Burnet, from the Committee on Private Land Claims, reported the following bill; which was read, and passed to a second reading: [Washington, 1830] 2 p. (S. 191) DNA.
                                    4270

---- A bill for the relief of the mayor and city council of Baltimore. December 16, 1829. Agreeably to notice given, Mr. Smith, of Maryland, asked and obtained leave to bring in the following bill; which was read, and passed to a second reading: December 17. --Read 2d time, and referred to the Committee of Claims.   January 5, 1830--Reported with an amendment, viz. strike out 2d section within brackets, and insert what follows in italics as section 2d. [Washington, 1830] 2 p. (S. 7) DNA.
                                    4271

---- A bill for the relief of the Mercantile Insurance Company, in Salem, Massachusetts. January 7, 1830. Mr. Silsbee, from the Committee on Finance, reported the following bill; which was read, and passed to a second reading: [Washington, 1830] 2 p. (S. 47) DNA.   4272

---- A bill for the relief of the Miami Exporting Company. April 19, 1830. Read twice, and committed to a Committee of the Whole House to-morrow. Mr. Crane, from the Committee of Claims, reported the following bill: [Washington, 1830] 1 p. (H. R. 434) DNA.   4273

---- A bill for the relief of the owners of the ship Alleghany, and their legal representatives. January 20, 1830. Read twice, and committed to a Committee of the Whole House to-morrow.

Mr. Archer, from the Committee on Foreign Affairs, reported the following bill: [Washington, 1830] 1 p. (H. R. 138) DNA.
4274

---- A bill for the relief of the personal representatives of Col. John Laurens. March 2, 1830. Read twice, and committed to a Committee of the Whole House to-morrow. Mr. Burges, from the Committee on Revolutionary Claims, reported the following bill: [Washington, 1830] 3 p. (H. R. 310) DNA.   4275

---- A bill for the relief of the president, directors, and company, of the Bank of Chillicothe. January 4, 1830. Read twice, and committed to a Committee of the Whole House to-morrow. Mr. Whittlesey, from the Committee of Claims, reported the following bill: [Washington, 1830] 1 p. (H. R. 69) DNA.   4276

---- A bill for the relief of the representative of Anthony Foreman. April 16, 1830. Read twice, and committed to the Committee of the Whole House to which is committed the bill from the Senate for the relief of sundry citizens of the United States who have lost property by the depredation of certain Indian tribes. Mr. Whittlesey, from the Committee of Claims, reported the following bill: [Washington, 1830] 2 p. (H. R. 425) DNA.
4277

---- A bill for the relief of the representatives of Elias Earle, deceased. January 5, 1830. Mr. Rowan, from the Committee on the Judiciary, reported the following bill; which was read, and passed to a second reading: [Washington, 1830] 1 p. (S. 37) DNA.   4278

---- A bill for the relief of the representatives of Reuben Wilkinson. March 26, 1830. Read twice, and committed to a Committee of the Whole House to-morrow. Mr. McDuffie, from the Committee of Ways and Means, reported the following bill: [Washington, 1830] 1 p. (H. R. 392) DNA.   4279

---- A bill for the relief of the securities of Amos Edwards. February 1, 1830. Mr. Rowan, from the committee on the Judiciary, reported the following bill; which was read, and passed to a second reading. [Washington, 1830] 1 p. (S. 75) DNA.
4280

---- A bill for the relief of the sureties of Amos Edwards. December 30, 1830. Read twice, and committed to a Committee of the whole House to-morrow. Mr. Daniel, from the Committee on the Judiciary, reported the following bill: [Washington, 1830] 1 p. (H. R. 522) DNA.   4281

---- A bill for the relief of the sureties of George Brown, deceased, late Collector of Internal Duties and Direct Tax for the first district in the state of Maryland. March 2, 1830. Read twice, and committed to a Committee of the Whole House to-morrow. Mr. Wickliffe, from the Committee on the Judiciary, reported the following bill: [Washington, 1830] 1 p. (H. R. 309) DNA.   4282

---- A bill for the relief of the sureties of William Gibbs, deceased, late a Paymaster in the army of the United States. April 7, 1830. Mr. McKinley, from the Committee on the Judiciary, reported the following bill; which was read, and passed to a second reading: [Washington, 1830] 1 p. (S. 171) DNA.   4283

---- A bill for the relief of the widow and heirs of Joseph Hulse, deceased. February 25, 1830. Read twice, and committed to a Committee of the Whole House to-morrow. Mr. Test, from the Committee on Private Land Claims, reported the following bill: [Washington, 1830] 1 p. (H. R. 289) DNA.   4284

---- A bill for the relief of the widows and orphans of the officers, seamen, and marines, of the sloop of war Hornet. February 9, 1830. Read twice, and committed to a Committee of the Whole House to-morrow. Mr. Dorsey, from the Committee on Naval Affairs, reported the following bill: [Washington, 1830] 1 p. (H. R. 218) DNA.   4285

---- A bill for the relief of the widows and orphans of the officers, seamen, and marines of the United States' schooner Wild Cat. March 29, 1830. Mr. Hayne, from the Committee on Naval Affairs, reported the following bill; which was read, and passed to a second reading: [Washington, 1830] 2 p. (S. 158) DNA.   4286

---- A bill for the relief of the widows and orphans of the officers, seamen, and marines, of the United States' schooner Wild Cat. May 18, 1830. Read twice, and committed to the Committee of the Whole House on the state of the Union. Mr. Miller, from the Committee on Naval Affairs, reported the following bill: [Washington, 1830] 1 p. (H. R. 473) DNA.   4287

---- A bill for the relief of Thomas Blackwell. January 29, 1830. Read twice, and committed to a Committee of the Whole House to-morrow. Mr. Young, from the Committee on Revolu-

tionary Claims, reported the following bill: [Washington, 1830] 1 p. (H. R. 173) DNA.   4288

---- A bill for the relief of Thomas Buford. January 4, 1830. Read twice, and committed to a Committee of the Whole House to-morrow. Mr. Drayton, from the Committee on Military Affairs, reported the following bill: [Washington, 1830] 1 p. (H. R. 65) DNA.   4289

---- A bill for the relief of Thomas Cooper, of South Carolina. February 3, 1830. Read, and passed to a second reading. February 4, 1830. Read second time, and referred to the Committee on the Judiciary. March 5, 1830. Reported without amendment. [Washington, 1830] 2 p. (S. 79) DNA.   4290

---- A bill for the relief of Thomas F. Cornell. February 17, 1830. Read twice, and committed to a Committee of the Whole House to-morrow. Mr. Clarke from the Committee on the Territories, reported the following bill: [Washington, 1830] 1 p. (H. R. 258) DNA.   4291

---- A bill for the relief of Thomas Fitzgerald. February 2, 1830. Mr. Marks, from the Committee on Pensions, reported the following bill; which was read, and passed to a second reading: [Washington, 1830] 1 p. (S. 78) DNA.   4292

---- A bill for the relief of Thomas L. Winthrop and others, Directors of an Association called the New England Mississippi Land Company. February 9, 1830. Mr. Rowan, from the Committee on the Judiciary, reported the following bill; which was read, and passed to a second reading:

[Washington, 1830] 2 p. (S. 88)
DNA.   4293

---- A bill for the relief of
Thomas Park. January 12, 1830.
Read twice, and committed to a
Committee of the Whole House
to-morrow. Mr. Goodenow,
from the Committee on Revolutionary Claims, reported the following bill: [Washington, 1830]
1 p. (H. R. 103) DNA.   4294

---- A bill for the relief of
Thomas Rhodes. April 28, 1830.
Mr. Bibb, from the Committee
on the Post Office and Post
Roads, reported the following
bill; which was read, and passed
to a second reading: [Washing-
ton, 1830] 1 p. (S. 184) DNA.
                              4295

---- A bill for the relief of
Thomas W. Newton, assignee of
Robert Crittenden. March 31,
1830. Read twice, and committed
to the Committee of the Whole
House to which is committed the
bill (H. R. No. 178) for the relief of George Ermatinger. Mr.
Whittlesey, from the Committee
of Claims, reported the following
bill: [Washington, 1830] 1 p.
(H. R. 399) DNA.   4296

---- A bill for the relief of
Thomas Wheatley. February 24,
1830. Read twice, and committed to a Committee of the Whole
House to-morrow. Mr. Whittlesey, from the Committee of
Claims, reported the following
bill: [Washington, 1830] 1 p.
(H. R. 281) DNA.   4297

---- A bill for the relief of
Thomas Wiggins. February 27,
1830. Mr. McKinley, from the
Committee on Public Lands, reported the following bill; which
was read, and passed to a second reading: [Washington, 1830]
2 p. (S. 115) DNA.   4298

---- A bill for the relief of Timothy Risley. February 26, 1830.
Read twice, and committed to a
Committee of the Whole House
to-morrow. Mr. Clay, from the
Committee on the Public Lands,
reported the following bill:
[Washington, 1830] 1 p. (H. R.
303) DNA.   4299

---- A bill for the relief of Vincent de Rivafinoli, and others.
March 10, 1830. Mr. Hayne,
from the Committee on the Judiciary, reported the following
bill; which was read, and passed
to a second reading: [Washing-
ton, 1830] 2 p. (S. 129) DNA.
                              4300

---- A bill for the relief of Wallace Robinson. January 11, 1830.
Read twice, and committed to a
Committee of the Whole House
to-morrow. Mr. Clay, from the
Committee on the Public Lands,
reported the following bill:
[Washington, 1830] 1 p. (H. R.
98) DNA.   4301

---- A bill for the relief of Whitford Gill. April 15, 1830. Read
twice, and committed to a Committee of the Whole House to-
morrow. Mr. Whittlesey, from
the Committee of Claims, reported the following bill: [Wash-
ington, 1830] 1 p. (H. R. 422)
DNA.   4302

---- A bill for the relief of Wilkins Tannehill. January 22,
1830. Read twice, and committed to a Committee of the Whole
House to-morrow. Mr. Whittlesey, from the Committee of
Claims, reported the following
bill: [Washington, 1830] 1 p.
(H. R. 147) DNA.   4303

---- A bill for the relief of William B. Mathews, trustee.
March 31, 1830. Mr. Rowan,
from the Committee on the Judi-

ciary, reported the following bill; which was read, and passed to a second reading: [Washington, 1830] 1 p. (S. 162) DNA. 4304

---- A bill for the relief of William Bradshaw, March 26, 1830. Read, and passed to a second reading. March 29, Read second time, and referred to the Committee on Public Lands. March 31, Reported without amendment. [Washington, 1830] 2 p. (S. 155) DNA. 4305

---- A bill for the relief of William Clower. April 19, 1830. Read twice, and committed to a Committee of the Whole House to-morrow. Mr. Johnson, from the Committee on the Post Office and Post Roads, reported the following bill: [Washington, 1830] 1 p. (H. R. 431) DNA. 4306

---- A bill for the relief of William D. King, James Daviess, and Genland Lincecum. March 2, 1830. Read twice, and committed to a Committee of the Whole House to-morrow. Mr. Whittlesey, from the Committee of Claims, reported the following bill: [Washington, 1830] 1 p. (H. R. 308) DNA. 4307

---- A bill for the relief of William Forsythe. March 22, 1830. Read twice, and committed to a Committee of the Whole House to-morrow. Mr. Whittlesey, from the Committee of Claims, reported the following bill: [Washington, 1830] 1 p. (H. R. 377) DNA. 4308

---- A bill for the relief of William Gallop. March 17, 1830. Read twice, and committed to a Committee of the Whole House to-morrow. Mr. Ham-

mons, from the Committee on Military Pensions, reported the following bill: [Washington, 1830] 1 p. (H. R. 362) DNA. 4309

---- A bill for the relief of William J. Quincy and Charles E. Quincy. February 15, 1830. Read twice, and committed to a Committee of the Whole House to-morrow. Mr. Dwight, from the Committee of Claims, reported the following bill: [Washington, 1830] 1 p. (H. R. 246) DNA. 4310

---- A bill for the relief of William Morrisson. January 8, 1830. Read twice, and committed to a Committee of the Whole House to-morrow. Mr. Whittlesey, from the Committee of Claims, reported the following bill: [Washington, 1830] 1 p. (H. R. 87) DNA. 4311

---- A bill for the relief of William Price. April 9, 1830. Read twice, and committed to a Committee of the Whole House to-morrow. Mr. Ford, from the Committee on Military Pensions, reported the following bill: [Washington, 1830] 1 p. (H. R. 414) DNA. 4312

---- A bill for the relief of William Stewart. May 11, 1830. Read twice, and committed to a Committee of the Whole House to-morrow. Mr. Hunt, from the Committee on the Public Lands, reported the following bill: [Washington, 1830] 1 p. (H. R. 465) DNA. 4313

---- A bill for the relief of William T. Carroll, Clerk of the Supreme Court of the

United States.   February 24,
1830.   Read twice, and committed to a Committee of the
Whole House to-morrow.   Mr.
McDuffie, from the Committee
of Ways and Means, reported
the following bill: [Washington,
1830]   1 p.   (H. R.   286) DNA.
                                    4314

---- A bill for the relief of
William Tharp.   April 19,
1830.   Read twice, and committed to the Committee of the
Whole House to which is committed the bill (H. R. No. 230) for
the relief of Elizabeth Williams.
Mr. Crane, from the Committee of Claims, reported the
following bill: [Washington,
1830]   2 p.   (H. R.   435)
DNA.   4315

---- A bill for the relief of William Blount.   April 14, 1830.
Read twice, and committed to a
Committee of the Whole House
to-morrow. Mr. Johnson, of Tennessee, from the select committee to which was referred the
case of Willie Blount, reported
the following bill: [Washington,
1830] 1 p.   (H. R.   421) DNA.
                                    4316

---- A bill for the relief of Wm.
H. Harrison.   April 23, 1830.
Read twice, and committed to a
Committee of the Whole House
to-morrow. Mr. Archer, from the
Committee on Foreign Affairs,
reported the following bill:
[Washington, 1830] 1 p.   (H. R.
437) DNA.   4317

---- A bill for the relief of
Woodson Wren, of Mississippi.
March 3, 1830. Read twice, and
referred to the Committee on the
Public Lands. March 10, 1830.
Reported without amendment.
[Washington, 1830] 2 p.   (S. 117)
DNA.   4318

---- A bill for the removal of
the Land Office established at
Chillicothe. February 8, 1830.
Read twice, and committed to a
Committee of the Whole House
to-morrow. Mr. Irvin, from the
Committee on the Public Lands,
reported the following bill:
[Washington, 1830] 1 p.   (H. R.
209) DNA.   4319

---- A bill for the security of
the Pea Patch Island; for the
construction of a new water tank;
and for graveling the parade at
Fort Delaware.   April 7, 1830.
Read twice, and committed to
the Committee of the Whole
House on the state of the Union.
Mr. Drayton, from the Committee on Military Affairs, reported
the following bill: [Washington,
1830] 1 p.   (H. R.   409) DNA.
                                    4320

---- A bill for the settlement of
the accounts of Samuel Sitgreaves.
January 11, 1830. Read twice,
and committed to a Committee of
the Whole House to-morrow. Mr.
Archer, from the Committee on
Foreign Affairs, reported the
following bill: [Washington,
1830]   1 p.   (H. R.   92) DNA.
                                    4321

---- A bill for the settlement of
the claim of the state of Delaware against the United States.
February 11, 1830. Read twice,
and committed to a Committee
of the Whole House to which is
committed the bill (No. 91) for
the settlement of the claim of
South Carolina. Mr. Drayton,
from the Committee on Military
Affairs, reported the following
bill: [Washington, 1830] 1 p.
(H. R.   231) DNA.   4322

---- A bill further to amend the
act, entitled "An act to reduce
into one, the several acts establishing and regulating the
Post Office Department."   Janu-

ary 18, 1830. Read twice, and committed to a Committee of the Whole House to-morrow. Mr. Johnson, from the Committee on the Post Office and Post Roads, reported the following bill: [Washington, 1830] 3 p. (H. R. 119) DNA. 4323

---- A bill further to define the duties of the Attorney General, and of the Solicitor of the Treasury. December 28, 1830. Read twice, and committed to the Committee of the Whole House on the state of the Union. Mr. Buchanan, from the Committee on the Judiciary, reported the following bill: [Washington, 1830] 2 p. (H. R. 521) DNA. 4324

---- A bill further to regulate the Patent Office, February 23, 1830. Mr. McKinley, from the Committee on the Judiciary, reported the following bill; which was read, and passed to a second reading: [Washington, 1830] 2 p. (S. 106) DNA. 4325

---- A bill further to regulate the transportation of merchandise on certain inland routes. March 15, 1830. Read twice, and committed to a Committee of the Whole House to-morrow. Mr. Cambreleng, from the Committee on Commerce, to which the subject had been referred, reported the following bill: [Washington, 1830] 3 p. (H. R. 350) DNA. 4326

---- A bill granting a pension to David M. Randolph. January 5, 1830. Mr. Holmes, from the Committee on Pensions, reported the following bill; which was read, and passed to a second reading: [Washington, 1830] 1 p. (S. 33) DNA. 4327

---- A bill granting a pension to Martin Miller. April 5, 1830.

Mr. Marks, from the Committee on Pensions, reported the following bill; which was read, and passed to the second reading: [Washington, 1830] 1 p. (S. 166) DNA. 4328

---- A bill granting a pension to the minor children of Peter Cabet, deceased. January 20, 1830. Read twice, and committed to a Committee of the Whole House to-morrow. Mr. Drayton, from the Committee on Military Affairs, reported the following bill: [Washington, 1830] 1 p. (H. R. 134) DNA. 4329

---- A bill granting a quantity of land to the territory of Arkansas, for the erection of a public building at the seat of government of said territory. January 26, 1830. Read twice, and committed to a Committee of the Whole House to-morrow. Mr. Cowles, from the Committee on the Territories, reported the following bill: [Washington, 1830] 2 p. (H. R. 158) DNA. 4330

---- A bill granting a township of land to Kenyon College, in Ohio. January 13, 1830. Mr. Kane, from the Committee on Public Lands, reported the following bill; which was read, and passed to a second reading: [Washington, 1830] 1 p. (S. 56) DNA. 4331

---- A bill granting a township of the public lands, in aid of the college of Louisiana. February 26, 1830. Mr. Livingston, from the Committee on Public Lands, reported the following bill; which was read, and passed to a second reading: [Washington, 1830] 1 p. (S. 114) DNA. 4332

---- A bill granting a township of the Public Lands in aid of the

Transylvania University, in Kentucky. February 24, 1830. Mr. Barton, from the Committee on Public Lands, reported the following bill; which was read, and passed to a second reading: [Washington, 1830] 1 p. (S. 108) DNA.   4333

---- A bill granting a township of the public lands in aid of the Transylvania University, in Kentucky. March 17, 1830. Read twice, and committed to the Committee of the Whole House on the state of the Union. Mr. Clarke, from the Select Committee to which the subject had been referred, reported the following bill: [Washington, 1830] 1 p. (H. R. 363) DNA.   4334

---- A bill granting certain lots, and parts of lots, to the Washington City Orphan Asylum. April 15, 1830. Mr. Chambers, from the Committee on the District of Columbia, reported the following bill; which was read, and passed to a second reading: [Washington, 1830] 1 p. (S. 180) DNA.   4335

---- A bill granting pensions to certain persons therein named. April 23, 1830. Read twice, and committed to a Committee of the Whole House to-morrow. Mr. Bates, of Massachusetts, from the Committee on Military Pensions, to which had been referred the petition of John Slaven, Thomas Sappington, Abraham Parker, William Mattheny, William Black, Jonah Garrison, and George Field, reported the following bill: [Washington, 1830] 2 p. (H. R. 439) DNA.   4336

---- A bill granting pensions to certain Revolutionary and Invalid soldiers and officers therein named. May 31, 1830. Read twice, and committed to a Com-

mittee of the Whole House to-morrow. Mr. Bockee, from the Committee on Military Pensions, reported the following bill: [Washington, 1830] 2 p. (H. R. 499) DNA.   4337

---- A bill granting pensions to certain Revolutionary and invalid soldiers therein mentioned. May 3, 1830. Read twice, and committed to the Committee of the Whole House to which is committed the bill (No. 362) for the relief of William Gallop. Mr. Bockee, from the Committee on Military Pensions, reported the following bill: [Washington, 1830] 2 p. (H. R. 454) DNA.   4338

---- A bill granting pensions to certain Revolutionary soldiers. May 25, 1830. Read twice, and committed to a Committee of the Whole House to-morrow. Mr. Ford, from the Committee on Military Pensions, reported the following bill: [Washington, 1830] 1 p. (H. R. 490) DNA.   4339

---- A bill granting pensions to Elisha James and Nathaniel Standish. May 25, 1830. Read twice, and committed to a Committee of the Whole House to-morrow. Mr. Bates, from the Committee on Military Pensions, reported the following bill: [Washington, 1830] 1 p. (H. R. 489) DNA.   4340

---- A bill granting pensions to Jared Cone, Hezekiah Hines, and William Kinney, soldiers of the Revolution. May 26, 1830. Read twice, and committed to a Committee of the Whole House to-morrow. Mr. Forward, from the Committee on Military Pensions, reported the following bill: [Washington, 1830] 1 p. (H. R. 491) DNA.   4341

---- A bill granting pensions to

Lester Morris, and others. May 21, 1830. Read twice, and committed to a Committee of the Whole House to-morrow. Mr. Bates, from the Committee on Military Pensions, reported the following bill: [Washington, 1830] 2 p. (H. R. 478) DNA.
4342

---- A bill granting pensions to Samuel H. Phillips, Cord Hazard, and John M'Creary, and to increase the pension of George W. Howard. February 1, 1830. Mr. Chambers, from the Committee on Pensions, reported the following bill; which was read, and passed to a second reading: [Washington, 1830] 2 p. (S. 76) DNA.
4343

---- A bill granting to the state of Ohio, upon certain conditions, all the lands of the United States within that state. January 28, 1830. Read twice, and committed to the Committee of the Whole House on the state of the Union. Mr. Irwin, from the Committee on the Public Lands, reported the following bill: [Washington, 1830] 5 p. (H. R. 171) DNA.
4344

---- A bill imposing regulations on sales at auction, for the further protection of the revenue. February 9, 1830. Read twice, and committed to a Committee of the Whole House to-morrow. Mr. Ingersoll, from the Committee of Ways and Means, to which the subject had been referred, reported the following bill: [Washington, 1830] 4 p. (H. R. 219) DNA.
4345

---- A bill in addition to an act passed the first of March, one thousand eight hundred and twenty-three, entitled "An act supplementary to, and to amend, an act to regulate the collection of duties on imports and tonnage,

passed second of March, one thousand seven hundred and ninety-nine, and for other purposes. March 30, 1830. Mr. Silsbee, from the Committee on Commerce, reported the following bill; which was read, and passed to a second reading: [Washington, 1830] 2 p. (S. 159) DNA.
4346

---- A bill in addition to "An act to promote the progress of useful arts, and to repeal the act heretofore made for that purpose," passed February twenty-first, one thousand seven hundred and ninety-three. March 22, 1830. Mr. Robbins, from the Joint Committee on the Library of Congress, reported the following bill; which was read, and passed to a second reading. [Washington, 1830] 1 p. (S. 143) DNA.
4347

---- A bill in addition to the acts concerning coins and the mint. January 11, 1830. Mr. Sanford, from the Select Committee to whom the subject was referred, reported the following bill; which was read, and passed to a second reading: [Washington, 1830] 2 p. (S. 49) DNA.
4348

---- A bill increasing the terms of the Judicial Courts of the United States for the Southern District of New York, and adding to the compensation of several District Judges of the United States. January 11, 1830. Mr. Rowan, from the Committee on the Judiciary, reported the following bill; which was read, and passed to a second reading: [Washington, 1830] 2 p. (S. 51) DNA.
4349

---- A bill making a re-appropriation of a sum heretofore appropriated for the suppression of the slave trade. May 11, 1830.

Read twice, and committed to the Committee of the Whole House on the state of the Union. Mr. McDuffie, from the Committee of Ways and Means, reported the following bill: [Washington, 1830] 1 p. (H. R. 466) DNA.   4350

---- A bill making additional appropriations for the diplomatic service during the year one thousand eight hundred and thirty. May 24, 1830. Read twice, and committed to the Committee of the Whole House on the state of the Union. Mr. Verplanck, from the Committee of Ways and Means, reported the following bill: [Washington, 1830] 1 p. (H. R. 484) DNA.   4351

---- A bill making an appropriation for building a Marine Hospital at or near Charleston, in South Carolina. February 4, 1830. Read twice, and committed to a Committee of the Whole House to-morrow. Mr. Cambreleng, from the Committee on Commerce, reported the following bill: [Washington, 1830] 2 p. (H. R. 194) DNA.   4352

---- A bill making an appropriation for public warehouses. March 6, 1830. Read twice, and committed to the Committee of the Whole House on the state of the Union. Mr. Cambreleng, from the Committee on Commerce, reported the following bill: [Washington, 1830] 2 p. (H. R. 329) DNA.   4353

---- A bill making an appropriation for the improvement of the navigation of the Kentucky river, near Frankfort, Kentucky. February 11, 1830. Read twice, and committed to a Committee of the Whole House to-morrow. Mr. Letcher, from the Committee on Internal Improvements, reported

the following bill: [Washington, 1830] 1 p. (H. R. 236) DNA.   4354

---- A bill making an appropriation for the Marine Corps. May 31, 1830. Read twice, and ordered to be engrossed, and read a third time to-morrow. Mr. McDuffie, from the Committee of Ways and Means, reported the following bill: [Washington, 1830] 1 p. (H. R. 496) DNA.   4355

---- A bill making an appropriation for the protection of the western frontiers of the United States. January 4, 1830. Read twice, and committed to a Committee of the Whole House to-morrow. Mr. Drayton, from the Committee on Military Affairs, reported the following bill: [Washington, 1830] 1 p. (H. R. 61) DNA.   4356

---- A bill making an appropriation to complete the road leading from Fooy's, opposite Memphis, in the state of Tennessee, to Little Rock, in the territory of Arkansas. January 13, 1830. Read twice, and committed to a Committee of the Whole House to-morrow. Mr. Hemphill, from the Committee on Internal Improvements, reported the following bill: [Washington, 1830] 2 p. (H. R. 111) DNA.   4357

---- A bill making appropriation for the purchase of books for the use of the Supreme Court of the United States. March 15, 1830. Read twice, and committed to the Committee of the Whole House on the state of the Union. Mr. Everett, from the Committee on the Library, reported the following bill: [Washington, 1830] 1 p. (H. R. 351) DNA.   4358

---- A bill making appropriations for building light-houses and light-boats, erecting beacons and monuments, and placing buoys on proper sites, and for improving harbors and directing surveys. February 27, 1830. Read twice, and committed to the Committee of the Whole House on the state of the Union. Mr. Newton, from the Committee on Commerce, reported the following bill: [Washington, 1830] 12 p. (H. R. 304) DNA. 4359

---- A bill making appropriations for building light-houses, light-boats, beacons, and monuments, placing buoys, and for improving harbors, and directing surveys. March 20, 1830. Read and committed to the Committee of the Whole House on the state of the Union, to which the said bill is committed. Mr. Cambreleng, from the Committee on Commerce, submitted the following as amendatory of the bill (H. R. No. 304) making appropriations for building light-houses, light-boats, beacons, and monuments, placing buoys, and for improving harbors, and directing surveys. [Washington, 1830] 12 p. (H. R. 304) DNA. 4360

---- A bill making appropriations for carrying into effect certain provisions of the treaty with the Cherokees West of the Mississippi. April 3, 1830. Read twice, and committed to the Committee of the Whole House on the state of the Union. Mr. Verplanck, from the Committee of Ways and Means, reported the following bill: [Washington, 1830] 2 p. (H. R. 404) DNA. 4361

---- A bill making appropriations for certain expenditures on account of the Engineer, Ordnance and Quartermaster's Departments. January 22, 1830. Read twice, and committed to a Committee of the Whole House tomorrow. Mr. Drayton, from the Committee on Military Affairs, reported the following bill: [Washington, 1830] 3 p. (H. R. 146) DNA. 4362

---- A bill making appropriations for certain fortifications for the year one thousand eight hundred and thirty. January 13, 1830. Read twice, and committed to the Committee of the Whole House on the State of the Union. Mr. McDuffie, from the Committee of Ways and Means, reported the following bill: [Washington, 1830] 1 p. (H. R. 110) DNA. 4363

---- A bill making appropriations for examinations and surveys, and also, for certain works of Internal Improvement. February 22, 1830. Read twice, and committed to the Committee of the Whole House on the state of the Union. Mr. McDuffie, from the Committee of Ways and Means, reported the following bill: [Washington, 1830] 2 p. (H. R. 279) DNA. 4364

---- A bill making appropriations for the completion and support of the Penitentiary in the District of Columbia, and for other purposes. March 12, 1830. Read twice, and committed to the Committee of the Whole House on the state of the Union. Mr. Powers, from the Committee for the District of Columbia, reported the following bill: [Washington, 1830] 3 p. (H. R. 343) DNA. 4365

---- A bill making appropriations for the improvement of certain harbors, and for removing obstructions at the mouths of certain rivers, for the year one thousand eight hundred and thirty.

February 12, 1830. Read twice, and committed to the Committee of the Whole House on the state of the Union. Mr. McDuffie, from the Committee of Ways and Means, reported the following bill: [Washington, 1830] 3 p. (H. R. 242) DNA.   4366

---- A bill making appropriations for the Indian Department, for the year one thousand eight hundred and thirty. January 26, 1830. Read twice, and committed to the Committee of the Whole House on the state of the Union. Mr. McDuffie, from the Committee of Ways and Means, reported the following bill: [Washington, 1830] 1 p. (H. R. 162) DNA.
                               4367
---- A bill making appropriations for the military service for the year one thousand eight hundred and thirty. January 21, 1830. Read twice, and committed to the Committee of the Whole House on the state of the Union. Mr. McDuffie, from the Committee of Ways and Means, reported the following bill: [Washington, 1830] 3 p. (H. R. 144) DNA.
                               4368
---- A bill making appropriations for the naval service for the year one thousand eight hundred and thirty. January 18, 1830. Read twice, and committed to a Committee of the Whole House on the State of the Union. Mr. McDuffie, from the Committee of Ways and Means, reported the following bill: [Washington, 1830] 4 p. (H. R. 129) DNA.
                               4369
---- A bill making appropriations for the payment of Revolutionary and Invalid Pensioners. January 8, 1830. Read twice, and committed to a Committee of the Whole House on the state of the Union. Mr. McDuffie, from the Committee of Ways

and Means, reported the following bill: [Washington, 1830] 1 p. (H. R. 90) DNA.   4370

---- A bill making appropriations for the public buildings, and for other purposes. April 5, 1830. Read twice, and committed to the Committee of the Whole House on the state of the Union. Mr. Verplanck, from the Committee on the Public Buildings, reported the following bill: [Washington, 1830] 3 p. (H. R. 407) DNA.   4371

---- A bill making appropriations for the support of government for the year one thousand eight hundred and thirty. January 12, 1830. Read twice, and committed to the Committee of the Whole House on the state of the Union. Mr. McDuffie, from the Committee of Ways and Means, reported the following bill: [Washington, 1830] 15 p. (H. R. 102) DNA.   4372

---- A bill making appropriations for the support of government for the year one thousand eight hundred and thirty-one. December 31, 1830. Read twice, and committed to the Committee of the Whole House on the state of the Union. Mr. Verplanck, from the Committee of Ways and Means, reported the following bill: [Washington, 1830] 16 p. (H. R. 528) DNA.   4373

---- A bill making appropriations to carry into effect certain Indian Treaties. February 22, 1830. Read twice, and committed to a Committee of the Whole House on the state of the Union. Mr. McDuffie, from the Committee of Ways and Means, reported the following bill: [Washington, 1830] 3 p. (H. R. 278) DNA.   4374

---- A bill making appropriations to carry into effect certain Indian Treaties, for the year one thousand eight hundred and thirty. March 25, 1830. Read twice, and committed to the Committee of the Whole House on the state of the Union. Mr. McDuffie, from the Committee of Ways and Means, reported the following bill: [Washington, 1830] 3 p. (H. R. 386) DNA. 4375

---- A bill making appropriations to carry into effect the Treaty of Butte des Mortes. March 19, 1830. Read twice, and committed to the Committee of the Whole House on the state of the Union. Mr. McDuffie, from the Committee of Ways and Means, reported the following bill: [Washington, 1830] 2 p. (H. R. 369) DNA. 4376

---- A bill making appropriations to pay the claims of certain Cherokees. April 7, 1830. Read twice, and committed to the Committee of the Whole House on the state of the Union. Mr. Verplanck, from the Committee of Ways and Means, reported the following bill: [Washington, 1830] 1 p. (H. R. 411) DNA. 4377

---- A bill making appropriations to pay the expenses incurred in holding certain Indian Treaties. February 26, 1830. Read twice, and committed to the Committee of the Whole House on the state of the Union. Mr. McDuffie, from the Committee of Ways and Means, reported the following bill: [Washington, 1830] 2 p. (H. R. 299) DNA. 4378

---- A bill making compensation to the Register and Receiver of public lands at Augusta, Mississippi, for certain services performed by them. December 30, 1830. Read twice, and committed to a Committee of the Whole House to-morrow. Mr. Wickliffe, from the Committee on the Public Lands, reported the following bill: [Washington, 1830] 1 p. (H. R. 525) DNA. 4379

---- A bill making further appropriations for the improvement of the navigation of the Ohio and Mississippi rivers, and their tributary streams, and for the deepening the channel at the mouth of the Mississippi river. April 23, 1830. Read twice, and committed to the Committee of the Whole House on the state of the Union. Mr. Wickliffe, from the select committee to which the subject had been referred, reported the following bill: [Washington, 1830] 2 p. (H. R. 440) DNA. 4380

---- A bill making further provision for the Military Academy at West Point. January 7, 1830. Read twice, and committed to a Committee of the Whole House to-morrow. Mr. Drayton, from the Committee on Military Affairs, reported the following bill: [Washington, 1830] 3 p. (H. R. 83) DNA. 4381

---- A bill more effectually to secure the accountability of agents of the government of the United States, resident in foreign countries, and to provide a certain and efficient method of ascertaining the legal amount of their claims. March 30, 1830. Read twice, and committed to a Committee of the Whole House to-morrow. Mr. De Witt, from the Committee on Retrenchment, reported the following bill: [Washington, 1830] 2 p. (H. R. 398) DNA. 4382

---- A bill prescribing the modes

of commencing, prosecuting, and deciding, controversies between States.   January 6, 1830. Read, and passed to a second reading. January 7, Read second time, and referred to Committee on the Judiciary. January 19, Reported without amendment. [Washington, 1830]   7 p. (S. 42) DNA.   4383

---- A bill providing for a further adjudication of the claims of the citizens of Georgia, under the fourth article of a treaty made with the Creek Indians, on the eighth day of January, one thousand eight hundred and twenty-one.   January 26, 1830. Read twice, and committed to a Committee of the Whole House to-morrow. Mr. Bell, from the Committee on Indian Affairs, reported the following bill: [Washington, 1830]   1 p. (H. R. 155) DNA.   4384

---- A bill providing for the election and admission of a delegate to the Congress of the United States from the District of Columbia. April 26, 1830. Read twice, and committed to the Committee of the Whole House on the state of the Union.   Mr. Powers, from the Committee for the District of Columbia, reported the following bill: [Washington, 1830]   4 p. (H. R. 442) DNA.   4385

---- A bill providing for the organization of the Ordnance Department. January 6, 1830. Read twice, and committed to a Committee of the Whole House to-morrow. Mr. Drayton, from the Committee on Military Affairs, reported the following bill: [Washington, 1830] 2 p. (H. R. 77) DNA.   4386

---- A bill providing for the relief of Matthews Flournoy and R. J. Ward, of the state of Missis-

sippi.   February 24, 1830. Read twice, and committed to a Committee of the Whole House to-morrow. Mr. Pettis, from the Committee on Private Land Claims, reported the following bill: [Washington, 1830]   1 p. (H. R. 284) DNA.   4387

---- A bill providing for the sale of certain town and village lots in the state of Missouri. May 27, 1830. Read twice, and committed to a Committee of the Whole House to-morrow. Mr. Pettis, from the Committee on Private Land Claims, reported the following bill: [Washington, 1830] 1 p. (H. R. 493) DNA.   4388

---- A bill providing for the settlement of the accounts of certain diplomatic functionaries. February 22, 1830. Read twice, and committed to the Committee of the Whole House to which is committed the bill to amend the act, entitled "An act fixing the compensation of Public Ministers, and Consuls residing on the coast of Barbary, and for other purposes." Mr. Archer, from the Committee on Foreign Affairs, reported the following bill: [Washington, 1830] 2 p. (H. R. 275) DNA.   4389

---- A bill regulating the duties, and providing for the compensation of Pursers in the Navy. February 18, 1830. Mr. Hayne, from the Committee on Naval Affairs, reported the following bill; which was read, and passed to a second reading: [Washington, 1830] 4 p. (S. 99) DNA.   4390

---- A bill relating to the Orphans' Courts in the District of Columbia. April 26, 1830. Read twice, and committed to the Committee of the Whole House on the state of the Union. Mr. Semmes, from the Committee for the District of Columbia, reported the following bill: [Washington, 1830] 1 p. (H. R. 443) DNA. 4391

---- A bill relating to the Privateer Pension Fund. February 9, 1830. Read twice, and committed to a Committee of the Whole House to-morrow. Mr. Dorsey, from the Committee on Naval Affairs, reported the following bill: [Washington, 1830] 2 p. (H. R. 217) DNA. 4392

---- A bill relative to militia fines within the District of Columbia. March 22, 1830. Mr. Barnard, from the Committee on the Militia, reported the following bill; which was read, and passed to a second reading. [Washington, 1830] 3 p. (S. 144) DNA. 4393

---- A bill relative to the plan of Detroit, in Michigan Territory. March 25, 1830. Read twice, and ordered to be engrossed, and read the third time to-morrow. Mr. Cowles, from the Committee on the Territories, reported the following bill: [Washington, 1830] 1 p. (H. R. 383) DNA. 4394

---- A bill requiring vessels in the bays and rivers of the United States to display a light in the night time. March 10, 1830. Mr. Woodbury, from the Committee on Commerce, reported the following bill: [Washington, 1830] 1 p. (S. 128) DNA. 4395

---- A bill supplemental to an act, passed on the thirty-first March, one thousand eight hundred and thirty, entitled "An act for the relief of purchasers of public lands, and for the suppresion of fraudulent practices at the public sales of lands of the United States. December 23, 1830. Read twice, and commit-

ted to a Committee of the Whole House to-morrow. Mr. Clay, from the Committee on the Public Lands, reported the following bill: [Washington, 1830] 2 p. (H. R. 510) DNA. 4396

---- A bill supplementary to, and declaratory of, the intent and meaning of the act of Congress, passed April 24th, 1816, entitled, "An act for 'organizing the General Staff, and making further provision for ' the Army of the United States." January 4, 1830. Read twice, and committed to a Committee of the Whole House to-morrow. Mr. Drayton, from the Committee on Military Affairs, reported the following bill: [Washington, 1830] 1 p. (H. R. 58) DNA. 4397

---- A bill supplementary to, and declaratory of the intent and meaning of the act of March 16th, 1802, entitled "An act fixing the Military Peace Establishment of the United States." January 4, 1830. Read twice, and committed to a Committee of the Whole House to-morrow. Mr. Drayton, from the Committee on Military Affairs, reported the following bill: [Washington, 1830] 1 p. (H. R. 60) DNA. 4398

---- A bill supplementary to the act, entitled "An act to authorize the citizens of the territories of Arkansas and Florida to elect their officers, and for other purposes." March 23, 1830. Read twice, and ordered to be engrossed, and read the third time to-morrow. Mr. Buchanan, from the Committee on the Judiciary, reported the following bill: [Washington, 1830] 1 p. (H. R. 380) DNA. 4399

---- A bill supplementary to the act, entitled "An act to authorize

the President of the United States
to run and mark a line dividing
the Territory of Florida from the
State of Georgia." February 13,
1830. Read twice, and committed to a Committee of the Whole
House to-morrow. Mr. Buchanan, from the Committee on the
Judiciary, reported the following
bill: [Washington, 1830] 2 p.
(H. R. 243) DNA.   4400

---- A bill supplementary to the
act, entitled "An act to incorporate the Subscribers to the Bank
of the United States." February
4, 1830. Read twice, and committed to a Committee of the
Whole House on Thursday next.
Mr. Buchanan, from the Committee on the Judiciary, to which
the subject had been referred,
reported the following bill:
[Washington, 1830] 2 p. (H. R.
193) DNA.   4401

---- A bill to abolish Brevet
rank in the Army of the United
States and in the Marine Corps.
February 1, 1830. Read twice,
and committed to a Committee of
the Whole House to-morrow. Mr.
Coulter, from the Committee on
Retrenchment, reported the following bill: [Washington, 1830]
1 p. (H. R. 190) DNA.   4402

---- A bill to abolish the Board
of Navy Commissioners, and to
transfer its duties to the Secretary of the Navy, and to regulate
the office of Naval Constructor.
January 15, 1830. Read twice,
and committed to the Committee
of the Whole House on the state
of the Union. Mr. Coulter,
from the Committee on Retrenchment, reported the following
bill: [Washington, 1830] 2 p.
(H. R. 115) DNA.   4403

---- A bill to abolish the office
of Major General in the Army

of the United States, and for
other purposes. January 29,
1830. Read twice, and committed to the Committee of the
Whole House on the state of the
Union. Mr. Coke, from the
Committee on Retrenchment, reported the following bill: [Wash-
ington, 1830] 1 p. (H. R. 183)
DNA.   4404

---- A bill to aid in the education of indigent deaf and dumb
persons. February 23, 1830.
Read twice, and committed to a
Committee of the Whole House
to-morrow. Mr. Goodenow, from
the Select Committee to which
the subject had been referred,
reported the following bill:
[Washington, 1830] 2 p. (H. R.
280) DNA.   4405

---- A bill to alter and amend
"An act to set apart and dispose
of certain public lands, for the
encouragement of the cultivation
of the vine and olive." January
13, 1830. Mr. McKinley, from
the Committee on Public Lands,
reported the following bill; which
was read, and passed to a second reading: [Washington, 1830]
2 p. (S. 55) DNA.   4406

---- A bill to alter and amend
the organization of the Corps of
Marines. February 5, 1830.
Read twice, and committed to a
Committee of the Whole House
to-morrow. Mr. Drayton, from
the Committee on Military Affairs, reported the following bill:
[Washington, 1830] 5 p. (H. R.
202) DNA.   4407

---- A bill to alter and amend
the organization of the Corps of
Marines, and for other purposes.
February 5, 1830. Read twice,
and committed to a Committee of
the Whole House to-morrow.
March 6, 1830. Re-printed by

order of the House of Representatives, with proposed amendments. Mr. Drayton, from the
Committee on Military Affairs,
reported the following bill:
[Washington, 1830] 5 p. (H. R.
202) DNA.   4408

---- A bill to alter and amend
the sixty-fifth article of the first
section of an act, entitled "An
act for establishing rules and
articles for the government of
the Armies of the United States,"
passed tenth April, one thousand
eight hundred and six. February 18, 1830. Read twice, and
ordered to be engrossed, and
read a third time to-morrow.
Mr. Drayton, from the Committee on Military Affairs, to which
the subject had been referred,
reported the following bill:
[Washington, 1830] 2 p. (H. R.
259) DNA.   4409

---- A bill to alter the bridge
and draw across the Potomac,
from Washington City to Alexandria. January 6, 1830. Mr.
Chambers, from the Committee
on the District of Columbia, reported the following bill; which
was read, and passed to a second reading. [Washington, 1830]
3 p. (S. 40) DNA.   4410

---- A bill to alter the terms of
credit on bonds given for duties
on goods, wares, and merchandise, imported into the United
States. January 7, 1830. Mr.
Smith, from the Committee on
Finance, reported the following
bill; which was read, and passed
to a second reading: [Washing-
ton, 1830] 1 p. (S. 44) DNA.
                               4411
---- A bill to alter the time of
holding the Circuit Court of the
United States for the District of
Maryland. January 4, 1830.
Read twice, and ordered to be

engrossed, and read the third
time to-morrow. Mr. Buchanan, from the Committee on the
Judiciary, to which the subject
had been referred, reported the
following bill: [Washington,
1830] 1 p. (H. R. 68) DNA.
                               4412
---- A bill to alter the time of
holding the distric [sic] court of
the United States, for the northern district of Alabama. December 27, 1830. Read twice,
and ordered to be engrossed,
and read the third time to-morrow. Mr. Buchanan, from the
Committee on the Judiciary, reported the following bill: [Wash-
ington, 1830] 1 p. (H. R. 514)
DNA.   4413

---- A bill to alter the time of
holding the sessions of the Legislative Council of the territory
of Florida. January 11, 1830.
Read twice, and ordered to be
engrossed, and read the third
time to-morrow. Mr. Clark,
from the Committee on the Judiciary, reported the following
bill: [Washington, 1830] 1 p.
(H. R. 101) DNA.   4414

---- A bill to amend "an act authorizing the state of Tennessee
to issue grants and perfect titles
to certain lands herein described,
and to settle the claims to the
vacant and unappropriated lands
within the same," passed 18th of
April, 1806. January 29, 1830.
Read twice, and committed to a
Committee of the Whole House
to-morrow. Mr. Crockett, from
the Select Committee, to which
the subject had been referred,
reported the following bill:
[Washington, 1830] 3 p. (H. R.
185) DNA.   4415

---- A bill to amend an act confirming certain land claims in
the Territory of Michigan. May

31, 1830. Read twice, and committed to a Committee of the
Whole House to-morrow. Mr.
Isacks, from the Committee on
the Public Lands, reported the following bill: [Washington, 1830]
1 p. (H. R. 497) DNA.   4416

---- A bill to amend an act, entitled "An act fixing the compensation of Public Ministers, and
of Consuls residing on the coast
of Barbary, and for other purposes." February 22, 1830.
Read twice, and committed to the
Committee of the Whole House on
the state of the Union. Mr.
Archer, from the Committee on
Foreign Affairs, reported the following bill: [Washington, 1830]
3 p. (H. R. 274) DNA.   4417

---- A bill to amend an act, entitled "An act for the benefit of
the incorporated Kentucky Asylum
for teaching the Deaf and Dumb,"
and to extend the time for selling the land granted by said act.
April 12, 1830. Read twice,
and ordered to be engrossed, and
read the third time to-morrow.
Mr. Baylor, from the select committee to which the subject had
been referred, reported the following bill: [Washington, 1830]
2 p. (H. R. 418) DNA.   4418

---- A bill to amend an act, entitled "An act for the relief of
purchasers of public lands that
have reverted for non-payment of
the purchase money," approved
May the twenty-third, one thousand eight hundred and twenty-
eight. January 6, 1830. Read
twice, and committed to a Committee of the Whole House to-
morrow. Mr. Isacks, from the
Committee on the Public Lands,
reported the following bill:
[Washington, 1830] 1 p. (H. R.
79) DNA.   4419

---- A bill to amend an act, entitled "An act in addition to the
acts prohibiting the slave trade,"
passed March third, one thousand eight hundred and nineteen.
April 7, 1830. Read twice, and
committed to the Committee of
the Whole House on the state of
the Union. Mr. Mercer, from
the select committee to which
the subject had been referred,
reported the following bill:
[Washington, 1830] 1 p. (H. R.
412) DNA.   4420

---- A bill to amend an act, entitled "An act to allow the citizens of the territory of Michigan to elect the members of their
Legislative Council, and for other
purposes." Approved 29th January, 1827. February 1, 1830.
Read twice, and committed to a
Committee of the Whole House
to-morrow. Mr. Clark, from
the Committee on the Territories, reported the following
bill: [Washington, 1830] 3 p.
(H. R. 189) DNA.   4421

---- A bill to amend an act, entitled "An act to provide for paying to the state of Illinois three
per cent. of the nett proceeds
arising from the sale of the public lands within the same." January 13, 1830. Mr. Rowan,
from the Committee on the Judiciary, reported the following
bill; which was read, and passed
to a second reading: [Washing-
ton, 1830] 1 p. (S. 58) DNA.
                             4422
---- A bill to amend an act, entitled "An act to regulate the
practice in the courts of the
United States for the district of
Louisiana." December 23, 1829.
Read, and passed to a second
reading. December 24, 1829.
Read second time, and referred
to the Committee on the Judiciary. March 31, 1830. Report-

ed, with the recommendation that the whole, after the enacting clause, be stricken out, and that what follows the bill be adopted in lieu thereof. [Washington, 1830] 5 p. (S. 20) DNA. 4423

---- A bill to amend "An act in alteration of the several acts imposing duties on Imports." January 27, 1830. Read twice, and committed to the Committee of the Whole House on the state of the Union. Mr. Mallary, from the Committee on Manufactures, reported the following bill: [Washington, 1830] 9 p. (H. R. 164) DNA. 4424

---- A bill to amend and consolidate the acts respecting Copyrights. January 21, 1830. Read twice, and committed to a Committee of the Whole House to-morrow. Mr. Ellsworth, from the Committee on the Judiciary, reported the following bill: [Washington, 1830] 9 p. (H. R. 145) DNA. 4425

---- A bill to amend and extend the provisions of the act, approved the twenty-ninth day of May, one thousand eight hundred and thirty, entitled "An act to grant pre-emption rights to settlers on the public lands." December 30, 1830. Read twice, and committed to the Committee of the Whole House on the state of the Union. Mr. Wickliffe, from the Committee on the Public Lands, reported the following bill: [Washington, 1830] 2 p. (H. R. 524) DNA. 4426

---- A bill to amend the act, entitled "An act for the relief of certain surviving officers and soldiers of the Army of the Revolution." January 14, 1830. Mr. Foot, from the Committee on Pensions, reported the following

bill; which was read, and passed to a second reading: [Washington, 1830] 1 p. (S. 60) DNA. 4427

---- A bill to amend the acts regulating the commercial intercourse between the United States and certain colonies of Great Britain. May 27, 1830. Read twice, and committed to a Committee of the Whole House this day. Mr. Cambreleng, from the Committee on Commerce, reported the following bill: [Washington, 1830] 3 p. (H. R. 495) DNA. 4428

---- A bill to amend the charter of Georgetown. February 11, 1830. Read twice, and committed to a Committee of the Whole House to-morrow. Mr. Washington, from the Committee for the District of Columbia, reported the following bill: [Washington, 1830] 1 p. (H. R. 233) DNA. 4429

---- A bill to amend the navigation laws of the United States. April 30, 1830. Mr. Gorham, to postpone indefinitely. Mr. Cambreleng, from the Committee on Commerce, reported the following bill: [Washington, 1830] 3 p. (H. R. 449) DNA. 4430

---- A bill to amend the several acts authorizing the registering and granting of licences to steam-boats, and to provide for the better security of the lives of passengers on board of vessels propelled in whole or in part by steam. May 4, 1830. Read twice, and committed to the Committee of the Whole House on the state of the Union. Mr. Wickliffe, from the Committee to which the subject had been referred, reported the following bill: [Washington, 1830] 5 p. (H. R. 458) DNA. 4431

---- A bill to amend the several
acts establishing a Territorial
Government in Florida. December 28, 1830. Read twice, and
committed to a Committee of the
Whole House to-morrow. Mr.
Clarke, from the Committee on
the Territories, reported the following bill: [Washington, 1830]
1 p. (H. R. 519) DNA.   4432

---- A bill to amend the several
acts respecting copy-rights. December 17, 1830. Read twice,
and committed to the Committee
of the Whole House on the state
of the Union. Mr. Ellsworth,
from the Committee on the Judiciary, to which was recommitted
the bill [H. R. 145] to amend and
consolidate the acts respecting
copy-rights, reported the same
with amendments. [Washington,
1830] 9 p. (H. R. 145) DNA.
                             4433
---- A bill to amend the twelfth
section of the act, entitled "An
act to establish the Judicial
Courts of the United States."
March 23, 1830. Read twice,
and referred to the Committee
on the Judiciary. March 26,
1830. Reported without amendment. [Washington, 1830] 2 p.
(S. 153) DNA.   4434

---- A bill to ascertain and mark
the line between the state of Alabama and the territory of Florida, and for other purposes. December 28, 1830. Read twice,
and ordered to be engrossed, and
read the third time to-morrow.
Mr. Wickliffe, from the Committee on the Public Lands, to which
the subject had been referred,
reported the following bill:
[Washington, 1830] 2 p. (H. R.
516) DNA.   4435

---- A bill to ascertain and survey the northern boundary of the
state of Illinois. December 22,

1830. Read twice, and committed to the Committee of the
Whole House to which is committed the bill (H. R. No. 181) for
ascertaining the latitude of the
southerly bend, or extreme of
lake Michigan, and of certain
other points, for the purpose,
thereafter, of fixing the true
northern boundary lines of the
States of Ohio and Illinois. Mr.
Duncan, from the Committee on
the Public Lands, reported the
following bill: [Washington, 1830]
2 p. (H. R. 508) DNA.   4436

---- A bill to authorize a change
in the disposal of the land granted for the construction of the
Illinois and Michigan Canal. February 16, 1830. Read twice,
and committed to a Committee of
the Whole House to-morrow. Mr.
Duncan, from the Committee on
the Public Lands, reported the
following bill: [Washington,
1830] 4 p. (H. R. 255) DNA.
                             4437
---- A bill to authorize a subscription for completing the Mail
Road from Baltimore to Wilmington. March 15, 1830. Read
twice, and committed to the Committee of the Whole House on the
State of the Union. Mr. Hemphill, from the Committee on Internal Improvements, reported
the following bill: [Washington,
1830] 3 p. (H. R. 352) DNA.
                             4438
---- A bill to authorize a subscription for stock, on the part
of the United States, in the
Louisville and Portland Canal
Company. January 26, 1830. --
Read, and passed to a second
reading. Feb. 2. --Read a second time, and referred to the
Committee on Roads and Canals.
Feb. 3. --Reported without
amendment. [Washington, 1830]
2 p. (S. 74) DNA.   4439

---- A bill to authorize a subscription for stock, on the part of the United States, in the Louisville and Portland Canal Company. March 13, 1830. Read twice, and committed to the Committee of the Whole House on the state of the Union. Mr. Letcher, from the Committee on Internal Improvements, reported the following bill: [Washington, 1830] 1 p. (H. R. 348) DNA.
4440

---- A bill to authorize a subscription for stock, on the part of the United States, in the Wheeling and Belmont Bridge Company. May 11, 1830. Read twice, and committed to a Committee of the Whole House to-morrow. Mr. Letcher, from the Committee on Internal Improvements, reported the following bill: [Washington, 1830] 2 p. (H. R. 467) DNA.
4441

---- A bill to authorize a subscription of stock in the Farmington Canal Company, and in the Hampshire and Hampden Canal Company. February 22, 1830. Read twice, and committed to a Committee of the Whole House to-morrow. Mr. Butman, from the Committee on Internal Improvements, reported the following bill: [Washington, 1830] 2 p. (H. R. 276) DNA.
4442

---- A bill to authorize a subscription of stock in the Farmington Canal Company, and in the Hampshire and Hampden Canal Company. May 22, 1830. Mr. Ruggles, from the Committee on Roads and Canals, reported the following bill; which was read, and passed to a second reading: [Washington, 1830] 2 p. (S. 193) DNA.
4443

---- A bill to authorize a subscription of stock in the Savan-

nah, Ogechee, and Alatamaha Canal Company. May 3, 1830. Read twice, and committed to a Committee of the Whole House to-morrow. Mr. Blair of Tennessee, from the Committee on Internal Improvements, reported the following bill: [Washington, 1830] 2 p. (H. R. 456) DNA.
4444

---- A bill to authorize a subscription to the stock of the Blackstone Canal Company. Mar. 15, 1830. Read twice, and committed to the Committee of the Whole House on the state of the Union. Mr. Butman, from the Committee on Internal Improvements, reported the following bill: [Washington, 1830] 1 p. (H. R. 353) DNA. 4445

---- A bill to authorize Surveyors, under the direction of the Secretary of the Treasury, to enrol and license ships or vessels to be employed in the coasting trade and fisheries. January 5, 1830. Read twice, and committed to a Committee of the Whole House to-morrow. Mr Newton, from the Committee on Commerce, to which the subject had been referred, reported the following bill: [Washington, 1830] 1 p. (H. R. 71) DNA.
4446

---- A bill to authorize the appointment of a marshal for the Northern District of the state of Alabama. January 18, 1830. Read, and passed to a second reading. January 19, 1830. Read a second time, and referred to the Committee on the Judiciary. February 1, 1830. Reported without amendment. [Washington, 1830] 1 p. (S. 66) DNA. 4447

---- A bill to authorize the Commissioners of the Sinking Fund to redeem the public debt of the

United States. January 7, 1830.
Mr. Smith, from the Committee
on Finance, reported the following bill; which was read, and
passed to a second reading:
[Washington, 1830] 1 p. (S. 45)
DNA.   4448

---- The bill to authorize the
Commissioners of the Sinking
Fund to redeem the public debt
of the United States, being under
consideration in Committee of
the Whole, Mr. Smith, of Maryland, offered the following amendment: February 19, 1830.
[Washington, 1830] 2 p. (S. 45)
DNA.   4449

---- A bill to authorize the construction of three schooners for
the naval service of the United
States. December 22, 1830.
Read twice, and committed to the
Committee of the Whole House on
the state of the Union. Mr. Hoffman, from the Committee on
Naval Affairs, reported the following bill: [Washington, 1830]
1 p. (H. R. 507) DNA.   4450

---- A bill to authorize the employment of an additional number
of clerks in the Treasury and
War Departments, and for other
purposes. May 3, 1830. Read
twice, and committed to the Committee of the Whole House on the
state of the Union. Mr. McDuffie, from the Committee of Ways
and Means, reported the following bill: [Washington, 1830] 2 p.
(H. R. 455) DNA.   4451

---- A bill to authorize the exchange of the sixteenth sections,
granted for the use of common
schools, which are unfit for cultivation, for other lands. January 11, 1830. Read twice, and
committed to a Committee of the
Whole House to-morrow. Mr.
Isacks, from the Committee on

the Public Lands, reported the
following bill: [Washington,
1830] 1 p. (H. R. 93) DNA.
                                  4452

---- A bill to authorize the executor of Stephen Tippett to locate a tract of land in the state
of Louisiana. February 8, 1830.
Mr. Kane, from the Committee
on Private Land Claims, reported the following bill; which was
read, and passed to a second
reading: [Washington, 1830] 1 p.
(S. 85) DNA.   4453

---- A bill to authorize the extension, construction, and use
of a lateral branch of the Baltimore and Ohio Rail Road, into
and within the District of Columbia. December 8, 1830. Read
twice, and committed to the
Committee of the Whole House
on the state of the Union. Mr.
Blair, of Tennessee, from the
Committee on Internal Improvement, reported the following
bill: [Washington, 1830] 6 p.
(H. R. 517) DNA.   4454

---- A bill to authorize the heirs
of Silence Elliot to institute a
suit or suits against the United
States, for lands in Boston.
March 11, 1830. Mr. Rowan,
from the Committee on the Judiciary, reported the following
bill; which was read, and passed
to a second reading: [Washing-
ton, 1830] 2 p. (S. 131) DNA.
                                  4455
---- A bill to authorize the improvement of a road through the
lands of the Chickasaw nation,
in the direction between Memphis
and Tuscumbia, in the state of
Alabama. March 15, 1830.
Read twice, and committed to a
Committee of the Whole House
to-morrow. Mr. Johnson, of
Kentucky, from the Committee
on the Post Office and Post
Roads, reported the following

bill: [Washington, 1830] 1 p.
(H. R. 354) DNA.   4456

---- A bill to authorize the inhabitants of the state of Louisiana to enter the back lands.
February 25, 1830. Read, and
passed to a second reading. February 26, 1830. Read second
time, and referred to the Committee on Public Lands. March
12, 1830. Reported without
amendment. [Washington, 1830]
3 p. (S. 110) DNA.   4457

---- A bill to authorize the
Judges of the Courts of Record
of the territory of Michigan to
appoint the clerks of their several courts. February 10, 1830.
Read twice, and committed to a
Committee of the Whole House to-
morrow. Mr. Shepard, from the
Committee on the Territories, to
which the subject had been referred, reported the following
bill: [Washington, 1830] 2 p.
(H. R. 226) DNA.   4458

---- A bill to authorize the Legislature of Missouri to sell the
lands reserved for schools, a
seminary of learning, and salt
springs, in that state. January 19,
1830. Read twice, and committed
to a Committee of the Whole
House to-morrow. Mr. Isacks,
from the Committee on the Public
Lands, reported the following bill:
[Washington, 1830] 3 p. (H. R.
131) DNA.   4459

---- A bill to authorize the
mounting and equipment of a part
of the Army of the United States.
March 5, 1830. Mr. Benton,
from the Committee on Military
Affairs, reported the following
bill: [Washington, 1830] 1 p.
(S. 119) DNA.   4460

---- A bill to authorize the payment of the claim of the state of

Massachusetts, for certain services of her militia during the
late war. January 5, 1830.
Read, and passed to a second
reading. January 6, 1830, Read
second time, and referred to the
Committee on Military Affairs.
March 8, 1830, Reported without
amendment. [Washington, 1830]
1 p. (S. 31) DNA.   4461

---- A bill to authorize the payment of the claim of the state of
Missouri for certain services of
her militia in the year one thousand eight hundred and twenty-
nine. May 7, 1830. Read twice,
and committed to the Committee
of the Whole House on the state
of the Union to which is referred
the bill (H. R. No. 415,) for the
payment of certain mounted volunteers of the Territory of Arkansas, while in the service of
the United States. Mr. Drayton,
from the Committee on Military
Affairs, reported the following
bill: [Washington, 1830] 2 p.
(H. R. 462) DNA.   4462

---- A bill to authorize the pre-
emption of one hundred and sixty
acres of land, for the town of
Helena, in the Territory of Michigan. February 22, 1830. Read
twice, and committed to the Committee of a Whole House to-morrow. Mr. Isacks, from the Committee on the Public Lands, reported the following bill: [Wash-
ington, 1830] 2 p. (H. R. 272)
DNA.   4463

---- A bill to authorize the
President of the United States to
cause the present site of the National Mint to be sold, and the
proceeds of the sale to be applied
to the extension of the establishment at its new location. March
5, 1830. Read twice, and committed to the Committee of the
Whole House on the state of the

Union. Mr. McDuffie, from the Committee of Ways and Means, reported the following bill: [Washington, 1830] 1 p. (H. R. 324) DNA.   4464

---- A bill to authorize the President of the United States to divide Indian Agencies in certain cases. January 11, 1830. Mr. White, from the Committee on Indian Affairs, reported the following bill; which was read, and passed to a second reading: [Washington, 1830] 1 p. (S. 50) DNA.   4465

---- A bill to authorize the President to appoint a Superintendent and Receiver at the Fever River lead mines, and for other purposes. January 27, 1830. Read twice, and committed to a Committee of the Whole House on the state of the Union. Mr. Duncan, from the Committee on the Public Lands, reported the following bill: [Washington, 1830] 3 p. (H. R. 166) DNA.   4466

---- A bill to authorize the reconveyance of a lot of land to the mayor and corporation of the city of New York. January 20, 1830. Read twice, and ordered to be engrossed, and read the third time to-morrow. Mr. Drayton, from the Committee on Military Affairs, reported the following bill: [Washington, 1830] 1 p. (H. R. 137) DNA.   4467

---- A bill to authorize the Register and Receiver of the St. Helena land district, in Louisiana, to receive evidence, and report upon certain claims to land mentioned therein. January 11, 1830. Read twice, and committed to a Committee of the Whole House to-morrow. Mr. Gurley, from the Committee on Private Land Claims, reported

the following bill: [Washington, 1830] 2 p. (H. R. 95) DNA.
                                  4468
---- A bill to authorize the Registers of the several Land Offices in Louisiana to enter lands in certain cases, and give to the purchasers thereof certificates for the same. February 18, 1830. Read twice, and committed to a Committee of the Whole House to-morrow. Mr. Test, from the Committee on Private Land Claims, to which the subject had been referred, reported the following bill: [Washington, 1830] 2 p. (H. R. 260) DNA.
                                  4469
---- A bill to authorize the Secretary of the Navy to make compensation to the heirs of Taliaferro Livingston and Francis W. Armstrong, for the maintenance of fifteen Africans illegally imported into the United States. April 12, 1830. Read twice, and referred to the Committee on Finance. April 22, 1830. Reported without amendment. Agreeably to notice given, Mr. King asked and obtained leave to bring in the following bill; which was read twice, by unanimous consent, and referred to the Committee on Finance: [Washington, 1830] 2 p. (S. 177) DNA.   4470

---- A bill to authorize the Secretary of War to purchase an additional quantity of land for the fortifications at Fort Washington, upon the river Potomac. February 4, 1830. Read twice, and committed to a Committee of the Whole House to-morrow. Mr. Drayton, from the Committee on Military Affairs, reported the following bill: [Washington, 1830] 2 p. (H. R. 192) DNA.
                                  4471
---- A bill to authorize the Secretary of War to purchase, sites and for the erection of a powder

magazine, arsenal, and other buildings, in the vicinity of Detroit, in the Territory of Michigan, and for other purposes. February 22, 1830. Mr. Barnard, from the Committee on Military Affairs, reported the following bill; which was read, and passed to a second reading: [Washington, 1830] 2 p. (S. 105) DNA. 4472

---- A bill to authorize the Secretary of War to sell the public land at Greenbush, in the state of New York, for the purposes therein mentioned. January 13, 1830. Mr. Marks, from the Committee on Agriculture, reported the following bill: which was read, and passed to a second reading: [Washington, 1830] 3 p. (S. 54) DNA. 4473

---- A bill to authorize the selection of certain school lands, in the Territory of Arkansas. February 22, 1830. Read twice, and committed to a Committee of the Whole House to-morrow. Mr. Isacks, from the Committee on the Public Lands, reported the following bill: [Washington, 1830] 2 p. (H. R. 270) DNA. 4474

---- A bill to authorize the state of Illinois to surrender a township of land granted to said state for a seminary of learning, and to locate other lands in lieu thereof. January 4, 1830. Mr. Kane, from the Committee on Public Lands, reported the following bill; which was read, and passed to a second reading: [Washington, 1830] 1 p. (S. 30) DNA. 4475

---- A bill to authorize the utate [sic] of Illinois to surrender a township of land granted to said State for a seminary of learning, and to locate other lands in lieu thereof. December 22, 1830. Read twice, and committed to the Committee of the Whole House to which is committed the bill (H. R. No. 93) to authorize the exchange of sixteenth sections granted for the use of common schools which are unfit for cultivation. Mr. Duncan, from the Committee on the Public Lands, reported the following bill: [Washington, 1830] 1 p. (H. R. 509) DNA. 4476

---- A bill to authorize the state of Indiana to make a road through the public lands, and making a grant of lands to aid the state in so doing. May 5, 1830. Mr. Hendricks, from the Committee on Roads and Canals, reported the following bill; which was read, and passed to a second reading: [Washington, 1830] 2 p. (S. 188) DNA. 4477

---- A bill to authorize the state of Indiana to sell her reserved salt springs. May 27, 1830. Read twice, and committed to the Committee of the Whole House to which is committed the bill (H. R. No. 131) to authorize the Legislature of the State of Missouri to sell the lands reserved for schools, a seminary of learning, and salt springs, in that State. Mr. Isacks, from the Committee on the Public Lands, reported the following bill: [Washington, 1830] 1 p. (H. R. 492) DNA. 4478

---- A bill to authorize the subscription of stock to the Delaware and Raritan Canal Company. April 16, 1830. Read twice, and committed to the Committee of the Whole House on the state of the Union. Mr. Hemphill, from the Committee on Internal Improvements, reported the following bill: [Washington, 1830]

1 p. (H. R. 428) DNA.   4479

---- A bill to authorize the subscription of stock to the Delaware and Raritan Canal Company.
April 24, 1830. Mr. Hendricks,
from the Committee on Roads
and Canals, reported the following bill; which was read, and
passed to a second reading:
[Washington, 1830] 2 p. (S. 183)
DNA.   4480

---- A bill to authorize the survey and opening of a road from
Mariana, in the territory of Florida, to Appalachicola bay, in the
aforesaid territory, and from
Quincy to the same place.
March 8, 1830. Printed by order
of the House of Representatives.
Mr. White of Florida, submitted
the following, which, when the
bill [H. R. No. 266] to provide for
certain surveys in Florida shall
be taken up for consideration, he
will move as an amendment of
the same. [Washington, 1830]
3 p. (H. R. 266) DNA.   4481

---- A bill to authorize the survey and opening of a road from
Washington, in the territory of
Arkansas, to Jackson, in the
aforesaid territory. March 3,
1830. Read twice, and committed to the Committee of the
Whole House on the state of the
Union. Mr. Letcher, from the
Committee on Internal Improvements, reported the following
bill: [Washington, 1830] 3 p.
(H. R. 321) DNA.   4482

---- A bill to authorize the surveying and making of a road
from La Plaisance Bay, in the
territory of Michigan, to inter-
sect the Chicago road. March 5,
1830. Read twice, and committed to a Committee of the Whole
House to-morrow. Mr. Letcher,
from the Committee on Internal

Improvements, reported the following bill: [Washington, 1830]
2 p. (H. R. 325) DNA.   4483

---- A bill to cause the Northern boundary line of the state of
Missouri to be better marked
and established, and to divide
certain land adjoining said boundary among the half breed Indians
of the Sac and Fox tribes. January 5, 1830. Mr. Benton, from
the Committee on Indian Affairs,
reported the following bill; which
was read, and passed to a second reading: [Washington, 1830]
2 p. (S. 34) DNA.   4484

---- A bill to change the port of
entry from New Iberia to Franklin, in the State of Louisiana.
February 5, 1830. Mr. Woodbury, from the Committee on
Commerce, reported the following bill; which was read, and
passed to a second reading:
[Washington, 1830] 1 p. (S. 81)
DNA.   4485

---- A bill to change the time
and place of holding the court for
the county of Crawford, in the
territory of Michigan. March 9,
1830. Read twice, and ordered
to be engrossed, and read a
third time to-morrow. Mr.
Clarke, from the Committee on
the Judiciary, reported the following bill: [Washington, 1830]
1 p. (H. R. 332) DNA.   4486

---- A bill to change the time
of holding the court of the United
States for the District of Mississippi. April 7, 1830. Read
twice, and referred to the Committee on the Judiciary. April 8,
1830. Reported no amendment.
[Washington, 1830] 2 p. (S. 172)
DNA.   4487

---- A bill to change the time
of holding the rule term of the

circuit court for the district of West Tennessee. December 17, 1830. Read twice, and ordered that it be engrossed, and read the third time on Monday next. Mr. Buchanan, from the Committee on the Judiciary, to which the subject had been referred, reported the following bill: [Washington, 1830] 2 p. (H. R. 502) DNA.   4488

---- A bill to compensate David Kilbourn, for services rendered by him to the United States during the late war. February 12, 1830. Read twice, and committed to a Committee of the Whole House to-morrow. Mr. Drayton, from the Committee on Military Affairs, reported the following bill: [Washington, 1830] 1 p. (H. R. 238) DNA.   4489

---- A bill to compensate Susan Decatur, widow and legal representative of Captain Stephen Decatur, deceased, and others. January 7, 1830. Read twice, and committed to a Committee of the Whole House to-morrow. Mr. Hoffman, from the Committee on Naval Affairs, reported the following bill: [Washington, 1830] 3 p. (H. R. 82) DNA.   4490

---- A bill to confirm certain claims to lands in the District of Jackson Court House, in the state of Mississippi. March 10, 1830. Mr. Ellis, from the Committee on Public Lands, reported the following bill; which was read twice, and laid on the table: [Washington, 1830] 4 p. (S. 126) DNA.   4491

---- A bill to confirm the claim of Isidore Moore, of Missouri. January 5, 1830. Mr. Barton, from the Committee on Private Land Claims, reported the following bill; which was read, and

passed to a second reading. [Washington, 1830] 2 p. (S. 35) DNA.   4492

---- A bill to construct a national road from Buffalo, in the state of New York, passing by the seat of the general government, in the District of Columbia, to New Orleans, in the state of Louisiana. January 7, 1830. Read twice, and committed to a Committee of the Whole House on the state of the Union. Mr. Hemphill, from the Committee on Internal Improvements, reported the following bill: [Washington, 1830] 5 p. (H. R. 86) DNA.   4493

---- A bill to construct a national road from Zanesville, in Ohio, to Florence, in Alabama. March 18, 1830. Read twice, and committed to the Committee of the Whole House on the state of the Union. Mr. Letcher, from the Committee on Internal Improvements, reported the following bill: [Washington, 1830] 5 p. (H. R. 366) DNA.   4494

---- A bill to continue in force "An act authorizing certain soldiers in the late war to surrender the bounty lands drawn by them, and to locate others in lieu thereof, and for other purposes." January 11, 1830. Read, and laid upon the table. January 14, 1830. Ordered to be engrossed, and read a third time to-morrow. Mr. Clay, from the Committee on the Public Lands, reported the following bill: [Washington, 1830] 1 p. (H. R 99) DNA.   4495

---- A bill to continue in force an act authorizing the importation and allowance of drawback on brandy in casks of a capacity not less than fifteen gallons. January 7, 1830. Mr. Smith, from the Committee on Finance, reported the following bill; which was read, and passed to a second reading: [Washington, 1830] 1 p. (S. 43) DNA.   4496

---- A bill to enable claimants to lands lying in the state of Missouri to prosecute to final judgment certain suits now depending in the district court for the district of Missouri. May 8, 1830. Read twice, and postpoined until Monday next. Mr. Test, from the Committee on Private Land Claims, reported the following bill: [Washington, 1830] 2 p. (H. R. 463) DNA.
4497
---- A bill to enable the President to extinguish Indian title within the state of Indiana. January 7, 1830. Mr. White, from the Committee on Indian Affairs, reported the following bill; which was read, and passed to a second reading: [Washington, 1830] 1 p. (S. 48) DNA.   4498

---- A bill to encourage ship building in the United States. May 20, 1830. Read twice, and committed to the Committee of the Whole House on the state of the Union. Mr. Cambreleng, from the Committee on Commerce reported the following bill: [Washington, 1830] 4 p. (H. R. 476) DNA.   4499

---- A bill to establish a land district in Illinois. February 16, 1830. Mr. Kane, from the Committee on Public Lands, reported the following bill; which was read, and passed to a second reading: [Washington, 1830] 2 p. (S. 94) DNA.   4500

---- A bill to establish a Land Office at Pensacola, in West Florida. January 18, 1830. Read twice, and committed to the Committee of the Whole House to

which is committed the bill to establish a Land Office at the Town of Belle Fonte, Jackson county, State of Alabama. Mr. Clay, from the Committee on the Public Lands, reported the following bill: [Washington, 1830] 1 p. (H. R. 121) DNA.   4501

---- A bill to establish a Land Office in the territory of Michigan, and for other purposes. February 8, 1830. Read twice, and committed to the Committee of the Whole House to which is committed the bill (No. 28) to establish a Land Office at the town of Bellefonte, in Jackson county, State of Alabama. Mr. Isacks, from the Committee on the Public Lands, reported the following bill: [Washington, 1830] 3 p. (H. R. 210) DNA.
4502
---- A bill to establish a port of delivery at Delaware City. March 19, 1830. Mr. Woodbury, from the Committee on Commerce, reported the following bill; which was read, and passed to a second reading: [Washington, 1830] 1 p. (S. 139) DNA.   4503

---- A bill to establish a port of delivery on Lake Pontchartrain. April 28, 1830. Read twice, and referred to the Committee on Commerce. May 3, 1830. Reported without amendment. Agreeably to notice given, Mr. Livingston asked and obtained leave to bring in the following bill: [Washington, 1830] 2 p. (S. 186) DNA.   4504

---- A bill to establish a town at St. Marks, and at the mouth of Appalachicola river, in Florida. March 31, 1830. Mr. Kane, from the Committee on Public Lands, reported the following bill; which was read, and passed to a second reading: [Washing-

ton, 1830] 2 p. (S. 161) DNA.
4505

---- A bill to establish a town
at St. Marks, and at the mouth
of Appalachicola river, in Florida.   March 31, 1830. Mr. Kane,
from the Committee on Public
Lands, reported the following
bill; which was read, and passed
to a second reading: [Washing-
ton, 1830] 3 p. (S. 161) DNA.
4506

---- A bill to establish an addi-
tional Land Office in the state of
Indiana.   February 8, 1830. Mr.
Barton, from the Committee on
Public Lands, reported the fol-
lowing bill; which was read, and
passed to a second reading:
[Washington, 1830] 2 p. (S. 83)
DNA.   4507

---- A bill to establish an additional Land Office in the state
of Indiana.   February 15, 1830.
Read twice, and committed to
the Committee of the Whole
House to which is committed the
bill (No. 28) to establish a Land
Office at the town of Bellefonte,
in Jackson county, State of Alabama.   Mr. Jennings, from the
Committee on the Public Lands,
reported the following bill:
[Washington, 1830] 2 p. (H. R.
254) DNA.   4508

---- A bill to establish certain
Post Offices, and to alter and
discontinue others, and for other
purposes.   April 14, 1830. Read
twice, and committed to the
Committee of the Whole House on
the state of the Union.   Mr.
Johnson, from the Committee on
the Post Office and Post Roads,
reported the following bill:
[Washington, 1830] 28 p. (H. R.
420) DNA.   4509

---- A bill to establish the office of Surgeon General of the
Navy.   February 16, 1830. Mr.

Hayne, from the Committee on
Naval Affairs, reported the fol-
lowing bill; which was read,
and passed to a second reading:
[Washington, 1830] 2 p. (S. 95)
DNA.   4510

---- A bill to exempt alum salt
from the payment of duty, and
to abolish the fishing bounties
and allowances.   March 8, 1830.
Agreeably to notice given, Mr.
Benton, asked and obtained leave
to bring in the following bill;
which was read, passed to a
second reading, and ordered to
be printed. [Washington, 1830]
1 p. (S. 123) DNA.   4511

---- A bill to exempt deserters,
in time of peace, from the punishment of death.   May 25, 1830.
Read twice, and ordered to be
engrossed, and read the third
time this day.   Mr. Drayton,
from the Committee on Military
Affairs, reported the following
bill: [Washington, 1830] 1 p.
(H. R. 487) DNA.   4512

---- A bill to exempt merchandise imported under certain circumstances, from the operation
of the act of the nineteenth of
May, one thousand eight hundred
and twenty-eight, entitled "An
act in alteration of the several
acts imposing duties on imports."
March 22, 1830. Mr. Smith, of
Maryland, from the Committee
on Finance, reported the following bill; which was read, and
passed to a second reading:
[Washington, 1830] 2 p. (S. 145)
DNA.   4513

---- A bill to extend the time
for commencing the improvement
of the navigation of the Tennessee river.   February 17, 1830,
Read twice, and referred to the
Committee on the Public Lands.
February 22, 1830. Reported

without amendment. [Washington, 1830] 1 p. (S. 97) DNA.
                                    4514

---- A bill to fix the salaries of the Judges of the territory of Michigan. March 17, 1830. Read twice, and committed to the Committee of the Whole House to which is committed the bill (H. R. 294) to fix the salary of the Governor and Judges of the Territory of Arkansas. Mr. Angel, from the Committee on the Territories, reported the following bill: [Washington, 1830] 1 p. (H. R. 359) DNA.   4515

---- A bill to fix the salary of the Governor and Judges of the territory of Arkansas. February 26, 1830. Read twice, and committed to a Committee of the Whole House to-morrow. Mr. Clarke, from the Committee on the Territories, reported the following bill: [Washington, 1830] 1 p. (H. R. 294) DNA.
                                    4516

---- A bill to graduate the price of Public Lands. January 11, 1830. Read twice, and committed to a Committee of the Whole House on the state of the Union. Mr. Duncan, from the Committee on the Public Lands, reported the following bill: [Washington, 1830] 4 p. (H. R. 96) DNA.
                                    4517

---- A bill to grant to the state of Alabama certain lands for the purpose of improving the navigation of the Coosa river, and to connect its waters with those of the Tennessee river by a canal. February 12, 1830. Mr. McKinley, from the Committee on Public Lands, reported the following bill; which was read, and passed to a second reading: [Washington, 1830] 3 p. (S. 92) DNA.   4518

---- A bill to grant to the state

of Ohio a quantity of land to aid in the making and repair of certain roads therein named. May 18, 1830. Read twice, and committed to the Committee of the Whole House on the state of the Union. Mr. Vinton, from the Committee on Internal Improvements, reported the following bill: [Washington, 1830] 2 p. (H. R. 472) DNA.   4519

---- A bill to grant to the state of Ohio certain lands for the support of schools in the Connecticut Western Reserve. February 13, 1830. Read twice, and committed to the Committee of the Whole House to which is committed the "bill (H. R. No. 93) to authorize the exchange of the sixteenth sections, granted for the use of common schools, which are unfit for cultivation." Mr. Irvin, from the Committee on the Public Lands, to which the subject had been referred, reported the following bill: [Washington, 1830] 2 p. (H. R. 244) DNA.   4520

---- A bill to improve Back Creek. February 25, 1830. Read twice, and committed to a Committee of the Whole House to-morrow. Mr. Hemphill, from the Committee on Internal Improvements, reported the following bill: [Washington, 1830] 1 p. (H. R. 293) DNA.   4521

---- A bill to improve the condition of the Army of the United States, and to prevent desertion. January 26, 1830. Read twice, and committed to a Committee of the Whole House to-morrow. Mr. Drayton from the Committee on Military Affairs, reported the following bill: [Washington, 1830] 3 p. (H. R. 152) DNA.   4522

---- A bill to improve the navigation of the Monongahela and Alle-

ghany rivers. April 14, 1830. Mr. Hendricks, from the Committee on Roads and Canals, reported the following bill; which was read, and passed to a second reading: [Washington, 1830] 1 p. (S. 179) DNA.
4523

---- A bill to incorporate an Insurance Company in Georgetown, in the District of Columbia. Reported by the Committee for the District of Columbia. March 9, 1830. Read twice, and committed to a Committee of the Whole House to-morrow. Mr. Washington, from the Committee for the District of Columbia, reported the following bill: [Washington, 1830] 7 p. (H. R. 334) DNA.
4524

---- A bill to incorporate the Alexandria Canal Company. January 29, 1830. Read twice, and committed to a Committee of the Whole House to-morrow. Mr. Hemphill, from the Committee on Internal Improvements, reported the following bill: [Washington, 1830] 19 p. (H. R. 184) DNA.
4525

---- A bill to increase the pay and the number of surgeons and assistant surgeons, in the Army of the United States. January 6, 1830. Read twice, and committed to a Committee of the Whole House to-morrow. Mr. Drayton, from the Committee on Military Affairs, reported the following bill: [Washington, 1830] 1 p. (H. R. 78) DNA.
4526

---- A bill to increase the pay of the Master Armorers in the service of the United States. January 4, 1830. Read twice, and committed to a Committee of the Whole House to-morrow. Mr. Drayton, from the Committee on Military Affairs, reported the following bill: [Washington, 1830] 1 p. (H. R. 62) DNA.
4527

---- A bill to increase the pension of Carey Clark. April 8, 1830. Mr. Marks, from the Committee on Pensions, reported the following bill; which was read, and passed to a second reading: [Washington, 1830] 1 p. (S. 173) DNA.
4528

---- A bill to increase the pension of Charles Larrabee. January 5, 1830. Mr. Holmes, from the Committee on Pensions, reported the following bill; which was read, and passed to a second reading: [Washington, 1830] 1 p. (S. 32) DNA.
4529

---- A bill to modify the duties on certain imported articles, and to repeal the duties on others. January 25, 1830. Mr. Smith, of Maryland, from the Committee on Finance, reported the following bill; which was read, and passed to a second reading: [Washington, 1830] 7 p. (S. 72) DNA.
4530

---- A bill to organize the several fire companies in the District of Columbia. February 17, 1830. Read the first time, and ordered to a second reading on Monday next. Mr. Varnum, from the Committee for the District of Columbia, reported the following bill: [Washington, 1830] 5 p. (H. R. 257) DNA.
4531

---- A bill to organize the several fire companies in the District of Columbia. December 21, 1830. Read twice, and committed to a Committee of the Whole House to-morrow. Mr. Doddridge, from the Committee for the District of Columbia, reported the following bill: [Washington, 1830] 5 p. (H. R. 503) DNA.
4532

---- A bill to place Charles Yeater on the Privateer Pension

list. February 9, 1830. Mr.
Woodbury, from the Committee
on Naval Affairs, reported the
following bill; which was read,
and passed to a second reading:
[Washington, 1830] 1 p. (S. 86)
DNA.   4533

---- A bill to prevent improper
allowances to the officers and
agents of the government, in the
settlement of their accounts. January 14, 1830. Read twice, and
committed to a Committee of the
Whole House to-morrow. Mr.
Wickliffe, from the Committee
on Retrenchment, reported the
following bill: [Washington, 1830]
1 p. (H. R. 113) DNA.   4534

---- A bill to prevent military
and naval officers from being dis-
missed the service at the pleasure of the President. March 23,
1830. Mr. Benton, from the select committee to whom the subject was referred, on the 16th
instant, reported the following
bill; which was read, and passed
to a second reading: [Washing-
ton, 1830] 1 p. (S. 151) DNA.
                              4535
---- A bill to prevent sutlers
from selling ardent or spirituous
liquors, and for other purposes.
February 8, 1830. Read twice,
and committed to a Committee of
the Whole House to-morrow. Mr.
Drayton, from the Committee on
Military Affairs, reported the following bill: [Washington, 1830]
1 p. (H. R. 211) DNA.   4536

---- A bill to prohibit the use of
secret service money in time of
peace, and for other purposes.
January 22, 1830. Read twice,
and committed to the Committee
of the Whole House on the state
of the Union. Mr. Wickliffe,
from the Committee on Retrenchment, reported the following bill:
[Washington, 1830] 2 p. (H. R.

148) DNA.   4537

---- A bill to protect the surveyors of the public lands of the
United States and to punish persons guilty of interrupting and
hindering, by force, surveyors
in the discharge of their duty.
May 17, 1830. Read twice, and
postponed until Wednesday next.
Mr. Wickliffe, from the Committee on the Judiciary, to which
the subject had been referred,
reported the following bill:
[Washington, 1830] 2 p. (H. R.
470) DNA.   4538

---- A bill to provide a more
suitable location for the Naval
Monument at the Navy Yard in
Washington. March 5, 1830.
Read twice, and committed to a
Committee of the Whole House
to-morrow. Mr. Miller, from
the Committee on Naval Affairs,
reported the following bill:
[Washington, 1830] 1 p. (H. R.
326) DNA.   4539

---- A bill to provide a system
of criminal law for the United
States. May 31, 1830. Agreeably to notice given, Mr. Livingston asked and obtained leave to
bring in the following bill; which
was read, and passed to a second reading: [Washington, 1830]
1 p. (S. 194) DNA.   4540

---- A bill to provide for an exchange of lands with the Indians
residing in any of the states or
territories, and for their removal West of the river Mississippi.
February 22, 1830. Mr. White,
from the Committee on Indian Affairs, reported the following bill;
which was read, and passed to a
second reading: [Washington,
1830] 3 p. (S. 102) DNA. 4541

---- A bill to provide for certain
surveys in Florida. February

19, 1830. Read twice, and committed to a Committee of the Whole House to-morrow. Mr. Hemphill, from the Committee on Internal Improvements, reported the following bill: [Washington, 1830] 2 p. (H. R. 266) DNA.
                                    4542

---- A bill to provide for completing the Navy Hospital at Norfolk and the Navy Asylum at Philadelphia, and to furnish them in part. January 28, 1830. Read twice, and committed to the Committee of the Whole House on the state of the Union. Mr. Hoffman, from the Committee on Naval Affairs, reported the following bill: [Washington, 1830] 1 p. (H. R. 170) DNA.   4543

---- A bill to provide for opening a road in Arkansas Territory, from Villemont, in the county of Chicot, to Little Rock. February 22, 1830. Read twice, and committed to the Committee of the Whole House to which is committed the bill (No. 111) making an appropriation to complete the road heading from Fooys, opposite Memphis, in Tennessee, to Little Rock, in Arkansas. Mr. Johnson, from the Committee on the Post Office and Post Roads, reported the following bill: [Washington, 1830] 3 p. (H. R. 273) DNA.   4544

---- A bill to provide for surveying certain lands in the territory of Arkansas. February 22, 1830. Read twice, and committed to a Committee of the Whole House to-morrow. Mr. Isacks, from the Committee on the Public Lands, reported the following bill: [Washington, 1830] 1 p. (H. R. 271) DNA.   4545

---- A bill to provide for taking the fifth census or enumeration of the inhabitants of the United States. January 15, 1830. Read twice, and committed to the Committee of the Whole House on the State of the Union. Mr. Storrs, from the Committee on the Judiciary, reported the following bill: [Washington, 1830] [17 p.] (H. R. 116) DNA.   4546

---- A bill to provide for taking the fifth census or enumeration of the inhabitants of the United States. January 15, 1830. Read twice, and committed to the Committee of the Whole House. February 3, 1830. Considered in Committee of the Whole, and progress made. February 4, 1830. Reported from Committee of the Whole with amendments. Further consideration postponed until Monday, the eighth of February, instant, and ordered to be printed. [Washington, 1830] 15 p. (H. R. 116) DNA.   4547

---- A bill to provide for the abolition of unnecessary duties, to relieve the people from sixteen millions of taxes, and to improve the condition of the agriculture, manufactures, commerce, and navigation, of the United States. March 8, 1830. Agreeably to notice given, Mr. Benton asked and obtained leave to bring in the following bill; which was read, passed to a second reading, and ordered to be printed. [Washington, 1830] 3 p. (S. 125) DNA.
                                    4548

---- A bill to provide for the adjustment of claims of persons entitled to indemnification under the convention between the United States and his Majesty the King of Denmark, of the twenty-eighth March, eighteen hundred and thirty, and for the distribution among such claimants of the sums to be paid by the Danish Government to that of the United States according to the stipulation of the said

convention. December 30, 1830.
Read twice, and committed to the
Committee of the Whole House on
the state of the Union. Mr.
Archer, from the Committee on
Foreign Affairs, reported the fol-
lowing bill: [Washington, 1830]
4 p. (H. R. 523) DNA.   4549

---- A bill to provide for the appointment of a Solicitor of the
Treasury. May 3, 1830. Agreeably to notice given, Mr. Webster asked and obtained leave to
bring in the following bill; which
was read, and passed to a second reading: [Washington, 1830]
5 p. (S. 187) DNA.   4550

---- A bill to provide for the appointment of Commissioners to
digest, prepare, and report to
Congress at the next session
thereof, a code of statute law,
civil and criminal, for the District of Columbia. March 19,
1830. Read twice, and committed to the Committee of the Whole
House on the state of the Union.
Mr. Powers, from the Committee
for the District of Columbia, reported the following bill: [Wash-
ington, 1830] 2 p. (H. R. 372)
DNA.   4551

---- A bill to provide for the distribution of a part of the revenues
of the United States among the
several States. May 6, 1830.
Mr. Dickerson, from the Select
Committee appointed on so much
of the President's message at the
commencement of the session as
relates to the disposition of the
surplus funds of the United States,
after the payment of the public
debt, reported the following bill;
which was read, and passed to a
second reading: [Washington,
1830] 1 p. (S. 190) DNA.
                            4552
---- A bill to provide for the
distribution of the duties of the

Commissioners of the Navy, and
for other purposes. March 23,
1830. Mr. Hayne, from the Committee on Naval Affairs, reported
the following bill; which was read,
and passed to a second reading:
[Washington, 1830] 4 p. (S. 152)
DNA.   4553

---- A bill to provide for the
final settlement of land claims in
Florida. February 5, 1830.
Read twice, and committed to a
Committee of the Whole House
to-morrow. Mr. Isacks, from
the Committee on the Public
Lands, reported the following
bill: [Washington, 1830] 4 p.
(H. R. 206) DNA.   4554

---- A bill to provide for the
further compensation of the Marshal of the District of Rhode Island. December 21, 1829.
Agreeably to notice given, Mr.
Knight asked and obtained leave
to bring in the following bill,
which was read, and passed to a
second reading. December 22. --
Read second time, and referred
to Committee on the Judiciary.
January 11, 1830. --Reported without amendment. [Washington,
1830] 1 p. (S. 12) DNA. 4555

---- A bill to provide for the improvement of the navigation of
Coosa river, in the state of Alabama, and to connect the waters
of said river Coosa with the
waters of the Tennessee river.
December 23, 1830. Read twice,
and committed to the Committee
of the Whole House on the state
of the Union. Mr. Blair, from
the Committee on Internal Improvement, reported the following
bill: [Washington, 1830] 3 p.
(H. R. 511) DNA.   4556

---- A bill to provide for the
legal adjudication and settlement
of the claims to land therein

mentioned. December 23, 1829.
Introduced by Mr. Johnston, of
Louisiana, on leave, and read.
December 24. --Read 2d time,
and referred to the Committee on
the Judiciary. January 5, 1830.
--Reported with an amendment,
viz: at the end of the 3d Section,
insert the words there printed in
italics. [Washington, 1830] 4 p.
(S. 21) DNA. 4557

---- A bill to provide for the
more effectual execution of the
ministerial duties of the Navy Department. January 28, 1830.
Read twice, and committed to the
Committee of the Whole House on
the state of the Union. Mr. Hoffman, from the Committee on Naval Affairs, reported the following
bill: [Washington, 1830] 3 p.
(H. R. 169) DNA. 4558

---- A bill to provide for the
payment of Joshua Kennedy, of
Alabama, for the losses sustained by him by the destruction
of his property, in the year one
thousand eight hundred and thirteen, by the hostile Creek Indians, in consequence of its having been occupied as a fort or
garrison, by the troops of the
United States. March 29, 1830.
Mr. White from the Committee
on Indian Affairs, reported the
following bill; which was read,
and passed to a second reading:
[Washington, 1830] 1 p. (S. 156)
DNA. 4559

---- A bill to provide for the
purchase of eighty copies of
Peters' condensed Reports of
cases in the Supreme Court of
the United States. February 12,
1830. Read twice, and committed to a Committee of the Whole
House to-morrow. Mr. Buchanan,
from the Committee on the Judiciary, reported the following bill:
[Washington, 1830] 2 p. (H. R.

237) DNA. 4560

---- A bill to provide for the re-
funding of money to purchasers
of public land, paid through error
of the officers of Land Offices.
April 30, 1830. Read twice, and
committed to a Committee of the
Whole House to-morrow. Mr.
Hunt, from the Committee on the
Public Lands, reported the following bill: [Washington, 1830] 2
p. (H. R. 448) DNA. 4561

---- A bill to provide for the
removal of the Indian tribes
within any of the states and territories, and for their permanent
settlement west of the river Mississippi. February 24, 1830.
Read twice, and committed to the
Committee of the Whole House
on the state of the Union. Mr.
Bell, from the Committee on Indian Affairs, to which was referred so much of the President's
message as relates to Indian affairs, and several memorials,
&c. upon the subject, reported
the following bill: [Washington,
1830] 4 p. (H. R. 287) DNA.
4562

---- A bill to provide for the
satisfaction of claims due to certain American citizens, for spoliations committed on their commerce, prior to the year eighteen hundred. February 22, 1830.
Mr. Livingston, from the Select
Committee appointed on the 22d
December last, reported the following bill; which was read, and
passed to a second reading:
[Washington, 1830] 4 p. (S. 103)
DNA. 4563

---- A bill to provide for the
survey and sale of certain lands
in the territory of Michigan.
May 24, 1830. Read twice, and
committed to the Committe of
the Whole House on the state of
the Union. Mr. Isacks, from

the Committee on the Public
Lands, reported the following
bill: [Washington, 1830] 2 p.
(H. R. 486) DNA.   4564

---- A bill to provide hereafter
for the payment of six thousand
dollars annually to the Seneca
Indians, and for other purposes.
May 22, 1830. Read twice, and
committed to the Committee of
the Whole House on the state of
the Union. Mr. Hubbard, from
the Committee on Indian Affairs,
reported the following bill:
[Washington, 1830] 2 p. (H. R.
481) DNA.   4565

---- A bill to provide more effectually for the national defence,
by organizing, arming, and establishing, a uniform Militia
throughout the United States, and
to provide for the discipline
thereof. January 27, 1830. Read
twice, and committed to the Committee of the Whole House on the
state of the Union. Mr. Thompson, of Georgia, from the Committee on the Militia, reported
the following bill: [Washington,
1830] 20 p. (H. R. 168) DNA.
                                     4566
---- A bill to quiet the titles of
certain purchasers of lands between the lines of Ludlow and Roberts, in the state of Ohio. January 20, 1830. Read twice, and
committed to a Committee of the
Whole House to-morrow. Mr.
Gurley, from the Committee on
Private Land Claims, to which the
subject had been referred, reported the following bill: [Washington,
1830] 2 p. (H. R. 141) DNA.
                                     4567
---- A bill to recompense the
heirs of Robert Fulton, deceased.
January 20, 1830. Mr. Barton,
from the Committee on Public
Lands, reported the following bill;
which was read, and passed to a
second reading: [Washington,

1830] 2 p. (S. 69) DNA.   4568

---- A bill to reduce and modify
the duties upon certain imported
articles, and to allow a drawback
on spirits distilled from foreign
molasses. February 5, 1830.
Read the first time, and second
reading objected to. Mr. McDuffie, from the Committee of Ways
and Means, reported the following bill: [Washington, 1830] 3 p.
(H. R. 208) DNA.   4569

---- A bill to reduce the duties
on coffee and tea. February 3,
1830. Read twice, and committed to the Committee of the Whole
House on the state of the Union.
Mr. McDuffie, from the Committee of Ways and Means, reported
the following bill: [Washington,
1830] 2 p. (H. R. 207) DNA.
                                     4570
---- A bill to reduce the duty on
molasses, and to allow a drawback on spirits distilled from foreign materials. May 21, 1830.
Read twice, and ordered to be
engrossed, and read the third
time to-morrow. Mr. McDuffie,
from the Committee of Ways and
Means, reported the following
bill: [Washington, 1830] 1 p.
(H. R. 479) DNA.   4571

---- A bill to reduce the duty on
salt. May 19, 1830. Read the
first time. May 20, 1830. Read
the second time; and ordered to
be engrossed, and read the third
time to-morrow. Mr. McDuffie,
from the Committee of Ways and
Means, reported the following
bill: [Washington, 1830] 1 p.
(H. R. 474) DNA.   4572

---- A bill to refund the moiety
of the forfeiture upon the schooner
Volant. January 5, 1830. Read
twice, and committed to a Committee of the Whole House to-
morrow. Mr. Verplanck, from

the Committee of Ways and Means, to which the subject had been referred, reported the following bill: [Washington, 1830] 1 p. (H. R. 73) DNA. 4573

---- A bill to regulate and fix the compensation of the clerks in the Department of State. January 20, 1830. Read twice, and committed to the Committee of the Whole House on the state of the Union. Mr. McDuffie, from the Committee of Ways and Means, reported the following bill: [Washington, 1830] 2 p. (H. R. 143) DNA. 4574

---- A bill to regulate the appointment of Cadets. March 23, 1830. Mr. Benton, from the select committee to whom the subject was referred, on the 16th instant, reported the following bill; which was read, and passed to a second reading: [Washington, 1830] 1 p. (S. 149) DNA. 4575

---- A bill to regulate the appointment of Midshipmen. March 23, 1830. Mr. Benton, from the select committee to whom the subject was referred, on the 16th instant, reported the following bill; which was read, and passed to a second reading: [Washington, 1830] 1 p. (S. 150) DNA. 4576

---- A bill to regulate the appointment of Postmasters. March 23, 1830. Mr. Benton, from the select committee to whom the subject was referred, on the sixteenth instant, reported the following bill; which was read, and passed to a second reading: [Washington, 1830] 1 p. (S. 148) DNA. 4577

---- A bill to regulate the foreign and coasting trade on the Northern and Northwestern frontiers of the United States, and for other purposes. March 19, 1830. Read twice, and committed to the Committee of the Whole House on the state of the Union. Mr. Cambreleng, from the Committee on Commerce, reported the following bill: [Washington, 1830] 3 p. (H. R. 376) DNA. 4578

---- A bill to regulate the future importation of raw hides and furs. March 8, 1830. Agreeably to notice given, Mr. Benton asked and obtained leave to bring in the following bill; which was read, ordered to lie on the table, and to be printed. [Washington, 1830] 2 p. (S. 124) DNA. 4579

---- A bill to regulate the pay and emoluments of the officers of the Army of the United States, and for other purposes. January 19, 1830. Read twice, and committed to a Committee of the Whole House to-morrow. December 16, 1830. Reprinted by order of the House of Representatives. Mr. Drayton, from the Committee on Military Affairs, reported the following bill: [Washington, 1830] 3 p. (H. R. 130) DNA. 4580

---- A bill to regulate the pay of the officers of the Army and Navy in certain cases. March 12, 1830. Read twice, and committed to the Committee of the Whole House on the state of the Union. Mr. Wickliffe, from the Committee on Retrenchment, reported the following bill: [Washington, 1830] 2 p. (H. R. 346) DNA. 4581

---- A bill to regulate the publication of the Laws of the United States, and of public advertisements. March 23, 1830. Mr. Benton, from the select committee to whom the subject was referred, on the 16th instant, re-

ported the following bill; which
was read, and passed to a second
reading: [Washington, 1830] 3 p.
(S. 146) DNA.   4582

---- A bill to reimburse Lieutenant Daniel Tyler for money advanced by him for the government of the United States. January 20, 1830. Read twice, and
committed to a Committee of the
Whole House to-morrow. Mr.
Drayton, from the Committee on
Military Affairs, reported the
following bill: [Washington, 1830]
1 p. (H. R. 136) DNA.   4583

---- A bill to relinquish the reversionary interest of the United
States in certain Indian reservations in the state of Alabama.
January 11, 1830. Read twice,
and committed to a Committee of
the Whole House to-morrow. Mr.
Clay, from the Committee on the
Public Lands, to which the subject had been referred, reported
the following bill: [Washington,
1830] 2 p. (H. R. 97) DNA.
                                4584
---- A bill to remit a part of the
duties on a cargo imported in
the brig Liberator. May 7, 1830.
Read twice, and committed to a
Committee of the Whole House
to-morrow. Mr. Verplanck,
from the Committee of Ways and
Means, reported the following
bill: [Washington, 1830] 1 p.
(H. R. 461) DNA.   4585

---- A bill to remit the duties
imposed upon certain articles
imported for the use of the Theological Seminary and Kenyon College, in Ohio. February 26,
1830. Read twice, and committed to a Committee of the Whole
House to-morrow. Mr. McDuffie,
from the Committee of Ways and
Means, reported the following
bill: [Washington, 1830] 1 p.
(H. R. 300) DNA.   4586

---- A bill to remit to George
and William Bangs the amount of
duties on certain goods destroyed
by fire. January 4, 1830. Read
twice, and committed to a Committee of the Whole House to-
morrow. Mr. Dwight, from the
Committee of Ways and Means,
reported the following bill:
[Washington, 1830] 1 p. (H. R.
66) DNA.   4587

---- A bill to remove the Land
Office from St. Stephen's to Mobile, in Alabama. March 19,
1830. Read twice, and committed to the Committee of the
Whole House to which is committed the bill (No. 290) to remove the Land Office from Sparta to Monticello, in Alabama.
Mr. Clay, from the Committee
on the Public Lands, reported
the following bill: [Washington,
1830] 1 p. (H. R. 368) DNA.
                                4588
---- A bill to remove the Land
Office from Sparta to Monticello,
in Alabama. February 25, 1830.
Read twice, and committed to a
Committee of the Whole House
to-morrow. Mr. Clay, from the
Committee on the Public Lands,
reported the following bill:
[Washington, 1830] 1 p. (H. R.
290) DNA.   4589

---- A bill to reorganize the establishment of the Attorney General, and erect it into an executive department. February 9,
1830. Mr. Rowan, from the
Committee on the Judiciary, reported the following bill; which
was read, and passed to a second reading: [Washington, 1830]
6 p. (S. 87) DNA.   4590

---- A bill to re-organize the
Navy of the United States. March
5, 1830. Mr. Hayne, from the
Committee on Naval Affairs, reported the following bill; which

was read, and passed to a second reading: [Washington, 1830] 5 p. (S. 120) DNA.   4591

---- A bill to repeal a part of an act, passed the twenty-sixth day of March, one thousand eight hundred and four, entitled "An act making provisions for the disposal of the public lands in the Indiana Territory, and for other purposes." February 11, 1830. Read twice, and committed to a Committee of the Whole House on the fourth day of March next. Mr. Lamar, from the Committee on Retrenchment, reported the following bill: [Washington, 1830] 1 p. (H.R. 234) DNA.   4592

---- A bill to repeal the proviso in the act for the relief of Philip Slaughter, passed the twenty-sixth May, one thousand eight hundred and twenty-eight. February 25, 1830. Read twice, and committed to a Committee of the Whole House to-morrow. Mr. Goodenow, from the Committee on Revolutionary Claims, reported the following bill: [Washington, 1830] 1 p. (H.R. 301) DNA.   4593

---- A bill to repeal the proviso in "An act to authorize masters of vessels in certain cases to clear out either at the Custom House of Petersburg, or that of Richmond." March 19, 1830. Mr. Woodbury, from the Committee on Commerce, reported the following bill; which was read, and passed to a second reading: [Washington, 1830] 1 p. (S. 140) DNA.   4594

---- A bill to repeal the tonnage duties upon ships and vessels of the United States, and upon certain foreign vessels. December 15. Read, and passed to a second reading. December 16. Read a second time, and referred to the Committee on Finance. January 28, 1830. Reported without amendment. [Washington, 1830] 2 p. (S. 2) DNA.   4595

---- A bill to revive and continue in force, for a limited time, the act, entitled "An act authorizing the payment of certain certificates." January 12, 1830. Read twice, and committed to a Committee of the Whole House to-morrow. Mr. Burges, from the Committee on Revolutionary Claims, reported the following bill: [Washington, 1830] 1 p. (H.R. 104) DNA.   4596

---- A bill to secure in office the faithful collectors and disbursers of the revenue, and to dispose defaulters. March 23, 1830. Mr. Benton, from the select committee to whom the subject was referred, on the 16th instant, reported the following bill; which was read, and passed to a second reading: [Washington, 1830] 2 p. (S. 147) DNA.   4597

---- A bill to vest in the state of Indiana certain lands within the limits of the canal grant. March 17, 1830. Mr. Hendricks, from the Committee on Roads and Canals, reported the following bill; which was read, and passed to a second reading. [Washington, 1830] 2 p. (S. 135) DNA.   4598

---- Boundary line--Florida and Georgia. (To accompany bill House of Representatives, No. 243.) February 13, 1830. Mr. Buchanan, from the Committee on the Judiciary, to which the subject had been referred, made the following report: Washington, Pr. by Duff Green, 1830. 8 p. (Rep. No. 191) DLC; NjR. 4599

---- Bowie, Kurtz, et al. Jan. 20, 1830. Mr. Everett, from the Committee on Foreign Affairs, to which was referred the case of the owners of the ship Alleghany, made the following report: Washington, Duff Green, 1830. 24 p. (Rep. No. 100) DLC; NjR.   4600

---- Brevet officers, Paymaster General, and Surgeon General. January 4, 1830. Read, and laid upon the table. Mr. Drayton, from the Committee on Military Affairs, to which the subject had been referred, made the following report: Washington, Duff Green, 1830. 3 p. (Rep. No. 47) DLC; NjR.   4601

---- Bridge across the Ohio. April 29, 1830. Read, and laid upon the table. Mr. Wickliffe, from the Committee on the Judiciary, to which the subject had been referred, made the following report: Washington, Duff Green, 1830. 1 p. (Rep. No. 387) DLC; NjR.   4602

---- Buzzard and Barnstable Bay Canal. Report and estimate on the Buzzard and Barnstable Canal, Massachusetts. Feb. 8, 1830. Printed by order of the House of Representatives. Washington, Pr. by Duff Green, 1830. 17 p. (Doc. No. 54) DLC; NjR.
                            4603
---- Cadets--Military academy. Letter from the Secretary of War, transmitting the information required by a resolution of the House of Representatives of the 26th Jan. last, on the subject of the Military Academy. March 15, 1830. Read, and laid upon the table. Washington, Pr. by Duff Green, 1830. 152 p. (Doc. No. 79) DLC; NjR.   4604

---- Canal, Atlantic to Gulf of

Mexico. Letter from the Secretary of War, transmitting an estimate of the cost of completing a survey, &c. of a Canal to connect the waters of the Atlantic and the Gulf of Mexico. Jan. 28, 1830. Referred to the Committee of Ways and Means. Washington, Pr. by Duff Green, 1830. 3 p. (Doc. No. 41) DLC; NjR.   4605

---- Canal--Boston Harbor to Narragansett Bay. Feb. 5, 1830. Read, laid upon the table, and ordered to be printed. Washington, Pr. by Duff Green, 1830. 1 p. (Doc. No. 62) DLC; NjR.
                            4606
---- Canal--Lake Michigan to Illinois River. Illinois to relinquish land and issue scrip. April 22, 1830. (To accompany Bill H. R. No. 255) Mr. Duncan, from the Committee on the Public Lands, to which the subject had been referred made the following report: Washington, Duff Green, 1830. 3 p. (Rep. No. 377) DLC; NjR.   4607

---- Canal--Tennessee and Coosa Rivers. Feb. 10, 1830. Read, and laid upon the table. Mr. Blair, of Tennessee, from the Committee on Internal Improvements, to which the subject had been referred, made the following report: Washington, Pr. by Duff Green, 1830. 2 p. (Rep. No. 180) DLC; NjR.   4608

---- Canal--Tennessee River to Mobile Bay. February 25, 1830. Printed by order of the House of Representatives. Memorial of the General Assembly of the state of Tennessee, upon the subject of a canal or rail road to connect the waters of Tennessee River and Mobile Bay. Washington, Pr. by Duff Green, 1830. 3 p. (Rep. No. 228) DLC;

NjR. 4609

---- Cape Fear River. Letter from the Secretary of War, transmitting a report in relation to the works on Cape Fear River. Feb. 1, 1830. Referred to the Committee on Commerce. Washington, Pr. by Duff Green, 1830. 3 p. (Doc. No. 44) DLC; NjR. 4610

---- Captain John Wood. Jan. 15, 1830. Mr. Clay, from the Committee on the Public Lands, to which was referred the case of Captain John Wood, made the following report: Washington, Duff Green, 1830. 1 p. (Rep. No. 82) DLC; NjR. 4611

---- Captain Thomas Paine. February 24, 1830. Mr. Overton, from the Committee of Ways and Means, made the following report: Washington, Pr. by Duff Green, 1830. 1 p. (Rep. No. 224) DLC; NjR. 4612

---- Case of James H. Peck. In Senate of the United States, December 21, 1830. Washington, Duff Green, 1830. 4 p. (Doc. No. 11) DLC; PU. 4613

---- ---- Substance of an argument delivered before the District Court of the United States. Dec. 22, 1830. Ordered that the following documents be printed for the use of the Senate. Washington, Duff Green, 1830. 30 p. (Doc. No. 12) DLC; PU. 4614

---- Case of Nathaniel Patten. Feb. 20, 1830. Printed by order of the House of Representatives. Washington, Duff Green, 1830. 6 p. (Rep. No. 59) DLC; NjR. 4615

---- Case of Stephen Olney. Jan. 5, 1830. Printed by order of the House of Representatives. Washington, Duff Green, 1830. 6 p. (Rep. No. 53) DLC; NjR. 4616

---- Case of Susan Decatur, et al. To accompany Bill H. R. 82. Jan. 7, 1830. Printed by order of the House of Representatives of the United States. Washington, Duff Green, 1830. 28 p. (Rep. No. 60) DLC; NjR. 4617

---- Catalogue of the Library of Congress. December, 1830. Washington, Pr. by D. Green, 1830. 258 p. DLC; TNJ; BrMus. 4618

---- Catalogue of the Library of the Department of State of the United States. May, 1830. [Washington, 1830] 150 p. DLC; MH. 4619

---- Certificates to Issue for lands in Louisiana, in certain cases. To accompany bill House Representatives No. 260. February 18, 1830. Printed by order of the House of Representatives. Washington, Pr. by Duff Green, 1830. 1 p. (Rep. No. 210) DLC; NjR. 4620

---- Charles Brown. Jan. 18, 1830. Mr. Chilton, from the Committee on Military Pensions, made the following report: Washington, Duff Green, 1830. 2 p. (Rep. No. 94) DLC; NjR. 4621

---- Charles Cassedy. May 7, 1830. Mr. Whittlesey, from the Committee of Claims, made the following report: Washington, Duff Green, 1830. 1 p. (Rep. No. 394) DLC; NjR. 4622

---- Charles Collins. Jan. 29, 1830. Mr. Verplanck, from the Committee of Ways and Means, made the following report: Washington, Duff Green, 1830. 1 p. (Rep. No. 136) DLC; NjR. 4623

---- Charles Josslyn's bail.
Feb. 8, 1830. Mr. Magee,
from the Committee on the Post
Office and Post Roads, made the
following report: Washington,
Duff Green, 1830. 2 p. (Rep.
No. 167) DLC; NjR.   4624

---- Charter of Georgetown. February 11, 1830. Mr. Washington, from the Committee for the
District of Columbia, to which
the subject had been referred,
made the following report: Washington, Pr. by Duff Green, 1830.
1 p. (Rep. No. 187) DLC; NjR.
                                  4625
---- Cherokee and other Indians.
Memorial of inhabitants of the
state of Massachusetts, in relation to the Cherokee and other
Indian tribes. March 1, 1830.
Read, and committed to the Committee of the Whole House on the
state of the Union. Washington,
Pr. by Duff Green, 1830. 7 p.
(Rep. No. 245) DLC; NjR. 4626

---- Cherokee Indians. Memorial
of a delegation of the Cherokee
Nation of Indians. May 10, 1830.
Read, and laid upon the table.
Washington, Duff Green, 1830.
4 p. (Rep. No. 397) DLC; NjR.
                                  4627
---- Chesapeake and Ohio Canal
Company. Memorial of the pres-
ident and directors of the Chesa-
peake and Ohio Canal Company.
May 24, 1830. Referred to the
Committee on Internal Improve-
ments, and ordered to be printed.
[Washington, Pr. by Duff
Green, 1830] 108 p. CSt;
CtY; DBRE; DIC; DLC; IU; M;
MB; MBAt; MWA; MiU-T; NN;
NRU; NjP; P.   4628

---- Chesapeake and Ohio Canal
west of the Alleghany. March 8,
1830. Read, and laid upon the
table. Mr. Hemphill, from the
Committee on Internal Improve-

ments, to which the subject had
been referred, made the following report: Washington, Pr. by
Duff Green, 1830. 2 p. (Rep.
No. 280) DLC; NjR.   4629

---- Children of Charles Comb,
&c. February 11, 1830. Mr. Foster, from the Committee on Private Land Claims, to which was
referred the case of the children,
&c. of Charles Comb, made the
following report: Washington,
Pr. by Duff Green, 1830. 1 p.
(Rep. No. 186) DLC; NjR. 4630

---- Claim of Delaware. February 11, 1830. Mr. Drayton,
from the Committee on Military
Affairs, to which the subject had
been referred, made the following report: Washington, Pr. by
Duff Green, 1830. 1 p. (Rep. No.
185) DLC; NjR.   4631

---- Claims of citizens of Georgia. Jan. 26, 1830. Mr.
Bell, from the Committee on Indian Affairs, to which the subject had been referred, made
the following report: Washington,
Duff Green, 1830. 2 p. (Rep.
No. 115) DLC; NjR.   4632

---- Clerks--Department of
State. Letter from the Secretary
of State transmitting a list of
names of the clerks employed in
the State Department during the
last year, and the compensation
of each. May 3, 1830. Read,
and laid upon the table. Washington, [Pr. by Duff Green]
1830. 3 p. (Doc. No. 97) DLC;
NjR.   4633

---- Clerks--General Post Office. Letter from the Postmaster General transmitting a statement of the names of the clerks
in the Post Office Department
during the year 1829, and the
compensation of each. May 20,

1830. Read, and laid upon the table. Washington [Pr. by Duff Green] 1830. 3 p. (Doc. No. 105) DLC; NjR.   4634

---- Clerks in the Treasury Department. Letter from the Secretary of the Treasury, transmitting a list of the names of the clerks employed in the Treasury Department, during the year 1829, and the compensation allowed to each.   Jan. 19, 1830. Read, and laid upon the table. Washington, Pr. by Duff Green, 1830. 10 p. (Doc. No. 28) DLC; NjR.   4635

---- Clerks in the War Department. Letter from the Secretary of War, transmitting a list of the names of the clerks employed in the War Department, during the year 1829, and the compensation allowed to each.   Jan. 19, 1830. Read, and laid upon the table. Washington, Pr. by Duff Green, 1830. 3 p. (Doc. No. 27) DLC; NjR.   4636

---- Clerks--Navy Department. Letter from the Secretary of the Navy, transmitting statements of the names of the clerks employed in the Navy Department during the year 1829, and the compensation allowed to each. Washington, Pr. by Duff Green, 1830. 2 p. (Doc. No. 20) DLC; NjR.   4637

---- Col. John Laurens--representatives of.   March 2, 1830. Mr. Burges, from the Committee on Revolutionary Claims, made the following report: Washington, Pr. by Duff Green, 1830. 20 p. (Rep. No. 257) DLC; NjR.   4638

---- Coleman Fisher.   March 16, 1830. Mr. Test, from the Committee on Private Land Claims, made the following report: Washington, Pr. by Duff Green, 1830. 1 p. (Rep. No. 296)   DLC;

NjR.   4639

---- Colin M'Lachlan.   February 15, 1830. Mr. Young, from the Committee on Revolutionary Claims, to which was referred the case of Colin M'Lachlan, made the following report: Washington, Pr. by Duff Green, 1830. 1 p. (Rep. No. 194) DLC; NjR.   4640

---- Colonial trade.   Message from the President of the United States upon the subject of providing by law for carrying into effect any provision which may be effected by the Minister of the United States with the British government, relating to the colonial trade, should the same be made known during the recess of Congress. May 26, 1830. Referred to the Committee on Commerce. Washington, [Pr. by Duff Green] 1830. 1 p. (Doc. No. 110) DLC; NjR.   4641

---- Columbian College. March 12, 1830. Mr. Varnum, from the Committee for the District of Columbia, to which the subject had been referred, made the following report: Washington, Pr. by Duff Green, 1830. 12 p. (Rep. No. 290) DLC; NjR.   4642

---- Commerce and navigation. Feb. 8, 1830.   Read, and referred to the Committee of the Whole House on the state of the Union. Mr. Cambreleng, from the Committee on Commerce, submitted the following report: Washington, Duff Green, 1830. 63 p. (Rep. No. 165) DLC; NjR.   4643

---- Commerce and navigation of the United States. Letter from the Secretary of the Treasury transmitting statements respecting the commerce and navigation of the United States, &c.

&c. February 5, 1830. Read, and ordered that 1,000 additional copies be printed. Washington, Pr. by Duff Green, 1830. 304 p. (Doc. No. 95) DLC; NjR.   4644

---- ---- Washington, Pr. by Duff Green, 1830. 304 p. (Doc. No. 49) DLC; NjR.   4645

---- The Committee on Finance, to which was recommitted the "Bill to alter the terms of credit on bonds given for duties on goods, wares, and merchandise, imported into the United States," report: That the whole thereof, after the enacting clause, be stricken out, and the following be inserted in lieu thereof: January 14, 1830. [Washington, 1830] 2 p. (S. 44) DNA.   4646

---- Compensation to officers of the Army of the U.S. Letter from the Secretary of War transmitting the information required by a resolution of the House of Representatives, of the 4th February last, in relation to the compensation of the officers of the Army of the United States. May 6, 1830. Read, and laid upon the table. Washington [Pr. by Duff Green] 1830. 139 p. (Doc. No. 99) DLC; NjR.   4647

---- Conaleskee, or challenge, James Ore, Giles M'Anulty, and George Stiggins. (With Bill No. 97) Jan. 11, 1830. Mr. Clay, from the Committee on the Public Lands, made the following report: Washington, Duff Green, 1830. 2 p. (Rep. No. 69) DLC; NjR.   4648

---- Condensed reports of cases in the Supreme Court of the United States. Containing the whole series of the decisions of the Court from its organization to the commencement of Peter's reports at January term 1827. ... Edited by Richard Peters Esq. From April term, 1791 to (January term, 1827, inclusive). Philadelphia, Pub. by John Grigg [Pr. by James Kay, Jun. & co.] 1830. 6 vols. CU-L; MH-L; NjP; PP; RPL; TxU-L.   4649

---- Constitution. [Broadside indicating the objectives and provisions of the Constitution.] Philadelphia, DeSilver [1830?] PU.   4650

---- The Constitution of the United States, arranged in lessons, with questions, (well adapted to the capacities of youth,) for the use of schools. By J. O'Conner, teacher. Philadelphia, Pub. for the author, J. Coates, Jr., pr., 1830. 110 p. PPL.   4651

---- Contingent expenses Ho. Reps. 1830. Letter from the clerk of the House of Representatives U.S. submitting a report of the expenditures of the appropriation for contingent expenses of the House for the year 1831. December 13, 1830. Read, and laid upon the table. Washington, Pr. by Duff Green, 1830. 5 p. (Doc. No. 5) DLC; NjR.   4652

---- Contingent expenses--military establishment, 1829. Jan. 7, 1830. Read, and laid upon the table. Washington, Pr. by Duff Green, 1830. 6 p. (Doc. No. 19) DLC; NjR.   4653

---- Contingent expenses Navy Department. Jan. 25, 1830. Read, and laid upon the table. Washington, Pr. by Duff Green, 1830. 23 p. (Doc. No. 35) DLC; NjR.   4654

---- Continuation of the Cumberland Road. Message from the President of the United States, transmitting a letter from the chief of the engineers, with surveys of two routes, for the continuation of the Cumberland Road. Feb. 12, 1830. Read, and referred to the Committee of Ways and Means. Washington, Pr. by Duff Green, 1830. 12 p. (Doc. No. 59) DLC; NjR. 4655

---- Contracts General Post Office, 1829. Letter from the Postmaster General, transmitting a statement of contracts for transporting the mail of the United States, made during the year 1829. March 12, 1830. Read, and laid upon the table. Washington, Pr. by Duff Green, 1830. 11 p. (Doc. No. 77) DLC; NjR. 4656

---- Contracts--War Department, 1829. Letter from the Secretary of War, transmitting statements of contracts made by the War Department during the year 1829. January 27, 1830. Read, and laid upon the table. March 30, 1830. Ordered to be printed. Washington, Pr. by Duff Green, 1830. 66 p. (Doc. No. 86) DLC; NjR. 4657

---- Copy-right. Dec. 17, 1830. Mr. Ellsworth, from the Committee on the Judiciary, to which was committed the bill (H. R. No. 145) to amend, and consolidate the acts respecting copy-rights, made the following report: Washington, Duff Green, 1830. 2 p. (Rep. No. 3) DLC; NjR. 4658

---- Creek Nation of Indians. Memorial of certain chiefs of the Creek Nation of Indians. Feb. 8, 1830. Read, and laid upon the table for one day. Washington, Duff Green, 1830. 5 p. (Rep. No. 169) DLC; NjR. 4659

---- Cumberland Road in Indiana.

Memorial of the legislature of Indiana, in relation to the Cumberland Road in that state. Feb. 8, 1830. Read, and referred to the Committee on Internal Improvements. Washington, Duff Green, 1830. 2 p. (Rep. No. 174) DLC; NjR. 4660

---- Cumberland Road. Jan. 27, 1830. Read, and referred to the Committee on Internal Improvement. Washington, Pr. by Duff Green, 1830. 21 p. (Doc. No. 36) DLC; NjR. 4661

---- ---- Letter from the Secretary of War transmitting, in pursuance of a resolution of the House of Representatives of the 16th instant, a report of the progress which has been made in the construction of the Cumberland Road, &c. &c. December 21, 1830. Read, and laid upon the table. Washington, Pr. by Duff Green, 1830. 14 p. (Doc. No. 12) DLC; NjR. 4662

---- ---- May 24, 1830. Mr. Vinton, from the Committee on Internal Improvements, made the following report: Washington, Duff Green, 1830. 2 p. (Rep. No. 410) DLC; NjR. 4663

---- Daniel Goodwin. March 19, 1830. Mr. Dickinson, from the Committee on Revolutionary Claims, made the following report: Washington, Duff Green, 1830. 3 p. (Rep. No. 314) DLC; NjR. 4664

---- Daniel Johnson. March 26, 1830. Mr. Drayton, from the Committee on Military Affairs, made the following report: Washington, Duff Green, 1830. 1 p. (Rep. No. 330) DLC; NjR. 4665

---- Daniel M'Duff. Jan. 6, 1830. Mr. Clay, from the Se-

lect Committee, to which had
been referred the case of Captain
Daniel M'Duff, made the following report: Washington, Duff
Green, 1830. 3 p. (Rep. No.
58) DLC; NjR.   4666

---- David Brooks. April 9,
1830. Mr. Bockee, from the
Committee on Military Pensions,
made the following report: Washington, Duff Green, 1830. 1 p.
(Rep. No. 353) DLC; NjR. 4667

---- David Kennard. May 14,
1830. Mr. Bockee, from the
Committee on Military Pensions,
made the following report: Washington, Duff Green, 1830. 1 p.
(Rep. No. 405) DLC; NjR. 4668

---- David Kilbourn. February
12, 1830. Mr. Drayton, from
the Committee on Military Affairs, to which had been referred
the case of David Kilbourn, made
the following report: Washington, Pr. by Duff Green, 1830.
2 p. (Rep. No. 189) DLC; NjR.
                             4669
---- David M. Lewis. December 28, 1829. Read, and laid
upon the table. February 15,
1830. Committed to a Committee of the Whole House to-morrow. Mr. McIntire, from the
Committee of Claims, made the
following report: Washington,
Pr. by Duff Green, 1830. 2 p.
(Rep. No. 201) DLC; NjR. 4670

---- David Rogers and sons.
Jan. 26, 1830. Mr. Inger-
soll, from the Committee of
Ways and Means, made the following report: Washington, Duff
Green, 1830. 1 p. (Rep. No.
114) DLC; NjR.   4671

---- The Declaration of independence, of July 4, 1776, and
the Constitution of the United
States, with the amendments.

Philadelphia, L. B. Clarke, 1830.
71 p. DLC; MB.   4672

---- Defence of northern frontier.
Letter from the Secretary of
War, in reply to a Resolution of
the House of Representatives,
relative to plans for the defence
of the northern frontier of the
United States, &c. &c. March
2, 1830. Read, and laid upon
the table. Washington, Pr. by
Duff Green, 1830. 1 p. (Doc. No.
67) DLC; NjR.   4673

---- Delinquent clerks--district
courts, U. S. Letter from the
Secretary of the Treasury transmitting the information required
by a resolution of the House of
Representatives of the 10th instant, in relation to moneys lost
by the government, or by individuals who have paid moneys
into the court, &c. &c. May 13,
1830. Read, and referred to the
Committee on the Judiciary.
Washington, [Pr. by Duff Green]
1830. 4 p. (Doc. No. 100) DLC;
NjR.   4674

---- Denison & Ely. March 26,
1830. Mr. Whittlesey, from the
Committee of Claims, made the
following report: Washington,
Duff Green, 1830. 5 p. (Rep.
No. 329) DLC; NjR.   4675

---- D'Honergue upon American
silk. Report of the Committee
on Agriculture on the growth and
manufacture of silk; to which is
annexed Essays on American silk,
with directions to farmers for
raising silk worms, by John d'-
Homergue, silk manufacturer and
Peter Stephen Duponceau, member of the A. Philosophical Society, ... Printed by order of
the House of Representatives.
Washington, Pr. by Duff Green,

1830. 88 p. (Doc. No. 126)
DLC; NjR. 4676

---- A digest of the treaties and
statutes of the United States, relating to commerce, navigation,
and revenue. Compiled at the
instance of the secretary of the
Treasury. By Thomas F. Gordon. Philadelphia, 1830. 12, 25,
302, 319, [273]-299, [190] p.
CLSU; CU; DLC; MH-L; Md;
MiD-B; MnU; NcD; OO. 4677

---- Directory of the the [!] 21st
Congress, first session... Wash-
ington, Sold at the bookstore of
Jonathan Elliot, 1830. 64 p.
PPL. 4678

---- Disbursements for certain
specific purposes. Letter from
the Secretary of the Treasury
transmitting, in compliance with
a resolution of the House of Representatives of the 26th of May
last, a statement of disbursements made, since the year 1789,
for fortifications, light-houses,
public debt, revolutionary and
other pensions, and internal improvements, &c. December 21,
1830. Read, and laid upon the
table. Washington, Pr. by Duff
Green, 1830. 32 p. (Doc. No.
11) DLC; NjR. 4679

---- Disbursements to the Indians.
Letter from the Secretary of War,
transmitting copies of accounts of
persons charged or trusted with
the disbursement of money, goods,
or effects, for the benefit of the
Indians, from the 1st Sept.,
1828, to 1st Sept., 1829, &c.
&c. Feb. 23, 1830. Read,
and laid upon the table. Washington, Pr. by Duff Green, 1830.
139 p. (Doc. No. 87) DLC; NjR.
4680

---- Doctor Eliakim Crosby.
May 8, 1828. Printed by order
of the House of Representatives.

March 3, 1830. Mr. Sterigere,
from the Committee on Private
Land Claims, to which was referred the petition of D. Eliakim
Crosby, made the following report: Washington, Pr. by Duff
Green, 1830. 2 p. (Rep. No.
262) DLC; NjR. 4681

---- Documents in relation to the
continuation of the Cumberland
Road in the states of Ohio and
Indiana (with Senate Bill No. 100)
February 22, 1830. Laid on the
table by Mr. Hendricks, and ordered to be printed. Washington, Pr. by Duff Green, 1830.
9 p. (Doc. No. 63) DLC; NjR.
4682

---- Dorothy Wells. February
15, 1830. Mr. Test, from the
Committee on Private Land
Claims, made the following report: Washington, Pr. by Duff
Green, 1830. 1 p. (Rep. No.
195) DLC; NjR. 4683

---- Draughtsman to the House
of Representatives. March 30,
1830. Read, and laid upon the
table. Mr. Wickliffe, from the
Committee on Retrenchment, to
which the subject had been referred, made the following report: Washington, Duff Green,
1830. 6 p. (Rep. No. 338)
DLC; NjR. 4684

---- Duties on imports, &c.
Letter from the Secretary of the
Treasury, transmitting a statement shewing the amount of duties accruing on goods imported,
and drawbacks payable, during
the years 1826, 1827, and 1828.
Jan. 19, 1830. Read, and
laid upon the table. Washington,
Pr. by Duff Green, 1830. 7 p.
(Doc. No. 29) DLC; NjR. 4685

---- Duty on salt. May 13, 1830.
Read, and laid upon the table.
Mr. Taliaferro submitted the fol-

lowing resolution. Washington,
Duff Green, 1830. 1 p. (Res.
No. 15) DLC; NjR.   4686

---- Eber Hubbard. March 12,
1830. Mr. Whittlesey, from the
Committee of Claims, to which
was referred the case of Eber
Hubbard, made the following report: Washington, Pr. by Duff
Green, 1830. 2 p. (Rep. No.
288) DLC; NjR.   4687

---- Edmund Brooke. February
26, 1830. Mr. Burges, from
the Committee on Revolutionary
Claims, to which was referred
the case of Edmund Brooke, made
the following report: Washington,
Pr. by Duff Green, 1830. 2 p.
(Rep. No. 236) DLC; NjR. 4688

---- Edward Lee. February 22,
1830. Mr. Whittlesey, from the
Committee of Claims, to which
was referred the case of Edward
Lee, made the following report:
Washington, Pr. by Duff Green,
1830. 2 p. (Rep. No. 217) DLC;
NjR.   4689

---- Eleanor Courts. February
26, 1830. Mr. Goodenow, from
the Committee on Revolutionary
Claims, to which was referred
the case of Eleanor Courts, widow of Richard Henly Courts,
made the following report: Washington, Pr. by Duff Green, 1830.
2 p. (Rep. No. 240) DLC; NjR.
                            4690
---- Elisha Ives.   Feb. 1,
1830. Mr. Whittlesey, from the
Committee of Claims, made the
following report: Washington,
Duff Green, 1830. 2 p. (Rep. No.
142) DLC; NjR.   4691

---- Elisha James.   May 25,
1830. Mr. Bates, from the Committee on Military Pensions, made
the following report: Washington,
Duff Green, 1830. 1 p. (Rep. No.

414) DLC; NjR.   4692

---- Elisha Tracy.   April 10,
1830. Read, and with the bill,
committed to a Committee of the
Whole House to-morrow. Mr.
McIntire, from the Committee of
Claims, to which was referred
the bill from the Senate, for the
relief of Elisha Tracy, made the
following report: Washington,
Duff Green, 1830. 3 p. (Rep.
No. 354) DLC; NjR.   4693

---- Elizabeth Dandridge. February 10, 1830. Mr. Young,
from the Committee on Revolutionary Claims, to which had
been referred the case of Elizabeth Dandridge, made the following report: Washington, Pr. by
Duff Green, 1830. 1 p. (Rep.
No. 182) DLC; NjR.   4694

---- Elizabeth Williams. February 11, 1830. Mr. Whittlesey,
from the Committee of Claims,
to which was referred the case
of Elizabeth Williams, made the
following report: Washington, Pr.
by Duff Green, 1830. 2 p. (Rep.
No. 188) DLC; NjR.   4695

---- Emoluments of officers of
the customs, &c. March 2, 1830.
Referred to the Committee on
Commerce. Washington, Pr. by
Duff Green, 1830. 15 p. (Doc.
No. 71) DLC; NjR.   4696

---- Entombment and statue of
Washington. Washington, Duff
Green, 1830. 9 p. (Rep. No. 318)
DLC; NjR.   4697

---- Ephraim F. Gilbert. February 24, 1830. Mr. McIntire,
from the Committee of Claims,
made the following report: Washington, Pr. by Duff Green, 1830.
4 p. (Rep. No. 226) DLC; NjR.
                            4698
---- Ephram Whitaker.   Jan.

26, 1830. Mr. Bockee, from
the Committee on Military Pensions, made the following report:
Washington, Duff Green, 1830.
2 p. (Rep. No. 117) DLC; NjR.
4699
---- Estimate of appropriations
for 1831. Letter from the Secretary of the Treasury transmitting an estimate of appropriations
for the year 1831. December 21,
1830. Referred to the Committee of Ways and Means. Washington, Pr. by Duff Green, 1830.
56 p. (Doc. No. 10) DLC; NjR.
4700
---- Eugene Borell. February
15, 1830. Mr. Test, from the
Committee on Private Land
Claims, made the following report: Washington, Pr. by Duff
Green, 1830. 2 p. (Rep. No.
199) DLC; NjR.   4701

---- Expenditure--Army proper.
Letter from the Secretary of War
transmitting the information required by a resolution of the
House of Representatives, in relation to the annual amount ex-
pended upon the army proper,
from the 3d March, 1821, to the
present time, &c. &c. May 29,
1830. Read, and laid upon the
table. Washington, [Pr. by Duff
Green] 1830. 8 p. (Doc. No.
120) DLC; NjR.   4702

---- Expenditure of appropriation
--Naval, 1829. Letter from the
Secretary of the Navy, transmitting a statement shewing the appropriation for the Naval service
for the year 1829; the expenditure
of the same, &c. &c.   Feb.
18, 1830. Referred to the Committee of Ways and Means.
Washington, Pr. by Duff Green,
1830. 4 p. (Doc. No. 65) DLC;
NjR.   4703

---- Expenditure--Treasury Department, 1829. April 6, 1830.

Read, and laid upon the table.
Mr. Leiper, from the Committee on Expenditures in the Treasury Department, made the following report: Washington, Duff
Green, 1830. 3 p. (Rep. No.
346) DLC; NjR.   4704

---- Expenditures--Navy Department. May 5, 1830. Read, and
laid upon the table. Mr. Augustine H. Shepperd, from the Committee on the Expenditures of
Navy Department, made the following report: Washington, Duff
Green, 1830. 3 p. (Rep. No.
393) DLC; NjR.   4705

---- Expenditures--State Department. April 27, 1830. Read,
and laid upon the table. Mr.
Earll, from the Committee on
the Expenditures of the State Department, made the following report: Washington, Duff Green,
1830. 17 p. (Rep. No. 384)
DLC; NjR.   4706

---- F. M. Arredondo. (With
bill H. R. No. 221) February 9,
1830. Mr. Archer, from the
Committee on Foreign Affairs,
made the following report: Washington, Pr. by Duff Green, 1830.
4 p. (Rep. No. 176) DLC; NjR.
4707
---- Farmington, and Hampshire
and Hampden, Canals. Statement
on the petition of the Farmington, and Hampshire and Hampden Canals. (To accompany bill
H. R. No. 276) February 22,
1830. Printed by order of the
House of Representatives. Washington, Pr. by Duff Green, 1830.
7 p. (Rep. No. 221) DLC; NjR.
4708
---- Farmington and Hampshire
Canal Company. April 2, 1830.
Printed by order of the House
of Representatives. Washington,
Duff Green, 1830. 2 p. (Rep.
No. 341) DLC; NjR.   4709

---- Farmington, &c. Canal Company. (To be annexed to Report no. 221) April 29, 1830. "Answer to the remonstrance of the Agent of the Connecticut River Company." Washington, Pr. by Duff Green, 1830. 3 p. DLC; NjR.   4710

---- Farrow and Harris. Letter from the Secretary of War, transmitting the information required by a resolution of the House of Representatives of the 10th instant, in relation to the settlement of the accounts of Farrow and Harris. May 14, 1830. Read, and laid upon the table. Washington [Pr. by Duff Green] 1830. 5 p. (Doc. No. 102) DLC; NjR.   4711

---- ---- March 19, 1830. Read, and committed to a Committee of the Whole House to-morrow. Mr. Whittlesey, from the Committee of Claims, to which was referred the case of Farrow and Harris, made the following report: Washington, Duff Green, 1830. 16 p. (Rep. No. 315) DLC; NjR.   4712

---- Fielding L. White. Feb. 1, 1830. Mr. Johnson, from the Committee on the Post Office and Post Roads, made the following report: Washington, Duff Green, 1830. 1 p. (Rep. No. 140) DLC; NjR.   4713

---- Fifth census. Message from the President of the United States suggesting the expediency of extending the time allowed by law for completing the fifth census. December 16, 1830. Read, and referred to a select committee, consisting of Messrs. Storrs of New York, Coulter, Bates, Gurley, Martindale, Grennell, and Holland. Washington, Pr. by Duff Green, 1830. 1 p. (Doc.

No. 8) DLC; NjR.   4714

---- Fire companies, District Columbia. February 17, 1830. Mr. Varnum, from the Committee for the District of Columbia, to which the subject had been referred, made the following report: Washington, Pr. by Duff Green, 1830. 1 p. (Rep. No. 207) DLC; NjR.   4715

---- Florida boundary. Message from the President of the United States, transmitting the information required by a resolution of the House of Representatives of the 27th ultimo, respecting the report of the Commissioners for running the line between the United States and Florida, under the Treaty of 1795. March 16, 1830. Read, and laid upon the table. Washington, Duff Green, 1830. 16 p. (Doc. No. 80) DLC; NjR.   4716

---- Fortifications. Letter from the Secretary of War, transmitting the information required by a resolution of the House of Representatives of the 27th ultimo, in relation to the appropriations for fortifications since 1815, &c. &c. March 9, 1830. Referred to the Committee on Military Affairs. Washington, Pr. by Duff Green, 1830. 5 p. (Doc. No. 75) DLC; NjR.   4717

---- Fortifications--Pea Patch Island. Message from the President of the United States, transmitting a report from the War Department, in relation to the fortifications at Pea Patch Island, &c. &c. March 31, 1830. Referred to the Committee on Military Affairs. Washington, Pr. by Duff Green, 1830. 3 p. (Doc. No. 88) DLC; NjR.   4718

---- Frances Moore.   Dec.

27, 1830. Read, and laid upon the table. Dec. 31, 1830. Printed by order of the House of Representatives. Mr. De Witt, from the Committee on Revolutionary Claims, made the following report: Washington, Duff Green, 1830. 4 p. (Rep. No. 15) DLC; NjR.   4719

---- Francis Larche. May 11, 1830. Read, and with the bill, committed to a Committee of the Whole House to-morrow. Mr. Whittlesey, from the Committee of Claims, to which was referred the bill from the Senate (No. 24) for the relief of Francis Larche, of New Orleans, made the following report: Washington, Duff Green, 1830. 3 p. (Rep. No. 401) DLC; NjR.   4720

---- Francis Preston. February 25, 1830. Reprinted by order of the House of Representatives. Washington, Pr. by Duff Green, 1830. 8 p. (Rep. No. 234) DLC; NjR.   4721

---- François Isidore Tuillier. Jan. 13, 1830. Mr. Gurley, from the Committee on Private Land Claims, made the following report: Washington, Duff Green, 1830. 1 p. (Rep. No. 77) DLC; NjR.   4722

---- Frederick Raymer. Jan. 4, 1830. Mr. Burges, from the Committee on Revolutionary Claims, made the following report: Washington, Duff Green, 1830. 1 p. (Rep. No. 46) DLC; NjR.   4723

---- Frontiers of Arkansas. Letter of the Secretary of War, in reply to a resolution of the House of Representatives, of the 17th ultimo, relative to the protection of the frontier of Arkansas. Jan. 6, 1830. Read,

and referred to the Committee on Military Affairs. Washington, Pr. by Duff Green, 1830. 1 p. (Doc. No. 17) DLC; NjR.   4724

---- Garret Fountain. February 9, 1830. Read, and committed to a committee of the Whole House to-morrow. Mr. Whittlesey, from the Committee of Claims, to which was referred the petition of Garret Fountain, made the following report: Washington, Pr. by Duff Green, 1830. 2 p. (Rep. No. 212) DLC; NjR.   4725

---- Gates Hoit. February 20, 1830. Mr. Drayton, from the Committee on Military Affairs, to which had been referred the petition of Gates Hoit, made the following report: Washington, Pr. by Duff Green, 1830. 1 p. (Rep. No. 214) DLC; NjR. 4726

---- Geo. Loyall vs. Tho. Newton--contested election. February 19, 1830. Read, and committed to a Committee of the Whole House on Tuesday next. Mr. Alston, from the Committee on Elections, to which the subject had been referred, made the following report: Washington, Pr. by Duff Green, 1830. 331 p. (Rep. No. 213) DLC; NjR.   4727

---- George and William Bangs. Jan. 4, 1830. Mr. Dwight, from the Committee of Ways and Means, to which was referred the case of George and William Bangs, made the following report: Washington, Duff Green, 1830. 1 p. (Rep. No. 44) DLC; NjR.   4728

---- George Brown--Sureties of. March 2, 1830. Mr. Wickliffe, from the Committee on the Judiciary, made the following report: Washington, Pr. by Duff Green,

1830. 2 p. (Rep. No. 250) DLC;
NjR.   4729

---- George E. Tingle. February 17, 1830. Mr. Clarke, from
the Committee on the Territories,
to which was referred the case
of George E. Tingle, made the
following report: Washington, Pr.
by Duff Green, 1830. 1 p. (Rep.
No. 205) DLC; NjR.   4730

---- George Ermatinger. Jan.
29, 1830. Mr. Whittlesey,
from the Committee of Claims,
made the following report: Washington, Duff Green, 1830. 1 p.
(Rep. No. 134) DLC; NjR. 4731

---- George Innes. February 15,
1830. Mr. Cambreleng, from
the Committee on Commerce,
made the following report: Washington, Pr. by Duff Green, 1830.
3 p. (Rep. No. 200) DLC; NjR.
                                4732
---- George Johnson. April 12,
1830. Read, and committed with
the bill, to a Committee of the
Whole House to-morrow. Mr.
Whittlesey, from the Committee
of Claims, to which was referred
the bill from the Senate, entitled
"An act for the relief of George
Johnson," made the following report: Washington, Duff Green,
1830. 6 p. (Rep. No. 356)
DLC; NjR.   4733

---- Georgia Legislature--elec-
tion of President. Feb. 1, 1830.
Read, and laid upon the table.
Washington, Duff Green, 1830. 2
p. (Rep. No. 147) DLC; NjR.
                                4734
---- Governor and judges of Arkansas. February 26, 1830. Mr.
Clarke, from the Committee on
the Territories, to which the
subject had been referred, made
the following report: Washington, Pr. by Duff Green, 1830.
2 p. (Rep. No. 235) DLC;

NjR.   4735

---- Governor Blount's Claim.
April 14, 1830. Mr. Johnson, of
Tennessee, from the select com-
mittee to which was referred the
case of Willie Blount, made the
following report: Washington,
Duff Green, 1830. 12 p. (Rep.
No. 362) DLC; NjR.   4736

---- Growth and manufacture of
silk. March 12, 1830. Mr.
Spencer, of New York, from the
Committee on Agriculture, to
which the subject had been referred, made the following report: Washington, Pr. by Duff
Green, 1830. 11 p. (Rep. No.
289) DLC; NjR.   4737

---- Hall of the House of Representatives U.S. Memorial of Robert Mills, of South Carolina.
Jan. 14, 1830.   Referred to the
Committee on the Public Buildings, and ordered to be printed.
Washington, Duff Green, 1830.
5 p. (Rep. No. 83) DLC; NjR.
                                4738
---- Harbor of Westbrook--Con-
necticut. Letter from the Secretary of War transmitting a survey and estimate for the improvement of the harbor of Westbrook,
in the state of Connecticut. February 16, 1830. Referred to the
Committee on Commerce. Washington, [Pr. by Duff Green] 1830.
4 p. (Doc. No. 124) DLC; NjR.
                                4739
---- Heirs of Doctor Kennedy.
April 9, 1830. Mr. Fry, from
the Committee on Revolutionary
Claims, made the following report: Washington, Duff Green,
1830. 1 p. (Rep. No. 351) DLC;
NjR.   4740

---- Heirs of John Dauphin.
March 16, 1830. Read, and laid
upon the table. Mr. Archer,
from the Committee on Foreign

Affairs, to which was referred the case of the heirs of John Dauphin, made the following report: Washington, Duff Green, 1830. 2 p. (Rep. No. 301) DLC; NjR.   4741

---- Heirs of John Ellis, deceased. Jan. 7, 1830. Mr. Gurley, from the Committee on Private Land Claims, to which was referred the case of the heirs of Col. John Ellis, made the following report: Washington, Duff Green, 1830. 3 p. (Rep. No. 62) DLC; NjR.   4742

---- Heirs of John Tuillier. Jan. 18, 1830. Mr. Gurley, from the Committee on Private Land Claims, to which was referred the case of the heirs of John Tuillier, made the following report: Washington, Duff Green, 1830. 1 p. (Rep. No. 86) DLC; NjR.   4743

---- Heirs of Le Gendre. Jan. 13, 1830. Mr. Gurley, from the Committee on Private Land Claims, made the following report: Washington, Duff Green, 1830. 1 p. (Rep. No. 75) DLC; NjR.   4744

---- Heirs of Peter Cabet. Jan. 20, 1830. Mr. Drayton, from the Committee on Military Affairs, made the following report: Washington, Duff Green, 1830. 1 p. (Rep. No. 99) DLC; NjR.   4745

---- Heirs of Robert Fulton. March 3, 1830. Mr. White, from the Select Committee to which had been referred the case of the heirs of Robert Fulton, deceased, made the following report: Washington, Pr. by Duff Green, 1830. 3 p. (Rep. No. 267) DLC; NjR.   4746

---- Heirs of Ulrich Reeser. Jan. 20, 1830. Mr. Wingate, from the Committee on Revolutionary Claims, to which had been referred the case of the heirs of Ulrich Reeser, made the following report: Washington, Duff Green, 1830. 1 p. (Rep. No. 104) DLC; NjR.   4747

---- Heirs of Widow Dupre. Jan. 13, 1830. Mr. Whittlesey, from the Committee of Claims, to which was referred the case of the heirs of Widow Dupré, made the following report: Washington, Duff Green, 1830. 2 p. (Rep. No. 73) DLC; NjR.   4748

---- The heirs of William Treadwell. Feb. 5, 1830. Mr. Burges, from the Committee on Revolutionary Claims, made the following report: Washington, Duff Green, 1830. 1 p. (Rep. No. 156) DLC; NjR.   4749

---- Henry Bull. Debenture on rum exported. Feb. 1, 1830. Referred to the Committee of Ways and Means. Mr. Pearce laid before the House the following letter; which was read, and ordered to be printed. Washington, Duff Green, 1830. 3 p. (Rep. No. 143) DLC; NjR.   4750

---- Henry Kilbourn. March 26, 1830. Mr. Crane, from the Committee of Claims, made the following report: Washington, Duff Green, 1830. 2 p. (Rep. No. 331) DLC; NjR.   4751

---- Henry Williams. Jan. 25, 1830. Mr. Whittlesey, from the Committee of Claims, to which was referred the case of Henry Williams, made the following report: Washington, Duff Green, 1830. 1 p. (Rep. No. 108) DLC; NjR.   4752

---- Holders of revolutionary
land warrants. March 22, 1830.
(To accompany bill H. R. No.
370) Washington, Pr. by Duff
Green, 1830. 2 p. (Doc. No.
82) DLC; NjR.   4753

---- The House being in Committee of the Whole on the state
of the Union, and having under
consideration the bill (No. 164)
entitled, "A bill to amend an act
in alteration of the several acts
imposing duties on imports," Mr.
McDuffie proposed to amend the
said bill by striking out all after
the first section, and in lieu
thereof inserting the following
amendment: April 25, 1830.
[Washington, 1830] 2 p. (H. R. 164)
DNA.   4754

---- Ichabod Ward. March 22,
1830. Mr. Young from the Committee on Revolutionary Claims,
made the following report: Washington, Duff Green, 1830. 1 p.
(Rep. No. 320) DLC; NjR.   4755

---- In Senate of the United
States. February 8, 1830. Read,
and ordered to be printed: Mr.
Foot made the following report:
The Committee of Claims, on the
petition of Ezra St. John, of
Erie, New York report: Washington, Pr. by Duff Green, 1830.
6 p. (Doc. No. 50) DLC; NjR.
                            4756

---- ---- February 8, 1830.
Read, and ordered to be printed.
Mr. Woodbury made the follow-
ing report: The Committee on
Naval Affairs, to which was re-
ferred the petition of Charles
Yeaton, ask leave to report:
Washington, Pr. by Duff Green,
1830. 1 p. (Doc. No. 51) DLC;
NjR.   4757

---- ---- February 9, 1830.
Read, and ordered to be printed.
Mr. Rowan made the following

report: The Committee on the
Judiciary, to whom was referred
the petition of Thomas L. Winthrop and others, directors of
an association called the New
England Mississippi Land Company, &c. report: Washington,
Pr. by Duff Green, 1830. 7 p.
(Doc. No. 52) DLC; NjR.   4758

---- ---- February 12, 1830.
Mr. McKinley made the following report: The Committee on
Public Lands, to which was referred the memorial of the legislature of the state of Alabama
... report: Washington, Pr. by
Duff Green, 1830. 7 p. (Doc.
No. 55) DLC; NjR.   4759

---- ---- February 17, 1830.
Read, and ordered to be printed.
Mr. Tazewell made the following
report: The Committee on Foreign Relations to which was referred a bill that passed the
House of Representatives on the
sixth of January, 1830, for the
relief of Alexander Scott... report: Washington, Pr. by Duff
Green, 1830. 3 p. (Doc. No. 57)
DLC; NjR.   4760

---- ---- February 22, 1830.
Mr. Livingston, from the Select
Committee appointed on 22d December last, made the following
report: Washington, Pr. by Duff
Green, 1830. 16 p. (Doc. No.
68) DLC; NjR.   4761

---- ---- February 22, 1830.
Read, and ordered to be printed.
Mr. White made the following
report: The Committee on Indian Affairs, to whom was referred that part of the President's message dated the eighth
day of December last, which relates to Indian Affairs... report:
Washington, Pr. by Duff Green,
1830. 9 p. (Doc. No. 61) DLC;
NjR.   4762

---- ---- February 23, 1830.
Read, and ordered to be printed.
Mr. Woodbury made the following report: The Joint Library
Committee, to whom was referred
the resolution "to postpone the
subscription, on the part of the
Senate, to the compilation of the
public documents proposed to be
printed by Gales and Seaton..."
report: Washington, Pr. by Duff
Green, 1830. 4 p. (Doc. No. 67)
DLC; NjR.   4763

---- ---- February 24, 1830.
Laid on the table, and ordered
to be printed. Mr. Foot, made
the following report: The Committee on Pensions, on the petition of Celestine T. Wilkinson
...report: Washington, Pr. by
Duff Green, 1830. 2 p. (Doc.
No. 71) DLC; NjR.   4764

---- ---- February 24, 1830.
Laid on the table, and ordered
to be printed. Mr. Foot made
the following report: The Committee on Pensions, to which has
been referred the petition of
Mrs. Caroline Langdon Eustis
and others...report: Washington,
Pr. by Duff Green, 1830. 1 p.
(Doc. No. 70) DLC; NjR.   4765

---- ---- February 24, 1830.
Laid upon the table, and ordered
to be printed. Mr. Foot made
the following report: The Committee on Pensions have had under consideration a resolution of
the Senate of the 17th instant
...report: Washington, Pr. by
Duff Green, 1830. 1 p. (Doc.
No. 69) DLC; NjR.   4766

---- ---- February 25, 1830.
Read, and ordered to be printed.
Mr. Smith of Maryland made the
following report: The Committee on Finance, to which was referred the petition of David
Beard, report: Washington, Pr.

by Duff Green, 1830. 2 p. (Doc.
No. 72) DLC; NjR.   4767

---- ---- March 4, 1830. Read,
and ordered to be printed. Mr.
Woodbury made the following report: The Committee on Commerce, to which was referred
a resolution on "the expediency
of extending the right of debenture to merchandise imported into Key West from other than foreign ports..." report: Washington, Pr. by Duff Green, 1830.
5 p. (Doc. No. 78) DLC; NjR.
                            4768
---- ---- March 5, 1830. Read,
and ordered to be printed. Mr.
Rowan, from the Committee on
the Judiciary, made the following report: The Committee on
the Judiciary, to whom was referred the petition of the representatives of Simeon Theus...
respectfully report: Washington,
Pr. by Duff Green, 1830. 10 p.
(Doc. No. 80) DLC; NjR.   4769

---- ---- March 11, 1830. Read,
and ordered to be printed. Mr.
Rowan made the following report: The Judiciary Committee
have had under consideration the
resolution instructing them to
inquire into the expediency of
erecting in Savannah, at the expense of the general government,
a suitable building for the ac-
commodation of the District
Court of the United States for
the District of Georgia...Wash-
ington, Pr. by Duff Green, 1830.
1 p. (Doc. No. 87) DLC; NjR.
                            4770
---- ---- March 11, 1830.
Read, and ordered to be printed.
Mr. Rowan made the following
report: The Judiciary Committee, to whom was referred the
petition of J. N. Cardozo...re-
port: Washington, Pr. by Duff
Green, 1830. 2 p. (Doc. No.
86) DLC; NjR.   4771

---- ---- March 15, 1830. Read, and ordered to be printed. Mr. Barton made the following report: The Committee on Public Lands, to whom was referred the petition of John Reily, report: Washington, Pr. by Duff Green, 1830. 2 p. (Doc. No. 89) DLC; NjR.   4772

---- ---- March 29, 1830. Ordered. That the report made to the House of Representatives on the 22d of May, 1826, by a select committee, on the subject of reorganizing the Executive Departments, be printed. Report of the select committee of the House of Representatives, on the subject of re-organizing the Executive Departments, made 22d May, 1826. Washington, Pr. by Duff Green, 1830. 13 p. (Doc. No. 109) DLC; NjR.   4773

---- ---- March 29, 1830. Read and ordered to be printed. Mr. Smith, of Maryland, made the following report: The Committee on Finance, to which was referred a resolution of the 30th December, 1829, directing the Committee to inquire into the expediency of establishing an uniform national currency for the United States, and to report thereon to the Senate, report: Washington, Pr. by Duff Green, 1830. 7, [1] p. (Doc. No. 104) DLC; DeGE; NjR.   4774

---- ---- March 29, 1830. Read, and ordered to be printed. Mr. White made the following report: the Committee of Indian Affairs, to whom was referred the memorial of Joshua Kennedy, praying indemnity for the destruction of property by the hostile Creek Indians, in the year 1813, ask leave to submit the following report: Washington, Pr. by Duff Green, 1830. 2 p. (Doc. No. 105)

DLC; NjR.   4775

---- ---- March 31, 1830. Read, and ordered to be printed. Mr. Tazewell made the following report: The Committee on Foreign Relations. to whom was referred a bill for the relief of Don Carlos Dehault Delassus, have had the same under their consideration, and now beg leave to report: Washington, Pr. by Duff Green, 1830. 2 p. (Doc. No. 119) DLC; NjR.   4776

---- ---- April 5, 1830. Ordered to be printed. Mr. Holmes submitted the following motions: Washington, Pr. by Duff Green, 1830. 2 p. (Doc. No. 114) DLC; NjR.   4777

---- ---- April 5, 1830. Read, and ordered to be printed. Mr. Burnet made the following report: The Committee, to whom was referred the memorial of the mayor, aldermen, and inhabitants of New Orleans, beg leave to report: Washington, Pr. by Duff Green, 1830. 2 p. (Doc. No. 113) DLC; NjR.   4778

---- ---- April 6, 1830. Ordered to be printed. Mr. Chase made the following report: The Committee on Pensions, to whom was referred the petition of Abraham Brownson, report: Washington, Pr. by Duff Green, 1830. 1 p. (Doc. No. 118) DLC; NjR.   4779

---- ---- April 6, 1830. Ordered to be printed. Mr. Chase made the following report: The Committee on Pensions, to whom was referred the petition of Ezekiel Woodworth, report: Washington, Pr. by Duff Green, 1830. 1 p. (Doc. No. 117) DLC; NjR.   4780

---- ---- April 6, 1830. Ordered to be printed. Mr. Chase

made the following report: The Committee on Pensions, to whom was referred the petition of Joseph Chamberlain, report: Washington, Pr. by Duff Green, 1830. 1 p. (Doc. No. 116) DLC; NjR.   4781

---- ---- April 6, 1830. Read, and ordered to be printed. Mr. Hayne made the following report: The Committee of Naval Affairs, to whom was referred the petition of Benjamin Pendleton, report: Washington, Pr. by Duff Green, 1830. 1 p. (Doc. No. 115) DLC; NjR.   4782

---- ---- April 8, 1830. Read, and ordered to be printed. Mr. Chase made the following report: The Committee on Revolutionary Pensions, to which was referred the resolution of the Senate of the 18th ultimo, instructing the committee to inquire into the expediency of granting a pension to Isaac Pinney, a Revolutionary soldier, report: Washington, Pr. by Duff Green, 1830. 2 p. (Doc. No. 121) DLC; NjR.   4783

---- ---- April 21, 1830. Read, and ordered to be printed. Mr. Barton made the following report: The Committee on Public Lands have considered the application of N. B. Tucker... and report: Washington, Pr. by Duff Green, 1830. 1 p. (Doc. No. 127) DLC; NjR.   4784

---- ---- April 22, 1830. Read, and ordered to be printed. Mr. McKinley made the following report: The Committee on Public Lands, to which was referred the memorial of John Smith T. by his attorney in fact, William Kelley... report: Washington, Pr. by Duff Green, 1830. 3 p. (Doc. No. 129) DLC; NjR.   4785

---- ---- April 23, 1830. Read, and ordered to be printed. Mr. King made the following report: The Committee of Finance, to which was referred the petition of Elizabeth Scott, assignee of Alexander Scott, Jr. report: Washington, Pr. by Duff Green, 1830. 1 p. (Doc. No. 130) DLC; NjR.   4786

---- ---- April 28, 1830. Read, and ordered to be printed. Mr. Bibb made the following report: The Committee on the Post Office and Post Roads, of the Senate, to whom was referred the petition of Thomas Rhodes, respectfully report: Washington, Pr. by Duff Green, 1830. 3 p. (Doc. No. 132) DLC; NjR. 4787

---- ---- May 5, 1830. Read, and ordered to be printed. Mr. Hendricks made the following report: The Committee on Roads and Canals, to whom were referred a resolution of the Senate, and a memorial of many citizens of Allen County in the state of Indiana... report: Washington, Pr. by Duff Green, 1830. 5 p. (Doc. No. 137) DLC; NjR.   4788

---- ---- May 6, 1830. Read, and ordered to be printed. Mr. Dickerson made the following report: The Committee to whom was referred so much of the President's message as respects the disposition of the surplus funds of the United States... report: Washington, Pr. by Duff Green, 1830. 4 p. (Doc. No. 139) DLC; NjR.   4789

---- ---- May 8, 1830. Ordered to be printed. Mr. Woodbury made the following report: The Committee on Commerce, to whom were referred two letters from the Engineer Department on the subject of a survey of the Wa-

bash River, ask leave to report:
Washington, Pr. by Duff Green,
1830. 1 p. (Doc. No. 140)
DLC; NjR.   4790

---- ---- May 14, 1830. Read,
and ordered to be printed. Mr.
Iredell made the following report: The Committee to audit
and control the Contingent Fund,
to whom was referred a resolution instructing them "to inquire
if any, and what, provision is
necessary to prevent unnecessary
expense for printing documents
ordered to be printed by the two
House of Congress" respectfully
report: Washington, Pr. by Duff
Green, 1830. 2 p. (Doc. No.
141) DLC; NjR.   4791

---- ---- May 18, 1830. Read,
and ordered to be printed. Mr.
Dickerson made the following report: The Committee on Manufactures, to whom were referred
the petitions of the re-manufac-
turers of iron, in all branches
of smiths' work, in the city and
county of Philadelphia, beg leave
to report: Washington, Pr. by
Duff Green, 1830. 4 p. (Doc.
No. 142) DLC; NjR.   4792

---- ---- May 24, 1830. Read,
and ordered to be printed. Mr.
Marks, from the Committee on
Agriculture, made the following
report: The Committee on Agriculture, to whom was referred
the memorial of a number of
farmers and graziers of Philadelphia, and some adjoining counties, in Pennsylvania, report:
Washington, Pr. by Duff Green,
1830. 8 p. (Doc. No. 143)
DLC; NjR.   4793

---- ---- 15th Dec. 1830.
Read, and ordered to be printed,
and that 1,000 additional copies
be furnished for the use of the
Senate. Mr. Sanford, from the

Select Committee appointed to
consider the state of the current
coins, and to report such amendments of the existing laws concerning coins, as may be deemed
expedient, made the following report: Washington, Duff Green,
1830. 14 p. (Doc. No. 3) DLC;
PU.   4794

---- ---- Dec. 15, 1830.
Read, and ordered to be printed.
Mr. Bell, from the Committee of
Claims, made the following re-
port: Washington, Duff Green,
1830. 16 p. (Doc. No. 4) DLC;
PU.   4795

---- ---- Dec. 16, 1830.
Read, and ordered to be printed.
Mr. Holmes made the following
report: Washington, Duff Green,
1830. 1 p. (Doc. No. 7) DLC;
PU.   4796

---- ---- Dec. 16, 1830.
Read, and ordered to be printed.
Mr. Johnston made the following
report: Washington, Duff Green,
1830. 2 p. (Doc. No. 8) DLC;
PU.   4797

---- ---- Dec. 17, 1830.
Mr. Foot made the following report: On the petition of John
Brunson, of Detroit, in the territory of Michigan, the Committee of Claims report: Washington, Duff Green, 1830. 1 p.
(Doc. No. 9) DLC; PU.   4798

---- ---- Dec. 24, 1830.
Read, and ordered to be printed.
Mr. Poindexter, from the Committee on Private Land Claims,
made the following report:
Washington, Duff Green, 1830.
3 p. (Doc. No. 13) DLC; PU.
                                 4799
---- Increase of the corps of
engineers. (See Document No.
36, of the first Session of the
Nineteenth Congress) Jan. 4,

1830. Document to accompany Bill No. 56, for the gradual increase of the Engineer Corps. Washington, Duff Green, 1830. 2 p. (Rep. No. 42) DLC; NjR. 4800

---- Index to bills of the House of Representatives. First session --Twenty-first Congress. [Washington, 1830] 24 p. DNA. 4801

---- Index to public documents. Feb. 10, 1830. Read, and postponed until 20th Feb. instant. Mr. Burges submitted, for the consideration of the House, the following resolution: Washington, Duff Green, 1830. 1 p. (Res. No. 5) DLC; NjR. 4802

---- Index to resolutions and bills of the Senate of the United States. First Session, Twenty-first Congress--1829-'30. [Washington, 1830] 16 p. DNA. 4803

---- Indian depredations in Georgia. Letter from the Secretary of War, transmitting the correspondence to depredations committed by the Creek Indians on the frontier inhabitants of that State. Jan. 11, 1830. Read, and laid upon the table. Jan. 14, 1830. Referred to the Committee on Indian Affairs. Washington, Pr. by Duff Green, 1830. 102 p. (Doc. No. 25) DLC; NjR. 4804

---- Indian treaties. Message from the President of the United States, transmitting copies of three treaties with Indian tribes, which have been duly ratified. Jan. 14, 1830. Referred to the Committee of Ways and Means. Washington, Pr. by Duff Green, 1830. 13 p. (Doc. No. 24) DLC; NjR. 4805

---- Indians. Laws of the colonial and state governments, relating to the Indian inhabitants.

March 19, 1830. Printed by order of the House of Representatives, and under the direction of the Committee on Indian Affairs. Washington, Duff Green, 1830. 52 p. (Rep. No. 319) DLC; NjR. 4806

---- ---- Memorial of the Indian Board for the emigration, preservation, and improvement of the Aborigines of America. February 22, 1830. Read, and laid upon the table. Washington, Pr. by Duff Green, 1830. 3 p. (Rep. No. 233) DLC; NjR. 4807

---- Indigent deaf and dumb. February 23, 1830. Mr. Goodenow, from the Select Committee to which the subject had been referred, made the following report: Washington, Pr. by Duff Green, 1830. 2 p. (Rep. No. 222) DLC; NjR. 4808

---- Intercourse with foreign nations. Jan. 27, 1830. Referred to the Committee on Foreign Affairs. Washington, Pr. by Duff Green, 1830. 20 p. (Doc. No. 37) DLC; NjR. 4809

---- Isaiah Townsend, et al., sureties of Dox. Jan. 25, 1830. Mr. Johnson, of Kentucky, from the Committee on the Post Office and Post Roads, to which was referred the petition of Isaiah Townsend et al., sureties of Gerrit L. Dox, made the following report: Washington, Duff Green, 1830. 6 p. (Rep. No. 109). DLC; NjR. 4810

---- J. N. Cardozo. March 17, 1830. Mr. Overton, from the Committee of Ways and Means, made the following report: Washington, Duff Green, 1830. 2 p. (Rep. No. 306) DLC; NjR. 4811

---- Jacob Wilderman. Jan.

4, 1830. Mr. Ramsey, from the
Committee of Claims, to which
was referred the case of Jacob
Wilderman, made the following
report: Washington, Duff Green,
1830. (Rep. No. 41) DLC; NjR.
                                4812
---- James Abbot.   Jan. 6,
1830. Mr. Whittlesey, from the
Committee of Claims, made the
following report: Washington,
Duff Green, 1830. 1 p. (Rep.
No. 55) DLC; NjR.   4813

---- James Barnett.   Jan. 26,
1830. Mr. Wingate, from the
Committee on the Revolutionary
Claims, made the following report: Washington, Duff Green,
1830. 1 p. (Rep. No. 120) DLC;
NjR.   4814

---- James Bradford.   March 16,
1830. Mr. Test, from the Committee on Private Land Claims,
made the following report: Washington, Pr. by Duff Green, 1830.
1 p. (Rep. No. 297) DLC; NjR.
                                4815
---- James Fisk.   Feb. 5,
1830. Mr. Ramsey, from the
Committee of Claims, made the
following report: Washington,
Duff Green, 1830. 2 p. (Rep. No.
157) DLC; NjR.   4816

---- James Gibbon.   March 2,
1830. Mr. Burges, from the
Committee on Revolutionary
Claims, made the following report: Washington, Pr. by Duff
Green, 1830. 1 p. (Rep. No.
251) DLC; NjR.   4817

---- James Gordon.   February
10, 1830. Mr. Goodenow, from
the Committee on Revolutionary
Claims, to which was referred
the case of James Gordon, made
the following report: Washington,
Pr. by Duff Green, 1830. 1 p.
(Rep. No. 179) DLC; NjR. 4818

---- James H. Peck.   April 29,
1830. Read, and laid upon the
table. Washington, Duff Green,
1830. 4 p. (Rep. No. 385) DLC;
NjR.   4819

---- ---- Letter from James H.
Peck, April 14, 1830. Read,
and committed to the Committee
of the Whole House on the state
of the Union. Washington, Duff
Green, 1830. 53 p. (Rep. No.
359) DLC; NjR.   4820

---- ---- Memorial of James H.
Peck, judge of the District Court
of the United States for the District of Missouri.   April 5, 1830.
Read, and laid upon the table.
Washington, Duff Green, 1830.
6 p. (Rep. No. 345) DLC; NjR.
                                4821
---- James L. Ridgeley, Adm'r
of Edward Moore.   To accompany bill H. R. No. 203.   Feb.
5, 1830. Printed by order of
the House of Representatives.
Washington, Duff Green, 1830.
2 p. (Rep. No. 159) DLC; NjR.
                                4822
---- James Linsey.   Jan. 4,
1830. Read, and laid upon the
table. Mr. Buchanan, from the
Committee on the Judiciary, to
which was referred the case of
James Linsey, made the following report: Washington, Duff
Green, 1830. 1 p. (Rep. No. 48)
DLC; NjR.   4823

---- James McCarty.   February
20, 1830. Mr. Ramsey, from
the Committee of Claims, to
which was referred the case of
James McCarty, made the following report: Washington, Pr. by
Duff Green, 1830. 2 p. (Rep.
No. 215) DLC; NjR.   4824

---- James Monroe. Letter from
James Monroe, late president of
the United States upon the subject of his claim upon the gener-

al government.   December 13,
1830.   Read, and referred to the
Committee of the Whole House to
which is committed the bill
(H. R. No. 330) for his relief.
Washington, Pr. by Duff Green,
1830.   13 p. (Doc. No. 6) DLC;
NjR.   4825

---- ---- March 6, 1830.   Mr.
Mercer, from the Select Committee to whom the subject had been
referred, made the following report: Washington, Pr. by Duff
Green, 1830.   27 p. (Rep. No.
276) DLC; NjR.   4826

---- James Porliers, et al.
Jan. 15, 1830.   Mr. Hunt, from
the Committee on the Public
Lands, to which was referred the
case of James Porliers et al.
made the following report: Washington, Duff Green, 1830. 1 p.
(Rep. No. 81) DLC; NjR.   4827

---- James Smith.   Jan. 8,
1830.   Mr. Whittlesey, from the
Committee of Claims, to which
was referred the case of James
Smith, made the following report:
Washington, Duff Green, 1830.
1 p. (Rep. No. 64) DLC; NjR.
                                 4828
---- James Soyer.   Mr. Burges,
from the Committee on Revolutionary Claims, to which was referred the case of James Soyer,
made the following report: Washington, Pr. by Duff Green, 1830.
1 p. (Rep. No. 275) DLC; NjR.
                                 4829
---- James W. Brannin, Chas.
Hughes, and Nath. Ford.   May
24, 1830.   Mr. Pettis, from the
Committee on Private Land
Claims, made the following report: Washington, Duff Green,
1830.   2 p. (Rep. No. 409) DLC;
NjR.   4830

---- Jane Muir.   March 17, 1830.
Mr. Whittlesey, from the Com-

mittee of Claims, to which was
referred the petition of Jane
Muir, made the following report:
Washington, Duff Green, 1830.
2 p.   (Rep. No. 303) DLC; NjR.
                                 4831
---- Jared E. Groce.   March
25, 1830.   Mr. Clay, from the
Committee on the Public Lands,
to which was referred the petition of Jared E. Groce, made
the following report: Washington, Duff Green, 1830. 1 p.
(Rep. No. 327) DLC; NjR. 4832

---- Jasper Parish.   Feb.
5, 1830.   Mr. Whittlesey, from
the Committee of Claims, made
the following report: Washington, Duff Green, 1830. 2 p.
(Rep. No. 163) DLC; NjR. 4833

---- Jean Marie Trahaud.
Jan. 18, 1830.   Mr. Gurley, from
the Committee on Private Land
Claims, made the following report: Washington, Pr. by Duff
Green, 1830.   49 p. (Doc. No.
89) DLC; NjR.   4834

---- ---- Jan. 18, 1830.
Mr. Gurley, from the Committee on Private Land Claims,
made the following report: Washington, Duff Green, 1830. 1 p.
(Rep. No. 89) DLC; NjR.   4835

---- Jeremiah Buckley--heirs of.
March 19, 1830.   Mr. Baylor,
from the Committee on Private
Land Claims, made the following
report: Washington, Duff Green,
1830.   2 p. (Rep. No. 316) DLC;
NjR.   4836

---- Jeremiah Walker.   Feb.
5, 1830.   Mr. Test, from
the Committee on Private Land
Claims, made the following report: Washington, Duff Green,
1830. 1 p. (Rep. No. 161) DLC;
NjR.   4837

---- Job Alvord. Jan. 20, 1830. Mr. Goodenow, from the Committee on Revolutionary Claims, made the following report: Washington, Duff Green, 1830. 1 p. (Rep. No. 102) DLC; NjR. 4838

---- John A. Parker. December 23, 1829. Read, and laid upon the table. February 15, 1830. Committed to a Committee of the Whole House to-morrow. Mr. Whittlesey, from the Committee of Claims, in the case of John A. Parker, report: Washington, Pr. by Duff Green, 1830. 2 p. (Rep. No. 202) DLC; NjR. 4839

---- John B. Timberlake and Robert B. Randolph. Letter from the Secretary of the Navy transmitting the information required by a resolution of the House of Representatives in relation to the accounts of John B. Timberlake and Robert B. Randolph. May 28, 1830. Read, and laid upon the table. Washington [Pr. by Duff Green] 1830. 60 p. (Doc. No. 116) DLC; NjR. 4840

---- John Balthrope. Dec. 20, 1830. Read, and concurred in by the House of Representatives. Mr. Drayton, from the Committee on Military Affairs, to which was referred the petition of John Balthrope, made the following report: Washington, Duff Green, 1830. 3 p. (Rep. No. 10) DLC; NjR. 4841

---- John Boone. May 3, 1830. Mr. Chilton, from the Committee on Military Pensions, made the following report: Washington, Duff Green, 1830. 1 p. (Rep. No. 350) DLC; NjR. 4842

---- ---- Washington, Duff Green, 1830. 1 p. (Rep. No. 390) DLC; NjR. 4843

---- John Bruce. February 27, 1830. Mr. Bates, from the Committee on Revolutionary Claims, to which had been referred the petition of John Bruce, administrator of Philip Bush, made the following report: Washington, Pr. by Duff Green, 1830. 3 p. (Rep. No. 243) DLC; NjR. 4844

---- John Brunson. May 17, 1830. Read, and with the bill, committed to a Committee of the Whole House to-morrow. Mr. Whittlesey, from the Committee of Claims, to which was referred the bill from the Senate (No. 93) for the relief of John Brunson, made the following report: Washington, Duff Green, 1830. 2 p. (Rep. No. 407) DLC; NjR. 4845

---- John Buhler. February 15, 1830. Mr. Test, from the Committee on Private Land Claims, made the following report: Washington, Pr. by Duff Green, 1830. 2 p. (Rep. No. 198) DLC; NjR. 4846

---- John Campbell--heirs of. March 5, 1830. Mr. Dickinson, from the Committee on Revolutionary Claims, to which was referred the case of the heirs of John Campbell, made the following report: Washington, Pr. by Duff Green, 1830. 4 p. (Rep. No. 273) DLC; NjR. 4847

---- John Conard. March 22, 1830. Mr. Buchanan, from the Committee on the Judiciary, made the following report: Washington, Duff Green, 1830. 1 p. (Rep. No. 323) DLC; NjR. 4848

---- John Donnell. February 17, 1830. Read, and laid upon the table. Mr. Ellsworth, from the Committee on the Judiciary, to which was referred the case of the representatives of John Donnell, deceased, made the following report: Washington, Pr. by Duff Green, 1830. 1 p. (Rep. No. 206) DLC; NjR.   4849

---- John F. Girod.   March 2, 1830.   Mr. Nuckolls, from the Committee on Private Land Claims, made the following report: Washington, Pr. by Duff Green, 1830. 2 p. (Rep. No. 252) DLC; NjR.   4850

---- John F. Ohl.   May 14, 1830. Mr. Gilmore, from the Committee of Ways and Means, made the following report: Washington, Duff Green, 1830.   2 p. (Rep. No. 406) DLC; NjR.   4851

---- John Fruge, of Louisiana. March 2, 1830. Mr. Test, from the Committee on Private Land Claims, made the following report: Washington, Pr. by Duff Green, 1830. 2 p. (Rep. No. 258) DLC; NjR.   4852

---- John Glass.   Jan. 18, 1830.   Mr. Clay, from the Committee on the Public Lands, made the following report: Washington, Duff Green, 1830. 1 p. (Rep. No. 87) DLC; NjR.   4853

---- John Good.   March 29, 1830.   Read, and committed to a Committee of the Whole House to-morrow. Mr. McIntire, from the Committee of Claims, made the following report: Washington, Duff Green, 1830. 3 p. (Rep. No. 334) DLC; NjR. 4854

---- John H. Thomas.   March 30, 1830.   Mr. Pettis, from the Committee on Private Land Claims, made the following report: Washington, Duff Green, 1830.   1 p. (Rep. No. 336) DLC; NjR.   4855

---- John H. Wendal.   Jan. 26, 1830.   Mr. Forward, from the Committee on Military Pensions, made the following report: Washington, Duff Green, 1830.   1 p. (Rep. No. 119) DLC; NjR.   4856

---- John Hayner.   Jan. 29, 1830.   Mr. Whittlesey, from the Committee of Claims, made the following report: Washington, Duff Green, 1830. 1 p. (Rep. No. 135) DLC; NjR.   4857

---- John Heard, assignee of Amasa Davis.   March 4, 1830. Mr. Verplanck, from the Committee of Ways and Means, to which was referred the case of John Heard, surviving assignee of Amasa Davis, made the following report: Washington, Pr. by Duff Green, 1830. 2 p. (Rep. No. 270) DLC; NjR. 4858

---- John Lord.   February 10, 1830.   Mr. Goodenow, from the Committee on Revolutionary Claims, made the following report: Washington, Pr. by Duff Green, 1830. 1 p. (Rep. No. 179) DLC; NjR.   4859

---- John McDonogh.   Jan. 11, 1830.   Mr. Gurley, from the Committee on Private Land Claims, to which was referred the case of John McDonogh, made the following report: Washington, Duff Green, 1830. 1 p. (Rep. No. 67) DLC; NjR. 4860

---- John M'Iver.   April 14, 1830.   Read, and laid upon the table. Mr. Whittlesey, from the Committee of Claims, to which had been referred the case of John M'Iver, made the following report: Washington, Duff Green, 1830. 2 p. (Rep. No. 363) DLC; NjR.   4861

---- John Moffitt.   Jan. 18,
1830.   Mr. Dickinson, from the
Committee on Revolutionary
Claims, made the following report: Washington, Duff Green,
1830.   1 p. (Rep. No. 91) DLC;
NjR.   4862

---- John O. Lay.   March 8,
1830.   Read, and committed to a
Committee on the Whole House
to-morrow.   Mr. Whittlesey,
from the Committee of Claims,
to which was referred the case
of John O. Lay, made the following report: Washington, Pr. by
Duff Green, 1830.   2 p. (Rep.
No. 278) DLC; NjR.   4863

---- John P. Cox.   Jan. 4,
1830.   Read, and, with the bill,
committed to a Committee of the
Whole House to-morrow.   Mr.
Whittlesey, from the Committee
of Claims, to which was referred the bill from the Senate
for the relief of the representatives of John P. Cox, made the
following report: Washington,
Duff Green, 1830. 1 p. (Rep. No.
52) DLC; NjR.   4864

---- John Robinson.   Jan. 29,
1830.   Mr. Burges, from the
Committee on Revolutionary
Claims, to which the subject had
been referred, made the follow-
ing report: Washington, Duff
Green, 1830. 1 p. (Rep. No. 131)
DLC; NjR.   4865

---- John Rodgers.   Dec. 28,
1830.   Read twice, and committed to a Committee of the Whole
House to-morrow.   Mr. Wm. L.
Storrs, from the Committee on
Indian Affairs, to which was referred the petition of John Rodgers, made the following report:
Washington, Duff Green, 1830.
1 p. (Rep. No. 12) DLC; NjR.
                                         4866
---- John Sapp.   February 15,

1830.   Mr. Whittlesey, from the
Committee of Claims, made the
following report: Washington, Pr.
by Duff Green, 1830. 1 p. (Rep.
No. 192) DLC; NjR.   4867

---- John Teel.   Jan. 29,
1830.   Mr. Burges, from the
Committee on Revolutionary
Claims, made the following report: Washington, Duff Green,
1830.   3 p. (Rep. No. 132) DLC;
NjR.   4868

---- John Wilson--heirs of.
March 27, 1830.   Mr. Brown,
from the Committee on Revolutionary Claims, made the following report: Washington, Duff
Green, 1830.   1 p. (Rep. No.
333) DLC; NjR.   4869

---- A joint resolution for amending the Constitution of the United
States, in relation to the election
of President and Vice-President.
February 1, 1830. Read twice,
and committed to a Committee of
the Whole on the state of the Union.   Mr. M'Duffie submitted the
following joint resolution: [Wash-
ington, 1830] 5 p. (H. R.) DNA.
                                         4870
---- Joint resolution in relation
to the transmission of public documents printed by order of either
House of Congress. December 27,
1830.   Read twice, and ordered
to be engrossed, and read the
third time to-morrow. Mr. Johnson, of Kentucky, from the Committee on the Post Office and
Post Roads, reported the following joint resolution: [Washington,
1830] 1 p. (H. R.) DNA.   4871

---- Joint resolution proposing
an amendment of the Constitution,
relative to the re-eligibility of
the President of the United States.
December 22, 1830. Read twice,
and committed to the Committee
of the Whole House on the state

of the Union. Mr. McDuffie submitted the following joint resolution: [Washington, 1830] 1 p. (H. R.) DNA.   4872

---- A joint resolution relative to the re-printing of certain documents. May 17, 1830. Mr. Woodbury, from the Joint Committee on the Library, reported the following resolution; which was read; and passed to a second reading: [Washington, 1830] 2 p. (S. 6) DNA.   4873

---- Joint rules. April 6, 1830. Read, and laid upon the table. Washington, Duff Green, 1830. 1 p. (Res. No. 11) DLC; NjR.
4874
---- Jonathan Lincoln, Adm'r of Sam'l B. Lincoln.   Dec. 17, 1830. Mr. Whittlesey, from the Committee of Claims, made the following report: Washington, Duff Green, 1830. 1 p. (Rep. No. 1) DLC; NjR.   4875

---- Jonathan M. Blaisdell. Jan. 26, 1830.   Read, and laid upon the table.   Jan. 29, 1830. Committed to a Committee of the Whole House to-morrow. Mr. Gilmore, from the Committee on Ways and Means, to which was referred the case of Jonathan M. Blaisdell, made the following report: Washington, Duff Green, 1830.   11 p. (Rep. No. 137) DLC; NjR.   4876

---- Jonathan Taylor and others. Jan. 29, 1830. Mr. Whittlesey, from the Committee of Claims, made the following report: Washington, Duff Green, 1830. 2 p. (Rep. No. 133) DLC; NjR.   4877

---- Jonathan Walton and John J. De Graff. April 27, 1830. Mr. Verplanck, from the Committee of Ways and Means, to which

was referred the case of Jonathan Walton and Company, made the following report: Washington, Duff Green, 1830. 3 p. (Rep. No. 383) DLC; NjR.   4878

---- Joseph Falconer.   Jan. 18, 1830. Mr. Dickinson, from the Committee on Revolutionary Claims, made the following report: Washington, Duff Green, 1830.   2 p. (Rep. No. 92) DLC; NjR.   4879

---- Joseph Jeans. April 14, 1830. Mr. Whittlesey, from the Committee of Claims, made the following report: Washington, Duff Green, 1830. 1 p. (Rep. No. 360) DLC; NjR.   4880

---- Joseph Young.   Feb. 5, 1830. Mr. Young, from the Committee on the Post Office and Post Roads, made the following report: Washington, Duff Green, 1830.   1 p. (Rep. No. 164) DLC; NjR.   4881

---- Joshua Kennedy.   March 25, 1830. Mr. Pettis, from the Committee on Private Land Claims, made the following report: Washington, Duff Green, 1830.   1 p. (Rep. No. 327) DLC; NjR.   4882

---- Josiah H. Webb. February 10, 1830. Mr. Johnson of Kentucky, from the Committee on the Post Office and Post Roads, made the following report: Washington, Pr. by Duff Green, 1830. 2 p. (Rep. No. 183) DLC; NjR. 4883

---- Jotham Lincoln, administrator of Samuel B.   Feb. 1, 1830. Mr. Crane, from the Committee of Claims, made the following report: Washington, Duff Green, 1830.   3 p. (Rep. No. 139) DLC; NjR.   4884

---- Journal of the House of Representatives of the United States; being the first session of the twenty-first Congress, begun and held at the city of Washington, Dec. 7, 1829, and in the fifty-fourth year of the independence of the United States. Washington, Duff Green, 1829 [i. e. 1830] 988 p. DLC; NjR.   4885

---- Journal of the Senate of the United States of America: being the first session of the twenty-first Congress; begun and held at the city of Washington, Dec. 7, 1829, and in the fifty-fourth year of the independence of the said United States. Washington, Pr. by Duff Green, 1829 [i. e. 1830] 577 p. DLC; NjR.   4886

---- Journals of Congress, 1774 to 1788.   Feb. 25, 1830. Read, and laid upon the table. Mr. Goodenow submitted the following resolution: Washington, Duff Green, 1830. 1 p. (Rep. No. 6) DLC; NjR.   4887

---- Judah Alden.   Jan. 18, 1830. Mr. Dickinson, from the Committee on Revolutionary Claims, made the following report: Washington, Duff Green, 1830. 1 p. (Rep. No. 90) DLC; NjR.   4888

---- Judge Peck.   March 23, 1830. Read, and committed to the Committee of the Whole House on the state of the Union. Washington, Duff Green, 1830. 53 p. (Rep. No. 325) DLC; NjR.   4889

---- Judge Superior Court--Arkansas. (With bill H. R. No. 112)   Jan. 14, 1830.   Mr. Storrs, of New York, from the Committee on the Judiciary, to which the subject had been referred, made the following report: Washington, Duff Green, 1830. 19 p. (Rep. No. 80) DLC; NjR.   4890

---- Judicial terms--Southern District, New York, &c.   April 12, 1830. Read, and committed to a Committee of the Whole House to-morrow. Washington, Duff Green, 1830. 1 p. (Rep. No. 355) DLC; NjR.   4891

---- Lands for education. March 18, 1830.   Mr. Hunt, from the select committee to which the subject had been referred made the following report: Washington, Duff Green, 1830. 8 p. (Rep. No. 312) DLC; NjR. 4892

---- Lands of U. S. in Tennessee. Letter from the Secretary of the Treasury, transmitting information in relation to the vacant lands belonging to the United States in Tennessee.   Jan. 7, 1830. Read, and referred to a Select Committee. Washington, Pr. by Duff Green, 1830. 6 p. (Doc. No. 18) DLC; NjR.   4893

---- Lands to officers, &c. -- Virginia state line.   May 13, 1830. Printed by order of the House of Representatives. Washington, Duff Green, 1830. 6 p. (Rep. No. 404) DLC; NjR. 4894

---- Laws for the District of Columbia. March 3, 1830. Read, and laid upon the table. Mr. Powers, from the Committee for the District of Columbia, to which the subject had been referred, made the following report: Washington, Pr. by Duff Green, 1830. 112 p. (Rep. No. 269) DLC; NjR.   4895

---- Legislature of Alabama. Memorial of the Legislature of the state of Alabama for relief to purchasers of public lands.

February 15, 1830. Read, and referred to the Committee of the Whole House to which is committed the bill (No. 49) to dispose of reverted and relinquished lands. Washington, Pr. by Duff Green, 1830. 4 p. (Rep. No. 204) DLC; NjR. 4896

---- Legislature of Georgia-- Tariff of 1828. Jan. 18, 1830. Read, and laid upon the table. Washington, Duff Green, 1830. 1 p. (Rep. No. 98) DLC; NjR. 4897

---- Letter from the Postmaster General relative to the case of John Fitzgerald, late Postmaster at Pensacola, removed, &c. April 30, 1830. Read, and ordered to be printed. Washington, Pr. by Duff Green, 1830. 1 p. (Doc. No. 133) DLC; NjR. 4898

---- Letter from the president of the Chesapeake and Ohio Canal Company, with proceedings of a meeting of that company, to the Hon. E. F. Chambers, chairman of the Committee on the District of Columbia. May 24, 1830. Read, and laid upon the table. Washington, Pr. by Duff Green, 1830. 3 p. (Doc. No. 144) DLC; NjR. 4899

---- Letter from the president of the Washington Turnpike Company, in relation to the recent survey of two routes for a road from Washington City to Frederick, in Maryland. February 11, 1830. Washington, Pr. by Duff Green, 1830. 4 p. (Doc. No. 54) DLC; NjR. 4900

---- Letter from the Secretary of State, transmitting a list of the name of persons to whom patents have been granted for the invention of any new and useful art or machine, manufacture, or composition of matter, or improvement thereon, from the 1st day of Jan. 1829, to the 1st day of Jan. 1830. Jan. 3, 1830. Read, and laid upon the table. Washington, Pr. by Duff Green, 1830. 33 p. (Doc. No. 16) DLC; NjR. 4901

---- Letter from the Secretary of the Navy, to Hon. R. Y. Hayne, chairman of the Committee on Naval Affairs, covering a plan for a Navy Peace Establishment. February 18, 1830. Laid on the table by Mr. Hayne, and ordered to be printed. Washington, Pr. by Duff Green, 1830. 12 p. (Doc. No. 58) DLC; NjR. 4902

---- Letter from the Secretary of the Navy, transmitting a statement of contracts made by the commissioners of the Navy during the year 1829. Jan. 19, 1830. Read, and laid upon the table. Washington, Pr. by Duff Green, 1830. 8 p. (Doc. No. 30) DLC; NjR. 4903

---- Letter from the Secretary of the Treasury to the Hon. S. Smith, chairman of the Committee on Finance. With statements showing the amounts of duties on articles enumerated in bill of Senate, No. 72, "to modify certain duties on merchandise imported, and to repeal the duties on others. March 10, 1830. Laid upon the table, and ordered to be printed. Washington, Pr. by Duff Green, 1830. 4 p. (Doc. No. 85) DLC; NjR. 4904

---- Letter from the Secretary of the Treasury transmitting his annual report on the finances. December 16, 1830. Read, and referred to the Committee of Ways and Means. Washington, Pr. by Duff Green, 1830. 143 p. (Doc. No. 7) DLC; NjR. 4905

---- Letter from the Secretary of the Treasury, with statements showing the appropriations, receipts, and expenditures and balances for each year, from 1789 to 1829, inclusive. April 13, 1830. Laid on the table by the chairman of the Committee on Finance, and ordered to be printed. Washington [Pr. by Duff Green] 1830. 7 p. (Doc. No. 90) DLC; NjR.   4906

---- Letter from the Secretary of the Treasury, with statements showing the appropriations, receipts, and expenditures and balances for each year, from 1789 to 1829, inclusive. April 13, 1830. Laid upon the table by the chairman of the Committee on Finance, and ordered to be printed. Washington, Pr. by Duff Green, 1830. 7 p. (Doc. No. 123) DLC; NjR.   4907

---- Letter from the Secretary of War to the chairman of the Committee on Internal Improvements, with the result of the examination of Back Creek, &c. In Senate, April 26, 1830. Laid on the table by Mr. Bernard, and ordered to be printed. December 21, 1830. Printed by order of the House of Representatives. 5 p. (Doc. No. 13) DLC; DeGE; NjR.   4908

---- ---- Washington, Pr. by Duff Green, 1830. 5 p. (Doc. No. 131) DLC; NjR.   4909

---- Letter from the Secretary of War, transmitting a survey and estimate for the improvement of the Harbor of Chicago, on Lake Michigan. March 2, 1830. Read, and referred to the Committee of the Whole House to which is committed the Bill H. R. No. 304. Washington, Pr. by Duff Green, 1830. 4 p. (Doc.

No. 69) DLC; NjR.   4910

---- Letter from the Secretary of War transmitting copies of the reports of H. M. Shreve and R. Delafield, on the improvement of the navigation of the Mississippi and Ohio rivers. December 16, 1830. Read, and referred to the Committee of the Whole House to which is referred the bill (H. R. no. 458) to amend the several acts authorizing the registering and granting licenses to steamboats and to provide for the better security of the lives of passengers on board of vessels propelled in whole or in part by steam. Washington, Pr. by Duff Green, 1830. 12 p. (Doc. No. 9) DLC; NjR.   4911

---- Levy Court--Calvert County. February 8, 1830. Read, and committed to a Committee of the Whole House tomorrow. Mr. Ramsey, from the Committee of Claims, to which was referred the case of the Levy Court of Calvert County, in the state of Maryland, made the following report: Washington, Pr. by Duff Green, 1830. 9 p. (Doc. No. 178) DLC; NjR.   4912

---- Lewis Anderson. Dec. 22, 1830. Mr. Whittlesey, from the Committee of Claims, made the following report: Washington, Duff Green, 1830. 1 p. (Rep. No. 8) DLC; NjR.   4913

---- Lewis Marks and Alexander O. Brodie. Feb. 5, 1830. Mr. Cambreleng, from the Committee on Commerce, made the following report: Washington, Duff Green, 1830. 1 p. (Rep. No. 160) DLC; NjR.   4914

---- Lewis Rouse. Jan. 25, 1830. Mr. McIntire, from the Committee of Claims, to which

had been referred the case of
Lewis Rouse, made the following
report: Washington, Duff Green,
1830. 4 p. (Rep. No. 110) DLC;
NjR.   4915

---- Lieutenant Charles Wilkes,
Jr. March 17, 1830. Mr.
White, from the Committee on
Naval Affairs, to which was re-
ferred the case of Lieutenant
Charles Wilkes, Jr. made the
following report: Washington,
Duff Green, 1830. 7 p. (Rep.
No. 305) DLC; NjR.   4916

---- Light-House--Point Lookout.
Letter from the Secretary of the
Treasury, transmitting the information required, in relation to
the erection of a beacon-light or
small light-house on Point Lookout.   Feb. 16, 1830. Read,
and laid upon the table. Washington, Pr. by Duff Green, 1830.
6 p. (Doc. No. 64) DLC; NjR.
                              4917
---- List of committees of the
Senate of the United States for
the second session, twenty-first
Congress, 1830-'31. December
31, 1830. Washington, Duff
Green, 1830. 3 p. (Doc. No. 15)
DLC; PU.   4918

---- List of reports to be made
to the House of Representatives
at the second session of the
twenty-first Congress by the executive departments. Prepared
by the clerk in obedience to a
standing order of the House of
Representatives. December 6,
1830. Washington, Pr. by Duff
Green, 1830. 19 p. (Doc. No.
1) DLC; NjR.   4919

---- Lobster fishery.   Jan.
13, 1830. Read, and laid upon
the table. Mr. Buchanan, from
the Committee on the Judiciary,
to which the subject had been referred, made the following re-

port: Washington, Duff Green,
1830. 1 p. (Rep. No. 79) DLC;
NjR.   4920

---- Loomis & Bassett. February 12, 1830. Mr. C. P. White,
from the Committee on Naval Affairs, to which was referred the
case of Loomis and Bassett,
made the following report:
Washington, Pr. by Duff Green,
1830. 3 p. (Rep. No. 190)
DLC; NjR.   4921

---- Ludlow's and Roberts' Lines.
To accompany bill of H. R. No.
141.   Jan. 20, 1830.   Re-
printed by order of the House of
Representatives. Washington,
Duff Green, 1830. 19 p. (Rep.
No. 103) DLC; NjR.   4922

---- Mail route--Louisville, Kentucky, to St. Louis. Resolution of the General Assembly of
the state of Indiana, relative to
the Western Mail Stage route,
from Louisville, in Kentucky to
St. Louis, in Missouri.   Feb.
8, 1830.   Read, and referred to the Committee on Internal Improvement. Washington,
Duff Green, 1830. 1 p. (Rep.
No. 173) DLC; NjR.   4923

---- Mail route Zaneville to
Florence. Letter from the Postmaster General, communicating
the information required by a
resolution of the House of Representatives of the 24th ultimo,
respecting the transportation of
the United States' mail from
Zaneville, Ohio, to Florence, in
Alabama. March 9, 1830. Read,
and laid upon the table. Washington, Pr. by Duff Green, 1830. 2
p. (Doc. No. 76) DLC; NjR.
                              4924
---- Maison Rouge and de Bas-
trop's Claims. April 6, 1830.
Reprinted by order of the House
of Representatives. Washington,

Duff Green, 1830. 12 p. (Rep.
No. 347) DLC; NjR.   4925

---- Major John Roberts.
Dec. 21, 1830. Mr. Dickinson, from the Committee on Revolutionary Claims, to which was
referred the case of Major John
Roberts, made the following report: Washington, Duff Green,
1830. 1 p. (Rep. No. 6) DLC;
NjR.   4926

---- Manuel del Barco.   Jan.
4, 1830. Read, and laid upon
the table. Mr. Buchanan, from
the Committee on the Judiciary,
to which had been referred the
case of Manuel del Barco, made
the following report: Washington, Duff Green, 1830. 1 p.
(Rep. No. 51) DLC; NjR.   4927

---- Marine hospital--Charles-
ton, S. C.   Feb. 4, 1830.
Mr. Cambreleng, from the Committee on Commerce, to which
the subject had been referred
made the following report: Washington, Duff Green, 1830. 4 p.
(Rep. No. 152) DLC; NjR. 4928

---- Marine rail-way, &c. Message from the President of the
United States in reply to a resolution of the House of Representatives, in relation to the erection
of a marine rail-way at the Navy
yard at Pensacola, &c. &c. May
13, 1830. Read, and referred
to the Committee on Naval Affairs. Washington [Pr. by Duff
Green] 1830. 10 p. (Doc. No.
101) DLC; NjR.   4929

---- Martha Yeomans.   Feb.
4, 1830. Mr. Dickinson, from
the Committee on Revolutionary
Claims, made the following report: Washington, Duff Green,
1830. 1 p. (Rep. No. 154) DLC;
NjR.   4930

---- Massachusetts claim.
Feb. 22, 1830. Read, and laid
upon the table, and ordered to be
printed. Washington, Pr. by
Duff Green, 1830. 5 p. (Rep.
No. 223) DLC; NjR.   4931

---- Massachusetts. Memorial
of inhabitants of Hampshire County, Massachusetts, in relation to
the Indian tribes. March 17, 1830.
Referred to the Committee of the
Whole House on the state of the
Union. Washington, Duff Green,
1830. 2 p. (Rep. No. 310) DLC;
NjR.   4932

---- Matilda B. Dunn.   February
19, 1830. Read, and laid upon
the table. February 20, 1830.
Committed to a Committee of the
Whole House tomorrow. Mr.
Drayton, from the Committee on
Military Affairs, made the follow-
ing report: Washington, Pr. by
Duff Green, 1830. 5 p. (Rep. No.
216) DLC; NjR.   4933

---- Matthews Flournoy and R.
J. Ward.   February 24, 1830.
Mr. Pettis, from the Committee
on Private Land Claims, made
the following report: Washington,
Pr. by Duff Green, 1830. 1 p.
(Rep. No. 225) DLC; NjR. 4934

---- Maysville Road. Message
from the President of the United
States returning to the House of
Representatives the enrolled bill
entitled "An act authorizing a
subscription of stock in the Maysville, Washington, Paris, and
Lexington Turnpike Road Company" with his objections thereto. May 27, 1830. Read, and
to-morrow at 12 o'clock assigned for the re-consideration
of the bill. Washington [Pr. by
Duff Green] 1830. 22 p. (Doc.
No. 113) DLC; NjR.   4935

---- Medal of the President liberator of Colombia. Feb. 9, 1830. Read, considered, and concurred in by the House. Mr. Archer, from the Committee on Foreign Affairs, to which was referred the message from the President of the United States, of the 19th ultimo, submitted the following report: Washington, Duff Green, 1830. 1 p. (Rep. No. 170) DLC; NjR. 4936

---- Memorial of a committee appointed by the corporation remonstrating against the grant of any of the public grounds in Washington for the endowment of any institution within or without its limits. April 20, 1830. Laid on the table, and ordered to be printed. Washington, Pr. by Duff Green, 1830. 2 p. (Doc. No. 126) DLC; NjR. 4937

---- Memorial of a deputation from the Creek nation of Indians, complaining that certain acts of the state of Alabama are in violation of the acts and ammunities guaranteed to their nation by treaty stipulations, with the United States, and praying relief. February 9, 1830. Ordered to lie on table and be printed. Washington, Pr. by Duff Green, 1830. 5 p. (Doc. No. 53) DLC; NjR. 4938

---- Memorial of American Colonization Society. The Committee to whom was referred the memorial of the American Colonization Society, have instructed their chairman to request the House to cause the memorial, and its accompanying documents, to be printed. March 6, 1830. Printed by order of the House of Representatives. Washington, Pr. by Duff Green, 1830. 29 p. (Rep. No. 277) DLC; NjR. 4939

---- Memorial of Charles Bull-

finch, on the subject of the Hall of the House of Representatives. Jan. 25, 1830. Referred to the Committee on the Public Buildings. Washington, Duff Green, 1830. 11 p. (Rep. No. 123) DLC; NjR. 4940

---- Memorial of Charles Cramer, et al. March 8, 1830. Referred to the Committee of Ways and Means. Washington, Pr. by Duff Green, 1830. 5 p. (Rep. No. 279) DLC; NjR. 4941

---- Memorial of citizens of Delaware residing in Wilmington, expressive of the sentiments entertained by them on the claims of the Indians to certain lands within the territorial limits of the United States. February 15, 1830. Referred to the Committee on Indian Affairs, and ordered to be printed. Washington, Pr. by Duff Green, 1830. 3 p. (Doc. No. 56) DLC; NjR. 4942

---- Memorial of Farnifold Green. Jan. 6, 1830. Referred to the Committee on Naval Affairs. Printed by order of the House of Representatives. Washington, Duff Green, 1830. 45 p. (Rep. No. 57) DLC; NjR. 4943

---- Memorial of inhabitants of Brunswick, Maine, praying that the southern Indians may not be removed from their present places of abode, without their free consent. March 15, 1830. Ordered to lie on the table and be printed. Washington, Pr. by Duff Green, 1830. 1 p. (Doc. No. 92) DLC; NjR. 4944

---- Memorial of inhabitants of Burlington County, New Jersey, praying that the Indians may be protected in their rights by the government: March 3, 1830. Ordered to lie on the table and

to be printed. Washington, Pr.
by Duff Green, 1830. 1 p. (Doc.
No. 77) DLC; NjR.   4945

---- Memorial of inhabitants of
Kennebunk, Maine, praying that
the Indians may be protected in
their rights, and in the possession of their lands, &c. March
17, 1830. Ordered to lie on the
table, and be printed. Washington, Pr. by Duff Green, 1830. 1
p. (Doc. No. 96) DLC; NjR.
                           4946
---- Memorial of inhabitants of
Sharon, Connecticut, praying that
government would extend its protection over certain Indian tribes,
&c. March 22, 1830. Ordered
to lie on the table and be printed.
Washington, Pr. by Duff Green,
1830. 3 p. (Doc. No. 101)
DLC; NjR.   4947

---- Memorial of Joshua Kennedy, of Mobile, praying Congress to indemnify him for losses
sustained during the Creek War.
March 15, 1830. Referred to the
Committee on Indian Affairs, and
ordered to be printed. Washington, Pr. by Duff Green, 1830.
4 p. (Doc. No. 94) DLC; NjR.
                           4948
---- Memorial of ladies, inhabitants of Pennsylvania, praying
that the Indians may be protected
in their rights and in the possession of their lands. March 3,
1830. Ordered to lie upon the
table, and be printed. Washington, Pr. by Duff Green, 1830.
2 p. (Doc. No. 76) DLC; NjR.
                           4949
---- Memorial of sundry citizens
of Farmington, Connecticut, praying that the Indians may be protected in their just rights, &c.
February 27, 1830. Referred to
the Committee on Indian Affairs,
and ordered to be printed. Washington, Pr. by Duff Green, 1830.
4 p. (Doc. No. 74) DLC;

NjR.   4950

---- Memorial of sundry inhabitants of Boston, Massachusetts,
that so much of the post office
laws as require the mail to be
transported on the Sabbath day,
may be repealed. April 13,
1830. Referred to the Committee on the Post Office and Post
Road and ordered to be printed.
Washington, Pr. by Duff Green,
1830. 4 p. (Doc. No. 124)
DLC; NjR.   4951

---- Memorial of sundry inhabitants of Salem, Massachusetts,
praying that duty on imported
molasses may be reduced to five
cents per gallon, and that a drawback to the same amount may be
allowed in the exportation of spirits distilled therefrom. March
15, 1830. Read, and ordered
to lie on the table, and be printed. Washington, Pr. by Duff
Green, 1830. 5 p. (Doc. No.
93) DLC; NjR.   4952

---- Memorial of sundry persons
engaged in ship building at Philadelphia, praying that a drawback
be granted on the exportation of
materials used in ship building.
April 20, 1830. Referred to the
Committee on Commerce, and
ordered to be printed. Washington, Pr. by Duff Green, 1830.
4 p. (Doc. No. 125) DLC; NjR.
                           4953
---- ... Memorial of the American Colonization Society... March
6, 1830. Printed by order of
the House of Representatives...
[Washington, D.C., 1830] 29 p.
MdBJ; OCl.   4954

---- Memorial of the Baltimore
and Ohio Rail Road Company, for
permission to extend a lateral
branch of their road to some
point within the District of Columbia.   Dec. 14, 1830.

Referred to the Committee on Roads and Canals. Dec. 15, 1830--Ordered to be printed. Washington, Duff Green, 1830. 2 p. (Doc. No. 5) DLC; PU.

4955

---- Memorial of the Baptist General Association of Pennsylvania for Missionary Purposes, approving the plan of settling the Indians to the west of the Mississippi, &c. February 2, 1830. Read, and ordered to be printed, and laid upon the table. Washington, Pr. by Duff Green, 1830. 2 p. (Doc. No. 64) DLC; NjR.

4956

---- Memorial of the Board of Managers of the New York Baptist Missionary Society, in favor of colonizing the Indians east of the Rocky Mountains, &c. February 19, 1830. Referred to the Committee on Indian Affairs, and ordered to be printed. Washington, Pr. by Duff Green, 1830. 1 p. (Doc. No. 59) DLC; NjR.

4957

---- Memorial of the Chamber of Commerce, and certain importing merchants of Philadelphia praying that the excess of duty under the tariff of 1828, beyond that of former tariffs... be remitted. March 12, 1830. Referred to the Committee on Finance, and ordered to be printed. Washington, Pr. by Duff Green, 1830. 3 p. (Doc. No. 88) DLC; NjR.

4958

---- Memorial of the Chamber of Commerce of New York, praying that the duties on teas and coffee may be reduced after the 31st March, 1832. March 15, 1830. Ordered to lie on the table and be printed. Washington, Pr. by Duff Green, 1830. 2 p. (Doc. No. 91) DLC; NjR.

4959

---- Memorial of the General Assembly of Indiana, praying

that the Indian title to certain lands within that state be extinguished, and that all the Indians residing therein be induced to emigrate westward. March 4, 1830. Ordered to lie on the table and be printed. Washington, Pr. by Duff Green, 1830. 1 p. (Doc. No. 79) DLC; NjR.

4960

---- Memorial of the General Assembly of Indiana, respecting the removal of the Indians beyond the Mississippi. March 8, 1830. Read, and committed to the Committee of the Whole House on the state of the Union. Washington, Pr. by Duff Green, 1830. 1 p. (Rep. No. 291) DLC; NjR.

4961

---- Memorial of the inhabitants of Chester County, Pennsylvania, praying that the act passed at the last session, for the removal of the Indians beyond the Mississippi, may be repealed, and that no treaty made under that law be confirmed. Dec. 31, 1830. Referred to the Committee on Indian Affairs, and ordered to be printed. Washington, Duff Green, 1830. 2 p. (Doc. No. 16) DLC; PU.

4962

---- Memorial of the inhabitants of Rahway, Woodbridge, &c., New Jersey praying that the government would extend its protection to the Southern Indians, &c. February 26, 1830. Laid on the table, and ordered to be printed. Washington, Pr. by Duff Green, 1830. 2 p. (Doc. No. 73) DLC; NjR.

4963

---- Memorial of the ladies of Burlington, New Jersey, praying that Congress would protect the Indians... February 23, 1830. Ordered to lie on the table. Washington, Pr. by Duff Green, 1830. 2 p. (Doc. No. 66) DLC;

NjR.   4964

---- Memorial of the legislative
council of the territory of Michigan, asking for an additional
body to the territory legislature.
Dec. 16, 1829. Referred
to the Committee on the Territories.   Feb. 1, 1830. Bill
reported, No. 189. Washington, Duff Green, 1830. 2 p.
(Rep. No. 141) DLC; NjR. 4965

---- Memorial of the manufacturers of salt in the county of
Kenhawa, Virginia, against the
repeal of the duty on imported
salt. April 30, 1830. Ordered
to be printed. Washington, Pr.
by Duff Green, 1830. 18 p.
(Doc. No. 134) DLC; NjR. 4966

---- Memorial of the officers of
the Revolutionary army who
served prior to March, 1780.
Dec. 17, 1830. Read, and
referred to a Select Committee,
consisting of Messrs. Verplanck,
Forward, Deberry, Campbell,
Hawkins, Cooper, and Everett.
Dec. 21, 1830. Printed by
order of the House of Representatives. Washington, Duff Green,
1830. 4 p. (Rep. No. 4) DLC;
NjR.   4967

---- Memorial of the president
and directors of the Chesapeake
and Ohio Canal Company, May
24, 1830. Read, and laid upon
the table. [Washington, Pr. by
Duff Green, 1830] 10 p. CSt;
CtY; DBRE; DLC; IU; M; MB;
MBAt; MH; MWA; MiU-T; N; NN;
NRU; NjP; P.   4968

---- Memorial of the representatives of the yearly meeting of
Friends or Quakers of Baltimore,
praying that government would extend its protection over certain
Indian tribes, &c. March 22,
1830. Ordered to lie on the
table and be printed. Washington, Pr. by Duff Green, 1830.
1 p. (Doc. No. 100) DLC; NjR.
                               4969

---- Memorial of William Kelly,
of Alabama, attorney of John
Smith T. in relation to the claim
of the said John Smith T. for
land from the United States. February 23, 1830. Referred to the
Committee on the Public Lands,
and ordered to be printed. Washington, Pr. by Duff Green, 1830.
4 p. (Doc. No. 65) DLC; NjR.
                               4970

---- Memorials of the Cherokee
Indians, signed by their representatives, and by 3,085 individuals of the Nation.   Feb. 15,
1830. Presented, and laid upon
the table. March 15, 1830.
Committed to the Committee of
the Whole House on the state of
the Union. Washington, Duff
Green, 1830. 9 p. (Rep. No.
311) DLC; NjR.   4971

---- Mesheck Browning.   Feb.
5, 1830.   Mr. Whittlesey,
from the Committee of Claims,
made the following report: Washington, Duff Green, 1830. 1 p.
(Rep. No. 155) DLC; NjR. 4972

---- Message from the President
of the United States, in compliance with a resolution of the Senate of the 3d March, shewing:
1st, quantity of public land appropriated to the several states;
2d, amount of disbursements
made within several states; and
3d, amount of exports from 1789
to 1828.   May 31, 1830. Read,
and ordered to be printed. Washington, Pr. by Duff Green, 1830.
7 p. (Doc. No. 145) DLC; NjR.
                               4973

---- Message from the President
of the United States to the two
Houses of Congress, at the commencement of the second session
of the twenty-first Congress.

Dec. 7, 1830. Printed by order of the Senate of the United States. Washington, Duff Green, 1830. 251 p. (Doc. No. 1) DLC; PU. 4974

---- Message from the President of the United States to the two houses of Congress at the commencement of the second session of the twenty-first Congress. December 7, 1830. Read, and committed to a Committee of the Whole House on the state of the Union. Washington, Pr. by Duff Green, 1830. 251 p. (Doc. No. 2) DLC; NjR. 4975

---- ---- Washington, Pr. by Duff Green, 1830. 24 p. DLC. 4976

---- Message from the President of the United States, with a report from the officers detailed to make a survey of the Dry Tortugas, and recommending it as an important station for Naval purposes, &c. March 30, 1830. Referred to the Committee on Naval Affairs. April 1, 1830. Ordered to be printed. Washington, Pr. by Duff Green, 1830. 5 p. (Doc. No. 111) DLC; NjR. 4977

---- Miami Exporting Company. April 19, 1830. Mr. Crane, from the Committee of Claims, made the following report: Washington, Duff Green, 1830. 6 p. (Rep. No. 373) DLC; NjR. 4978

---- Michael Lewis. Jan. 26, 1830. Mr. Miller, from the Committee on Naval Affairs, made the following report: Washington, Duff Green, 1830. 1 p. (Rep. No. 116) DLC; NjR. 4979

---- Miles King. Letter from the Secretary of the Navy transmitting the information required by a resolution of the House of Representatives of the 15th instant, in relation to the accounts of Miles King. May 28, 1830. Read, and laid upon the table. Washington [Pr. by Duff Green] 1830. 104 p. (Doc. No. 115) DLC; NjR. 4980

---- ---- Mr. Tazewell's opinion to Mr. King, in the bread case. [To be annexed to the report from the Secretary of the Navy on the 27th May, 1830, in relation to the accounts of Miles King.] Washington [Pr. by Duff Green] 1830. 7 p. (Doc. No. 115) DLC; NjR. 4981

---- Military and invalid pensioners. Letter from the Secretary of War, in reply to a resolution of the House of Representatives, respecting military and invalid pensioners. Feb. 10, 1830. Read, and laid upon the table. Washington, Pr. by Duff Green, 1830. 2 p. (Doc. No. 58) DLC; NjR. 4982

---- Military peace establishment. Jan. 18, 1830. Mr. Vance, from the Committee on Military Affairs, to which the subject had been referred, made the following report: Washington, Duff Green, 1830. 4 p. (Rep. No. 85) DLC; NjR. 4983

---- Militia of the United States. Letter from the Secretary of War, transmitting abstract of the returns of the Militia of the United States. Feb. 5, 1830. Read, and laid upon the table. Washington, Pr. by Duff Green, 1830. 9 p. (Doc. No. 50) DLC; NjR. 4984

---- Ministerial duties--Navy Department. (To accompany bill H. R. 169) Letter from the Secretary of the Navy, to the chairman of the Committee on naval affairs, in relation to the ministerial duties of the officers of

the Navy Department.   Jan.
28, 1830.   Laid before the House
by the Chairman of the Committee, and ordered to be printed.
Washington, Pr. by Duff Green,
1830.   2 p. (Doc. No. 39) DLC;
NjR.   4985

---- Mint of the United States.
Letter from the Secretary of the
Treasury transmitting statements
showing the operations of the
mint during the year 1829.   May
26, 1830.   Referred to the Committee of Ways and Means.
Washington [Pr. by Duff Green]
1830.   7 p. (Doc. No. 112)
DLC; NjR.   4986

---- Mint United States. March 5,
1830.   Mr. McDuffie, from the
Committee of Ways and Means, to
which the subject had been referred,
made the following report: Washington, Pr. by Duff Green, 1830.
1 p. (Rep. No. 272) DLC; NjR.
                              4987
---- Mississippi.   Resolution of
the legislature of the state of
Mississippi, upon the subject of
the tariff, Colonization Society,
and internal improvements.
March 15, 1830.   Read, and laid
upon the table. Washington, Duff
Green, 1830.   2 p. (Rep. No.
300) DLC; NjR; PPL.   4988

---- Mr. Barnard, from the Committee on the Militia, to whom was
referred the bill from the House of
Representatives, entitled "An act
for the better organization of the
militia of the District of Columbia,"
reported the same with the following amendment: May 22, 1830.
[Washington, 1830] 49 p. (H.R.
235) DNA.   4989

---- Mr. Cambreleng, from the
Committee on Commerce, to
which was recommitted the bill,
entitled "A bill to regulate the
foreign and coasting trade on the

northern and northwestern frontiers of the United States, and
for other purposes," reported
the same with amendments. December 30, 1930.   Read twice,
and committed to the Committee
of the Whole House on the state
of the Union. [Washington,
1830] 2 p. (H.R. 376) DNA.
                              4990
---- Mr. Cambreleng, from the
Committee on Commerce, to
which was referred the bill from
the Senate, (No. 26) entitled "An
act allowing the duties on foreign
merchandise imported into Louisville, Pittsburg, Cincinnati, St.
Louis, Natchez, and Nashville,
to be secured and paid at those
places," reported the same with
the following amendments: April
22, 1830.   Committed to the
Committee of the Whole House
on the state of the Union. [Wash-
ington, 1830] 5 p. (S. 26) DNA.
                              4991
---- Mr. Chilton's resolutions,
upon the subject of internal improvements, distribution of surplus revenue, and reduction of
duties on necessaries of life.
February 9, 1830. Read, and
laid on the table. [Washington,
1830] 2 p. (H.R. 6) DNA. 4992

---- Mr. Clay, from the Committee on Public Lands, to which
had been referred the bill from
the Senate, (No. 55,) entitled,
"An act to alter and amend an
act to set apart and dispose of
certain public lands, for the encouragement of the cultivation of
the vine and olive;" reported the
same with the following amendment.   April 22, 1830. [Wash-
ington, 1830] 1 p. (S. 55) DNA.
                              4993
---- Mr. Clay, from the Committee on the Public Lands, to
whom was referred the bill from
the Senate, entitled "An act for
the relief of purchasers of pub-

lic lands," reported the same with an amendment. March 4, 1830. Read, and committed to a Committee of the Whole House to which is committed the bill (H. R. No. 49) to dispose of reverted and relinquished lands. [Washington, 1830] 4 p. (S. 28) DNA. 4994

---- Mr. Daniel, submitted the following, which, when the "bill establishing Circuit Courts, and abridging the jurisdiction of the District Courts, in the districts of Indiana, Illinois, Missouri, Mississippi, the Eastern district of Louisiana, and the Southern district of Alabama," shall be taken up for consideration, he will move as an amendment. February 10, 1830. Read, and committed to the Committee of the Whole House to which the said bill is committed. [Washington, 1830] 2 p. (H. R. 37) DNA. 4995

---- Mr. De Witt, from the Committee on Retrenchment, submitted the following resolution: Jan. 25, 1830. Read, and postponed until Thursday next, 28th instant. Washington, Duff Green, 1830. 2 p. (Rep. No. 113) DLC; NjR. 4996

---- Mr. Drayton, from the Committee on Military Affairs, reported the following amendments to the bill to regulate the pay and emoluments of the officers of the Army of the United States, and for other purposes. January 19, 1830. Read twice, and committed to a Committee of the Whole House to-morrow. December 16, 1830. Reprinted by order of the House of Representatives. December 24, 1830. [Washington, 1830] 6 p. (H. R. 130) DNA. 4997

---- Mr. Drayton, from the Committee on Military Affairs,

to which was referred the bill from the Senate, entitled "An act to authorize the payment of the claim of the State of Massachusetts for certain services of her militia during the late war," reported the same with the following amendments: April 24, 1830. Read, and committed to the Committee of the Whole House on the state of the Union. [Washington, 1830] 2 p. (S. 31) DNA. 4998

---- Mr. Mercer, from the select committee, to which the subject had been referred, submitted, for the consideration of the House, the following resolutions: April 7, 1830. Read twice, and committed to the Committee of the Whole House on the state of the Union. [Washington, 1830] 2 p. (H. R. 8) DNA. 4999

---- Mr. Miller, from the Committee on Naval Affairs, to which was referred the bill from the Senate, entitled "An act to establish the office of Surgeon General of the Navy," reported the same with the following amendments: April 29, 1830. [Washington, 1830] 2 p. (S. 95) DNA. 5000

---- Mr. Pettis submitted the following, which, when the bill (H. R. No. 96) to graduate the price of the public lands shall be taken up for consideration, he will move as an amendment. December 10, 1830. [Washington, 1830] 3 p. (H. R. 96) DNA. 5001

---- Mr. Richardson submitted the following, which, when the bill (H. R. No. 86) to construct a national road from Buffalo, in the State of New York, passing by the seat of Government, in the District of Columbia, to New Orleans, in the state of Louisiana, shall be taken up for consideration, he will move as an amendment. February 25, 1830. [Washington, 1830] 1 p. (H. R. 86) DNA.   5002

---- Mr. Rowan, from the Committee on the Judiciary, reported the bill, entitled "An act concerning judgments in the Courts of the United States within the State of New York," with the following amendment: April 10, 1830. [Washington, 1830] 2 p. (H. R. 331) DNA.   5003

--- Mr. Sevier submitted the following, which, when the bill from the Senate, No. 19, entitled "An act to grant pre-emption rights to settlers on the Public Lands," shall be taken up for consideration, he will move as an amendment: February 22, 1830. Read, and laid on the table. [Washington, 1830] 1 p. (S. 19) DNA.   5004

---- Mr. Wilde submitted the following, which, when the bill [H. R. No. 243,) supplementary to the act, entitled "An act to authorize the President of the United States to run and mark a line dividing the Territory of Florida from the State of Georgia," shall be taken up for consideration, he will move as an amendment. January 19, 1831. Read, and committed to the Committee of the Whole House on the state of the Union to which the said bill is committed. [Washington, 1830] 2 p. (H. R. 243) DNA.   5005

---- Mr. Woodbury, from the Committee on Commerce, reported the bill entitled, "An act for the more effectual collection of the impost duties," with the following amendments: May 17, 1830. [Washington, 1830] 1 p. (H. R. 164) DNA.   5006

---- Mr. Woodbury, from the Committee on Commerce, to which was referred the bill from the House of Representatives, entitled "An act making appropriations for building light-houses, light-boats, beacons, and monuments, placing buoys, and for improving harbors, and directing surveys," reported the same with the following amendments: April 20, 1830. [Washington, 1830] 5 p. (H. R. 304) DNA.   5007

---- Moritz Furst.   Jan. 18, 1830. Read, and committed to a Committee of the Whole House to-morrow. Mr. Whittlesey, from the Committee of Claims, to which was referred the case of Moritz Furst, made the following report: Washington, Duff Green, 1830. 5 p. (Rep. No. 84) DLC; NjR.   5008

---- Moses Adams.   May 11, 1830. Read, and committed to a Committee of the Whole House to-morrow. Mr. Forward, from the Committee on Military Pensions, made the following report: Washington, Duff Green, 1830. 4 p. (Rep. No. 402) DLC; NjR.
5009
---- Motion by Mr. Barton, concerning appointments and removals by the executive. March 23, 1830--submitted. March 26, 1830--considered, and postponed to, and made the order of the day for the 5th of April next. Washington, Pr. by Duff Green, 1830. 1 p. (Doc. No. 103) DLC; NjR.   5010

---- Mounted force.   April 8, 1830. Printed by order of the House of Representatives. Washington, Duff Green, 1830. 1 p. (Rep. No. 350) DLC; NjR. 5011

---- Nancy Davis.   March 22, 1830. Mr. Young, from the

Committee on Revolutionary
Claims, to which was referred
the case of Nancy Davis, made
the following report: Washington,
Duff Green, 1830. 1 p. (Rep.
No. 324) DLC; NjR.   5012

---- Nathaniel Bird. March 11,
1830. Mr. Burges, from the
Committee on Revolutionary
Claims, to which was referred
the petition of Nathaniel Bird,
made the following report: Washington, Pr. by Duff Green, 1830.
1 p. (Rep. No. 286) DLC; NjR.
                                     5013
---- Nathaniel Childers.   Jan.
26, 1830. Read, and committed
to a Committee of the Whole
House to-morrow. Mr. Whittlesey, from the Committee of
Claims, to which had been referred the case of Nathaniel Childers, made the following report:
Washington, Duff Green, 1830.
2 p. (Rep. No. 121) DLC; NjR.
                                     5014
---- ---- March 29, 1830. Mr.
Whittlesey, from the Committee
of Claims, made the following report: Washington, Duff Green,
1830.   4 p. (Rep. No. 335) DLC;
NjR.   5015

---- Nathaniel Standish.   May 25,
1830. Mr. Bates, from the Committee on Military Pensions,
made the following report: Washington, Duff Green, 1830. 1 p.
(Rep. No. 413) DLC; NjR. 5016

---- Navigation Ohio and Mississippi Rivers. (To accompany
bill H. R. No. 440) April 23,
1830. Mr. Wickliffe, from the
select committee to which the
subject had been referred, made
the following report: Washington,
Duff Green, 1830. 4 p. (Rep.
No. 379) DLC; NjR.   5017

---- Navy hospital, Norfolk, and
Asylum, Philadelphia. Docu-

ments to accompany bill H. R.
No. 170.   Navy Department,
Jan. 18, 1830. Washington, Pr.
by Duff Green, 1830. 18 p. (Doc.
No. 40) DLC; NjR.   5018

---- Navy United States--three
schooners.   (To accompany bill
H. R. No. 507.) December 22,
1830. Printed by order of the
House of Representatives. Washington, Pr. by Duff Green, 1830.
3 p. (Doc. No. 14) DLC; NjR.
                                     5019
---- Navy yard--Portsmouth, Virginia. Letter from the Secretary
of the Navy in reply to a resolution of the House of Representatives of the 29th ultimo, requiring information of the probable
loss of property to the United
States, by changing the site of
the Navy Yard at Portsmouth,
Virginia, for one more eligible.
May 6, 1830. Read, and laid upon the table. Washington [Pr. by
Duff Green] 1830. 2 p. (Doc.
No. 98) DLC; NjR.   5020

---- New Jersey.   Petition of
inhabitants of Rahway and Wood-
bridge, &c. &c. in relation to
the Cherokee and other Indians.
March 1, 1830. Referred to the
Committee of the Whole on bill
No. 287. Washington, Pr. by
Duff Green, 1830. 2 p. (Rep.
No. 256) DLC; NjR.   5021

---- New York.   Memorial of the
board of managers of the New
York Babtist [sic] Missionary Society. March 2, 1830. Referred
to the Committee of the Whole
House on the state of the Union on
bill No. 287. Washington, Pr.
by Duff Green, 1830. 2 p. (Rep.
No. 247) DLC; NjR.   5022

---- Officers and soldiers of the
Revolution. Letter from the Secretary of War, in reply to a resolution of the House of Represent-

atives of the 14th instant, in relation to the number of the surviving Revolutionary Officers, &c.
&c.   Jan. 19, 1830.   Read,
and laid upon the table. Washington, Pr. by Duff Green, 1830.
2 p. (Doc. No. 32) DLC; NjR.
                                    5023

---- Official documents, etc. in
relation to the Bank of the United
States. House of Representatives
of the United States, April 13,
1830. Steubenville, Pr. by subscription, by Jas. Wilson, [1830]
60 p. CSmH; MH-BA; WHi.
                                    5024

---- Ohio and Mississippi River.
Memorial of sundry citizens of
Louisville, Kentucky, praying for
the improvement of the navigation
of the Ohio and Mississippi
Rivers. Washington, Duff Green,
1830. 2 p. (Rep. No. 337) DLC;
NjR.   5025

---- Ohio. Memorial of citizens
of the county of Miami, in the
state of Ohio, in relation to the
Indian Tribes. March 17, 1830.
Referred to the Committee of the
Whole House on the state of the
Union. Washington, Duff Green,
1830. 1 p. (Rep. No. 302) DLC;
NjR.   5026

---- ---- Memorial of inhabitants of Brown County in the state
of Ohio, in relation to the Cherokee Indians. February 22, 1830.
Read, and laid upon the table.
Washington, Pr. by Duff Green,
1830. 2 p. (Rep. No. 263) DLC;
NjR.   5027

---- ---- Memorial of the ladies
of Steubenville, Ohio. Against
the forcible removal of the Indians without the limits of the
United States. February 15,
1830. Read, and ordered that
it lie one day upon the table.
Washington, Pr. by Duff Green,
1830. 2 p. (Rep. No. 209)

DLC; NjR.   5028

---- ---- Petition of inhabitants
of Greene, Trumbull County,
Ohio, on behalf of the Indians.
February 22, 1830. Read, and
laid upon the table. Washington,
Pr. by Duff Green, 1830. 2 p.
(Doc. No. 265) DLC; NjR.   5029

---- ---- Resolution of the Ohio
legislature, on the subject of
domestic manufactures. March
15, 1830. 1 p. (Rep. No. 299)
DLC; NjR.   5030

---- ---- Titles to Sec. 8, 11,
26, 29: Thirteenth Township, &c.
&c. May 24, 1830. Read, and
laid upon the table. Mr. Irvine,
from the Committee on the Public Lands, to which the subject
had been referred, made the following report: Washington, Duff
Green, 1830. 2 p. (Rep. No.
411) DLC; NjR.   5031

---- Operations of the Mint--
1829. Message from the President of the United States, transmitting a report of the Director
of the Mint, for the year 1829.
Feb. 9, 1830.   Read, and
laid upon the table. Washington,
Pr. by Duff Green, 1830. 2 p.
(Doc. No. 56) DLC; NjR.   5032

---- Oppressive duties. Jan.
27, 1830.   Read, and committed to a Committee of the
Whole House on the state of the
Union. Mr. Drayton submitted
the following resolution: Washington, Duff Green, 1830. 1 p.
(Res. No. 4) DLC; NjR.   5033

---- Organizing militia. Jan.
27, 1830. With Bill No. 167.
Mr. Thompson, of Georgia, from
the Committee on the Militia,
made the following report: Washington, Duff Green, 1830. 4 p.
(Rep. No. 126) DLC; NjR.   5034

---- ... P. S. Du Ponceau - flag of American silk... Mr. Spencer, of New York, from the Committee on Agriculture, to which was referred the letter of Peter S. Du Ponceau, Esq., presenting to the House a flag of American silk and manufacture, made the following report... [Washington, 1830] 9 p. DLC; DeGE; NjR.
5035

---- Parker McCobb. May 7, 1830. Mr. Verplanck, from the Committee of Ways and Means, made the following report: Washington, Duff Green, 1830. 1 p. (Rep. No. 395) DLC; NjR.
5036

---- Passengers arriving in the U.S. in 1829. Letter from the Secretary of State transmitting the annual statement of the number and description of passengers arriving in the United States on ship board during the year ending on the 30th of September, 1829. May 28, 1830. Read, and laid upon the table. Washington [Pr. by Duff Green] 1830. 39 p. (Doc. No. 114) DLC; NjR. 5037

---- Patent Office. Jan. 27, 1830. Referred to the Committee on the Judiciary. Washington, Pr. by Duff Green, 1830. 14 p. (Doc. No. 38) DLC; NjR. 5038

---- Patents to issue to foreigners, not residents. March 15, 1830. Read, and committed to a Committee of the Whole House to-morrow. Mr. Buchanan, from the Committee on the judiciary, to which the subject had been referred, made the following report: Washington, Pr. by Duff Green, 1830. 1 p. (Rep. No. 292) DLC; NjR. 5039

---- Patrick Green. April 19, 1830. Mr. Johnson, of Kentucky, from the Committee on

the Post Office and Post Roads, made the following report: Washington, Duff Green, 1830. 3 p. (Rep. No. 372) DLC; NjR.
5040

---- Pay, &c. of Naval Officers and agents. Letter from the Secretary of the Navy transmitting the information required by a resolution of the House of Representatives of the 4th of February last, respecting the pay, emoluments, and allowances to officers and agents in the Naval service of the United States. May 29, 1830. Read, and laid upon the table. Washington [Pr. by Duff Green] 1830. 93 p. (Doc. No. 121) DLC; NjR. 5041

---- Pay, &c. Officers Marine Corps. May 25, 1830. Printed by order of the House of Representatives. Washington [Pr. by Duff Green] 1830. 15 p. (Doc. No. 107) DLC; NjR. 5042

---- Penitentiary--Washington City. Message from the President of the United States, transmitting the annual report of the inspectors of the penitentiary in the District of Columbia. February 1, 1830. Read, and laid upon the table. Washington, Pr. by Duff Green, 1830. 12 p. (Doc. No. 46) DLC; NjR. 5043

---- Pennsylvania--Chamber of Commerce, Philadelphia. Reduction of duties on tea and coffee. March 8, 1830. Referred to the Committee of the Whole House on the state of the Union. Washington, Pr. by Duff Green, 1830. 2 p. (Rep. No. 283) DLC; NjR.
5044

---- Pennsylvania--dealers in tea and coffee, Philadelphia. March 8, 1830. Referred to the Committee of the Whole House on the state of the Union. Washington, Pr. by Duff Green, 1830.

2 p. (Rep. No. 282) DLC; NjR. 5045

---- Pennsylvania. Memorial of inhabitants of lower Dublin, Philadelphia County, in relation to the Southern Indians. March 1, 1830. Referred to the Committee of the Whole House on the state of the Union on bill 287. Washington, Pr. by Duff Green, 1830. 2 p. (Rep. No. 254) DLC; NjR. 5046

---- ---- Memorial of inhabitants of Montgomery County, in relation to the Cherokee Indians. March 1, 1830. Referred to the Committee of the Whole House on bill No. 287. Washington, Pr. by Duff Green, 1830. 2 p. (Rep. No. 255) DLC; NjR. 5047

---- Memorial of inhabitants of Montgomery County, in relation to the Cherokees and other Indians. February 22, 1830. Read, and laid upon the table. Washington, Pr. by Duff Green, 1830. 2 p. (Rep. No. 261) DLC; NjR. 5048

---- ---- Memorial of ship carpenters, smiths, rope makers, and others, employed or connected in ship building, in the city of Philadelphia. April 19, 1830. Referred to the Committee of the Whole House on the state of the Union. Washington, Duff Green, 1830. 5 p. (Rep. No. 369) DLC; DeGE; NjR. 5049

---- ---- Memorial of the Baptist General Association of Pennsylvnia for missionary purposes (with bill H. R. No. 287) March 2, 1830. Read, and committed to the Committee of the Whole House on the state of the Union. Washington, Pr. by Duff Green, 1830. 2 p. (Rep. No. 253) DLC; NjR. 5050

---- ---- Memorial of the inhabitants of Pittsburgh, relative to protecting Indians in Georgia.

Feb. 22, 1830. Read, and laid upon the table for one day. Washington, Pr. by Duff Green, 1830. 7 p. (Rep. No. 265) DLC; NjR. 5051

---- Pensacola Bar. Feb. 5, 1830. Ordered to be printed. Memoir and estimate on the improvement of the Bar of Pensacola. (Transmitting to the House of Representatives by the Secretary of War. Washington, Pr. by Duff Green, 1830. 4 p. (Doc. No. 48) DLC; NjR. 5052

---- Percia Tupper. March 22, 1830. Mr. Lea, from the Committee of Claims, made the following report: Washington, Duff Green, 1830. 3 p. (Rep. No. 322) DLC; NjR. 5053

---- Peter Bargy, Jr. et al. March 2, 1830. Mr. Whittlesey, from the Committee of Claims, made the following report: Washington, Pr. by Duff Green, 1830. 3 p. (Rep. No. 247) DLC; NjR. 5054

---- Peter Bonnefit. March 9, 1830. Read, and laid upon the table. Mr. Archer, from the Committee on Foreign Affairs, to which was referred the case of Peter Bonnefit, made the following report: Washington, Pr. by Duff Green, 1830. 2 p. (Rep. No. 284) DLC; NjR. 5055

---- Peter Gasney. Jan. 8, 1830. Mr. Whittlesey, from the Committee of Claims, to which was referred the case of Peter Gasney, made the following report: Washington, Duff Green, 1830. 1 p. (Rep. No. 65) DLC; NjR. 5056

---- Peter Peck. May 19, 1830. Read, and with an accompanying bill for his relief, committed to the Committee of the Whole

House to which is committed the bill for the relief of John Sapp. Mr. Whittlesey, from the Committee of Claims, made the following report: Washington, Duff Green, 1830. 1 p. (Rep. No. 408) DLC; NjR.   5057

---- Peter Yarnell and Samuel Mitchell. May 11, 1830. Read, and committed to the Committee of the Whole House to which is committed the report of the Committee of Claims on the petition of John O. Lay. Mr. Whittlesey, from the Committee of Claims, to which had been referred the case of Peter Yarnell and Samuel Mitchell, made the following report: Washington, Duff Green, 1830. 1 p. (Rep. No. 400) DLC; NjR.   5058

---- Petition of citizens of Louisville, Kentucky, praying for an appropriation for improving the navigation of the Ohio River. Dec. 24, 1830.   Referred to the Committee on Internal Improvements. Washington, Duff Green, 1830. 3 p. (Rep. No. 11) DLC; NjR.   5059

---- Petition of sundry remanufacturers of iron, residing in Philadelphia, praying that the duty on certain descriptions of iron may be so modified as to afford to them an adequate protection in their business. March 2, 1830. Referred to the Committee on Manufactures, and ordered to be printed. Washington, Pr. by Duff Green, 1830. 7 p. (Doc. No. 75) DLC; NjR.   5060

---- Philip and Eliphalet Greely. April 26, 1830. Mr. Gilmore, from the Committee of Ways and Means, made the following report: Washington, Duff Green, 1830. 1 p. (Rep. No. 382) DLC; NjR.   5061

---- Philip Slaughter. February 26, 1830. Mr. Goodenow, from the Committee on Revolutionary Claims, to which was referred the case of Philip Slaughter, made the following report: Washington, Pr. by Duff Green, 1830. 1 p. (Rep. No. 239) DLC; NjR. 5062

---- A plan of Congress hall, with the names of the members and officers, numbered so as to shew their seats:--21st Congress. 2d session. [Washington, D. C.] Wm. Greer, pr., 1830. 1 p. DLC.   5063

---- Post Office establishment. April 14, 1830. Committed to the Committee of the Whole House on the state of the Union. Mr. Conner, from the Committee on the Post Office and Post Roads, made the following report: Washington, Duff Green, 1830. 6 p. (Rep. No. 361) DLC; NjR. 5064

---- Pre-emption to certain persons in Florida. To accompany bill H. R. No. 206. February 5, 1830. Reprinted by order of the House of Representatives. Mr. Isacks, from the Committee on the Public Lands, to which the subject had been referred, made the following report: Washington, Duff Green, 1830. 1 p. (Rep. No. 162) DLC; NjR.   5065

---- Presidential election. February 1, 1830. Read, and referred to the Committee of the Whole House on the state of the Union, to which the above mentioned resolution is committed, Mr. Haynes submitted the following, which, when the joint resolution submitted by Mr. McDuffie, for amending the Constitution of the United States, relative to the election of President and Vice President, shall be taken up for consideration, he will

move as an amendment. [Washington, 1830] 2 p. (H. R.) DNA.
5066

---- Print rules--Jefferson's manual, &c. April 15, 1830. Read, and laid upon the table. Mr. DeWitt submitted the following resolution: Washington, Duff Green, 1830. 1 p. (Res. No. 13) DLC; NjR.
5067

---- Private land claims--Florida. Letter from the Secretary of the Treasury, transmitting a report (final) on private land claims in East Florida. Jan. 15, 1830. Read and referred to the Committee on Public Lands. Feb. 5, 1830. Printed by order of the House of Representatives. Washington, Pr. by Duff Green, 1830. 159 p. (Doc. No. 51) DLC; NjR.
5068

---- Privateer Pension Fund. Feb. 9, 1830. Mr. Dorsey, from the Committee on Naval Affairs, made the following report: Washington, Duff Green, 1830. 8 p. (Rep. No. 175) DLC; NjR.
5069

---- Protest of North Carolina against the Hopewell Treaty with the Cherokees, &c. March 29, 1830. Laid on the table by Mr. White, and ordered to be printed. Washington, Pr. by Duff Green, 1830. 6 p. (Doc. No. 108) DLC; NjR.
5070

---- [January term, 1830] The Providence Bank vs. Thos. G. Pitman, general treasurer of the state of Rhode Island et al. Argument of council on the part of the state. [Washington? 1830] 22 p. RHi.
5071

---- Public buildings--Arkansas. Jan. 26, 1830. Mr. Cowles, from the Committee on the Territories, to which the subject had been referred, made the following report: Washington, Duff Green, 1830. 1 p. (Rep. No. 118) DLC; NjR.
5072

---- Public Buildings. Jan. 4, 1830. Read, and laid upon the table. Washington, Pr. by Duff Green, 1830. 1 p. (Doc. No. 15) DLC; NjR.
5073

---- Public land sold during the year ending on 30th September, 1830. Letter from the Secretary of the Treasury transmitting a report from the Commissioner of the General Land Office of the lands sold in the several states and territories during the year ending on the 30th September, 1830, &c. &c. December 31, 1830. Read, and laid upon the table. Washington, Pr. by Duff Green, 1830. 2 p. (Doc. No. 19) DLC; NjR.
5074

---- Public ministers and consuls. (To accompany bill H. R. Nos. 274 and 275) February 22, 1830. Mr. Archer, from the Committee on Foreign Affairs, to which the subject had been referred, made the following report: Washington, Pr. by Duff Green, 1830. 6 p. (Rep. No. 220) DLC; NjR.
5075

---- R. S. Hackley. March 16, 1830. Mr. Archer, from the Committee on Foreign Affairs, made the following report: Washington, Pr. by Duff Green, 1830. 11 p. (Rep. No. 298) DLC; NjR.
5076

---- Rapport sur la culture et manufacture de la soie, fait... par M. Spencer, au nom du Comite, d'agriculture, le 12 mars, 1830. Philadelphia, Kay, 1830. 20 p. PPAmP.
5077

---- Ratio of Representation, &c. To accompany Bill H. R. No. 167.

Jan. 27, 1830. Mr. Storrs, from the Select Committee to which the subject had been referred, made the following report: Washington, Duff Green, 1830. 3 p. (Rep. No. 127) DLC; NjR. 5078

---- Receipts and expenditures--Post Office Department. Letter from the Postmaster General transmitting, in compliance with a resolution of the House of Representatives of the 26th instant, a statement showing the receipts and expenditures of the Post Office Department for the last two quarters of 1829 [i. e. 1828] and the first quarter of 1829 [sic] May 29, 1830. Read, and laid upon the table. Washington [Pr. by Duff Green] 1830. 2 p. (Doc. No. 118) DLC; NjR. 5079

---- Register of debates in Congress, comprising the leading debates and incidents...Washington, D. C., Gales & Seaton, 1830-1837. 10 vols. in 20. CSmH. 5080

---- A register of officers and agents, civil, military, and naval, in the service of the United States, on the 30th of September, 1829; together with the names, force, and condition of all the ships and vessels belonging to the United States, and when and where built. Prepared at the Department of State... Washington City, Pr. by William A. Davis, Pennsylvania Avenue, 1830. 148, 224 p. DeGE; MB. 5081

---- Re-manufacture of iron. Petition of inhabitants of the city and county of Philadelphia concerned in the re-manufacture of iron. March 2, 1830. Referred to the Committee of the Whole House on the state of the Union. Washington, Pr. by Duff Green, 1830. 6 p. (Rep. No. 266) DLC;

NjR. 5082

---- Removal of Indians. February 24, 1830. Accompanied by a bill (No. 287) which was twice read and committed to a Committee of the Whole House on the State of the Union...and ten thousand copies of report and bill ordered to be printed. Mr. Bell, from the Committee on Indian Affairs, made the following report: Washington, Pr. by Duff Green, 1830. 32 p. (Rep. No. 227) DLC; NjR. 5083

---- Remove Indians--west of the Mississippi. Message of the President of the United States transmitting, in compliance with a resolution of the House of Representatives, of the 18th ultimo, a report in relation to the expenses of removing and supporting the Indians west of the Mississippi. April 14, 1830. Read, and laid upon the table. Washington [Pr. by Duff Green] 1830. 9 p. (Doc. No. 91) DLC; NjR. 5084

---- Report and remonstrance of the legislature of Georgia in relation to the Indian tribes within that state, and acts of certain states, extending jurisdiction over the Indian tribes within their limits, &c. In Senate of the United States, March 8, 1830. Ordered to be printed. Washington, Pr. by Duff Green, 1830. 13 p. (Doc. No. 98) DLC; GU-De; NjR. 5085

--- Report and resolves of the legislature of Massachusetts, relative to the claims of that state for militia services during the late war. February 22, 1830. Read, and referred to the Committee on Military Affairs, and ordered to be printed. Washington, Pr. by Duff Green, 1830. 6 p. (Doc. No. 60) DLC; NjR. 5086

---- Report from the Postmaster General in compliance with a resolution of the Senate, showing the number of deputy postmasters removed by that department between 4th March, 1829, and 22d March, 1830. March 24, 1830. Read, and ordered to be printed. Washington, Pr. by Duff Green, 1830. 1 p. (Doc. No. 106) DLC; NjR.
5087

---- Report from the Postmaster General in reply to certain resolutions of the Senate of the 10th April, relating to that department. May 5, 1830. Read, and ordered to be printed. Washington, Pr. by Duff Green, 1830. 19 p. (Doc. No. 136) DLC; NjR.   5088

---- Report from the Secretary of the Navy, in compliance with a resolution of the Senate, concerning the subject of dispensing with the Marine Corps in the naval service of the United States. March 24, 1830. Read, and referred to the Committee on Naval Affairs, and ordered to be printed. Washington, Pr. by Duff Green, 1830. 20 p. (Doc. No. 102) DLC; NjR.   5089

---- Report from the Secretary of the Treasury in compliance with a resolution of the Senate of the 17th instant, in relation to the expenditures of the government in 1828 and 1829. April 21, 1830. Read, and ordered to be printed. Washington, Pr. by Duff Green, 1830. 2 p. (Doc. No. 128) DLC; NjR.   5090

---- Report from the Secretary of the Treasury (in compliance with a resolution of the Senate, of the 29th December, 1828) respecting the relative value of gold and silver, &c. May 4, 1830. Read, and ordered to be printed, and that 1,000 additional copies be sent to the Senate.

Washington, Pr. by Duff Green, 1830. 118 p. (Doc. No. 135) DLC; NjR.   5091

---- Report from the Secretary of the Treasury (in compliance with a resolution of the Senate, of the 29th of December, 1828) respecting the relative value of gold and silver, &c. May 29, 1830. Printed by order of the House of Representatives. Washington [Pr. by Duff Green] 1830. 118 p. (Doc. No. 117) DLC; DeGE; NjR.   5092

---- Report from the Secretary of the Treasury in compliance with a resolution of the Senate of the 22d January, 1829, in relation to the "sum of about one million dollars" described in the annual report in the finances as "funds not considered as effective" &c. March 10, 1830. Read, and ordered to be printed. Washington, Pr. by Duff Green, 1830. 11 p. (Doc. No. 84) DLC; NjR.   5093

---- Report from the Secretary of the Treasury in compliance with a resolution of the Senate of the 26th March, relative to land returned as "Swamp Land" in Florida, &c. May 5, 1830. Read, and ordered to be printed. Washington, Pr. by Duff Green, 1830. 4 p. (Doc. No. 138) DLC; NjR.   5094

---- Report from the Secretary of the Treasury in compliance with a resolution of the Senate of the 23d of April, with statements shewing the amount of expenditures for 1828 and 1829 incurred for outfits of ministers, chargé d'affaires, treaties with Indians, &c., for which no appropriations were made. May 31, 1830. Read, and ordered to be printed. Washington, Pr. by Duff Green,

1830. 11 p. (Doc. No. 146)
DLC; NjR.   5095

---- Report from the Secretary
of the Treasury (in compliance
with a resolution of the Senate)
showing the number of subordin-
ate officers of the customs removed from office since the fourth
of March last, and the numbers
increased and diminished in each
district. April 8, 1830. Read,
and ordered to be printed. Washington, Pr. by Duff Green, 1830.
2 p. (Doc. No. 120) DLC; NjR.
                                 5096

---- Report from the Secretary
of the Treasury, in part compliance with a resolution of the Senate, showing the expenditures for
1828 and 1829, under each head
of appropriation, &c. April 13,
1830. Read, and ordered to be
printed. Washington, Pr. by
Duff Green, 1830. 25 p. (Doc.
No. 122) DLC; NjR.   5097

---- Report from the Secretary
of the Treasury in reply to two
resolutions of the Senate, with
the copy, bond, and account of
money advanced to the late Marshal of Key West, and copy of
bond, by Collector of that port,
with gross amount of revenue in
that district for 1828 and 1829.
April 1, 1830. Read, and ordered to be printed. Washington,
Pr. by Duff Green, 1830. 5 p.
(Doc. No. 112) DLC; NjR. 5098

---- Report from the Secretary
of the Treasury, with statements
of the amount that would be re-
turnable, should the bill to refund, in certain cases, the difference between the tariff of 1828
and that previously existing, become a law.   Dec. 20, 1830.
Read, and ordered to be printed.
Washington, Duff Green, 1830. 4
p. (Doc. No. 10) DLC; PU.
                                 5099

---- Report from the Secretary
of War in answer to a resolution
of the Senate, in relation to desertion on the army.   February
22, 1830. Washington, Pr. by
Duff Green, 1830. 16 p. (Doc.
No. 62) DLC; NjR.   5100

---- Report from the Secretary
of War in reply to a resolution
of the Senate of the 25th of January last, showing the progress
made in civilizing the Indians for
the last eight years, and their
present condition.   1830, March
26--read.   1830, March 30--
ordered to be printed, with the
accompanying documents, and two
letters from Abram A. Heard
and Calab Starr, which were laid
on the table the 29th inst. by Mr.
White. Washington, Pr. by Duff
Green, 1830. 22 p. (Doc. No.
110) DLC; NjR.   5101

---- ...Report from the Secretary of War... shewing the result
of an examination, made by order
of that department, of the route
for a road from Washington to
Fredricktown by way of New Market, and also by Rockville.
[Washington, 1830] 6 p. [Senate
Doc. 44]   5102

---- Report of Joint Committee
and resolution of the legislature
of Maine, on the subject of the
claims of that state on account of
militia services during the late
war.   March 29, 1830. Ordered
to lie on the table and be printed.
Washington, Pr. by Duff Green,
1830. 4 p. (Doc. No. 107) DLC;
NjR.   5103

---- Report of the Committee of
the U.S. House of Representatives
on the petition against the transportation of the Sunday mails.
Philadelphia, Pub. by J. Marot.
A Waldie, pr. [1830] 1 p. DLC.
                                 5104

---- Report of the Committee on Commerce and Navigation... Mr. Cambreleng, from the Committee on Commerce, submitted the following report... [New York, Pr. by J. M. Danforth, for the merchants of New York, 1830] 63 p. DeGE. 5105

---- Report of the Secretary of the Navy, in reply to a resolution of the Senate, relative to the mode of relieving United States' vessels on foreign stations, and the means taken for the return to the United States of seamen whose terms of service expire abroad, &c. Dec. 29, 1830. Read, and ordered to be printed. Washington, Duff Green, 1830. 2 p. (Doc. No. 14) DLC; PU. 5106

---- Report of the Secretary of the Treasury, in reply to a resolution of the Senate relative to procuring a site for, and building a custom house and warehouse at Mobile. March 9, 1830. Read, and referred to the Committee of Commerce, and ordered to be printed. Washington, Pr. by Duff Green, 1830. 2 p. (Doc. No. 82) DLC; NjR. 5107

---- Report of the Secretary of the Treasury in reply to a resolution of the Senate, showing the amount received from sales of public land since 1st January, 1828, and expenses of each land office. March 10, 1830. Read, and ordered to be printed. Washington, Pr. by Duff Green, 1830. 7 p. (Doc. No. 84) DLC; NjR. 5108

---- Report of the Secretary of the Treasury, on the state of the finances, for 1830. December 16, 1830. Read, and ordered to be printed, and that fifteen hundred additional copies be printed for the use of the Senate. Washington, Duff Green, 1830. 143 p.

(Doc. No. 6) DLC; PU. 5109

---- Report of the Secretary of War in reply to a resolution of the Senate of the 24th of February last, relative to the barracks of the United States at Greenbush, New York, and the inexpediency of preserving them, &c. March 8, 1830. Read, and ordered to be printed. Washington, Pr. by Duff Green, 1830. 2 p. (Doc. No. 81) DLC; NjR. 5110

---- Report (on) so much of the President's message as relates to the commerce of the United States with foreign nations, the amendment of the laws to prevent smuggling and the establishment of warehouses... [New York, Pr. by J. M. Danforth, 1830] 63 p. MH-BA. 5111

---- ... Report: the Committee on finance, to which was referred a resolution of the 30th December, 1829, directing the committee to inquire into the expediency of establishing an uniform national currency for the United States, and to report thereon to the Senate... [Washington, 1830] 7 [1] p. CSmH; DLC. 5112

---- Reservation--Seneca tribe of Indians. Letter from the Secretary of War, transmitting information, in relation to the wishes of the Seneca tribe of Indians to sell a reservation of land, called the Seneca Reservation, in the state of Ohio. Feb. 3, 1830. Referred to the Committee on Indian Affairs. Washington, Pr. by Duff Green, 1830. 3 p. (Doc. No. 47) DLC; NjR. 5113

---- Resolution directing the clerks of the District and Superior Courts of the United States to transmit to the Department of State all returns of enumerations of the inhabitants of the United States, on file in their respective offices. May 22, 1830. Mr. Grundy, introduced the following resolution; which was read and passed to a second reading: [Washington, 1830] 1 p. (S. 7) DNA. 5114

---- Resolution for obtaining the aggregate returns of former enumerations of the population of the United States. May 22, 1830. Read. [Washington, 1830] 1 p. (H. R. 3) DNA. 5115

---- Resolution granting the use of the books in the Library of Congress, to the Heads of Departments, to certain Officers of Congress, and to Ex-Presidents of the United States. January 4, 1830. Read, and passed to a second reading. [Washington, 1830] 1 p. (H. R. 2) DNA. 5116

---- Resolution of the General Assembly of Ohio, declaring the tariff law of 1828 to be constitutional, and calculated to protect the industry of the country against the policy and legislation of foreign nations, and concurring with the resolution of Pennsylvania on the same subject. March 15, 1830. Ordered to lie on the table and be printed. Washington, Pr. by Duff Green, 1830. 1 p. (Doc. No. 90) DLC; NjR. 5117

---- Resolution of the legislature of Indiana stating that certain alternate sections of land on the margin of the Wabash and Erie Canal fell within Indian reservations, and praying that a law be passed granting other sections in lieu thereof. March 1, 1830. Referred to the Committee on Roads and Canals. March 17, 1830. Bill reported (No. 135) and resolution ordered to be printed. Washington, Pr. by

Duff Green, 1830. 2 p. (Doc. No. 97) DLC; NjR. 5118

---- Resolution proposing an amendment to the Constitution of the United States, as it respects the election of President and Vice President of the United States. March 15, 1830. Referred to a select committee, consisting of Messrs. Benton, Webster, Hayne, Tazewell, and Woodbury. March 23, 1830. Reported without amendment. [Washington, 1830] 4 p. (S. 4) DNA. 5119

---- Resolution proposing an amendment to the Constitution of the United States, as it respects the periods to which any person can be elected President of the United States. December 29, 1830. Agreeably to notice given, Mr. Dickerson asked and obtained leave to bring in the following resolution; which was read, and passed to a second reading. [Washington, 1830] 1 p. (S. 1) DNA. 5120

---- Resolution relative to printing and distributing Public Documents. January 6, 1830, Agreeably to notice given, Mr. Woodbury asked and obtained leave to bring in the following Resolution; which was read, and passed to a second reading. January 7, 1830, Read a second time, and referred to Committee on Contingent Fund. February 9, Reported with the following amendment: [Washington, 1830] 7 p. (S. 3) DNA. 5121

---- Resolution requiring annual reports to be made to Congress, in relation to applications for pensions. March 31, 1830. Read twice, and referred to the Committee on Pensions. 2 p. (H. R. 3) DNA. 5122

---- Resolved, That the bill
from the House of Representatives, entitled "An act to provide
for taking the fifth Census or
enumeration of the inhabitants of
the United States," do pass, with
the following amendments: March
1830. [Washington, 1830] 5 p.
(H. R. 116) DNA.   5123

---- Retrenchment. March 18,
1830. Read, and laid upon the
table. Mr. Forward submitted
the following resolutions: Washington, Duff Green, 1830. 1 p.
(Rep. No. 8) DLC; NjR.   5124

---- Richard G. Morriss. March
6, 1830. Mr. Burges, from the
Committee on Revolutionary
Claims, to which was referred
the case of Richard G. Morriss,
made the following report: Washington, Pr. by Duff Green, 1830.
2 p. (Rep. No. 274) DLC; NjR.
                                5125
---- Richard Hardesty. May 12,
1830. Read, and committed to a
Committee of the Whole House
to-morrow. Mr. Whittlesey,
from the Committee of Claims,
made the following report: Washington, Duff Green, 1830. 2 p.
(Rep. No. 403) DLC; NjR. 5126

---- Richard Livingston.
Feb. 9, 1830. Mr. Dickinson,
from the Committee on Revolutionary Claims, made the following report: Washington, Duff
Green, 1830. 2 p. (Rep. No.
172) DLC; NjR.   5127

---- Richard W. Steele. March
23, 1830. Mr. Foster, from
the Committee on Private Land
Claims, to which had been referred the case of Richard W.
Steele, made the following report:
Washington, Duff Green, 1830.
1 p. (Rep. No. 326) DLC; NjR.
                                5128
---- Richard Wall.   Jan. 25,

1830. Read, and committed to
a Committee of the Whole House
to-morrow. Mr. Goodenow, from
the Committee on Revolutionary
Claims, to which was referred
the case of Richard Wall, made
the following report: Washington,
Duff Green, 1830. 2 p. (Rep.
No. 111) DLC; NjR.   5129

---- Road--Chicot County to Little Rock. February 22, 1830.
Mr. Johnson of Kentucky, from
the Committee on the Post Office and Post Roads, made the
following report: Washington,
Pr. by Duff Green, 1830. 2 p.
(Rep. No. 218) DLC; NjR. 5130

---- Road--Memphis and Tuscumbia (with bill H. R. No. 354).
March 15, 1830. Mr. Johnson,
of Kentucky, from the Committee on the Post Office and Post
Roads, to which the subject had
been referred, made the following report: Washington, Pr. by
Duff Green, 1830. 1 p. (Rep.
No. 293) DLC; NjR.   5131

---- Road--Uniontown, Pittsburg,
Presque Isle. February 15,
1830. Read, and laid upon the
table. Mr. Hemphill, from the
Committee on Internal Improvements, to which the subject had
been referred, made the following report: Washington, Pr. by
Duff Green, 1830. 2 p. (Rep.
No. 196) DLC; NjR.   5132

---- Roanoke Inlet. March 19,
1830. Read, and referred to the
Committee on Commerce. Mr.
William B. Shepard, from the
select committee to which the
subject had been referred, made
the following report: Washington, Duff Green, 1830. 4 p.
(Rep. No. 317) DLC; NjR. 5133

---- ---- Mr. William B. Shepard, from the select committee

to which was referred memorials, &c. from the state of North Carolina, in relation to the navigation of Roanoke Inlet, submitted the following resolution. 1830. 1 p. (Res. No. 9) DLC; NjR.
5134

---- Robert A. Forsythe. March 10, 1830. Mr. Whittlesey, from the Committee of Claims, to which was referred the case of Robert A. Forsythe, made the following report: Washington, Pr. by Duff Green, 1830. 2 p. (Rep. No. 285) DLC; NjR.
5135

---- Robert Eaton. March 18, 1830. Mr. Gilmore, from the Committee of Ways and Means, to which was referred the case of Robert Eaton, made the following report: Washington, Duff Green, 1830. 1 p. (Rep. No. 309) DLC; NjR.
5136

---- Robert Kaine, of Buffalo, N.Y. March 31, 1830. Mr. Lent, from the Committee of Claims, made the following report: Washington, Duff Green, 1830. 1 p. (Rep. No. 340) DLC; NjR.
5137

---- Robert Smart. April 15, 1830. Mr. McIntire, from the Committee of Claims, to which had been referred the case of Robert Smart, made the following report: Washington, Duff Green, 1830. 3 p. (Rep. No. 366) DLC; NjR.
5138

---- Roger Enos. April 5, 1830. Mr. Verplanck, from the Committee of Ways and Means, made the following report: Washington, Duff Green, 1830. 1 p. (Rep. No. 345) DLC; NjR.
5139

---- Salaries--judges of Michigan. March 17, 1830. Mr. Angel, from the Committee on the Territories, to which the subject

had been referred, made the following report: Washington, Duff Green, 1830. 3 p. (Rep. No. 304) DLC; NjR.
5140

---- Sales of public lands--Alabama. Memorial of the legislature of Alabama, praying for a postponement of the sales of Public Lands in the county of Jackson, in said state. Washington, Duff Green, 1830. 2 p. (Rep. No. 97) DLC; NjR.
5141

---- Sale of U. States' lands in Ohio to that state. Jan. 28, 1830. Mr. Irwin from the committee on the Public Lands, to which the subject had been referred, made the following report: Washington, Duff Green, 1830. 2 p. (Rep. No. 128) DLC; NjR.
5142

---- Salt works--United States. Letter from the Secretary of the Treasury, transmitting a report of the number and nature of the salt works established in the United States, &c. &c. Feb. 8, 1830. Read, and laid upon the table. Washington, Pr. by Duff Green, 1830. 77 p. (Doc. No. 55) DLC; NjR.
5143

--- Samuel Demarest. Feb. 1, 1830. Read, and committed to a Committee of the Whole House to-morrow. Mr. Whittlesey, from the Committee of Claims, to which had been referred the case of Samuel Demarest, made the following report: Washington, Duff Green, 1830. 2 p. (Rep. No. 138) DLC; NjR.
5144

---- Samuel Holgate. Jan. 13, 1830. Read, and committed to a Committee of the Whole House to-morrow. Mr. Crane, from the Committee of Claims, to which was referred the case of Samuel Holgate, made the following report: Washington, Duff Green, 1830. 2 p. (Rep. No. 78) DLC; NjR.   5145

---- Samuel Keep. April 15, 1830. Mr. Crane, from the Committee of Claims, made the following report: Washington, Duff Green, 1830. 2 p. (Rep. No. 365) DLC; NjR.   5146

---- Samuel Meeker. February 19, 1830. Read, and laid upon the table. February 25, 1830. Committed to a Committee of Claims, to which was referred the case of Samuel Meeker... Washington, Pr. by Duff Green, 1830. 3 p. (Rep. No. 244) DLC; NjR.   5147

---- Samuel Sitgreaves. Jan. 11, 1830. Mr. Archer, from the Committee on Foreign Affairs, to which had been referred the case of Samuel Sitgreaves, made the following report: Washington, Duff Green, 1830. 9 p. (Rep. No. 105) DLC; NjR.   5148

---- Samuel Sprigg. Jan. 27, 1830. Mr. Gurley, from the Committee on Private Land Claims, made the following report: Washington, Duff Green, 1830. 3 p. (Rep. No. 124) DLC; NjR.   5149

---- Samuel Wagstaff. May 5, 1830. Mr. Whittlesey, from the Committee of Claims, made the following report: Washington, Duff Green, 1830. 2 p. (Rep. No. 392) DLC; NjR.   5150

---- Samuel Ward. February 27, 1830. Mr. Burges, from the Committee on Revolutionary Claims, to which was referred the case of Samuel Ward, made the following report: Washington, Pr. by Duff Green, 1830. 2 p. (Rep. No. 242) DLC; NjR.   5151

---- Samuel Watson and George Hoppas. February 25, 1830. Mr. Test, from the Committee on Private Land Claims, to which was referred the case of Samuel Watson and George Hoppas, made the following report: Washington, Pr. by Duff Green, 1830. 1 p. (Rep. No. 231) DLC; NjR.   5152

---- Sandy and Beaver Canal. April 12, 1830. Read, and laid upon the table. Washington, Duff Green, 1830. 10 p. (Rep. No. 357) DLC; NjR.   5153

---- Sarah Easton and Dorothy Storer. Jan. 29, 1830. Mr. Burges, from the Committee on Revolutionary Claims, to which was referred the case of Sarah Easton and Dorothy Storer, made the following report: Washington, Duff Green, 1830. 7 p. (Rep. No. 130) DLC; NjR.   5154

---- Savannah River. Letter from the Secretary of the Treasury transmitting the information required by a resolution of the House of Representatives of the 6th ultimo, in relation to disbursements which have been made in removing obstructions in the Savannah River, under the authority of the act of 18th May, 1826, &c. &c. May 20, 1830. Read, and laid upon the table. Washington, [Pr. by Duff Green] 1830. 59 p. (Doc. No. 106) DLC; NjR.   5155

---- School lands, Salines, &c. in Missouri. (With Bill H. R. 131) Jan. 19, 1830. Printed by order of the House of Representatives. Washington, Duff Green, 1830. 3 p. (Rep. No. 96) DLC; NjR.   5156

---- Seamen of the United States. Letter from the Secretary of State transmitting an abstract of

American seamen in the several districts of the United States for 1829. April 15, 1830. Read, and laid upon the table. Washington, [Pr. by Duff Green] 1830. 12 p. (Doc. No. 92) DLC; NjR. 5157

---- The Select Committee of the Senate to whom was referred the bill from the House of Representatives, entitled "An act to establish a uniform rule for the computation of the mileage of members of Congress, and for other purposes," report the following amendments: February 10, 1830. [Washington, 1830] 1 p. (H. R. 19) DNA. 5158

---- Senate amendments to Bill H. R. No. 116. March 15, 1830. Mr. Storrs, from the Select Committee to which was referred the amendments of the Senate to the bill (H. R. No. 116) to provide for taking the fifth census, or enumeration of the inhabitants of the United States, made the following report: Washington, Pr. by Duff Green, 1830. 4 p. (Rep. No. 295) DLC; NjR. 5159

---- Settlements on public lands, &c. Letter from the Secretary of the Treasury transmitting the information required by a resolution of the House of Representatives, in relation to settlements on the public lands, &c. May 26, 1830. Read, and laid upon the table. Washington [Pr. by Duff Green] 1830. 6 p. (Doc. No. 109) DLC; NjR. 5160

---- Sick and disabled seamen-- Marine hospital, &c. &c. March 2, 1830. Read, and referred to the Committee on Commerce. Washington, Pr. by Duff Green, 1830. 27 p. (Doc. No. 68) DLC; NjR. 5161

---- Sick and disabled seamen-- Providence, Rhode Island. Letter from the Secretary of the Treasury, in reply to a resolution of the House of Representatives of the 6th instant, in relation to providing for sick and disabled seamen in Providence, Rhode Island, and providing for the erection of a Marine hospital in said district, &c. &c. &c. April 27, 1830. Read, and laid upon the table. Washington, [Pr. by Duff Green] 1830. 20 p. (Doc. No. 96) DLC; NjR. 5162

---- Silas Wright, Jr. vs. George Fisher. Jan. 19, 1830. Read, and committed to a Committee of the Whole House on Tuesday next. Mr. Alston, from the Committee on Elections, to which the subject had been referred, made the following report: Washington, Duff Green, 1830. 2 p. (Rep. No. 95) DLC; NjR. 5163

---- Simeon C. Whittier, Dec. 30, 1830. Read, and with the bill, committed to a Committee of the Whole House to-morrow. Mr. Verplanck, from the Committee of Ways and Means, to which was referred the bill from the Senate (No. 3) for the relief of Simeon C. Whittier, made the following report: Washington, Duff Green, 1830. 1 p. (Rep. No. 14) DLC; NjR. 5164

---- Simeon Theus. March 2, 1830. Mr. Overton, from the Committee of Ways and Means, made the following report: Washington, Pr. by Duff Green, 1830. 13 p. (Rep. No. 260) DLC; NjR. 5165

---- Skinner's Grand Basin-- Water for public buildings, &c. March 8, 1830. Read, and so much thereof as relates to the system of Internal Improvements referred to the Committee on Internal Improvements, the residue to the Committee for the District of Columbia. Washington, Pr. by Duff Green, 1830. 5 p. (Rep. No. 281) DLC; NjR. 5166

---- Skinner's Grand Central Basin. April 20, 1830. Read, and referred to the Committee on Internal Improvements. Mr. Taliaferro, from the Committee for the District of Columbia, to which had been referred, in part, the letter from Mr. Skinner, upon the subject of a central canal basin in the city of Washington, made the following report: Washington, Duff Green, 1830. 1 p. (Rep. No. 375) DLC; NjR. 5167

---- ---- April 22, 1830. Read, and laid upon the table. Mr. Craig, of Virginia, from the Committee on Internal Improvements, to which the subject had been referred, made the following report: Washington, Duff Green, 1830. 1 p. (Rep. No. 376) DLC; NjR. 5168

---- Slave Trade. (To accompany bill H.R. No. 412) April 7, 1830. Mr. Mercer, from the select committee to which the subject had been referred, made the following report: Washington, Duff Green, 1830. 293 p. (Rep. No. 348) DLC; NjR. 5169

---- Society of Christian Indians. Message from the President of the United States, on the subject of an appropriation to pay the annuity due by the United States to the Society of Christian Indians. Jan. 22, 1830. Referred to the Committee on Indian Affairs. Washington, Pr. by Duff Green, 1830. 2 p. (Doc. No. 34) DLC; NjR. 5170

---- Soldiers of the revolution. Jan. 8, 1830. Read, and laid upon the table. Washington, Duff Green, 1830. 1 p. (Res. No. 2) DLC; NjR. 5171

---- South Carolina Claims. Jan. 11, 1830. Mr. Drayton, from the Committee on Military Affairs, to which was referred the claim of the State of South Carolina against the United States, made the following report: Washington, Duff Green, 1830. 71 p. (Rep. No. 66) DLC; NjR. 5172

---- Southern Indians. Petition of the Yearly Meeting of Friends of New England. March 1, 1830. Read, and committed to the Committee of the Whole House to which is committed the bill (No. 287) to provide for the removal of the Indian tribes within any of the states and territories, and for their permanent settlement west of the river Mississippi. Washington, Pr. by Duff Green, 1830. 3 p. (Rep. No. 246) DLC; NjR. 5173

---- Specific appropriations. Feb. 3, 1830. Read, and referred to the Committee of the Whole House on the state of the Union to which is committed the Bill (No. 102) making appropriations for the support of Government for the year 1830. Mr. Wickliffe, from the Committee on Retrenchment, submitted the following report: Washington, Duff Green, 1830. 2 p. (Rep. No. 150) DLC; NjR. 5174

---- Specification of a patent for an improved cooking grate, intended chiefly for cooking by means of anthracite coal. Granted to Thomas Vinton...October 31, 1829. With remarks by the editor of the Journal of the Franklin Institute. From the Journal of the Franklin Institute, for March, 1830. Philadelphia, 1830. 7 p. MB.   5175

---- Stafford and Yates. April 29, 1830. Read, and laid upon the table. Mr. Conner, from the Committee on the Post Office and Post Roads, to which was recommitted the report of the said committee, in the case of Stafford and Yates, of the 25th of January, last, made the following report: Washington, Duff Green, 1830. 3 p. (Rep. No. 388) DLC; NjR.   5176

---- Stafford and Yates, sureties of Southwick. Jan. 25, 1830. Read, and committed to a Committee of the Whole House tomorrow. Mr. Conner, from the Committee on the Post Office and Post Roads, to which was referred the petition of Stafford and Yates sureties of Solomon Southwick, made the following report: Washington, Duff Green, 1830. 3 p. (Rep. No. 112) DLC; NjR.   5177

---- Steam boats and steam vessels. May 4, 1830. Mr. Wickliffe submitted the following resolution. Washington, Duff Green, 1830. 1 p. (Rep. No. 14) DLC; NjR.   5178

---- Stephen Hook. February 22, 1830. Mr. Crane, from the Committee of Claims, made the following report: Washington, Pr. by Duff Green, 1830. 3 p. (Rep. No. 219) DLC; NjR.   5179

---- Stockholders, &c. Bank United States. May 26, 1830. Read, and ordered to lie upon the table for one day. Washington, Duff Green, 1830. 2 p. (Res. No. 16) DLC; NjR.   5180

---- Street--Capitol to executive offices. To accompany bill H. R. No. 224. February 10, 1830. Mr. Powers, from the Committee for the District of Columbia, to which the subject had been referred, made the following report: Washington, Pr. by Duff Green, 1830. 15 p. (Rep. No. 184) DLC; NjR.   5181

---- Sugar Cane. Jan. 13, 1830. Read, and laid upon the table. Mr. Spender submitted the following resolution: Washington, Duff Green, 1830. 1 p. (Res. No. 3) DLC; NjR.   5182

---- Sugar imported. Letter from the Secretary of the Treasury communicating the information required by a resolution of the House of Representatives of the 14th instant, in relation to brown sugars imported into the United States, from 30th September, 1815, &c. &c. December 31, 1830. Read, and laid upon the table. Washington, Pr. by Duff Green, 1830. 6 p. (Doc. No. 18) DLC; NjR.   5183

---- Sunday mail. Letter from the Postmaster General, transmitting (in obedience to a resolution of the House of Representatives of the 24th ultimo,) a statement of the post routes within the United States, on which the mail is transported on Sunday. March 4, 1830. Read, and laid upon the table. Washington, Pr. by Duff Green, 1830. 9 p. (Doc. No. 73) DLC; NjR.   5184

---- ---- March 4, 1830. Read, and committed to the Committee of the Whole House on the state of the Union. March 5, 1830. Printed by order of the House of Representatives. Mr. Johnson, of Kentucky, from the Committee on the Post Office and Post

Roads, to which had been referred petitions and remon-
strances against the transportation and opening of the public
mail on the Sabbath day, made
the following report: Washington,
Pr. by Duff Green, 1830. 8 p.
(Rep. No. 271) DLC; NjR. 5185

---- Supreme Court of the United
States. Charles F. Sibbald, et
al. vs. The United States. On
appeal. [1830] 2 p. PPL. 5186

---- Survey--Cumberland River.
February 10, 1830. Read, and
laid upon the table. Mr. Blair,
from the Committee on Internal
Improvements, to which the subject had been referred, made the
following report: Washington,
Pr. by Duff Green, 1830. 1 p.
(Rep. No. 181) DLC; NjR. 5187

---- Survey--Flat Beach. Letter
from the Secretary of War, transmitting a copy of a report of the
engineer appointed to survey Flat
Beach, on Tucker's Island, at
Egg Harbor, in New Jersey, with
an estimate of the expense of se-
curing the harbor. March 16,
1830. Referred to the Committee
on Commerce. Washington, Pr.
by Duff Green, 1830. 3 p. (Doc.
No. 81) DLC; NjR.   5188

---- Survey--Narraganset Bay,
&c. &c. Letter from the Secretary of War, transmitting surveys
and reports of the water of Nar-
raganset Bay and the Harbor of
Newport, Rhode Island, with a
view to the establishment of a
Naval Depot. Jan. 14, 1830.
Read, and laid upon the table.
Washington, Pr. by Duff Green,
1830. 11 p. (Doc. No. 21) DLC;
NjR.   5189

---- Survey of Connecticut River,
&c. March 15, 1830. Read, and
laid upon the table. Mr. Butman,

from the Committee on Internal
Improvements, to which the sub-
ject had been referred, made the
following report: Washington,
Pr. by Duff Green, 1830. 1 p.
(Rep. No. 294) DLC; NN; NjR.
                               5190

---- Survey of Sandy Bay, Massachusetts. Message from the
President of the United States
transmitting a report of a survey
of Sandy Bay, in the state of Massachusetts. April 24, 1830.
Read, and laid upon the table.
Washington [Pr. by Duff Green]
1830. 5 p. (Doc. No. 95) DLC;
NjR.   5191

---- Survey of the harbor of St.
Augustine. Message from the
President of the United States
transmitting a copy of the report
of a survey of the harbor of St.
Augustine. April 22, 1830. Read,
and laid upon the table. Washington, [Pr. by Duff Green] 1830.
11 p. (Doc. No. 93) DLC; NjR.
                               5192

---- Survey--Penobscot River.
Message from the President of
the United States, transmitting a
copy of the report on survey made
of the ship channel of Penobscot
river, &c. &c. March 19, 1830.
Read, and laid upon the table.
Washington, Pr. by Duff Green,
1830. 3 p. (Doc. No. 82) DLC;
NjR.   5193

---- Survey--River Thames,
Conn. Letter from the Secretary
of War transmitting a copy of a
report of the engineer appointed
to make a survey of the River
Thames in the state of Connecticut. March 9, 1830. Referred
to the Committee on Commerce.
Washington [Pr. by Duff Green]
1830. 7 p. (Doc. No. 125) DLC;
NjR.   5194

---- Surveyors of public lands.
Message from the President of

the United States recommending that provision be made by law for the punishment of person guilty of interrupting the surveyors of the public lands when engaged in the performance of the duties of their office. May 13, 1830. Referred to the Committee on the judiciary. May 17, 1830. Printed by order of the House of Representatives. Washington [Pr. by Duff Green] 1830. 4 p. (Doc. No. 103) DLC; NjR. 5195

---- Surveys for roads. April 12, 1830. Read, and laid upon the table. Mr. Hemphill submitted the following resolution: Washington, Duff Green, 1830. 1 p. (Res. No. 12) DLC; NjR. 5196

---- Surveys--Naval depots. Letter from the Secretary of the Navy in reply to a resolution of the House of Representatives of the 14th instant, in relation to the reports of the survey of certain ports and harbors, with a view to the establishment of Naval depots. December 23, 1830. Read, and laid upon the table. Washington, Pr. by Duff Green, 1830. 3 p. (Doc. No. 16) DLC; NjR. 5197

---- Susanna McHugh. February 15, 1830. Mr. Test, from the Committee on Private Land Claims, made the following report: Washington, Pr. by Duff Green, 1830. 1 p. (Rep. No. 197) DLC; NjR. 5198

---- Sylvester Havens. March 12, 1830. Mr. Crane, from the Committee of Claims, to which was referred the case of Sylvester Havens, made the following report: Washington, Pr. by Duff Green, 1830. 3 p. (Rep. No. 287) DLC; NjR. 5199

---- Tariff. Jan. 5, 1830.

Read, and laid upon the table. Mr. Mallary, from the Committee on Manufactures, made the following report: Washington, Duff Green, 1830. 3 p. (Rep. No. 54) DLC; NjR. 5200

---- Tariff of 1828. Feb. 1, 1830. Read, and referred to the Committee of the Whole House to which is committed the report of the Committee on Manufactures upon the subject of the Tariff. Washington, Duff Green, 1830. 2 p. (Rep. No. 146) DLC; NjR. 5201

---- Tennessee to issue grants. To accompany bill H.R. 185. Jan. 29, 1830. Mr. Crockett, from the Select Committee to which the subject had been referred, made the following report: Washington, Duff Green, 1830. 2 p. (Rep. No. 137) DLC; NjR. 5202

---- Territory of Huron. Jan. 6, 1830. Mr. Clark, from the Committee on the Territories, to which the subject had been referred, made the following report: Washington, Duff Green, 1830. 8 p. (Rep. No. 56) DLC; NjR. 5203

---- Thomas Blackwell. Jan. 29, 1830. Mr. Young, from the Committee on Revolutionary Claims, to which was referred the case of Thomas Blackwell, made the following report: Washington, Duff Green, 1830. 2 p. (Rep. No. 129) DLC; NjR. 5204

---- Thomas Buford. Jan. 4, 1830. Mr. Drayton, from the Committee on Military Affairs, made the following report: Washington, Duff Green, 1830. 1 p. (Rep. No. 43) DLC; NjR. 5205

---- Thomas Cooper. Petition of Thomas Cooper, President of

the South Carolina College, praying that he may be refunded the
amount of a fine which he paid to
the United States, by reason of a
conviction under the sedition law.
Feb. 1, 1830.   Referred to
the Committee on the Judiciary.
Washington, Pr. by Duff Green,
1830.   6 p. (Rep. No. 149) DLC;
NjR.   5206

---- Thomas F. Cornell.
Feb.   17, 1830.   Mr. Clarke,
from the Committee on the Territories, to which was referred
the case of Thomas F. Cornell,
made the following report: Washington, Pr. by Duff Green, 1830.
2 p. (Rep. No. 208) DLC; NjR.
                                5207
---- Thomas F. Hunt.   May 29,
1830.   Read, and laid upon the
table. Mr. McIntire, from the
Committee of Claims, to which
was referred the case of Thomas
F. Hunt, made the following report: Washington, Duff Green,
1830.   5 p. (Rep. No. 419)
DLC; NjR.   5208

---- Thomas Park.   Jan. 12,
1830.   Mr. Goodenow, from the
Committee on Revolutionary
Claims, to which was referred
the case of Thomas Park, made
the following report: Washington,
Duff Green, 1830. 2 p. (Rep.
No. 72) DLC; NjR.   5209

---- Thomas W. Newton, assignee
of Robert Crittenden.   March 31,
1830.   Mr. Whittlesey, from the
Committee of Claims, made the
following report: Washington,
Duff Green, 1830. 1 p. (Rep.
No. 339) DLC; NjR.   5210

---- Timothy D. and Robert A.
Pettigrew.   April 16, 1830.
Read, and committed to a Committee of the Whole House to-
morrow.   Mr. Hubbard, from
the Committee on Indian Affairs,

to which had been referred the
case of Timothy D. Pettigrew,
and Robert A. Pettigrew, made
the following report: Washing-
ton, Duff Green, 1830. 3 p.
(Rep. No. 368) DLC; NjR.
                                5211
---- Timothy Risley.   February
26, 1830.   Mr. Clay, from the
Committee on the Public Lands,
to which was referred the case
of Timothy Risley, made the
following report: Washington,
Pr. by Duff Green, 1830. 1 p.
(Rep. No. 238) DLC; NjR.
                                5212
---- To accompany Bill H. R.
No. 54.   Jan. 14, 1830.
Printed by order of the House of
Representatives.   Washington,
Pr. by Duff Green, 1830. 1 p.
(Doc. No. 26) DLC; NjR.   5213

---- (To be annexed to report
213)   March 5, 1830.   Printed by
order of the House of Representatives.   [Washington, 1830] 9 p.
DLC; NjR.   5214

---- (To be annexed to the report of the Committee of Claims
in the case of Peter Bargy, et
al.)   April 28, 1830.   "To the
honorable the Senate and House
of Representatives of the United
States in Congress assembled:"
Washington, Pr. by Duff Green,
1830.   23 p. (Rep. No. 248)
DLC; NjR.   5215

---- Transylvania University.
March 17, 1830.   Mr. Clarke,
from the Select Committee to
which the subject had been referred, made the following report: Washington, Duff Green,
1830. 2 p. (Rep. No. 308) DLC;
NjR.   5216

---- Treasury statements. 1st.
Contracts made in 1829.   2d.
Payments, miscellaneous claims.
3d. Payments &c. collectors

revenue. 4th. Payments, sick and disabled seamen. February 9, 1830. Read, and laid upon the table. Washington, Pr. by Duff Green, 1830. 12 p. (Doc. No. 57) DLC; NjR.   5217

---- Treaty with Denmark. Message from the President of the United States transmitting copies of a convention between the United States and Denmark, concluded the 28th of March, 1830. December 13, 1830. Referred to the Committee on Foreign Affairs. Washington, Pr. by Duff Green, 1830. 7 p. (Doc. No. 3) DLC; NjR.   5218

---- Turnpike Road in Tennessee. Resolutions of the legislature of the state of Tennessee in relation to the construction of a turnpike road from the Virginia line to the Mississippi River. February 25, 1830. Read, and referred to the Committee of the Whole House on the state of the Union, to which is committed the bill (H.R. No. 285) authorizing a subscription of stock in the Maysville, Washington, Paris, and Lexington Turnpike Road Company. Washington, Pr. by Duff Green, 1830. 1 p. (Rep. No. 230) DLC; NjR.   5219

---- Unexpended balances. Mr. M'Duffie, from the Committee of Ways and Means, laid before the House the following statement of unexpended balances of appropriations, on the 31st of December 1829. January 30, 1830. Printed by order of the House of Representatives. Washington, Pr. by Duff Green, 1830. 11 p. (Doc. No. 42) DLC; NjR.   5220

---- United States and Colombia. Message from the President of the United States, transmitting information on the subject of the relations between the government of the United States and Colombia. Jan. 19, 1830. Referred to the Committee on Foreign Affairs. Washington, Pr. by Duff Green, 1830. 2 p. (Doc. No. 31) DLC; NjR.   5221

---- United States Bank. Resolutions of the General Assembly of the state of Tennessee, in relation to re-chartering the Bank of the United States. February 25, 1830. Read, and laid upon the table. Washington, Pr. by Duff Green, 1830. 3 p. (Rep. No. 243) DLC; NjR.   5222

---- Unproductive post roads. Letter from the Postmaster General, transmitting a list of unproductive post roads, &c. March 2, 1830. Read, and referred to the Committee on the Post Office and Post Roads. Washington, Pr. by Duff Green, 1830. 15 p. (Doc. No. 70) DLC; NjR.   5223

---- Upon the subject of Navy yards. Letter from the Secretary of the Navy, transmitting a report of the Commissioners of the Navy, upon the subject of Navy Yards. Feb. 1, 1830. Referred to the Committee on Naval Affairs. Washington, Pr. by Duff Green, 1830. 3 p. (Doc. No. 43) DLC; NjR.   5224

---- Vessels sunk for defence of Baltimore. (To accompany bill H.R. No. 191) Feb. 1, 1830. Printed by order of the House of Representatives. Washington, Duff Green, 1830. 20 p. (Rep. No. 144) DLC; NjR.   5225

---- Virginia. Memorial of the Wheeling Bridge Company. March 12, 1830. Referred to the Committee of Internal Improvements. Washington, Duff Green, 1830. 5 p. (Rep. No. 349) DLC;

NjR. 5226

---- W. C. Daniel, vs. Bargy, Norton, and Wolverton. May 26, 1830. Referred to the Committee of the Whole House to which is committed the bill (H. R. No. 307) for the relief of Peter Bargy, Jr., Stephen Norton, and Hiram Wolverton. Washington, Duff Green, 1830. 16 p. (Rep. No. 415) DLC; NjR. 5227

---- Wallace Robinson. Jan. 11, 1830. Mr. Clay, from the Committee on the Public Lands, to which was referred the case of Wallace Robinson, made the following report: Washington, Duff Green, 1830. 1 p. (Rep. No. 70) DLC; NjR. 5228

---- Walter Livingston. Jan. 18, 1830. Mr. Wingate, from the Committee on Revolutionary Claims, made the following report: Washington, Duff Green, 1830. 22 p. (Rep. No. 93) DLC; NjR. 5229

---- Warehouses. (To accompany bill H. R. No. 329) Letter from the Secretary of the Treasury, on the subject of public warehouses. March 6, 1830. Laid before the House by the chairman of the Committee on Commerce, and ordered to be printed. Washington, Pr. by Duff Green, 1830. 1 p. (Doc. No. 74) DLC; NjR. 5230

---- Washburn vs. Ripley. To be annexed to the report of the Committee of Elections in the case of Reuel Washburn, vs. James W. Ripley. Jan. 22, 1830. Printed by order of the House of Representatives. Washington, Duff Green, 1830. 44 p. (Rep. No. 88) DLC; NjR. 5231

---- Water for the Capitol.

Feb. 2, 1830. Referred to the Committee on the Public Buildings. Washington, Duff Green, 1830. 1 p. (Rep. No. 145) DLC; NjR. 5232

---- ---- Letter from Robert Mills to the Chairman of the Committee on the Public Buildings, upon the subject of providing a supply of water for the use of the Capitol. April 5, 1830. Printed by order of the House of Representatives. Washington, Duff Green, 1830. 4 p. (Rep. No. 344) DLC; NjR. 5233

---- Wheeling and Belmont Bridge Company. May 11, 1830. Mr. Letcher, from the Committee on Internal Improvements, made the following report: Washington, Duff Green, 1830. 1 p. (Rep. No. 399) DLC; NjR. 5234

---- Whitford Gill. April 15, 1830. Mr. Whittlesey, from the Committee of Claims, to which was referred the case of Whitford Gill, made the following report: Washington, Duff Green, 1830. 2 p. (Rep. No. 364) DLC; NjR. 5235

---- Widow and heirs of Joseph Hulse. February 25, 1830. Mr. Test, from the Committee on Private Land Claims, made the following report: Washington, Pr. by Duff Green, 1830. 1 p. (Rep. No. 232) DLC; NjR. 5236

---- Wilkins Tannehill. Jan. 22, 1830. Mr. Whittlesey, from the Committee of Claims, to which had been referred the case of Wilkins Tannehill, made the following report: Washington, Duff Green, 1830. 2 p. (Rep. No. 107) DLC; NjR. 5237

---- William B. Lawrence. Message from the President of the

United States, transmitting the information required by a resolution of the House of Representatives, of the 9th instant, in relation to the accounts of William B. Lawrence, as Chargé des Affairs of the United States to Great Britain.   Feb. 19, 1830.   Referred to the Committee on Foreign Affairs. Washington, Pr. by Duff Green, 1830. 14 p. (Doc. No. 66) DLC; NjR.
5238

---- William Carter--heirs of. March 26, 1830. Mr. Brown, from the Committee on Revolutionary Claims, made the following report: Washington, Duff Green, 1830. 2 p. (Rep. No. 332) DLC; NjR.   5239

---- William Clower.   April 19, 1830. Mr. Johnson, from the Committee on the Post Office and Post Roads, made the following report: Washington, Duff Green, 1830. 1 p. (Rep. No. 371) DLC; NjR.   5240

---- William D. King, et al. March 2, 1830. Mr. Whittlesey, from the Committee of Claims, made the following report: Washington, Pr. by Duff Green, 1830. 1 p. (Rep. No. 249) DLC; NjR.
5241

---- William Forsythe.   March 22, 1830. Mr. Whittlesey, from the Committee of Claims, made the following report: Washington, Duff Green, 1830. 2 p. (Rep. No. 321) DLC; NjR.   5242

---- William Gallop.   March 17, 1830. Mr. Hammons, from the Committee on Military Pensions, made the following report: Washington, Duff Green, 1830. 1 p. (Rep. No. 307) DLC; NjR.
5243

---- William Gibbs.   May 7, 1830. Read, and with the bill, committed to a Committee of the Whole House to-morrow.   Mr. Whittlesey, from the Committee of Claims, to which was referred the bill from the Senate, (No. 171) entitled "An act for the relief of the sureties of William Gibbs. deceased, late a Paymaster in the army of the U. S." submitted the following report: Washington, Duff Green, 1830. 4 p. (Rep. No. 396) DLC; NjR.   5244

---- William H. Harrison. April 23, 1830. Mr. Archer, from the Committee on Foreign Affairs, made the following report: Washington, Duff Green, 1830. 1 p. (Rep. No. 378) DLC; NjR. 5245

---- William Henry. March 2, 1830. Read, and laid upon the table.   Mr. Irvin, from the Committee on the Public Lands, to which was referred the case of William Henry, made the following report: Washington, Pr. by Duff Green, 1830. 2 p. (Rep. No. 259) DLC; NjR.   5246

---- William Morrisson.   Jan. 8, 1830. Mr. Whittlesey, from the Committee of Claims, to which was referred the case of William Morrisson, made the following report: Washington, Duff Green, 1830. 1 p. (Rep. No. 63) DLC; NjR.   5247

---- William Price.   April 9, 1830. Mr. Ford, from the Committee on Military Pensions, made the following report: Washington, Duff Green, 1830. 2 p. (Rep. No. 352) DLC; NjR.   5248

---- William Saunders, et al. Jan. 11, 1830. Mr. Bouldin, from the Committee on the Judiciary, to which was referred the case of William Saunders, et al. made the following report. Washington, Duff Green, 1830. 1 p. (Rep.

No. 71) DLC; NjR.   5249

---- William Stewart. May 11,
1830. Mr. Hunt, from the Committee on the Public Lands, made
the following report: Washington,
Duff Green, 1830. 1 p. (Rep. No.
398) DLC; NjR.   5250

---- William Tharp. April 19,
1830. Mr. Crane, from the
Committee of Claims, made the
following report: Washington,
Duff Green, 1830. 3 p. (Rep. No.
374) DLC; NjR.   5251

---- William Vawters. March 19,
1830. Mr. Brown, from the
Committee on Revolutionary
Claims, made the following report: Washington, Duff Green,
1830. 1 p. (Rep. No. 313) DLC;
NjR.   5252

---- Military Academy, West
Point, N. Y.
Catalogue of the library of the
U. S. Military Academy at West-
Point. May 1830. New York, Pr.
by J. Desnoues, 1830. 132 p.
MHi; NWM; PPAmP.   5253

The United States reader. See
Darby, William.

United States' spelling book, with
appropriate reading lessons: being an easy standard for spelling,
reading and pronouncing the English language, according to the
rules established by John Walker,
in his critical and pronouncing
dictionary. By sundry experienced teachers. 30th ed. Pittsburgh, Pr. and pub. by Cramer
and Spear, 1830. 156 p. PPins.
                         5254
The United States working man's
almanack and farmer's and mechanic's every day book for 1831.
Boston, Charles Ellms [1830] 18
l. DLC; InU; MB; MWA; N;
RPB.   5255

Upton, Samuel, 1784-1842.
An oration delivered in Bluehill, July 5, 1830. Published by
request of the citizens. Bluehill,
Beacon Press, B. F. Bond, pr.,
1830. 16 p. Williamson: 10,093.
                         5256

V

The valedictory poem. See Warren, George Washington.

Valpy, Richard, 1754-1836.
The elements of Greek grammar, by R. Valpy... With additions by C. Anthon...4th ed.
New York, Collins and Co., etc.
1830. vi, 322 p. DLC; NCH;
NSyU; OO; PPiW; PV.   5257

Van der Kemp, Francis Adrian,
1752-1829.
Catalogue of... Library... sold
July 15, 1830 at J. L. Cunning-
ham's auction room, Boston.
Cambridge, 1830. 29 p. MHi.
                         5258
[Vandewater, Robert J.]
The tourist; or, Pocket manu-
al for travelers on the Hudson
River, the western canal, and
stage road; comprising also the
routes to Lebanon, Ballston, and
Saratoga Springs. New York, J.
& J. Harper, 1830. 59 p. CSt;
CoD; CtSoP; DeGE; IU; MB; MH;
NBuG; NIC; NN; VtU; WHi. 5259

Varle's Self-instructor; no. 2.
Being an expositor of all the terms
and figures, used in the preceding number: giving not only plain
intelligible definitions of the several words, but instructive remarks on the different objects,
adapted to the comprehension of
the youthful learner. Baltimore,
Pr. by William Wooddy, 1830.
58 p. MdBJ; OMC.   5260

Vauquelin, Louis Nicolas, 1763-

1829.

Dictionary of chemistry, containing the principles and modern theories of the science, with its application to the arts, manufactures, and medicine... Translated from Le dictionnaire de chimie, approuvé par Vauquelin... With additions and notes by Mrs. Almira H. Lincoln... New York, G. & C. & H. Carvill [Sleight & Robinson, prs.] 1830. 531, [1] p. DeGE; IGK; MBC; NCH; NNF; PU.   5261

Vedder, Nicholas I., compiler.

A new and choice selection of psalms and hymns and spiritual songs, designed for the Christian's companion through life. Selected from various authors, by Nicholas I. Vedder. Stereotyped by Oliver Wells, & co. Cincinnati, Pr. and pub. by N. & G. Guilford, 1830. 218, [6] p. KyLoF.   5262

Velpeau, Alfred Armand Louis Marie, 1795-1867.

Treatise on surgical anatomy ... Translated from the French with notes by J. W. Sterling, M.D. New York, Samuel Wood and sons; R. & G. S. Wood, prs., 1830. 2 vols. DLC; GU-M; IaU; LNOP; MBCo; MdBJ-W; NBuU-M; NRAM; NbU-M; PPC; PU; ViU.   5263

Vergilius Maro, Publius.

P. Virgilii Maronis Opera. Interpretatione et notis illustravit Carolus Rualus, Soc. Jesu. Jussu Christianissimi regis, ad usum serenissimi delphini. Editio sexta in America stereotypis impressa; cum novissima parisiensi diligenter collata, caeterisque hactenus editis longe emendatioc. Huic editioni accessit clavis Virgiliana. E. stereotypis A.D. & G. Bruce fabricatis, Novi-Eboraci. Philadelphia, Pub.

by Joseph Allen. Sold by J. Grigg, 1830. xxii, [3], 567, [1], 106 p. THi.   5264

---- Publius Virgilius Maro. Bucolica, Georgica, et Aeneis... Cura B. A. Gould... Bostoniae, Hilliard, Gray, Little, et Wilkins [Stereotyped at the Boston Type and Stereotype Foundry] 1830. 491 p. ICU; MB; MeHi.   5265

Vermont.

(Vermont State Officers, Councellors and Representatives and their address) His Excellency Samuel C. Crafts, etc., Montpelier [1830] Bdsd. Not located.   5266

---- Journal of the General Assembly of the state of Vermont at their session begun and held at Montpelier, Washington County, on Thursday, 8th October, A.D. 1829. Woodstock, Pr. by Rufus Colton, 1830. 224 p. Mi.   5267

The Vermont Anti-Masonic almanac for 1831. By Samuel Hemenway, Jr. Woodstock, Hemenway & Holbrook, prs. [1830] 18 l. DLC; MWA; NHi; VtHi; VtU.   5268

Vermont Bible Society.

Eighteenth annual report of the Vermont Bible Society, communicated at their meeting at Montpelier, October 20, 1830. Montpelier, Pr. by E. P. Walton, & Co., Watchman Office, 1830. 15 p. CSmH; IEG; VtMiS; WHi.   5269

Vermont Colonization Society.

Eleventh annual report of the Vermont Colonization Society, communicated at their meeting at Montpelier, October 20, 1830. Montpelier, Pr. by E. P. Walton, 1830. 8 p. Not located. 5270

Vermont Domestic Missionary Society.

Annual report of the Vermont

Domestic Missionary Society,
presented at Rutland,   Sept.
16, 1830.   Burlington, Foote &
Stacy [1830] 24 p. Nh.   5271

Vermont State Convention.
    Sir: It is deemed by our
friends in different sections of
the state, indispensably necessary that a State Convention
should be holden, composed of
delegates from the several counties for the purpose of forming
a ticket for state officers...
Burlington, June 15th, 1830. 1 p.
DLC.   5272

Vermont. State Normal School,
Castleton.
    Prospectus. Castleton, Vt.,
February 1830. [n.p., 1830] 7 p.
N.   5273

Verplanck, Gulian Crommelin,
1786-1870.
    An address delivered before
the Philolexian and Peithologian
Societies, August 2, 1830; on the
evening preceding the annual commencement of Columbia College.
New York, G. & C. & H. Carvill
[Ludwig & Tolefree, prs.] 1830.
39 p. CSmH; DLC; LNHT; MdHi;
MoS; NCH; NIC; NNC; PHi;
PPAmP; PPL; RPB; WHi.   5274

Very, Nathaniel.
    Nathaniel Very's renunciation
of Free Masonry, with his answers
to several masonic queries of the
day. Worcester, Spooner & Church,
pr., 1830. 16 p. DLC; MB; MH;
MWA; WHi.   5275

The vestal. See Gray, Thomas.

Vesuvius Fire Co., Boston.
    Constitution & by laws. Bos-
ton, 1830. MB.   5276

The veterinary surgeon. See
Badcock, John.

[Vethake, Henry] 1792-1866.

    A reply to "A narrative of the
proceedings of the Board of Trustees of Dickinson College from
1821 to 1830." [Princeton, N.J.,
W. D'Hart, 1830] 11 p. DLC;
MnHi; PHi; PPL; PPPrHi. 5277

A view and description of the
Eastern Penitentiary. See Smith,
George W.

A view of some of the leading
doctrines of the Methodist Episcopal Church in their influence
on Christian experience. New
Haven, Baldwin & Treadway,
1830. 24 p. CtHC.   5278

A view of the economy of Methodism from the most approved
authorities. First pub. in
the Christian Spectator, September 1829. New Haven, Pr. by
Hezekiah Howe, 1830. 24 p.
MBC; MH-AH; PPL.   5279

Views of interesting places in the
Holy Land. See Rosenmueller,
Ernst F. C.

A village pastor. See Advice to
the young Christian.

Vincennes. Grand Menagerie.
    The proprietor of the Grand
Menagerie returns his sincere
thanks to the citizens of this
town and its vicinity for...pa-
tronage...and wishes to inform
them that he shall continue to
exhibit the same for about two
months.... Vincennes, January
4, 1830. Bdsd. In.   5280

Vincent, Thomas.
    Christ's sudden and certain
appearances to judgment. By
Thomas Vincent,...also an account of the destruction of Jerusalem; an absolute and irresistible proof of the divine origin
of Christianity. Published by J.
Locken, Philadelphia [S. Pro-

basco, pr.] 1830. 407 p. GDC;
InU; KyDC; LNB; MeB; MoSU;
NbOP; NjR; O.   5281

Vindex, pseud. See Truth advocated.

A vindication of the Cherokee
claims. See Hare, Robert.

The vine. See American Tract
Society, N. Y.

Virginia.
   Acts passed at a General Assembly of the Commonwealth of
Virginia begun and held at the
Capitol... on Monday, the seventh
day of December... one thousand
eight hundred and twenty-nine.
Richmond, Pr. by Thomas Ritchie, 1830. 151 p. Vi.   5282

---- Bill of rights. A declaration of rights made by the representatives of the good people of
Virginia, assembled in full and
free convention; which rights do
pertain to them, and their pos-
terity, as the basis and foundation of goverment. Unanimously
adopted June 12th, 1776. [Fol-
lowed by] An amended constitution or form of government for
Virginia. Adopted January 14th,
1830. 14 p. DLC; PPL; Vi.
                                 5283
---- A collection of all acts and
parts of act, of the General Assembly of Virginia, from October, 1784, down to the session
of 1829-30, inclusive, relative to
the James River company. Together with an appendix, containing the regulations of the president and directors of the said
company, for the superintendence
and preservation of the improvements under their direction.
Richmond, Pr. by S. Shepherd &
Co. , 1830. 104, 14, xxvii p.
DLC.   5284

---- ... Constitution of Virginia
... [Richmond, 1830] CSmH.
                                 5285
---- Fourteenth annual report of
the Board of Public Works, to
the General Assembly of Virginia.
22d January, 1830. Richmond,
Pr. by Thomas Ritchie, 1830.
50 p. (Doc. no. 16) Vi.   5286

---- ---- [With returns and reports of internal improvement
companies] Richmond, Pr. by
Samuel Shepherd & Co. , 1830.
108 p. Vi.   5287

---- Journal of the House of
Delegates of the Commonwealth
of Virginia, begun and held at the
capitol,... on Monday, the seventh day of December, one thousand eight hundred and twenty-
nine. Richmond, Pr. by Thomas Ritchie, 1829 [i. e. 1830]
195 p. Vi.   5288

---- Journal of the Senate of the
commonwealth of Virginia, begun
and held at the capitol... on Monday the seventh day of December,
in the year one thusand eight
hundred and twenty-nine. Richmond, Pr. by John Warrock,
1829 [i. e. 1830] 120 p. Vi.
                                 5289
---- A list of accounts remain-
ing open on the books of the Auditor's office on the 30th September 1829... Richmond, Pr. by
Thomas Ritchie, 1830. 31 p.
(Doc. No. 19)   5290

---- Proceedings and debates of
the Virginia convention, begun
and held in the city of Richmond,
October 5, 1829-January 15,
1830. Winchester, Pr. and pub.
by Samuel H. Davis, 1830. 124
p. "Issued weekly as a supplement to the Winchester Republican, Oct. 30, 1829 to April 16,
1830, in 30 numbers, four pages
each, except no. 2, eight pages,

including supplement." Vi. 5291

---- Proceedings and debates of
the Virginia state convention of
1829-30. To which are subjoined, the new constitution of
Virginia, and the votes of the
people... Richmond, Pr. by Samuel Shepherd & co. for Ritchie
& Cook, 1830. iv, 919, [1] p.
CSmH; DLC; MA; PPL.   5292

---- Reports of cases argued
and determined in the court of
appeals, and in the General
Court of Virginia. By Benjamin
Watkins Leigh. Vol. 1. Richmond,
Pr. by Samuel Shepard & Co.,
1830. xii, 632 p. Vi.   5293

Virginia and North Carolina almanack for 1831. By David Richardson. Richmond, John Warrock
[1830] 18 l. DLC; MWA (two varieties); NcU; ViHi; ViLxV. 5294

The Virginia and North-Carolina
pocket almanack and farmers'
companion for 1831. By David
Richardson. Richmond, John
Warrock [1830] 18 l. ViW. 5295

Virginia. University.
A catalogue of the officers and
matriculates of the University of
Virginia, session 1829-30. Charlottesville, Va., Pr. by Carr &
Elliott, 1830. 11 p. PPAmP;
PPL; PPPrHi; Vi; ViU; ViW.
                           5296
---- University of Virginia. 183-
By a law of the University of
Virginia, it becomes my duty at
the end of every month, to transmit to the parent or guardian of
each student, a list containing the
number of times his son or ward
has been absent from the lectures... [Charlottesville, 183-]
2 p. DLC.   5297

Visits to the Blessed Sacrament
and to the Blessed Virgin, for

every day in the month. Trans-
lated from the Italian of Liguori.
Baltimore, Pub. by F. Lucas,
Jr. [183-?] 285 p. DGU; MdBS.
                           5298
Der Volksfreund und Hägers-
tauner Calender auf 1831. Von
Carl F. Egelmann. Hägerstaun:
Johann Gruber [1830] 15 l. InU
(impf); MWA (two varieties); N;
NjR; PHi; PPL; PYHi.   5299

Volney, Constantin François
Chasseboeuf comte de, 1757-
1820.
Volney's ruins: or, Meditation on the revolutions of empires. Translated under the immediate inspection of the author
from the sixth Paris edition. To
which is added. The law of nature, and a short biographical
notice, by Count Daru; also The
controversy between Dr. Priestly
and Volney... Boston [Dixon &
Sickels] 1830. 216 p. NNG;
OClWHi.   5300

Voltaire, Francois Marie Arouet
de, 1694-1778.
Histoire de Charles XII. Roi
de Suede par Voltaire.... 2d ed.
Revue et Corrigee. Edition stereotype. Boston, Carter & Hendee, 1830. [3], 285 p. IaHi.
                           5301
---- ---- 3d ed. New York,
Charles D. Behr, 1830. 285 p.
MiU; WBB.   5302

---- The philosophical dictionary
of M. de Voltaire, with a life of
the author. From the most approved London ed. New York, G.
H. Evans, 1830. 215, [4] p. MH;
OHi; WHi.   5303

Von Dunderhead, Messrs., pseud.
The budget; or, Humble at-
tempts at immortality. By Messrs.
Von Dunderhead... Hallowell [Me.]
Glazier, Masters & co., 1830.
199 p. CSmH; DLC; MB; MH;

NjP; PU. 5304

A voyage to the Island of Philosophers. See Woodruff, Sylvester.

W

Waddell, Thomas.
Letters to the editors of the Catholic Miscellany illustrating the papal doctrine of intention; the opus operatium; Roman infallibility and the knavery of papish writers. New York, Protestant Press, 1830. 71 p. ICU; MBC; N; NHC; PPPrHi. 5305

The wages of sin; or, Strictures on the life and death of George Swearingen. Winchester, Samuel H. Davis, 1830. Winchester Republican, January 15, 1830. Not. loc. 5306

Wainwright, Jonathan Mayhew, 1793-1854.
A sermon, preached in Grace Church, New-York... September 19, 1830, on occasion of the death of the Right Rev. John Henry Hobart... to which are appended, some particulars of the bishop's last illness, by the Rev. F. H. Cuming. New York, Pub. by T. & J. Swords, Pr. by Edward J. Swords, 1830. 31 p. CtHT; MB; MBAt; MBNEH; MH; N; NGH; NjR; PHi; RPB; WHi. 5307

Waite, Daniel.
An address delivered before the Mutual Humane Working Class Association, March 15, 1830. Providence, Marshall & Hammond, prs., 1830. 8 p. RHi. 5308

Waite, George.
The surgeon-dentist's anatomical and physiological manual... Philadelphia, E. L. Carey and A. Hart [Thomas Kite, pr.] 1830. xii, 210, 6 p. CSmH; CSt-L;

MoSW-D; NIC; NNNAM; OC; PPC. 5309

Wakefield, Samuel, 1799-1895.
The American repository of sacred music, containing a great variety of Psalm and hymn tunes, original and selected; together with a plain introduction to the rudiments of music. Pittsburgh, Pr. and pub. by Cramer & Spear, 1830. 30, [2] p. RPB. 5310

Waldoborough, Me.
New Meeting-House, so-called, in Waldoboro'. [Waldoboro, 1830] 8 p. MMeT. 5311

Walker, Amasa, 1799-1875.
An oration delivered at Stoughton, Mass., July 5, 1830. In commemoration of the 54th anniversary of American Independence. Boston, John Marsh and William Souther [Waitt & Dow's, pr.] 1830. 31 p. DLC; MB; MH; PHi. 5312

Walker, David, 1785-1830.
Walker's appeal, in four articles; together with a preamble, to the colored citizens of the world... 2d ed., with corrections, &c. Boston, D. Walker, 1830. 80 p. DLC; MH; MHi. 5313

---- ---- 3d and last ed., with additional notes, corr., &c. Boston, Rev. and pub. by David Walker, 1830. 88 p. DLC; MB; MH; MWA; MdBP; MiD-B; NN; NNUT; OClWHi; PHi; PPAmP. 5314

Walker, James.
...On the Exclusive System. By James Walker. 2d ed. Printed for the American Unitarian Association. Boston, Gray and Bowen [Pr. by I. R. Butts] 1830. 34, [1] p. (1st series. No. 39) ICMe; IEG; MBAU; MH-AH; MHi; MMeT; MNF; MeBaT; N; OClWHi. 5315

Walker, James Scott.

An accurate description of the Liverpool and Manchester Railway, the tunnel, the bridges, and other works throughout the line; with a sketch of the objects which it presents interesting to the traveller or tourist. Repub. by the standing committee appointed by the inhabitants of Paterson, to forward the application for a rail-road from this place to the Hudson River, opposite New-York. Paterson, N. J., D. Burnett, 1830. 33, [1] p. CSmH; CtY; DBRE; DIC; MiU-T; N; NN. 5316

Walker, John.

An expostulary address to the members of the Methodist Society in Ireland. Belchertown, Wilson, 1830. 28 p. ICN; MH-AH. 5317

Walker, John, 1732-1807.

... Walker's critical pronouncing dictionary, and expositor of the English language, abridged... New-York, Sold by Collins & Hannay, J. A. Burtis, E. Bliss, C. Bartlett, G. C. Morgan, W. B. Gilley, and J. Allen. G. F. Bunce, pr., 1830. 528 p. (At head of title: Standard edition, with the author's last corrections.) KWiU. 5318

---- ---- Sandbornton, H. H., Pr. and pub. by N. Howland, 1830. (At head of title: Stereotype edition) 413 p. NhHi. 5319

Walker, Joseph.

An examination of the New Testament evidence on the mode of Baptism. Norway, Me., Pr. at the Observer Office by Wm. E. Goodnow, 1830. 24 p. MBC; MeHi; NNUT; PPPrHi. 5320

Walker, S. C.

The new Latin reader: containing the Latin text for the purpose of recitation; accompan-

ied with a key... for the use of beginners in the study of the Latin language. By S. C. Walker, 2d ed. Boston, Richardson, Lord and Holbrook, 1830. 196, 54 p. CtSoP; ICU; KyU; MH; NNC; OCHP. 5321

Walker, Timothy.

An address, delivered at the opening of the Charlestown Lyceum, January 5, 1830. Cambridge, Hilliard & Borwn, 1830. 24 p. M; MB; MH; MHi; MiD-B; OCHP; PU; RPB; BrMus. 5322

Wall, W.

A conference between two men that had doubts about infant baptism. New York, Protestant Episcopal Tract Society, 1830. 38 p. NNG. 5323

Walsh, Robert, 1784-1859.

Antimasonry. [Philadelphia?] 1830. 32 p. (Reprinted from American Quarterly Review, March, 1830.) MB. 5324

---- Notice of Brazil in 1828 and 1829. Boston, Richardson, Lord & Holbrook; New York, G. & C. & H. Carvill [etc., etc.] 1830. 2 v. IU. 5325

---- Review of "A narrative of the anti-Masonic excitement in the western part of the state of New York during the years 1826, 1827, 1828, and part of 1829. By Henry Brown, Batavia, N. Y." Portland, 1830. 32 p. Williamson: 10, 255. 5326

Walter Colyton; a tale. See Smith, Horatio.

Walton's Vermont register and farmer's almanac for 1831. By Zadock Thompson. Montpelier, E. P. Walton & Co. [1830] 72 l. CLU; InU; M; MB; MHi; MWA; N; NHi; NhHi; NjJ; OCLloyd;

OO; VtHi; VtU; WHi.   5327

Walz, E. L.
    Vollständige erklärung des cal-
enders, mit einem fasslichen unterricht über die himmelskörper,
insbesondere über die sonne und
der sich um sie bewegenden plan-
eten. In drey abtheilungen... Von
E. L. Walz... Reading, Johann
Ritter und comp., 1830. viii, 1 l.,
[3]-315 p. DLC; MH; MiU; MiU-
C; PHi; PLFM; PPG; PPL;
PPeSchw; PU.   5328

Wardlaw, Gilbert, 1798?-1873.
    Education for the Christian
ministry; an address, delivered
at the annual meeting of the committee and friends of the Black-
burn Theological Academy, held
June 24th, 1830. Manchester, Pr.
by J. Clarke, 1830. 2 p. l.,
[3]-19 p., 1 l. DLC.   5329

---- The testimony of Scripture
to the obligations and especially
of prayer for the gift of Holy
Spirit... Boston, Pub. by Peirce
and Williams, 1830. iv, 142, [6]
p. CBPac; CtHC; GDC; ICMcC;
IEG; IaHi; MBAt; MBC; MH;
MoSpD; NCH; NbOP; PPPrHi.
                           5330
---- ---- 2d American ed. Windsor, P. Merrifield and J. C. Allen; Pr. at the Chronicle Press,
1830. iv, 101 p. CtSoP; MBC;
Vt.   5331

Wardlaw, Ralph.
    Two Essays: I. On the Assur-
ance of Faith. II. On the extent
of the atonement and universal
pardon, in which the views of T.
Erskine are particularly examined.
New York, Jonathan Leavitt;
Crocker & Brewster, Boston
[Clayton & Van Norden, prs.]
1830. xxiii, [1], 261 p. MBC;
MH-AH; MWiW; MeBaT; NNUT;
PPLT; RP; RPA.   5332

Ware, Henry, 1794-1843.
    The connexion between the du-
ties of the pulpit and the pastor-
al office. An introductory ad-
dress delivered to the members
of the Theological School in Cam-
bridge, October 18 and 25, 1830.
Cambridge, Pub. by Hilliard &
Brown [Pr. by E. W. Metcalf &
Co.] 1830. 28 p. CBPac; ICMe;
MB; MBAU; MBC; MH-AH; MHi;
MdHi; MiD-B; NCH; NN; NjR;
PPAmP; PPL; PPPrHi; RPB;
WHi; BrMus.   5333

---- A farewell address to the
Second Church and Society in Bos-
ton, delivered October 4, 1830.
Boston, I. R. Butts, 1830. 12 p.
CBPac; CtHC; ICMe; MB; MBAU;
MH-AH; MMeT; RPB.   5334

---- Three important questions
answered relating to the Christian name... 4th ed. Boston,
1830. CtHC; MB; MH-AH. 5335

[Warren, George Washington]
1813-1883.
    The valedictory poem before
the class of 1830, delivered in
the college chapel, July 13. Cambridge, 1830. 16 p. CSmH; DLC;
MB; MH; OCHP.   5336

Warren, Henry.
    An address delivered at St.
Albans, July 5, 1830. Norridge-
wock, Pr. by Thomas J. Copeland, 1830. 31 p. MeLB.   5337

Warren, John Collins, 1778-1856.
    On the influence of the climate
of St. Augustine, Florida, on pul-
monary affections... Philadelphia,
Pr. by Joseph R. A. Skerrett,
1830. 8 p. ScU.   5338

Was Dr. Watts a believer in the
Supreme Divinity of Jesus Christ?
Boston, Pr. for the Massachusetts Evangelical Book & Pamphlet Society by Peirce & Williams

[1830?] 8 p. BrMus.   5339

Washington, George, 1732-1799.
Washington's farewell address
to the people of the United States,
September 19, 1796. Philadelphia,
Thomas T. Ash, A. Waldie, pr.
[1830] 55 p. CSmH; PPL.   5340

Washington, D. C.
Laws of the corporation of the
city of Washington: passed by
the twenty-seventh council. Pr. by
order of the council. Washington,
Pr. by Way & Gideon, 1830. 46,
6 p. IN-SC.   5341

---- Association of Mechanics.
Address of the Association
of Mechanics and other working
men of the city of Washington, to
the operatives throughout the
United States. Washington, Pr.
at the office of the National Journal by Wm. Duncan, 1830. 15 p.
DLC.   5342

---- Address of the mechanics and
other working men of Washington
City, to their fellow-citizens.
[Washington, D. C., 1830] 1 p.
DLC.   5343

---- Citizens.
To the Honorable the Senate
and House of Representatives of
the United States, in Congress assembled. The memorial of the
undersigned, citizens of Washington, respectfully showeth. That,
on the 15th May, 1820, your honorable bodies passed "An act to
incorporate the inhabitants of the
city of Washington, and to repeal
all acts heretofore passed for
that purpose..." [Washington,
1830] 2 p. DLC.   5344

---- First Unitarian Church.
Order of services, at the ordination of the Rev. Cazneay Palfrey, as pastor of the First Uni-

tarian Church in the City of
Washington, October 5, 1830.
1 p. DLC.   5345

Washington almanac for 1831.
By Nathan Bassett. Baltimore,
Cushing & Sons [1830] 18 l.
WvU.   5346

Washington & Baltimore Turnpike
Road Company.
Letter from the president of
the Washington and Baltimore
Turnpike Road Company, enclos-
ing an abstract, &c. Annapolis,
Pr. by Jeremiah Hughes, 1830.
[4] p. MdHi.   5347

Washington City Chronicle, Washington, D. C.
1830. Address of the carriers
of The Washington City Chronicle,
to its patrons. January 1, 1830.
[Washington, D. C., 1830] 1 p.
DLC.   5348

The Washington directory, showing the name, occupation, and
residence, of each head of a family & person in business, together with other useful information.
City of Washington, Pr. and pub.
by S. A. Elliot, 1830. 22, [7]-
107, [1] p. DLC.   5349

Washington monument. [Balti-
more] Pr. by James Young
[183-?] 1 p. DLC.   5350

The watchman's address... January 1, 1830. [Boston, 1830]
Bdsd. MB.   5351

Waterbury, Jared Bell, 1799-
1876.
The brighter age: a poem.
Boston, Crocker & Brewster,
1830. 94 p. CSmH; ICU; IU; MB;
MH; MWH; MiD; PU; TxU. 5352

---- Influence of religion on national prosperity. A sermon, delivered in Portsmouth, N. H. Ap-

ril 1, 1830, being the day of annual fast. Portsmouth, Pub. by John W. Shepard. Miller & Brewster, prs., 1830. 28 p. CSmH; DLC; MB; MH; MiD-B; N; NbU; Nh; WHi. 5353

Waterville College.
Catalogue of the officers and students of Waterville College, and of the Clinical School of Medicine, at Woodstock, connected with the College, 1830-1. Hallowell, Glazier, Masters & Co., prs., 1830. 12 p. DLC; MH; MeHi. 5354

Watervliet, N.Y. United Society.
Catalogue of medicinal plants and vegetable medicines, prepared in the United Society, Watervliet, N.Y. ...Orders to be directed to Watervliet, N.Y. Albany, Pr. by Packard and Van Benthuysen, 1830. 8 p. OClWHi. 5355

Watkins, Oliver.
Trial and a sketch of the life of Oliver Watkins, now under sentence of death in Brooklyn (Con.) jail, for the murder of his wife, March 22, 1829. The facts of his history obtained in part from his own mouth and partly from the testimony of others. Providence, H.H. Brown, pr., 1830. 36 p. DLC; MH-L; PP; RHi; RPB. 5356

Watson, John Fanning, 1780-1860.
Annals of Philadelphia, being a collection of memoirs... To which is added an appendix, containing olden time researches and reminiscences of New York City ... Philadelphia, E. L. Carey & A. Hart; New York, G. & C. & H. Carvill [Billmeyer, pr.] 1830. xii, 740, 78 p. CSmH; CtMW; DLC; ICU; IU; MH; MHi; MdHi; MoSpD; NR; NhHi; NjR; O; OCHP; OHi; PHi; PSC-Hi; PP;

PPL; PU; ScC; ScSoh; THi; WHi. 5357
---- ---- Philadelphia, For sale by Uriah Hunt, 1830. [4], xii, 740, 78, viii (index added) PPL. 5358

Watson, Richard.
Theological institutes; or, A view of the evidences, doctrines, morals, and institutions of Christianity...Stereotyped ed. New York, Pr. and pub. by J. & J. Harper, 1830. 454 p. ArCH; CtHT; GAU; ICU; NNUT; OMC; PPiW; ViRUT. 5359

Watterston, George.
Gallery of American portraits. Washington, Pub. by Pishey Thompson, A. Rothwell, pr., 1830. 123 p. NbU; PPL. 5360

Watts, Isaac, 1674-1748.
An arrangement of the psalms, hymns and spiritual songs, of the Rev. Isaac Watts, D.D. including (what no other volume contains) all his hymns, with which the vacancies in the first book were filled up in 1786, and also those in 1793. Now collated, with each of the doctor's own editions: to which are subjoined, Indexes, very much enlarged, both of Scriptures and of subjects. By John Rippon, D.D. Philadelphia, Pub. and for sale by David Clark, 1830. xxxvi p. hymns numbered 1-718, but pages not numbered. ViRU.
See also: Rippon, John. 5361

---- The cradle hymn, with the morning and evening hymns, by I. Watts... New York, Illman & Pilbrow [183-] 13 l. DLC. 5362
---- Watts' Divine songs for the use of young children. With handsome engravings. New-Haven, S. Babcock; Charleston, S. Babcock & Co., Sidney's press, 1830. 23 p. CtHi;

CtY. 5363

---- Hymns and spiritual songs. In three books. 1. Collected from the Scriptures. 2. Composed on divine subjects. 3. Prepared for the Lord's supper... Elizabethtown, N. J., Pub. by T. O. Sayre, 1830. 246 p. DLC; NjP; OO. 5364

---- ---- New London, W. & J. Bolles, 1830. 190 p. N; NNUT; PPeSchw. 5365

---- ---- Philadelphia, R. W. Pomeroy, 1830. 240 p. DLC; NcA-S. 5366

---- The improvement of the mind. By Isaac Watts, D. D. with corrections, questions and supplement. By Joseph Emerson... Rev. stereotype ed. Boston, Pub. by James Loring [1830] 234 p. NNC. 5367

The way of living in a method and by rule or A regular way of employing our time. New York, New York Protestant Episcopal Tract Society, 1830. 8 p. NNG. 5368

The way to be good and happy. Wendell, Mass., J. Metcalf, 1830. 1 p. l., [5]-18 p. DLC. 5369

Wayland, Francis, 1796-1865. The certain triumph of the redeemer. A sermon delivered in the Murray Street Church, on the evening of May 9, 1830. New York, Henry C. Sleight, Pr. by Sleight & Robinson, 1830. 39, [1] p. MH-AH; NRAB; RHi; RPB; BrMus. 5370

---- Encouragements to religious efforts: a sermon delivered at the request of the American Sunday School Union, May 25, 1830. Published at the request of the Board of Managers of the American Sunday School Union. Phila-delphia, American Sunday School Union, 1830. 72 p. CtHC; CtSoP; CtY; DLC; GDC; IU; KyDC; LNHT; MB; MBC; MeB; MeHi; MiD-B; NCH; NNG; NjPT; NjR; OClWHi; P; PHC; PHi; PPAmP; PPPrHi; RHi; RPB; WHi; BrMus. 5371

---- An introductory address delivered in Boston before the convention of teachers and other friends of education. August 19th, 1830. Boston, Hilliard, Gray, Little and Wilkins, 1830. 24 p. ICU; MiU; RPB. 5372

Wayne, James Moore, 1790-1867. Speech of James M. Wayne, of Georgia, on the bill to provide for the removal of the Indians west of the Mississippi. Delivered in the House of Representatives of the United States, May 24, 1830. Washington, Duff Green, pr., 1830. 16 p. DLC. 5373

... "We must live." New York, Pub. by the American Tract Society [183-?] 16 p. CSmH. 5374

Webb, Edwin. An oration, pronounced in the Methodist Episcopal Church, Hempstead, July 5, 1830, being the 54th anniversary of American Independence... Pr. at the Office of the Long Island Telegraph: by Le Fevre| & Hutchinson, 1830. 14 p. NBLiHi; NSmb; NjQ. 5375

Webb, James Watson. Albany, January 13, 1830. To the members of the Legislature of the state of New York. During my absence from New-York, I have been grossly assailed by the conductors of the New-York press ... [Albany, 1830] Bdsd. NN. 5376

Webster, Daniel, 1782-1852. Extracts from the writings and speeches of Daniel Webster, and from a paper sustained by his

endorsements, called the Massachusetts Journal. [n. p. , 183-?]
16 p. CSmH. 5377

---- ... Mr. Webster's second
speech. Second speech of Mr.
Webster on Mr. Foot's resolution.
In Senate Jan. 20, 1830. 2 p.
At head of title: Supplement. DLC.
5378

---- Second speech of Hon. Daniel
Webster, delivered in the Senate
of the United States, January 26,
1830. With a sketch of the preced-
ing debate on the resolution of Mr.
Foot, respecting the sale, &c. of
public lands. Boston, Carter &
Hendee, 1830. xvi, 76 p. CSmH;
DLC; ICN; KWiU; MBC; MH-AH;
MHi; MMeT; MeB; MiD-B; N;
NNUT; OCHP; PPL; PU. 5379

---- Speech of Daniel Webster, in
reply to Mr. Hayne, of South Carolina: the resolution offered by Mr.
Foot, of Connecticut, relative to
the public lands, being under consideration. Delivered in the Senate, January 26, 1830. [1830?]
32p. CSmH; DLC; NcU; PPL.
5380

---- ---- Cincinnati, Pr. by Lodge,
L'Hommedieu & Hammond, 1830.
40 p. InHi; OCLaw; BrMus. 5381

---- ---- New York, Pr. by Elliott
& Palmer, 1830. 72 p. ICU; IU;
MB; PHi. 5382

---- ---- Washington, Pr. by
Gales & Seaton, 1830. 76 p.
CSmH; DLC. 5383

---- ---- Washington, Pr. by
Gales & Seaton, 1830. 96 p. CSmH;
DLC; PPL (two varieties, 1: "Ah,
Sir" passage on p. 96; 2: Without
this passage) 5384

---- Speech of Daniel Webster,
on the subject of the public lands,
&c. delivered in the Senate of

the United States, January 20,
1830. Washington, Pr. by Gales
& Seaton, 1830. 28 p. CSmH;
DLC; DeGE; PPL. 5385

---- Speeches and forensic argu-
ments. Boston, Perkins & Mar-
vin, and Gray & Bowen. New
York, Jonathan Leavitt, 1830.
520 p. AMob; CtMW; DLC;
GMM; Ky; LNHT; LU; MB; MBC;
MH; MHi; MeHi; MoS; NNLI;
NhHi; Nj; OClWHi; PHi; PPL;
RPB; ScCliJ; ScU; TN. 5386

---- [Supplement containing second part of Mr. Webster's speech
in reply to Hayne. Jan. 28?
1830] 2 p. DLC. 5387

Webster, Noah, 1758-1843.
An American dictionary of the
English language; exhibiting the
origin, orthography, pronunciation, and definitions of words...
3d ed. New York, Pub. by S.
Converse, Stereotyped at the Boston Type and Stereotype Foundry,
1830. xxiii, [1], 1011 p. DLC;
PPL. 5388

---- ---- 5th ed. New York, S.
Converse, 1830. xxiii, [1], 1011
p. KyU; MH; PP; ViU; BrMus.
5389

---- The American spelling book,
containing the rudiments of the
English language, for the use of
schools in the United States. The
revised impression with latest
corrections. Concord, N. H. ,
Pub. by Horatio Hill & Co. ,
1830. 168 p. MH; NhM. 5390

---- Biography for the use of
schools. By N. Webster, LL. D.
New Haven, Pr. by H. Howe,
1830. 214 p. Ct; DLC; MB;
MHi. 5391

---- A brief view 1. Of errors
and obscurities in the common
version of the scriptures...

2. Of errors and defects in class-books used in seminaries of learning... 3. A few plagiarisms, showing the way in which books may be made, by those who use borrowed capital. [n. p., 183-?] 24 p. DLC.   5392

---- A dictionary of the English language: abridged from the American dictionary, for the use of primary schools and the counting house. New-York, White, Gallaher, & White, 1830. 4 p. l., 532 p.   CSmH; CtHT-W; DLC; MH; Nj.   5393

---- The elementary spelling book; Being an improvement on the American spelling book. Philadelphia, Pub. by Kimber & Sharpless, Stereotyped by A. Chandler, 1830. 168 p. KTW; RPB.   5394

[----] The prompter; or a commentary on common sayings and subjects: which are full of common sense, the best sense in the world. Cleaveland, Pub. by R. Pew & Co. David B. M'Lain, pr., 1830. 88, [2] p. OCl; OClWHi.   5395

---- Series of books for systematic instruction in the English language. A description of Noah Webster's school books together with, "discrepancies of English orthography." New Haven, Baldwin & Treadway [H. Howe, pr.] 1830. 16 p. CtHi; CtY; MH; MWA; PPAmP.   5396

Webster's calendar: or the Albany almanack for 1831. By Edwin E. Prentiss. Albany, Webster & Skinners [1830] 18 1. Ct; MWA; MiU-C; MnU; N; NBuHi; NHi; NN; WHi.   5397

---- ---- Albany, Webster & Skinners [1830] 2d ed. 18 1.

MWA; NHi.   5398

Weems, Mason Locke, 1759-1825.
    The life of George Washington; with curious anecdotes... Philadelphia, J. Allen, 1830. 228 p. CSmH; DGU; OHi; PHi.   5399

[Weld, Theodore Dwight] 1803-1895.
    The Bible against slavery... An inquiry into the patriarchal and Mosaic systems on the subject of human rights. [New York? 183-?] 74 p. DLC; MH.   5400

The Well spent sou; or, Bibles for the poor Negroes. Translated from the French by Jacob Porter. New-Haven, Pr. by Baldwin & Treadway, 1830. 16 p. CBPac; CSmH; MB; MBC; MH-AH; PPL.   5401

Weller, George, ed.
    Tracts on several important topics of religion. Collected and edited by George Weller... Philadelphia, Pr. and pub. by J. Harding, 1830. 2 vols. CtHT; ICU; IU; Md; MeBaT; MoS; NBuDD; NNG; RNR; TCU.   5402

Wells, Mrs. Anna Maria (Foster) 1795?-1868.
    Poems and juvenile sketches. Boston, Carter, Hendee & Babcock [Waitt & Dow, prs.] 1830. 104 p. CtHi; DLC; ICU; IaU; LU; MBC; MH; NNP; NbU; OO; PU; RPB; TxU; BrMus.   5403

Wenceslaus, Clement, bp.
    Proofs of the true church. In two parts, by Clement Wenceslaus, Archbishop and Elector of Treves, and Bishop of Augsburg. Translated from the French. Boston, Pub. by William Smith for the editors of "The Jesuit." 1830. 223 p. DCU; DGU; MBC; MdW.   5404

Wesley, John, 1703-1791.
Des Christen handbuch, eine
abhandlung uber Christliche voll-
kommenheit; mit anweisungen
diesen zustand zu erlangen.
Hauptsachlich zusammengetragen
aus den werken des Ehrw. Hrn.
Joh. Wesley. Aus dem Englisch-
en ubersetzt-Erste auflage. Harrisburg, Gedruckt und herausgegeben von John T. Bobbs, 1830.
216 p. MiU-C; PPLT.   5405

---- The works of John Wesley.
In ten volumes, containing the
extracts of the Rev. John Wes-
ley's journal. New York, J.
& J. Harper, 1830. 10 v.
MWA.   5406

West, George Montgomery.
Address of the Rev. George
Montgomery West, A. M., Chaplain to the Bishop of Ohio, on
the completion of his mission to
Europe, delivered before the Rt.
Rev. Philander Chase... [Gam-
bier?] 1830. 9 p. MH; OCHP.
                           5407
West, William, 1770-1854.
Tavern anecdotes, and reminiscences of the origin of signs,
coffee-houses, &c. intended as a
laugh-book for citizens and their
country cousins, by one of the old
school. New York, S. & D. A.
Forbes, 1830. 208 p. PU.   5408

West-Chester County (N. Y.) Temperance Society.
First report of the West-Chester County Temperance Society,
presented at the annual meeting
at White-Plains, August 12, 1830.
Together with the address of the
president. New York, Ludwig &
Tolefree, 1830. 12 p. ScCC.
                           5409
[Westcott, Hampton]
Sir, The following statement
was prepared by me some days
ago... [concerns controversey between R. Dillon Drake, Charles

H. Duryee, etc.] [Philadelphia,
1830] [12 p.] PPL.   5410

The Western agriculturist, and
practical farmer's guide. Prepared under the superintendence
of the Hamilton County Agricultural Society. Cincinnati, Robinson and Fairbank, 1830. 367 p.
DLC; ICN; IU; InU; KyLxT; NcD;
O; OC; OCHP; OHi.   5411

Western almanac for 1831. By
Oliver Loud. Cleveland, Henry
Bolles [1830] 12 l. OClWHi.
                           5412
The Western almanac, for the
states of Ohio, Kentucky, and In-
diana for 1831. By Oner R.
Powell. Cincinnati, W. Conclin
[1830] 12 l. MWA; OClWHi.
                           5413
Western almanack for 1831. Ba-
tavia, A. P. Parker [1830] 12 l.
DLC; NRMA.   5414

---- Fredonia, Henry C. Frisbee [1830] DLC (11 l.)   5415

---- Le Roy; Elisha Starr
[1830] 12 l. CSmH; NRMA. 5416

---- Rochester, E. Peck & Co.
[1830] 12 l. MWA; N; NR;
NRHi; NRU; NUtHi.   5417

---- Watertown, Knowlton &
Rice [1830] 12 l. MWA.   5418

The Western almanack, for the
States of Ohio, Kentucky, and In-
diana for 1831. Cincinnati, Geo.
T. Williamson. [1830] 12 l.
KyBgW; MWA; OClWHi.   5419

---- Issue with 24 l. OMC. 5420

The Western farmer's almanac
for 1831. By Rev. John Taylor.
Pittsburgh, H. Holdship & Son;
D. and M. Maclean, prs. [1830]
18 l. DLC; ICHi; InU; MWA; NN;
OClWHi; OMC; PHi; PPi.   5421

---- Issue with added "Magazine." 36 l. MWA; PPi.   5422

Western Rail-road Corporation.
   [Articles which will be brought over the Western Rail-way from the towns west of Boston.] n. p. [1830] 1 sheet. DBRE; M. 5423

Western Reserve College, Hudson.
   Catalogue of books belonging to the library of Western Reserve College. [n. p., 1830?] 18 p. OClW; OClWHi.   5424

Westfield Academy, Westfield, Mass.
   Catalogue of the trustees, instructors & students of Westfield Academy, for the year, ending Nov. 1830. [Westfield] Office of the Westfield Register, 1830. 16 p. MH.   5425

Weston, John E.
   Claims of the poor; discourse before the Female Benevolent Society of Charlestown, and the Female Charitable Society of East Cambridge. Boston, 1830. 16 p. MBC; MH-AH; RPB.   5426

Wetmore, Prosper Montgomery, 1798-1876.
   Lexington, with other fugitive poems. New York, G. & C. & H. Carvill [Ludwig & Tolefree, prs.] 1830. 87, [1] p. CSmH; CtHT; DLC; ICU; MB; MH; MiU-C; NCH; NN; NNS; Nh; NjP; NjR; OO; RNR; RP; TxU; BrMus. 5427

Wheaton, Nathaniel Sheldon, 1792-1862.
   A journal of a residence in London; including excursions through various parts of England; and a short tour in France and Scotland; in the years 1823 and 1824... Hartford, H. & F. J. Huntington; New York, G. & C. & H. Carvill; etc., etc., 1830. 520 p.   Philemon Canfield,

pr.] CSmH; Ct; CtHT; CtHi; DLC; KyLx; MB; MBC; MdBP; NGH; NNS; PPL; PU; RPB; TxDaM.   5428

Whelpley, Samuel A. N.
   A compend of history from earliest times. General view of the present state of the world, with respect to civilization, religion & government. New York, Collins & Hannay, publisher [W. E. Dean, pr.] 1830. 352 p. CtMW; GU; ICN; MeLB; NGH; OO; PLFM; ViU.   5429

Whelpley, Samuel W.
   Address delivered before the Peace Society of Hartford County, in the Centre Church, Hartford. By... pastor of the First Ecclesiastical Society, East Windsor. Hartford, Pr. by Philemon Canfield, 1830. 32 p. CtHi; ICT; MBAt; MBC.   5430

Whig Committee of Vigilance.
   [Undated circular letter urging all voters to go to the polls.] [n. p., ca. 1830] Bdsd. DeGE.   5431

Whipple, Francis Putnam.
   Rules for the pronunciation of the Latin and Greek languages, etc., to which are added tables exhibiting a systematic order of parsing those languages. Middlebury, Pr. by O. & J. Miner, 1830. 19, [1] p. CoU; MB; N; VtHi; BrMus.   5432

White, Daniel Appleton.
   An address, delivered at Ipswich, before the Essex County Lyceum, at their first annual meeting, May 5, 1830. Salem, Foote & Brown, prs., 1830. 60 p. CSmH; DLC; IaHi; In; M; MBAt; MBC; MH-AH; MHi; MeB; MiD-B; MnU; MoSpD; N; NNS; NNUT; NjR; P; PPAmP; RPB; BrMus.
                          5433

White, Hugh.

Cosmogenia... Watertown, N. Y., Pub. for the proprietor, by E. E. Camp, 1830. 34 p. OClWHi; PBa; WHi.   5434

White, Samuel.
  History of the American troops during the late war under the command of Colonels Fenton and Campbell. Baltimore, Samuel White, publisher [B. Edes, pr.] 1830. 107 p. ICN; IHi; IaHA; MB; MnM; NIC; NN; NhHi; OC; OkHi; PHC; PHi; RHi; T.   5435

White, William.
  A sermon on early piety, delivered in the Philadelphia House of Refuge, on Sunday, June 4th, 1829. Philadelphia, Jesper Harding, pr., 1830. 16 p. MH; NGH; NNG; OMC; PHC; PHi; PPPrHi.
                            5436
[----] Three letters to the Editor of the American Quarterly Review. Extracted from the Protestant Episcopalian for October, 1830. 15 p. MB; MBC; MdHi; PHi; PPL.   5437

The white kitten. A sequel to 'Mary and her cat.' Boston, Pub. by Munroe and Francis [1830] 35 p. PPL.   5438

Whitecross, John.
  The Assembly's shorter catechism, illustrated with appropriate anecdotes; chiefly designed to assist parents and Sabbath school teachers in the instruction of youth. By John Whitecross, Teacher, Edinburgh. New Bedford, Stephen S. Smith, 1830. 180 p. CSmH; MDeeP; MWA; NN.
                            5439
---- ---- New York, Pub. by Jonathan Leavitt; Boston, Crocker & Brewster, 1830. iv, 183 p. NNC-T; PPPrHi.   5440

[Whiting, Henry]
  The age of steam, by ____

Anonymous, esq. Detroit, 1830. 16 p. On verso of t. p., at bottom right: [Pr. at the Journal Office.] MiD-B.   5441

[----] ---- (On verso of t. p., at bottom left: Printed at the Journal Office.) MiD-B.   5442

Whiting, Nathan.
  Bible history, illustrated by engravings, on the manners and customs of the ancients, together with some historical scenes explained and made familiar. New Haven, Prepared and pub. by Nathan Whiting [183-?] 286 p., 1 l. CtY.   5443

Whiting, Samuel.
  The elementary reader: being a collection of original reading lessons, for common schools... New York, Pr. and pub. by Mahlon Day, 1830. 180 p. CtHT-W.
                            5444
Whitman, Bernard, 1796-1834.
  Christian salvation. A discourse delivered in Wilton, N. H., January 13, 1830, at the ordination of Rev. Stephen A. Barnard ... Boston, Isaac R. Butts [Pr. by I. R. Butts, Boston] 1830. 44 p. CBPac; ICMcC; MH-AH; MMeT; OCHP; PPL; RPB. 5445

---- ---- 2d ed. Boston, James Munroe & Co. [Press of I. R. Butts] 1830. (American Unitarian Society. 1st Series. No. 33.) ICMe; ICU; MBAt; MH-AH; MHi; MMeT-Hi.   5446

---- Two letters to the Rev. Moses Stuart; on the subject of religious liberty. By Bernard Whitman. Boston, Pub. by Gray and Bowen [Cambridge, E. W. Metcalf & Co., prs.] 1830. 165, [1] p. CBPac; CSmH; CtHC; CtHT; ICN; IU; MB; MH-AH; MHi; MeB; MiU-C; OCHP; OkU; PPAmP; PPPrHi; RPB; WHi;

BrMus.   5447

Whitman, Nathaniel, 1785-1869.
"Being defamed, we entreat."
... Boston, Wells & Lilly, 1830.
20 p. CtY; DLC; ICN; MB;
MBAt; MH; MHi; MWA; MiD-B;
RPB; WHi; BrMus.   5448

Whittemore, Thomas, 1800-1861.
An examination of Dr. Beecher's sermon against Universalism. Delivered in the Town-
house in Dorchester Mass. Sunday evening, March 28, 1830.
Boston, Pub. at the Trumpet
Office, [1830?] 36 p. NcD;
BrMus.   5449

---- Modern history of Univer-
salism from the era of the re-
formation, to the present time...
Boston, Pub. by the author
[Power Press] 1830. 458 p.
CBPac; CSmH; Ct; ICN; KWiU;
MB; MBAt; MH-AH; MMet-Hi;
MeBaT; NR; NhHi; NjR; OHi; OO;
PHi; RNR; RPB; PU; THi;
BrMus.   5450

---- A sermon, delivered at the
dedication of the Universalist
Meeting House, in Dedham,
Mass. Thursday, January 14,
1830. Boston, Pr. by G. W.
Bazin, 1830. 21, [2] p. ICMe;
MB; MMeT-Hi; MWA; MiD-B;
RPB; BrMus.   5451

---- A sermon, on the parable
of the rich man and Lazarus...
3d ed. Boston, Pr. by G. W.
Bazin, Trumpet Office, 1830.
24 p. MMeT; MWA; PPL.   5452

Whittingham, William Rollinson,
ed., 1805-1879.
Standard works adopted to the
use of the Protestant Episcopal
Church in the United States. New
York, Pub. by Protestant Epis-
copal Press, 1830. 3 vols.
CBCDS; CtHT; GDC; ICU; KyU;

MdHi; NNG; NSyU; NT.   5453

Whittlesey, Frederick.
Report. On the abduction and
murder of William Morgan, and
on the conduct and measures of
the Masonic fraternity to prevent
convictions, &c. [Philadelphia?
1830] 18 p. CSmH.   5454

Who is your representative? or
Imposter exposed. To the free
and independent voters of Baltimore... [Signed] Poker. [Balti-
more, 183-] 1 p. DLC.   5455

The whole art of legerdemain,
or Hocus-pocus laid open and
explained by those renowned masters Sena Sama, Hamed Ben-Ali,
etc., with full instructions how
to perform the various tricks on
cards, dice, birds, eggs, rings,
&c. (Nickerson's ed.) Baltimore, C. V. Nickerson, 1830.
64+ p. MH.   5456

Whyte, James.
Sermons on doctrinal and
practical subjects by the Rev.
James White,... Philadelphia,
Pub. for the benefit of the au-
thor's family, and for sale by
Towar & Hogan, 1830. 379 p.
ICMcC; IaDuU; KKcB; NSchU.
                          5457
Wickliffe, pseud. See Baptist,
Edward.

Wickliffe, Robert, 1775-1859.
An oration delivered on the
22nd February 1830, at the re-
quest of the Union Philosophical
Society of Transylvania Univer-
sity. Lexington [Ky.], Pr. by
Thomas Smith, 1830. 8 p.
CSmH; OOxM.   5458

---- Speech by Robert Wickliffe,
in the Senate of Ky., upon the
tariff and internal improvements;
and in response to certain resolutions from South Carolina.

Frankfort, Ky., Pr. by J. H. Holeman, 1830. 59 p. ICU; PHi. 5459

---- To the freemen of Fayette County. Fellow Citizens, [text begins] [Lexington, 1830?] Bdsd. [An appeal for election to the Kentucky legislature.] KyLx. 5460

Wigham, John.
Christian instruction in a discourse as between a mother and her daughter. Philadelphia, To be had of Thomas Kite, 1830. 16 p. (No. 6) InRE. 5461

Wilberforce, William, 1759-1833.
A practical view of the prevailing religious system of professed Christians, in the higher and middle classes, contrasted with real Christianity. From a late London ed. ...New York, American Tract Society [183-?] 375, 96 p. (Evangelical family library; issued with J. Flavel's The touchstone of sincerity) DLC; KU; MH; NbOM; NcD; OO; ViU. 5462

Wilbraham Academy.
Catalogue of the officers and students of the Wesleyan Academy, Wilbraham, Mass. Spring term, April, 1830. [Springfield? 1830] 8 p. MB. 5463

Wilbur, Hervey, 1787-1852.
Elements of astronomy, descriptive and physical: in which the general phenomena of the heavenly bodies and the theory of the tides are familiarly explained ... The work is... intended for schools, academies...and for private reading. 2d. ed., with an appendix of problems on the globes and useful tables. New-Haven, Pub. by Durrie & Peck, 1830. 144 p. CtHi; CtMW; MBC; MH; MeHi; MoSU; NNC; NjC. 5464

---- A lexicon of useful knowledge, for the use of schools and libraries, with several hundred engravings... New York, White, Gallaher & White [Sleight & Robinson, prs.] 1830. 295 p. CSmH; MBAt; TNJ; WHi; BrMus. 5465

Wilde, Richard Henry.
Speech of Mr. Wilde, of Georgia, on the bill for removing the Indians from the East to the West side of the Mississippi. Delivered in the House of Representatives, on the 20th May, 1830. Washington, Pr. by Gales & Seaton, 1830. 66 p. CSmH; DLC; PPL. 5466

Wilkins, John Hubbard.
Elements of astronomy, illustrated with plates, for the use of schools and academies, with questions... Stereotype ed. Boston, Hilliard, Gray, Little, and Wilkins, 1830. viii, 152 p. CLSU; CtMW; GU; ICU; MH; NNE; OClWHi; OMC; OO. 5467

Wilkinson, Edward, 1728-1809.
Wisdom, a poem. Providence, H. H. Brown, pr., 1830. 23 p. DLC; MB; MNBedf; NNC; RHi; RPB; TxU. 5468

Willard, Emma.
History of the United States, or Republic of America: exhibited in connexion with its chronology and progressive geography; by means of a series of maps... 3d ed., rev. and corr. New York, White, Gallaher & White, 1830. xl, 424, xliv p. IHi; Me; NNC; PU. 5469

Willard, Joseph, 1798-1865.
An address to the members of the bar of Worcester County, Massachusetts, October 2, 1829 ... Lancaster, Carter, Andrews, and company, prs., 1830. 144 p. CSmH; PPL. 5470

[Willard, Samuel] 1776-1859.

The general class-book, or
Interesting lessons in prose and
verse. Greenfield, A. Phelps.
For sale also by Richardson,
Lord & Holbrook, Hilliard, Gray
& Co. Peirce & Williams. Bos-
ton, S. Butler, 1830. 324 p.
CtHT-W; MNF.   5471

---- Rhetoric, or The principles
of elocution and rhetorical composition. Boston, Leonard C.
Bowles, 1830. 198 p. ICU;
MDeeP; MH; OO.   5472

---- Sacred poetry and music
reconciled; or, A collection of
hymns... Boston, Leonard C.
Bowles. Sold also by Gray &
Bowen, and by Richardson, Lord
& Holbrook, Press of Minot
Pratt, 1830. 360 p. CBPac;
MBAU; MBAt; MBC; MH-AH;
MHi; NB; NNUT; RPB; TxU.
                             5473
[----] Secondary lessons, or The
improved reader! intended as a
sequel to the Franklin primer...
10th ed. Greenfield, Mass., Pr.
and pub. by A. Phelps, 1830.
186 p. CtHT-W.   5474

[----] ----11th ed. Greenfield,
Mass., Pr. and pub. by A.
Phelps, 1830. 186 p. CtHT-W.
                             5475
Willetts, Jacob.
    Book-keeping, by single entry.
[rev. ed.] Poughkeepsie [N. Y.]
Pr. and pub. by P. Potter, 1830.
12 p., 1 1., 4 numb. 1., 21 p.
CSmH; NP.   5476

William and Mary College. Wil-
liamsburg, Va.
    Laws and regulations of the
College of William and Mary, in
Virginia. Richmond, Pr. by
Thomas W. White, 1830. 23 p.
MBC; MH; Vi; ViW.   5477

Williams, Catherine (Arnold),
1790-1872.

Tales; national and revolutionary. By Mrs. Catherine R. Williams, author of Religion at
home, Original poems, etc.
Providence, H. H. Brown, pr.,
1830. 216 p. CU; CtY; DLC;
ICN; ICU; IU; MB; MH; MWA;
PU; RHi; RPB.   5478

Williams, Charles James Blasins.
    A rational exposition of the
physical signs of the diseases of
the lungs and pleura; illustrating
their pathology, and facilitating
their diagnosis. Philadelphia,
Carey & Lea, 1830. 203, [1] p.,
1 1. DLC; ICJ; IU-M; LU-Med;
MB; MdUM; MoU; NIC; NRAM;
NcU; OCGHM; PPC; PU; TNJ.
                             5479
Williams, John.
    ...The life and actions of
Alexander the great. New York,
Pr. by J. & J. Harper, 1830.
351 p. (Harper's stereotype ed.)
MA; MH; MdBP; MoSU; NGH;
NNF; NNS; NhHi; NjR; RPB;
TNJ.   5480

Williams, John Bickerton, 1792-
1855.
    Memoirs of the life, charac-
ter, and writings of the Rev.
Matthew Henry... From the 3d
London ed. Boston Peirce &
Williams; Philadelphia, Towar &
Hogan, 1830. 335, [1], xii p.
CBPac; CtMW; GDC; ICU; InGrD;
KyDC; MB; MBC; MH-AH; NGH;
NbOM; NcMHi; NhHi; NjP; OO;
PHi; PU; RPB; ViAlTh; WBB.
                             5481
Williams, N. W.
    An address, delivered at the
organization of the Hopkinton Ab-
stinence Society, Nov. 12, 1829.
Concord, Pr. by Moses G. At-
wood, 1830. 12 p. MWA.   5482

Williams, Peter.
    A discourse delivered in St.
Philip's Church, for the benefit
of the colored community of Wil-

berforce, in Upper Canada, on
the fourth of July, 1830. New-
York, Pr. by G. F. Bunce, 1830.
16 p. NGH; NN.   5483

Williams, Samuel, 1743-1817.
A history of the American revolution; intended as a reading
book for schools. By Samuel Williams... 10th stereotype ed. New-
Haven, Durrie & Peck, 1830.
204 p. CtHi; CtY.   5484

---- ---- 11th stereotyped ed.
New-Haven, Pub. by William
Storer, jr., Baldwin & Treadway,
pr., 1830. 204 p. CtHi.   5485

---- ---- 12th stereotype ed.
New Haven, Pub. by Wm. Storer,
Jun., Pr. at the Journal Office,
1830. 204 p. CtHi.   5486

Williams College.
Catalogue of the officers and
students of Williams College,
and the Berkshire Medical Institution, connected with it. 1830-
31. [Williamstown, R. Bannister? 1830] 20 p. DNLM; MWiW;
NNNAM.   5487

---- Celebration of American in-
dependence. Williams College,
July 5, 1830. [Williamstown, R.
Bannister? 1830] 4 p. MWiW.
                                  5488
---- Commencement, Williams
College, September 1, 1830.
[Williamstown, R. Bannister?
1830] 4 p. MWiW.   5489

---- Exhibition of the Junior
class. Williams College, May
18, 1830. [Williamstown, R.
Bannister? 1830] 2 l. MWiW.
                                  5490
---- Senior exhibition. Williams
College, December 28, 1830.
[Williamstown, R. Bannister?
1830] 2 l. MWiW.   5491

---- Adelphic Union.

Exhibition of the Adelphic Un-
ion Society. Williams College,
August 4, 1830. [Williamstown,
R. Bannister? 1830] 4 p.
MWiW.   5492

Williams College Temperance Society.
Temperance Society of William College [n.p., 183-?] Bdsd.
CSmH.   5493

Williamson, J. D.
Intemperance reproved. A
discourse [on Is. XIX.4], etc.
[Albany? 1830?] BrMus.   5494

Willig's Pocket companion; containing a selection of songs, airs,
waltzes, marches, &c. arranged
for the German flute, violin or
patent flageolet. Philadelphia,
1830. 166 p. PHi.   5495

Willis, Thomas.
A short account of the reli-
gious exercise and experience of
Betty, an Indian woman... New
York, Samuel Wood & Sons, 1830.
23 p. PPRF.   5496

Willison, John, 1680-1750.
The afflicted man's companion;
or, A directory for persons and
families, afflicted by sickness or
any other distress, and directions
to the sick, both under and after
affliction... 2d Pittsburgh ed.,
to which is annexed A friendly
visit to the house of mourning.
By the Rev. Richard Cecil...
Pittsburgh, Pub. by Luke Loomis
& Co., D. & M. Maclean, prs.,
1830. 252 p. GDC; NN; PPi.
                                  5497
---- The balm of Gilead for heal-
ing a diseased land; with The
glory of the ministration of the
spirit; and a scripture prophecy
of the increase of Christ's Kingdom and the destruction of anti-
Christ. Opened and applied in
twelve sermons upon several

texts. Pittsburgh, Pub. by Luke Loomis & Co., Pr. by Johnston & Stockton, 1830. 260 p. 2d Pittsburgh ed. CSansS; ICU; MA; MnU; PPPrHi; PPiPT. 5498

---- A sacramental catechism; or, A familiar instructor for young communicants. Plainly unfolding the nature of the covenant of grace, with the two seals, thereof, baptism and the Lord's supper. Pittsburgh, Pub. by Luke Loomis, D. & M. Maclean, prs., 1830. 269, [6] p. GDC; MoU; OClWHi; P; PPi; PPiPT. 5499

---- The young communicants catechism. New York, Pr. and pub. by John C. Totten, 1830. iv, 92 p. MAJ; MB; MH; MH-AH. 5500

Willits, John H.
An elementary treatise of natural philosophy; designed for the use of students. Philadelphia, Uriah Hunt, 1830. viii, 470, 2, 24 p. CSt; In; MiD; MiU; OU; P; PHi; PP; PSC-Hi; PU-P. 5501

Wilmsen, Friedrich Phillipp, 1770-1831.
Der Deutsche Kinderfreund, ein Lesebuch fur Volksschulen. Erste Amerikanische Auflage nach der sechzigsten Europaischen. Vermehrt mit geographischen Zusatzen und einer kurzen deutschen Sprachlehre fur Americanisch deutsche Volksschulen. Gedruckt auf Veraustaltung einer Committee der St. Michaels u. Zions-Gemeinde. Philadelphia, Pr. by Gossler u. Blumer, 1830. Seidensticker p. 247. CtY; PHi; PPG; PU. 5502

Wilson, Daniel, bp. of Calcutta, 1778-1858.
The evidences of Christianity: stated in a popular and practical manner, in a course of lectures

... Boston, Crocker & Brewster, 1830. xvi, 26-410, [2] p. CBPac; IU; KyLoP; MBC; NBuDD; NNG; NbCrD. 5503

Wilson, James Patriot.
A free conversation on the unpardonable sin: wherein the blasphemy against the Holy Spirit, the final apostasy, and the sin unto death, are shown to have been originally distinct. Philadelphia, Towar, J. & D. M. Hogan; [etc., etc.] 1830. 171, [1] p. CSansS; DLC; GDC; ICU; IEG; PPPrHi. 5504

Wilson, William.
A manual of instruction for infants' schools, with an engraved sketch of the area of an infants' school-room and playground, -of the abacus, of a scheme of instruction, and the tables of numbers. New York, G. & C. & H. Carvill; stereotyped by Wm. Hagar and company, 1830. 222, [6] p. NjR; PWW. 5505

Winchell, R.
The sacred songster, or Divine songs for the conference meetings, and for the private devotions of the pious. Cincinnati, Pr. at the Chronicle office, 1830. 212 p. IU. 5506

[Winchester, George]
Address to the mayor & city council, on the trade of the Susquehanna, and the rail road to that river. Baltimore, Pr. by Lucas and Deaver, 1830. 24 p. CtY; MH-BA; MdHi; NNE; OCHP; PHi; PPL. 5507

Windsor, Vermont. First Congregational Church.
The confession of faith and covenant of the First Congregational Church in the East Parish of Windsor, Vt. Windsor, Pr.

at the Chronicle Press, 1830.
8 p. CSmH; MBC; MiD-B; NN.
5508
[Winslow, Hubbard] 1799-1864.
An evangelical view of the nature and means of regeneration;
comprising a review of "Dr. Tyler's Strictures," by Evangelus
Pacificus. Boston, Perkins &
Marvin, 1830. 40 p. CtHT-W;
IEG; IU; MB; MBC; MH-AH;
MeBaT; NCH; Nh; OO; PPPrHi.
5509
[----] Examination of Dr. Tyler's
vindication of his "Strictures" on
the Christian Spectator, by Evangelus Pacificus. Boston, Perkins & Marvin, 1830. 56 p.
CSansS; Ct; CtHC; IU; MB; MBC;
MH-AH; MeBaT; NCH; NNG; OO;
PPL; PPPrHi.   5510

Winter, Mary.
Alton Park; or Conversations
on religious and moral subjects;
chiefly designed for the amusement and instruction of young
ladies. Philadelphia, Pub. by
Eugene Cummiskey [c. 183-] 406
p. DLC.   5511

[Wirt, Mrs. Elizabeth Washington (Gamble)] 1784-1857.
Flora's dictionary. By a
lady... Baltimore, F. Lucas
[1830?] [192] p. DLC; MdHi;
MnU; NNG; OC; PP-W; RPA.
5512
Wirt, William, 1772-1834.
An address delivered before
the Peithessophian and Philo-
clean Societies of Rutgers College.
Delivered and published at the request of the Peithessophian Society. New Brunswick, N. J.,
Rutgers press, Terhune & Letson, prs., 1830. 34 p. CSmH;
DLC; PPL.   5513

---- ---- 2d ed. New Brunswick,
N. J., Rutger's press, Terhune
& Letson, prs., 1830. 34 p.
CSmH; DLC; MB; MH-AH; MdHi;

MiD-B; N; NNG; NNUT; NbU;
Nj; NjN; NjR; PHC; PHi; PPAmP;
PPL; PPPrHi; PU; TNJ; WHi;
BrMus.   5514

---- Argument delivered at Annapolis, by William Wirt, Esq.,
late attorney general of the
United States, before the chancellor of Maryland, on the 19th and
20th days of August, 1829, in
support of a motion to dissolve
an injunction obtained by the Baltimore and Ohio Rail-Road Company against the Chesapeake and
Ohio Canal Company. Washington, Pr. by Gales & Seaton,
1830. 206 p. DIC; DLC; MH-
BA; MWA; NN.   5515

---- An opinion on the claims
for improvements, by the state
of Georgia on the Cherokee Nation, under the treaties of 1817
and 1828. New Echota, Pr. for
the Cherokee Nation at the office
of the Cherokee Phoenix and Indians' advocate, Jno. F. Wheeler,
pr., 1830. 22, 6 p. CSmH; GMW;
Md; NN; PPL; WHi.   5516

---- Opinion on the right of the
State of Georgia to extend her
laws over the Cherokee nation...
Baltimore, F. Lucas, jr., 1830.
29 p. ICN; ICU; MH-L; MdBP;
MdHi; PHi; WHi.   5517

---- ---- New Echota [Ga.] Pr.
for the Cherokee Nation at the
office of the Cherokee Phoenix
and Indians' Advocate, Jno. F.
Wheeler, pr., 1830. 27 p. DLC;
MH-L; NN; PPL; WHi; BrMus.
5518
The wise boys; or The entertaining histories of Fred. Fore-
thought, Matt. Merrythought,
Luke Lovebook, and Ben. Bee.
New York, E. Dunigan [183-?]
42 p. MH.   5519

Wisner, Benjamin Blydenburg,
1794-1835.
Benefits and claims of Sabbath
schools. A sermon delivered in
the Old South Church, in Boston,
on the morning and afternoon of
the Sabbath, January 17, 1830.
Boston, Perkins & Marvin, 1830.
28 p. MB; MBAt; MBC; MH-AH;
N; Nh; OO; WHi; BrMus. 5520

---- The history of the Old
South Church in Boston, in four
sermons, delivered May 9, &
16, 1830, being the first and second Sabbaths after the completion
of a century from the first occu-
pancy of the present meeting
house. Boston, Crocker & Brewster, 1830. 122 p. CBPac;
CSmH; CtHT; GDC; ICN; LNHT;
MB; MBAt; MBC; MH-AH; MHi;
MiD-B; NCH; NhHi; NjP; NjR;
OCHP; OClWHi; PHi; PPPrHi;
RHi; RPB; WHi; BrMus. 5521

Wisner, William, 1782-1871.
A letter from Rev. William
Wisner to a clerical friend, on
the theological views of Dr.
Taylor. Hartford, Conn., Edw.
Hopkins, 1830, 16 p. CBPac;
CSmH; IU; MBC; NcMHi; OClW;
OO; PPPrHi. 5522

Wistar, Caspar, 1761-1818.
A system of anatomy for the
use of students of medicine...
5th ed. With notes and additions
by William Edmonds Horner...
Philadelphia, Carey & Lea, 1830.
2 v. GDC; KyLxT; MeB; NNNAM;
NRAM; OCGHM; OClW; PPC; PU;
RNR; RPM; TxU. 5523

Witherspoon, John, 1723-1794.
Treatises on justification and
regeneration. With an introduc-
tory essay, by William Wilber-
force... Amherst, J. S. & C.
Adams, [etc., etc.] 1830. 264 p.
CBPac; ICN; MBC; MiU; NNUT;
NbOP; OMC. 5524

Withington, Leonard.
A sermon. Delivered at New-
bury... August 22, and... [at] Newburyport, August 29, 1830. Newburyport, Pr. by W. & J. Gilman, 1830. 16 p. CtSoP; MBC;
MeBaT; NjR. 5525

Woburn Agricultural & Mechanic
Association.
Charter and by-laws of the
Association. Boston, J. Howe,
1830. 14 p. MH. 5526

Wolcott, Eliza, 1795-1832.
The two sisters' poems and
memoirs. Composed by Eliza
and Sarah G. Wolcott, of Con-
necticut. New-Haven, Baldwin
& Treadway, prs., 1830. 174 p.
CSmH; CtHi; CtY; DLC; ICN;
MWA; NNC; PU; TxU. 5527

The woman of the town; or Authentic memoirs of Phebe Phillips... New-York, Pr. for the
booksellers, 1830. 24 p. DLC;
NN. 5528

The wonderful cure of Naaman.
See American Tract Society,
N. Y.

The wonderful exploits of Guy,
Earl of Warwick. With original
plates. Philadelphia, Wm. H.
Morgan [c 1830] 8 l. PP.
5529

Wonders! Descriptive of some of
the most remarkable of Nature
and art. Providence, Pub. by
A. S. Beckwith [1830] 12 l. PPL.
5530

Wood, James.
The parable of the ten virgins.
Illustrated in six sermons... Pub.
by J. S. & C. Adams & Co.,
Amherst, Mass. Mark Newman,
Andover. J. Leavitt, New York,
1830. 132 p. GDC; ICMcC; MA;
MB; MBC; MDeeP; MH-AH;
MeBaT. 5531

Wood, John.
Account of the Edinburgh sessional school... 2d ed. Boston, Repr. by Munroe & Francis, 1830. 204 p. GDC; LNHT; MB; MH; MH-AH; MeB; OSW; PU; RPB.   5532

Wood, W. W.
Sketches of China: with illustrations from original drawings. Philadelphia, Carey & Lea, [Skerrett, pr.] 1830. 250, [2] p. CU; DLC; GU; LN; MH; MdBE; MeBaT; MiD; NNG; Nj; PPL; PU; RPA; ViL.   5533

Woodbridge, William Channing, 1794-1845.
Rudiments of geography on a new plan... Accompanied with an atlas, exhibiting the prevailing religions, forms of government, ...and the comparative size of towns, rivers, and mountains. ...13th ed., from the 3d imp. ed., with corr. Hartford, Oliver D. Cooke & Co., 1830. 208 p. Ct; CtHi; NjR; PPL.   5534

---- Woodbridge school atlas, to accompany the Rudiments of geography. Atlas on a new plan exhibiting the prevailing religious forms of government, degrees of civilization, comparative size of towns, rivers and mountains... Hartford, Oliver D. Cooke & Co., 1830. 10 l. incl. 13 col. maps. MH (accompanying text wanting)
                                 5535

Woodbury, Levi, 1789-1851.
Speech of Mr. Woodbury, of New Hampshire, in the Senate of the United States, February 23, 1830, on Mr. Foot's resolution, proposing an inquiry into the expediency of abolishing the office of surveyor general of public lands... [Washington, 1830] 15 p. CSmH.   5536

---- ---- 2d ed. Washington, Pr.

by D. Green, 1830. 38 p. DLC.
                                 5537
Woodhouselee, Alexander Fraser Tytler, 1747-1813.
Elements of general history, ancient and modern. By Alexander Fraser Tytler. With a continuation, terminating at the demise of King George III, 1820. By Rev. Edward Nares, D.D. ...to which are added a succinct history of the United States; with addition and alterations. By an American gentleman. ...Adapted for the use of schools and academies, by an experienced teacher. Stereotyped by T.H. Carter & co., Boston. Concord, N.H., Pr. and pub. by H. Hill & co., 1830. 527, 44, [2] p. (Questions for the examination of scholars in Tytler's Elements, 44 p. at end.) CtMW; DLC; IEG; InU; KyBgW; LU; MH; MWH; MdU; MoSU; MoSpD; NRU-W; NT; NjP; OC; P; PLFM; PPL; PV; TU; TxU-T; WHi.   5538

[Woodruff, Sylvester]
A voyage to the Island of Philosophers, by Caesario San Blas, bachelor. Part 1st, containing an account of the Island and its inhabitants, together with the incidents which accurred [sic] there, during the sojourn of the writer ... [Albany?] 1830. [2], 53 p. NN.   5539

Woods, Leonard, 1774-1854.
Letters to Rev. Nathaniel W. Taylor, D.D. By Leonard Woods, D.D. Andover, Pub. by Mark Newman, Flagg & Gould, prs., 1830. 114 p. CBPac; CtHT; CtY-D; ICN; MB; MBC; MH-AH; MeB; MiD-B; NCH; Nh; OClWHi; OO; PHi; PPL; PPPrHi; RPB; BrMus.   5540

---- The province of reason in matters of religion, a sermon delivered by request in the Murray Street Church, in the city of New York, May 16, 1830. New York, Henry C. Sleight, Pr. by Sleight and Robinson, 1830. [2], 32 p. CBPac; CoU; ICN; MBC; MH; N; OMC; PPPrHi.   5541

---- A sermon preached at Haverhill, Mass. in rememberance of Mrs. Harriet Newell, wife of the Rev. Samuel Newell, missionary to India, who died at the Isle of France, Nov. 30th, 1812, aged 19 years. To which are added memoirs of her life. ... 9th ed. Baltimore, Pub. for Abel Brown, 1830. 238 p. CSmH; Ct; ICT; MB; NHC; NhHi; NjR; PPL; PW.   5542

Wood's almanac for 1831. By Joshua Sharp. New York, Samuel Wood & Sons; R. & G. S. Wood, prs. [1830] 18 l. DLC; MWA; NHi; OClWHi.   5543

Woodworth, Samuel, 1785-1842.
   Melodies, duets, trios, songs, and ballads, pastoral, amatory, sentimental, patriotic, religious, and miscellaneous. Together with metrical epistles, tales and recitations. By Samuel Woodworth. 2d ed., comprising many late productions never before published. New-York, Pub. for the author, by Elliot & Palmer, 1830. 3 p. l., [5]-288 p. DLC; MnU; RPA; BrMus.   5544

---- Ode for the celebration of the French revolution in the city of New-York, November 25, 1830. Written at the request of the printers of New-York, by Samuel Woodworth, printer. Tune-Marseillaise hymn. Stereotyped by James Conner, Franklin Bldg. [1830] 1 p. DLC; PHi.   5545

Woolman, John.
   Considerations on the keeping of negroes; recommended to the professors of Christianity of every denomination... 1st printed in the year 1754. Philadelphia, Pub. by the Tract Association of Friends, and to be had at their depository... [183-?] CSmH.
                                      5546

Worcester, Joseph Emerson, 1784-1865.
   A comprehensive pronouncing and explanatory dictionary of the English language, with pronouncing vocabularies of classical and scripture proper names. Burlington, Chauncey Goodrich, 1830. 400 p. MH; NjR; OClWHi. 5547

---- Elements of geography, ancient and modern: ...By J. E. Worcester. ... Boston, Hilliard, Gray, Little, and Wilkins, 1830. xi, [1], 271 p. IaHi; MB; MH; MHi; MWHi; Nh.   5548

---- Elements of history, ancient and modern: with historical charts. ...Boston, Hilliard, Gray, Little and Wilkins, 1830. xii, 403 p. ICU; MDeeP; MH; Nh; WvU.   5549

---- ... An epitome of geography, with an atlas. Boston, Hilliard, Gray, Little, and Wilkins, 1830. 162 p. DLC.   5550

---- An historical atlas, containing the following charts... 4th ed. Boston, Hilliard, Gray, Little & Wilkins. Cambridge, E. W. Metcalf & Co., prs. to the University, 1830. 1 l., 12 charts. DeWi; MB; MNF; MNS; NNC; NjP; OO; PP; PPL; RPB.   5551

---- Outlines of Scripture geography, with an Atlas. Boston, Hilliard, Gray, Little & Wilkins, 1830. 54 p. MB; NCH; RPB.
                                      5552

Worcester, Noah.
  The atoning sacrifice, a dis-
play of love not wrath. 2d ed.
Cambridge, Hilliard & Brown,
1830. 247 p. IEG; MBAU; MBC;
MH-AH; MMeT-Hi; NNUT. 5553

Worcester, Samuel, 1793-1844.
  A first book of geography.
Boston, Pub. by Crocker &
Brewster, 1830. 92 p. MH. 5554

---- A second book for reading
and spelling. Boston, Richardson, Lord, & Holbrook, 1830.
108 p. DLC.   5555

---- Spelling-book. Boston,
Crocker & Brewster, etc., etc.
1830. CtHT-W; MH.   5556

Worcester, Samuel Austin, 1798-
1859, comp.
  Cherokee hymns, compiled
from several authors and revised. By S. A. Worcester and
E. Boudinott... Printed for the
American Board of Commissioners for Foreign Missions. 2d ed.
enl. New Echota, J. F. Wheeler,
pr., 1830. 34, [2] p. DLC.
                              5557
Worcester County Colonization
Society.
  Report made at an adjourned
meeting of the friends of the
American Colonization Society, in
Worcester County, held in Worcester, December 8, 1830, by a
committee appointed for that purpose, with the proceedings of the
meeting, etc. Worcester, Pr.
by S. H. Colton & Co., 1830.
20 p. CLSU; DLC; M; MBC; MH;
MHi; MWA; MdBJ; MnHi; N;
OClWHi; PHi; RP; TNJ; WHi;
BrMus.   5558

The world turned upside down.
Hartford, Pub. by Henry Benton,
1830. [24] p. CtHi.   5559

Wrangham, Francis, ed.

The pleiad, A series of
abridgments from seven distinguished writers on the evidences
of Christianity. Philadelphia,
Thomas Kite, 1830. 224 p.
KyLoS; MdW; PU.   5560

The wreath. A collection of poems from celebrated English authors. Hartford [Conn.], Pub.
by Silas Andrus, 1830. 252 p.
InU; KyLoS; NCanHi.   5561

Wright, Akins.
  A history of the principal and
most distinguished martyrs in
the different ages of the world;
giving an account of their birth,
life, sufferings and death; and
particularly their dying words in
testimony of that religion which
they professed. By Akins Wright.
Illustrated with copper-plate engravings. Cincinnati, Pub. by
R. Houck, Pr. at the Chronicle office, 1830. 502 p. In;
KyLo; KyLx; MoK; OClWHi; OSW;
TxDaM.   5562

[Wright, Alfred, 1788-1853]
  Chahta holisso. [Choctaw
spelling and reading book.] Boston, Pr. by Crocker & Brewster,
1830. 108 p. CtY; NN.   5563

The writing master. See Hewett,
D.

Wylie, Andrew.
  A discourse on education, delivered before the Legislature of
the state of Indiana, at the request of the joint committees on
education, by A. Wylie. Published in pursuance of a vote of
the House of Representatives,
January 17, 1830. Smith & Bolton, state prs., 1830. 23 p. In;
InU; NNU.   5564

---- Religion and state; not
church and state. A sermon, on
Psalm 11, 10-12. Delivered,

July fourth 1830. In the hall of
the Indiana college, Bloomington;
by the Rev. A. Wylie, D.D.
president of the college, and published by request of the students.
Bloomington, Pr. by McCollough
& Co. [1830] 16 p. In; InU; PHi;
PU. 5565

Wyman, Rufus.
Discourse on mental philosophy
as connected with mental disease,
delivered before the Massachusetts Medical Society, June 2,
1830. Boston, Daily Advertiser,
1830. 24 p. MBAt; MH; MHi;
NCH; NNNAM; OC. 5566

Wynantz, Wilhelm.
Predigten ueber höchst wich-
tige Gegenstände des Christenthums... Lancaster, Gedruckt
bey Johann Bär, 1830. [1], 297,
[3] p. PHi; PPG; PPL;
PPPeSchW. 5567

Wzokhilain, Peter Paul.
Wawasi lagidamwoganek mdala
chowagidamwoganal tabtagil, on-
kawodokodozwal wji pobatami
kidwogan. P. P. Wzokhilain.
Boston, Pr. by Crocker & Brewster, 1830. 35 p. DLC; MB; NN.
5568
---- Wobanaki kinzowi awighigan,
P. P. Wzokhilain, kizitokw.
Boston, Pr. by Crocker & Brewster, 1830. 90 p., 1 l. DLC;
MB; MBAt; MH; MHi; MeU; NN.
5569

X Y Z

Xenophon.
Xenophon's expedition of Cyrus, with English notes, prepared for the use of schools and
colleges, with a life of the author. By Charles Dexter Cleveland... Boston, Hilliard, Gray,
Little & Wilkins. [Cambridge,
E. W. Metcalf & co.] 1830. xv,
320 p. DLC; ICMcC; MB; NNC;

NjR. 5570

---- ... Xenophontis De cyri in-
stitutione Libri octo. Ex recen-
sione ex cum notis Thomae Hutchinson, A.M. Philadelphia,
Pub. by John Grigg, 1830. 500 p.
CtHT; LRuL; ScCC. 5571

The Yahoo; a satirical rhapsody
... New York, Pr. and pub. by
H. Simpson, 1830. xxvii, [1],
136 p. 1 l. CSmH (attributed to
Wm. Watts); ICN (attributed to
Redivivus Lucien, pseud.) 5572

Yale, Charles.
Outlines of general history, in
three parts: I. Ancient history.
II. Modern history. III. American history. Designed for the
use of schools and academies,
by Charles Yale. Rochester,
N.Y., Pr. by E. Peck & Co.,
1830. 308 p. NRHi. 5573

Yale, Cyrus.
Life of the Rev. Jeremiah
Hallock, late pastor of the Con-
gregational Church in Canton,
Connecticut... [2d ed.] Hartford,
D. F. Robinson & co., Peter B.
Gleason & co., prs., 1830.
292 p. Ct; CtHi; ICMcC; MB;
MH-AH; Me; NCH; OMC; PHi;
PPL; RPB. 5574

Yale University.
Catalogue of the officers and
students in Yale College. New
Haven, Baldwin & Treadway,
1830. 21 p. CtHT-W; CtSoP;
MeB; OClW. 5575

---- Circular explanatory of the
recent proceedings of the sophomore class, in Yale College.
New-Haven, August, 1830. [New
Haven? 1830] 15 p. CtHi; CtY.
5576
---- A circular of the recent
proceedings of the sophomore
class in Yale College. New

Haven, August, 1830. 15 p. Ct;
MB; MBC; N.   5577

---- Reports on the instruction
in Yale College. Submitted by a
committee of the corporation and
the academical faculty. New
Haven, H. Howe, 1830. 56 p. Ct;
DLC; MB; MH; MeBaT; N; OClW;
WHi.   5578

---- [Begin] Yale College, August
7th, 1830. On Saturday, the 31st
of July ... [Circular of the faculty
of Yale College, apropos of the
"conic sections rebellion." New
Haven? 1830] 2 l. Pr. on p.
[2-3,] of folded sheet; p. [1, 4]
blank. CtY.   5579

No entry.   5580

Yamacraw Intemperance Society.
Rules and regulations for the
"Yamacraw Intemperance Society." Founded Dec. 20, 1830.
1 p. DLC.   5581

The Yankee, or Farmer's alman-
ack for 1831. By Thomas Spof-
ford. Boston, Willard Felt &
Co.; New York, David Felt
[1830] 18 l. CLU; CtY; DLC;
InU; MB; MBAt; MH; MHi;
MWA; NBLiHi; NHi; Nh; NjR;
OMC; OClWHi; PPL; RP; WHi.
                               5582

Yates, Andrew J.
The citizen's guide: compre-
hending the constitutions of the
United States and the state of
New York; together with chapters
eleventh and twelfth of the Re-
vised statutes... Utica, Press of
W. Williams, 1830. 121 p. CtY;
DLC; LU; N; NCH; NNC; NUt;
NjR; TxU.   5583

A year in Spain. See Mackenzie, Alexander Slidell.

Youmans, Jonathan.
The Christian remembrancer,
or Short reflections upon the
faith, life, and conduct of a real
Christian. 2d ed. New York, Pr.
by Sleight & Robinson, 1830.
214 p. MMeT-Hi; RPB.   5584

Young, Alexander, 1800-1854.
An address delivered at the
ordination of the Rev. William
Newell, as pastor of the First
Parish in Cambridge, May 19,
1830. Cambridge, Pub. by Hil-
liard & Brown, 1830. 16 p. DLC;
MBAU; MBC; MH-AH; MHi;
MWA; MiD-B; OClWHi; BrMus.
                               5585

---- Christianity designed and
adapted to be a universal reli-
gion. Discourse delivered at
the ordination of the Rev. James
W. Thompson, as pastor of the
South Congregational Society, in
Natick, Feb. 17, 1830. Boston,
Gray & Bowen, 1830. 76 p.
CBPac; CSmH; DLC; ICN; MB;
MBAU; MBAt; MH-AH; MHi;
MWA; NNC; OClWHi; OO; RPB;
BrMus.   5586

---- Evangelical Unitarianism;
adapted to the poor and unlearned.
No. 37. Printed for The American Unitarian Association. Boston, Gray & Bowen [I. R. Butts,
pr.] 1830. 28 p. CBPac; ICMe;
MBAU; MBAt; MBC; MH-AH;
MMeT-Hi; MeB; N; NNC; WHi.
                               5587

Young, Edward, 1683-1765.
The complaint: or Night
thoughts by Edward Young. Hartford, Conn., Pub. by Silas Andrus, 1830. 324 p. CtHi; IaB.
                               5588

---- Night thoughts on life, death,
and immortality... Philadelphia,
Pub. by Stoddart & Atherton, 1830.
301 p. (Added t. p. dated 1821) CtW;
MB; MdHi; NcA-S; ViU; WU. 5589

Young, James, comp.

A history of the most interesting events in the history and progress of Methodism in Europe and America. A Dagget, H. Howe, pr., 1830. 443 p. MH-AH.
5590

Young, James Hamilton.
The tourist's pocket map of Pennsylvania, exhibiting its internal improvements, roads, distances, &c. By J. H. Young. Philadelphia, S. Augustus Mitchell [1830] P.   5591

Young, John Clarke, 1803-1857.
Address of Rev. John C. Young, delivered at his inauguration as president of Centre College. Danville, Nov. 18, 1830. Lexington, Ky., Pr. by T. T. Skillman, 1830. 11, [1] p. DLC; KyBgW; KyLoF; MH-AH; NjP; PHi; PPPrHi.   5592

A young American. See Mackenzie, Alexander Slidell.

The young child's prayer book. See Palfrey, John Gorham.

The young emigrants. See Sedgwick, Susan Ann Livingston (Ridley).

Young Gentlemen's Society.
Constitution of the Young Gentlemen's Society in Cornwall; with the catalogue of their library, Oct. 1829. Middlebury, From the Press of the American, 1830. 15 p.   5593

The young lady's book: a manual of elegant recreations, exercises, and pursuits. Boston, A. Bowen, and Carter & Hendee; Philadelphia, Carey & Lea [1830] 3 p. l., [9]-504 p. 1 l. CU; DLC; ICU; LNHT; MB; RPB.
5594

Young Men's Bible Society of Baltimore.
The tenth report of the Young Men's Bible Society of Baltimore, auxiliary to the American Bible Society. Also the ninth report of the Ladies' Branch Bible Society, presented at their annual meeting, Nov. 16, 1829. Baltimore, Pr. by Lucas & Deaver, 1830. 31 p. MdHi.   5595

---- The eleventh report of the Young Men's Bible Society of Baltimore, auxiliary to the American Bible Society; also the tenth report of the Ladies' Branch Bible Society, presented at their annual meeting November 29, 1830. With an Appendix. Baltimore, Pr. by Sands & Neilson, 1830. 36 p. MdHi.   5596

Young Men's Bible Society of Frederick County, Md.
Proceedings... [Frederick City? Md., 1830] 20 p. CSmH.
5597

Young Men's Temperance Society, New Haven.
Second annual report of the Young Men's Temperance Society of New Haven, Auxiliary to the New-Haven County Temperance Society. New Haven, Baldwin & Treadway, 1830. 12 p. CtY.
5598

Youthful dialogues. By a teacher. Philadelphia [1830?] BrMus.
5599

Youthful stories... New-York, Pr. & sold by Mahlon Day at the New Juvenile Book-store [183-?] 16 p. NN.   5600

The youth's director; or Familiar instructions for young people which will be found useful also to persons of every sex, age and condition in life; illustrated with a number of historical traits and edifying examples. Translated from the French. 1st American ed. Boston, Pub. by William Smith for the editors of "The Jesuit." 1830. [4], 328 p.

MiDSH. 5601

The youth's instructor and Sabbath school and Bible class assistant. New Series. New-York, Pub. by J. Emory and B. Waugh, for the Methodist Episcopal Church, J. Collord, pr., 1830. 4 v. MB; MiD-B. 5602

Youth's keepsake, a Christmas and New Year's gift for young people. Boston, Carter and Hendee [Waitt & Dow, prs.] 1830. 210 p. MB; NNC; PPL; WHi. 5603

Youth's Mariner's Bible Society, Boston.
First annual report of the Youth's Mariner's Bible Society, Boston. Presented at the annual meeting, May 31, 1830. Boston, T. R. Marvin, pr., 1830. 8 p. NjR. 5604

The youth's prayer book. See Palfrey, John Gorham.

Youth's Tract Society.
Fourth annual report of the Youth's Tract Society; Read at the annual meeting, held on Monday evening, October 18, 1830. Philadelphia, William F. Geddes, pr., 1830. 23 p. PHi. 5605

[Zavala, Lorenzo de] 1788-1836.
Juicio imparcial sobre los acontecimientos de Mexico, en 1828 y 1829. New-York, C. S. Van Winkle, 1830. 48 p. CSmH; DLC; KHi; MHi; NN; PPL; BrMus. 5606

Zilia: A poem. In three cantos. New York, G. & C. & H. Carvill, 1830. 54 p. CSmH; GHi; MB; NbU; PHi; TxU; BrMus. 5607

Zimmerman, John G., 1720-1795
Solitude. By John G. Zimmerman. With the life of the author... In two parts. Charlestown, G. Davidson, 1830. 408 p. MB; MDeeP; MeBa; OO; WBB. 5608

[Zschokke, Heinrich] 1771-1848.
Abaellino, the bravo of Venice. Translated from the German by M. G. Lewis. Stereotyped by D. Watson, Woodstock. Woodstock, Pr. by David Watson, 1830. 159 p. VtMiS. 5609